MW00334822

The Complete Lojban Language

John Woldemar Cowan

A Logical Language Group Publication

Version 1.1, Generated 2016-04-12

Table of Contents
1. Lojban As We Mangle It In Lojbanistan: About This Book 9
  1.1. What is Lojban? 9
  1.2. What is this book? 10
  1.3. What are the typographical conventions of this book? 10
  1.4. Disclaimers 11
  1.5. Acknowledgements and Credits 11
  1.6. Informal Bibliography 12
  1.7. Captions to Pictures 12
  1.8. Boring Legalities 13
2. A Quick Tour of Lojban Grammar, With Diagrams 15
  2.1. The concept of the bridi 15
  2.2. Pronunciation 16
  2.3. Words that can act as sumti 17
  2.4. Some words used to indicate selbri relations 17
  2.5. Some simple Lojban bridi 18
  2.6. Variant bridi structure 19
  2.7. Varying the order of sumti 20
  2.8. The basic structure of longer utterances 21
  2.9. tanru 21
  2.10. Description sumti 23
  2.11. Examples of brivla 24
  2.12. The sumti di'u and la'e di'u 24
  2.13. Possession 25
  2.14. Vocatives and commands 25
  2.15. Questions 26
  2.16. Indicators 28
  2.17. Tenses 29
  2.18. Lojban grammatical terms 30
3. The Hills Are Alive With The Sounds Of Lojban 33
  3.1. Orthography 33
  3.2. Basic Phonetics 34
  3.3. The Special Lojban Characters 35
  3.4. Diphthongs and Syllabic Consonants 36
  3.5. Vowel Pairs 38
  3.6. Consonant Clusters 38
  3.7. Initial Consonant Pairs 39
  3.8. Buffering Of Consonant Clusters 40
  3.9. Syllabication And Stress 41
  3.10. IPA For English Speakers 44
  3.11. English Analogues For Lojban Diphthongs 46
  3.12. Oddball Orthographies 47
4. The Shape Of Words To Come: Lojban Morphology 49
  4.1. Introductory 49
  4.2. cmavo 50
  4.3. brivla 52
  4.4. gismu 53
  4.5. lujvo 54
  4.6. rafsi 56
  4.7. fu'ivla 60
  4.8. cmene 63
  4.9. Rules for inserting pauses 66
  4.10. Considerations for making lujvo 67

4.11. The lujvo-making algorithm 68
4.12. The lujvo scoring algorithm 69
4.13. lujvo-making examples 70
4.14. The gismu creation algorithm 71
4.15. Cultural and other non-algorithmic gismu 73
4.16. rafsi fu'ivla: a proposal 76
5. "Pretty Little Girls' School": The Structure Of Lojban selbri 79
5.1. Lojban content words: brivla 79
5.2. Simple tanru 80
5.3. Three-part tanru grouping with bo 82
5.4. Complex tanru grouping 83
5.5. Complex tanru with ke and ke'e 84
5.6. Logical connection within tanru 85
5.7. Linked sumti: be-bei-be'o 88
5.8. Inversion of tanru: co 91
5.9. Other kinds of simple selbri 93
5.10. selbri based on sumti: me 95
5.11. Conversion of simple selbri 96
5.12. Scalar negation of selbri 98
5.13. Tenses and bridi negation 100
5.14. Some types of asymmetrical tanru 101
5.15. Some types of symmetrical tanru 107
5.16. "Pretty little girls' school": forty ways to say it 108
6. To Speak Of Many Things: The Lojban sumti 115
6.1. The five kinds of simple sumti 115
6.2. The three basic description types 116
6.3. Individuals and masses 119
6.4. Masses and sets 121
6.5. Descriptors for typical objects 122
6.6. Quantified sumti 123
6.7. Quantified descriptions 124
6.8. Indefinite descriptions 127
6.9. sumti-based descriptions 127
6.10. sumti qualifiers 128
6.11. The syntax of vocative phrases 130
6.12. Lojban names 132
6.13. Pro-sumti summary 134
6.14. Quotation summary 136
6.15. Number summary 136
7. Brevity Is The Soul Of Language: Pro-sumti And Pro-bridi 139
7.1. What are pro-sumti and pro-bridi? What are they for? 139
7.2. Personal pro-sumti: the mi-series 140
7.3. Demonstrative pro-sumti: the ti-series 141
7.4. Utterance pro-sumti: the di'u-series 142
7.5. Assignable pro-sumti and pro-bridi: the ko'a-series and the broda-series 144
7.6. Anaphoric pro-sumti and pro-bridi: the ri-series and the go'i-series 146
7.7. Indefinite pro-sumti and pro-bridi: the zo'e-series and the co'e-series 150
7.8. Reflexive and reciprocal pro-sumti: the vo'a-series 152
7.9. sumti and bridi questions: ma and mo 153
7.10. Relativized pro-sumti: ke'a 154
7.11. Abstraction focus pro-sumti: ce'u 154
7.12. Bound variable pro-sumti and pro-bridi: the da-series and the bu'a-series 155
7.13. Pro-sumti and pro-bridi cancelling 155
7.14. The identity predicate: du 156

7.15. lujvo based on pro-sumti...156
7.16. KOhA cmavo by series 157
7.17. GOhA and other pro-bridi by series 158
7.18. Other cmavo discussed in this chapter 159
8. Relative Clauses, Which Make sumti Even More Complicated....................161
8.1. What are you pointing at?..161
8.2. Incidental relative clauses...163
8.3. Relative phrases 165
8.4. Multiple relative clauses: zi'e..168
8.5. Non-veridical relative clauses: voi..169
8.6. Relative clauses and descriptors..170
8.7. Possessive sumti 172
8.8. Relative clauses and complex sumti: vu'o..173
8.9. Relative clauses in vocative phrases...175
8.10. Relative clauses within relative clauses...176
8.11. Index of relative clause cmavo...177
9. To Boston Via The Road Go I, With An Excursion Into The Land Of Modals.....179
9.1. Introductory 179
9.2. Standard bridi form: cu..180
9.3. Tagging places: FA...182
9.4. Conversion: SE..185
9.5. Modal places: FIhO, FEhU 187
9.6. Modal tags: BAI...188
9.7. Modal sentence connection: the causals 189
9.8. Other modal connections 192
9.9. Modal selbri 194
9.10. Modal relative phrases; Comparison...195
9.11. Mixed modal connection...198
9.12. Modal conversion: JAI...199
9.13. Modal negation..200
9.14. Sticky modals..201
9.15. Logical and non-logical connection of modals 201
9.16. CV'V cmavo of selma'o BAI with irregular forms...........................202
9.17. Complete table of BAI cmavo with rough English equivalents 203
10. Imaginary Journeys: The Lojban Space/Time Tense System 207
10.1. Introductory 207
10.2. Spatial tenses: FAhA and VA..209
10.3. Compound spatial tenses 210
10.4. Temporal tenses: PU and ZI...211
10.5. Interval sizes: VEhA and ZEhA...213
10.6. Vague intervals and non-specific tenses 215
10.7. Dimensionality: VIhA 215
10.8. Movement in space: MOhI 216
10.9. Interval properties: TAhE and roi 217
10.10. Event contours: ZAhO and re'u...219
10.11. Space interval modifiers: FEhE..222
10.12. Tenses as sumti tcita...223
10.13. Sticky and multiple tenses: KI..225
10.14. Story time 227
10.15. Tenses in subordinate bridi 229
10.16. Tense relations between sentences 230
10.17. Tensed logical connectives...232
10.18. Tense negation...234
10.19. Actuality, potentiality, capability: CAhA 235

10.20. Logical and non-logical connections between tenses 237
10.21. Sub-events...238
10.22. Conversion of sumti tcita: JAI 239
10.23. Tenses versus modals 240
10.24. Tense questions: cu'e 242
10.25. Explicit magnitudes..243
10.26. Finally (an exercise for the much-tried reader) 244
10.27. Summary of tense selma'o 244
10.28. List of spatial directions and direction-like relations 245
11. Events, Qualities, Quantities, And Other Vague Words: On Lojban Abstraction............247
11.1. The syntax of abstraction 247
11.2. Event abstraction 248
11.3. Types of event abstractions 250
11.4. Property abstractions...251
11.5. Amount abstractions 253
11.6. Truth-value abstraction: jei 254
11.7. Predication/sentence abstraction 255
11.8. Indirect questions 256
11.9. Minor abstraction types...258
11.10. Lojban sumti raising 259
11.11. Event-type abstractors and event contour tenses 260
11.12. Abstractor connection 261
11.13. Table of abstractors 262
12. Dog House And White House: Determining lujvo Place Structures....................263
12.1. Why have lujvo?..263
12.2. The meaning of tanru: a necessary detour 264
12.3. The meaning of lujvo...266
12.4. Selecting places...267
12.5. Symmetrical and asymmetrical lujvo..267
12.6. Dependent places 269
12.7. Ordering lujvo places. 271
12.8. lujvo with more than two parts. 272
12.9. Eliding SE rafsi from seltau 273
12.10. Eliding SE rafsi from tertau 274
12.11. Eliding KE and KEhE rafsi from lujvo 274
12.12. Abstract lujvo..275
12.13. Implicit-abstraction lujvo 277
12.14. Anomalous lujvo 279
12.15. Comparatives and superlatives...280
12.16. Notes on gismu place structures...283
13. Oooh! Arrgh! Ugh! Yecch! Attitudinal and Emotional Indicators 285
13.1. What are attitudinal indicators?...285
13.2. Pure emotion indicators 287
13.3. Propositional attitude indicators 289
13.4. Attitudes as scales..292
13.5. The space of emotions 294
13.6. Emotional categories..294
13.7. Attitudinal modifiers 295
13.8. Compound indicators 298
13.9. The uses of indicators..299
13.10. Attitude questions; empathy; attitude contours 300
13.11. Evidentials 302
13.12. Discursives..304
13.13. Miscellaneous indicators...307

13.14. Vocative scales 309
13.15. A sample dialogue...311
13.16. Tentative conclusion 314
14. If Wishes Were Horses: The Lojban Connective System 317
14.1. Logical connection and truth tables 317
14.2. The Four basic vowels...319
14.3. The six types of logical connectives 319
14.4. Logical connection of bridi 320
14.5. Forethought bridi connection 322
14.6. sumti connection...324
14.7. More than two propositions 325
14.8. Grouping of afterthought connectives 326
14.9. Compound bridi 328
14.10. Multiple compound bridi 330
14.11. Termset logical connection..332
14.12. Logical connection within tanru 333
14.13. Truth questions and connective questions 335
14.14. Non-logical connectives 338
14.15. More about non-logical connectives...341
14.16. Interval connectives and forethought non-logical connection 343
14.17. Logical and non-logical connectives within mekso 346
14.18. Tenses, modals, and logical connection 347
14.19. Abstractor connection and connection within abstractions 350
14.20. Constructs and appropriate connectives 351
14.21. Truth functions and corresponding logical connectives 351
14.22. Rules for making logical and non-logical connectives 352
14.23. Locations of other tables 352
15. "No" Problems: On Lojban Negation...353
15.1. Introductory 353
15.2. bridi negation..354
15.3. Scalar Negation 357
15.4. selbri and tanru negation 360
15.5. Expressing scales in selbri negation 363
15.6. sumti negation...365
15.7. Negation of minor grammatical constructs 366
15.8. Truth questions 367
15.9. Affirmations 369
15.10. Metalinguistic negation forms...370
15.11. Summary – Are All Possible Questions About Negation Now Answered? 373
16. "Who Did You Pass On The Road? Nobody": Lojban And Logic 375
16.1. What's wrong with this picture?...375
16.2. Existential claims, prenexes, and variables 376
16.3. Universal claims..378
16.4. Restricted claims: da poi 379
16.5. Dropping the prenex 380
16.6. Variables with generalized quantifiers...381
16.7. Grouping of quantifiers 382
16.8. The problem of "any" 384
16.9. Negation boundaries 385
16.10. bridi negation and logical connectives...388
16.11. Using naku outside a prenex 389
16.12. Logical Connectives and DeMorgan's Law 392
16.13. selbri variables...394
16.14. A few notes on variables 395

16.15. Conclusion...395
17. As Easy As A-B-C? The Lojban Letteral System And Its Uses.........................397
    17.1. What's a letteral, anyway? 397
    17.2. A to Z in Lojban, plus one 398
    17.3. Upper and lower cases 399
    17.4. The universal bu 400
    17.5. Alien alphabets...400
    17.6. Accent marks and compound lerfu words 402
    17.7. Punctuation marks 403
    17.8. What about Chinese characters? 403
    17.9. lerfu words as pro-sumti 404
    17.10. References to lerfu 405
    17.11. Mathematical uses of lerfu strings 406
    17.12. Acronyms..407
    17.13. Computerized character codes...408
    17.14. List of all auxiliary lerfu-word cmavo 409
    17.15. Proposed lerfu words – introduction 409
    17.16. Proposed lerfu words for the Greek alphabet.....................................409
    17.17. Proposed lerfu words for the Cyrillic alphabet...................................410
    17.18. Proposed lerfu words for the Hebrew alphabet...................................410
    17.19. Proposed lerfu words for some accent marks and multiple letters 411
    17.20. Proposed lerfu words for radio communication 412
18. lojbau mekso: Mathematical Expressions in Lojban.......................................413
    18.1. Introductory 413
    18.2. Lojban numbers...414
    18.3. Signs and numerical punctuation 414
    18.4. Special numbers 416
    18.5. Simple infix expressions and equations 417
    18.6. Forethought operators (Polish notation, functions).............................419
    18.7. Other useful selbri for mekso bridi 421
    18.8. Indefinite numbers 422
    18.9. Approximation and inexact numbers 424
    18.10. Non-decimal and compound bases 426
    18.11. Special mekso selbri 428
    18.12. Number questions..431
    18.13. Subscripts...431
    18.14. Infix operators revisited 432
    18.15. Vectors and matrices 433
    18.16. Reverse Polish notation..434
    18.17. Logical and non-logical connectives within mekso 435
    18.18. Using Lojban resources within mekso 437
    18.19. Other uses of mekso 438
    18.20. Explicit operator precedence...440
    18.21. Miscellany..440
    18.22. Four score and seven: a mekso problem 441
    18.23. mekso selma'o summary...442
    18.24. Complete table of VUhU cmavo, with operand structures..................443
    18.25. Complete table of PA cmavo: digits, punctuation, and other numbers...............443
    18.26. Table of MOI cmavo, with associated rafsi and place structures 444
19. Putting It All Together: Notes on the Structure of Lojban Texts....................447
    19.1. Introductory...447
    19.2. Sentences: I 447
    19.3. Paragraphs: NIhO...448
    19.4. Topic-comment sentences: ZOhU...449

19.5. Questions and answers 451
19.6. Subscripts: XI 453
19.7. Utterance ordinals: MAI 455
19.8. Attitude scope markers: FUhE/FUhO... 456
19.9. Quotations: LU, LIhU, LOhU, LEhU 457
19.10. More on quotations: ZO, ZOI... 458
19.11. Contrastive emphasis: BAhE... 460
19.12. Parenthesis and metalinguistic commentary: TO, TOI, SEI........... 461
19.13. Erasure: SI, SA, SU... 463
19.14. Hesitation: Y... 465
19.15. No more to say: FAhO 465
19.16. List of cmavo interactions.. 466
19.17. List of Elidable Terminators... 466
20. A Catalogue of selma'o.. 467
    20.1. 467
21. Formal Grammars... 489
    21.1. EBNF Grammar of Lojban.. 489
    21.2. EBNF Cross-Reference 494
Lojban Word Glossary 505
General Index 527
Lojban Words Index 571
Examples Index... 581

Chapter 1
Lojban As We Mangle It In Lojbanistan: About This Book

coi lojban.   *coi rodo*

1.1 What is Lojban?

Lojban (pronounced "LOZH-bahn") is a constructed language. Previous versions of the language were called "Loglan" by Dr. James Cooke Brown, who founded the Loglan Project and started the development of the language in 1955. The goals for the language were first described in the open literature in the article "Loglan", published in *Scientific American*, June, 1960. Made well-known by that article and by occasional references in science fiction (most notably in Robert Heinlein's novel *The Moon Is A Harsh Mistress*) and computer publications, Loglan and Lojban have been built over four decades by dozens of workers and hundreds of supporters, led since 1987 by The Logical Language Group (who are the publishers of this book).

There are thousands of artificial languages (of which Esperanto is the best-known), but Loglan/ Lojban has been engineered to make it unique in several ways. The following are the main features of Lojban:

- Lojban is designed to be used by people in communication with each other, and possibly in the future with computers.
- Lojban is designed to be neutral between cultures.
- Lojban grammar is based on the principles of predicate logic.
- Lojban has an unambiguous yet flexible grammar.
- Lojban has phonetic spelling, and unambiguously resolves its sounds into words.
- Lojban is simple compared to natural languages; it is easy to learn.

- Lojban's 1300 root words can be easily combined to form a vocabulary of millions of words.
- Lojban is regular; the rules of the language are without exceptions.
- Lojban attempts to remove restrictions on creative and clear thought and communication.
- Lojban has a variety of uses, ranging from the creative to the scientific, from the theoretical to the practical.
- Lojban has been demonstrated in translation and in original works of prose and poetry.

1.2 What is this book?

This book is what is called a "reference grammar". It attempts to expound the whole Lojban language, or at least as much of it as is understood at present. Lojban is a rich language with many features, and an attempt has been made to discover the functions of those features. The word "discover" is used advisedly; Lojban was not "invented" by any one person or committee. Often, grammatical features were introduced into the language long before their usage was fully understood. Sometimes they were introduced for one reason, only to prove more useful for other reasons not recognized at the time.

By intention, this book is complete in description but not in explanation. For every rule in the formal Lojban grammar (given in Chapter 21 (p. 489)), there is a bit of explanation and an example somewhere in the book, and often a great deal more than a bit. In essence, Chapter 2 (p. 15) gives a brief overview of the language, Chapter 21 (p. 489) gives the formal structure of the language, and the chapters in between put semantic flesh on those formal bones. I hope that eventually more grammatical material founded on (or even correcting) the explanations in this book will become available.

Nevertheless, the publication of this book is, in one sense, the completion of a long period of language evolution. With the exception of a possible revision of the language that will not even be considered until five years from publication date, and any revisions of this book needed to correct outright errors, the language described in this book will not be changing by deliberate act of its creators any more. Instead, language change will take place in the form of new vocabulary – Lojban does not yet have nearly the vocabulary it needs to be a fully usable language of the modern world, as Chapter 12 (p. 263) explains – and through the irregular natural processes of drift and (who knows?) native-speaker evolution. (Teach your children Lojban!) You can learn the language described here with assurance that (unlike previous versions of Lojban and Loglan, as well as most other artificial languages) it will not be subject to further fiddling by language-meisters.

It is probably worth mentioning that this book was written somewhat piecemeal. Each chapter began life as an explication of a specific Lojban topic; only later did these begin to clump together into a larger structure of words and ideas. Therefore, there are perhaps not as many cross-references as there should be. However, I have attempted to make the index as comprehensive as possible.

Each chapter has a descriptive title, often involving some play on words; this is an attempt to make the chapters more memorable. The title of Chapter 1 (p. 9) (which you are now reading), for example, is an allusion to the book *English As We Speak It In Ireland*, by P. W. Joyce, which is a sort of informal reference grammar of Hiberno-English. "Lojbanistan" is both an imaginary country where Lojban is the native language, and a term for the actual community of Lojban-speakers, scattered over the world. Why "mangle"? As yet, nobody in the real Lojbanistan speaks the language at all well, by the standards of the imaginary Lojbanistan; that is one of the circumstances this book is meant to help remedy.

1.3 What are the typographical conventions of this book?

Each chapter is broken into numbered sections; each section contains a mixture of expository text, numbered examples, and possibly tables.

The reader will notice a certain similarity in the examples used throughout the book. One chapter after another rings the changes on the self-same sentences:

Example 1.1

mi	klama	le	zarci
I	go-to	that-which-I-describe-as-a	store.

I go to the store.

will become wearisomely familiar before Chapter 21 (p. 489) is reached. This method is deliberate; I have tried to use simple and (eventually) familiar examples wherever possible, to avoid obscuring new grammatical points with new vocabulary. Of course, this is not the method of a textbook, but this book is not a textbook (although people have learned Lojban from it and its predecessors). Rather, it is intended both for self-learning (of course, at present would-be Lojban teachers must be self-learners) and to serve as a reference in the usual sense, for looking up obscure points about the language.

It is useful to talk further about Example 1.1 (p. 10) for what it illustrates about examples in this book. Examples usually occupy three lines. The first of these is in Lojban (in italics), the second in a word-by-word literal translation of the Lojban into English (in boldface), and the third in colloquial English. The second and third lines are sometimes called the "literal translation" and the "colloquial translation" respectively. Sometimes, when clarity is not sacrificed thereby, one or both are omitted. If there is more than one Lojban sentence, it generally means that they have the same meaning.

Words are sometimes surrounded by square brackets. In Lojban texts, these enclose optional grammatical particles that may (in the context of the particular example) be either omitted or included. In literal translations, they enclose words that are used as conventional translations of specific Lojban words, but don't have exactly the meanings or uses that the English word would suggest. In Chapter 3 (p. 33), square brackets surround phonetic representations in the International Phonetic Alphabet.

Many of the tables, especially those placed at the head of various sections, are in three columns. The first column contains Lojban words discussed in that section; the second column contains the grammatical category (represented by an UPPER CASE Lojban word) to which the word belongs, and the third column contains a brief English gloss, not necessarily or typically a full explanation. Other tables are explained in context.

A few Lojban words are used in this book as technical terms. All of these are explained in Chapter 2 (p. 15), except for a few used only in single chapters, which are explained in the introductory sections of those chapters.

1.4 Disclaimers

It is necessary to add, alas, that the examples used in this book do not refer to any existing person, place, or institution, and that any such resemblance is entirely coincidental and unintentional, and not intended to give offense.

When definitions and place structures of gismu, and especially of lujvo, are given in this book, they may differ from those given in the English-Lojban dictionary (which, as of this writing, is not yet published). If so, the information given in the dictionary supersedes whatever is given here.

1.5 Acknowledgements and Credits

Although the bulk of this book was written for the Logical Language Group (LLG) by John Cowan, who is represented by the occasional authorial "I", certain chapters were first written by others and then heavily edited by me to fit into this book.

In particular: Chapter 2 (p. 15) is a fusion of originally separate documents, one by Athelstan, and one by Nora Tansky LeChevalier and Bob LeChevalier; Chapter 3 (p. 33) and Chapter 4 (p. 49) were originally written by Bob LeChevalier with contributions by Chuck Barton; Chapter 12 (p. 263) was originally written (in much longer form) by Nick Nicholas; the dialogue near the end of Chapter 13 (p. 285) was contributed by Nora Tansky LeChevalier; Chapter 15 (p. 353) and parts of Chapter 16 (p. 375) were originally by Bob LeChevalier; and the YACC grammar in Chapter 21 (p. 489) is the work of several hands, but is primarily by Bob LeChevalier and Jeff Taylor. The BNF grammar, which is also in Chapter 21 (p. 489), was originally written by me, then rewritten by Clark Nelson, and finally touched up by me again.

The research into natural languages from which parts of Chapter 5 (p. 79) draw their material was performed by Ivan Derzhanski. LLG acknowledges his kind permission to use the fruits of his research.

The pictures in this book were drawn by Nora Tansky LeChevalier, except for the picture appearing in Chapter 4 (p. 49), which is by Sylvia Rutiser Rissell.

The index was made by Nora Tansky LeChevalier.

I would like to thank the following people for their detailed reviews, suggestions, comments, and early detection of my embarrassing errors in Lojban, logic, English, and cross-references: Nick Nicholas, Mark Shoulson, Veijo Vilva, Colin Fine, And Rosta, Jorge Llambias, Iain Alexander, Paulo S. L. M. Barreto, Robert J. Chassell, Gale Cowan, Karen Stein, Ivan Derzhanski, Jim Carter, Irene Gates, Bob LeChevalier, John Parks-Clifford (also known as "pc"), and Nora Tansky LeChevalier.

Nick Nicholas (NSN) would like to thank the following Lojbanists: Mark Shoulson, Veijo Vilva, Colin Fine, And Rosta, and Iain Alexander for their suggestions and comments; John Cowan, for his extensive comments, his exemplary trailblazing of Lojban grammar, and for solving the *manskapi* dilemma for NSN; Jorge Llambias, for his even more extensive comments, and for forcing NSN to think more than he was inclined to; Bob LeChevalier, for his skeptical overview of the issue, his encouragement, and for scouring all Lojban text his computer has been burdened with for lujvo; Nora Tansky LeChevalier, for writing the program converting old rafsi text to new rafsi text, and sparing NSN from embarrassing errors; and Jim Carter, for his dogged persistence in analyzing lujvo algorithmically, which inspired this research, and for first identifying the three lujvo classes.

Of course, the entire Loglan Project owes a considerable debt to James Cooke Brown as the language inventor, and also to several earlier contributors to the development of the language. Especially noteworthy are Doug Landauer, Jeff Prothero, Scott Layson, Jeff Taylor, and Bob McIvor. Final responsibility for the remaining errors and infelicities is solely mine.

1.6 Informal Bibliography

The founding document for the Loglan Project, of which this book is one of the products, is *Loglan 1: A Logical Language* by James Cooke Brown (4th ed. 1989, The Loglan Institute, Gainesville, Florida, U.S.A.). The language described therein is not Lojban, but is very close to it and may be considered an ancestral version. It is regrettably necessary to state that nothing in this book has been approved by Dr. Brown, and that the very existence of Lojban is disapproved of by him.

The logic of Lojban, such as it is, owes a good deal to the American philosopher W. v.O. Quine, especially *Word and Object* (1960, M.I.T. Press). Much of Quine's philosophical writings, especially on observation sentences, reads like a literal translation from Lojban.

The theory of negation expounded in Chapter 15 (p. 353) is derived from a reading of Laurence Horn's work *A Natural History of Negation*.

Of course, neither Brown nor Quine nor Horn is in any way responsible for the uses or misuses I have made of their works.

Depending on just when you are reading this book, there may be three other books about Lojban available: a textbook, a Lojban/English dictionary, and a book containing general information about Lojban. You can probably get these books, if they have been published, from the same place where you got this book. In addition, other books not yet foreseen may also exist.

1.7 Captions to Pictures

The following examples list the Lojban caption, with a translation, for the picture at the head of each chapter. If a chapter's picture has no caption, "(none)" is specified instead.

Chapter 1	*coi .lojban.*
	Greetings, O Lojban!
	coi rodo
	Greetings, all-of you
Chapter 2	(none)
Chapter 3	*.i .ai .i .ai .o*
	[untranslatable]
Chapter 4	*jbobliku*
	Lojbanic-blocks
Chapter 5	(none)

Chapter 6	*lei*		*re*	*nanmu*	*cu*	*bevri*	*le*	*re*	*nanmu*
	The-mass-of		**two**	**men**		**carry**	**the**	**two**	**men**

Two men (jointly) carry two men (both of them).

Chapter 7	*ma*		*drani*		*danfu*
	[What-sumti]		**is-the-correct**		**type-of-answer?**

	.i	*di'e*
		The-next-sentence.

	.i	*di'u*		*.i*	*dei*
		The-previous-sentence.			**This-sentence.**

	.i	*ri*		*.i*	*do'i*
		The-previous-sentence.			**An-unspecified-utterance.**

Chapter 8	*ko*	*viska*	*re*	*prenu*	*poi*	*bruna*	*la*	*santas.*
	[You!]	**see**	**two**	**persons**	**who-are**	**brothers-of**	**Santa.**	

Chapter 9	(none)

Chapter 10	*za'o*	*klama*
	[superfective]	**come/go**

Something goes (or comes) for too long.

Chapter 11	*le*	*si'o*	*kunti*
	The	**concept-of**	**emptiness**

Chapter 12	(none)

Chapter 13	*.oi*	*ro'i*	*ro'a*	*ro'o*
	[Pain!]	**[emotional]**	**[social]**	**[physical]**

Chapter 14	(none)

Chapter 15	*mi*	*na'e*		*lumci*	*le*	*karce*
	I	**other-than**		**wash**	**the**	**car**

I didn't wash the car.

Chapter 16	*drata*	*mupli*	*pe'u*	*.djan.*
	another	**example**	**[please]**	**John**

Another example, John, please!

Chapter 17	*zai*	*xanlerfu*	*by.*	*ly.*	*.obu*	*jy*	*by.*	*.abu*	*ny.*
	[Shift]	**hand-letters**	**l**	**o**	**j**		**b**	**a**	**n**

"Lojban" in a manual alphabet

Chapter 18	*no*	*no*
	0	**0**

Chapter 19	(none)
Chapter 20	(none)
Chapter 21	(none)

1.8 Boring Legalities

For information, contact: The Logical Language Group, 2904 Beau Lane, Fairfax VA 22031-1303 USA. Telephone: 703-385-0273. Email address: llg-board@lojban.org. Web Address: http://www.lojban.org.

Chapter 2
A Quick Tour of Lojban Grammar, With Diagrams

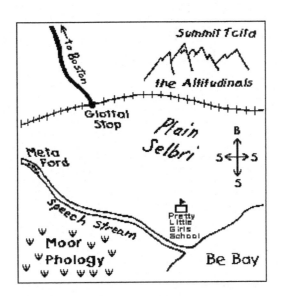

2.1 The concept of the bridi

This chapter gives diagrammed examples of basic Lojban sentence structures. The most general pattern is covered first, followed by successive variations on the basic components of the Lojban sentence. There are many more capabilities not covered in this chapter, but covered in detail in later chapters, so this chapter is a "quick tour" of the material later covered more slowly throughout the book. It also introduces most of the Lojban words used to discuss Lojban grammar.

Let us consider John and Sam and three statements about them:

Example 2.1
> John is the father of Sam.

Example 2.2
> John hits Sam.

Example 2.3
> John is taller than Sam.

These examples all describe relationships between John and Sam. However, in English, we use the noun "father" to describe a static relationship in Example 2.1 (p. 15), the verb "hits" to describe an active relationship in Example 2.2 (p. 15), and the adjective "taller" to describe an attributive relationship in Example 2.3 (p. 15). In Lojban we make no such grammatical distinctions; these three sentences, when expressed in Lojban, are structurally identical. The same part of speech is used to represent the relationship. In formal logic this whole structure is called a "predication"; in Lojban it is called a *bridi*, and the central part of speech is the *selbri*. Logicians refer to the things thus related as "arguments", while Lojbanists call them *sumti*. These Lojban terms will be used for the rest of the book.

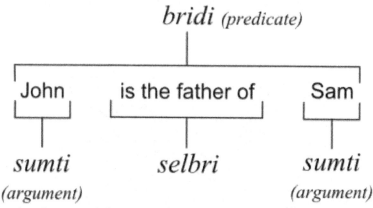

In a relationship, there are a definite number of things being related. In English, for example, "give" has three places: the donor, the recipient and the gift. For example:

Example 2.4

    John gives Sam the book.

and

Example 2.5

    Sam gives John the book.

mean two different things because the relative positions of "John" and "Sam" have been switched. Further,

Example 2.6

    The book gives John Sam.

seems strange to us merely because the places are being filled by unorthodox arguments. The relationship expressed by "give" has not changed.

In Lojban, each selbri has a specified number and type of arguments, known collectively as its "place structure". The simplest kind of selbri consists of a single root word, called a *gismu*, and the definition in a dictionary gives the place structure explicitly. The primary task of constructing a Lojban sentence, after choosing the relationship itself, is deciding what you will use to fill in the sumti places.

This book uses the Lojban terms *bridi*, *sumti*, and *selbri*, because it is best to come to understand them independently of the English associations of the corresponding words, which are only roughly similar in meaning anyhow.

The Lojban examples in this chapter (but not in the rest of the book) use boldface (as well as the usual italics) for selbri, to help you to tell them apart.

2.2 Pronunciation

Detailed pronunciation and spelling rules are given in Chapter 3 (p. 33), but what follows will keep the reader from going too far astray while digesting this chapter.

Lojban has six recognized vowels: *a, e, i, o, u* and *y*. The first five are roughly pronounced as "a" as in "father", *e* as in "let", *i* as in "machine", *o* as in "dome" and *u* as in "flute". *y* is pronounced as the sound called "schwa", that is, as the unstressed "a" as in "about" or "around".

Twelve consonants in Lojban are pronounced more or less as their counterparts are in English: *b, d, f, k, l, m, n, p, r, t, v* and *z*. The letter *c*, on the other hand is pronounced as the "sh" in "hush", while *j* is its voiced counterpart, the sound of the "s" in "pleasure". *g* is always pronounced as it is in "gift", never as in "giant". *s* is as in "sell", never as in "rose". The sound of *x* is not found in English in normal words. It is found as "ch" in Scottish "loch", as "j" in Spanish "junta", and as „ch" in German „Bach"; it also appears in the English interjection "yecchh!". It gets easier to say as you practice it. The letter *r* can be trilled, but doesn't have to be.

The Lojban diphthongs *ai*, *ei*, *oi*, and *au* are pronounced much as in the English words "sigh", "say", "boy", and "how". Other Lojban diphthongs begin with an *i* pronounced like English "y" (for example, *io* is pronounced "yo") or else with a *u* pronounced like English "w" (for example, *ua* is pronounced "wa").

Lojban also has three "semi-letters": the period, the comma and the apostrophe. The period represents a glottal stop or a pause; it is a required stoppage of the flow of air in the speech stream. The apostrophe sounds just like the English letter "h". Unlike a regular consonant, it is not found at the beginning or end of a word, nor is it found adjacent to a consonant; it is only found between two vowels. The comma has no sound associated with it, and is used to separate syllables that might ordinarily run together. It is not used in this chapter.

Stress falls on the next to the last syllable of all words, unless that vowel is *y*, which is never stressed; in such words the third-to-last syllable is stressed. If a word only has one syllable, then that syllable is not stressed.

All Lojban words are pronounced as they are spelled: there are no silent letters.

2.3 Words that can act as sumti

Here is a short table of single words used as sumti. This table provides examples only, not the entire set of such words, which may be found in Section 7.16 (p. 157).

mi	I/me, we/us
do	you
ti	this, these
ta	that, those
tu	that far away, those far away
zo'e	unspecified value (used when a sumti is unimportant or obvious)

Lojban sumti are not specific as to number (singular or plural), nor gender (masculine/feminine/neutral). Such distinctions can be optionally added by methods that are beyond the scope of this chapter.

The cmavo *ti*, *ta*, and *tu* refer to whatever the speaker is pointing at, and should not be used to refer to things that cannot in principle be pointed at.

Names may also be used as sumti, provided they are preceded with the word *la*:

la meris.	the one/ones named Mary
la djan.	the one/ones named John

Other Lojban spelling versions are possible for names from other languages, and there are restrictions on which letters may appear in Lojban names: see Section 6.12 (p. 132) for more information.

2.4 Some words used to indicate selbri relations

Here is a short table of some words used as Lojban selbri in this chapter:

vecnu	x1 (seller) sells x2 (goods) to x3 (buyer) for x4 (price)
tavla	x1 (talker) talks to x2 (audience) about x3 (topic) in language x4
sutra	x1 (agent) is fast at doing x2 (action)
blari'o	x1 (object/light source) is blue-green
melbi	x1 (object/idea) is beautiful to x2 (observer) by standard x3
cutci	x1 is a shoe/boot for x2 (foot) made of x3 (material)
bajra	x1 runs on x2 (surface) using x3 (limbs) in manner x4 (gait)
klama	x1 goes/comes to x2 (destination) from x3 (origin point) via x4 (route) using x5 (means of transportation)

pluka	x1 pleases/is pleasing to x2 (experiencer) under conditions x3
gerku	x1 is a dog of breed x2
kurji	x1 takes care of x2
kanro	x1 is healthy by standard x2
stali	x1 stays/remains with x2
zarci	x1 is a market/store/shop selling x2 (products) operated by x3 (storekeeper)

Each selbri (relation) has a specific rule that defines the role of each sumti in the bridi, based on its position. In the table above, that order was expressed by labeling the sumti positions as x1, x2, x3, x4, and x5.

Like the table in Section 2.3 (p. 17), this table is far from complete: in fact, no complete table can exist, because Lojban allows new words to be created (in specified ways) whenever a speaker or writer finds the existing supply of words inadequate. This notion is a basic difference between Lojban (and some other languages such as German and Chinese) and English; in English, most people are very leery of using words that "aren't in the dictionary". Lojbanists are encouraged to invent new words; doing so is a major way of participating in the development of the language. Chapter 4 (p. 49) explains how to make new words, and Chapter 12 (p. 263) explains how to give them appropriate meanings.

2.5 Some simple Lojban bridi

Let's look at a simple Lojban bridi. The place structure of the gismu *tavla* is

Example 2.7

> x1 talks to x2 about x3 in language x4

where the "x" es with following numbers represent the various arguments that could be inserted at the given positions in the English sentence. For example:

Example 2.8

> John talks to Sam about engineering in Lojban.

has "John" in the x1 place, "Sam" in the x2 place, "engineering" in the x3 place, and "Lojban" in the x4 place, and could be paraphrased:

Example 2.9

> Talking is going on, with speaker John and listener Sam and subject matter engineering and language Lojban.

The Lojban bridi corresponding to Example 2.7 (p. 18) will have the form

Example 2.10

> *x1* [*cu*] *tavla* *x2* *x3* *x4*

The word *cu* serves as a separator between any preceding sumti and the selbri. It can often be omitted, as in the following examples.

Example 2.11

> *mi* *tavla* *do* *zo'e* *zo'e*

> I talk to you about something in some language.

Example 2.12

> *do* *tavla* *mi* *ta* *zo'e*

> You talk to me about that thing in a language.

Example 2.13

> *mi* *tavla* *zo'e* *tu* *ti*

> I talk to someone about that thing yonder in this language.

(Example 2.13 (p. 18) is a bit unusual, as there is no easy way to point to a language; one might point to a copy of this book, and hope the meaning gets across!)

When there are one or more occurrences of the cmavo *zo'e* at the end of a bridi, they may be omitted, a process called "ellipsis". Example 2.11 (p. 18) and Example 2.12 (p. 18) may be expressed thus:

Example 2.14

mi	*tavla*	*do*

I talk to you (about something in some language).

Example 2.15

do	*tavla*	*mi*	*ta*

You talk to me about that thing (in some language).

Note that Example 2.13 (p. 18) is not subject to ellipsis by this direct method, as the *zo'e* in it is not at the end of the bridi.

2.6 Variant bridi structure

Consider the sentence

Example 2.16

mi	[cu]	*vecnu*	*ti*	*ta*	*zo'e*
seller-x1	-	**sells**	**goods-sold-x2**	**buyer-x3**	**price-x4**
I	-	**sell**	**this**	**to that**	**for some price.**

I sell this-thing/these-things to that-buyer/those-buyers.
(the price is obvious or unimportant)

Example 2.16 (p. 19) has one sumti (the x1) before the selbri. It is also possible to put more than one sumti before the selbri, without changing the order of sumti:

Example 2.17

mi	*ti*	[cu]	*vecnu*	*ta*
seller-x1	**goods-sold-x2**	-	**sells**	**buyer-x3**
I	**this**	-	**sell**	**to that.**

(translates as stilted or poetic English)
I this thing do sell to that buyer.

Example 2.18

mi	*ti*	*ta*	[cu]	*vecnu*
seller-x1	**goods-sold-x2**	**buyer-x3**	-	**sells**
I	**this**	**to that**	-	**sell**

(translates as stilted or poetic English)
I this thing to that buyer do sell.

Example 2.16 (p. 19) through Example 2.18 (p. 19) mean the same thing. Usually, placing more than one sumti before the selbri is done for style or for emphasis on the sumti that are out-of-place from their normal position. (Native speakers of languages other than English may prefer such orders.)

If there are no sumti before the selbri, then it is understood that the x1 sumti value is equivalent to *zo'e*; i.e. unimportant or obvious, and therefore not given. Any sumti after the selbri start counting from x2.

Example 2.19

ta	[cu]	*melbi*	
object/idea-x1	-	**is-beautiful**	**(to someone by some standard)**
That/Those	-	**is/are beautiful.**	

That is beautiful.
Those are beautiful.

when the x1 is omitted, becomes:

Example 2.20

	melbi	
unspecified-x1	is-beautiful	to someone by some standard

Beautiful!

It's beautiful!

Omitting the x1 adds emphasis to the selbri relation, which has become first in the sentence. This kind of sentence is termed an observative, because it is often used when someone first observes or takes note of the relationship, and wishes to quickly communicate it to someone else. Commonly understood English observatives include "Smoke!" upon seeing smoke or smelling the odor, or "Car!" to a person crossing the street who might be in danger. Any Lojban selbri can be used as an observative if no sumti appear before the selbri.

The word *cu* does not occur in an observative; *cu* is a separator, and there must be a sumti before the selbri that needs to be kept separate for *cu* to be used. With no sumti preceding the selbri, *cu* is not permitted. Short words like *cu* which serve grammatical functions are called *cmavo* in Lojban.

2.7 Varying the order of sumti

For one reason or another you may want to change the order, placing one particular sumti at the front of the bridi. The cmavo *se*, when placed before the last word of the selbri, will switch the meanings of the first and second sumti places. So

Example 2.21

mi	*tavla*	*do*	*ti*

I talk to you about this.

has the same meaning as

Example 2.22

do	*se tavla*	*mi*	*ti*

You are talked to by me about this.

The cmavo *te*, when used in the same location, switches the meanings of the first and the third sumti places.

Example 2.23

mi	*tavla*	*do*	*ti*

I talk to you about this.

has the same meaning as

Example 2.24

ti	*te tavla*	*do*	*mi*

This is talked about to you by me.

Note that only the first and third sumti have switched places; the second sumti has remained in the second place.

The cmavo *ve* and *xe* switch the first and fourth sumti places, and the first and fifth sumti places, respectively. These changes in the order of places are known as "conversions", and the *se*, *te*, *ve*, and *xe* cmavo are said to convert the selbri.

More than one of these operators may be used on a given selbri at one time, and in such a case they are evaluated from left to right. However, in practice they are used one at a time, as there are better tools for complex manipulation of the sumti places. See Section 9.4 (p. 185) for details.

The effect is similar to what in English is called the "passive voice". In Lojban, the converted selbri has a new place structure that is renumbered to reflect the place reversal, thus having effects when such a conversion is used in combination with other constructs such as *le selbri [ku]* (see Section 2.10 (p. 23)).

2.8 The basic structure of longer utterances

People don't always say just one sentence. Lojban has a specific structure for talk or writing that is longer than one sentence. The entirety of a given speech event or written text is called an utterance. The sentences (usually, but not always, bridi) in an utterance are separated by the cmavo *ni'o* and *i.* These correspond to a brief pause (or nothing at all) in spoken English, and the various punctuation marks like period, question mark, and exclamation mark in written English. These separators prevent the sumti at the beginning of the next sentence from being mistaken for a trailing sumti of the previous sentence.

The cmavo *ni'o* separates paragraphs (covering different topics of discussion). In a long text or utterance, the topical structure of the text may be indicated by multiple *ni'o* s, with perhaps *ni'oni'oni'o* used to indicate a chapter, *ni'oni'o* to indicate a section, and a single *ni'o* to indicate a subtopic corresponding to a single English paragraph.

The cmavo *i* separates sentences. It is sometimes compounded with words that modify the exact meaning (the semantics) of the sentence in the context of the utterance. (The cmavo *xu*, discussed in Section 2.15 (p. 26), is one such word – it turns the sentence from a statement to a question about truth.) When more than one person is talking, a new speaker will usually omit the *i* even though she/he may be continuing on the same topic.

It is still O.K. for a new speaker to say the *i* before continuing; indeed, it is encouraged for maximum clarity (since it is possible that the second speaker might merely be adding words onto the end of the first speaker's sentence). A good translation for *i* is the "and" used in run-on sentences when people are talking informally: "I did this, and then I did that, and ..., and ...".

2.9 tanru

When two gismu are adjacent, the first one modifies the second, and the selbri takes its place structure from the rightmost word. Such combinations of gismu are called *tanru*. For example,

Example 2.25

    sutra tavla

has the place structure

Example 2.26

    x1 is a fast type-of talker to x2 about x3 in language x4
    x1 talks fast to x2 about x3 in language x4

When three or more gismu are in a row, the first modifies the second, and that combined meaning modifies the third, and that combined meaning modifies the fourth, and so on. For example

Example 2.27

    sutra tavla cutci

has the place structure

Example 2.28

    s1 is a fast-talker type of shoe worn by s2 of material s3

That is, it is a shoe that is worn by a fast talker rather than a shoe that is fast and is also worn by a talker.

Note especially the use of "type-of" as a mechanism for connecting the English translations of the two or more gismu; this convention helps the learner understand each tanru in its context. Creative interpretations are also possible, however:

Example 2.29

bajra	*cutci*
runner	**shoe**

most probably refers to shoes suitable for runners, but might be interpreted in some imaginative instances as "shoes that run (by themselves?)". In general, however, the meaning of a tanru is determined by the literal meaning of its components, and not by any connotations or figurative meanings. Thus

Example 2.30

sutra	tavla
fast	**talker**

would not necessarily imply any trickery or deception, unlike the English idiom, and a

Example 2.31

jikca	toldi
social	**butterfly**

must always be an insect with large brightly-colored wings, of the family *Lepidoptera*.

The place structure of a tanru is always that of the final component of the tanru. Thus, the following has the place structure of *klama*:

Example 2.32

mi	[cu]	sutra klama	la meris.
I	**-**	**quickly-go**	**to Mary.**

With the conversion *se klama* as the final component of the tanru, the place structure of the entire selbri is that of *se klama*: the x1 place is the destination, and the x2 place is the one who goes:

Example 2.33

mi	[cu]	sutra	se klama	la meris.
I	**-**	**quickly**	**am-gone-to**	**by Mary.**

The following example shows that there is more to conversion than merely switching places, though:

Example 2.34

la tam.	[cu]	melbi tavla	la meris.
Tom	**-**	**beautifully-talks**	**to Mary.**
Tom	**-**	**is a beautiful-talker**	**to Mary.**

has the place structure of *tavla*, but note the two distinct interpretations.

Now, using conversion, we can modify the place structure order:

Example 2.35

la meris.	[cu]	melbi se tavla	la tam.
Mary	**-**	**is beautifully-talked-to**	**by Tom.**
Mary	**-**	**is a beautiful-audience**	**for Tom.**

and we see that the modification has been changed so as to focus on Mary's role in the bridi relationship, leading to a different set of possible interpretations.

Note that there is no place structure change if the modifying term is converted, and so less drastic variation in possible meanings:

Example 2.36

la tam.	[cu]	tavla melbi	la meris.
Tom	**-**	**is talkerly-beautiful**	**to Mary.**

Example 2.37

la tam.	[cu]	se tavla melbi	la meris.
Tom	**-**	**is audiencely-beautiful**	**to Mary.**

and we see that the manner in which Tom is seen as beautiful by Mary changes, but Tom is still the one perceived as beautiful, and Mary, the observer of beauty.

2.10 Description sumti

Often we wish to talk about things other than the speaker, the listener and things we can point to. Let's say I want to talk about a talker other than *mi*. What I want to talk about would naturally fit into the first place of *tavla*. Lojban, it turns out, has an operator that pulls this first place out of a selbri and converts it to a sumti called a "description sumti". The description sumti *le tavla ku* means "the talker", and may be used wherever any sumti may be used.

For example,

Example 2.38

mi	tavla	do	le tavla	[ku]

means the same as

Example 2.39

    I talk to you about the talker

where "the talker" is presumably someone other than me, though not necessarily.

Similarly *le sutra tavla ku* is "the fast talker", and *le sutra te tavla ku* is "the fast subject of talk" or "the subject of fast talk". Which of these related meanings is understood will depend on the context in which the expression is used. The most plausible interpretation within the context will generally be assumed by a listener to be the intended one.

In many cases the word *ku* may be omitted. In particular, it is never necessary in a description at the end of a sentence, so:

Example 2.40

mi	tavla	do	le tavla
I	talk-to	you	about-the talker

means exactly the same thing as Example 2.38 (p. 23).

There is a problem when we want to say "The fast one is talking." The "obvious" translation *le sutra tavla* turns out to mean "the fast talker", and has no selbri at all. To solve this problem we can use the word *cu*, which so far has always been optional, in front of the selbri.

The word *cu* has no meaning, and exists only to mark the beginning of the selbri within the bridi, separating it from a previous sumti. It comes before any other part of the selbri, including other cmavo like *se* or *te*. Thus:

Example 2.41

    le sutra tavla
    The fast talker

Example 2.42

le sutra	cu	tavla
The fast one	-	is talking.

Example 2.43

    le sutra se tavla
    The fast talked-to one

Example 2.44

le sutra	cu	se tavla
The fast one	-	is talked to.

Consider the following more complex example, with two description sumti.

Example 2.45

mi	[cu]	tavla	le vecnu	[ku]	le blari'o	[ku]
I	-	talk-to	the seller	-	about the blue-green-thing.	-

The sumti *le vecnu* contains the selbri *vecnu*, which has the "seller" in the x1 place, and uses it in this sentence to describe a particular "seller" that the speaker has in mind (one that he or she probably expects the listener will also know about). Similarly, the speaker has a particular blue-green thing in mind, which is described using *le* to mark *blari'o*, a selbri whose first sumti is something blue-green.

It is safe to omit both occurrences of *ku* in Example 2.45 (p. 23), and it is also safe to omit the *cu*.

2.11 Examples of brivla

The simplest form of selbri is an individual word. A word which may by itself express a selbri relation is called a *brivla*. The three types of brivla are gismu (root words), lujvo (compounds), and fu'ivla (borrowings from other languages). All have identical grammatical uses. So far, most of our selbri have been gismu or tanru built from gismu.

gismu:

Example 2.46

mi	*[cu]*	*klama*	*ti*	*zo'e*	*zo'e*	*ta*
Go-er	-	goes	destination	origin	route	means.

I go here (to this) using that means (from somewhere via some route).

lujvo:

Example 2.47

ta	*[cu]*	*blari'o*
That	-	is-blue-green.

fu'ivla:

Example 2.48

ti	*[cu]*	*djarspageti*
This	-	is-spaghetti.

Some cmavo may also serve as selbri, acting as variables that stand for another selbri. The most commonly used of these is *go'i*, which represents the main bridi of the previous Lojban sentence, with any new sumti or other sentence features being expressed replacing the previously expressed ones. Thus, in this context:

Example 2.49

ta	*[cu]*	*go'i*
That	-	too/same-as-last selbri.

That (is spaghetti), too.

2.12 The sumti *di'u* and *la'e di'u*

In English, I might say "The dog is beautiful", and you might reply "This pleases me." How do you know what "this" refers to? Lojban uses different expressions to convey the possible meanings of the English:

Example 2.50

le gerku	*[ku]*	*cu*	*melbi*

The dog is beautiful.

The following three sentences all might translate as "This pleases me."

Example 2.51

ti	*[cu]*	*pluka*	*mi*

This (the dog) pleases me.

Example 2.52

di'u	*[cu]*	*pluka*	*mi*

This (the last sentence) pleases me (perhaps because it is grammatical or sounds nice).

Example 2.53

> *la'e di'u* | *[cu]* | *pluka* | *mi*

> This (the meaning of the last sentence; i.e. that the dog is beautiful) pleases me.

Example 2.53 (p. 25) uses one sumti to point to or refer to another by inference. It is common to write *la'edi'u* as a single word; it is used more often than *di'u* by itself.

2.13 Possession

"Possession" refers to the concept of specifying an object by saying who it belongs to (or with). A full explanation of Lojban possession is given in Chapter 8 (p. 161). A simple means of expressing possession, however, is to place a sumti representing the possessor of an object within the description sumti that refers to the object: specifically, between the *le* and the selbri of the description:

Example 2.54

> *le mi gerku* | *cu* | *sutra*
> **The of-me dog** | - | **is fast.**

> My dog is fast.

In Lojban, possession doesn't necessarily mean ownership: one may "possess" a chair simply by sitting on it, even though it actually belongs to someone else. English uses possession casually in the same way, but also uses it to refer to actual ownership or even more intimate relationships: "my arm" doesn't mean "some arm I own" but rather "the arm that is part of my body". Lojban has methods of specifying all these different kinds of possession precisely and easily.

2.14 Vocatives and commands

You may call someone's attention to the fact that you are addressing them by using *doi* followed by their name. The sentence

Example 2.55

> *doi djan.*

means "Oh, John, I'm talking to you". It also has the effect of setting the value of *do*; *do* now refers to "John" until it is changed in some way in the conversation. Note that Example 2.55 (p. 25) is not a bridi, but it is a legitimate Lojban sentence nevertheless; it is known as a "vocative phrase".

Other cmavo can be used instead of *doi* in a vocative phrase, with a different significance. For example, the cmavo *coi* means "hello" and *co'o* means "good-bye". Either word may stand alone, they may follow one another, or either may be followed by a pause and a name. (Vocative phrases with *doi* do not need a pause before the name.)

Example 2.56

> *coi.* | *djan.*
> **Hello,** | **John.**

Example 2.57

> *co'o.* | *djan.*
> **Good-bye,** | **John.**

Commands are expressed in Lojban by a simple variation of the main bridi structure. If you say

Example 2.58

> *do* | *tavla*
> **You** | **are-talking.**

you are simply making a statement of fact. In order to issue a command in Lojban, substitute the word *ko* for *do*. The bridi

Example 2.59

> *ko* | *tavla*

instructs the listener to do whatever is necessary to make Example 2.58 (p. 25) true; it means "Talk!" Other examples:

Example 2.60

> *ko* ⋮ *sutra*

> Be fast!

The *ko* need not be in the x1 place, but rather can occur anywhere a sumti is allowed, leading to possible Lojban commands that are very unlike English commands:

Example 2.61

> *mi* ⋮ *tavla* ⋮ *ko*

> Be talked to by me.
> Let me talk to you.

The cmavo *ko* can fill any appropriate sumti place, and can be used as often as is appropriate for the selbri:

Example 2.62

> *ko* ⋮ *kurji* ⋮ *ko*

and

Example 2.63

> *ko* ⋮ *ko* ⋮ *kurji*

both mean "You take care of you" and "Be taken care of by you", or to put it colloquially, "Take care of yourself".

2.15 Questions

There are many kinds of questions in Lojban: full explanations appear in Section 19.5 (p. 451) and in various other chapters throughout the book. In this chapter, we will introduce three kinds: sumti questions, selbri questions, and yes/no questions.

The cmavo *ma* is used to create a sumti question: it indicates that the speaker wishes to know the sumti which should be placed at the location of the *ma* to make the bridi true. It can be translated as "Who?" or "What?" in most cases, but also serves for "When?", "Where?", and "Why?" when used in sumti places that express time, location, or cause. For example:

Example 2.64

ma	*tavla*	*do*	*mi*
Who?	**talks**	**to-you**	**about-me.**

> Who is talking to you about me?

The listener can reply by simply stating a sumti:

Example 2.65

> *la djan.*

> John (is talking to you about me).

Like *ko*, *ma* can occur in any position where a sumti is allowed, not just in the first position:

Example 2.66

do	*[cu]*	*tavla*	*ma*
You	**-**	**talk**	**to what/whom?**

A *ma* can also appear in multiple sumti positions in one sentence, in effect asking several questions at once.

Example 2.67

ma	[cu]	tavla	ma
What/Who	**-**	**talks**	**to what/whom?**

The two separate *ma* positions ask two separate questions, and can therefore be answered with different values in each sumti place.

The cmavo *mo* is the selbri analogue of *ma*. It asks the respondent to provide a selbri that would be a true relation if inserted in place of the *mo*:

Example 2.68

do	[cu]	mo
You	**-**	**are-what/do-what?**

A *mo* may be used anywhere a brivla or other selbri might. Keep this in mind for later examples. Unfortunately, by itself, *mo* is a very non-specific question. The response to the question in Example 2.68 (p. 27) could be:

Example 2.69

> *mi* [cu] *melbi*
>
> I am beautiful.

or:

Example 2.70

> *mi* [cu] *tavla*
>
> I talk.

Clearly, *mo* requires some cooperation between the speaker and the respondent to ensure that the right question is being answered. If context doesn't make the question specific enough, the speaker must ask the question more specifically using a more complex construction such as a tanru (see Section 2.9 (p. 21)).

It is perfectly permissible for the respondent to fill in other unspecified places in responding to a *mo* question. Thus, the respondent in Example 2.70 (p. 27) could have also specified an audience, a topic, and/or a language in the response.

Finally, we must consider questions that can be answered "Yes" or "No", such as

Example 2.71

> Are you talking to me?

Like all yes-or-no questions in English, Example 2.71 (p. 27) may be reformulated as

Example 2.72

> Is it true that you are talking to me?

In Lojban we have a word that asks precisely that question in precisely the same way. The cmavo *xu*, when placed in front of a bridi, asks whether that bridi is true as stated. So

Example 2.73

xu	do	tavla	mi
Is-it-true-that	**you**	**are-talking**	**to-me?**

is the Lojban translation of Example 2.71 (p. 27).

The answer "Yes" may be given by simply restating the bridi without the *xu* question word. Lojban has a shorthand for doing this with the word *go'i*, mentioned in Section 2.11 (p. 24). Instead of a negative answer, the bridi may be restated in such a way as to make it true. If this can be done by substituting sumti, it may be done with *go'i* as well. For example:

Example 2.74

> *xu* *do* *kanro*
>
> Are you healthy?

can be answered with

Example 2.75

> *mi* | *kanro*

I am healthy.

or

Example 2.76

> *go'i*

I am healthy.

(Note that *do* to the questioner is *mi* to the respondent.)

or

Example 2.77

> *le tavla* | *cu* | *kanro*

The talker is healthy.

or

Example 2.78

> *le tavla* | *cu* | *go'i*

The talker is healthy.

A general negative answer may be given by *na go'i*. *na* may be placed before any selbri (but after the *cu*). It is equivalent to stating "It is not true that ..." before the bridi. It does not imply that anything else is true or untrue, only that that specific bridi is not true. More details on negative statements are available in Chapter 15 (p. 353).

2.16 Indicators

Different cultures express emotions and attitudes with a variety of intonations and gestures that are not usually included in written language. Some of these are available in some languages as interjections (i.e. "Aha!", "Oh no!", "Ouch!", "Aahh!", etc.), but they vary greatly from culture to culture.

Lojban has a group of cmavo known as "attitudinal indicators" which specifically covers this type of commentary on spoken statements. They are both written and spoken, but require no specific intonation or gestures. Grammatically they are very simple: one or more attitudinals at the beginning of a bridi apply to the entire bridi; anywhere else in the bridi they apply to the word immediately to the left. For example:

Example 2.79

> *.ie* | *mi* | *[cu]* | *klama*
>
> **Agreement!** | **I** | **-** | **go.**

Yep! I'll go.

Example 2.80

> *.ei* | *mi* | *[cu]* | *klama*
>
> **Obligation!** | **I** | **-** | **go.**

I should go.

Example 2.81

> *mi* | *[cu]* | *klama* | *le melbi*
>
> **I** | **-** | **go** | **to-the beautiful-thing**
>
> *.ui* | *[ku]*
>
> **and I am happy because it is the beautiful thing I'm going to** | **-**

Not all indicators indicate attitudes. Discursives, another group of cmavo with the same grammatical rules as attitudinal indicators, allow free expression of certain kinds of commentary about the main utterances. Using discursives allows a clear separation of these so-called "metalinguistic" features from the underlying statements and logical structure. By comparison, the English words "but" and "also", which discursively indicate contrast or an added weight of example, are logically equivalent to "and", which does not have a discursive content. The average English-speaker does not think about, and may not even realize, the paradoxical idea that "but" basically means "and".

Example 2.82

mi	[cu]	klama	.i	do	[cu]	stali
I	-	go.		You	-	stay.

Example 2.83

mi	[cu]	klama	.i	ji'a	do	[cu]	stali	
I	-	go.		In addition,	you	-	stay.	added weight

Example 2.84

mi	[cu]	klama	.i	ku'i	do	[cu]	stali	
I	-	go.		However,	you	-	stay.	contrast

Another group of indicators are called "evidentials". Evidentials show the speaker's relationship to the statement, specifically how the speaker came to make the statement. These include *za'a* (I directly observe the relationship), *pe'i* (I believe that the relationship holds), *ru'a* (I postulate the relationship), and others. Many American Indian languages use this kind of words.

Example 2.85

pe'i	do	[cu]	melbi
I opine!	You	-	are beautiful.

Example 2.86

za'a	do	[cu]	melbi
I directly observe!	You	-	are beautiful.

2.17 Tenses

In English, every verb is tagged for the grammatical category called tense: past, present, or future. The sentence

Example 2.87

John went to the store

necessarily happens at some time in the past, whereas

Example 2.88

John is going to the store

is necessarily happening right now.

The Lojban sentence

Example 2.89

la djan.	[cu]	klama	le zarci
John	-	goes/went/will-go	to-the store

serves as a translation of either Example 2.87 (p. 29) or Example 2.88 (p. 29), and of many other possible English sentences as well. It is not marked for tense, and can refer to an event in the past, the present or the future. This rule does not mean that Lojban has no way of representing the time of an event. A close translation of Example 2.87 (p. 29) would be:

Example 2.90

la djan.	pu	klama	le zarci
John	[past]	goes	to-the store

where the tag *pu* forces the sentence to refer to a time in the past. Similarly,

Example 2.91

la djan.	ca	klama	le zarci
John	**[present]**	**goes**	**to-the store**

necessarily refers to the present, because of the tag *ca*. Tags used in this way always appear at the very beginning of the selbri, just after the *cu*, and they may make a *cu* unnecessary, since tags cannot be absorbed into tanru. Such tags serve as an equivalent to English tenses and adverbs. In Lojban, tense information is completely optional. If unspecified, the appropriate tense is picked up from context.

Lojban also extends the notion of "tense" to refer not only to time but to space. The following example uses the tag *vu* to specify that the event it describes happens far away from the speaker:

Example 2.92

do	vu vecnu	zo'e
You	**yonder sell**	**something-unspecified.**

In addition, tense tags (either for time or space) can be prefixed to the selbri of a description, producing a tensed sumti:

Example 2.93

le pu bajra	[ku]	cu	tavla
The earlier/former/past runner	**-**	**-**	**talked/talks.**

(Since Lojban tense is optional, we don't know when he or she talks.)

Tensed sumti with space tags correspond roughly to the English use of "this" or "that" as adjectives, as in the following example, which uses the tag *vi* meaning "nearby":

Example 2.94

le vi bajra	[ku]	cu	tavla
The nearby runner	**-**	**-**	**talks.**

This runner talks.

Do not confuse the use of *vi* in Example 2.94 (p. 30) with the cmavo *ti*, which also means "this", but in the sense of "this thing".

Furthermore, a tense tag can appear both on the selbri and within a description, as in the following example (where *ba* is the tag for future time):

Example 2.95

le vi tavla	[ku]	cu	ba klama
The here talker	**-**	**-**	**[future] goes.**

The talker who is here will go.
This talker will go.

2.18 Lojban grammatical terms

Here is a review of the Lojban grammatical terms used in this chapter, plus some others used throughout this book. Only terms that are themselves Lojban words are included: there are of course many expressions like "indicator" in Chapter 16 (p. 375) that are not explained here. See the Index for further help with these.

bridi	predication; the basic unit of Lojban expression; the main kind of Lojban sentence; a claim that some objects stand in some relationship, or that some single object has some property.
sumti	argument; words identifying something which stands in a specified relationship to something else, or which has a specified property. See Chapter 6 (p. 115).
selbri	logical predicate; the core of a bridi; the word or words specifying the relationship between the objects referred to by the sumti. See Chapter 5 (p. 79).

cmavo	one of the Lojban parts of speech; a short word; a structural word; a word used for its grammatical function.
brivla	one of the Lojban parts of speech; a content word; a predicate word; can function as a selbri; is a gismu, a lujvo, or a fu'ivla. See Chapter 4 (p. 49).
gismu	a root word; a kind of brivla; has associated rafsi. See Chapter 4 (p. 49).
lujvo	a compound word; a kind of brivla; may or may not appear in a dictionary; does not have associated rafsi. See Chapter 4 (p. 49) and Chapter 12 (p. 263).
fu'ivla	a borrowed word; a kind of brivla; may or may not appear in a dictionary; copied in a modified form from some non-Lojban language; usually refers to some aspect of culture or the natural world; does not have associated rafsi. See Chapter 4 (p. 49).
rafsi	a word fragment; one or more is associated with each gismu; can be assembled according to rules in order to make lujvo; not a valid word by itself. See Chapter 4 (p. 49).
tanru	a group of two or more brivla, possibly with associated cmavo, that form a selbri; always divisible into two parts, with the first part modifying the meaning of the second part (which is taken to be basic). See Chapter 5 (p. 79).
selma'o	a group of cmavo that have the same grammatical use (can appear interchangeably in sentences, as far as the grammar is concerned) but differ in meaning or other usage. See Chapter 20 (p. 467).

Chapter 3
The Hills Are Alive With The Sounds Of Lojban

.i .ai .i .ai .o

3.1 Orthography

Lojban is designed so that any properly spoken Lojban utterance can be uniquely transcribed in writing, and any properly written Lojban can be spoken so as to be uniquely reproduced by another person. As a consequence, the standard Lojban orthography must assign to each distinct sound, or phoneme, a unique letter or symbol. Each letter or symbol has only one sound or, more accurately, a limited range of sounds that are permitted pronunciations for that phoneme. Some symbols indicate stress (speech emphasis) and pause, which are also essential to Lojban word recognition. In addition, everything that is represented in other languages by punctuation (when written) or by tone of voice (when spoken) is represented in Lojban by words. These two properties together are known technically as "audio-visual isomorphism".

Lojban uses a variant of the Latin (Roman) alphabet, consisting of the following letters and symbols:

'	,	.	a	b	c	d	e	f	g	i	j	k
l	m	n	o	p	r	s	t	u	v	x	y	z

omitting the letters "h", "q", and "w".

The alphabetic order given above is that of the ASCII coded character set, widely used in computers. By making Lojban alphabetical order the same as ASCII, computerized sorting and searching of Lojban text is facilitated.

Capital letters are used only to represent non-standard stress, which can appear only in the representation of Lojbanized names. Thus the English name "Josephine", as normally pronounced, is Lojbanized as *DJOsefin.*, pronounced ['dʒosɛfinʔ]. (See Section 3.2 (p. 34) for an explanation of the

33

symbols within square brackets.) Technically, it is sufficient to capitalize the vowel letter, in this case *O*, but it is easier on the reader to capitalize the whole syllable.

Without the capitalization, the ordinary rules of Lojban stress would cause the *se* syllable to be stressed. Lojbanized names are meant to represent the pronunciation of names from other languages with as little distortion as may be; as such, they are exempt from many of the regular rules of Lojban phonology, as will appear in the rest of this chapter.

3.2 Basic Phonetics

Lojban pronunciations are defined using the International Phonetic Alphabet, or IPA, a standard method of transcribing pronunciations. By convention, IPA transcriptions are always within square brackets: for example, the word "cat" is pronounced (in General American pronunciation) [kæt]. Section 3.10 (p. 44) contains a brief explanation of the IPA characters used in this chapter, with their nearest analogues in English, and will be especially useful to those not familiar with the technical terms used in describing speech sounds.

The standard pronunciations and permitted variants of the Lojban letters are listed in the table below. The descriptions have deliberately been made a bit ambiguous to cover variations in pronunciation by speakers of different native languages and dialects. In all cases except *r* the first IPA symbol shown represents the preferred pronunciation; for *r*, all of the variations (and any other rhotic sound) are equally acceptable.

Letter	IPA	X-SAMPA	Description
'	[h]	[h]	an unvoiced glottal spirant
,	-	-	the syllable separator
.	[ʔ]	[?]	a glottal stop or a pause
a	[a], [ɑ]	[a], [A]	an open vowel
b	[b]	[b]	a voiced bilabial stop
c	[ʃ], [s̺]	[S], [s`]	an unvoiced coronal sibilant
d	[d]	[d]	a voiced dental/alveolar stop
e	[ɛ], [e]	[E], [e]	a front mid vowel
f	[f], [ɸ]	[f], [p\]	an unvoiced labial fricative
g	[g]	[g]	a voiced velar stop
i	[i]	[i]	a front close vowel
j	[ʒ], [z̺]	[Z], [z`]	a voiced coronal sibilant
k	[k]	[k]	an unvoiced velar stop
l	[l], [l̩]	[l], [l=]	a voiced lateral approximant (may be syllabic)
m	[m], [m̩]	[m], [m=]	a voiced bilabial nasal (may be syllabic)
n	[n], [n̩], [ŋ], [ŋ̍]	[n], [n=], [N], [N=]	a voiced dental or velar nasal (may be syllabic)
o	[o], [ɔ]	[o], [O]	a back mid vowel
p	[p]	[p]	an unvoiced bilabial stop
r	[r], [ɹ], [ɾ], [ʀ], [r̩], [ɻ], [ɽ], [ʁ]	[r], [r\], [4], [R\], [r=], [r\=], [4=], [R\=]	a rhotic sound
s	[s]	[s]	an unvoiced alveolar sibilant
t	[t]	[t]	an unvoiced dental/alveolar stop
u	[u]	[u]	a back close vowel
v	[v], [β]	[v], [B]	a voiced labial fricative
x	[x]	[x]	an unvoiced velar fricative
y	[ə]	[@]	a central mid vowel
z	[z]	[z]	a voiced alveolar sibilant

The Lojban sounds must be clearly pronounced so that they are not mistaken for each other. Voicing and placement of the tongue are the key factors in correct pronunciation, but other subtle differences will develop between consonants in a Lojban-speaking community. At this point these are the only mandatory rules on the range of sounds.

Note in particular that Lojban vowels can be pronounced with either rounded or unrounded lips; typically *o* and *u* are rounded and the others are not, as in English, but this is not a requirement; some people round *y* as well. Lojban consonants can be aspirated or unaspirated. Palatalizing of consonants, as found in Russian and other languages, is not generally acceptable in pronunciation, though a following *i* may cause it.

The sounds represented by the letters *c*, *g*, *j*, *s*, and *x* require special attention for speakers of English, either because they are ambiguous in the orthography of English (*c*, *g*, *s*), or because they are strikingly different in Lojban (*c*, *j*, *x*). The English "c" represents three different sounds, [k] in "cat" and [s] in "cent", as well as the [ʃ] of "ocean". Similarly, English "g" can represent [g] as in "go", [dʒ] as in "gentle", and [ʒ] as in the second "g" in "garage" (in some pronunciations). English "s" can be either [s] as in "cats", [z] as in "cards", [ʃ] as in "tension", or [ʒ] as in "measure". The sound of Lojban *x* doesn't appear in most English dialects at all.

There are two common English sounds that are found in Lojban but are not Lojban consonants: the "ch" of "church" and the "j" of "judge". In Lojban, these are considered two consonant sounds spoken together without an intervening vowel sound, and so are represented in Lojban by the two separate consonants: *tc* (IPA [tʃ]) and *dj* (IPA [dʒ]). In general, whether a complex sound is considered one sound or two depends on the language: Russian views "ts" as a single sound, whereas English, French, and Lojban consider it to be a consonant cluster.

3.3 The Special Lojban Characters

The apostrophe, period, and comma need special attention. They are all used as indicators of a division between syllables, but each has a different pronunciation, and each is used for different reasons:

The apostrophe represents a phoneme similar to a short, breathy English "h", (IPA [h]). The letter "h" is not used to represent this sound for two reasons: primarily in order to simplify explanations of the morphology, but also because the sound is very common, and the apostrophe is a visually lightweight representation of it. The apostrophe sound is a consonant in nature, but is not treated as either a consonant or a vowel for purposes of Lojban morphology (word-formation), which is explained in Chapter 4 (p. 49). In addition, the apostrophe visually parallels the comma and the period, which are also used (in different ways) to separate syllables.

The apostrophe is included in Lojban only to enable a smooth transition between vowels, while joining the vowels within a single word. In fact, one way to think of the apostrophe is as representing an unvoiced vowel glide.

As a permitted variant, any unvoiced fricative other than those already used in Lojban may be used to render the apostrophe: IPA [θ] is one possibility. The convenience of the listener should be regarded as paramount in deciding to use a substitute for [h].

The period represents a mandatory pause, with no specified length; a glottal stop (IPA [ʔ]) is considered a pause of shortest length. A pause (or glottal stop) may appear between any two words, and in certain cases – explained in detail in Section 4.9 (p. 66) – must occur. In particular, a word beginning with a vowel is always preceded by a pause, and a word ending in a consonant is always followed by a pause.

Technically, the period is an optional reminder to the reader of a mandatory pause that is dictated by the rules of the language; because these rules are unambiguous, a missing period can be inferred from otherwise correct text. Periods are included only as an aid to the reader.

A period also may be found apparently embedded in a word. When this occurs, such a written string is not one word but two, written together to indicate that the writer intends a unitary meaning for the compound. It is not really necessary to use a space between words if a period appears.

The comma is used to indicate a syllable break within a word, generally one that is not obvious to the reader. Such a comma is written to separate syllables, but indicates that there must be no pause between them, in contrast to the period. Between two vowels, a comma indicates that some type of glide may be necessary to avoid a pause that would split the two syllables into separate words. It is always legal to use the apostrophe (IPA [h]) sound in pronouncing a comma. However, a comma cannot be pronounced as a pause or glottal stop between the two letters separated by the comma, because that pronunciation would split the word into two words.

Otherwise, a comma is usually only used to clarify the presence of syllabic *l*, *m*, *n*, or *r* (discussed later). Commas are never required: no two Lojban words differ solely because of the presence or placement of a comma.

Here is a somewhat artificial example of the difference in pronunciation between periods, commas and apostrophes. In the English song about Old MacDonald's Farm, the vowel string which is written as "ee-i-ee-i-o" in English could be Lojbanized with periods as:

Example 3.1

> .i.ai.i.ai.o
> [ʔi ʔaj ʔi ʔaj ʔo]
> Ee! Eye! Ee! Eye! Oh!

However, this would sound clipped, staccato, and unmusical compared to the English. Furthermore, although Example 3.1 (p. 36) is a string of meaningful Lojban words, as a sentence it makes very little sense. (Note the use of periods embedded within the written word.)

If commas were used instead of periods, we could represent the English string as a Lojbanized name, ending in a consonant:

Example 3.2

> .i,ai,i,ai,on.
> [ʔi jaj ji jaj jon?]

The commas represent new syllable breaks, but prohibit the use of pauses or glottal stop. The pronunciation shown is just one possibility, but closely parallels the intended English pronunciation.

However, the use of commas in this way is risky to unambiguous interpretation, since the glides might be heard by some listeners as diphthongs, producing something like

Example 3.3

> .i,iai,ii,iai,ion.

which is technically a different Lojban name. Since the intent with Lojbanized names is to allow them to be pronounced more like their native counterparts, the comma is allowed to represent vowel glides or some non-Lojbanic sound. Such an exception affects only spelling accuracy and the ability of a reader to replicate the desired pronunciation exactly; it will not affect the recognition of word boundaries.

Still, it is better if Lojbanized names are always distinct. Therefore, the apostrophe is preferred in regular Lojbanized names that are not attempting to simulate a non-Lojban pronunciation perfectly. (Perfection, in any event, is not really achievable, because some sounds simply lack reasonable Lojbanic counterparts.)

If apostrophes were used instead of commas in Example 3.2 (p. 36), it would appear as:

Example 3.4

> .i'ai'i'ai'on.
> [ʔi hai hi hai hon?]

which preserves the rhythm and length, if not the exact sounds, of the original English.

3.4 Diphthongs and Syllabic Consonants

There exist 16 diphthongs in the Lojban language. A diphthong is a vowel sound that consists of two elements, a short vowel sound and a glide, either a labial (IPA [w]) or palatal (IPA [j]) glide, that either precedes (an on-glide) or follows (an off-glide) the main vowel. Diphthongs always constitute a single syllable.

For Lojban purposes, a vowel sound is a relatively long speech-sound that forms the nucleus of a syllable. Consonant sounds are relatively brief and normally require an accompanying vowel sound in order to be audible. Consonants may occur at the beginning or end of a syllable, around the vowel, and there may be several consonants in a cluster in either position. Each separate vowel sound constitutes a distinct syllable; consonant sounds do not affect the determination of syllables.

The six Lojban vowels are *a*, *e*, *i*, *o*, *u*, and *y*. The first five vowels appear freely in all kinds of Lojban words. The vowel *y* has a limited distribution: it appears only in Lojbanized names, in the Lojban names of the letters of the alphabet, as a glue vowel in compound words, and standing alone as a space-filler word (like English "uh" or "er").

The Lojban diphthongs are shown in the table below. (Variant pronunciations have been omitted, but are much as one would expect based on the variant pronunciations of the separate vowel letters: *ai* may be pronounced [ɑj], for example.)

Letters	IPA	Description
ai	[aj]	an open vowel with palatal off-glide
ei	[ɛj]	a front mid vowel with palatal off-glide
oi	[oj]	a back mid vowel with palatal off-glide
au	[aw]	an open vowel with labial off-glide
ia	[ja]	an open vowel with palatal on-glide
ie	[jɛ]	a front mid vowel with palatal on-glide
ii	[ji]	a front close vowel with palatal on-glide
io	[jo]	a back mid vowel with palatal on-glide
iu	[ju]	a back close vowel with palatal on-glide
ua	[wa]	an open vowel with labial on-glide
ue	[wɛ]	a front mid vowel with labial on-glide
ui	[wi]	a front close vowel with labial on-glide
uo	[wo]	a back mid vowel with labial on-glide
uu	[wu]	a back close vowel with labial on-glide
iy	[jə]	a central mid vowel with palatal on-glide
uy	[wə]	a central mid vowel with labial on-glide

(Approximate English equivalents of most of these diphthongs exist: see Section 3.11 (p. 46) for examples.)

The first four diphthongs above (*ai*, *ei*, *oi*, and *au*, the ones with off-glides) are freely used in most types of Lojban words; the ten following ones are used only as stand-alone words and in Lojbanized names and borrowings; and the last two (*iy* and *uy*) are used only in Lojbanized names.

The syllabic consonants of Lojban, [l̩], [m̩], [n̩], and [r̩], are variants of the non-syllabic [l], [m], [n], and [r] respectively. They normally have only a limited distribution, appearing in Lojban names and borrowings, although in principle any *l*, *m*, *n*, or *r* may be pronounced syllabically. If a syllabic consonant appears next to a *l*, *m*, *n*, or *r* that is not syllabic, it may not be clear which is which:

Example 3.5

> brlgan.
> [br̩l gan]
> or
> [brl̩ gan]

is a hypothetical Lojbanized name with more than one valid pronunciation; however it is pronounced, it remains the same word.

Syllabic consonants are treated as consonants rather than vowels from the standpoint of Lojban morphology. Thus Lojbanized names, which are generally required to end in a consonant, are allowed to end with a syllabic consonant. An example is *rl.*, which is an approximation of the English name "Earl", and has two syllabic consonants.

Syllables with syllabic consonants and no vowel are never stressed or counted when determining which syllables to stress (see Section 3.9 (p. 41)).

3.5 Vowel Pairs

Lojban vowels also occur in pairs, where each vowel sound is in a separate syllable. These two vowel sounds are connected (and separated) by an apostrophe. Lojban vowel pairs should be pronounced continuously with the [h] sound between (and not by a glottal stop or pause, which would split the two vowels into separate words).

All vowel combinations are permitted in two-syllable pairs with the apostrophe separating them; this includes those which constitute diphthongs when the apostrophe is not included.

The Lojban vowel pairs are:

a'a	a'e	a'i	a'o	a'u	a'y
e'a	e'e	e'i	e'o	e'u	e'y
i'a	i'e	i'i	i'o	i'u	i'y
o'a	o'e	o'i	o'o	o'u	o'y
u'a	u'e	u'i	u'o	u'u	u'y
y'a	y'e	y'i	y'o	y'u	y'y

Vowel pairs involving *y* appear only in Lojbanized names. They could appear in cmavo (structure words), but only .y'y. is so used – it is the Lojban name of the apostrophe letter (see Section 17.2 (p. 398)).

When more than two vowels occur together in Lojban, the normal pronunciation pairs vowels from the left into syllables, as in the Lojbanized name:

Example 3.6

> meiin.
>
> mei,in.

Example 3.6 (p. 38) contains the diphthong *ei* followed by the vowel *i*. In order to indicate a different grouping, the comma must always be used, leading to:

Example 3.7

> me,iin.

which contains the vowel *e* followed by the diphthong *ii*. In rough English representation, Example 3.6 (p. 38) is "May Een", whereas Example 3.7 (p. 38) is "Meh Yeen".

3.6 Consonant Clusters

A consonant sound is a relatively brief speech-sound that precedes or follows a vowel sound in a syllable; its presence either preceding or following does not add to the count of syllables, nor is a consonant required in either position for any syllable. Lojban has seventeen consonants: for the purposes of this section, the apostrophe is not counted as a consonant.

An important distinction dividing Lojban consonants is that of voicing. The following table shows the unvoiced consonants and the corresponding voiced ones:

UNVOICED	VOICED
p	b
t	d
k	g
f	v
c	j
s	z
x	-

The consonant *x* has no voiced counterpart in Lojban. The remaining consonants, *l*, *m*, *n*, and *r*, are typically pronounced with voice, but can be pronounced unvoiced.

Consonant sounds occur in languages as single consonants, or as doubled, or as clustered combinations. Single consonant sounds are isolated by word boundaries or by intervening vowel sounds from other consonant sounds. Doubled consonant sounds are either lengthened like [s] in

English "hiss", or repeated like [k] in English "backcourt". Consonant clusters consist of two or more single or doubled consonant sounds in a group, each of which is different from its immediate neighbor. In Lojban, doubled consonants are excluded altogether, and clusters are limited to two or three members, except in Lojbanized names.

Consonants can occur in three positions in words: initial (at the beginning), medial (in the middle), and final (at the end). In many languages, the sound of a consonant varies depending upon its position in the word. In Lojban, as much as possible, the sound of a consonant is unrelated to its position. In particular, the common American English trait of changing a "t" between vowels into a "d" or even an alveolar tap (IPA [ɾ]) is unacceptable in Lojban.

Lojban imposes no restrictions on the appearance of single consonants in any valid consonant position; however, no consonant (including syllabic consonants) occurs final in a word except in Lojbanized names.

Pairs of consonants can also appear freely, with the following restrictions:

1. It is forbidden for both consonants to be the same, as this would violate the rule against double consonants.
2. It is forbidden for one consonant to be voiced and the other unvoiced. The consonants *l*, *m*, *n*, and *r* are exempt from this restriction. As a result, *bf* is forbidden, and so is *sd*, but both *fl* and *vl*, and both *ls* and *lz*, are permitted.
3. It is forbidden for both consonants to be drawn from the set *c, j, s, z*.
4. The specific pairs *cx, kx, xc, xk*, and *mz* are forbidden.

These rules apply to all kinds of words, even Lojbanized names. If a name would normally contain a forbidden consonant pair, a *y* can be inserted to break up the pair:

Example 3.8
djeimyz.
[dʒɛj məz?]
James

The regular English pronunciation of "James", which is [dʒɛjmz], would Lojbanize as *djeimz.*, which contains a forbidden consonant pair.

3.7 Initial Consonant Pairs

The set of consonant pairs that may appear at the beginning of a word (excluding Lojbanized names) is far more restricted than the fairly large group of permissible consonant pairs described in Section 3.6 (p. 38). Even so, it is more than English allows, although hopefully not more than English-speakers (and others) can learn to pronounce.

There are just 48 such permissible initial consonant pairs, as follows:

```
bl  br
cf  ck  cl  cm  cn  cp  cr  ct
dj  dr  dz
fl  fr
gl  gr
jb  jd  jg  jm  jv
kl  kr
ml  mr
pl  pr
sf  sk  sl  sm  sn  sp  sr  st
tc  tr  ts
vl  vr
xl  xr
zb  zd  zg  zm  zv
```

Lest this list seem almost random, a pairing of voiced and unvoiced equivalent vowels will show significant patterns which may help in learning:

pl	pr					fl	fr
bl	br					vl	vr
cp	cf	ct	ck	cm	cn	cl	cr
jb	jv	jd	jg	jm			
sp	sf	st	sk	sm	sn	sl	sr
zb	zv	zd	zg	zm			
tc	tr	ts				kl	kr
dj	dr	dz				gl	gr
ml	mr					xl	xr

Note that if both consonants of an initial pair are voiced, the unvoiced equivalent is also permissible, and the voiced pair can be pronounced simply by voicing the unvoiced pair. (The converse is not true: *cn* is a permissible initial pair, but *jn* is not.)

Consonant triples can occur medially in Lojban words. They are subject to the following rules:

1. The first two consonants must constitute a permissible consonant pair;
2. The last two consonants must constitute a permissible initial consonant pair;
3. The triples *ndj*, *ndz*, *ntc*, and *nts* are forbidden.

Lojbanized names can begin or end with any permissible consonant pair, not just the 48 initial consonant pairs listed above, and can have consonant triples in any location, as long as the pairs making up those triples are permissible. In addition, names can contain consonant clusters with more than three consonants, again requiring that each pair within the cluster is valid.

3.8 Buffering Of Consonant Clusters

Many languages do not have consonant clusters at all, and even those languages that do have them often allow only a subset of the full Lojban set. As a result, the Lojban design allows the use of a buffer sound between consonant combinations which a speaker finds unpronounceable. This sound may be any non-Lojbanic vowel which is clearly separable by the listener from the Lojban vowels. Some possibilities are IPA [ɪ], [ɨ], [ʊ], or even [ɣ], but there probably is no universally acceptable buffer sound. When using a consonant buffer, the sound should be made as short as possible. Two examples showing such buffering (we will use [ɪ] in this chapter) are:

Example 3.9
> vrusi
> ['vru si]
> or
> [vɪ 'ru si]

Example 3.10
> .AMsterdam.
> [?am ster dam?]
> or
> ['?a mɪ sɪ tɛ rɪ da mɪ?]

When a buffer vowel is used, it splits each buffered consonant into its own syllable. However, the buffering syllables are never stressed, and are not counted in determining stress. They are, in effect, not really syllables to a Lojban listener, and thus their impact is ignored.

Here are more examples of unbuffered and buffered pronunciations:

Example 3.11
> klama
> ['kla ma]
> [kɪ 'la ma]

Example 3.12

    xapcke

    ['xap ʃkɛ]

    ['xa pɪ ʃkɛ]

    ['xa pɪ ʃɪ kɛ]

In Example 3.12 (p. 41), we see that buffering vowels can be used in just some, rather than all, of the possible places: the second pronunciation buffers the *pc* consonant pair but not the *ck*. The third pronunciation buffers both.

Example 3.13

    ponyni'u

    [po nə 'ni hu]

Example 3.13 (p. 41) cannot contain any buffering vowel. It is important not to confuse the vowel *y*, which is pronounced [ə], with the buffer, which has a variety of possible pronunciations and is never written. Consider the contrast between

Example 3.14

    bongynanba

    [boŋ gə 'nan ba]

an unlikely Lojban compound word meaning "bone bread" (note the use of [ŋ] as a representative of *n* before *g*) and

Example 3.15

    bongnanba

    [boŋ 'gnan ba]

a possible borrowing from another language (Lojban borrowings can only take a limited form). If Example 3.15 (p. 41) were pronounced with buffering, as

Example 3.16

    [boŋ gɪ 'nan ba]

it would be very similar to Example 3.14 (p. 41). Only a clear distinction between *y* and any buffering vowel would keep the two words distinct.

Since buffering is done for the benefit of the speaker in order to aid pronounceability, there is no guarantee that the listener will not mistake a buffer vowel for one of the six regular Lojban vowels. The buffer vowel should be as laxly pronounced as possible, as central as possible, and as short as possible. Furthermore, it is worthwhile for speakers who use buffers to pronounce their regular vowels a bit longer than usual, to avoid confusion with buffer vowels. The speakers of many languages will have trouble correctly hearing any of the suggested buffer vowels otherwise. By this guideline, Example 3.16 (p. 41) would be pronounced

Example 3.17

    [boːŋ gɪ 'naːn baː]

with lengthened vowels.

3.9 Syllabication And Stress

A Lojban word has one syllable for each of its vowels, diphthongs, and syllabic consonants (referred to simply as "vowels" for the purposes of this section.) Syllabication rules determine which of the consonants separating two vowels belong to the preceding vowel and which to the following vowel. These rules are conventional only; the phonetic facts of the matter about how utterances are syllabified in any language are always very complex.

A single consonant always belongs to the following vowel. A consonant pair is normally divided between the two vowels; however, if the pair constitute a valid initial consonant pair, they are normally both assigned to the following vowel. A consonant triple is divided between the first and second consonants. Apostrophes and commas, of course, also represent syllable breaks. Syllabic consonants usually appear alone in their syllables.

It is permissible to vary from these rules in Lojbanized names. For example, there are no definitive rules for the syllabication of names with consonant clusters longer than three consonants. The comma is used to indicate variant syllabication or to explicitly mark normal syllabication.

Here are some examples of Lojban syllabication:

Example 3.18

    pujenaicajeba

    pu,je,nai,ca,je,ba

This word has no consonant pairs and is therefore syllabified before each medial consonant.

Example 3.19

    ninmu

    nin,mu

This word is split at a consonant pair.

Example 3.20

    fitpri

    fit,pri

This word is split at a consonant triple, between the first two consonants of the triple.

Example 3.21

    sairgoi

    sair,goi

    sai,r,goi

This word contains the consonant pair *rg*; the *r* may be pronounced syllabically or not.

Example 3.22

    klezba

    klez,ba

    kle,zba

This word contains the permissible initial pair *zb*, and so may be syllabicated either between *z* and *b* or before *zb*.

Stress is a relatively louder pronunciation of one syllable in a word or group of words. Since every syllable has a vowel sound (or diphthong or syllabic consonant) as its nucleus, and the stress is on the vowel sound itself, the terms "stressed syllable" and "stressed vowel" are largely interchangeable concepts.

Most Lojban words are stressed on the next-to-the-last, or penultimate, syllable. In counting syllables, however, syllables whose vowel is *y* or which contain a syllabic consonant (*l*, *m*, *n*, or *r*) are never counted. (The Lojban term for penultimate stress is *da'amoi terbasna*.) Similarly, syllables created solely by adding a buffer vowel, such as [ɪ], are not counted.

There are actually three levels of stress – primary, secondary, and weak. Weak stress is the lowest level, so it really means no stress at all. Weak stress is required for syllables containing *y*, a syllabic consonant, or a buffer vowel.

Primary stress is required on the penultimate syllable of Lojban content words (called *brivla*). Lojbanized names may be stressed on any syllable, but if a syllable other than the penultimate is stressed, the syllable (or at least its vowel) must be capitalized in writing. Lojban structural words (called *cmavo*) may be stressed on any syllable or none at all. However, primary stress may not be used in a syllable just preceding a brivla, unless a pause divides them; otherwise, the two words may run together.

Secondary stress is the optional and non-distinctive emphasis used for other syllables besides those required to have either weak or primary stress. There are few rules governing secondary stress, which typically will follow a speaker's native language habits or preferences. Secondary stress can be used for contrast, or for emphasis of a point. Secondary stress can be emphasized at any level up to primary stress, although the speaker must not allow a false primary stress in brivla, since errors in word resolution could result.

The following are Lojban words with stress explicitly shown:

Example 3.23
> dikyjvo
> DI,ky,jvo

(In a fully-buffered dialect, the pronunciation would be: ['di kə ʒɪ vo].) Note that the syllable *ky* is not counted in determining stress. The vowel *y* is never stressed in a normal Lojban context.

Example 3.24
> .armstrong.
> .ARM,strong.

This is a Lojbanized version of the name "Armstrong". The final *g* must be explicitly pronounced. With full buffering, the name would be pronounced:

Example 3.25
> ['ʔa rɪ mɪ sɪ tɪ ro nɪ gɪ?]

However, there is no need to insert a buffer in every possible place just because it is inserted in one place: partial buffering is also acceptable. In every case, however, the stress remains in the same place: on the first syllable.

The English pronunciation of "Armstrong", as spelled in English, is not correct by Lojban standards; the letters "ng" in English represent a velar nasal (IPA [ŋ]) which is a single consonant. In Lojban, *ng* represents two separate consonants that must both be pronounced; you may not use [ŋ] to pronounce Lojban *ng*, although [ŋg] is acceptable. English speakers are likely to have to pronounce the ending with a buffer, as one of the following:

Example 3.26
> ['ʔarm stron gɪ?]
> or
> ['ʔarm stroŋ gɪ?]
> or even
> ['ʔarm stro nɪg?]

The normal English pronunciation of the name "Armstrong" could be Lojbanized as:

Example 3.27
> .ARMstron.

since Lojban *n* is allowed to be pronounced as the velar nasal [ŋ].

Here is another example showing the use of *y*:

Example 3.28
> bisydja
> BI,sy,dja
> BI,syd,ja

This word is a compound word, or lujvo, built from the two affixes *bis* and *dja*. When they are joined, an impermissible consonant pair results: *sd*. In accordance with the algorithm for making lujvo, explained in Section 4.11 (p. 68), a *y* is inserted to separate the impermissible consonant pair; the *y* is not counted as a syllable for purposes of stress determination.

Example 3.29

    da'udja
    da'UD,ja
    da'U,dja

These two syllabications sound the same to a Lojban listener – the association of unbuffered consonants in syllables is of no import in recognizing the word.

Example 3.30

    e'u bridi
    e'u BRI,di
    E'u BRI,di
    e'U.BRI,di

In Example 3.30 (p. 44), *e'u* is a cmavo and *bridi* is a brivla. Either of the first two pronunciations is permitted: no primary stress on either syllable of *e'u*, or primary stress on the first syllable. The third pronunciation, which places primary stress on the second syllable of the cmavo, requires that – since the following word is a brivla – the two words must be separated by a pause. Consider the following two cases:

Example 3.31

    le re nobli prenu
    le re NObli PREnu

Example 3.32

    le re no bliprenu
    le re no bliPREnu

If the cmavo *no* in Example 3.32 (p. 44) were to be stressed, the phrase would sound exactly like the given pronunciation of Example 3.31 (p. 44), which is unacceptable in Lojban: a single pronunciation cannot represent both.

3.10 IPA For English Speakers

There are many dialects of English, thus making it difficult to define the standardized symbols of the IPA in terms useful to every reader. All the symbols used in this chapter are repeated here, in more or less alphabetical order, with examples drawn from General American. In addition, some attention is given to the Received Pronunciation of (British) English. These two dialects are referred to as GA and RP respectively. Speakers of other dialects should consult a book on phonetics or their local television sets.

[']	An IPA indicator of primary stress; the syllable which follows ['] receives primary stress.
[ʔ]	An allowed variant of Lojban .. This sound is not usually considered part of English. It is the catch in your throat that sometimes occurs prior to the beginning of a word (and sometimes a syllable) which starts with a vowel. In some dialects, like Cockney and some kinds of American English, it is used between vowels instead of "t": "bottle" [boʔl]. The English interjection "uh-oh!" almost always has it between the syllables.
[ː]	A symbol indicating that the previous vowel is to be spoken for a longer time than usual. Lojban vowels can be pronounced long in order to make a greater contrast with buffer vowels.
[a]	The preferred pronunciation of Lojban *a*. This sound doesn't occur in GA, but sounds somewhat like the "ar" of "park", as spoken in RP or New England American. It is pronounced further forward in the mouth than [ɑ].
[ɑ]	An allowed variant of Lojban *a*. The "a" of GA "father". The sound [a] is preferred because GA speakers often relax an unstressed [ɑ] into a schwa [ə], as in the usual pronunciations of "about" and "sofa". Because schwa is a distinct vowel in Lojban, English speakers must either learn to avoid this shift or to use [a] instead: the Lojban word for "sofa" is *sfofa*, pronounced [sfofa] or [sfofɑ] but never [sfofə] which would be the non-word *sfofy*.

44

[æ]	Not a Lojban sound. The "a" of English "cat".
[b]	The preferred pronunciation of Lojban *b*. As in English "boy", "sober", or "job".
[β]	An allowed variant of Lojban *v*. Not an English sound; the Spanish "b" or "v" between vowels. This sound should not be used for Lojban *b*.
[d]	The preferred pronunciation of Lojban *d*. As in English "dog", "soda", or "mad".
[ɛ]	The preferred pronunciation of Lojban *e*. The "e" of English "met".
[e]	An allowed variant of Lojban *e*. This sound is not found in English, but is the Spanish "e", or the tense «e» of Italian. The vowel of English "say" is similar except for the off-glide: you can learn to make this sound by holding your tongue steady while saying the first part of the English vowel.
[ə]	The preferred pronunciation of Lojban *y*. As in the "a" of English "sofa" or "about". Schwa is generally unstressed in Lojban, as it is in English. It is a totally relaxed sound made with the tongue in the middle of the mouth.
[f]	The preferred pronunciation of Lojban *f*. As in "fee", "loafer", or "chef".
[ɸ]	An allowed variant of Lojban *f*. Not an English sound; the Japanese "f" sound.
[g]	The preferred pronunciation of Lojban *g*. As in English "go", "eagle", or "dog".
[h]	The preferred pronunciation of the Lojban apostrophe sound. As in English "aha" or the second "h" in "oh, hello".
[i]	The preferred pronunciation of Lojban *i*. Essentially like the English vowel of "pizza" or "machine", although the English vowel is sometimes pronounced with an off-glide, which should not be present in Lojban.
[ɪ]	A possible Lojban buffer vowel. The "i" of English "bit".
[ɨ]	A possible Lojban buffer vowel. The "u" of "just" in some varieties of GA, those which make the word sound more or less like "jist". Also Russian «y» as in «byt'» (to be); like a schwa [ə], but higher in the mouth.
[j]	Used in Lojban diphthongs beginning or ending with *i*. Like the "y" in English "yard" or "say".
[k]	The preferred pronunciation of Lojban *k*. As in English "kill", "token", or "flak".
[l]	The preferred pronunciation of Lojban *l*. As in English "low", "nylon", or "excel".
[l̩]	The syllabic version of Lojban *l*, as in English "bottle" or "middle".
[m]	The preferred pronunciation of Lojban *m*. As in English "me", "humor", or "ham".
[m̩]	The syllabic version of Lojban *m*. As in English "catch 'em" or "bottom".
[n]	The preferred pronunciation of Lojban *n*. As in English *no*, "honor", or "son".
[n̩]	The syllabic version of Lojban *n*. As in English "button".
[ŋ]	An allowed variant of Lojban *n*, especially in Lojbanized names and before *g* or *k*. As in English "sing" or "singer" (but not "finger" or "danger").
[ŋ̩]	An allowed variant of Lojban syllabic *n*, especially in Lojbanized names.
[o]	The preferred pronunciation of Lojban *o*. As in the French « haute (cuisine) » or Spanish "como". There is no exact English equivalent of this sound. The nearest GA equivalent is the "o" of "dough" or "joke", but it is essential that the off-glide (a [w]-like sound) at the end of the vowel is not pronounced when speaking Lojban. The RP sound in these words is [əw] in IPA terms, and has no [o] in it at all; unless you can speak with a Scots, Irish, or American accent, you may have trouble with this sound.
[ɔ]	An allowed variant of Lojban *o*, especially before *r*. This sound is a shortened form of the "aw" in GA "dawn" (for those people who don't pronounce "dawn" and "Don" alike; if you do, you may have trouble with this sound). In RP, but not GA, it is the "o" of "hot".
[p]	The preferred pronunciation of Lojban *p*. As in English "pay", "super", or "up".
[r]	One version of Lojban *r*. Not an English sound. The Spanish "rr" and the Scots "r", a tongue-tip trill.
[ɹ]	One version of Lojban *r*. As in GA "right", "baron", or "car". Not found in RP.

[ɾ]	One version of Lojban *r*. In GA, appears as a variant of "t" or "d" in the words "metal" and "medal" respectively. A tongue-tip flap.
[ʀ]	One version of Lojban *r*. Not an English sound. The French or German « r » in « reine » or „rot" respectively. A uvular trill.
[ɹ̩], [ɻ̩], [ɾ̩], [ʀ̩]	Syllabic versions of the above. [ɻ̩] appears in the GA (but not RP) pronunciation of "bird".
[s]	The preferred pronunciation of Lojban *s*. As in English "so", "basin", or "yes".
[ʃ]	The preferred pronunciation of Lojban *c*. The "sh" of English "ship", "ashen", or "dish".
[ʂ]	An allowed variant of Lojban *c*. Not an English sound. The Hindi retroflex "s" with dot below, or Klingon "S".
[t]	The preferred pronunciation of Lojban *t*. As in English "tea", "later", or "not". It is important to avoid the GA habit of pronouncing the "t" between vowels as [d] or [ɾ].
[θ]	Not normally a Lojban sound, but a possible variant of Lojban '. The "th" of English "thin" (but not "then").
[v]	The preferred pronunciation of Lojban *v*. As in English "voice", "savor", or "live".
[w]	Used in Lojban diphthongs beginning or ending with *u*. Like the "w" in English "wet" [wɛt] or "cow" [kaw].
[x]	The preferred pronunciation of Lojban *x*. Not normally an English sound, but used in some pronunciations of "loch" and "Bach"; "gh" in Scots "might" and "night". The German „Ach-Laut". To pronounce [x], force air through your throat without vibrating your vocal chords; there should be lots of scrape.
[ʏ]	A possible Lojban buffer vowel. Not an English sound: the „ü" of German „hübsch".
[z]	The preferred pronunciation of Lojban *z*. As in English "zoo", "hazard", or "fizz".
[ʒ]	The preferred pronunciation of Lojban *j*. The "si" of English "vision", or the consonant at the end of GA "garage".
[ʐ]	An allowed variant of Lojban *j*. Not an English sound. The voiced version of [ʂ].

3.11 English Analogues For Lojban Diphthongs

Here is a list of English words that contain diphthongs that are similar to the Lojban diphthongs. This list does not constitute an official pronunciation guide; it is intended as a help to English-speakers.

Lojban	English
ai	"pie"
ei	"pay"
oi	"boy"
au	"cow"
ia	"yard"
ie	"yes"
ii	"ye"
io	"yodel" (in GA only)
iu	"unicorn" or "few"
ua	"suave"
ue	"wet"
ui	"we"
uo	"woe" (in GA only)
uu	"woo"
iy	"million" (the "io" part, that is)
uy	"was" (when unstressed)

3.12 Oddball Orthographies

The following notes describe ways in which Lojban has been written or could be written that differ from the standard orthography explained in the rest of this chapter. Nobody needs to read this section except people with an interest in the obscure. Technicalities are used without explanation or further apology.

There exists an alternative orthography for Lojban, which is designed to be as compatible as possible (but no more so) with the orthography used in pre-Lojban versions of Loglan. The consonants undergo no change, except that *x* is replaced by *h*. The individual vowels likewise remain unchanged. However, the vowel pairs and diphthongs are changed as follows:

- *ai, ei, oi, au* become *ai, ei, oi, ao*.
- *ia* through *iu* and *ua* through *uu* remain unchanged.
- *a'i, e'i, o'i* and *a'o* become *a,i, e,i, o,i* and *a,o*.
- *i'a* through *i'u* and *u'a* through *u'u* are changed to *ia* through *iu* and *ua* through *uu* in lujvo and cmavo other than attitudinals, but become *i,a* through *i,u* and *u,a* through *u,u* in names, fu'ivla, and attitudinal cmavo.
- All other vowel pairs simply drop the apostrophe.

The result of these rules is to eliminate the apostrophe altogether, replacing it with comma where necessary, and otherwise with nothing. In addition, names and the cmavo *i* are capitalized, and irregular stress is marked with an apostrophe (now no longer used for a sound) following the stressed syllable.

Three points must be emphasized about this alternative orthography:

- It is not standard, and has not been used.
- It does not represent any changes to the standard Lojban phonology; it is simply a representation of the same phonology using a different written form.
- It was designed to aid in a planned rapprochement between the Logical Language Group and The Loglan Institute, a group headed by James Cooke Brown. The rapprochement never took place.

There also exists a Cyrillic orthography for Lojban which was designed when the introductory Lojban brochure was translated into Russian. It uses the "а", "б", "в", "г", "д", "е", "ж", "з", "и", "к", "л", "м", "н", "о", "п", "р", "с", "т", "у", "ф", "х", and "ш" in the obvious ways. The Latin letter "y" is mapped onto the hard sign "ъ", as in Bulgarian. The apostrophe, comma, and period are unchanged. Diphthongs are written as vowel pairs, as in the Roman representation.

Finally, an orthography using the Tengwar of Féanor, a fictional orthography invented by J. R. R. Tolkien and described in the Appendixes to *The Lord Of The Rings*, has been devised for Lojban. The following mapping, which closely resembles that used for Westron, will be meaningful only to those who have read those appendixes. In brief, the tincotéma and parmatéma are used in the conventional ways; the calmatéma represents palatal consonants, and the quessetéma represents velar consonants.

tinco	calma	ando	anga
t	-	*d*	-
thule	harma	anto	anca
-	*c*	-	*j*
numen	noldo	ore	anna
n	-	*r*	*i*
parma	quesse	umbar	ungwe
p	*k*	*b*	*g*
formen	hwesta	ampa	unque
f	*x*	*v*	-
malta	nwalme	vala	vilya
m	-	*u*	-

The letters "vala" and "anna" are used for *u* and *i* only when those letters are used to represent glides. Of the additional letters, *r*, *l*, *s*, and *z* are written with "rómen", "lambe", "silme", and "áre"/ "esse" respectively; the inverted forms are used as free variants.

Lojban, like Quenya, is a vowel-last language, so tehtar are read as following the tengwar on which they are placed. The conventional tehtar are used for the five regular vowels, and the dot below for *y*. The Lojban apostrophe is represented by "halla". There is no equivalent of the Lojban comma or period.

Chapter 4
The Shape Of Words To Come: Lojban Morphology

jbobliku

4.1 Introductory

Morphology is the part of grammar that deals with the form of words. Lojban's morphology is fairly simple compared to that of many languages, because Lojban words don't change form depending on how they are used. English has only a small number of such changes compared to languages like Russian, but it does have changes like "boys" as the plural of "boy", or "walked" as the past-tense form of "walk". To make plurals or past tenses in Lojban, you add separate words to the sentence that express the number of boys, or the time when the walking was going on.

However, Lojban does have what is called "derivational morphology": the capability of building new words from old words. In addition, the form of words tells us something about their grammatical uses, and sometimes about the means by which they entered the language. Lojban has very orderly rules for the formation of words of various types, both the words that already exist and new words yet to be created by speakers and writers.

A stream of Lojban sounds can be uniquely broken up into its component words according to specific rules. These so-called "morphology rules" are summarized in this chapter. (However, a detailed algorithm for breaking sounds into words has not yet been fully debugged, and so is not presented in this book.) First, here are some conventions used to talk about groups of Lojban letters, including vowels and consonants.

1. V represents any single Lojban vowel except *y*; that is, it represents *a, e, i, o,* or *u*.
2. VV represents either a diphthong, one of the following:

    ai ┊ *ei* ┊ *oi* ┊ *au*

or a two-syllable vowel pair with an apostrophe separating the vowels, one of the following:

a'a	a'e	a'i	a'o	a'u
e'a	e'e	e'i	e'o	e'u
i'a	i'e	i'i	i'o	i'u
o'a	o'e	o'i	o'o	o'u
u'a	u'e	u'i	u'o	u'u

3. C represents a single Lojban consonant, not including the apostrophe, one of *b, c, d, f, g, j, k, l, m, n, p, r, s, t, v, x,* or *z* . Syllabic *l, m, n,* and *r* always count as consonants for the purposes of this chapter.

4. CC represents two adjacent consonants of type C which constitute one of the 48 permissible initial consonant pairs:

pl	pr					fl	fr	
bl	br					vl	vr	
cp	cf	ct	ck	cm	cn	cl	cr	
jb	jv	jd	jg	jm				
sp	sf	st	sk	sm	sn	sl	sr	
zb	zv	zd	zg	zm				
tc	tr	ts						
dj	dr	dz				kl	kr	
ml	mr					gl	gr	
						xl	xr	

5. C/C represents two adjacent consonants which constitute one of the permissible consonant pairs (not necessarily a permissible initial consonant pair). The permissible consonant pairs are explained in Section 3.6 (p. 38). In brief, any consonant pair is permissible unless it: contains two identical letters, contains both a voiced (excluding *r, l, m, n*) and an unvoiced consonant, or is one of certain specified forbidden pairs.

6. C/CC represents a consonant triple. The first two consonants must constitute a permissible consonant pair; the last two consonants must constitute a permissible initial consonant pair.

Lojban has three basic word classes – parts of speech – in contrast to the eight that are traditional in English. These three classes are called cmavo, brivla, and cmene. Each of these classes has uniquely identifying properties – an arrangement of letters that allows the word to be uniquely and unambiguously recognized as a separate word in a string of Lojban, upon either reading or hearing, and as belonging to a specific word-class.

They are also functionally different: cmavo are the structure words, corresponding to English words like "and", "if", "the" and "to"; brivla are the content words, corresponding to English words like "come", "red", "doctor", and "freely"; cmene are proper names, corresponding to English "James", "Afghanistan", and "Pope John Paul II".

4.2 cmavo

The first group of Lojban words discussed in this chapter are the cmavo. They are the structure words that hold the Lojban language together. They often have no semantic meaning in themselves, though they may affect the semantics of brivla to which they are attached. The cmavo include the equivalent of English articles, conjunctions, prepositions, numbers, and punctuation marks. There are over a hundred subcategories of cmavo, known as *selma'o*, each having a specifically defined grammatical usage. The various selma'o are discussed throughout Chapter 5 (p. 79) to Chapter 19 (p. 447) and summarized in Chapter 20 (p. 467).

Standard cmavo occur in four forms defined by their word structure. Here are some examples of the various forms:

V-form	.a	.e	.i	.o	.u
CV-form	ba	ce	di	fo	gu
VV-form	.au	.ei	.ia	o'u	u'e
CVV-form	ki'a	pei	mi'o	coi	cu'u

In addition, there is the cmavo *.y.* (remember that *y* is not a V), which must have pauses before and after it.

A simple cmavo thus has the property of having only one or two vowels, or of having a single consonant followed by one or two vowels. Words consisting of three or more vowels in a row, or a single consonant followed by three or more vowels, are also of cmavo form, but are reserved for experimental use: a few examples are *ku'a'e*, *sau'e*, and *bai'ai*. All CVV cmavo beginning with the letter *x* are also reserved for experimental use. In general, though, the form of a cmavo tells you little or nothing about its grammatical use.

"Experimental use" means that the language designers will not assign any standard meaning or usage to these words, and words and usages coined by Lojban speakers will not appear in official dictionaries for the indefinite future. Experimental-use words provide an escape hatch for adding grammatical mechanisms (as opposed to semantic concepts) the need for which was not foreseen.

The cmavo of VV-form include not only the diphthongs and vowel pairs listed in Section 4.1 (p. 49), but also the following ten additional diphthongs:

.ia	.ie	.ii	.io	.iu
.ua	.ue	.ui	.uo	.uu

In addition, cmavo can have the form *Cy*, a consonant followed by the letter *y*. These cmavo represent letters of the Lojban alphabet, and are discussed in detail in Chapter 17 (p. 397).

Compound cmavo are sequences of cmavo attached together to form a single written word. A compound cmavo is always identical in meaning and in grammatical use to the separated sequence of simple cmavo from which it is composed. These words are written in compound form merely to save visual space, and to ease the reader's burden in identifying when the component cmavo are acting together.

Compound cmavo, while not visually short like their components, can be readily identified by two characteristics:

1. They have no consonant pairs or clusters, and
2. They end in a vowel.

For example:

Example 4.1
> .iseci'i
> .i se ci'i

Example 4.2
> punaijecanai
> pu nai je ca nai

Example 4.3
> ki'e.u'e
> ki'e .u'e

The cmavo *u'e* begins with a vowel, and like all words beginning with a vowel, requires a pause (represented by .) before it. This pause cannot be omitted simply because the cmavo is incorporated into a compound cmavo. On the other hand,

Example 4.4
> *ki'e'u'e*

is a single cmavo reserved for experimental purposes: it has four vowels.

Example 4.5
> cy.ibu.abu
> cy. .ibu .abu

Again the pauses are required (see Section 4.9 (p. 66)); the pause after *cy.* merges with the pause before *.ibu.*

There is no particular stress required in cmavo or their compounds. Some conventions do exist that are not mandatory. For two-syllable cmavo, for example, stress is typically placed on the first vowel; an example is

Example 4.6

> .e'o ko ko kurji
> .E'o ko ko KURji

This convention results in a consistent rhythm to the language, since brivla are required to have penultimate stress; some find this esthetically pleasing.

If the final syllable of one word is stressed, and the first syllable of the next word is stressed, you must insert a pause or glottal stop between the two stressed syllables. Thus

Example 4.7

> *le re nanmu*

can be optionally pronounced

Example 4.8

> le RE. NANmu

since there are no rules forcing stress on either of the first two words; the stress on *re*, though, demands that a pause separate *re* from the following syllable *nan* to ensure that the stress on *nan* is properly heard as a stressed syllable. The alternative pronunciation

Example 4.9

> LE re NANmu

is also valid; this would apply secondary stress (used for purposes of emphasis, contrast or sentence rhythm) to *le*, comparable in rhythmical effect to the English phrase "THE two men". In Example 4.8 (p. 52), the secondary stress on *re* would be similar to that in the English phrase "the TWO men".

Both cmavo may also be left unstressed, thus:

Example 4.10

> le re NANmu

This would probably be the most common usage.

4.3 brivla

Predicate words, called *brivla*, are at the core of Lojban. They carry most of the semantic information in the language. They serve as the equivalent of English nouns, verbs, adjectives, and adverbs, all in a single part of speech.

Every brivla belongs to one of three major subtypes. These subtypes are defined by the form, or morphology, of the word – all words of a particular structure can be assigned by sight or sound to a particular type (cmavo, brivla, or cmene) and subtype. Knowing the type and subtype then gives you, the reader or listener, significant clues to the meaning and the origin of the word, even if you have never heard the word before.

The same principle allows you, when speaking or writing, to invent new brivla for new concepts "on the fly"; yet it offers people that you are trying to communicate with a good chance to figure out your meaning. In this way, Lojban has a flexible vocabulary which can be expanded indefinitely.

All brivla have the following properties:

1. always end in a vowel;
2. always contain a consonant pair in the first five letters, where *y* and apostrophe are not counted as letters for this purpose (see Section 4.6 (p. 56).);
3. always are stressed on the next-to-the-last (penultimate) syllable; this implies that they have two or more syllables.

The presence of a consonant pair distinguishes brivla from cmavo and their compounds. The final vowel distinguishes brivla from cmene, which always end in a consonant. Thus *da'amei* must be a compound cmavo because it lacks a consonant pair; *lojban.* must be a name because it lacks a final vowel.

Thus, *bisycla* has the consonant pair *sc* in the first five non- *y* letters even though the *sc* actually appears in the form of *sy.*. Similarly, the word *ro'inre'o* contains *nr* in the first five letters because the apostrophes are not counted for this purpose.

The three subtypes of brivla are:

1. gismu, the Lojban primitive roots from which all other brivla are built;
2. lujvo, the compounds of two or more gismu; and
3. fu'ivla (literally "copy-word"), the specialized words that are not Lojban primitives or natural compounds, and are therefore borrowed from other languages.

4.4 gismu

The gismu, or Lojban root words, are those brivla representing concepts most basic to the language. The gismu were chosen for various reasons: some represent concepts that are very familiar and basic; some represent concepts that are frequently used in other languages; some were added because they would be helpful in constructing more complex words; some because they represent fundamental Lojban concepts (like *cmavo* and *gismu* themselves).

The gismu do not represent any sort of systematic partitioning of semantic space. Some gismu may be superfluous, or appear for historical reasons: the gismu list was being collected for almost 35 years and was only weeded out once. Instead, the intention is that the gismu blanket semantic space: they make it possible to talk about the entire range of human concerns.

There are about 1350 gismu. In learning Lojban, you need only to learn most of these gismu and their combining forms (known as *rafsi*) as well as perhaps 200 major cmavo, and you will be able to communicate effectively in the language. This may sound like a lot, but it is a small number compared to the vocabulary needed for similar communications in other languages.

All gismu have very strong form restrictions. Using the conventions defined in Section 4.1 (p. 49), all gismu are of the forms CVC/CV or CCVCV. They must meet the rules for all brivla given in Section 4.3 (p. 52); furthermore, they:

1. always have five letters;
2. always start with a consonant and end with a single vowel;
3. always contain exactly one consonant pair, which is a permissible initial pair (CC) if it's at the beginning of the gismu, but otherwise only has to be a permissible pair (C/C);
4. are always stressed on the first syllable (since that is penultimate).

The five letter length distinguishes gismu from lujvo and fu'ivla. In addition, no gismu contains '.

With the exception of five special brivla variables, *broda*, *brode*, *brodi*, *brodo*, and *brodu*, no two gismu differ only in the final vowel. Furthermore, the set of gismu was specifically designed to reduce the likelihood that two similar sounding gismu could be confused. For example, because *gismu* is in the set of gismu, *kismu, xismu, gicmu, gizmu,* and *gisnu* cannot be.

Almost all Lojban gismu are constructed from pieces of words drawn from other languages, specifically Chinese, English, Hindi, Spanish, Russian, and Arabic, the six most widely spoken natural languages. For a given concept, words in the six languages that represent that concept were written in Lojban phonetics. Then a gismu was selected to maximize the recognizability of the Lojban word for speakers of the six languages by weighting the inclusion of the sounds drawn from each language by the number of speakers of that language. See Section 4.14 (p. 71) for a full explanation of the algorithm.

Here are a few examples of gismu, with rough English equivalents (not definitions):

Example 4.11

> *creka*
>
> shirt

Example 4.12

lijda

religion

Example 4.13

blanu

blue

Example 4.14

mamta

mother

Example 4.15

cukta

book

Example 4.16

patfu

father

Example 4.17

nanmu

man

Example 4.18

ninmu

woman

A small number of gismu were formed differently; see Section 4.15 (p. 73) for a list.

4.5 lujvo

When specifying a concept that is not found among the gismu (or, more specifically, when the relevant gismu seems too general in meaning), a Lojbanist generally attempts to express the concept as a tanru. Lojban tanru are an elaboration of the concept of "metaphor" used in English. In Lojban, any brivla can be used to modify another brivla. The first of the pair modifies the second. This modification is usually restrictive – the modifying brivla reduces the broader sense of the modified brivla to form a more narrow, concrete, or specific concept. Modifying brivla may thus be seen as acting like English adverbs or adjectives. For example,

Example 4.19

skami pilno

is the tanru which expresses the concept of "computer user".

The simplest Lojban tanru are pairings of two concepts or ideas. Such tanru take two simpler ideas that can be represented by gismu and combine them into a single more complex idea. Two-part tanru may then be recombined in pairs with other tanru, or with individual gismu, to form more complex or more specific ideas, and so on.

The meaning of a tanru is usually at least partly ambiguous: *skami pilno* could refer to a computer that is a user, or to a user of computers. There are a variety of ways that the modifier component can be related to the modified component. It is also possible to use cmavo within tanru to provide variations (or to prevent ambiguities) of meaning.

Making tanru is essentially a poetic or creative act, not a science. While the syntax expressing the grouping relationships within tanru is unambiguous, tanru are still semantically ambiguous, since the rules defining the relationships between the gismu are flexible. The process of devising a new tanru is dealt with in detail in Chapter 5 (p. 79).

4.5 lujvo

To express a simple tanru, simply say the component gismu together. Thus the binary metaphor "big boat" becomes the tanru

Example 4.20

> *barda bloti*

representing roughly the same concept as the English word "ship".

The binary metaphor "father mother" can refer to a paternal grandmother ("a father-ly type of mother"), while "mother father" can refer to a maternal grandfather ("a mother-ly type of father"). In Lojban, these become the tanru

Example 4.21

> *patfu mamta*

and

Example 4.22

> *mamta patfu*

respectively.

The possibility of semantic ambiguity can easily be seen in the last case. To interpret Example 4.22 (p. 55), the listener must determine what type of motherliness pertains to the father being referred to. In an appropriate context, *mamta patfu* could mean not "grandfather" but simply "father with some motherly attributes", depending on the culture. If absolute clarity is required, there are ways to expand upon and explain the exact interrelationship between the components; but such detail is usually not needed.

When a concept expressed in a tanru proves useful, or is frequently expressed, it is desirable to choose one of the possible meanings of the tanru and assign it to a new brivla. For Example 4.19 (p. 54), we would probably choose "user of computers", and form the new word

Example 4.23

> *sampli*

Such a brivla, built from the rafsi which represent its component words, is called a *lujvo*. Another example, corresponding to the tanru of Example 4.20 (p. 55), would be:

Example 4.24

> *bralo'i*
> "big-boat"
> ship

The lujvo representing a given tanru is built from units representing the component gismu. These units are called *rafsi* in Lojban. Each rafsi represents only one gismu. The rafsi are attached together in the order of the words in the tanru, occasionally inserting so-called "hyphen" letters to ensure that the pieces stick together as a single word and cannot accidentally be broken apart into cmavo, gismu, or other word forms. As a result, each lujvo can be readily and accurately recognized, allowing a listener to pick out the word from a string of spoken Lojban, and if necessary, unambiguously decompose the word to a unique source tanru, thus providing a strong clue to its meaning.

The lujvo that can be built from the tanru *mamta patfu* in Example 4.22 (p. 55) is

Example 4.25

> *mampa'u*

which refers specifically to the concept "maternal grandfather". The two gismu that constitute the tanru are represented in *mampa'u* by the rafsi *mam-* and *-pa'u*, respectively; these two rafsi are then concatenated together to form *mampa'u*.

Like gismu, lujvo have only one meaning. When a lujvo is formally entered into a dictionary of the language, a specific definition will be assigned based on one particular interrelationship between the terms. (See Chapter 12 (p. 263) for how this has been done.) Unlike gismu, lujvo may have more than one form. This is because there is no difference in meaning between the various rafsi for a gismu when

55

they are used to build a lujvo. A long rafsi may be used, especially in noisy environments, in place of a short rafsi; the result is considered the same lujvo, even though the word is spelled and pronounced differently. Thus the word *brivla*, built from the tanru *bridi valsi*, is the same lujvo as *brivalsi*, *bridyvla*, and *bridyvalsi*, each of which uses a different combination of rafsi.

When assembling rafsi together into lujvo, the rules for valid brivla must be followed: a consonant cluster must occur in the first five letters (excluding *y* and ʼ), and the lujvo must end in a vowel.

A *y* (which is ignored in determining stress or consonant clusters) is inserted in the middle of the consonant cluster to glue the word together when the resulting cluster is either not permissible or the word is likely to break up. There are specific rules describing these conditions, detailed in Section 4.6 (p. 56).

An *r* (in some cases, an *n*) is inserted when a CVV-form rafsi attaches to the beginning of a lujvo in such a way that there is no consonant cluster. For example, in the lujvo

Example 4.26
> *soirsai*
> from *sonci sanmi*
> "soldier meal"
> field rations

the rafsi *soi-* and *-sai* are joined, with the additional *r* making up the *rs* consonant pair needed to make the word a brivla. Without the *r*, the word would break up into *soi sai*, two cmavo. The pair of cmavo have no relation to their rafsi lookalikes; they will either be ungrammatical (as in this case), or will express a different meaning from what was intended.

Learning rafsi and the rules for assembling them into lujvo is clearly seen to be necessary for fully using the potential Lojban vocabulary.

Most important, it is possible to invent new lujvo while you speak or write in order to represent a new or unfamiliar concept, one for which you do not know any existing Lojban word. As long as you follow the rules for building these compounds, there is a good chance that you will be understood without explanation.

4.6 rafsi

Every gismu has from two to five rafsi, each of a different form, but each such rafsi represents only one gismu. It is valid to use any of the rafsi forms in building lujvo – whichever the reader or listener will most easily understand, or whichever is most pleasing – subject to the rules of lujvo making. There is a scoring algorithm which is intended to determine which of the possible and legal lujvo forms will be the standard dictionary form (see Section 4.12 (p. 69)).

Each gismu always has at least two rafsi forms; one is the gismu itself (used only at the end of a lujvo), and one is the gismu without its final vowel (used only at the beginning or middle of a lujvo). These forms are represented as CVC/CV or CCVCV (called "the 5-letter rafsi"), and CVC/C or CCVC (called "the 4-letter rafsi") respectively. The dashes in these rafsi form representations show where other rafsi may be attached to form a valid lujvo. When lujvo are formed only from 4-letter and 5-letter rafsi, known collectively as "long rafsi", they are called "unreduced lujvo".

Some examples of unreduced lujvo forms are:

Example 4.27
> *mamtypatfu*
> from *mamta patfu*
> "mother father" or "maternal grandfather"

Example 4.28
> *lerfyliste*
> from *lerfu liste*
> "letter list" or a "list of letters"
> (letters of the alphabet)

Example 4.29

> *nancyprali*
> from *nanca prali*
> "year profit" or "annual profit"

Example 4.30

> *prunyplipe*
> from *pruni plipe*
> "elastic (springy) leap" or "spring" (the verb)

Example 4.31

> *vancysanmi*
> from *vanci sanmi*
> "evening meal" or "supper"

In addition to these two forms, each gismu may have up to three additional short rafsi, three letters long. All short rafsi have one of the forms CVC, CCV, or CVV. The total number of rafsi forms that are assigned to a gismu depends on how useful the gismu is, or is presumed to be, in making lujvo, when compared to other gismu that could be assigned the rafsi.

For example, *zmadu* ("more than") has the two short rafsi *zma* and *mau* (in addition to its unreduced rafsi *zmad* and *zmadu*), because a vast number of lujvo have been created based on *zmadu*, corresponding in general to English comparative adjectives ending in "-er" such as "whiter" (Lojban *labmau*). On the other hand, *bakri* ("chalk") has no short rafsi and few lujvo.

There are at most one CVC-form, one CCV-form, and one CVV-form rafsi per gismu. In fact, only a tiny handful of gismu have both a CCV-form and a CVV-form rafsi assigned, and still fewer have all three forms of short rafsi. However, gismu with both a CVC-form and another short rafsi are fairly common, partly because more possible CVC-form rafsi exist. Yet CVC-form rafsi, even though they are fairly easy to remember, cannot be used at the end of a lujvo (because lujvo must end in vowels), so justifying the assignment of an additional short rafsi to many gismu.

The intention was to use the available "rafsi space"- the set of all possible short rafsi forms – in the most efficient way possible; the goal is to make the most-used lujvo as short as possible (thus maximizing the use of short rafsi), while keeping the rafsi very recognizable to anyone who knows the source gismu. For this reason, the letters in a rafsi have always been chosen from among the five letters of the corresponding gismu. As a result, there are a limited set of short rafsi available for assignment to each gismu. At most seven possible short rafsi are available for consideration (of which at most three can be used, as explained above).

Here are the only short rafsi forms that can possibly exist for gismu of the form CVC/CV, like *sakli*. The digits in the second column represent the gismu letters used to form the rafsi.

CVC	123	-*sak*-
CVC	124	-*sal*-
CVV	12'5	-*sa'i*-
CVV	125	-*sai*-
CCV	345	-*kli*-
CCV	132	-*ska*-

(The only actual short rafsi for *sakli* is -*sal*-.)

For gismu of the form CCVCV, like *blaci*, the only short rafsi forms that can exist are:

CVC	134	-*bac*-
CVC	234	-*lac*-
CVV	13'5	-*ba'i*-
CVV	135	-*bai*-
CVV	23'5	-*la'i*-
CVV	235	-*lai*-
CCV	123	-*bla*-

(In fact, *blaci* has none of these short rafsi; they are all assigned to other gismu. Lojban speakers are not free to reassign any of the rafsi; the tables shown here are to help understand how the rafsi were chosen in the first place.)

There are a few restrictions: a CVV-form rafsi without an apostrophe cannot exist unless the vowels make up one of the four diphthongs *ai*, *ei*, *oi*, or *au*; and a CCV-form rafsi is possible only if the two consonants form a permissible initial consonant pair (see Section 4.1 (p. 49)). Thus *mamta*, which has the same form as *salci*, can only have *mam*, *mat*, and *ma'a* as possible rafsi: in fact, only *mam* is assigned to it.

Some cmavo also have associated rafsi, usually CVC-form. For example, the ten common numerical digits, which are all CV form cmavo, each have a CVC-form rafsi formed by adding a consonant to the cmavo. Most cmavo that have rafsi are ones used in composing tanru.

The term for a lujvo made up solely of short rafsi is "fully reduced lujvo". Here are some examples of fully reduced lujvo:

Example 4.32

> *cumfri*
> from *cumki lifri*
> "possible experience"

Example 4.33

> *klezba*
> from *klesi zbasu*
> "category make"

Example 4.34

> *kixta'a*
> from *krixa tavla*
> "cry-out talk"

Example 4.35

> *sniju'o*
> from *sinxa djuno*
> "sign know"

In addition, the unreduced forms in Example 4.27 (p. 56) and Example 4.28 (p. 56) may be fully reduced to:

Example 4.36

> *mampa'u*
> from *mamta patfu*
> "mother father" or "maternal grandfather"

Example 4.37

> *lerste*
> from *lerfu liste*
> "letter list" or a "list of letters"

As noted above, CVC-form rafsi cannot appear as the final rafsi in a lujvo, because all lujvo must end with one or two vowels. As a brivla, a lujvo must also contain a consonant cluster within the first five letters – this ensures that they cannot be mistaken for compound cmavo. Of course, all lujvo have at least six letters since they have two or more rafsi, each at least three letters long; hence they cannot be confused with gismu.

When attaching two rafsi together, it may be necessary to insert a hyphen letter. In Lojban, the term "hyphen" always refers to a letter, either the vowel *y* or one of the consonants *r* and *n*. (The letter *l* can also be a hyphen, but is not used as one in lujvo.)

4.6 rafsi

The y-hyphen is used after a CVC-form rafsi when joining it with the following rafsi could result in an impermissible consonant pair, or when the resulting lujvo could fall apart into two or more words (either cmavo or gismu).

Thus, the tanru *pante tavla* ("protest talk") cannot produce the lujvo *patta'a*, because *tt* is not a permissible consonant pair; the lujvo must be *patyta'a*. Similarly, the tanru *mudri siclu* ("wooden whistle") cannot form the lujvo *mudsiclu*; instead, *mudysiclu* must be used. (Remember that *y* is not counted in determining whether the first five letters of a brivla contain a consonant cluster: this is why.)

The y-hyphen is also used to attach a 4-letter rafsi, formed by dropping the final vowel of a gismu, to the following rafsi. (This procedure was shown, but not explained, in Example 4.27 (p. 56) to Example 4.31 (p. 57).)

The lujvo forms *zunlyjamfu*, *zunlyjma*, *zuljamfu*, and *zuljma* are all legitimate and equivalent forms made from the tanru *zunle jamfu* ("left foot"). Of these, *zuljma* is the preferred one since it is the shortest; it thus is likely to be the form listed in a Lojban dictionary.

The r-hyphen and its close relative, the n-hyphen, are used in lujvo only after CVV-form rafsi. A hyphen is always required in a two-part lujvo of the form CVV-CVV, since otherwise there would be no consonant cluster.

An r-hyphen or n-hyphen is also required after the CVV-form rafsi of any lujvo of the form CVV-CVC/CV or CVV-CCVCV since it would otherwise fall apart into a CVV-form cmavo and a gismu. In any lujvo with more than two parts, a CVV-form rafsi in the initial position must always be followed by a hyphen. If the hyphen were to be omitted, the supposed lujvo could be broken into smaller words without the hyphen: because the CVV-form rafsi would be interpreted as a cmavo, and the remainder of the word as a valid lujvo that is one rafsi shorter.

An n-hyphen is only used in place of an r-hyphen when the following rafsi begins with *r*. For example, the tanru *rokci renro* ("rock throw") cannot be expressed as *ro'ire'o* (which breaks up into two cmavo), nor can it be *ro'irre'o* (which has an impermissible double consonant); the n-hyphen is required, and the correct form of the hyphenated lujvo is *ro'inre'o*. The same lujvo could also be expressed without hyphenation as *rokre'o*.

There is also a different way of building lujvo, or rather phrases which are grammatically and semantically equivalent to lujvo. You can make a phrase containing any desired words, joining each pair of them with the special cmavo *zei*. Thus,

Example 4.38

> *bridi zei valsi*

is the exact equivalent of *brivla* (but not necessarily the same as the underlying tanru *bridi valsi*, which could have other meanings.) Using *zei* is the only way to get a cmavo lacking a rafsi, a cmene, or a fu'ivla into a lujvo:

Example 4.39

> *xy. zei kantu*
> X ray

Example 4.40

> *kulnr,farsi zei lolgai*
> "Farsi floor-cover"
> Persian rug

Example 4.41

> *na'e zei .a zei na'e zei by. livgyterbilma*
> "non-A, non-B liver-disease"
> non-A, non-B hepatitis

Example 4.42

> *.cerman. zei jamkarce*
> "Sherman war-car"
> Sherman tank

Example 4.41 (p. 59) is particularly noteworthy because the phrase that would be produced by removing the *zei* from it doesn't end with a brivla, and in fact is not even grammatical. As written, the example is a tanru with two components, but by adding a *zei* between *by.* and *livgyterbilma* to produce

Example 4.43

   na'e zei .a zei na'e zei by. zei livgyterbilma
   non-A-non-B-hepatitis

the whole phrase would become a single lujvo. The longer lujvo of Example 4.43 (p. 60) may be preferable, because its place structure can be built from that of *bilma*, whereas the place structure of a lujvo without a brivla must be constructed ad hoc.

Note that rafsi may not be used in *zei* phrases, because they are not words. CVV rafsi look like words (specifically cmavo) but there can be no confusion between the two uses of the same letters, because cmavo appear only as separate words or in compound cmavo (which are really just a notation for writing separate but closely related words as if they were one); rafsi appear only as parts of lujvo.

4.7 fu'ivla

The use of tanru or lujvo is not always appropriate for very concrete or specific terms (e.g. "brie" or "cobra"), or for jargon words specialized to a narrow field (e.g. "quark", "integral", or "iambic pentameter"). These words are in effect names for concepts, and the names were invented by speakers of another language. The vast majority of words referring to plants, animals, foods, and scientific terminology cannot be easily expressed as tanru. They thus must be borrowed (actually "copied") into Lojban from the original language.

There are four stages of borrowing in Lojban, as words become more and more modified (but shorter and easier to use). Stage 1 is the use of a foreign name quoted with the cmavo *la'o* (explained in full in Section 19.10 (p. 458)):

Example 4.44

   me la'o ly. spaghetti .ly.

is a predicate with the place structure "x1 is a quantity of spaghetti".

Stage 2 involves changing the foreign name to a Lojbanized name, as explained in Section 4.8 (p. 63):

Example 4.45

   me la spagetis.

One of these expedients is often quite sufficient when you need a word quickly in conversation. (This can make it easier to get by when you do not yet have full command of the Lojban vocabulary, provided you are talking to someone who will recognize the borrowing.)

Where a little more universality is desired, the word to be borrowed must be Lojbanized into one of several permitted forms. A rafsi is then usually attached to the beginning of the Lojbanized form, using a hyphen to ensure that the resulting word doesn't fall apart.

The rafsi categorizes or limits the meaning of the fu'ivla; otherwise a word having several different jargon meanings in other languages would require the word-inventor to choose which meaning should be assigned to the fu'ivla, since fu'ivla (like other brivla) are not permitted to have more than one definition. Such a Stage 3 borrowing is the most common kind of fu'ivla.

Finally, Stage 4 fu'ivla do not have any rafsi classifier, and are used where a fu'ivla has become so common or so important that it must be made as short as possible. (See Section 4.16 (p. 76) for a proposal concerning Stage 4 fu'ivla.)

The form of a fu'ivla reliably distinguishes it from both the gismu and the cmavo. Like cultural gismu, fu'ivla are generally based on a word from a single non-Lojban language. The word is "borrowed" (actually "copied", hence the Lojban tanru *fukpi valsi*) from the other language and Lojbanized – the phonemes are converted to their closest Lojban equivalent and modifications are made as necessary to make the word a legitimate Lojban fu'ivla-form word. All fu'ivla:

1.   must contain a consonant cluster in the first five letters of the word; if this consonant cluster
         is at the beginning, it must either be a permissible initial consonant pair, or a longer cluster

such that each pair of adjacent consonants in the cluster is a permissible initial consonant pair: *spraile* is acceptable, but not *ktraile* or *trkaile*;

2. must end in one or more vowels;

3. must not be gismu or lujvo, or any combination of cmavo, gismu, and lujvo; furthermore, a fu'ivla with a CV cmavo joined to the front of it must not have the form of a lujvo (the so-called "slinku'i test", not discussed further in this book);

4. cannot contain *y*, although they may contain syllabic pronunciations of Lojban consonants;

5. like other brivla, are stressed on the penultimate syllable.

Note that consonant triples or larger clusters that are not at the beginning of a fu'ivla can be quite flexible, as long as all consonant pairs are permissible. There is no need to restrict fu'ivla clusters to permissible initial pairs except at the beginning.

This is a fairly liberal definition and allows quite a lot of possibilities within "fu'ivla space". Stage 3 fu'ivla can be made easily on the fly, as lujvo can, because the procedure for forming them always guarantees a word that cannot violate any of the rules. Stage 4 fu'ivla require running tests that are not simple to characterize or perform, and should be made only after deliberation and by someone knowledgeable about all the considerations that apply.

Here is a simple and reliable procedure for making a non-Lojban word into a valid Stage 3 fu'ivla:

1. Eliminate all double consonants and silent letters.

2. Convert all sounds to their closest Lojban equivalents. Lojban *y*, however, may not be used in any fu'ivla.

3. If the last letter is not a vowel, modify the ending so that the word ends in a vowel, either by removing a final consonant or by adding a suggestively chosen final vowel.

4. If the first letter is not a consonant, modify the beginning so that the word begins with a consonant, either by removing an initial vowel or adding a suggestively chosen initial consonant.

5. Prefix the result of steps 1-5 with a 4-letter rafsi that categorizes the fu'ivla into a "topic area". It is only safe to use a 4-letter rafsi; short rafsi sometimes produce invalid fu'ivla. Hyphenate the rafsi to the rest of the fu'ivla with an r-hyphen; if that would produce a double *r*, use an n-hyphen instead; if the rafsi ends in *r* and the rest of the fu'ivla begins with *n* (or vice versa), or if the rafsi ends in "r" and the rest of the fu'ivla begins with "tc", "ts", "dj", or "dz" (using "n" would result in a phonotactically impermissible cluster), use an l-hyphen. (This is the only use of l-hyphen in Lojban.)

   Alternatively, if a CVC-form short rafsi is available it can be used instead of the long rafsi.

6. Remember that the stress necessarily appears on the penultimate (next-to-the-last) syllable.

In this section, the hyphen is set off with commas in the examples, but these commas are not required in writing, and the hyphen need not be pronounced as a separate syllable.

Here are a few examples:

Example 4.46

> spaghetti (from English or Italian)
> *spageti* (Lojbanize)
> *cidj,r,spageti* (prefix long rafsi)
> *dja,r,spageti* (prefix short rafsi)

where *cidj-* is the 4-letter rafsi for *cidja*, the Lojban gismu for "food", thus categorizing *cidjrspageti* as a kind of food. The form with the short rafsi happens to work, but such good fortune cannot be relied on: in any event, it means the same thing.

Example 4.47

> Acer (the scientific name of maple trees)
> *acer* (Lojbanize)
> *xaceru* (add initial consonant and final vowel)
> *tric,r,xaceru* (prefix rafsi)
> *ric,r,xaceru* (prefix short rafsi)

where *tric-* and *ric-* are rafsi for *tricu*, the gismu for "tree". Note that by the same principles, "maple sugar" could get the fu'ivla *saktrxaceru*, or could be represented by the tanru *tricrxaceru sakta*. Technically, *ricrxaceru* and *tricrxaceru* are distinct fu'ivla, but they would surely be given the same meanings if both happened to be in use.

Example 4.48

> brie (from French)
> *bri* (Lojbanize)
> *cirl,r,bri* (prefix rafsi)

where *cirl-* represents *cirla* ("cheese").

Example 4.49

> cobra
> *kobra* (Lojbanize)
> *sinc,r,kobra* (prefix rafsi)

where *sinc-* represents *since* ("snake").

Example 4.50

> quark
> *kuark* (Lojbanize)
> *kuarka* (add final vowel)
> *sask,r,kuarka* (prefix rafsi)

where *sask-* represents *saske* ("science"). Note the extra vowel *a* added to the end of the word, and the diphthong *ua*, which never appears in gismu or lujvo, but may appear in fu'ivla.

Example 4.51

> 자모 (from Korean)
> *djamo* (Lojbanize)
> *lerf,r,djamo* (prefix rafsi)
> *ler,l,djamo* (prefix rafsi)

where *ler-* represents *lerfu* ("letter"). Note the l-hyphen in "lerldjamo", since "lerndjamo" contains the forbidden cluster "ndj".

The use of the prefix helps distinguish among the many possible meanings of the borrowed word, depending on the field. As it happens, *spageti* and *kuarka* are valid Stage 4 fu'ivla, but *xaceru* looks like a compound cmavo, and *kobra* like a gismu.

For another example, "integral" has a specific meaning to a mathematician. But the Lojban fu'ivla *integrale*, which is a valid Stage 4 fu'ivla, does not convey that mathematical sense to a non-mathematical listener, even one with an English-speaking background; its source – the English word "integral" – has various other specialized meanings in other fields.

Left uncontrolled, *integrale* almost certainly would eventually come to mean the same collection of loosely related concepts that English associates with "integral", with only the context to indicate (possibly) that the mathematical term is meant.

The prefix method would render the mathematical concept as *cmacrntegrale*, if the *i* of *integrale* is removed, or something like *cmacrnintegrale*, if a new consonant is added to the beginning; *cmac-* is the rafsi for *cmaci* ("mathematics"). The architectural sense of "integral" might be conveyed with *dinjrnintegrale* or *tarmrnintegrale*, where *dinju* and *tarmi* mean "building" and "form" respectively.

Here are some fu'ivla representing cultures and related things, shown with more than one rafsi prefix:

Example 4.52
> *bang,r,blgaria*
> Bulgarian (in language)

Example 4.53
> *kuln,r,blgaria*
> Bulgarian (in culture)

Example 4.54
> *gugd,r,blgaria*
> Bulgaria (the country)

Example 4.55
> *bang,r,kore,a*
> Korean (the language)

Example 4.56
> *kuln,r,kore,a*
> Korean (the culture)

Note the commas in Example 4.55 (p. 63) and Example 4.56 (p. 63), used because *ea* is not a valid diphthong in Lojban. Arguably, some form of the native name "Chosen" should have been used instead of the internationally known "Korea"; this is a recurring problem in all borrowings. In general, it is better to use the native name unless using it will severely impede understanding: "Navajo" is far more widely known than "Dine'e".

4.8 cmene

Lojbanized names, called *cmene*, are very much like their counterparts in other languages. They are labels applied to things (or people) to stand for them in descriptions or in direct address. They may convey meaning in themselves, but do not necessarily do so.

Because names are often highly personal and individual, Lojban attempts to allow native language names to be used with a minimum of modification. The requirement that the Lojban speech stream be unambiguously analyzable, however, means that most names must be modified somewhat when they are Lojbanized. Here are a few examples of English names and possible Lojban equivalents:

Example 4.57
> *djim.*
> Jim

Example 4.58
> *djein.*
> Jane

Example 4.59
> *.arnold.*
> Arnold

Example 4.60
> *pit.*
> Pete

Example 4.61
> *katrinas.*
> Katrina

Example 4.62

> *kat,r,in.*
> Catherine

(Note that syllabic *r* is skipped in determining the stressed syllable, so Example 4.62 (p. 64) is stressed on the *ka*.)

Example 4.63

> *katis.*
> Cathy

Example 4.64

> *keit.*
> Kate

Names may have almost any form, but always end in a consonant, and are followed by a pause. They are penultimately stressed, unless unusual stress is marked with capitalization. A name may have multiple parts, each ending with a consonant and pause, or the parts may be combined into a single word with no pause. For example,

Example 4.65

> *djan. braun.*

and

Example 4.66

> *djanbraun.*

are both valid Lojbanizations of "John Brown".

The final arbiter of the correct form of a name is the person doing the naming, although most cultures grant people the right to determine how they want their own name to be spelled and pronounced. The English name "Mary" can thus be Lojbanized as *meris.*, *maris.*, *meiris.*, *merix.*, or even *marys.*. The last alternative is not pronounced much like its English equivalent, but may be desirable to someone who values spelling over pronunciation. The final consonant need not be an *s*; there must, however, be some Lojban consonant at the end.

Names are not permitted to have the sequences *la*, *lai*, or *doi* embedded in them, unless the sequence is immediately preceded by a consonant. These minor restrictions are due to the fact that all Lojban cmene embedded in a speech stream will be preceded by one of these words or by a pause. With one of these words embedded, the cmene might break up into valid Lojban words followed by a shorter cmene. However, break-up cannot happen after a consonant, because that would imply that the word before the *la*, or whatever, ended in a consonant without pause, which is impossible.

For example, the invalid name *laplas.* would look like the Lojban words *la plas.*, and *ilanas.* would be misunderstood as *.i la nas.*. However, *NEderlants.* cannot be misheard as *NEder lants.*, because *NEder* with no following pause is not a possible Lojban word.

There are close alternatives to these forbidden sequences that can be used in Lojbanizing names, such as *ly*, *lei*, and *dai* or *do'i*, that do not cause these problems.

Lojban cmene are identifiable as word forms by the following characteristics:

1. They must end in one or more consonants. There are no rules about how many consonants may appear in a cluster in cmene, provided that each consonant pair (whether standing by itself, or as part of a larger cluster) is a permissible pair.

2. They may contain the letter y as a normal, non-hyphenating vowel. They are the only kind of Lojban word that may contain the two diphthongs *iy* and *uy*.

3. They are always followed in speech by a pause after the final consonant, written as ..

4. They may be stressed on any syllable; if this syllable is not the penultimate one, it must be capitalized when writing. Neither names nor words that begin sentences are capitalized in Lojban, so this is the only use of capital letters.

4.8 cmene

Names meeting these criteria may be invented, Lojbanized from names in other languages, or formed by appending a consonant onto a cmavo, a gismu, a fu'ivla or a lujvo. Some cmene built from Lojban words are:

Example 4.67

> *pav.*
>
> the One
>
> from the cmavo *pa*, with rafsi *pav*, meaning "one"

Example 4.68

> *sol.*
>
> the Sun
>
> from the gismu *solri*, meaning "solar", or actually "pertaining to the Sun"

Example 4.69

> *ralj.*
>
> Chief (as a title)
>
> from the gismu *ralju*, meaning "principal".

Example 4.70

> *nol.*
>
> Lord/Lady
>
> from the gismu *nobli*, with rafsi *nol*, meaning "noble".

To Lojbanize a name from the various natural languages, apply the following rules:

1. Eliminate double consonants and silent letters.
2. Add a final *s* or *n* (or some other consonant that sounds good) if the name ends in a vowel.
3. Convert all sounds to their closest Lojban equivalents.
4. If possible and acceptable, shift the stress to the penultimate (next-to-the-last) syllable. Use commas and capitalization in written Lojban when it is necessary to preserve non-standard syllabication or stress. Do not capitalize names otherwise.
5. If the name contains an impermissible consonant pair, insert a vowel between the consonants: *y* is recommended.
6. No cmene may have the syllables *la*, *lai*, or *doi* in them, unless immediately preceded by a consonant. If these combinations are present, they must be converted to something else. Possible substitutions include *ly*, *ly'i*, and *dai* or *do'i*, respectively.

There are some additional rules for Lojbanizing the scientific names (technically known as "Linnaean binomials" after their inventor) which are internationally applied to each species of animal or plant. Where precision is essential, these names need not be Lojbanized, but can be directly inserted into Lojban text using the cmavo *la'o*, explained in Section 19.10 (p. 458). Using this cmavo makes the already lengthy Latinized names at least four syllables longer, however, and leaves the pronunciation in doubt. The following suggestions, though incomplete, will assist in converting Linnaean binomals to valid Lojban names. They can also help to create fu'ivla based on Linnaean binomials or other words of the international scientific vocabulary. The term "back vowel" in the following list refers to any of the letters *a*, *o*, or *u*; the term "front vowel" correspondingly refers to any of the letters *e*, *i*, or *y*.

1. Change double consonants other than *cc* to single consonants.
2. Change *cc* before a front vowel to *kc*, but otherwise to *k*.
3. Change *c* before a back vowel and final *c* to *k*.
4. Change *ng* before a consonant (other than *h*) and final *ng* to *n*.
5. Change *x* to *z* initially, but otherwise to *ks*.
6. Change *pn* to *n* initially.
7. Change final *ie* and *ii* to *i*.
8. Make the following idiosyncratic substitutions:

aa	a
ae	e
ch	k
ee	i
eigh	ei
ew	u
igh	ai
oo	u
ou	u
ow	au
ph	f
q	k
sc	sk
w	u
y	i

However, the diphthong substitutions should not be done if the two vowels are in two different syllables.

9. Change "h" between two vowels to ', but otherwise remove it completely. If preservation of the "h" seems essential, change it to *x* instead.

10. Place ' between any remaining vowel pairs that do not form Lojban diphthongs.

Some further examples of Lojbanized names are:

English	"Mary"	*meris.* or *meiris.*
English	"Smith"	*smit.*
English	"Jones"	*djonz.*
English	"John"	*djan.* or *jan.* (American) or *djon.* or *jon.* (British)
English	"Alice"	*.alis.*
English	"Elise"	*.eLIS.*
English	"Johnson"	*djansn.*
English	"William"	*.uiliam.* or *.uil,iam.*
English	"Brown"	*braun.*
English	"Charles"	*tcarlz.*
French	"Charles"	*carl.*
French	"De Gaulle"	*dyGOL.*
German	"Heinrich"	*xainrix.*
Spanish	"Joaquin"	*xuaKIN.*
Russian	"Svetlana"	*sfietlanys.*
Russian	"Khrushchev"	*xrucTCOF.*
Hindi	"Krishna"	*kricnas.*
Polish	"Lech Walesa"	*lex. va,uensas.*
Spanish	"Don Quixote"	*don. kicotes.* or modern Spanish: *don. kixotes.* or Mexican dialect: *don. ki'otes.*
Chinese	"Mao Zedong"	*maudzydyn.*
Japanese	"Fujiko"	*fudjikos.* or *fujikos.*

4.9 Rules for inserting pauses

Summarized in one place, here are the rules for inserting pauses between Lojban words:

1. Any two words may have a pause between them; it is always illegal to pause in the middle of a word, because that breaks up the word into two words.

2. Every word ending in a consonant must be followed by a pause. Necessarily, all such words are cmene.

3. Every word beginning with a vowel must be preceded by a pause. Such words are either cmavo, fu'ivla, or cmene; all gismu and lujvo begin with consonants.

4. Every cmene must be preceded by a pause, unless the immediately preceding word is one of the cmavo *la*, *lai*, *la'i*, or *doi* (which is why those strings are forbidden in cmene). However, the situation triggering this rule rarely occurs.

5. If the last syllable of a word bears the stress, and a brivla follows, the two must be separated by a pause, to prevent confusion with the primary stress of the brivla. In this case, the first word must be either a cmavo or a cmene with unusual stress (which already ends with a pause, of course).

6. A cmavo of the form "Cy" must be followed by a pause unless another "Cy"-form cmavo follows.

7. When non-Lojban text is embedded in Lojban, it must be preceded and followed by pauses. (How to embed non-Lojban text is explained in Section 19.10 (p. 458).)

4.10 Considerations for making lujvo

Given a tanru which expresses an idea to be used frequently, it can be turned into a lujvo by following the lujvo-making algorithm which is given in Section 4.11 (p. 68).

In building a lujvo, the first step is to replace each gismu with a rafsi that uniquely represents that gismu. These rafsi are then attached together by fixed rules that allow the resulting compound to be recognized as a single word and to be analyzed in only one way.

There are three other complications; only one is serious.

The first is that there is usually more than one rafsi that can be used for each gismu. The one to be used is simply whichever one sounds or looks best to the speaker or writer. There are usually many valid combinations of possible rafsi. They all are equally valid, and all of them mean exactly the same thing. (The scoring algorithm given in Section 4.12 (p. 69) is used to choose the standard form of the lujvo – the version which would be entered into a dictionary.)

The second complication is the serious one. Remember that a tanru is ambiguous – it has several possible meanings. A lujvo, or at least one that would be put into the dictionary, has just a single meaning. Like a gismu, a lujvo is a predicate which encompasses one area of the semantic universe, with one set of places. Hopefully the meaning chosen is the most useful of the possible semantic spaces. A possible source of linguistic drift in Lojban is that as Lojbanic society evolves, the concept that seems the most useful one may change.

You must also be aware of the possibility of some prior meaning of a new lujvo, especially if you are writing for posterity. If a lujvo is invented which involves the same tanru as one that is in the dictionary, and is assigned a different meaning (or even just a different place structure), linguistic drift results. This isn't necessarily bad. Every natural language does it. But in communication, when you use a meaning different from the dictionary definition, someone else may use the dictionary and therefore misunderstand you. You can use the cmavo *za'e* (explained in Section 19.11 (p. 460)) before a newly coined lujvo to indicate that it may have a non-dictionary meaning.

The essential nature of human communication is that if the listener understands, then all is well. Let this be the ultimate guideline for choosing meanings and place structures for invented lujvo.

The third complication is also simple, but tends to scare new Lojbanists with its implications. It is based on Zipf's Law, which says that the length of words is inversely proportional to their usage. The shortest words are those which are used more; the longest ones are used less. Conversely, commonly used concepts will be tend to be abbreviated. In English, we have abbreviations and acronyms and jargon, all of which represent complex ideas that are used often by small groups of people, so they shortened them to convey more information more rapidly.

Therefore, given a complicated tanru with grouping markers, abstraction markers, and other cmavo in it to make it syntactically unambiguous, the psychological basis of Zipf's Law may compel the lujvo-maker to drop some of the cmavo to make a shorter (technically incorrect) tanru, and then use that tanru to make the lujvo.

This doesn't lead to ambiguity, as it might seem to. A given lujvo still has exactly one meaning and place structure. It is just that more than one tanru is competing for the same lujvo. But more than one meaning for the tanru was already competing for the "right" to define the meaning of the lujvo. Someone has to use judgment in deciding which one meaning is to be chosen over the others.

If the lujvo made by a shorter form of tanru is in use, or is likely to be useful for another meaning, the decider then retains one or more of the cmavo, preferably ones that set this meaning apart from the shorter form meaning that is used or anticipated. As a rule, therefore, the shorter lujvo will be used for a more general concept, possibly even instead of a more frequent word. If both words are needed, the simpler one should be shorter. It is easier to add a cmavo to clarify the meaning of the more complex term than it is to find a good alternate tanru for the simpler term.

And of course, we have to consider the listener. On hearing an unknown word, the listener will decompose it and get a tanru that makes no sense or the wrong sense for the context. If the listener realizes that the grouping operators may have been dropped out, he or she may try alternate groupings, or try inserting an abstraction operator if that seems plausible. (The grouping of tanru is explained in Chapter 5 (p. 79); abstraction is explained in Chapter 11 (p. 247).) Plausibility is the key to learning new ideas and to evaluating unfamiliar lujvo.

4.11 The lujvo-making algorithm

The following is the current algorithm for generating Lojban lujvo given a known tanru and a complete list of gismu and their assigned rafsi. The algorithm was designed by Bob LeChevalier and Dr. James Cooke Brown for computer program implementation. It was modified in 1989 with the assistance of Nora LeChevalier, who detected a flaw in the original "tosmabru test".

Given a tanru that is to be made into a lujvo:

1. Choose a 3-letter or 4-letter rafsi for each of the gismu and cmavo in the tanru except the last.
2. Choose a 3-letter (CVV-form or CCV-form) or 5-letter rafsi for the final gismu in the tanru.
3. Join the resulting string of rafsi, initially without hyphens.
4. Add hyphen letters where necessary. It is illegal to add a hyphen at a place that is not required by this algorithm. Right-to-left tests are recommended, for reasons discussed below.
   a. If there are more than two words in the tanru, put an r-hyphen (or an n-hyphen) after the first rafsi if it is CVV-form. If there are exactly two words, then put an r-hyphen (or an n-hyphen) between the two rafsi if the first rafsi is CVV-form, unless the second rafsi is CCV-form (for example, *saicli* requires no hyphen). Use an r-hyphen unless the letter after the hyphen is *r*, in which case use an n-hyphen. Never use an n-hyphen unless it is required.
   b. Put a y-hyphen between the consonants of any impermissible consonant pair. This will always appear between rafsi.
   c. Put a y-hyphen after any 4-letter rafsi form.
5. Test all forms with one or more initial CVC-form rafsi – with the pattern "CVC ... CVC + X" – for "tosmabru failure". X must either be a CVCCV long rafsi that happens to have a permissible initial pair as the consonant cluster, or is something which has caused a y-hyphen to be installed between the previous CVC and itself by one of the above rules.
   The test is as follows:
   a. Examine all the C/C consonant pairs up to the first y-hyphen, or up to the end of the word in case there are no y-hyphens.
      These consonant pairs are called "joints".
   b. If all of those joints are permissible initials, then the trial word will break up into a cmavo and a shorter brivla. If not, the word will not break up, and no further hyphens are needed.
   c. Install a y-hyphen at the first such joint.

Note that the "tosmabru test" implies that the algorithm will be more efficient if rafsi junctures are tested for required hyphens from right to left, instead of from left to right; when the test is required, it cannot be completed until hyphenation to the right has been determined.

4.12 The lujvo scoring algorithm

This algorithm was devised by Bob and Nora LeChevalier in 1989. It is not the only possible algorithm, but it usually gives a choice that people find preferable. The algorithm may be changed in the future. The lowest-scoring variant will usually be the dictionary form of the lujvo. (In previous versions, it was the highest-scoring variant.)

1. Count the total number of letters, including hyphens and apostrophes; call it **L**.
2. Count the number of apostrophes; call it **A**.
3. Count the number of y-, r-, and n-hyphens; call it **H**.
4. For each rafsi, find the value in the following table. Sum this value over all rafsi; call it **R**:

CVC/CV (final)	(-sarji)	1
CVC/C	(-sarj-)	2
CCVCV (final)	(-zbasu)	3
CCVC	(-zbas-)	4
CVC	(-nun-)	5
CVV with an apostrophe	(-ta'u-)	6
CCV	(-zba-)	7
CVV with no apostrophe	(-sai-)	8

5. Count the number of vowels, not including y, call it **V**.

The score is then:

$$(1000 * L) - (500 * A) + (100 * H) - (10 * R) - V$$

In case of ties, there is no preference. This should be rare. Note that the algorithm essentially encodes a hierarchy of priorities: short words are preferred (counting apostrophes as half a letter), then words with fewer hyphens, words with more pleasing rafsi (this judgment is subjective), and finally words with more vowels are chosen. Each decision principle is applied in turn if the ones before it have failed to choose; it is possible that a lower-ranked principle might dominate a higher-ranked one if it is ten times better than the alternative.

Here are some lujvo with their scores (not necessarily the lowest scoring forms for these lujvo, nor even necessarily sensible lujvo):

Example 4.71

> *zbasai*
> *zba + sai*
> $(1000 * 6) - (500 * 0) + (100 * 0) - (10 * 15) - 3 = 5847$

Example 4.72

> *nunynau*
> *nun + y + nau*
> $(1000 * 7) - (500 * 0) + (100 * 1) - (10 * 13) - 3 = 6967$

Example 4.73

> *sairzbata'u*
> *sai + r + zba + ta'u*
> $(1000 * 11) - (500 * 1) + (100 * 1) - (10 * 21) - 5 = 10385$

Example 4.74

> *zbazbasysarji*
> *zba + zbas + y + sarji*
> $(1000 * 13) - (500 * 0) + (100 * 1) - (10 * 12) - 4 = 12976$

4.13 lujvo-making examples

This section contains examples of making and scoring lujvo. First, we will start with the tanru *gerku zdani* ("dog house") and construct a lujvo meaning "doghouse", that is, a house where a dog lives. We will use a brute-force application of the algorithm in Section 4.12 (p. 69), using every possible rafsi.

The rafsi for *gerku* are:

-ger-, *-ge'u-*, *-gerk-*, *-gerku*

The rafsi for *zdani* are:

-zda-, *-zdan-*, *-zdani.*

Step 1 of the algorithm directs us to use *-ger-*, *-ge'u-* and *-gerk-* as possible rafsi for *gerku*; Step 2 directs us to use *-zda-* and *-zdani* as possible rafsi for *zdani*. The six possible forms of the lujvo are then:

ger -zda
ger -zdani
ge'u -zda
ge'u -zdani
gerk -zda
gerk -zdani

We must then insert appropriate hyphens in each case. The first two forms need no hyphenation: *ge* cannot fall off the front, because the following word would begin with *rz*, which is not a permissible initial consonant pair. So the lujvo forms are *gerzda* and *gerzdani*.

The third form, *ge'u-zda*, needs no hyphen, because even though the first rafsi is CVV, the second one is CCV, so there is a consonant cluster in the first five letters. So *ge'uzda* is this form of the lujvo.

The fourth form, *ge'u-zdani*, however, requires an r-hyphen; otherwise, the *ge'u-* part would fall off as a cmavo. So this form of the lujvo is *ge'urzdani*.

The last two forms require y-hyphens, as all 4-letter rafsi do, and so are *gerkyzda* and *gerkyzdani* respectively.

The scoring algorithm is heavily weighted in favor of short lujvo, so we might expect that *gerzda* would win. Its **L** score is 6, its **A** score is 0, its **H** score is 0, its **R** score is 12, and its **V** score is 3, for a final score of 5878. The other forms have scores of 7917, 6367, 9506, 8008, and 10047 respectively. Consequently, this lujvo would probably appear in the dictionary in the form *gerzda*.

For the next example, we will use the tanru *bloti klesi* ("boat class") presumably referring to the category (rowboat, motorboat, cruise liner) into which a boat falls. We will omit the long rafsi from the process, since lujvo containing long rafsi are almost never preferred by the scoring algorithm when there are short rafsi available.

The rafsi for *bloti* are *-lot-*, *-blo-*, and *-lo'i-*; for *klesi* they are *-kle-* and *-lei-*. Both these gismu are among the handful which have both CVV-form and CCV-form rafsi, so there is an unusual number of possibilities available for a two-part tanru:

lotkle	*blokle*	*lo'ikle*
lotlei	*blolei*	*lo'irlei*

Only *lo'irlei* requires hyphenation (to avoid confusion with the cmavo sequence *lo'i lei*). All six forms are valid versions of the lujvo, as are the six further forms using long rafsi; however, the scoring algorithm produces the following results:

lotkle	5878
blokle	5858
lo'ikle	6367
lotlei	5867
blolei	5847
lo'irlei	7456

So the form *blolei* is preferred, but only by a tiny margin over *blokle*; "lotlei" and "lotkle" are only slightly worse; *lo'ikle* suffers because of its apostrophe, and *lo'irlei* because of having both apostrophe and hyphen.

Our third example will result in forming both a lujvo and a name from the tanru *logji bangu girzu*, or "logical-language group" in English. ("The Logical Language Group" is the name of the publisher of this book and the organization for the promotion of Lojban.)

The available rafsi are *-loj-* and *-logj-*; *-ban-*, *-bau-*, and *-bang-*; and *-gri-* and *-girzu*, and (for name purposes only) *-gir-* and *-girz-*. The resulting 12 lujvo possibilities are:

loj -ban -gri	*loj -bau -gri*	*loj -bang -gri*
logj -ban -gri	*logj -bau -gri*	*logj -bang -gri*
loj -ban -girzu	*loj -bau -girzu*	*loj -bang -girzu*
logj -ban -girzu	*logj -bau -girzu*	*logj -bang -girzu*

and the 12 name possibilities are:

loj -ban -gir	*loj -bau -gir*	*loj -bang -gir*
logj -ban -gir	*logj -bau -gir*	*logj -bang -gir*
loj -ban -girz	*loj -bau -girz*	*loj -bang -girz*
logj -ban -girz	*logj -bau -girz*	*logj -bang -girz*

After hyphenation, we have:

lojbangri	*lojbaugri*	*lojbangygri*
logjybangri	*logjybaugri*	*logjybangygri*
lojbangirzu	*lojbaugirzu*	*lojbangygirzu*
logjybangirzu	*logjybaugirzu*	*logjybangygirzu*
lojbangir	*lojbaugir*	*lojbangygir*
logjybangir	*logjybaugir*	*logjybangygir*
lojbangirz	*lojbaugirz*	*lojbangygirz*
logjybangirz	*logjybaugirz*	*logjybangygirz*

The only fully reduced lujvo forms are *lojbangri* and *lojbaugri*, of which the latter has a slightly lower score: 8827 versus 8796, respectively. However, for the name of the organization, we chose to make sure the name of the language was embedded in it, and to use the clearer long-form rafsi for *girzu*, producing *lojbangirz*.

Finally, here is a four-part lujvo with a cmavo in it, based on the tanru *nakni ke cinse ctuca* or "male (sexual teacher)". The *ke* cmavo ensures the interpretation "teacher of sexuality who is male", rather than "teacher of male sexuality". Here are the possible forms of the lujvo, both before and after hyphenation:

nak -kem -cin -ctu	*nakykemcinctu*
nak -kem -cin -ctuca	*nakykemcinctuca*
nak -kem -cins -ctu	*nakykemcinsyctu*
nak -kem -cins -ctuca	*nakykemcinsyctuca*
nakn -kem -cin -ctu	*naknykemcinctu*
nakn -kem -cin -ctuca	*naknykemcinctuca*
nakn -kem -cins -ctu	*naknykemcinsyctu*
nakn -kem -cins -ctuca	*naknykemcinsyctuca*

Of these forms, *nakykemcinctu* is the shortest and is preferred by the scoring algorithm. On the whole, however, it might be better to just make a lujvo for *cinse ctuca* (which would be *cinctu*) since the sex of the teacher is rarely important. If there was a reason to specify "male", then the simpler tanru *nakni cinctu* ("male sexual-teacher") would be appropriate. This tanru is actually shorter than the four-part lujvo, since the *ke* required for grouping need not be expressed.

4.14 The gismu creation algorithm

The gismu were created through the following process:

1. At least one word was found in each of the six source languages (Chinese, English, Hindi, Spanish, Russian, Arabic) corresponding to the proposed gismu. This word was rendered into Lojban phonetics rather liberally: consonant clusters consisting of a stop and the corresponding fricative were simplified to just the fricative (*tc* became *c*, *dj* became *j*) and

non-Lojban vowels were mapped onto Lojban ones. Furthermore, morphological endings were dropped. The same mapping rules were applied to all six languages for the sake of consistency.

2. All possible gismu forms were matched against the six source-language forms. The matches were scored as follows:

    a. If three or more letters were the same in the proposed gismu and the source-language word, and appeared in the same order, the score was equal to the number of letters that were the same. Intervening letters, if any, did not matter.

    b. If exactly two letters were the same in the proposed gismu and the source-language word, and either the two letters were consecutive in both words, or were separated by a single letter in both words, the score was 2. Letters in reversed order got no score.

    c. Otherwise, the score was 0.

3. The scores were divided by the length of the source-language word in its Lojbanized form, and then multiplied by a weighting value specific to each language, reflecting the proportional number of first-language and second-language speakers of the language. (Second-language speakers were reckoned at half their actual numbers.) The weights were chosen to sum to 1.00. The sum of the weighted scores was the total score for the proposed gismu form.

4. Any gismu forms that conflicted with existing gismu were removed. Obviously, being identical with an existing gismu constitutes a conflict. In addition, a proposed gismu that was identical to an existing gismu except for the final vowel was considered a conflict, since two such gismu would have identical 4-letter rafsi.

    More subtly: If the proposed gismu was identical to an existing gismu except for a single consonant, and the consonant was "too similar" based on the following table, then the proposed gismu was rejected.

proposed gismu	existing gismu
b	p, v
c	j, s
d	t
f	p, v
g	k, x
j	c, z
k	g, x
l	r
m	n
n	m
p	b, f
r	l
s	c, z
t	d
v	b, f
x	g, k
z	j, s

See Section 4.4 (p. 53) for an example.

5. The gismu form with the highest score usually became the actual gismu. Sometimes a lower-scoring form was used to provide a better rafsi. A few gismu were changed in error as a result of transcription blunders (for example, the gismu *gismu* should have been *gicmu*, but it's too late to fix it now).

The language weights used to make most of the gismu were as follows:

Chinese	0.36
English	0.21
Hindi	0.16
Spanish	0.11
Russian	0.09
Arabic	0.07

reflecting 1985 number-of-speakers data. A few gismu were made much later using updated weights:

Chinese	0.347
Hindi	0.196
English	0.160
Spanish	0.123
Russian	0.089
Arabic	0.085

(English and Hindi switched places due to demographic changes.)

Note that the stressed vowel of the gismu was considered sufficiently distinctive that two or more gismu may differ only in this vowel; as an extreme example, *bradi*, *bredi*, *bridi*, and *brodi* (but fortunately not *brudi*) are all existing gismu.

4.15 Cultural and other non-algorithmic gismu

The following gismu were not made by the gismu creation algorithm. They are, in effect, coined words similar to fu'ivla. They are exceptions to the otherwise mandatory gismu creation algorithm where there was sufficient justification for such exceptions. Except for the small metric prefixes and the assignable predicates beginning with *brod-*, they all end in the letter *o*, which is otherwise a rare letter in Lojban gismu.

The following gismu represent concepts that are sufficiently unique to Lojban that they were either coined from combining forms of other gismu, or else made up out of whole cloth. These gismu are thus conceptually similar to lujvo even though they are only five letters long; however, unlike lujvo, they have rafsi assigned to them for use in building more complex lujvo. Assigning gismu to these concepts helps to keep the resulting lujvo reasonably short.

broda	1st assignable predicate
brode	2nd assignable predicate
brodi	3rd assignable predicate
brodo	4th assignable predicate
brodu	5th assignable predicate
cmavo	structure word (from *cmalu valsi*)
lojbo	Lojbanic (from *logji bangu*)
lujvo	compound word (from *pluja valsi*)
mekso	Mathematical EXpression

It is important to understand that even though *cmavo*, *lojbo*, and *lujvo* were made up from parts of other gismu, they are now full-fledged gismu used in exactly the same way as all other gismu, both in grammar and in word formation.

The following three groups of gismu represent concepts drawn from the international language of science and mathematics. They are used for concepts that are represented in most languages by a root which is recognized internationally.

Small metric prefixes (values less than 1):

decti	.1	deci
centi	.01	centi
milti	.001	milli
mikri	10^{-6}	micro
nanvi	10^{-9}	nano

picti	10^{-12}	pico
femti	10^{-15}	femto
xatsi	10^{-18}	atto
zepti	10^{-21}	zepto
gocti	10^{-24}	yocto

Large metric prefixes (values greater than 1):

dekto	10	deka
xecto	100	hecto
kilto	1000	kilo
megdo	10^6	mega
gigdo	10^9	giga
terto	10^{12}	tera
petso	10^{15}	peta
xexso	10^{18}	exa
zetro	10^{21}	zetta
gotro	10^{24}	yotta

Other scientific or mathematical terms:

delno	candela
kelvo	kelvin
molro	mole
radno	radian
sinso	sine
stero	steradian
tanjo	tangent
xampo	ampere

The gismu *sinso* and *tanjo* were only made non-algorithmically because they were identical (having been borrowed from a common source) in all the dictionaries that had translations. The other terms in this group are units in the international metric system; some metric units, however, were made by the ordinary process (usually because they are different in Chinese).

Finally, there are the cultural gismu, which are also borrowed, but by modifying a word from one particular language, instead of using the multi-lingual gismu creation algorithm. Cultural gismu are used for words that have local importance to a particular culture; other cultures or languages may have no word for the concept at all, or may borrow the word from its home culture, just as Lojban does. In such a case, the gismu algorithm, which uses weighted averages, doesn't accurately represent the frequency of usage of the individual concept. Cultural gismu are not even required to be based on the six major languages.

The six Lojban source languages:

jungo	Chinese (from "Zhong [1] guo [2]")
glico	English
xindo	Hindi
spano	Spanish
rusko	Russian
xrabo	Arabic

Seven other widely spoken languages that were on the list of candidates for gismu-making, but weren't used:

bengo	Bengali
porto	Portuguese
baxso	Bahasa Melayu/Bahasa Indonesia
ponjo	Japanese (from "Nippon")
dotco	German (from „Deutsch")
fraso	French (from « Français »)
xurdo	Urdu

(Urdu and Hindi began as the same language with different writing systems, but have now become somewhat different, principally in borrowed vocabulary. Urdu-speakers were counted along with Hindi-speakers when weights were assigned for gismu-making purposes.)

Countries with a large number of speakers of any of the above languages (where the meaning of "large" is dependent on the specific language):

English:

merko	American
brito	British
skoto	Scottish
sralo	Australian
kadno	Canadian

Spanish:

gento	Argentinian
mexno	Mexican

Russian:

softo	Soviet/USSR
vukro	Ukrainian

Arabic:

filso	Palestinian
jerxo	Algerian
jordo	Jordanian
libjo	Libyan
lubno	Lebanese
misro	Egyptian (from "Mizraim")
morko	Moroccan
rakso	Iraqi
sadjo	Saudi
sirxo	Syrian

Bahasa Melayu/Bahasa Indonesia:

bindo	Indonesian
meljo	Malaysian

Portuguese:

brazo	Brazilian

Urdu:

kisto	Pakistani

The continents (and oceanic regions) of the Earth:

bemro	North American (from *berti merko*)
dzipo	Antarctican (from *cadzu cipni*)
ketco	South American (from "Quechua")
friko	African
polno	Polynesian/Oceanic
ropno	European
xazdo	Asiatic

A few smaller but historically important cultures:

latmo	Latin/Roman
srito	Sanskrit
xebro	Hebrew/Israeli/Jewish
xelso	Greek (from «Hellas»)

Major world religions:

budjo	Buddhist
dadjo	Taoist
muslo	Islamic/Moslem
xriso	Christian

A few terms that cover multiple groups of the above:

jegvo	Jehovist (Judeo-Christian-Moslem)
semto	Semitic
slovo	Slavic
xispo	Hispanic (New World Spanish)

4.16 rafsi fu'ivla: a proposal

The list of cultures represented by gismu, given in Section 4.15 (p. 73), is unavoidably controversial. Much time has been spent debating whether this or that culture "deserves a gismu" or "must languish in fu'ivla space". To help defuse this argument, a last-minute proposal was made when this book was already substantially complete. I have added it here with experimental status: it is not yet a standard part of Lojban, since all its implications have not been tested in open debate, and it affects a part of the language (lujvo-making) that has long been stable, but is known to be fragile in the face of small changes. (Many attempts were made to add general mechanisms for making lujvo that contained fu'ivla, but all failed on obvious or obscure counterexamples; finally the general *zei* mechanism was devised instead.)

The first part of the proposal is uncontroversial and involves no change to the language mechanisms. All valid Type 4 fu'ivla of the form CCVVCV would be reserved for cultural brivla analogous to those described in Section 4.15 (p. 73). For example,

Example 4.75

> *tci'ile*

> Chilean

is of the appropriate form, and passes all tests required of a Stage 4 fu'ivla. No two fu'ivla of this form would be allowed to coexist if they differed only in the final vowel; this rule was applied to gismu, but does not apply to other fu'ivla or to lujvo.

The second, and fully experimental, part of the proposal is to allow rafsi to be formed from these cultural fu'ivla by removing the final vowel and treating the result as a 4-letter rafsi (although it would contain five letters, not four). These rafsi could then be used on a par with all other rafsi in forming lujvo. The tanru

Example 4.76

tci'ile	*ke*	*canre*	*tutra*
Chilean	**type-of-(**	**sand**	**territory)**

Chilean desert

could be represented by the lujvo

Example 4.77

> *tci'ilykemcantutra*

which is an illegal word in standard Lojban, but a valid lujvo under this proposal. There would be no short rafsi or 5-letter rafsi assigned to any fu'ivla, so no fu'ivla could appear as the last element of a lujvo.

4.16 rafsi fu'ivla: a proposal

The cultural fu'ivla introduced under this proposal are called *rafsi fu'ivla*, since they are distinguished from other Type 4 fu'ivla by the property of having rafsi. If this proposal is workable and introduces no problems into Lojban morphology, it might become standard for all Type 4 fu'ivla, including those made for plants, animals, foodstuffs, and other things.

Chapter 5
"Pretty Little Girls' School": The Structure Of Lojban selbri

5.1 Lojban content words: brivla

At the center, logically and often physically, of every Lojban bridi is one or more words which constitute the selbri. A bridi expresses a relationship between things: the selbri specifies which relationship is referred to. The difference between:

Example 5.1

do	mamta	mi
You	**are-a-mother-of**	**me**

You are my mother

and

Example 5.2

do	patfu	mi
You	**are-a-father-of**	**me.**

You are my father.

lies in the different selbri.

The simplest kind of selbri is a single Lojban content word: a brivla. There are three different varieties of brivla: those which are built into the language (the gismu), those which are derived from combinations of the gismu (the lujvo), and those which are taken (usually in a modified form) from other languages (the fu'ivla). In addition, there are a few cmavo that can act like brivla; these are mentioned in Section 5.9 (p. 93), and discussed in full in Chapter 7 (p. 139).

For the purposes of this chapter, however, all brivla are alike. For example,

Example 5.3

ta	bloti
That	is-a-boat.

That is a boat.

Example 5.4

ta	brablo
That	is-a-large-boat.

That is a ship.

Example 5.5

ta	blotrskunri
That	is-a-(boat)-schooner.

That is a schooner.

illustrate the three types of brivla (gismu, lujvo, and fu'ivla respectively), but in each case the selbri is composed of a single word whose meaning can be learned independent of its origins.

The remainder of this chapter will mostly use gismu as example brivla, because they are short. However, it is important to keep in mind that wherever a gismu appears, it could be replaced by any other kind of brivla.

5.2 Simple tanru

Beyond the single brivla, a selbri may consist of two brivla placed together. When a selbri is built in this way from more than one brivla, it is called a tanru, a word with no single English equivalent. The nearest analogue to tanru in English are combinations of two nouns such as "lemon tree". There is no way to tell just by looking at the phrase "lemon tree" exactly what it refers to, even if you know the meanings of "lemon" and "tree" by themselves. As English-speakers, we must simply know that it refers to "a tree which bears lemons as fruits". A person who didn't know English very well might think of it as analogous to "brown tree" and wonder, "What kind of tree is lemon-colored?"

In Lojban, tanru are also used for the same purposes as English adjective-noun combinations like "big boy" and adverb-verb combinations like "quickly run". This is a consequence of Lojban not having any such categories as "noun", "verb", "adjective", or "adverb". English words belonging to any of these categories are translated by simple brivla in Lojban. Here are some examples of tanru:

Example 5.6

tu	pelnimre	tricu
That-yonder	is-a-lemon	tree.

That is a lemon tree.

Example 5.7

la	djan.	barda	nanla
That-named	John	is-a-big	boy.

John is a big boy.

Example 5.8

mi	sutra	bajra
I	quick	run

I quickly run./I run quickly.

Note that *pelnimre* is a lujvo for "lemon"; it is derived from the gismu *pelxu*, yellow, and *nimre*, citrus. Note also that *sutra* can mean "fast/quick" or "quickly" depending on its use:

Example 5.9

mi	sutra
I	am-fast/quick

shows *sutra* used to translate an adjective, whereas in Example 5.8 (p. 80) it is translating an adverb. (Another correct translation of Example 5.8 (p. 80), however, would be "I am a quick runner".)

There are special Lojban terms for the two components of a tanru, derived from the place structure of the word *tanru*. The first component is called the *seltau*, and the second component is called the *tertau*.

The most important rule for use in interpreting tanru is that the tertau carries the primary meaning. A *pelnimre tricu* is primarily a tree, and only secondarily is it connected with lemons in some way. For this reason, an alternative translation of Example 5.6 (p. 80) would be:

Example 5.10

That is a lemon type of tree.

This "type of" relationship between the components of a tanru is fundamental to the tanru concept. We may also say that the seltau modifies the meaning of the tertau:

Example 5.11

That is a tree which is lemon-ish (in the way appropriate to trees)

would be another possible translation of Example 5.6 (p. 80). In the same way, a more explicit translation of Example 5.7 (p. 80) might be:

Example 5.12

John is a boy who is big in the way that boys are big.

This "way that boys are big" would be quite different from the way in which elephants are big; big-for-a-boy is small-for-an-elephant.

All tanru are ambiguous semantically. Possible translations of:

Example 5.13

ta	klama	jubme
That	is-a-goer	type-of-table.

include:

That is a table which goes (a wheeled table, perhaps).
That is a table owned by one who goes.
That is a table used by those who go (a sports doctor's table?).
That is a table when it goes (otherwise it is a chair?).

In each case the object referred to is a "goer type of table", but the ambiguous "type of" relationship can mean one of many things. A speaker who uses tanru (and pragmatically all speakers must) takes the risk of being misunderstood. Using tanru is convenient because they are short and expressive; the circumlocution required to squeeze out all ambiguity can require too much effort.

No general theory covering the meaning of all possible tanru exists; probably no such theory can exist. However, some regularities obviously do exist:

Example 5.14

do	barda	prenu
You	are-a-large	person.

Example 5.15

do	cmalu	prenu
You	are-a-small	person.

are parallel tanru, in the sense that the relationship between *barda* and *prenu* is the same as that between *cmalu* and *prenu*. Section 5.14 (p. 101) and Section 5.15 (p. 107) contain a partial listing of some types of tanru, with examples.

5.3 Three-part tanru grouping with *bo*

The following cmavo is discussed in this section:

bo	BO	closest scope grouping

Consider the English sentence:

Example 5.16

> That's a little girls' school.

What does it mean? Two possible readings are:

Example 5.17

> That's a little school for girls.

Example 5.18

> That's a school for little girls.

This ambiguity is quite different from the simple tanru ambiguity described in Section 5.2 (p. 80). We understand that "girls' school" means "a school where girls are the students", and not "a school where girls are the teachers" or "a school which is a girl" (!). Likewise, we understand that "little girl" means "girl who is small". This is an ambiguity of grouping. Is "girls' school" to be taken as a unit, with "little" specifying the type of girls' school? Or is "little girl" to be taken as a unit, specifying the type of school? In English speech, different tones of voice, or exaggerated speech rhythm showing the grouping, are used to make the distinction; English writing usually leaves it unrepresented.

Lojban makes no use of tones of voice for any purpose; explicit words are used to do the work. The cmavo *bo* (which belongs to selma'o BO) may be placed between the two brivla which are most closely associated. Therefore, a Lojban translation of Example 5.17 (p. 82) would be:

Example 5.19

ta	cmalu	nixli	bo	ckule
That	**is-a-small**	**girl**	**-**	**school.**

Example 5.18 (p. 82) might be translated:

Example 5.20

ta	cmalu	bo	nixli	ckule
That	**is-a-small**	**-**	**girl**	**school.**

The *bo* is represented in the literal translation by a bracketed hyphen (not to be confused with the bare hyphen used as a placeholder in other glosses) because in written English a hyphen is sometimes used for the same purpose: "a big dog-catcher" would be quite different from a "big-dog catcher" (presumably someone who catches only big dogs).

Analysis of Example 5.19 (p. 82) and Example 5.20 (p. 82) reveals a tanru nested within a tanru. In Example 5.19 (p. 82), the main tanru has a seltau of *cmalu* and a tertau of *nixli bo ckule*; the tertau is itself a tanru with *nixli* as the seltau and *ckule* as the tertau. In Example 5.20 (p. 82), on the other hand, the seltau is *cmalu bo nixli* (itself a tanru), whereas the tertau is *ckule*. This structure of tanru nested within tanru forms the basis for all the more complex types of selbri that will be explained below.

What about Example 5.21 (p. 82)? What does it mean?

Example 5.21

ta	cmalu	nixli	ckule
That	**is-a-small**	**girl**	**school.**

The rules of Lojban do not leave this sentence ambiguous, as the rules of English do with Example 5.16 (p. 82). The choice made by the language designers is to say that Example 5.21 (p. 82) means the same as Example 5.20 (p. 82). This is true no matter what three brivla are used: the leftmost two are always grouped together. This rule is called the "left-grouping rule". Left-grouping in seemingly ambiguous structures is quite common – though not universal – in other contexts in Lojban.

5.4 Complex tanru grouping

Another way to express the English meaning of Example 5.19 (p. 82) and Example 5.20 (p. 82), using parentheses to mark grouping, is:

Example 5.22

ta	cmalu		nixli	bo	ckule
That	is-a-small	type-of	(girl	type-of	school).

Example 5.23

ta	cmalu	bo	nixli		ckule
That	is-a-(small	type-of	girl)	type-of	school.

Because "type-of" is implicit in the Lojban tanru form, it has no Lojban equivalent.

Note: It is perfectly legal, though pointless, to insert *bo* into a simple tanru:

Example 5.24

ta	klama	bo	jubme
That	is-a-goer	-	table.

is a legal Lojban bridi that means exactly the same thing as Example 5.13 (p. 81), and is ambiguous in exactly the same ways. The cmavo *bo* serves only to resolve grouping ambiguity: it says nothing about the more basic ambiguity present in all tanru.

5.4 Complex tanru grouping

If one element of a tanru can be another tanru, why not both elements?

Example 5.25

do	mutce	bo	barda	gerku	bo	kavbu
You	are-a-(very	type-of	large)	(dog	type-of	capturer).

You are a very large dog-catcher.

In Example 5.25 (p. 83), the selbri is a tanru with seltau *mutce bo barda* and tertau *gerku bo kavbu*. It is worth emphasizing once again that this tanru has the same fundamental ambiguity as all other Lojban tanru: the sense in which the "dog type-of capturer" is said to be "very type-of large" is not precisely specified. Presumably it is his body which is large, but theoretically it could be one of his other properties.

We will now justify the title of this chapter by exploring the ramifications of the phrase "pretty little girls' school", an expansion of the tanru used in Section 5.3 (p. 82) to four brivla. (Although this example has been used in the Loglan Project almost since the beginning – it first appeared in Quine's book *Word and Object* (1960) – it is actually a mediocre example because of the ambiguity of English "pretty"; it can mean "beautiful", the sense intended here, or it can mean "very". Lojban *melbi* is not subject to this ambiguity: it means only "beautiful".)

Here are four ways to group this phrase:

Example 5.26

ta	melbi		cmalu		nixli		ckule
That	is-a-((pretty	type-of	little)	type-of	girl)	type-of	school.

That is a school for girls who are beautifully small.

Example 5.27

ta	melbi		cmalu	nixli	bo	ckule
That	is-a-(pretty	type-of	little)	(girl	type-of	school).

That is a girls' school which is beautifully small.

Example 5.28

ta	melbi		cmalu	bo	nixli		ckule
That	is-a-(pretty	type-of	(little	type-of	girl))	type-of	school.

That is a school for small girls who are beautiful.

Example 5.29

ta	melbi		cmalu	bo	nixli	bo	ckule
That	is-a-pretty	type-of	(little	type-of	(girl	type-of	school)).

That is a small school for girls which is beautiful.

Example 5.29 (p. 84) uses a construction which has not been seen before: *cmalu bo nixli bo ckule*, with two consecutive uses of *bo* between brivla. The rule for multiple *bo* constructions is the opposite of the rule when no *bo* is present at all: the last two are grouped together. Not surprisingly, this is called the "right-grouping rule", and it is associated with every use of *bo* in the language. Therefore,

Example 5.30

ta	cmalu	bo	nixli	bo	ckule
That	is-a-little	type-of	(girl	type-of	school).

means the same as Example 5.19 (p. 82), not Example 5.20 (p. 82). This rule may seem peculiar at first, but one of its consequences is that *bo* is never necessary between the first two elements of any of the complex tanru presented so far: all of Example 5.26 (p. 83) through Example 5.29 (p. 84) could have *bo* inserted between *melbi* and *cmalu* with no change in meaning.

5.5 Complex tanru with *ke* and *ke'e*

The following cmavo are discussed in this section:

ke	KE	start grouping
ke'e	KEhE	end grouping

There is, in fact, a fifth grouping of "pretty little girls' school" that cannot be expressed with the resources explained so far. To handle it, we must introduce the grouping parentheses cmavo, *ke* and *ke'e* (belonging to selma'o KE and KEhE respectively). Any portion of a selbri sandwiched between these two cmavo is taken to be a single tanru component, independently of what is adjacent to it. Thus, Example 5.26 (p. 83) can be rewritten in any of the following ways:

Example 5.31

ta	ke	melbi	cmalu	ke'e	nixli	ckule
That	is-a-(	pretty	little	)	girl	school.

Example 5.32

ta	ke	ke	melbi	cmalu	ke'e	nixli	ke'e	ckule
That	is-a-(	(	pretty	little	)	girl	)	school.

Example 5.33

ta	ke	ke	ke	melbi	cmalu	ke'e	nixli	ke'e	ckule	ke'e
That	is-a-(	(	(	pretty	little	)	girl	)	school	).

Even more versions could be created simply by placing any number of *ke* cmavo at the beginning of the selbri, and a like number of *ke'e* cmavo at its end. Obviously, all of these are a waste of breath once the left-grouping rule has been grasped. However, the following is equivalent to Example 5.28 (p. 83) and may be easier to understand:

Example 5.34

ta		melbi		ke	cmalu		nixli	ke'e			ckule
That	is-a-(	pretty	type-of	(	little	type-of	girl	)	)	type-of	school.

Likewise, a *ke* and *ke'e* version of Example 5.27 (p. 83) would be:

Example 5.35

ta	melbi		cmalu	ke	nixli		ckule	[ke'e]
That	is-a-(pretty	type-of	little)	(	girl	type-of	school	).

The final *ke'e* is given in square brackets here to indicate that it can be elided. It is always possible to elide *ke'e* at the end of the selbri, making Example 5.35 (p. 84) as terse as Example 5.27 (p. 83).

Now how about that fifth grouping? It is

Example 5.36

ta	melbi		ke	cmalu		nixli			ckule	[ke'e]
That	is-a-pretty	type-of	(	(little	type-of	girl	)	type-of	school	).

That is a beautiful school for small girls.

Example 5.36 (p. 85) is distinctly different in meaning from any of Examples 4.2 through 4.5. Note that within the *ke...ke'e* parentheses, the left-grouping rule is applied to *cmalu nixli ckule*.

It is perfectly all right to mix *bo* and *ke...ke'e* in a single selbri. For instance, Example 5.29 (p. 84), which in pure *ke...ke'e* form is

Example 5.37

ta	melbi		ke	cmalu
That	is-a-pretty	type-of	(	little

	ke	nixli		ckule	[ke'e]	[ke'e]
type-of	(	girl	type-of	school	)	).

can equivalently be expressed as:

Example 5.38

ta	melbi		ke	cmalu		nixli	bo	ckule	[ke'e]
That	is-a-pretty	type-of	(	little	type-of-(	girl	type-of	school	)).

and in many other different forms as well.

5.6 Logical connection within tanru

The following cmavo are discussed in this section:

je	JA	tanru logical "and"
ja	JA	tanru logical "or"
joi	JOI	mixed mass "and"
gu'e	GUhA	tanru forethought logical "and"
gi	GI	forethought connection separator

Consider the English phrase "big red dog". How shall this be rendered as a Lojban tanru? The naive attempt:

Example 5.39

barda		xunre		gerku
(big	type-of	red)	type-of	dog

will not do, as it means a dog whose redness is big, in whatever way redness might be described as "big". Nor is

Example 5.40

barda		xunre	bo	gerku
big	type-of	(red	type-of	dog)

much better. After all, the straightforward understanding of the English phrase is that the dog is big as compared with other dogs, not merely as compared with other red dogs. In fact, the bigness and redness are independent properties of the dog, and only obscure rules of English adjective ordering prevent us from saying "red big dog".

The Lojban approach to this problem is to introduce the cmavo *je*, which is one of the many equivalents of English "and". A big red dog is one that is both big and red, and we can say:

Example 5.41

barda	je	xunre		gerku
(big	and	red)	type-of	dog

Of course,

Example 5.42

xunre	je	barda		gerku
(red	**and**	**big)**	**type-of**	**dog**

is equally satisfactory and means the same thing. As these examples indicate, joining two brivla with *je* makes them a unit for tanru purposes. However, explicit grouping with *bo* or *ke...ke'e* associates brivla more closely than *je* does:

Example 5.43

barda	je	pelxu	bo	xunre	gerku
(big	**and**	**(yellow**	**type-of**	**red))**	**dog**

barda	je	ke	pelxu		xunre	ke'e	gerku
(big	**and**	**(**	**yellow**	**type-of**	**red)**	**)**	**dog**

big yellowish-red dog

With no grouping indicators, we get:

Example 5.44

barda	je	pelxu		xunre		gerku
((big	**and**	**yellow)**	**type-of**	**red)**	**type-of**	**dog**

biggish- and yellowish-red dog

which again raises the question of Example 5.39 (p. 85): what does "biggish-red" mean?

Unlike *bo* and *ke...ke'e*, *je* is useful as well as merely legal within simple tanru. It may be used to partly resolve the ambiguity of simple tanru:

Example 5.45

ta	blanu	je	zdani
that	**is-blue**	**and**	**is-a-house**

definitely refers to something which is both blue and is a house, and not to any of the other possible interpretations of simple *blanu zdani*. Furthermore, *blanu zdani* refers to something which is blue in the way that houses are blue; *blanu je zdani* has no such implication – the blueness of a *blanu je zdani* is independent of its houseness.

With the addition of *je*, many more versions of "pretty little girls' school" are made possible: see Section 5.16 (p. 108) for a complete list.

A subtle point in the semantics of tanru like Example 5.41 (p. 85) needs special elucidation. There are at least two possible interpretations of:

Example 5.46

ta	melbi		je	nixli		ckule
That	**is-a-(beautiful**		**and**	**girl)**	**type-of**	**school.**

It can be understood as:

Example 5.47

That is a girls' school and a beautiful school.

or as:

Example 5.48

That is a school for things which are both girls and beautiful.

The interpretation specified by Example 5.47 (p. 86) treats the tanru as a sort of abbreviation for:

Example 5.49

ta	ke	melbi		ckule	ke'e	je	ke	nixli		ckule	[ke'e]
That	**is-a-(**	**beautiful**	**type-of**	**school**	**)**	**and**	**(**	**girl**	**type-of**	**school**	**)**

5.6 Logical connection within tanru

whereas the interpretation specified by Example 5.48 (p. 86) does not. This is a kind of semantic ambiguity for which Lojban does not compel a firm resolution. The way in which the school is said to be of type "beautiful and girl" may entail that it is separately a beautiful school and a girls' school; but the alternative interpretation, that the members of the school are beautiful and girls, is also possible. Still another interpretation is:

Example 5.50

> That is a school for beautiful things and also for girls.

so while the logical connectives help to resolve the meaning of tanru, they by no means compel a single meaning in and of themselves.

In general, logical connectives within tanru cannot undergo the formal manipulations that are possible with the related logical connectives that exist outside tanru; see Section 14.12 (p. 333) for further details.

The logical connective *je* is only one of the fourteen logical connectives that Lojban provides. Here are a few examples of some of the others:

Example 5.51

> le ⋮ bajra ⋮ cu ⋮ jinga ⋮ ja ⋮ te ⋮ jinga
>
> the runner(s) is/are winner(s) or loser(s).

Example 5.52

> | blanu | naja | lenku | skapi |
> |---|---|---|---|
> | **(blue** | **only-if** | **cold)** | **skin** |
>
> skin which is blue only if it is cold

Example 5.53

> | xamgu | jo | tordu | nuntavla |
> |---|---|---|---|
> | **(good** | **if-and-only-if** | **short)** | **speech** |
>
> speech which is good if (and only if) it is short

Example 5.54

> | vajni | ju | pluka | nuntavla |
> |---|---|---|---|
> | **(important** | **whether-or-not** | **pleasing)** | **event-of-talking** |
>
> speech which is important, whether or not it is pleasing

In Example 5.51 (p. 87), *ja* is grammatically equivalent to *je* but means "or" (more precisely, "and/or"). Likewise, *naja* means "only if" in Example 5.52 (p. 87), *jo* means "if and only if" in Example 5.53 (p. 87), and *ju* means "whether or not" in Example 5.54 (p. 87).

Now consider the following example:

Example 5.55

> | ricfu | je | blanu | jabo | crino |
> |---|---|---|---|---|
> | **rich** | **and** | **(blue** | **or** | **green)** |

which illustrates a new grammatical feature: the use of both *ja* and *bo* between tanru components. The two cmavo combine to form a compound whose meaning is that of *ja* but which groups more closely; *jabo* is to *ja* as plain *bo* is to no cmavo at all. However, both *ja* and *jabo* group less closely than *bo* does:

Example 5.56

> | ricfu | je | blanu | jabo | crino | bo | blanu |
> |---|---|---|---|---|---|---|
> | **rich** | **and** | **(blue** | **or** | **green** | - | **blue)** |
>
> rich and (blue or greenish-blue)

An alternative form of Example 5.55 (p. 87) is:

Example 5.57

ricfu	*je*	*ke*	*blanu*	*ja*	*crino*	*[ke'e]*
rich	**and**	**(**	**blue**	**or**	**green**	**)**

In addition to the logical connectives, there are also a variety of non-logical connectives, grammatically equivalent to the logical ones. The only one with a well-understood meaning in tanru contexts is *joi*, which is the kind of "and" that denotes a mixture:

Example 5.58

ti	*blanu*	*joi*	*xunre*	*bolci*
This	**is-a-(blue**	**and**	**red)**	**ball.**

The ball described is neither solely red nor solely blue, but probably striped or in some other way exhibiting a combination of the two colors. Example 5.58 (p. 88) is distinct from:

Example 5.59

ti	*blanu*	*xunre*	*bolci*

This is a bluish-red ball

which would be a ball whose color is some sort of purple tending toward red, since *xunre* is the more important of the two components. On the other hand,

Example 5.60

ti	*blanu*	*je*	*xunre*	*bolci*
This	**is-a-(blue**	**and**	**red)**	**ball**

is probably self-contradictory, seeming to claim that the ball is independently both blue and red at the same time, although some sensible interpretation may exist.

Finally, just as English "and" has the variant form "both ... and", so *je* between tanru components has the variant form *gu'e...gi*, where *gu'e* is placed before the components and *gi* between them:

Example 5.61

gu'e	*barda*	*gi*	*xunre*		*gerku*
(both	**big**	**and**	**red)**	**type-of**	**dog**

is equivalent in meaning to Example 5.41 (p. 85). For each logical connective related to *je*, there is a corresponding connective related to *gu'e...gi* in a systematic way.

The portion of a *gu'e...gi* construction before the *gi* is a full selbri, and may use any of the selbri resources including *je* logical connections. After the *gi*, logical connections are taken to be wider in scope than the *gu'e...gi*, which has in effect the same scope as *bo*:

Example 5.62

gu'e	*barda*	*je*	*xunre*	*gi*	*gerku*	*ja*	*mlatu*
(both	**(big**	**and**	**red)**	**and**	**dog)**	**or**	**cat**

something which is either big, red, and a dog, or else a cat

leaves *mlatu* outside the *gu'e...gi* construction. The scope of the *gi* arm extends only to a single brivla or to two or more brivla connected with *bo* or *ke...ke'e*.

5.7 Linked sumti: *be- bei- be'o*

The following cmavo are discussed in this section:

be	BE	linked sumti marker
bei	BEI	linked sumti separator
be'o	BEhO	linked sumti terminator

The question of the place structures of selbri has been glossed over so far. This chapter does not attempt to treat place structure issues in detail; they are discussed in Chapter 9 (p. 179). One grammatical structure related to places belongs here, however. In simple sentences such as Example 5.1

(p. 79), the place structure of the selbri is simply the defined place structure of the gismu *mamta*. What about more complex selbri?

For tanru, the place structure rule is simple: the place structure of a tanru is always the place structure of its tertau. Thus, the place structure of *blanu zdani* is that of *zdani*: the x1 place is a house or nest, and the x2 place is its occupants.

What about the places of *blanu*? Is there any way to get them into the act? In fact, *blanu* has only one place, and this is merged, as it were, with the x1 place of *zdani*. It is whatever is in the x1 place that is being characterized as blue-for-a-house. But if we replace *blanu* with *xamgu*, we get:

Example 5.63

ti	xamgu	zdani
This	is-a-good	house.

This is a good (for someone, by some standard) house.

Since *xamgu* has three places (x1, the good thing; x2, the person for whom it is good; and x3, the standard of goodness), Example 5.63 (p. 89) necessarily omits information about the last two: there is no room for them. Room can be made, however!

Example 5.64

ti	xamgu	be	do	bei	mi	[be'o]	zdani
This	is-a-good	(for	you	by-standard	me)		house.

This is a house that is good for you by my standards.

Here, the gismu *xamgu* has been followed by the cmavo *be* (of selma'o BE), which signals that one or more sumti follows. These sumti are not part of the overall bridi place structure, but fill the places of the brivla they are attached to, starting with x2. If there is more than one sumti, they are separated by the cmavo *bei* (of selma'o BEI), and the list of sumti is terminated by the elidable terminator *be'o* (of selma'o BEhO).

Grammatically, a brivla with sumti linked to it in this fashion plays the same role in tanru as a simple brivla. To illustrate, here is a fully fleshed-out version of Example 5.19 (p. 82), with all places filled in:

Example 5.65

ti	cmalu	be	le	ka	canlu
This	is-a-small	(in-dimension	the	property-of	volume

bei	lo'e	ckule	be'o
by-standard	the-typical	school)	

nixli	be	li	mu
(girl	(of-years	the-number	five

bei	lo	merko	be'o	bo	ckule
by-standard	some	American-thing)			school)

la	bryklyn.
in-that-named	Brooklyn

loi	pemci
with-subject	poems

le	mela	nu,IORK.	prenu
for-audience-the	among-that-named	New-York	persons

le	jecta
with-operator-the	state.

This is a school, small in volume compared to the typical school, pertaining to five-year-old girls (by American standards), in Brooklyn, teaching poetry to the New York community and operated by the state.

Here the three places of *cmalu*, the three of *nixli*, and the four of *ckule* are fully specified. Since the places of *ckule* are the places of the bridi as a whole, it was not necessary to link the sumti which follow *ckule*. It would have been legal to do so, however:

Example 5.66

mi	klama	be	le	zarci	bei	le	zdani	[be'o]
I	go	(	to-the	market		from-the	house	).

means the same as

Example 5.67

mi	klama	le	zarci	le	zdani
I	go	to-the	market	from-the	house.

No matter how complex a tanru gets, the last brivla always dictates the place structure: the place structure of

Example 5.68

	melbi	je	cmalu	nixli	bo	ckule
a	(pretty	and	little)	(girl		school)

a school for girls which is both beautiful and small

is simply that of *ckule*. (The sole exception to this rule is discussed in Section 5.8 (p. 91).)

It is possible to precede linked sumti by the place structure ordering tags *fe*, *fi*, *fo*, and *fu* (of selma'o FA, discussed further in Section 9.3 (p. 182)), which serve to explicitly specify the x2, x3, x4, and x5 places respectively. Normally, the place following the *be* is the x2 place and the other places follow in order. If it seems convenient to change the order, however, it can be accomplished as follows:

Example 5.69

ti	xamgu	be	fi	mi	bei	fe	do	[be'o]	zdani
This	is-a-good	(	by-standard	me		for	you	)	house.

which is equivalent in meaning to Example 5.64 (p. 89). Note that the order of *be*, *bei*, and *be'o* does not change; only the inserted *fi* tells us that *mi* is the x3 place (and correspondingly, the inserted *fe* tells us that *do* is the x2 place). Changing the order of sumti is often done to match the order of another language, or for emphasis or rhythm.

Of course, using FA cmavo makes it easy to specify one place while omitting a previous place:

Example 5.70

ti	xamgu	be	fi	mi	[be'o]	zdani
This	is-a-good	(	by-standard	me	)	house.

This is a good house by my standards.

Similarly, sumti labeled by modal or tense tags can be inserted into strings of linked sumti just as they can into bridi:

Example 5.71

ta	blanu	be	ga'a	mi	[be'o]	zdani
That	is-a-blue	(	to-observer	me	)	house.

That is a blue, as I see it, house.

The meaning of Example 5.71 (p. 90) is slightly different from:

Example 5.72

ta	blanu	zdani	ga'a	mi
That	is-a-blue	house	to-observer	me.

That is a blue house, as I see it.

See discussions in Chapter 9 (p. 179) of modals and in Chapter 10 (p. 207) of tenses for more explanations.

The terminator *be'o* is almost always elidable: however, if the selbri belongs to a description, then a relative clause following it will attach to the last linked sumti unless *be'o* is used, in which case it will attach to the outer description:

Example 5.73

le	xamgu	be	do	noi	barda	cu	zdani
The	good-thing	for	you	(who	are-large)		is-a-house.

Example 5.74

le	xamgu	be	do	be'o	noi	barda	cu	zdani
The	(good-thing	for	you	)	(which	is-large)		is-a-house

(Relative clauses are explained in Chapter 8 (p. 161).)

In other cases, however, *be'o* cannot be elided if *ku* has also been elided:

Example 5.75

le	xamgu	be	le	ctuca	[ku]	be'o	zdani
the	good	(for	the	teacher)			house

requires either *ku* or *be'o*, and since there is only one occurrence of *be*, the *be'o* must match it, whereas it may be confusing which occurrence of *le* the *ku* terminates (in fact the second one is correct).

5.8 Inversion of tanru: *co*

The following cmavo is discussed in this section:

co	CO	tanru inversion marker

The standard order of Lojban tanru, whereby the modifier precedes what it modifies, is very natural to English-speakers: we talk of "blue houses", not of "houses blue". In other languages, however, such matters are differently arranged, and Lojban supports this reverse order (tertau before seltau) by inserting the particle *co*. Example 5.76 (p. 91) and Example 5.77 (p. 91) mean exactly the same thing:

Example 5.76

ta	blanu	zdani
That	is-a-blue	type-of-house.

That is a blue house.

Example 5.77

ta	zdani	co	blanu
That	is-a-house	of-type	blue.

That is a blue house.

This change is called "tanru inversion". In tanru inversion, the element before *co* (*zdani* in Example 5.77 (p. 91)) is the tertau, and the element following *co* (*blanu*) in Example 5.77 (p. 91)) is the seltau.

The meaning, and more specifically, the place structure, of a tanru is not affected by inversion: the place structure of *zdani co blanu* is still that of *zdani*. However, the existence of inversion in a selbri has a very special effect on any sumti which follow that selbri. Instead of being interpreted as filling places of the selbri, they actually fill the places (starting with x2) of the seltau. In Section 5.7 (p. 88), we saw how to fill interior places with *be...bei...be'o*, and in fact Example 5.78 (p. 91) and Example 5.79 (p. 92) have the same meaning:

Example 5.78

mi	klama	be	le	zarci	bei	le	zdani	be'o	troci
I	am-a-(goer	to	the	market	from	the	house	)	type-of-trier.

I try to go to the market from the house.

Example 5.79

mi	troci	co	klama	le	zarci	le	zdani
I	**am-a-trier**	**of-type**	**(goer**	**to-the**	**market**	**from-the**	**house).**

I try to go to the market from the house.

Example 5.79 (p. 92) is a less deeply nested construction, requiring fewer cmavo. As a result it is probably easier to understand.

Note that in Lojban "trying to go" is expressed using *troci* as the tertau. The reason is that "trying to go" is a "going type of trying", not a "trying type of going". The trying is more fundamental than the going – if the trying fails, we may not have a going at all.

Any sumti which precede a selbri with an inverted tanru fill the places of the selbri (i.e., the places of the tertau) in the ordinary way. In Example 5.79 (p. 92), *mi* fills the x1 place of *troci co klama*, which is the x1 place of *troci*. The other places of the selbri remain unfilled. The trailing sumti *le zarci* and *le zdani* do not occupy selbri places, despite appearances.

As a result, the regular mechanisms (involving selma'o VOhA and GOhI, explained in Chapter 7 (p. 139)) for referring to individual sumti of a bridi cannot refer to any of the trailing places of Example 5.79 (p. 92), because they are not really "sumti of the bridi" at all.

When inverting a more complex tanru, it is possible to invert it only at the most general modifier-modified pair. The only possible inversion of Example 5.19 (p. 82), for instance, is:

Example 5.80

ta	nixli	[bo]	ckule	co	cmalu
That	**(is-a-girl**	**type-of**	**school)**	**of-type**	**little.**

That's a girls' school which is small.

Note that the *bo* of Example 5.19 (p. 82) is optional in Example 5.80 (p. 92), because *co* groups more loosely than any other cmavo used in tanru, including none at all. Not even *ke...ke'e* parentheses can encompass a *co*:

Example 5.81

ta	cmalu		ke	nixli		ckule	[ke'e]	co	melbi
That	**is-a-(little**	**type-of**	**(**	**girl**	**type-of**	**school**	**))**	**of-type**	**pretty.**

That's a small school for girls which is beautiful.

In Example 5.81 (p. 92), the *ke'e* is automatically inserted before the *co* rather than at its usual place at the end of the selbri. As a result, there is a simple and mechanical rule for removing *co* from any selbri: change "A co B" to "ke B ke'e A". (At the same time, any sumti following the selbri must be transformed into *be...bei...be'o* form and attached following B.) Therefore,

Example 5.82

ckule	co	melbi	nixli
school	**of-type**	**pretty**	**girl**

school for beautiful girls

means the same as:

Example 5.83

ke	melbi	nixli	ke'e	ckule
(	**pretty**	**girl**	**)**	**school**

Multiple *co* cmavo can appear within a selbri, indicating multiple inversions: a right-grouping rule is employed, as for *bo*. The above rule can be applied to interpret such selbri, but all *co* cmavo must be removed simultaneously:

Example 5.84

ckule	co	nixli	co	cmalu
school	**of-type**	**(girl**	**of-type**	**little)**

becomes formally

Example 5.85

ke	ke	cmalu	ke'e	nixli	ke'e	ckule
(	(	**little**	)	**girl**	)	**school**

which by the left-grouping rule is simply

Example 5.86

cmalu	nixli	ckule
little	**girl**	**school**

school for little girls

As stated above, the selbri places, other than the first, of

Example 5.87

mi	klama	co	sutra
I	**am-a-goer**	**of-type**	**quick**

I go quickly

cannot be filled by placing sumti after the selbri, because any sumti in that position fill the places of *sutra*, the seltau. However, the tertau places (which means in effect the selbri places) can be filled with *be*:

Example 5.88

mi	klama	be	le	zarci	be'o	co	sutra
I	**am-a-goer**	(	**to-the**	**store**	)	**of-type**	**quick.**

I go to the store quickly.

5.9 Other kinds of simple selbri

The following cmavo are discussed in this section:

go'i	GOhA	repeats the previous bridi
du	GOhA	equality
nu'a	NUhA	math operator to selbri
moi	MOI	changes number to ordinal selbri
mei	MOI	changes number to cardinal selbri
nu	NU	event abstraction
kei	KEI	terminator for NU

So far we have only discussed brivla and tanru built up from brivla as possible selbri. In fact, there are a few other constructions in Lojban which are grammatically equivalent to brivla: they can be used either directly as selbri, or as components in tanru. Some of these types of simple selbri are discussed at length in Chapter 7 (p. 139), Chapter 11 (p. 247), and Chapter 18 (p. 413); but for completeness these types are mentioned here with a brief explanation and an example of their use in selbri.

The cmavo of selma'o GOhA (with one exception) serve as pro-bridi, providing a reference to the content of other bridi; none of them has a fixed meaning. The most commonly used member of GOhA is probably *go'i*, which amounts to a repetition of the previous bridi, or part of it. If I say:

Example 5.89

la	djan.	klama	le	zarci
That-named	**John**	**goes-to**	**the**	**market.**

you may retort:

Example 5.90

la	djan.	go'i	troci
That-named	John	[repeat-last]	are-a-trier.

John tries to.

Example 5.90 (p. 94) is short for:

Example 5.91

la	djan.	klama	be	le	zarci	be'o		troci
That-named	John	is-a-goer	(	to-the	market	)	type-of	trier.

because the whole bridi of Example 5.89 (p. 93) has been packaged up into the single word *go'i* and inserted into Example 5.90 (p. 94).

The exceptional member of GOhA is *du*, which represents the relation of identity. Its place structure is:

x1 is identical with x2, x3, ...

for as many places as are given. More information on selma'o GOhA is available in Chapter 7 (p. 139).

Lojban mathematical expressions (mekso) can be incorporated into selbri in two different ways. Mathematical operators such as *su'i*, meaning "plus", can be transformed into selbri by prefixing them with *nu'a* (of selma'o NUhA). The resulting place structure is:

x1 is the result of applying (the operator) to arguments x2, x3, etc.

for as many arguments as are required. (The result goes in the x1 place because the number of following places may be indefinite.) For example:

Example 5.92

li	vo	nu'a su'i	li	re	li	re
The-number	4	is-the-sum-of	the-number	2	and-the-number	2.

A possible tanru example might be:

Example 5.93

mi	jimpe	tu'a	loi	nu'a su'i	nabmi
I	understand	something-about	the-mass-of	is-the-sum-of	problems.

I understand addition problems.

More usefully, it is possible to combine a mathematical expression with a cmavo of selma'o MOI to create one of various numerical selbri. Details are available in Section 18.11 (p. 428). Here are a few tanru:

Example 5.94

la	prim.	palvr.	pamoi	cusku
That-named	Preem	Palver	is-the-1-th	speaker.

Preem Palver is the first speaker.

Example 5.95

la	an,iis.	joi	la	.asun.
That-named	Anyi	massed-with	that-named	Asun

bruna	remei
are-a-brother	type-of-twosome.

Anyi and Asun are two brothers.

Finally, an important type of simple selbri which is not a brivla is the abstraction. Grammatically, abstractions are simple: a cmavo of selma'o NU, followed by a bridi, followed by the elidable terminator *kei* of selma'o KEI. Semantically, abstractions are an extremely subtle and powerful feature of Lojban whose full ramifications are documented in Chapter 11 (p. 247). A few examples:

Example 5.96

ti	nu	zdile	kei	kumfa
This	is-an-event-of	amusement		room.

This is an amusement room.

Example 5.96 (p. 95) is quite distinct in meaning from:

Example 5.97

ti	zdile	kumfa
This	is-an-amuser	room.

which suggests the meaning "a room that amuses someone".

5.10 selbri based on sumti: *me*

The following cmavo are discussed in this section:

me	ME	changes sumti to simple selbri
me'u	MEhU	terminator for *me*

A sumti can be made into a simple selbri by preceding it with *me* (of selma'o ME) and following it with the elidable terminator *me'u* (of selma'o MEhU). This makes a selbri with the place structure

x1 is one of the referents of "[the sumti]"

which is true of the thing, or things, that are the referents of the sumti, and not of anything else. For example, consider the sumti

Example 5.98

le	ci	nolraitru
the	three	noblest-governors

the three kings

If these are understood to be the Three Kings of Christian tradition, who arrive every year on January 6, then we may say:

Example 5.99

la	BALtazar.	cu	me	le ci nolraitru
That-named	Balthazar		is-one-of-the-referents-of	"the three kings."

Balthazar is one of the three kings.

and likewise

Example 5.100

| la | kaspar. | cu | me | le | ci | nolraitru |

Caspar is one of the three kings.

and

Example 5.101

| la | melxi,or. | cu | me | le | ci | nolraitru |

Melchior is one of the three kings.

If the sumti refers to a single object, then the effect of *me* is much like that of *du*:

Example 5.102

do	du	la	djan.
You	are-identical-with	that-named	"John."

You are John.

means the same as

Example 5.103

do	me	la djan.
You	**are-the-referent-of**	**"that-named 'John'."**

You are John.

It is common to use *me* selbri, especially those based on name sumti using *la*, as seltau. For example:

Example 5.104

ta	me	lai kraislr.		[me'u]	karce
That	**(is-a-referent-of**	**"the-mass-named 'Chrysler"**	**)**		**car.**

That is a Chrysler car.

The elidable terminator *me'u* can usually be omitted. It is absolutely required only if the *me* selbri is being used in an indefinite description (a type of sumti explained in Section 6.8 (p. 127)), and if the indefinite description is followed by a relative clause (explained in Chapter 8 (p. 161)) or a sumti logical connective (explained in Section 14.6 (p. 324)). Without a *me'u*, the relative clause or logical connective would appear to belong to the sumti embedded in the *me* expression. Here is a contrasting pair of sentences:

Example 5.105

re	me	le	ci	nolraitru	.e	la	djan.	[me'u]	cu	blabi

Two of the group "the three kings and John" are white.

Example 5.106

re	me	le	ci	nolraitru	me'u	.e	la	djan.	cu	blabi

Two of the three kings, and John, are white.

In Example 5.105 (p. 96) the *me* selbri covers the three kings plus John, and the indefinite description picks out two of them that are said to be white: we cannot say which two. In Example 5.106 (p. 96), though, the *me* selbri covers only the three kings: two of them are said to be white, and so is John.

Finally, here is another example requiring *me'u*:

Example 5.107

ta	me la'e le se cusku be do	me'u		cukta
That	**is-a-(what-you-said)**		**type-of**	**book.**

That is the kind of book you were talking about.

There are other sentences where either *me'u* or some other elidable terminator must be expressed:

Example 5.108

le	me le ci nolraitru	[ku]	me'u	nunsalci
the	**(the three kings)**			**type-of-event-of-celebrating**

the Three Kings celebration

requires either *ku* or *me'u* to be explicit, and (as with *be'o* in Section 5.7 (p. 88)) the *me'u* leaves no doubt which cmavo it is paired with.

5.11 Conversion of simple selbri

Conversion is the process of changing a selbri so that its places appear in a different order. This is not the same as labeling the sumti with the cmavo of FA, as mentioned in Section 5.7 (p. 88), and then rearranging the order in which the sumti are spoken or written. Conversion transforms the selbri into a distinct, though closely related, selbri with renumbered places.

In Lojban, conversion is accomplished by placing a cmavo of selma'o SE before the selbri:

Example 5.109

mi	prami	do

I love you.

is equivalent in meaning to:

Example 5.110

do	se	prami	mi
You	[swap x1 and x2]	love	me.

You are loved by me.

Conversion is fully explained in Section 9.4 (p. 185). For the purposes of this chapter, the important point about conversion is that it applies only to the following simple selbri. When trying to convert a tanru, therefore, it is necessary to be careful! Consider Example 5.111 (p. 97):

Example 5.111

la	.alis.	cu	cadzu	klama	le	zarci
That-named	Alice		is-a-walker	type-of-goer-to	the	market.
That-named	Alice		walkingly	goes-to	the	market.

Alice walks to the market.

To convert this sentence so that *le zarci* is in the x1 place, one correct way is:

Example 5.112

le	zarci	cu	se
The	market		is-a-[swap x1/x2]
The	market		

ke	cadzu	klama	[ke'e]	la	.alis.
(	walker	type-of-goer-to	)	that-named	Alice.
	is-walkingly	gone-to-by		that-named	Alice.

The *ke...ke'e* brackets cause the entire tanru to be converted by the *se*, which would otherwise convert only *cadzu*, leading to:

Example 5.113

le	zarci	cu	se	cadzu
The	market		(is-a-[swap x1/x2]	walker)
The	market			is-a-walking-surface

klama	la	.alis.
type-of-goer-to	that-named	Alice.
type-of-goer-to	that-named	Alice.

whatever that might mean. An alternative approach, since the place structure of *cadzu klama* is that of *klama* alone, is to convert only the latter:

Example 5.114

le	zarci	cu	cadzu	se klama	la	.alis.
The	market		walkingly	is-gone-to-by	that-named	Alice.

But the tanru in Example 5.114 (p. 97) may or may not have the same meaning as that in Example 5.111 (p. 97); in particular, because *cadzu* is not converted, there is a suggestion that although Alice is the goer, the market is the walker. With a different sumti as x1, this seemingly odd interpretation might make considerable sense:

Example 5.115

la	djan.	cu	cadzu	se klama	la	.alis
That-named	John		walkingly	is-gone-to-by	that-named	Alice

suggests that Alice is going to John, who is a moving target.

There is an alternative type of conversion, using the cmavo *jai* of selma'o JAI optionally followed by a modal or tense construction. Grammatically, such a combination behaves exactly like conversion using SE. More details can be found in Section 9.12 (p. 199).

5.12 Scalar negation of selbri

Negation is too large and complex a topic to explain fully in this chapter; see Chapter 15 (p. 353). In brief, there are two main types of negation in Lojban. This section is concerned with so-called "scalar negation", which is used to state that a true relation between the sumti is something other than what the selbri specifies. Scalar negation is expressed by cmavo of selma'o NAhE:

Example 5.116

la	.alis.	cu	na'e	ke	cadzu	klama	[ke'e]	le	zarci
That-named	Alice		non-	(	walkingly	goes-to	)	the	market.

Alice doesn't walk to the market.

meaning that Alice's relationship to the market is something other than that of walking there. But if the *ke* were omitted, the result would be:

Example 5.117

la	.alis.	cu	na'e	cadzu	klama	le	zarci
That-named	Alice		non-	walkingly	goes-to	the	market.

Alice doesn't walk to the market.

meaning that Alice does go there in some way (*klama* is not negated), but by a means other than that of walking. Example 5.116 (p. 98) negates both *cadzu* and *klama*, suggesting that Alice's relation to the market is something different from walkingly-going; it might be walking without going, or going without walking, or neither.

Of course, any of the simple selbri types explained in Section 5.9 (p. 93) may be used in place of brivla in any of these examples:

Example 5.118

la	djonz.	cu	na'e	pamoi	cusku
That-named	Jones		is-non-	1st	speaker

Jones is not the first speaker.

Since only *pamoi* is negated, an appropriate inference is that he is some other kind of speaker.

Here is an assortment of more complex examples showing the interaction of scalar negation with *bo* grouping, *ke* and *ke'e* grouping, logical connection, and sumti linked with *be* and *bei*:

Example 5.119

mi	na'e	sutra	cadzu	be	fi	le	birka	be'o	klama	le	zarci
I	((non-	quickly)	(walking		using	the	arms	))	go-to	the	market.

I go to the market, walking using my arms other than quickly.

In Example 5.119 (p. 98), *na'e* negates only *sutra*. Contrast Example 5.120 (p. 98):

Example 5.120

mi	na'e	ke	sutra	cadzu	be	fi	le	birka	[be'o]
I	non-	(	quickly	(walking		using	the	arms	)

ke'e	klama	le	zarci
)	go-to	the	market.

I go to the market, other than by walking quickly on my arms.

Now consider Example 5.121 (p. 99) and Example 5.122 (p. 99), which are equivalent in meaning, but use *ke* grouping and *bo* grouping respectively:

5.12 Scalar negation of selbri

Example 5.121

mi	sutra	cadzu	be	fi	le	birka	be'o
I	(quickly	(walking		using	the	arms	)

je	masno	klama	le	zarci
and	slowly)	go-to	the	market.

I go to the market, both quickly walking using my arms and slowly.

Example 5.122

mi	ke	sutra	cadzu	be	fi	le	birka	[be'o]	ke'e
I	(	(quickly	(walking		using	the	arms	)	)

je	masno	klama	le	zarci
and	slowly)	go-to	the	market.

I go to the market, both quickly walking using my arms and slowly.

However, if we place a *na'e* at the beginning of the selbri in both Example 5.121 (p. 99) and Example 5.122 (p. 99), we get different results:

Example 5.123

mi	na'e	sutra	cadzu	be	fi	le	birka	be'o
I	((non-	quickly)	(walking		using	the	arms	)

je	masno	klama	le	zarci
and	slowly)	go-to	the	market.

I go to the market, both walking using my arms other than quickly, and also slowly.

Example 5.124

mi	na'e	ke	sutra	cadzu	be	fi	le	birka	[be'o]	ke'e
I	(non	(	quickly	(walking		using	the	arms)		)

je	masno	klama	le	zarci
and	slowly)	go-to	the	market.

I go to the market, both other than quickly walking using my arms, and also slowly.

The difference arises because the *na'e* in Example 5.124 (p. 99) negates the whole construction from *ke* to *ke'e*, whereas in Example 5.123 (p. 99) it negates *sutra* alone.

Beware of omitting terminators in these complex examples! If the explicit *ke'e* is left out in Example 5.124 (p. 99), it is transformed into:

Example 5.125

mi	na'e	ke	sutra	cadzu	be	fi	le	birka	be'o
I	non-	(	quickly	((walking		using	the	arms)	)

je	masno	klama	[ke'e]	le	zarci
and	slowly)	go-to	)	the	market.

I do something other than quickly both going to the market walking using my arms and slowly going to the market.

And if both *ke'e* and *be'o* are omitted, the results are even sillier:

Example 5.126

mi	na'e	ke	sutra	cadzu	be	fi	le	birka	je	masno
I	non	(	quickly	walk		on-my	(the	arm-type	and	slow)

klama	[be'o]	[ke'e]	le	zarci
goers	)	)	on-the	market.

I do something other than quickly walking using the goers, both arm-type and slow, relative-to the market.

In Example 5.126 (p. 99), everything after *be* is a linked sumti, so the place structure is that of *cadzu*, whose x2 place is the surface walked upon. It is less than clear what an "arm-type goer" might be. Furthermore, since the x3 place has been occupied by the linked sumti, the *le zarci* following the selbri falls into the nonexistent x4 place of *cadzu*. As a result, the whole example, though grammatical, is complete nonsense. (The bracketed Lojban words appear where a fluent Lojbanist would understand them to be implied.)

Finally, it is also possible to place *na'e* before a *gu'e...gi* logically connected tanru construction. The meaning of this usage has not yet been firmly established.

5.13 Tenses and bridi negation

A bridi can have cmavo associated with it which specify the time, place, or mode of action. For example, in

Example 5.127

mi	pu	klama	le	zarci
I	[past]	go-to	the	market.

I went to the market.

the cmavo *pu* specifies that the action of the speaker going to the market takes place in the past. Tenses are explained in full detail in Chapter 10 (p. 207). Tense is semantically a property of the entire bridi; however, the usual syntax for tenses attaches them at the front of the selbri, as in Example 5.127 (p. 100). There are alternative ways of expressing tense information as well. Modals, which are explained in Chapter 9 (p. 179), behave in the same way as tenses.

Similarly, a bridi may have the particle *na* (of selma'o NA) attached to the beginning of the selbri to negate the bridi. A negated bridi expresses what is false without saying anything about what is true. Do not confuse this usage with the scalar negation of Section 5.12 (p. 98). For example:

Example 5.128

la	djonz.	na	pamoi	cusku
That-named	Jones	(Not!)	is-the-first	speaker

It is not true that Jones is the first speaker.
Jones isn't the first speaker.

Jones may be the second speaker, or not a speaker at all; Example 5.128 (p. 100) doesn't say. There are other ways of expressing bridi negation as well; the topic is explained fully in Chapter 15 (p. 353).

Various combinations of tense and bridi negation cmavo are permitted. If both are expressed, either order is permissible with no change in meaning:

Example 5.129

mi	na	pu	klama	le	zarci

It is false that I went to the market.
I didn't go to the market.

It is also possible to have more than one *na*, in which case pairs of *na* cmavo cancel out:

Example 5.130

mi	na	na	klama	le	zarci

It is false that it is false that I go to the market.
I go to the market.

It is even possible, though somewhat pointless, to have multiple *na* cmavo and tense cmavo mixed together, subject to the limitation that two adjacent tense cmavo will be understood as a compound tense, and must fit the grammar of tenses as explained in Chapter 10 (p. 207).

Example 5.131

mi	na	pu	na	ca	klama	le	zarci
I	[not]	[past]	[not]	[present]	go-to	the	market

It is not the case that in the past it was not the case that in the present I went to the market.
I didn't not go to the market.
I went to the market.

Tense, modal, and negation cmavo can appear only at the beginning of the selbri. They cannot be embedded within it.

5.14 Some types of asymmetrical tanru

This section and Section 5.15 (p. 107) contain some example tanru classified into groups based on the type of relationship between the modifying seltau and the modified tertau. All the examples are paralleled by compounds actually observed in various natural languages. In the tables which follow, each group is preceded by a brief explanation of the relationship. The tables themselves contain a tanru, a literal gloss, an indication of the languages which exhibit a compound analogous to this tanru, and (for those tanru with no English parallel) a translation.

Here are the 3-letter abbreviations used for the various languages (it is presumed to be obvious whether a compound is found in English or not, so English is not explicitly noted):

Aba	Abazin	Chi	Chinese	Ewe	Ewe	Fin	Finnish
Geo	Georgian	Gua	Guarani	Hop	Hopi	Hun	Hungarian
Imb	Imbabura Quechua	Kar	Karaitic	Kaz	Kazakh	Kor	Korean
Mon	Mongolian	Qab	Qabardian	Que	Quechua	Rus	Russian
Skt	Sanskrit	Swe	Swedish	Tur	Turkish	Udm	Udmurt

Any lujvo or fu'ivla used in a group are glossed at the end of that group.

The tanru discussed in this section are asymmetrical tanru; that is, ones in which the order of the terms is fundamental to the meaning of the tanru. For example, *junla dadysli*, or "clock pendulum", is the kind of pendulum used in a clock, whereas *dadysli junla*, or "pendulum clock", is the kind of clock that employs a pendulum. Most tanru are asymmetrical in this sense. Symmetrical tanru are discussed in Section 5.15 (p. 107).

The tertau represents an action, and the seltau then represents the object of that action:

Table 5.1. Example tanru

pinsi nunkilbra	pencil sharpener	Hun	
zgike nunctu	music instruction	Hun	
mirli nunkalte	deer hunting	Hun	
finpe nunkalte	fish hunting	Tur,Kor,Udm,Aba	fishing
smacu terkavbu	mousetrap	Tur,Kor,Hun,Udm,Aba	
zdani turni	house ruler	Kar	host
zerle'a nunte'a	thief fear	Skt	fear of thieves
cevni zekri	god crime	Skt	offense against the gods

Table 5.2. Mini-Glossary

nunkilbra	sharpness-apparatus
nunctu	event-of-teaching
nunkalte	event-of-hunting
terkavbu	trap
zerle'a	crime-taker
nunte'a	event-of-fearing

The tertau represents a set, and the seltau the type of the elements contained in that set:

Table 5.3. Example tanru

zdani lijgri	house row		
selci lamgri	cell block		
karda mulgri	card pack	Swe	
rokci derxi	stone heap	Swe	
tadni girzu	student group	Hun	
remna girzu	human-being group	Qab	group of people
cpumi'i lijgri	tractor column	Qab	
cevni jenmi	god army	Skt	
cevni prenu	god folk	Skt	

Table 5.4. Mini-Glossary

lijgri	line-group
lamgri	adjacent-group
mulgri	complete-group
cpumi'i	pull-machine

Conversely: the tertau is an element, and the seltau represents a set in which that element is contained. Implicitly, the meaning of the tertau is restricted from its usual general meaning to the specific meaning appropriate for elements in the given set. Note the opposition between *zdani lijji* in the previous group, and *linji zdani* in this one, which shows why this kind of tanru is called "asymmetrical".

Table 5.5. Example tanru

carvi dirgo	raindrop	Tur,Kor,Hun,Udm,Aba
linji zdani	row house	

The seltau specifies an object and the tertau a component or detail of that object; the tanru as a whole refers to the detail, specifying that it is a detail of that whole and not some other.

Table 5.6. Example tanru

junla dadysli	clock pendulum	Hun	
purdi vorme	garden door	Qab	
purdi bitmu	garden wall	Que	
moklu skapi	mouth skin	Imb	lips
nazbi kevna	nose hole	Imb	nostril
karce xislu	automobile wheel	Chi	
jipci pimlu	chicken feather	Chi	
vinji rebla	airplane tail	Chi	

Table 5.7. Mini-Glossary

dadysli	hang-oscillator

Conversely: the seltau specifies a characteristic or important detail of the object described by the tertau; objects described by the tanru as a whole are differentiated from other similar objects by this detail.

Table 5.8. Example tanru

pixra cukta	picture book		
kerfa silka	hair silk	Kar	velvet
plise tapla	apple cake	Tur	
dadysli junla	pendulum clock	Hun	

Table 5.9. Mini-Glossary

dadysli	hang-oscillator

The tertau specifies a general class of object (a genus), and the seltau specifies a sub-class of that class (a species):

Table 5.10. Example tanru

ckunu tricu	pine tree	Hun,Tur,Hop

5.14 Some types of asymmetrical tanru

The tertau specifies an object of possession, and the seltau may specify the possessor (the possession may be intrinsic or otherwise). In English, these compounds have an explicit possessive element in them: "lion's mane", "child's foot", "noble's cow".

Table 5.11. Example tanru

cinfo kerfa	lion mane	Kor,Tur,Hun,Udm,Qab	
verba jamfu	child foot	Swe	
nixli tuple	girl leg	Swe	
cinfo jamfu	lion foot	Que	
danlu skapi	animal skin	Ewe	
ralju zdani	chief house	Ewe	
jmive munje	living world	Skt	
nobli bakni	noble cow	Skt	
nolraitru ralju	king chief	Skt	emperor

Table 5.12. Mini-Glossary

nolraitru	nobly-superlative-ruler

The tertau specifies a habitat, and the seltau specifies the inhabitant:

Table 5.13. Example tanru

lanzu tumla	family land	

The tertau specifies a causative agent, and the seltau specifies the effect of that cause:

Table 5.14. Example tanru

kalselvi'i gapci	tear gas	Hun	
terbi'a jurme	disease germ	Tur	
fenki litki	crazy liquid	Hop	whisky
pinca litki	urine liquid	Hop	beer

Table 5.15. Mini-Glossary

kalselvi'i	eye-excreted-thing
terbi'a	disease

Conversely: the tertau specifies an effect, and the seltau specifies its cause.

Table 5.16. Example tanru

djacu barna	water mark	Chi

The tertau specifies an instrument, and the seltau specifies the purpose of that instrument:

Table 5.17. Example tanru

taxfu dadgreku	garment rack	Chi	
tergu'i ti'otci	lamp shade	Chi	
xirma zdani	horse house	Chi	stall
nuzba tanbo	news board	Chi	bulletin board

Table 5.18. Mini-Glossary

dadgreku	hang-frame
tergu'i	source of illumination
ti'otci	shadow-tool

More vaguely: the tertau specifies an instrument, and the seltau specifies the object of the purpose for which that instrument is used:

Table 5.19. Example tanru

cpina rokci	pepper stone	Que	stone for grinding pepper
jamfu djacu	foot water	Skt	water for washing the feet
grana mudri	post wood	Skt	wood for making a post
moklu djacu	mouth water	Hun	water for washing the mouth
lanme gerku	sheep dog		dog for working sheep

The tertau specifies a product from some source, and the seltau specifies the source of the product:

Table 5.20. Example tanru

moklu djacu	mouth water	Aba,Qab	saliva
ractu mapku	rabbit hat	Rus	
jipci sovda	chicken egg	Chi	
sikcurnu silka	silkworm silk	Chi	
mlatu kalci	cat feces	Chi	
bifce lakse	bee wax	Chi	beeswax
cribe rectu	bear meat	Tur,Kor,Hun,Udm,Aba	
solxrula grasu	sunflower oil	Tur,Kor,Hun,Udm,Aba	
bifce jisra	bee juice	Hop	honey
tatru litki	breast liquid	Hop	milk
kanla djacu	eye water	Kor	tear

Table 5.21. Mini-Glossary

sikcurnu	silk-worm
solxrula	solar-flower

Conversely: the tertau specifies the source of a product, and the seltau specifies the product:

Table 5.22. Example tanru

silna jinto	salt well	Chi
kolme terkakpa	coal mine	Chi
ctile jinto	oil well	Chi

Table 5.23. Mini-Glossary

terkakpa	source of digging

The tertau specifies an object, and the seltau specifies the material from which the object is made. This case is especially interesting, because the referent of the tertau may normally be made from just one kind of material, which is then overridden in the tanru.

Table 5.24. Example tanru

rokci cinfo	stone lion		
snime nanmu	snow man	Hun	
kliti cipni	clay bird		
blaci kanla	glass eye	Hun	
blaci kanla	glass eye	Que	spectacles
solji sicni	gold coin	Tur	
solji junla	gold watch	Tur,Kor,Hun	
solji djine	gold ring	Udm,Aba,Que	
rokci zdani	stone house	Imb	
mudri zdani	wood house	Ewe	wooden house
rokci bitmu	stone wall	Ewe	
solji carce	gold chariot	Skt	
mudri xarci	wood weapon	Skt	wooden weapon
cmaro'i dargu	pebble road	Chi	
sudysrasu cutci	straw shoe	Chi	

Table 5.25. Mini-Glossary

cmaro'i	small-rock
sudysrasu	dry-grass

Note: the two senses of *blaci kanla* can be discriminated as:

Table 5.26. Example tanru

blaci kanla bo tarmi	glass (eye shape)	glass eye
blaci kanla bo sidju	glass (eye helper)	spectacles

5.14 Some types of asymmetrical tanru

The tertau specifies a typical object used to measure a quantity and the seltau specifies something measured. The tanru as a whole refers to a given quantity of the thing being measured. English does not have compounds of this form, as a rule.

Table 5.27. Example tanru

tumla spisa	land piece	Tur	piece of land
tcati kabri	tea cup	Kor,Aba	cup of tea
nanba spisa	bread piece	Kor	piece of bread
bukpu spisa	cloth piece	Udm,Aba	piece of cloth
djacu calkyguzme	water calabash	Ewe	calabash of water

Table 5.28. Mini-Glossary

calkyguzme	shell-fruit, calabash

The tertau specifies an object with certain implicit properties, and the seltau overrides one of those implicit properties:

Table 5.29. Example tanru

kensa bloti	spaceship		
bakni verba	cattle child	Ewe	calf

The seltau specifies a whole, and the tertau specifies a part which normally is associated with a different whole. The tanru then refers to a part of the seltau which stands in the same relationship to the whole seltau as the tertau stands to its typical whole.

Table 5.30. Example tanru

kosta degji	coat finger	Hun	coat sleeve
denci genja	tooth root	Imb	
tricu stedu	tree head	Imb	treetop

The tertau specifies the producer of a certain product, and the seltau specifies the product. In this way, the tanru as a whole distinguishes its referents from other referents of the tertau which do not produce the product.

Table 5.31. Example tanru

silka curnu	silkworm	Tur,Hun,Aba

The tertau specifies an object, and the seltau specifies another object which has a characteristic property. The tanru as a whole refers to those referents of the tertau which possess the property.

Table 5.32. Example tanru

sonci manti	soldier ant		
ninmu bakni	woman cattle	Imb	cow
mamta degji	mother finger	Imb	thumb
cifnu degji	baby finger	Imb	pinky
pacraistu zdani	hell house	Skt	
fagri dapma	fire curse	Skt	curse destructive as fire

Table 5.33. Mini-Glossary

pacraistu	evil-superlative-site

As a particular case (when the property is that of resemblance): the seltau specifies an object which the referent of the tanru resembles.

Table 5.34. Example tanru

grutrceraso jbama	cherry bomb		
solji kerfa	gold hair	Hun	golden hair
kanla djacu	eye water	Kar	spring
bakni rokci	bull stone	Mon	boulder

Table 5.35. Mini-Glossary

grutrceraso	fu'ivla for "cherry" based on Linnean name

The seltau specifies a place, and the tertau an object characteristically located in or at that place.

Table 5.36. Example tanru

ckana boxfo	bed sheet	Chi	
mrostu mojysu'a	tomb monument	Chi	tombstone
jubme tergusni	table lamp	Chi	
foldi smacu	field mouse	Chi	
briju ci'ajbu	office desk	Chi	
rirxe xirma	river horse	Chi	hippopotamus
xamsi gerku	sea dog	Chi	seal
cagyce'u zdani	village house	Skt	

Table 5.37. Mini-Glossary

mrostu	dead-site
mojysu'a	remember-structure
ci'ajbu	write-table
cagyce'u	farm-community

Specifically: the tertau is a place where the seltau is sold or made available to the public.

Table 5.38. Example tanru

cidja barja	food bar	Chi	restaurant
cukta barja	book bar	Chi	library

The seltau specifies the locus of application of the tertau.

Table 5.39. Example tanru

kanla velmikce	eye medicine	Chi	
jgalu grasu	nail oil	Chi	nail polish
denci pesxu	tooth paste	Chi	

Table 5.40. Mini-Glossary

velmikce	treatment used by doctor

The tertau specifies an implement used in the activity denoted by the seltau.

Table 5.41. Example tanru

me la pinpan. bolci	Ping-Pong ball	Chi

The tertau specifies a protective device against the undesirable features of the referent of the seltau.

Table 5.42. Example tanru

carvi mapku	rain cap	Chi	
carvi taxfu	rain garment	Chi	raincoat
vindu firgai	poison mask	Chi	gas mask

Table 5.43. Mini-Glossary

firgai	face-cover

The tertau specifies a container characteristically used to hold the referent of the seltau.

Table 5.44. Example tanru

cukta vasru	book vessel	Chi	satchel
vanju kabri	wine cup	Chi	
spatrkoka lanka	coca basket	Que	
rismi dakli	rice bag	Ewe,Chi	
tcati kabri	tea cup	Chi	
ladru botpi	milk bottle	Chi	
rismi patxu	rice pot	Chi	
festi lante	trash can	Chi	
bifce zdani	bee house	Kor	beehive
cladakyxa'i zdani	sword house	Kor	sheath
manti zdani	ant nest	Gua	anthill

Table 5.45. Mini-Glossary

spatrkoka	fu'ivla for "coca"
cladakyxa'i	(long-knife)-weapon

The seltau specifies the characteristic time of the event specified by the tertau.

Table 5.46. Example tanru

vensa djedi	spring day	Chi
crisa citsi	summer season	Chi
cerni bumru	morning fog	Chi
critu lunra	autumn moon	Chi
dunra nicte	winter night	Chi
nicte ckule	night school	Chi

The seltau specifies a source of energy for the referent of the tertau.

Table 5.47. Example tanru

dikca tergusni	electric lamp	Chi
ratni nejni	atom energy	Chi
brife molki	windmill	Tur,Kor,Hun,Udm,Aba

Table 5.48. Mini-Glossary

tergusni	illumination-source

Finally, some tanru which don't fall into any of the above categories.

Table 5.49. Example tanru

ladru denci	milk tooth	Tur,Hun,Udm,Qab
kanla denci	eye tooth	

It is clear that "tooth" is being specified, and that "milk" and "eye" act as modifiers. However, the relationship between *ladru* and *denci* is something like "tooth which one has when one is drinking milk from one's mother", a relationship certainly present nowhere except in this particular concept. As for *kanla denci*, the relationship is not only not present on the surface, it is hardly possible to formulate it at all.

5.15 Some types of symmetrical tanru

This section deals with symmetrical tanru, where order is not important. Many of these tanru can be expressed with a logical or non-logical connective between the components.

The tanru may refer to things which are correctly specified by both tanru components. Some of these instances may also be seen as asymmetrical tanru where the seltau specifies a material. The connective *je* is appropriate:

Table 5.50. Example tanru

cipnrstrigi pacru'i	owl demon	Skt	
nolraitru prije	royal sage	Skt	
remna nakni	human-being male	Qab	man
remna fetsi	human-being female	Qab	woman
sonci tolvri	soldier coward	Que	
panzi nanmu	offspring man	Ewe	son
panzi ninmu	offspring woman	Ewe	daughter
solji sicni	gold coin	Tur	
solji junla	gold watch	Tur,Kor,Hun	
solji djine	gold ring	Udm,Aba,Que	
rokci zdani	stone house	Imb	
mudri zdani	wooden house	Ewe	
rokci bitmu	stone wall	Ewe	
solji carce	gold chariot	Skt	
mudri xarci	wooden weapon	Skt	
zdani tcadu	home town	Chi	

107

Table 5.51. Mini-Glossary

cipnrstrigi	fu'ivla for "owl" based on Linnean name
pacru'i	evil-spirit
tolvri	opposite-of-brave

The tanru may refer to all things which are specified by either of the tanru components. The connective *ja* is appropriate:

Table 5.52. Example tanru

nunji'a nunterji'a	victory defeat	Skt	victory or defeat
donri nicte	day night	Skt	day and night
lunra tarci	moon stars	Skt	moon and stars
patfu mamta	father mother	Imb,Kaz,Chi	parents
tuple birka	leg arm	Kaz	extremity
nuncti nunpinxe	eating drinking	Udm	cuisine
bersa tixnu	son daughter	Chi	children

Table 5.53. Mini-Glossary

nunji'a	event-of-winning
nunterji'a	event-of-losing
nuncti	event-of-eating
nunpinxe	event-of-drinking

Alternatively, the tanru may refer to things which are specified by either of the tanru components or by some more inclusive class of things which the components typify:

Table 5.54. Example tanru

curnu jalra	worm beetle	Mon	insect
jalra curnu	beetle worm	Mon	insect
kabri palta	cup plate	Kaz	crockery
jipci gunse	hen goose	Qab	housefowl
xrula tricu	flower tree	Chi	vegetation

The tanru components specify crucial or typical parts of the referent of the tanru as a whole:

Table 5.55. Example tanru

tumla vacri	land air	Fin	world
moklu stedu	mouth head	Aba	face
sudysrasu cunmi	hay millet	Qab	agriculture
gugde ciste	state system	Mon	politics
prenu so'imei	people multitude	Mon	masses
djacu dertu	water earth	Chi	climate

Table 5.56. Mini-Glossary

sudysrasu	dry-grass
so'imei	manysome

5.16 "Pretty little girls' school": forty ways to say it

The following examples show every possible grouping arrangement of *melbi cmalu nixli ckule* using *bo* or *ke...ke'e* for grouping and *je* or *jebo* for logical connection. Most of these are definitely not plausible interpretations of the English phrase "pretty little girls' school", especially those which describe something which is both a girl and a school.

Examples Example 5.26 (p. 83), Example 5.27 (p. 83), Example 5.28 (p. 83), Example 5.29 (p. 84), and Example 5.36 (p. 85) are repeated here as Examples Example 5.132 (p. 109), Example 5.140 (p. 110), Example 5.148 (p. 110), Example 5.156 (p. 111), and Example 5.164 (p. 112) respectively. The seven examples following each of these share the same grouping pattern, but differ in the presence or absence of *je* at each possible site. Some of the examples have more than one Lojban version. In that case, they differ only in grouping mechanism, and are always equivalent in meaning.

5.16 "Pretty little girls' school": forty ways to say it

The logical connective *je* is associative: that is, "A and (B and C)" is the same as "(A and B) and C". Therefore, some of the examples have the same meaning as others. In particular, Example 5.139 (p. 109), Example 5.147 (p. 110), Example 5.155 (p. 111), Example 5.163 (p. 112), and Example 5.171 (p. 113) all have the same meaning because all four brivla are logically connected and the grouping is simply irrelevant. Other equivalent forms are noted in the examples themselves. However, if *je* were replaced by *naja* or *jo* or most of the other logical connectives, the meanings would become distinct.

It must be emphasized that, because of the ambiguity of all tanru, the English translations are by no means definitive – they represent only one possible interpretation of the corresponding Lojban sentence.

Example 5.132

melbi		*cmalu*		*nixli*		*ckule*
((pretty	type-of	little)	type-of	girl)	type-of	school

school for girls who are beautifully small

Example 5.133

melbi	*je*	*cmalu*		*nixli*		*ckule*
((pretty	and	little)	type-of	girl)	type-of	school

school for girls who are beautiful and small

Example 5.134

melbi	*bo*	*cmalu*	*je*	*nixli*		*ckule*
((pretty	type-of	little)	and	girl)	type-of	school

school for girls and for beautifully small things

Example 5.135

ke	*melbi*		*cmalu*		*nixli*	*ke'e*	*je*	*ckule*
((	pretty	type-of	little)	type-of	girl	)	and	school

thing which is a school and a beautifully small girl

Example 5.136

melbi	*je*	*cmalu*	*je*	*nixli*		*ckule*
((pretty	and	little)	and	girl)	type-of	school

school for things which are beautiful, small, and girls
Note: same as Example 5.152 (p. 111)

Example 5.137

melbi	*bo*	*cmalu*	*je*	*nixli*	*je*	*ckule*
((pretty	type-of	little)	and	girl)	and	school

thing which is beautifully small, a school, and a girl
Note: same as Example 5.145 (p. 110)

Example 5.138

ke	*melbi*	*je*	*cmalu*		*nixli*	*ke'e*	*je*	*ckule*
((	pretty	and	little)	type-of	girl	)	and	school

thing which is a school and a girl who is both beautiful and small

Example 5.139

melbi	*je*	*cmalu*	*je*	*nixli*	*je*	*ckule*
((pretty	and	little)	and	girl)	and	school

thing which is beautiful, small, a girl, and a school

Example 5.140

melbi			cmalu		nixli	bo	ckule
(pretty	type-of	little)	type-of	(girl	type-of	school)

girls' school which is beautifully small

Example 5.141

melbi	je	cmalu		nixli	bo	ckule
(pretty	and	little)	type-of	(girl	type-of	school)

girls' school which is beautiful and small

Example 5.142

melbi			cmalu		nixli	je	ckule
(pretty	type-of	little)	type-of	(girl	and	school)

something which is a girl and a school which is beautifully small

Example 5.143

melbi	bo	cmalu	je	nixli	bo	ckule
(pretty	type-of	little)	and	(girl	type-of	school)

something which is beautifully small and a girls' school

Example 5.144

melbi	je	cmalu		nixli	je	ckule
(pretty	and	little)	type-of	(girl	and	school)

a pretty and little type of thing which is both a girl and a school

Example 5.145

melbi	bo	cmalu	je	nixli	jebo	ckule
(pretty	type-of	little)	and	(girl	and	school)

thing which is beautifully small, a school, and a girl

Note: same as Example 5.137 (p. 109)

Example 5.146

melbi	jebo	cmalu	je	nixli	bo	ckule
(pretty	and	little)	and	(girl	type-of	school)

thing which is beautiful and small and a girl's school

Note: same as Example 5.161 (p. 112)

Example 5.147

melbi	jebo	cmalu	je	nixli	jebo	ckule
(pretty	and	little)	and	(girl	and	school)

thing which is beautiful, small, a girl, and a school

Example 5.148

melbi			cmalu	bo	nixli		ckule
(pretty	type-of	(little	type-of	girl))	type-of	school

school for beautiful girls who are small

Example 5.149

melbi			cmalu	je	nixli		ckule
(pretty	type-of	(little	and	girl))	type-of	school

school for beautiful things which are small and are girls

Example 5.150

melbi	je	cmalu	bo	nixli		ckule
(pretty	and	(little	type-of	girl))	type-of	school

school for things which are beautiful and are small girls

Example 5.151

ke	melbi		cmalu	bo	nixli	ke'e	je	ckule
	melbi	bo	cmalu	bo	nixli		je	ckule
(	pretty	type-of	(little	type-of	girl	))	and	school

thing which is a school and a small girl who is beautiful

Example 5.152

melbi	je	cmalu	jebo	nixli		ckule
(pretty	and	(little	and	girl))	type-of	school

school for things which are beautiful, small, and girls

Note: same as Example 5.136 (p. 109)

Example 5.153

melbi	je	cmalu	bo	nixli	je	ckule
(pretty	and	(little	type-of	girl))	and	school

thing which is beautiful, a small girl, and a school

Note: same as Example 5.169 (p. 113)

Example 5.154

ke	melbi		cmalu	je	nixli	ke'e	je	ckule
(	pretty	type-of	(little	and	girl	))	and	school

thing which is beautifully small, a beautiful girl, and a school

Example 5.155

melbi	je	cmalu	jebo	nixli	je	ckule
(pretty	and	(little	and	girl))	and	school

thing which is beautiful, small, a girl, and a school

Example 5.156

melbi		cmalu	bo	nixli	bo	ckule		
melbi	ke	cmalu	ke	nixli		ckule	[ke'e]	[ke'e]
pretty	type-of	(little	type-of	(girl	type-of	school	)	)

small school for girls which is beautiful

Example 5.157

melbi	ke	cmalu		nixli	je	ckule	[ke'e]
pretty	type-of	(little	type-of	(girl	and	school	))

small thing, both a girl and a school, which is beautiful

Example 5.158

melbi		cmalu	je	nixli	bo	ckule
pretty	type-of	(little	and	(girl	type-of	school))

thing which is beautifully small and a girls' school that is beautiful

Example 5.159

melbi	je		cmalu	bo		nixli	bo		ckule		
melbi	je	ke	cmalu			nixli	bo		ckule	[ke'e]	
melbi	je	ke	cmalu	ke		nixli			ckule	[ke'e]	[ke'e]
pretty	**and**	**(**	**little**	**type-of**	**(girl**	**type-of**	**school**	**)**		**)**	

thing which is beautiful and a small type of girls' school

Example 5.160

melbi			cmalu	je		nixli	jebo	ckule	
melbi			cmalu	je	ke	nixli	je	ckule	[ke'e]
pretty	**type-of**	**(little**	**and**	**(**	**girl**	**and**	**school**	**))**	

thing which is beautifully small, a beautiful girl, and a beautiful school

Note: same as Example 5.168 (p. 113)

Example 5.161

melbi	je		cmalu	jebo	nixli	bo		ckule	
melbi	je	ke	cmalu	je	nixli	bo		ckule	[ke'e]
pretty	**and**	**(**	**little**	**and**	**(girl**	**type-of**	**school**	**))**	

thing which is beautiful, small and a girls' school

Note: same as Example 5.146 (p. 110)

Example 5.162

melbi	je	ke	cmalu		nixli	je	ckule	[ke'e]
pretty	**and**	**(**	**little**	**type-of**	**(girl**	**and**	**school**	**))**

beautiful thing which is a small girl and a small school

Example 5.163

melbi	jebo	cmalu	jebo	nixli	jebo	ckule	
pretty	**and**	**(little**	**and**	**(girl**	**and**	**school))**	

thing which is beautiful, small, a girl, and a school

Example 5.164

melbi	ke	cmalu		nixli		ckule	[ke'e]
pretty	**type-of**	**((little**	**type-of**	**girl)**	**type-of**	**school**	**)**

beautiful school for small girls

Example 5.165

melbi	ke	cmalu	je	nixli		ckule	[ke'e]
pretty	**type-of**	**((little**	**and**	**girl)**	**type-of**	**school**	

beautiful school for things which are small and are girls

Example 5.166

melbi	ke	cmalu	bo	nixli	je	ckule	[ke'e]
pretty	**type-of**	**((little**	**type-of**	**girl)**	**and**	**school**	**)**

beautiful thing which is a small girl and a school

Example 5.167

melbi	je	ke	cmalu		nixli	ckule	[ke'e]
pretty	**and**	**((**	**little**	**type-of**	**girl)**	**type-of**	**school**	**)**

thing which is beautiful and a school for small girls

5.16 "Pretty little girls' school": forty ways to say it

Example 5.168

melbi		cmalu	je	nixli	je	ckule
pretty	**type-of**	**((little**	**and**	**girl)**	**and**	**school)**

thing which is beautifully small, a beautiful girl, and a beautiful school

Note: same as Example 5.160 (p. 112)

Example 5.169

melbi	je	ke	cmalu	bo	nixli	je	ckule	[ke'e]
pretty	**and**	**((**	**little**	**type-of**	**girl)**	**and**	**school**	**)**

thing which is beautiful, a small girl and a school

Note: same as Example 5.153 (p. 111)

Example 5.170

melbi	je	ke	cmalu	je	nixli		ckule	[ke'e]
pretty	**and**	**((**	**little**	**and**	**girl)**	**type-of**	**school**	**)**

thing which is beautiful and is a small school and a girls' school

Example 5.171

melbi	je	ke	cmalu	je	nixli	je	ckule	[ke'e]
pretty	**and**	**((**	**little**	**and**	**girl)**	**and**	**school**	**)**

thing which is beautiful, small, a girl, and a school

Chapter 6
To Speak Of Many Things: The Lojban sumti

lei re nanmu cu bevri le re nanmu

6.1 The five kinds of simple sumti

If you understand anything about Lojban, you know what a sumti is by now, right? An argument, one of those things that fills the places of simple Lojban sentences like:

Example 6.1

mi	*klama*	*le*	*zarci*
I	go-to	the	market

In Example 6.1 (p. 115), *mi* and *le zarci* are the sumti. It is easy to see that these two sumti are not of the same kind: *mi* is a pro-sumti (the Lojban analogue of a pronoun) referring to the speaker, whereas *le zarci* is a description which refers to something described as being a market.

There are five kinds of simple sumti provided by Lojban:

1. descriptions like *le zarci*, which usually begin with a descriptor (called a *gadri* in Lojban) such as *le*;
2. pro-sumti, such as *mi*;
3. names, such as *la lojban.*, which usually begin with *la*;
4. quotations, which begin with *lu, le'u, zo*, or *zoi*;
5. pure numbers, which usually begin with *li*.

Here are a few examples of each kind of sumti:

115

Example 6.2

e'osai	ko	sarji	la	lojban.
[request] [!]	You [imperative]	support	that-named	Lojban.

Please support Lojban!

Example 6.2 (p. 116) exhibits *ko*, a pro-sumti; and *la lojban.*, a name.

Example 6.3

mi	cusku	lu	e'osai	li'u	le	tcidu
I	express	[quote]	[request] [!]	[unquote]	to-the	reader.

I express "Please!" to the reader.

Example 6.3 (p. 116) exhibits *mi*, a pro-sumti; *lu e'osai li'u*, a quotation; and *le tcidu*, a description.

Example 6.4

ti	mitre	li	ci
This	measures-in-meters	the-number	three.

This is three meters long.

Example 6.4 (p. 116) exhibits *ti*, a pro-sumti; and *li ci*, a number.

Most of this chapter is about descriptions, as they have the most complicated syntax and usage. Some attention is also given to names, which are closely interwoven with descriptions. Pro-sumti, numbers, and quotations are described in more detail in Chapter 7 (p. 139), Chapter 18 (p. 413), and Chapter 19 (p. 447) respectively, so this chapter only gives summaries of their forms and uses. See Section 6.13 (p. 134) through Section 6.15 (p. 136) for these summaries.

6.2 The three basic description types

The following cmavo are discussed in this section:

le	LE	the, the one(s) described as
lo	LE	some, some of those which really are
la	LA	the one(s) named
ku	KU	elidable terminator for LE, LA

The syntax of descriptions is fairly complex, and not all of it can be explained within the confines of this chapter: relative clauses, in particular, are discussed in Chapter 8 (p. 161). However, most descriptions have just two components: a descriptor belonging to selma'o LE or LA, and a selbri. (The difference between selma'o LE and selma'o LA is not important until Section 6.12 (p. 132).) Furthermore, the selbri is often just a single brivla. Here is an elementary example:

Example 6.5

le	zarci
one-or-more-specific-things-each-of-which-I-describe-as	being-a-market

the market

The long gloss for *le* is of course far too long to use most of the time, and in fact *le* is quite close in meaning to English "the". It has particular implications, however, which "the" does not have.

The general purpose of all descriptors is to create a sumti which might occur in the x1 place of the selbri belonging to the description. Thus *le zarci* conveys something which might be found in the x1 place of *zarci*, namely a market.

The specific purpose of *le* is twofold. First, it indicates that the speaker has one or more specific markets in mind (whether or not the listener knows which ones they are). Second, it also indicates that the speaker is merely describing the things he or she has in mind as markets, without being committed to the truth of that description.

Example 6.6

le		zarci	cu	barda
One-or-more-specific-things-which-I-describe-as		"markets"		is/are-big.

The market is big.
The markets are big.

Note that English-speakers must state whether a reference to markets is to just one ("the market") or to more than one ("the markets"). Lojban requires no such forced choice, so both colloquial translations of Example 6.6 (p. 117) are valid. Only the context can specify which is meant. (This rule does not mean that Lojban has no way of specifying the number of markets in such a case: that mechanism is explained in Section 6.7 (p. 124).)

Now consider the following strange-looking example:

Example 6.7

le		nanmu	cu	ninmu
One-or-more-specific-things-which-I-describe-as		"men"		is/are-women.

The man is a woman.
The men are women.

Example 6.7 (p. 117) is not self-contradictory in Lojban, because *le nanmu* merely means something or other which, for my present purposes, I choose to describe as a man, whether or not it really is a man. A plausible instance would be: someone we had assumed to be a man at a distance turned out to be actually a woman on closer observation. Example 6.7 (p. 117) is what I would say to point out my observation to you.

In all descriptions with *le*, the listener is presumed to either know what I have in mind or else not to be concerned at present (perhaps I will give more identifying details later). In particular, I might be pointing at the supposed man or men: Example 6.7 (p. 117) would then be perfectly intelligible, since *le nanmu* merely clarifies that I am pointing at the supposed man, not at a landscape, or a nose, which happens to lie in the same direction.

The second descriptor dealt with in this section is *lo*. Unlike *le*, *lo* is nonspecific:

Example 6.8

lo		zarci
one-or-more-of-all-the-things-which-really		are-markets

a market
some markets

Again, there are two colloquial English translations. The effect of using *lo* in Example 6.8 (p. 117) is to refer generally to one or more markets, without being specific about which. Unlike *le zarci*, *lo zarci* must refer to something which actually is a market (that is, which can appear in the x1 place of a truthful bridi whose selbri is *zarci*). Thus

Example 6.9

lo		nanmu	cu	ninmu
That-which-really-is		a-man		is-a-woman.

Some man is a woman.
Some men are women.

must be false in Lojban, given that there are no objects in the real world which are both men and women. Pointing at some specific men or women would not make Example 6.9 (p. 117) true, because those specific individuals are no more both-men-and-women than any others. In general, *lo* refers to whatever individuals meet its description.

The last descriptor of this section is *la*, which indicates that the selbri which follows it has been dissociated from its normal meaning and is being used as a name. Like *le* descriptions, *la* descriptions are implicitly restricted to those I have in mind. (Do not confuse this use of *la* with its use before regular Lojbanized names, which is discussed in Section 6.12 (p. 132).) For example:

Example 6.10

la	cribe	pu	finti	le	lisri
That-named	"bear"	[past]	creates	the	story.

Bear wrote the story.

In Example 6.10 (p. 118), *la cribe* refers to someone whose naming predicate is *cribe*, i.e. "Bear". In English, most names don't mean anything, or at least not anything obvious. The name "Frank" coincides with the English word "frank", meaning "honest", and so one way of translating "Frank ate some cheese" into Lojban would be:

Example 6.11

la	stace	pu	citka	lo	cirla
That-named	"Honest/Frank"	[past]	eats	some	cheese.

English-speakers typically would not do this, as we tend to be more attached to the sound of our names than their meaning, even if the meaning (etymological or current) is known. Speakers of other languages may feel differently. (In point of fact, "Frank" originally meant "the free one" rather than "the honest one".)

It is important to note the differences between Example 6.10 (p. 118) and the following:

Example 6.12

le	cribe	pu	finti	le	lisri
One-or-more-specific-things-which-I-describe-as	bears	[past]	creates	the	story.

The bear(s) wrote the story.

Example 6.13

lo	cribe	pu	finti	le	lisri
One-or-more-of-the-things-which-really	are-bears	[past]	creates	the	story.

A bear wrote the story.
Some bears wrote the story.

Example 6.12 (p. 118) is about a specific bear or bearlike thing(s), or thing(s) which the speaker (perhaps whimsically or metaphorically) describes as a bear (or more than one); Example 6.13 (p. 118) is about one or more of the really existing, objectively defined bears. In either case, though, each of them must have contributed to the writing of the story, if more than one bear (or "bear") is meant.

(The notion of a "really existing, objectively defined bear" raises certain difficulties. Is a panda bear a "real bear"? How about a teddy bear? In general, the answer is "yes". Lojban gismu are defined as broadly as possible, allowing tanru and lujvo to narrow down the definition. There probably are no necessary and sufficient conditions for defining what is and what is not a bear that can be pinned down with complete precision: the real world is fuzzy. In borderline cases, *le* may communicate better than *lo*.)

So while Example 6.10 (p. 118) could easily be true (there is a real writer named "Greg Bear"), and Example 6.12 (p. 118) could be true if the speaker is sufficiently peculiar in what he or she describes as a bear, Example 6.13 (p. 118) is certainly false.

Similarly, compare the following two examples, which are analogous to Example 6.12 (p. 118) and Example 6.13 (p. 118) respectively:

Example 6.14

le	remna	pu	finti	le	lisri
Those-described-as	a-human	[past]	writes	that-described-as	a-story.

The human being(s) wrote the story.

Example 6.15

lo	remna	pu	finti	le	lisri
That-which-really-is	**a-human**	**[past]**	**writes**	**that-described-as**	**a-story.**

A human being wrote the story.
Some human beings wrote the story.

Example 6.14 (p. 118) says who the author of the story is: one or more particular human beings that the speaker has in mind. If the topic of conversation is the story, then Example 6.14 (p. 118) identifies the author as someone who can be pointed out or who has been previously mentioned; whereas if the topic is a person, then *le remna* is in effect a shorthand reference to that person. Example 6.15 (p. 119) merely says that the author is human.

The elidable terminator for all descriptions is *ku*. It can almost always be omitted with no danger of ambiguity. The main exceptions are in certain uses of relative clauses, which are discussed in Section 8.6 (p. 170), and in the case of a description immediately preceding the selbri. In this latter case, using an explicit *cu* before the selbri makes the *ku* unnecessary. There are also a few other uses of *ku*: in the compound negator *naku* (discussed in Chapter 16 (p. 375)) and to terminate place-structure, tense, and modal tags that do not have associated sumti (discussed in Chapter 9 (p. 179) and Chapter 10 (p. 207)).

6.3 Individuals and masses

The following cmavo are discussed in this section:

lei	LE	the mass I describe as
loi	LE	part of the mass of those which really are
lai	LA	the mass of those named

All Lojban sumti are classified by whether they refer to one of three types of objects, known as "individuals", "masses", and "sets". The term "individual" is misleading when used to refer to more than one object, but no less-confusing term has as yet been found. All the descriptions in Section 6.1 (p. 115) and Section 6.2 (p. 116) refer to individuals, whether one or more than one. Consider the following example:

Example 6.16

le	prenu	cu	bevri	le	pipno
One-or-more-of-those-I-describe-as	**persons**		**carry**	**the**	**piano.**

The person(s) carry the piano.

(Of course the second *le* should really get the same translation as the first, but I am putting the focus of this discussion on the first *le*, the one preceding *prenu*. I will assume that there is only one piano under discussion.)

Suppose the context of Example 6.16 (p. 119) is such that you can determine that I am talking about three persons. What am I claiming? I am claiming that each of the three persons carried the piano. This claim can be true if the persons carried the piano one at a time, or in turns, or in a variety of other ways. But in order for Example 6.16 (p. 119) to be true, I must be willing to assert that person 1 carried the piano, and that person 2 carried the piano, and that person 3 carried the piano.

But suppose I am not willing to claim that. For in fact pianos are heavy, and very few persons can carry a piano all by themselves. The most likely factual situation is that person 1 carried one end of the piano, and person 2 the other end, while person 3 either held up the middle or else supervised the whole operation without actually lifting anything. The correct way of expressing such a situation in Lojban is:

Example 6.17

lei	prenu	cu	bevri	le	pipno
The-mass-of-one-or-more-of-those-I-describe-as	**persons**		**carry**	**the**	**piano.**

The person(s) carry the piano.

Here the same three persons are treated not as individuals, but as a so-called "mass entity", or just "mass". A mass has the properties of each individual which composes it, and may have other properties of its own as well. This can lead to apparent contradictions. Thus suppose in the piano-moving example above that person 1 has fair skin, whereas person 2 has dark skin. Then it is correct to say that the person-mass has both fair skin and dark skin. Using the mass descriptor *lei* signals that ordinary logical reasoning is not applicable: contradictions can be maintained, and all sorts of other peculiarities may exist. However, we can safely say that a mass inherits only the component properties that are relevant to it; it would be ludicrous to say that a mass of two persons is of molecular dimensions, simply because some of the parts (namely, the molecules) of the persons are that small.

The descriptors *loi* and *lai* are analogous to *lo* and *la* respectively, but refer to masses either by property (*loi*) or by name (*lai*). A classic example of *loi* use is:

Example 6.18

loi		*cinfo*	*cu*	*xabju*	*le*	*fi'ortu'a*
Part-of-the-mass-of-those-which-really		**are-lions**		**dwell-in**	**the**	**African-land.**

The lion dwells in Africa.
Lions dwell in Africa.

The difference between *lei* and *loi* is that *lei cinfo* refers to a mass of specific individuals which the speaker calls lions, whereas *loi cinfo* refers to some part of the mass of all those individuals which actually are lions. The restriction to "some part of the mass" allows statements like Example 6.18 (p. 120) to be true even though some lions do not dwell in Africa – they live in various zoos around the world. On the other hand, Example 6.18 (p. 120) doesn't actually say that most lions live in Africa: equally true is

Example 6.19

loi		*glipre*
Part-of-the-mass-of-those-which-really		**are-English-persons**

cu	*xabju*	*le*	*fi'ortu'a*
dwell-in	**the**	**African-land.**	

The English dwell in Africa.

since there is at least one English person living there. Section 6.4 (p. 121) explains another method of saying what is usually meant by "The lion lives in Africa" which does imply that living in Africa is normal, not exceptional, for lions.

Note that the Lojban mass articles are sometimes translated by English plurals (the most usual case), sometimes by English singulars (when the singular is used to express typicalness or abstraction), and sometimes by singulars with no article:

Example 6.20

loi		*matne*	*cu*	*ranti*
Part-of-the-mass-of-that-which-really-is		**a-quantity-of-butter**		**is-soft.**

Butter is soft.

Of course, some butter is hard (for example, if it is frozen butter), so the "part-of" implication of *loi* becomes once again useful. The reason this mechanism works is that the English words like "butter", which are seen as already describing masses, are translated in Lojban by non-mass forms. The place structure of *matne* is "x1 is a quantity of butter from source x2", so the single English word "butter" is translated as something like "a part of the mass formed from all the quantities of butter that exist". (Note that the operation of forming a mass entity does not imply, in Lojban, that the components of the mass are necessarily close to one another or even related in any way other than conceptually. Masses are formed by the speaker's intention to form a mass, and can in principle contain anything.)

The mass name descriptor *lai* is used in circumstances where we wish to talk about a mass of things identified by a name which is common to all of them. It is not used to identify a mass by a single name peculiar to it. Thus the mass version of Example 6.9 (p. 117),

Example 6.21

lai	cribe	pu	finti	le	vi	cukta
The-mass-of-those-named	**"bear"**	**[past]**	**creates**	**the**	**nearby**	**book.**

The Bears wrote this book.

in a context where *la cribe* would be understood as plural, would mean that either Tom Bear or Fred Bear (to make up some names) might have written the book, or that Tom and Fred might have written it as collaborators. Using *la* instead of *lai* in Example 6.21 (p. 121) would give the implication that each of Tom and Fred, considered individually, had written it.

6.4 Masses and sets

The following cmavo are discussed in this section:

le'i	LE	the set described as
lo'i	LE	the set of those which really are
la'i	LA	the set of those named

Having said so much about masses, let us turn to sets. Sets are easier to understand than masses, but are more rarely used. Like a mass, a set is an abstract object formed from a number of individuals; however, the properties of a set are not derived from any of the properties of the individuals that compose it.

Sets have properties like cardinality (how many elements in the set), membership (the relationship between a set and its elements), and set inclusion (the relationship between two sets, one of which – the superset – contains all the elements of the other – the subset). The set descriptors *le'i*, *lo'i* and *la'i* correspond exactly to the mass descriptors *lei*, *loi*, and *lai* except that normally we talk of the whole of a set, not just part of it. Here are some examples contrasting *lo*, *loi*, and *lo'i*:

Example 6.22

lo	ratcu	cu	bunre
One-or-more-of-those-which-really-are	**rats**		**are-brown.**

Some rats are brown.

Example 6.23

loi	ratcu	cu	cmalu
Part-of-the-mass-of-those-which-really-are	**rats**		**are-small.**

Rats are small.

Example 6.24

lo'i	ratcu	cu	barda
The-set-of	**rats**		**is-large.**

There are a lot of rats.

The mass of rats is small because at least one rat is small; the mass of rats is also large; the set of rats, though, is unquestionably large – it has billions of members. The mass of rats is also brown, since some of its components are; but it would be incorrect to call the set of rats brown – brown-ness is not the sort of property that sets possess.

Lojban speakers should generally think twice before employing the set descriptors. However, certain predicates have places that require set sumti to fill them. For example, the place structure of *fadni* is:

x1 is ordinary/common/typical/usual in property x2 among the members of set x3

Why is it necessary for the x3 place of *fadni* to be a set? Because it makes no sense for an individual to be typical of another individual: an individual is typical of a group. In order to make sure that the bridi containing *fadni* is about an entire group, its x3 place must be filled with a set:

Example 6.25

mi	fadni	zo'e	lo'i	lobypli
I	am-ordinary	in-property [unspecified]	among-the-set-of	Lojban-users.

I am a typical Lojban user.

Note that the x2 place has been omitted; I am not specifying in exactly which way I am typical – whether in language knowledge, or age, or interests, or something else. If *lo'i* were changed to *lo* in Example 6.25 (p. 122), the meaning would be something like "I am typical of some Lojban user", which is nonsense.

6.5 Descriptors for typical objects

The following cmavo are discussed in this section:

lo'e	LE	the typical
le'e	LE	the stereotypical

As promised in Section 6.3 (p. 119), Lojban has a method for discriminating between "the lion" who lives in Africa and "the Englishman" who, generally speaking, doesn't live in Africa even though some Englishmen do. The descriptor *lo'e* means "the typical", as in

Example 6.26

lo'e	cinfo	cu	xabju	le	fi'ortu'a
The-typical	lion		dwells-in	the	African-land.

The lion dwells in Africa.

What is this "typical lion"? Surely it is not any particular lion, because no lion has all of the "typical" characteristics, and (worse yet) some characteristics that all real lions have can't be viewed as typical. For example, all real lions are either male or female, but it would be bizarre to suppose that the typical lion is either one. So the typical lion has no particular sex, but does have a color (golden brown), a residence (Africa), a diet (game), and so on. Likewise we can say that

Example 6.27

lo'e	glipre	cu	xabju
The-typical	English-person		dwells-in

le	fi'ortu'a	na.e	le	gligugde
the	African-land	(Not!) and	the	English-country.

The typical English person dwells not in Africa but in England.

The relationship between *lo'e cinfo* and *lo'i cinfo* may be explained thus: the typical lion is an imaginary lion-abstraction which best exemplifies the set of lions. There is a similar relationship between *le'e* and *le'i*:

Example 6.28

le'e	xelso	merko	cu	gusta	ponse
The-stereotypical	Greek-type-of	American		is-a-restaurant-type-of	owner.

Lots of Greek-Americans own restaurants.

Here we are concerned not with the actual set of Greek-Americans, but with the set of those the speaker has in mind, which is typified by one (real or imaginary) who owns a restaurant. The word "stereotypical" is often derogatory in English, but *le'e* need not be derogatory in Lojban: it simply suggests that the example is typical in the speaker's imagination rather than in some objectively agreed-upon way. Of course, different speakers may disagree about what the features of "the typical lion" are (some would include having a short intestine, whereas others would know nothing of lions' intestines), so the distinction between *lo'e cinfo* and *le'e cinfo* may be very fine.

Furthermore,

Example 6.29

le'e	skina	cu	se finti	ne'i	la	xali,uyd.
The-stereotypical	**movie**		**is-invented**	**in**	**that-named**	**Hollywood.**

is probably true to an American, but might be false (not the stereotype) to someone living in India or Russia.

Note that there is no naming equivalent of *lo'e* and *le'e*, because there is no need, as a rule, for a "typical George" or a "typical Smith". People or things who share a common name do not, in general, have any other common attributes worth mentioning.

6.6 Quantified sumti

The following cmavo are discussed in this section:

ro	PA	all of/each of
su'o	PA	at least (one of)

Quantifiers tell us how many: in the case of quantifiers with sumti, how many things we are talking about. In Lojban, quantifiers are expressed by numbers and mathematical expressions: a large topic discussed in some detail in Chapter 18 (p. 413). For the purposes of this chapter, a simplified treatment will suffice. Our examples will employ either the simple Lojban numbers *pa*, *re*, *ci*, *vo*, and *mu*, meaning "one", "two", "three", "four", "five" respectively, or else one of four special quantifiers, two of which are discussed in this section and listed above. These four quantifiers are important because every Lojban sumti has either one or two of them implicitly present in it – which one or two depends on the particular kind of sumti. There is more explanation of implicit quantifiers later in this section. (The other two quantifiers, *piro* and *pisu'o*, are explained in Section 6.7 (p. 124).)

Every Lojban sumti may optionally be preceded by an explicit quantifier. The purpose of this quantifier is to specify how many of the things referred to by the sumti are being talked about. Here are some simple examples contrasting sumti with and without explicit quantifiers:

Example 6.30

do	cadzu	le	bisli
You	**walk-on**	**the**	**ice.**

Example 6.31

re	do	cadzu	le	bisli
Two-of	**you**	**walk-on**	**the**	**ice.**

The difference between Example 6.30 (p. 123) and Example 6.31 (p. 123) is the presence of the explicit quantifier *re* in the latter example. Although *re* by itself means "two", when used as a quantifier it means "two-of". Out of the group of listeners (the number of which isn't stated), two (we are not told which ones) are asserted to be "walkers on the ice". Implicitly, the others (if any) are not walkers on the ice. In Lojban, you cannot say "I own three shoes" if in fact you own four shoes. Numbers need never be specified, but if they are specified they must be correct.

(This rule does not mean that there is no way to specify a number which is vague. The sentence

Example 6.32

mi	ponse	su'o	ci	cutci
I	**possess**	**at-least**	**three**	**shoes.**

is true if you own three shoes, or four, or indeed any larger number. More details on vague numbers appear in the discussion of mathematical expressions in Chapter 18 (p. 413).)

Now consider Example 6.30 (p. 123) again. How many of the listeners are claimed to walk on the ice? The answer turns out to be: all of them, however many that is. So Example 6.30 (p. 123) and Example 6.33 (p. 123):

Example 6.33

ro	do	cadzu	le	bisli
All-of	**you**	**walk-on**	**the**	**ice.**

turn out to mean exactly the same thing. This is a safe strategy, because if one of my listeners doesn't turn out to be walking on the ice, I can safely claim that I didn't intend that person to be a listener! And in fact, all of the personal pro-sumti such as *mi* and *mi'o* and *ko* obey the same rule. We say that personal pro-sumti have a so-called "implicit quantifier" of *ro* (all). This just means that if no quantifier is given explicitly, the meaning is the same as if the implicit quantifier had been used.

Not all sumti have *ro* as the implicit quantifier, however. Consider the quotation in:

Example 6.34

mi	*cusku*	*lu*	*do*	*cadzu*	*le*	*bisli*	*li'u*
I	express	[quote]	you	walk-on	the	ice	[unquote].

I say, "You walk on the ice."

What is the implicit quantifier of the quotation *lu do cadzu le bisli li'u*? Surely not *ro*. If *ro* were supplied explicitly, thus:

Example 6.35

mi	*cusku*	*ro*	*lu*	*do*	*cadzu*	*le*	*bisli*	*li'u*
I	express	all-of	[quote]	you	walk-on	the	ice	[unquote].

the meaning would be something like "I say every occurrence of the sentence 'You walk on the ice'". Of course I don't say every occurrence of it, only some occurrences. One might suppose that Example 6.34 (p. 124) means that I express exactly one occurrence, but it is more Lojbanic to leave the number unspecified, as with other sumti. We can say definitely, however, that I say it at least once.

The Lojban cmavo meaning "at least" is *su'o*, and if no ordinary number follows, *su'o* means "at least once". (See Example 6.32 (p. 123) for the use of *su'o* with an ordinary number). Therefore, the explicitly quantified version of Example 6.34 (p. 124) is

Example 6.36

mi	*cusku*	*su'o*	*lu*	*do*	*cadzu*	*le*	*bisli*	*li'u*
I	express	at-least-one-of	[quote]	you	walk-on	the	ice	[unquote].

I say one or more instances of "You walk on the ice".
I say "You walk on the ice".

If an explicit ordinary number such as *re* were to appear, it would have to convey an exact expression, so

Example 6.37

mi	*cusku*	*re*	*lu*	*do*	*cadzu*	*le*	*bisli*	*li'u*
I	express	two-of	[quote]	you	walk-on	the	ice	[unquote].

means that I say the sentence exactly twice, neither more nor less.

6.7 Quantified descriptions

The following cmavo are discussed in this section:

piro	PA	the whole of
pisu'o	PA	a part of

Like other sumti, descriptions can be quantified. When a quantifier appears before a description, it has the same meaning as one appearing before a non-description sumti: it specifies how many things, of all those referred to by the description, are being talked about in this particular bridi. Suppose that context tells us that *le gerku* refers to three dogs. Then we can say that exactly two of them are white as follows:

Example 6.38

re	*le*	*gerku*	*cu*	*blabi*
Two-of	the	dogs		are-white.

Two of the dogs are white.

6.7 Quantified descriptions

When discussing descriptions, this ordinary quantifier is called an "outer quantifier", since it appears outside the description. But there is another possible location for a quantifier: between the descriptor and the selbri. This quantifier is called an "inner quantifier", and its meaning is quite different: it tells the listener how many objects the description selbri characterizes.

For example, the context of Example 6.38 (p. 124) supposedly told us that *le gerku* referred to some three specific dogs. This assumption can be made certain with the use of an explicit inner quantifier:

Example 6.39

re	le	ci	gerku	cu	blabi
Two-of	**the**	**three**	**dogs**		**are-white.**

Two of the three dogs are white.

(As explained in the discussion of Example 6.32 (p. 123), simple numbers like those in Example 6.39 (p. 125) must be exact: it therefore follows that the third dog cannot be white.)

You may also specify an explicit inner quantifier and leave the outer quantifier implicit:

Example 6.40

le	ci	gerku	cu	blabi
The	**three**	**dogs**		**are-white.**

The three dogs are white.

There are rules for each of the 11 descriptors specifying what the implicit values for the inner and outer quantifiers are. They are meant to provide sensible default values when context is absent, not necessarily to prescribe hard and fast rules. The following table lists the implicit values:

le:	ro le su'o	all of the at-least-one described as
lo:	su'o lo ro	at least one of all of those which really are
la:	ro la su'o	all of the at least one named
lei:	pisu'o lei su'o	some part of the mass of the at-least-one described as
loi:	pisu'o loi ro	some part of the mass of all those that really are
lai:	pisu'o lai su'o	some part of the mass of the at-least-one named
le'i:	piro le'i su'o	the whole of the set of the at-least-one described as
lo'i:	piro lo'i ro	the whole of the set of all those that really are
la'i:	piro la'i su'o	the whole of the set of the at-least-one named
le'e:	ro le'e su'o	all the stereotypes of the at-least-one described as
lo'e:	su'o lo'e ro	at least one of the types of all those that really are

When examined for the first time, this table looks dreadfully arbitrary. In fact, there are quite a few regularities in it. First of all, the la-series (that is, the descriptors *la*, *lai*, and *la'i*) and the le-series (that is, the descriptors *le*, *lei*, *le'i*, and *le'e*) always have corresponding implicit quantifiers, so we may subsume the la-series under the le-series for the rest of this discussion: "le-series cmavo" will refer to both the le-series proper and to the la-series.

The rule for the inner quantifier is very simple: the lo-series cmavo (namely, *lo*, *loi*, *lo'i*, and *lo'e*) all have an implicit inner quantifier of *ro*, whereas the le-series cmavo all have an implicit inner quantifier of *su'o*.

Why? Because lo-series descriptors always refer to all of the things which really fit into the x1 place of the selbri. They are not restricted by the speaker's intention. Descriptors of the le-series, however, are so restricted, and therefore talk about some number, definite or indefinite, of objects the speaker has in mind – but never less than one.

Understanding the implicit outer quantifier requires rules of greater subtlety. In the case of mass and set descriptors, a single rule suffices for each: reference to a mass is implicitly a reference to some part of the mass; reference to a set is implicitly a reference to the whole set. Masses and sets are inherently singular objects: it makes no sense to talk about two distinct masses with the same components, or two distinct sets with the same members. Therefore, the largest possible outer quantifier for either a set description or a mass description is *piro*, the whole of it.

(Pedantically, it is possible that the mass of water molecules composing an ice cube might be thought of as different from the same mass of water molecules in liquid form, in which case we might talk about *re lei djacu*, two masses of the water-bits I have in mind.)

Why "*pi-*"? It is the Lojban cmavo for the decimal point. Just as *pimu* means ".5", and when used as a quantifier specifies a portion consisting of five tenths of a thing, *piro* means a portion consisting of the all-ness – the entirety – of a thing. Similarly, *pisu'o* specifies a portion consisting of at least one part of a thing, i.e. some of it.

Smaller quantifiers are possible for sets, and refer to subsets. Thus *pimu le'i nanmu* is a subset of the set of men I have in mind; we don't know precisely which elements make up this subset, but it must have half the size of the full set. This is the best way to say "half of the men"; saying *pimu le nanmu* would give us a half-portion of one of them instead! Of course, the result of *pimu le'i nanmu* is still a set; if you need to refer to the individuals of the subset, you must say so (see *lu'a* in Section 6.10 (p. 128)).

The case of outer quantifiers for individual descriptors (including *le, lo, la,* and the typical descriptors *le'e* and *lo'e*) is special. When we refer to specific individuals with *le*, we mean to refer to all of those we have in mind, so *ro* is appropriate as the implicit quantifier, just as it is appropriate for *do*. Reference to non-specific individuals with *lo*, however, is typically to only some of the objects which can be correctly described, and so *su'o* is the appropriate implicit quantifier, just as for quotations.

From the English-speaking point of view, the difference in structure between the following example using *le*:

Example 6.41

[ro]	le	ci	gerku	cu	blabi
[All-of]	those-described-as	three	dogs		are-white.

The three dogs are white.

and the corresponding form with *lo*:

Example 6.42

ci	lo	[ro]	gerku	cu	blabi
Three-of	those-which-are	[all]	dogs		are-white.

Three dogs are white.

looks very peculiar. Why is the number *ci* found as an inner quantifier in Example 6.41 (p. 126) and as an outer quantifier in Example 6.42 (p. 126)? The number of dogs is the same in either case. The answer is that the *ci* in Example 6.41 (p. 126) is part of the specification: it tells us the actual number of dogs in the group that the speaker has in mind. In Example 6.42 (p. 126), however, the dogs referred to by ... *lo gerku* are all the dogs that exist: the outer quantifier then restricts the number to three; which three, we cannot tell. The implicit quantifiers are chosen to avoid claiming too much or too little: in the case of *le*, the implicit outer quantifier *ro* says that each of the dogs in the restricted group is white; in the case of *lo*, the implicit inner quantifier simply says that three dogs, chosen from the group of all the dogs there are, are white.

Using exact numbers as inner quantifiers in lo-series descriptions is dangerous, because you are stating that exactly that many things exist which really fit the description. So examples like

Example 6.43

[so'o]	lo	ci	gerku	cu	blabi
[some-of]	those-which-really-are	three	dogs		are-white.

are semantically anomalous; Example 6.43 (p. 126) claims that some dog (or dogs) is white, but also that there are just three dogs in the universe!

Nevertheless, inner quantifiers are permitted on *lo* descriptors for consistency's sake, and may occasionally be useful.

Note that the inner quantifier of *le*, even when exact, need not be truthful: *le ci nanmu* means "what I describe as three men", not "three of what I describe as men". This follows from the rule that what is described by a *le* description represents the speaker's viewpoint rather than the objective way things are.

6.8 Indefinite descriptions

By a quirk of Lojban syntax, it is possible to omit the descriptor *lo*, but never any other descriptor, from a description like that of Example 6.42 (p. 126); namely, one which has an explicit outer quantifier but no explicit inner quantifier. The following example:

Example 6.44

ci	gerku	[ku]	cu	blabi
Three-of-those-which-are	dogs			are-white.

Three dogs are white.

is equivalent in meaning to Example 6.42 (p. 126). Even though the descriptor is not present, the elidable terminator *ku* may still be used. The name "indefinite description" for this syntactic form is historically based: of course, it is no more and no less indefinite than its counterpart with an explicit *lo*. Indefinite descriptions were introduced into the language in order to imitate the syntax of English and other natural languages.

Indefinite descriptions must fit this mold exactly: there is no way to make one which does not have an explicit outer quantifier (thus *gerku cu blabi* is ungrammatical), or which has an explicit inner quantifier (thus *reboi ci gerku cu blabi* is also ungrammatical – *re ci gerku cu blabi* is fine, but means "23 dogs are white").

Note: Example 6.32 (p. 123) also contains an indefinite description, namely *su'o ci cutci*; another version of that example using an explicit *lo* would be:

Example 6.45

mi	ponse	su'o	ci	lo	cutci
I	possess	at-least	three	things-which-really-are	shoes

I own three (or more) shoes.

6.9 sumti-based descriptions

As stated in Section 6.2 (p. 116), most descriptions consist of just a descriptor and a selbri. (In this chapter, the selbri have always been single gismu, but of course any selbri, however complex, can be employed in a description. The syntax and semantics of selbri are explained in Chapter 5 (p. 79).) In the intervening sections, inner and outer quantifiers have been added to the syntax. Now it is time to discuss a description of a radically different kind: the sumti-based description.

A sumti-based description has a sumti where the selbri would normally be, and the inner quantifier is required – it cannot be implicit. An outer quantifier is permitted but not required.

A full theory of sumti-based descriptions has yet to be worked out. One common case, however, is well understood. Compare the following:

Example 6.46

re	do	cu	nanmu
Two-of	you		are-men.

Example 6.47

le	re	do	cu	nanmu
The	two-of	you		are-men.

Example 6.46 (p. 127) simply specifies that of the group of listeners, size unknown, two are men. Example 6.47 (p. 127), which has the sumti-based description *le re do*, says that of the two listeners, all (the implicit outer quantifier *ro*) are men. So in effect the inner quantifier *re* gives the number of individuals which the inner sumti *do* refers to.

Here is another group of examples:

Example 6.48

re	le	ci	cribe	cu	bunre
Two-of	the	three	bears		are-brown.

Example 6.49

le	re	le	ci	cribe	cu	bunre
The	two-of	the	three	bears		are-brown.

Example 6.50

pa	le	re	le	ci	cribe	cu	bunre
One-of	the	two-of	the	three	bears		is-brown.

In each case, *le ci cribe* restricts the bears (or alleged bears) being talked of to some group of three which the speaker has in mind. Example 6.48 (p. 128) says that two of them (which two is not stated) are brown. Example 6.49 (p. 128) says that a specific pair of them are brown. Example 6.50 (p. 128) says that of a specific pair chosen from the original three, one or the other of that pair is brown.

6.10 sumti qualifiers

The following cmavo are discussed in this section:

la'e	LAhE	something referred to by
lu'e	LAhE	a reference to
tu'a	LAhE	an abstraction involving
lu'a	LAhE	an individual/member/component of
lu'i	LAhE	a set formed from
lu'o	LAhE	a mass formed from
vu'i	LAhE	a sequence formed from
na'ebo	NAhE+BO	something other than
to'ebo	NAhE+BO	the opposite of
no'ebo	NAhE+BO	the neutral form of
je'abo	NAhE+BO	that which indeed is
lu'u	LUhU	elidable terminator for LAhE and NAhE+BO

Well, that's quite a list of cmavo. What are they all about?

The above cmavo and compound cmavo are called the "sumti qualifiers". All of them are either single cmavo of selma'o LAhE, or else compound cmavo involving a scalar negation cmavo of selma'o NAhE immediately followed by *bo* of selma'o BO. Syntactically, you can prefix a sumti qualifier to any sumti and produce another simple sumti. (You may need to add the elidable terminator *lu'u* to show where the qualified sumti ends.)

Semantically, sumti qualifiers represent short forms of certain common special cases. Suppose you want to say "I see 'The Red Pony'", where "The Red Pony" is the title of a book. How about:

Example 6.51

mi	viska	lu	le	xunre	cmaxirma	li'u
I	see	[quote]	the	red	small-horse	[unquote].

But Example 6.51 (p. 128) doesn't work: it says that you see a piece of text "The Red Pony". That might be all right if you were looking at the cover of the book, where the words "The Red Pony" are presumably written. (More precisely, where the words *le xunre cmaxirma* are written – but we may suppose the book has been translated into Lojban.)

What you really want to say is:

Example 6.52

mi	viska	le	selsinxa
I	see	the	thing-represented-by

be	lu	le	xunre	cmaxirma	li'u
	[quote]	the	red	small-horse	[unquote].

6.10 sumti qualifiers

The x2 place of *selsinxa* (the x1 place of *sinxa*) is a sign or symbol, and the x1 place of *selsinxa* (the x2 place of *sinxa*) is the thing represented by the sign. Example 6.52 (p. 128) allows us to use a symbol (namely the title of a book) to represent the thing it is a symbol of (namely the book itself).

This operation turns out to be needed often enough that it's useful to be able to say:

Example 6.53

mi	viska	la'e	lu	le	xunre	cmaxirma	li'u	[lu'u]
I	see	the-referent-of	[quote]	the	red	small-horse	[unquote]	-.

So when *la'e* is prefixed to a sumti referring to a symbol, it produces a sumti referring to the referent of that symbol. (In computer jargon, *la'e* dereferences a pointer.)

By introducing a sumti qualifier, we correct a false sentence (Example 6.51 (p. 128)), which too closely resembles its literal English equivalent, into a true sentence (Example 6.53 (p. 129)), without having to change it overmuch; in particular, the structure remains the same. Most of the uses of sumti qualifiers are of this general kind.

The sumti qualifier *lu'e* provides the converse operation: it can be prefixed to a sumti referring to some thing to produce a sumti referring to a sign or symbol for the thing. For example,

Example 6.54

mi	pu	cusku	lu'e	le	vi	cukta
I	[past]	express	a-symbol-for	the	nearby	book.

I said the title of this book.

The equivalent form not using a sumti qualifier would be:

Example 6.55

mi	pu	cusku	le	sinxa	be	le	vi	cukta
I	[past]	express	the	symbol-for		the	nearby	book.

which is equivalent to Example 6.54 (p. 129), but longer.

The other sumti qualifiers follow the same rules. The cmavo *tu'a* is used in forming abstractions, and is explained more fully in Section 11.11 (p. 260). The triplet *lu'a*, *lu'i*, and *lu'o* convert between individuals, sets, and masses; *vu'i* belongs to this group as well, but creates a sequence, which is similar to a set but has a definite order. (The set of John and Charles is the same as the set of Charles and John, but the sequences are different.) Here are some examples:

Example 6.56

mi	troci	tu'a	le	vorme
I	try	some-abstraction-about	the	door.

I try (to open) the door.

Example 6.56 (p. 129) might mean that I try to do something else involving the door; the form is deliberately vague.

Most of the following examples make use of the cmavo *ri*, belonging to selma'o KOhA. This cmavo means "the thing last mentioned"; it is equivalent to repeating the immediately previous sumti (but in its original context). It is explained in more detail in Section 7.6 (p. 146).

Example 6.57

lo'i	ratcu	cu	barda
The-set-of	rats		is-large.

.iku'i	lu'a	ri	cmalu
But	some-members-of	it-last-mentioned	are-small.

The set of rats is large, but some of its members are small.

Example 6.58

lo	ratcu	cu	cmalu	.iku'i	lu'i	ri	barda
Some	rats		are-small.	But	the-set-of	them-last-mentioned	is-large.

Some rats are small, but the set of rats is large.

Example 6.59

mi	ce	do	girzu
I	in-a-set-with	you	are-a-set.

.i	lu'o	ri	gunma
	The-mass-of	it-last-mentioned	is-a-mass.

.i	vu'i	ri	porsi
	The-sequence-of	it-last-mentioned	is-a-sequence

The set of you and me is a set. The mass of you and me is a mass. The sequence of you and me is a sequence.

(Yes, I know these examples are a bit silly. This set was introduced for completeness, and practical examples are as yet hard to come by.)

Finally, the four sumti qualifiers formed from a cmavo of NAhE and *bo* are all concerned with negation, which is discussed in detail in Chapter 15 (p. 353). Here are a few examples of negation sumti qualifiers:

Example 6.60

mi	viska	na'ebo	le	gerku
I	see	something-other-than	the	dog.

This compound, *na'ebo*, is the most common of the four negation sumti qualifiers. The others usually only make sense in the context of repeating, with modifications, something already referred to:

Example 6.61

mi	nelci	loi	glare	cidja
I	like	part-of-the-mass-of	hot-type-of	food.

.ije	do	nelci	to'ebo	ri
And	you	like	the-opposite-of	the-last-mentioned.

.ije	la	djein.	nelci	no'ebo	ra
And	that-named	Jane	likes	the-neutral-value-of	something-mentioned.

I like hot food, and you like cold food, and Jane likes lukewarm food.

(In Example 6.61 (p. 130), the sumti *ra* refers to some previously mentioned sumti other than that referred to by *ri*. We cannot use *ri* here, because it would signify *la djein.*, that being the most recent sumti available to *ri*. See more detailed explanations in Section 7.6 (p. 146).)

6.11 The syntax of vocative phrases

Vocative phrases are not sumti, but are explained in this chapter because their syntax is very similar to that of sumti. Grammatically, a vocative phrase is one of the so-called "free modifiers" of Lojban, along with subscripts, parentheses, and various other constructs explained in Chapter 19 (p. 447). They can be placed after many, but not all, constructions of the grammar: in general, after any elidable terminator (which, however, must not then be elided!), at the beginnings and ends of sentences, and in many other places.

The purpose of a vocative phrase is to indicate who is being addressed, or to indicate to that person that he or she ought to be listening. A vocative phrase begins with a cmavo of selma'o COI or DOI, all of which are explained in more detail in Section 13.14 (p. 309). Sometimes that is all there is to the phrase:

Example 6.62

> *coi*
> **[greetings]**
>
> Hello.

Example 6.63

> *je'e*
> **[acknowledgement]**
>
> Uh-huh.
> Roger!

In these cases, the person being addressed is obvious from the context. However, a vocative word (more precisely, one or more cmavo of COI, possibly followed by *doi*, or else just *doi* by itself) can be followed by one of several kinds of phrases, all of which are intended to indicate the addressee. The most common case is a name:

Example 6.64

> *coi.* | *djan.*
> **[greetings]** | **John.**
>
> Hello, John.

A pause is required (for morphological reasons) between a member of COI and a name. You can use *doi* instead of a pause:

Example 6.65

> *coi* | *doi* | *djan.*
> **[greetings]** | **O** | **John.**
>
> Hello, John.

means exactly the same thing and does not require a pause. Using *doi* by itself is like just saying someone's name to attract his or her attention:

Example 6.66

> *doi* | *djan.*
> **O** | **John.**
>
> John!

In place of a name, a description may appear, lacking its descriptor, which is understood to be *le*:

Example 6.67

> *coi* | *xunre* | *pastu* | *nixli*
> **Hello,** | **(red-type-of** | **dress)-type-of** | **girl.**
>
> Hello, girl with the red dress!

The listener need not really be a *xunre pastu nixli*, as long as she understands herself correctly from the description. (Actually, only a bare selbri can appear; explicit quantifiers are forbidden in this form of vocative, so the implicit quantifiers *su'o le ro* are in effect.)

Finally, a complete sumti may be used, the most general case.

Example 6.68

> *co'o* | *la* | *bab.* | *.e* | *la* | *noras.*
> **[partings]** | **that-named** | **Bob** | **and** | **that-named** | **Nora.**
>
> Goodbye, Bob and Nora.

Example 6.67 (p. 131) is thus the same as:

Example 6.69

coi	le	xunre	pastu	nixli
Hello,	**the-one-described-as**	**(red-type-of**	**dress)-type-of**	**girl!**

and Example 6.66 (p. 131) is the same as:

Example 6.70

doi	la	djan.
O	**that-named**	**John!**

Finally, the elidable terminator for vocative phrases is *do'u* (of selma'o DOhU), which is rarely needed except when a simple vocative word is being placed somewhere within a bridi. It may also be required when a vocative is placed between a sumti and its relative clause, or when there are a sequence of so-called "free modifiers" (vocatives, subscripts, utterance ordinals – see Chapter 18 (p. 413) – metalinguistic comments – see Section 19.12 (p. 461) – or reciprocals – see Chapter 19 (p. 447)) which must be properly separated.

The meaning of a vocative phrase that is within a sentence is not affected by its position in the sentence: thus Example 6.70 (p. 132) and Example 6.71 (p. 132) mean the same thing:

Example 6.71

doi	djan.	ko	klama	mi
O	**John**	**you [imperative]**	**go-to**	**me.**

John, come to me!

Example 6.72

ko	klama	mi	doi	djan.
You [imperative]	**go-to**	**me**	**O**	**John.**

Come to me, John!

As usual for this chapter, the full syntax of vocative phrases has not been explained: relative clauses, discussed in Chapter 8 (p. 161), make for more possibilities.

6.12 Lojban names

Names have been used freely as sumti throughout this chapter without too much explanation. The time for the explanation has now come.

First of all, there are two different kinds of things usually called "names" when talking about Lojban. The naming predicates of Section 6.2 (p. 116) are just ordinary predicates which are being used in a special sense. In addition, though, there is a class of Lojban words which are used only to name things: these can be recognized by the fact that they end in a consonant followed by a pause. Some examples:

Example 6.73

djan.	meris.	djein.	.alis.
John.	**Mary.**	**Jane.**	**Alice.**

(Note that *.alis.* begins as well as ends with a pause, because all Lojban words beginning with a vowel must be preceded by a pause. See Chapter 4 (p. 49) for more information.)

Names of this kind have two basic uses in Lojban: when used in a vocative phrase (see Section 6.11 (p. 130)) they indicate who the listener is or should be. When used with a descriptor of selma'o LA, namely *la*, *lai*, or *la'i*, they form sumti which refer to the persons or things known by the name.

Example 6.74

la	djonz.	klama	le	zarci
Those-named	**Jones**	**go-to**	**the**	**store.**

The Joneses go to-the store.

6.12 Lojban names

Example 6.75

lai	djonz.	klama	le	zarci
The-mass-of-those-named	Jones	goes-to	the	store.

The Joneses go to the store.

In Example 6.74 (p. 132), the significance is that all the persons (perhaps only one) I mean to refer to by the name *djonz.* are going to the store. In Example 6.75 (p. 133), the Joneses are massified, and only some part of them needs to be going. Of course, by *djonz.* I can mean whomever I want: that person need not use the name *djonz.* at all.

The sumti in Example 6.74 (p. 132) and Example 6.75 (p. 133) operate exactly like the similar uses of *la* and *lai* in Example 6.10 (p. 118) and Example 6.21 (p. 121) respectively. The only difference is that these descriptors are followed by Lojban name-words. And in fact, the only difference between descriptors of selma'o LA (these three) and of selma'o LE (all the other descriptors) is that the former can be followed by name-words, whereas the latter cannot.

There are certain limitations on the form of name-words in Lojban. In particular, they cannot contain the letter-sequences (or sound-sequences) *la*, *lai*, or *doi* unless a consonant immediately precedes within the name. Reciprocally, every name not preceded by *la*, *lai*, *la'i*, or *doi* must be preceded by a pause instead:

Example 6.76

coi	.djan.
[greetings]	John.

Hello, John.

Example 6.77

zo	.djan.	cmene	mi
The-word	"John"	is-the-name-of	me.

My name is John.

In Example 6.76 (p. 133) and Example 6.77 (p. 133), *.djan.* appears with a pause before it as well as after it, because the preceding word is not one of the four special cases. These rules force names to always be separable from the general word-stream.

Unless some other rule prevents it (such as the rule that *zo* is always followed by a single word, which is quoted), multiple names may appear wherever one name is permitted, each with its terminating pause:

Example 6.78

doi	djan. pol. djonz.	le	bloti	cu	klama	fi la	niuport. niuz.
O	John Paul Jones	the	boat		goes	from-that-named	Newport News.

John Paul Jones, the boat comes (to somewhere) from Newport News.

A name may not contain any consonant combination that is illegal in Lojban words generally: the "impermissible consonant clusters" of Lojban morphology (explained in Section 3.6 (p. 38)). Thus *djeimz.* is not a valid version of "James" (because *mz* is invalid): *djeimyz* will suffice. Similarly, *la* may be replaced by *ly*, *lai* by *ly'i*, *doi* by *do'i* or *dai*. Here are a few examples:

Example 6.79

Doyle	*doi,l	do'il or dai,l
Lyra	*lairas	ly'iras
Lottie	*latis	LYtis. or lotis.
(American pronunciation)		

Names may be borrowed from other languages or created arbitrarily. Another common practice is to use one or more rafsi, arranged to end with a consonant, to form a name: thus the rafsi *loj-* for *logji* (logical) and *ban-* for *bangu* (language) unite to form the name of this language:

Example 6.80

lojban.

Lojban

When borrowing names from another language which end in a vowel, or when turning a Lojban brivla (all of which end in vowels) into a name, the vowel may be removed or an arbitrary consonant added. It is common (but not required) to use the consonants *s* or *n* when borrowing vowel-final names from English; speakers of other languages may wish to use other consonant endings.

The implicit quantifier for name sumti of the form *la* followed by a name is *su'o*, just as for *la* followed by a selbri.

6.13 Pro-sumti summary

The Lojban pro-sumti are the cmavo of selma'o KOhA. They fall into several classes: personal, definable, quantificational, reflexive, back-counting, indefinite, demonstrative, metalinguistic, relative, question. More details are given in Chapter 7 (p. 139); this section mostly duplicates information found there, but adds material on the implicit quantifier of each pro-sumti.

The following examples illustrate each of the classes. Unless otherwise noted below, the implicit quantification for pro-sumti is *ro* (all). In the case of pro-sumti which refer to other sumti, the *ro* signifies "all of those referred to by the other sumti": thus it is possible to restrict, but not to extend, the quantification of the other sumti.

Personal pro-sumti (*mi, do, mi'o, mi'a, ma'a, do'o, ko*) refer to the speaker or the listener or both, with or without third parties:

Example 6.81

mi	prami	do
I	love	you.

The personal pro-sumti may be interpreted in context as either representing individuals or masses, so the implicit quantifier may be *pisu'o* rather than *ro*: in particular, *mi'o, mi'a, ma'a,* and *do'o* specifically represent mass combinations of the individuals (you and I, I and others, you and I and others, you and others) that make them up.

Definable pro-sumti (*ko'a, ko'e, ko'i, ko'o, ko'u, fo'a, fo'e, fo'i, fo'o, fo'u*) refer to whatever the speaker has explicitly made them refer to. This reference is accomplished with *goi* (of selma'o GOI), which means "defined-as".

Example 6.82

le	cribe	goi	ko'a	cu	xekri	.i	ko'a	citka	le	smacu
The	bear	defined-as	it-1		is-black.		It-1	eats	the	mouse.

Quantificational pro-sumti (*da, de, di*) are used as variables in bridi involving predicate logic:

Example 6.83

ro	da	poi	prenu
All	somethings-1	which	are-persons

cu	prami	pa	de	poi	finpe
	love	one	something-2	which	is-a-fish.

All persons love a fish (each his/her own).

(This is not the same as "All persons love a certain fish"; the difference between the two is one of quantifier order.) The implicit quantification rules for quantificational pro-sumti are particular to them, and are discussed in detail in Chapter 16 (p. 375). Roughly speaking, the quantifier is *su'o* (at least one) when the pro-sumti is first used, and *ro* (all) thereafter.

Reflexive pro-sumti (*vo'a, vo'e, vo'i, vo'o, vo'u*) refer to the same referents as sumti filling other places in the same bridi, with the effect that the same thing is referred to twice:

Example 6.84

le	cribe	cu	batci	vo'a
The	bear		bites	what-is-in-the-x1-place.

The bear bites itself.

Back-counting pro-sumti (*ri, ra, ru*) refer to the referents of previous sumti counted backwards from the pro-sumti:

Example 6.85

mi	klama	la	frankfurt.	ri
I	go-to	that-named	Frankfurt	from-the-referent-of-the-last-sumti

I go from Frankfurt to Frankfurt (by some unstated route).

Indefinite pro-sumti (*zo'e, zu'i, zi'o*) refer to something which is unspecified:

Example 6.86

mi	klama	la	frankfurt.
I	go-to	that-named	Frankfurt

zo'e	zo'e	zo'e
from-unspecified	via-unspecified	by-means-unspecified.

The implicit quantifier for indefinite pro-sumti is, well, indefinite. It might be *ro* (all) or *su'o* (at least one) or conceivably even *no* (none), though *no* would require a very odd context indeed.

Demonstrative pro-sumti (*ti, ta, tu*) refer to things pointed at by the speaker, or when pointing is not possible, to things near or far from the speaker:

Example 6.87

ko	muvgau
You [imperative]	move

ti	ta	tu
this-thing	from-that-nearby-place	to-that-further-away-place.

Move this from there to over there!

Metalinguistic pro-sumti (*di'u, de'u, da'u, di'e, de'e, da'e, dei, do'i*) refer to spoken or written utterances, either preceding, following, or the same as the current utterance.

Example 6.88

li	re	su'i	re	du	li	vo
The-number	two	plus	two	equals	the-number	four.

.i	la'e	di'u	jetnu
	The-referent-of	the-previous-utterance	is-true.

The implicit quantifier for metalinguistic pro-sumti is *su'o* (at least one), because they are considered analogous to *lo* descriptions: they refer to things which really are previous, current, or following utterances.

The relative pro-sumti (*ke'a*) is used within relative clauses (see Chapter 8 (p. 161) for a discussion of relative clauses) to refer to whatever sumti the relative clause is attached to.

Example 6.89

mi	viska	le	mlatu	ku	poi	zo'e
I	see	the	cat(s)		such-that	something-unspecified

zbasu	ke'a	loi	slasi
makes	it/them-(the-cats)	from-a-mass-of	plastic.

I see the cat(s) made of plastic.

The question pro-sumti (*ma*) is used to ask questions which request the listener to supply a sumti which will make the question into a truth:

Example 6.90

do	klama	ma
You	go-to	what-sumti?

Where are you going?

The implicit quantifier for the question pro-sumti is *su'o* (at least one), because the listener is only being asked to supply a single answer, not all correct answers.

In addition, sequences of lerfu words (of selma'o BY and related selma'o) can also be used as definable pro-sumti.

6.14 Quotation summary

There are four kinds of quotation in Lojban: text quotation, words quotation, single-word quotation, non-Lojban quotation. More information is provided in Chapter 19 (p. 447).

Text quotations are preceded by *lu* and followed by *li'u*, and are an essential part of the surrounding text: they must be grammatical Lojban texts.

Example 6.91

mi	cusku	lu	mi'e	.djan.	li'u
I	say	the-text [quote]	I-am	John	[unquote].

I say "I'm John".

Words quotations are quotations of one or more Lojban words. The words need not mean anything, but they must be morphologically valid so that the end of the quotation can be discerned.

Example 6.92

mi	cusku	lo'u	li mi	le'u
I	say	the-words [quote]	li mi	[unquote].

I say "*li mi*".

Note that the translation of Example 6.92 (p. 136) does not translate the Lojban words, because they are not presumed to have any meaning (in fact, they are ungrammatical).

Single-word quotation quotes a single Lojban word. Compound cmavo are not allowed.

Example 6.93

mi	cusku	zo	.ai
I	say	the-word	ai.

Non-Lojban quotation can quote anything, Lojban or not, even non-speech such as drum talk, whistle words, music, or belching. A Lojban word which does not appear within the quotation is used before and after it to set it off from the surrounding Lojban text.

Example 6.94

mi	cusku	zoi	kuot.	I'm John	.kuot
I	express	[non-Lojban]	<	I'm John	>.

I say "I'm John".

The implicit quantifier for all types of quotation is *su'o* (at least one), because quotations are analogous to *lo* descriptions: they refer to things which actually are words or sequences of words.

6.15 Number summary

The sumti which refer to numbers consist of the cmavo *li* (of selma'o LI) followed by an arbitrary Lojban mekso, or mathematical expression. This can be anything from a simple number up to the most complicated combination of numbers, variables, operators, and so on. Much more information on numbers is given in Chapter 18 (p. 413). Here are a few examples of increasing complexity:

Example 6.95

li	vo
the-number	**four**

4

Example 6.96

li	re	su'i	re
the-number	**two**	**plus**	**two**

2 + 2

Example 6.97

li	.abu	bi'epi'i	xy.	bi'ete'a	re	su'i	by.	bi'epi'i	xy.	su'i	cy.
the-number	**a**	**times**	**x**	**to-power**	**2**	**plus**	**b**	**times**	**x**	**plus**	**c**

$ax^2 + bx + c$

An alternative to *li* is *me'o*, also of selma'o LI. Number expressions beginning with *me'o* refer to the actual expression, rather than its value. Thus Example 6.95 (p. 137) and Example 6.96 (p. 137) above have the same meaning, the number four, whereas

Example 6.98

me'o	vo
the-expression	**four**

"4"

and

Example 6.99

me'o	re	su'i	re
the-expression	**two**	**plus**	**two**

"2+2"

refer to different pieces of text.

The implicit quantifier for numbers and mathematical expressions is *su'o*, because these sumti are analogous to *lo* descriptions: they refer to things which actually are numbers or pieces of text. In the case of numbers (with *li*), this is a distinction without a difference, as there is only one number which is 4; but there are many texts "4", as many as there are documents in which that numeral appears.

Chapter 7
Brevity Is The Soul Of Language: Pro-sumti And Pro-bridi

7.1 What are pro-sumti and pro-bridi? What are they for?

Speakers of Lojban, like speakers of other languages, require mechanisms of abbreviation. If every time we referred to something, we had to express a complete description of it, life would be too short to say what we have to say. In English, we have words called "pronouns" which allow us to replace nouns or noun phrases with shorter terms. An English with no pronouns might look something like this:

Example 7.1

> Speakers of Lojban, like speakers of other languages, require mechanisms of abbreviation. If every time speakers of Lojban referred to a thing to which speakers of Lojban refer, speakers of Lojban had to express a complete description of what speakers of Lojban referred to, life would be too short to say what speakers of Lojban have to say.

Speakers of this kind of English would get mightily sick of talking. Furthermore, there are uses of pronouns in English which are independent of abbreviation. There is all the difference in the world between:

Example 7.2

> John picked up a stick and shook it.

and

Example 7.3

> John picked up a stick and shook a stick.

Example 7.3 (p. 139) does not imply that the two sticks are necessarily the same, whereas Example 7.2 (p. 139) requires that they are.

In Lojban, we have sumti rather than nouns, so our equivalent of pronouns are called by the hybrid term "pro-sumti". A purely Lojban term would be *sumti cmavo*: all of the pro-sumti are cmavo belonging to selma'o KOhA. In exactly the same way, Lojban has a group of cmavo (belonging to selma'o GOhA) which serve as selbri or full bridi. These may be called "pro-bridi" or *bridi cmavo*. This chapter explains the uses of all the members of selma'o KOhA and GOhA. They fall into a number of groups, known as series: thus, in selma'o KOhA, we have among others the mi-series, the ko'a-series, the da-series, and so on. In each section, a series of pro-sumti is explained, and if there is a corresponding series of pro-bridi, it is explained and contrasted. Many pro-sumti series don't have pro-bridi analogues, however.

A few technical terms: The term "referent" means the thing to which a pro-sumti (by extension, a pro-bridi) refers. If the speaker of a sentence is James, then the referent of the word "I" is James. On the other hand, the term "antecedent" refers to a piece of language which a pro-sumti (or pro-bridi) implicitly repeats. In

Example 7.4

John loves himself

the antecedent of "himself" is "John"; not the person, but a piece of text (a name, in this case). John, the person, would be the referent of "himself". Not all pro-sumti or pro-bridi have antecedents, but all of them have referents.

7.2 Personal pro-sumti: the mi-series

The following cmavo are discussed in this section:

mi	KOhA	mi-series	I, me
do	KOhA	mi-series	you
mi'o	KOhA	mi-series	you and I
mi'a	KOhA	mi-series	I and others, we but not you
ma'a	KOhA	mi-series	you and I and others
do'o	KOhA	mi-series	you and others
ko	KOhA	mi-series	you-imperative

The mi-series of pro-sumti refer to the speaker, the listener, and others in various combinations. *mi* refers to the speaker and perhaps others for whom the speaker speaks; it may be a Lojbanic mass. *do* refers to the listener or listeners. Neither *mi* nor *do* is specific about the number of persons referred to; for example, the foreman of a jury may refer to the members of the jury as *mi*, since in speaking officially he represents all of them.

The referents of *mi* and *do* are usually obvious from the context, but may be assigned by the vocative words of selma'o COI, explained in Section 13.14 (p. 309). The vocative *mi'e* assigns *mi*, whereas all of the other vocatives assign *do*.

Example 7.5

mi'e	.djan.	doi	frank.	mi	cusku	lu		mi	bajra	li'u			do
I-am	John,	O	Frank,	I	express	[quote]		I	run	[unquote]		to	you

I am John, Frank; I tell you "I run".

The cmavo *mi'o*, *mi'a*, *ma'a*, and *do'o* express various combinations of the speaker and/or the listener and/or other people:

mi'o includes only the speaker and the listener but no one else;
mi'a includes the speaker and others but excludes the listener;
do'o includes the listener and others but excludes the speaker;
ma'a includes all three: speaker, listener, others.

All of these pro-sumti represent masses. For example, *mi'o* is the same as *mi joi do*, the mass of me and you considered jointly.

In English, "we" can mean *mi* or *mi'o* or *mi'a* or even *ma'a*, and English-speakers often suffer because they cannot easily distinguish *mi'o* from *mi'a*:

Example 7.6

> We're going to the store.

Does this include the listener or not? There's no way to be sure.

Finally, the cmavo *ko* is logically equivalent to *do*; its referent is the listener. However, its use alters an assertion about the listener into a command to the listener to make the assertion true:

Example 7.7

do	*klama*	*le*	*zarci*
You	go-to	the	store.

becomes:

Example 7.8

ko	*klama*	*le*	*zarci*
You [imperative]	go-to	the	store.

Make "you go to the store" true!
Go to the store!

In English, the subject of a command is omitted, but in Lojban, the word *ko* must be used. However, *ko* does not have to appear in the x1 place:

Example 7.9

mi	*viska*	*ko*
I	see	you-[imperative]

Make "I see you" true!
Be seen by me!

In Example 7.9 (p. 141), it is necessary to make the verb passive in English in order to convey the effect of *ko* in the x2 place. Indeed, *ko* does not even have to be a sumti of the main bridi:

Example 7.10

mi	*viska*	*le*	*prenu*	*poi*	*prami*	*ko*
I	see	the	person	that	loves	you-[imperative]

Make "I see the person that loves you" true!
Be such that the person who loves you is seen by me!
Show me the person who loves you!

As mentioned in Section 7.1 (p. 139), some pro-sumti series have corresponding pro-bridi series. However, there is no equivalent of the mi-series among pro-bridi, since a person isn't a relationship.

7.3 Demonstrative pro-sumti: the ti-series

The following cmavo are discussed in this section:

ti	KOhA	ti-series	this here, a nearby object
ta	KOhA	ti-series	that there, a medium-distant object
tu	KOhA	ti-series	that yonder, a far-distant object

It is often useful to refer to things by pointing to them or by some related non-linguistic mechanism. In English, the words "this" and "that" serve this function among others: "this" refers to something pointed at that is near the speaker, and "that" refers to something further away. The Lojban pro-sumti of the ti-series serve the same functions, but more narrowly. The cmavo *ti*, *ta*, and *tu* provide only the pointing function of "this" and "that"; they are not used to refer to things that cannot be pointed at.

There are three pro-sumti of the ti-series rather than just two because it is often useful to distinguish between objects that are at more than two different distances. Japanese, among other languages, regularly does this. Until the 16th century, English did too; the pronoun "that" referred to something at a medium distance from the speaker, and the now-archaic pronoun "yon" to something far away.

In conversation, there is a special rule about *ta* and *tu* that is often helpful in interpreting them. When used contrastingly, *ta* refers to something that is near the listener, whereas *tu* refers to something far from both speaker and listener. This makes for a parallelism between *ti* and *mi*, and *ta* and *do*, that is convenient when pointing is not possible; for example, when talking by telephone. In written text, on the other hand, the meaning of the ti-series is inherently vague; is the writer to be taken as pointing to something, and if so, to what? In all cases, what counts as "near" and "far away" is relative to the current situation.

It is important to distinguish between the English pronoun "this" and the English adjective "this" as in "this boat". The latter is not represented in Lojban by *ti*:

Example 7.11

le	ti	bloti
the	**this**	**boat**

does not mean "this boat" but rather "this one's boat", "the boat associated with this thing", as explained in Section 8.7 (p. 172). A correct Lojban translation of Example 7.11 (p. 142) is

Example 7.12

le	vi	bloti
the	**here**	**boat**

the nearby boat

using a spatial tense before the selbri *bloti* to express that the boat is near the speaker. (Tenses are explained in full in Chapter 10 (p. 207).) Another correct translation would be:

Example 7.13

ti	noi	bloti
this-thing	**which-incidentally**	**is-a-boat**

There are no demonstrative pro-bridi to correspond to the ti-series: you can't point to a relationship.

7.4 Utterance pro-sumti: the di'u-series

The following cmavo are discussed in this section:

di'u	KOhA	di'u-series	the previous utterance
de'u	KOhA	di'u-series	an earlier utterance
da'u	KOhA	di'u-series	a much earlier utterance
di'e	KOhA	di'u-series	the next utterance
de'e	KOhA	di'u-series	a later utterance
da'e	KOhA	di'u-series	a much later utterance
dei	KOhA	di'u-series	this very utterance
do'i	KOhA	di'u-series	some utterance

The cmavo of the di'u-series enable us to talk about things that have been, are being, or will be said. In English, it is normal to use "this" and "that" for this (indeed, the immediately preceding "this" is an example of such a usage):

Example 7.14

You don't like cats.

That is untrue.

Here "that" does not refer to something that can be pointed to, but to the preceding sentence "You don't like cats". In Lojban, therefore, Example 7.14 (p. 142) is rendered:

Example 7.15

do	na	nelci	loi	mlatu
You	(Not!)	like	the-mass-of	cats

.i	di'u	jitfa	jufra
.	The-previous-utterance	is-a-false	sentence.

Using *ta* instead of *di'u* would cause the listener to look around to see what the speaker of the second sentence was physically pointing to.

As with *ti*, *ta*, and *tu*, the cmavo of the di'u-series come in threes: a close utterance, a medium-distance utterance, and a distant utterance, either in the past or in the future. It turned out to be impossible to use the *i/ a/ u* vowel convention of the demonstratives in Section 7.3 (p. 141) without causing collisions with other cmavo, and so the di'u-series has a unique *i/ e/ a* convention in the first vowel of the cmavo.

Most references in speech are to the past (what has already been said), so *di'e*, *de'e*, and *da'e* are not very useful when speaking. In writing, they are frequently handy:

Example 7.16

la	saimn.	cusku	di'e
That-named	Simon	expresses	the-following-utterance.

Simon says:

Example 7.16 (p. 143) would typically be followed by a quotation. Note that although presumably the quotation is of something Simon has said in the past, the quotation utterance itself would appear after Example 7.16 (p. 143), and so *di'e* is appropriate.

The remaining two cmavo, *dei* and *do'i*, refer respectively to the very utterance that the speaker is uttering, and to some vague or unspecified utterance uttered by someone at some time:

Example 7.17

dei	jetnu	jufra
This-utterance	is-a-true	sentence.

What I am saying (at this moment) is true.

Example 7.18

do'i	jetnu	jufra
Some-utterance	is-a-true	sentence.

That's true (where "that" is not necessarily what was just said).

The cmavo of the di'u-series have a meaning that is relative to the context. The referent of *dei* in the current utterance is the same as the referent of *di'u* in the next utterance. The term "utterance" is used rather than "sentence" because the amount of speech or written text referred to by any of these words is vague. Often, a single bridi is intended, but longer utterances may be thus referred to.

Note one very common construction with *di'u* and the cmavo *la'e* (of selma'o LAhE; see Section 6.10 (p. 128)) which precedes a sumti and means "the thing referred to by (the sumti)":

Example 7.19

mi	prami	la	djein.	.i	mi	nelci	la'e	di'u
I	love	that-named	Jane.	And	I	like	the-referent-of	the-last-utterance.

I love Jane, and I like that.

The effect of *la'e di'u* in Example 7.19 (p. 143) is that the speaker likes, not the previous sentence, but rather the state of affairs referred to by the previous sentence, namely his loving Jane. This cmavo compound is often written as a single word: *la'edi'u*. It is important not to mix up *di'u* and *la'edi'u*, or the wrong meaning will generally result:

Example 7.20

mi	prami	la	djein.	.i	mi	nelci	di'u
I	love	that-named	Jane.	And	I	like	the-last-utterance.

says that the speaker likes one of his own sentences.

There are no pro-bridi corresponding to the di'u-series.

7.5 Assignable pro-sumti and pro-bridi: the ko'a-series and the broda-series

The following cmavo and gismu are discussed in this section:

ko'a	KOhA	ko'a-series	it-1
ko'e	KOhA	ko'a-series	it-2
ko'i	KOhA	ko'a-series	it-3
ko'o	KOhA	ko'a-series	it-4
ko'u	KOhA	ko'a-series	it-5
fo'a	KOhA	ko'a-series	it-6
fo'e	KOhA	ko'a-series	it-7
fo'i	KOhA	ko'a-series	it-8
fo'o	KOhA	ko'a-series	it-9
fo'u	KOhA	ko'a-series	it-10
broda	BRIVLA	broda-series	is-thing-1
brode	BRIVLA	broda-series	is-thing-2
brodi	BRIVLA	broda-series	is-thing-3
brodo	BRIVLA	broda-series	is-thing-4
brodu	BRIVLA	broda-series	is-thing-5
goi	GOI		pro-sumti assignment
cei	CEI		pro-bridi assignment

The discussion of personal pro-sumti in Section 7.2 (p. 140) may have seemed incomplete. In English, the personal pronouns include not only "I" and "you" but also "he", "she", "it", and "they". Lojban does have equivalents of this latter group: in fact, it has more of them than English does. However, they are organized and used very differently.

There are ten cmavo in the ko'a-series, and they may be assigned freely to any sumti whatsoever. The English word "he" can refer only to males, "she" only to females (and ships and a few other things), "it" only to inanimate things, and "they" only to plurals; the cmavo of the ko'a-series have no restrictions at all. Therefore, it is almost impossible to guess from the context what ko'a-series cmavo might refer to if they are just used freely:

Example 7.21

la	.alis.	klama	le	zarci	.i	ko'a	blanu
That-named	Alice	goes-to	the	store	.	It-1	is-blue.

The English gloss "it-1", plus knowledge about the real world, would tend to make English-speakers believe that *ko'a* refers to the store; in other words, that its antecedent is *le zarci*. To a Lojbanist, however, *la .alis.* is just as likely an antecedent, in which case Example 7.21 (p. 144) means that Alice, not the store, is blue.

To avoid this pitfall, Lojban employs special syntax, using the cmavo *goi*:

Example 7.22

la	.alis.	klama	le	zarci
That-named	Alice	goes-to	the	store

.i	ko'a	goi	la	.alis.	cu	blanu
.	It-1,	also-known-as	that-named	Alice	,	is-blue.

Syntactically, *goi la .alis.* is a relative phrase (relative phrases are explained in Chapter 8 (p. 161)). Semantically, it says that *ko'a* and *la .alis.* refer to the same thing, and furthermore that this is true because *ko'a* is being defined as meaning *la .alis.*. It is equally correct to say:

7.5 Assignable pro-sumti and pro-bridi: the ko'a-series and the broda-series

Example 7.23

la	.alis.	klama	le	zarci
That-named	**Alice**	**goes-to**	**the**	**store**

.i	la	.alis.	goi	ko'a	cu	blanu
.	**That-named**	**Alice,**	**also-known-as**	**it-1,**		**is-blue.**

in other words, *goi* is symmetrical. There is a terminator, *ge'u* (of selma'o GEhU), which is almost always elidable. The details are in Section 8.3 (p. 165).

The afterthought form of *goi* shown in Example 7.22 (p. 144) and Example 7.23 (p. 145) is probably most common in speech, where we do not know until part way through our utterance that we will want to refer to Alice again. In writing, though, *ko'a* may be assigned at the point where Alice is first mentioned. An example of this forethought form of *goi* is:

Example 7.24

la	.alis.	goi	ko'a	klama	le	zarci	.i	ko'a	cu	blanu
That-named	**Alice,**	**also-known-as**	**it-1,**	**goes-to**	**the**	**store**	**.**	**It-1**		**is-blue.**

Again, *ko'a goi la .alis.* would have been entirely acceptable in Example 7.24 (p. 145). This last form is reminiscent of legal jargon: "The party of the first part, hereafter known as Buyer, ...".

Just as the ko'a-series of pro-sumti allows a substitute for a sumti which is long or complex, or which for some other reason we do not want to repeat, so the broda-series of pro-bridi allows a substitute for a selbri or even a whole bridi:

Example 7.25

> ti slasi je mlatu bo cidja lante gacri cei broda .i le crino broda cu barda .i le xunre broda cu cmalu
>
> These are plastic cat-food can covers or thingies. The green thingy is large. The red thingy is small.

The pro-bridi *broda* has as its antecedent the selbri *slasi je mlatu bo cidja lante gacri*. The cmavo *cei* performs the role of *goi* in assigning *broda* to this long phrase, and *broda* can then be used just like any other brivla. (In fact, *broda* and its relatives actually *are* brivla: they are gismu in morphology, although they behave exactly like the members of selma'o GOhA. The reasons for using gismu rather than cmavo are buried in the Loglan Project's history.)

Note that pro-bridi are so called because, even though they have the grammar of selbri, their antecedents are whole bridi. In the following rather contrived example, the antecedent of *brode* is the whole bridi *mi klama le zarci*:

Example 7.26

mi	klama	cei	brode	le	zarci	.i	do	brode
I	**go-to**	**(which-is**	**claim-1)**	**the**	**store**	**.**	**You**	**claim-1.**

I go to the store. You, too.

In the second bridi, *do brode* means *do klama le zarci*, because *brode* carries the x2 sumti of *mi klama le zarci* along with it. It also potentially carries the x1 sumti as well, but the explicit x1 sumti *do* overrides the *mi* of the antecedent bridi. Similarly, any tense or negation that is present in the antecedent is also carried, and can be overridden by explicit tense or negation cmavo on the pro-bridi. These rules hold for all pro-bridi that have antecedents.

Another use of *broda* and its relatives, without assignment, is as "sample gismu":

Example 7.27

	broda		ke	brode		brodi	
a	**thing-1**	**type-of**	**(**	**thing-2**	**type-of**	**thing-3**	**)**

represents an abstract pattern, a certain kind of tanru. (Historically, this use was the original one.)

As is explained in Section 17.9 (p. 404), the words for Lojban letters, belonging to selma'o BY and certain related selma'o, are also usable as assignable pro-sumti. The main difference between letter pro-sumti and ko'a-series pro-sumti is that, in the absence of an explicit assignment, letters are taken to refer to the most recent name or description sumti beginning with the same letter:

Example 7.28

mi	viska	le	gerku	.i	gy.	cusku	zo	arf.
I	see	the	dog	.	D	expresses	the-word	"Arf!"	.

The Lojban word *gerku* begins with *g*, so the antecedent of *gy.*, the cmavo for the letter *g*, must be *le gerku*. In the English translation, we use the same principle to refer to the dog as "D". Of course, in case of ambiguity, *goi* can be used to make an explicit assignment.

Furthermore, *goi* can even be used to assign a name:

Example 7.29

le	ninmu	goi	la	sam.	cu	klama	le	zarci
The	woman	also-known-as	that-named	Sam		goes-to	the	store.

The woman, whom I'll call Sam, goes to the store.

This usage does not imply that the woman's name is Sam, or even that the speaker usually calls the woman "Sam". "Sam" is simply a name chosen, as if at random, for use in the current context only.

7.6 Anaphoric pro-sumti and pro-bridi: the ri-series and the go'i-series

The following cmavo are discussed in this section:

ri	KOhA	ri-series	(repeats last sumti)
ra	KOhA	ri-series	(repeats previous sumti)
ru	KOhA	ri-series	(repeats long-ago sumti)
go'i	GOhA	go'i-series	(repeats last bridi)
go'a	GOhA	go'i-series	(repeats previous bridi)
go'u	GOhA	go'i-series	(repeats long-ago bridi)
go'e	GOhA	go'i-series	(repeats last-but-one bridi)
go'o	GOhA	go'i-series	(repeats future bridi)
nei	GOhA	go'i-series	(repeats current bridi)
no'a	GOhA	go'i-series	(repeats outer bridi)
ra'o	RAhO		pro-cmavo update

The term "anaphora" literally means "repetition", but is used in linguistics to refer to pronouns whose significance is the repetition of earlier words, namely their antecedents. Lojban provides three pro-sumti anaphora, *ri*, *ra*, and *ru*; and three corresponding pro-bridi anaphora, *go'i*, *go'a*, and *go'u*. These cmavo reveal the same vowel pattern as the ti-series, but the "distances" referred to are not physical distances, but distances from the anaphoric cmavo to its antecedent.

The cmavo *ri* is the simplest of these; it has the same referent as the last complete sumti appearing before the *ri*:

Example 7.30

la	.alis.	sipna	ne'i	le	ri	kumfa
That-named	Alice	sleeps	in	the	of- [repeat-last-sumti]	room.

Alice sleeps in her room.

The *ri* in Example 7.30 (p. 146) is equivalent to repeating the last sumti, which is *la .alis.*, so Example 7.30 (p. 146) is equivalent to:

Example 7.31

la	.alis.	sipna	ne'i	le	la	.alis.	kumfa
That-named	Alice	sleeps	in	the	of-	that-named	Alice	room.

Alice sleeps in Alice's room.

Note that *ri* does not repeat *le ri kumfa*, because that sumti is not yet complete when *ri* appears. This prevents *ri* from getting entangled in paradoxes of self-reference. (There are plenty of other ways to do that!) Note also that sumti within other sumti, as in quotations, abstractions, and the like, are counted in the order of their beginnings; thus a lower level sumti like *la alis.* in Example 7.31 (p. 146) is considered to be more recent than a higher level sumti that contains it.

Certain sumti are ignored by *ri*; specifically, most of the other cmavo of KOhA, and the almost-grammatically-equivalent lerfu words of selma'o BY. It is simpler just to repeat these directly:

Example 7.32

mi	prami	mi
I	love	me.

I love myself.

However, the cmavo of the ti-series can be picked up by *ri*, because you might have changed what you are pointing at, so repeating *ti* may not be effective. Likewise, *ri* itself (or rather its antecedent) can be repeated by a later *ri*; in fact, a string of *ri* cmavo with no other intervening sumti always all repeat the same sumti:

Example 7.33

la	djan.	viska	le	tricu	.i
That-named	John	sees	the	tree.	

ri		se jadni	le		ri	jimca
[repeat-last]		is-adorned-by	the	of-	[repeat-last]	branch.

John sees the tree. It is adorned by its branches.

Here the second *ri* has as antecedent the first *ri*, which has as antecedent *le tricu*. All three refer to the same thing: a tree.

To refer to the next-to-last sumti, the third-from-last sumti, and so on, *ri* may be subscripted (subscripts are explained in Section 19.6 (p. 453)):

Example 7.34

lo	smuci	.i	lo	forca	.i	la		rik.	pilno	rixire
A	spoon.		A	fork.		That-named	Rick	uses	[repeat-next-to-last].

.i	la		.alis.	pilno	riximu
	That-named	Alice	uses	[repeat-fifth-from-last].

Here *rixire*, or "ri-sub-2", skips *la rik.* to reach *lo forca*. In the same way, *riximu*, or "ri-sub-5", skips *la .alis.*, *rixire*, *la rik.*, and *lo forca* to reach *lo smuci*. As can clearly be seen, this procedure is barely practicable in writing, and would break down totally in speech.

Therefore, the vaguer *ra* and *ru* are also provided. The cmavo *ra* repeats a recently used sumti, and *ru* one that was further back in the speech or text. The use of *ra* and *ru* forces the listener to guess at the referent, but makes life easier for the speaker. Can *ra* refer to the last sumti, like *ri*? The answer is no if *ri* has also been used. If *ri* has not been used, then *ra* might be the last sumti. Likewise, if *ra* has been used, then any use of *ru* would repeat a sumti earlier than the one *ra* is repeating. A more reasonable version of Example Example 7.34 (p. 147), but one that depends more on context, is:

Example 7.35

lo	smuci	.i	lo	forca	.i	la		rik.	pilno	ra
A	spoon.		A	fork.		That-named	Rick	uses	[some-previous-thing].

.i	la		.alis.	pilno	ru
	That-named	Alice	uses	[some-more-remote-thing].

In Example 7.35 (p. 147), the use of *ra* tells us that something other than *la rik.* is the antecedent; *lo forca* is the nearest sumti, so it is probably the antecedent. Similarly, the antecedent of *ru* must be something even further back in the utterance than *lo forca*, and *lo smuci* is the obvious candidate.

The meaning of *ri* must be determined every time it is used. Since *ra* and *ru* are more vaguely defined, they may well retain the same meaning for a while, but the listener cannot count on this behavior. To make a permanent reference to something repeated by *ri*, *ra*, or *ru*, use *goi* and a ko'a-series cmavo:

Example 7.36

la	.alis.	klama	le	zarci
That-named	Alice	goes-to	the	store

.i	ri		goi		ko'a	blanu
.	It-last-mentioned		also-known-as		it-1	is-blue.

allows the store to be referred to henceforth as *ko'a* without ambiguity. Example 7.36 (p. 148) is equivalent to Example 7.21 (p. 144) and eliminates any possibility of *ko'a* being interpreted by the listener as referring to Alice.

The cmavo *go'i*, *go'a*, and *go'u* follow exactly the same rules as *ri*, *ra*, and *ru*, except that they are pro-bridi, and therefore repeat bridi, not sumti – specifically, main sentence bridi. Any bridi that are embedded within other bridi, such as relative clauses or abstractions, are not counted. Like the cmavo of the broda-series, the cmavo of the go'i-series copy all sumti with them. This makes *go'i* by itself convenient for answering a question affirmatively, or for repeating the last bridi, possibly with new sumti:

Example 7.37

xu	zo	.djan.	cmene	do	.i	go'i
[True-false?]	The-word	"John"	is-the-name-of	you?		[repeat last bridi].

Is John your name? Yes.

Example 7.38

mi	klama	le	zarci	.i	do	go'i
I	go-to	the	store	.	You	[repeat last bridi].

I go to the store . You, too.

Note that Example 7.38 (p. 148) means the same as Example 7.26 (p. 145), but without the bother of assigning an actual broda-series word to the first bridi. For long-term reference, use *go'i cei broda* or the like, analogously to *ri goi ko'a* in Example 7.36 (p. 148).

The remaining four cmavo of the go'i-series are provided for convenience or for achieving special effects. The cmavo *go'e* means the same as *go'ixire*: it repeats the last bridi but one. This is useful in conversation:

Example 7.39

A:	mi	ba		klama	le	zarci
A:	I	[future]		go-to	the	store.

A: I am going to the store.

B:	mi	nelci	le	si'o		mi	go'i
B:	I	like	the	concept-of		I	[repeat-last-bridi].

B: I like the idea of my going.

A:	do	go'e
A:	You	[repeat-last-bridi-but-one].

A: You'll go, too.

Here B's sentence repeats A's within an abstraction (explained in Chapter 11 (p. 247)): *le si'o mi go'i* means *le si'o mi klama le zarci*. Why must B use the word *mi* explicitly to replace the x1 of *mi klama le zarci*, even though it looks like *mi* is replacing *mi*? Because B's *mi* refers to B, whereas A's *mi* refers to A. If B said:

Example 7.40

mi nelci le si'o go'i

that would mean:

I like the idea of your going to the store.

148

7.6 Anaphoric pro-sumti and pro-bridi: the ri-series and the go'i-series

The repetition signalled by *go'i* is not literally of words, but of concepts. Finally, A repeats her own sentence, but with the x1 changed to *do*, meaning B. Note that in Example 7.39 (p. 148), the tense *ba* (future time) is carried along by both *go'i* and *go'e*.

Descriptions based on go'i-series cmavo can be very useful for repeating specific sumti of previous bridi:

Example 7.41

le	xekri	mlatu	cu	klama	le	zarci	.i	le
The	black	cat		goes-to	the	store.		That-described-as-the-x1-place-of

go'i		cu	cadzu	le	bisli
[repeat-last-bridi]			walks-on	the	ice.

The black cat goes to the store. It walks on the ice.

Here the *go'i* repeats *le xekri mlatu cu klama le zarci*, and since *le* makes the x1 place into a description, and the x1 place of this bridi is *le xekri mlatu*, *le go'i* means *le xekri mlatu*.

The cmavo *go'o*, *nei*, and *no'a* have been little used so far. They repeat respectively some future bridi, the current bridi, and the bridi that encloses the current bridi (*no'a*, unlike the other members of the go'i- series, can repeat non-sentence bridi). Here are a few examples:

Example 7.42

mi	nupre	le	nu	mi	go'o
I	promise	the	event-of	I	[repeat-future-bridi].

.i	ba	dunda	le	djini		le	bersa
	[Future]	give	the	money	to	the	son

.i	ba	dunda	le	zdani		le	tixnu
	[Future]	give	the	house	to	the	daughter

I promise to do the following: Give the money to my son. Give the house to my daughter.

(Note: The Lojban does not contain an equivalent of the *my* in the colloquial English; it leaves the fact that it is the speaker's son and daughter that are referred to implicit. To make the fact explicit, use *le bersa/tixnu be mi*.)

For good examples of *nei* and *no'a*, we need nested bridi contexts:

Example 7.43

mi	se	pluka	le	nu	do	pensi	le	nu
I		am-pleased-by	the	event-of	(you	think-about	the	(event-of

nei		kei	pu	le	nu	do	zukte
[main-bridi]		)	before	the	(event-of	your	acting).

I am pleased that you thought about whether I would be pleased (about ...) before you acted.

Example 7.44

mi	ba	klama	ca	le	nu	do	no'a
I	[future]	go	[present]	the	event-of	you	[repeats outer bridi]

I will go when you do.

Finally, *ra'o* is a cmavo that can be appended to any go'i-series cmavo, or indeed any cmavo of selma'o GOhA, to signal that pro-sumti or pro-bridi cmavo in the antecedent are to be repeated literally and reinterpreted in their new context. Normally, any pro-sumti used within the antecedent of the pro-bridi keep their meanings intact. In the presence of *ra'o*, however, their meanings must be reinterpreted with reference to the new environment. If someone says to you:

Example 7.45

mi ba lumci le mi karce

I will wash my car.

you might reply either:

Example 7.46

mi go'i

I will wash your car.

or:

Example 7.47

mi go'i ra'o

I will wash my car.

The *ra'o* forces the second *mi* from the original bridi to mean the new speaker rather than the former speaker. This means that *go'e ra'o* would be an acceptable alternative to *do go'e* in B's statement in Example 7.39 (p. 148).

The anaphoric pro-sumti of this section can be used in quotations, but never refer to any of the supporting text outside the quotation, since speakers presumably do not know that they may be quoted by someone else.

However, a *ri*-series or *go'a*-series reference within a quotation can refer to something mentioned in an earlier quotation if the two quotations are closely related in time and context. This allows a quotation to be broken up by narrative material without interfering with the pro-sumti within it. Here's an example:

Example 7.48

la	djan.	cusku	lu	mi	klama	le	zarci	li'u
That-named	**John**	**says**	**[quote]**	**I**	**go-to**	**the**	**store**	**[unquote].**

.i	la	.alis.	cusku	lu	mi	go'i	li'u
	That-named	**Alice**	**says**	**[quote]**	**I**	**[repeat]**	**[unquote].**

John says, "I am going to the store." Alice says, "Me too."

Of course, there is no problem with narrative material referring to something within a quotation: people who quote, unlike people who are quoted, are aware of what they are doing.

7.7 Indefinite pro-sumti and pro-bridi: the zo'e-series and the co'e-series

The following cmavo are discussed in this section:

zo'e	KOhA	zo'e-series	the obvious value
zu'i	KOhA	zo'e-series	the typical value
zi'o	KOhA	zo'e-series	the nonexistent value
co'e	GOhA	co'e-series	has the obvious relationship

The cmavo of the zo'e-series represent indefinite, unspecified sumti. The cmavo *zo'e* represents an elliptical value for this sumti place; it is the optional spoken place holder when a sumti is skipped without being specified. Note that the elliptical value is not always the typical value. The properties of ellipsis lead to an elliptical sumti being defined as "whatever I want it to mean but haven't bothered to figure out, or figure out how to express".

The cmavo *zu'i*, on the other hand, represents the typical value for this place of this bridi:

Example 7.49

mi	klama	le	bartu	be	le	zdani
I	**go-to**	**the**	**outside**	**of**	**the**	**house**	**from**

le	nenri	be	le	zdani	zu'i		zu'i
the	**inside**	**of**	**the**	**house**	**[by-typical-route]**		**[by-typical-means]**

In Example 7.49 (p. 150), the first *zu'i* probably means something like "by the door", and the second *zu'i* probably means something like "on foot", those being the typical route and means for leaving a house. On the other hand, if you are at the top of a high rise during a fire, neither *zu'i* is appropriate. It's also common to use *zu'i* in "by standard" places.

Finally, the cmavo *zi'o* represents a value which does not even exist. When a bridi fills one of its places with *zi'o*, what is really meant is that the selbri has a place which is irrelevant to the true relationship the speaker wishes to express. For example, the place structure of *zbasu* is:

actor x1 makes x2 from materials x3

Consider the sentence

Living things are made from cells.

This cannot be correctly expressed as:

Example 7.50

loi	*jmive*	*cu*	*se zbasu*	*[zo'e]*	*fi*	*loi*	*selci*
The-mass-of	**living-things**		**is-made**	**[by-something]**	**from**	**the-mass-of**	**cells**

because the *zo'e*, expressed or understood, in Example 7.50 (p. 151) indicates that there is still a "maker" in this relationship. We do not generally suppose, however, that someone "makes" living things from cells. The best answer is probably to find a different selbri, one which does not imply a "maker": however, an alternative strategy is to use *zi'o* to eliminate the maker place:

Example 7.51

loi	*jmive*	*cu*
The-mass-of	**living-things**	

se zbasu	*zi'o*		*loi*	*selci*
is-made	**[without-maker]**	**from**	**the-mass-of**	**cells.**

Note: The use of *zi'o* to block up, as it were, one place of a selbri actually creates a new selbri with a different place structure. Consider the following examples:

Example 7.52

mi	*zbasu*	*le*	*dinju*		*loi*		*mudri*
I	**make**	**the**	**building**	**from**	**some-of-the-mass-of**		**wood.**

I make the building out of wood.

Example 7.53

zi'o		*zbasu*	*le*	*dinju*		*loi*		*mudri*
[without-maker]	**makes**	**the**	**building**	**from**	**some-of-the-mass-of**		**wood.**

The building is made out of wood.

Example 7.54

mi	*zbasu*	*zi'o*		*loi*		*mudri*
I	**make**	**[without-thing-made]**	**from**	**some-of-the-mass-of**		**wood.**

I build using wood.

Example 7.55

mi	*zbasu*	*le*	*dinju*	*zi'o*
I	**make**	**the**	**building**	**[without-material].**

I make the building.

If Example 7.52 (p. 151) is true, then Example 7.53 (p. 151) through Example 7.55 (p. 151) must be true also. However, Example 7.51 (p. 151) does not correspond to any sentence with three regular (non- *zi'o*) sumti.

The pro-bridi *co'e* (which by itself constitutes the co'e-series of selma'o GOhA) represents the elliptical selbri. Lojban grammar does not allow the speaker to merely omit a selbri from a bridi, although any or all sumti may be freely omitted. Being vague about a relationship requires the use of *co'e* as a selbri place-holder:

Example 7.56

mi	troci	le	nu	mi	co'e	le	vorme
I	try	the	event-of	my	[doing-the-obvious-action]	to-the	door.

I try the door.

The English version means, and the Lojban version probably means, that I try to open the door, but the relationship of opening is not actually specified; the Lojbanic listener must guess it from context. Lojban, unlike English, makes it clear that there is an implicit action that is not being expressed.

The form of *co'e* was chosen to resemble *zo'e*; the cmavo *do'e* of selma'o BAI (see Section 9.6 (p. 188)) also belongs to the same group of cmavo.

Note that *do'i*, of the di'u-series, is also a kind of indefinite pro-sumti: it is indefinite in referent, but is restricted to referring only to an utterance.

7.8 Reflexive and reciprocal pro-sumti: the vo'a-series

The following cmavo are discussed in this section:

vo'a	KOhA	vo'a-series	x1 of this bridi
vo'e	KOhA	vo'a-series	x2 of this bridi
vo'i	KOhA	vo'a-series	x3 of this bridi
vo'o	KOhA	vo'a-series	x4 of this bridi
vo'u	KOhA	vo'a-series	x5 of this bridi
soi	SOI		reciprocity
se'u	SEhU		soi terminator

The cmavo of the vo'a-series are pro-sumti anaphora, like those of the ri-series, but have a specific function. These cmavo refer to the other places of the same bridi; the five of them represent up to five places. The same vo'a-series cmavo mean different things in different bridi. Some examples:

Example 7.57

mi lumci vo'a

I wash myself

Example 7.58

mi klama le zarci vo'e

I go to the store from itself [by some route unspecified].

To refer to places of neighboring bridi, constructions like *le se go'i ku* do the job: this refers to the 2nd place of the previous main bridi, as explained in Section 7.6 (p. 146).

The cmavo of the vo'a-series are also used with *soi* (of selma'o SOI) to precisely express reciprocity, which in English is imprecisely expressed with a discursive phrase like "vice versa":

Example 7.59

mi	prami	do	soi	vo'a	vo'e
I	love	you	[reciprocity]	[x1 of this bridi]	[x2 of this bridi].

I love you and vice versa (swapping "I" and "you").

The significance of *soi vo'a vo'e* is that the bridi is still true even if the x1 (specified by *vo'a*) and the x2 (specified by *vo'e*) places are interchanged. If only a single sumti follows *soi*, then the sumti immediately preceding *soi* is understood to be one of those involved:

Example 7.60

mi	prami	do	soi	vo'a
I	love	you	[reciprocity]	[x1 of this bridi].

again involves the x1 and x2 places.

Of course, other places can be involved, and other sumti may be used in place of vo'a-series cmavo, provided those other sumti can be reasonably understood as referring to the same things mentioned in the bridi proper. Here are several examples that mean the same thing:

Example 7.61

> mi bajykla ti ta soi vo'e -
> mi bajykla ti ta soi vo'e vo'i
> soi vo'e vo'i mi bajykla ti ta

> I runningly-go to this from that and vice versa (to that from this).

The elidable terminator for *soi* is *se'u* (selma'o SEhU), which is normally needed only if there is just one sumti after the *soi*, and the *soi* construction is not at the end of the bridi. Constructions using *soi* are free modifiers, and as such can go almost anywhere. Here is an example where *se'u* is required:

Example 7.62

mi	bajykla	ti	soi	vo'i	se'u	ta
I	runningly-go-to	this	[reciprocity]	[x3 of this bridi]		from	that

> I runningly-go to this from that and vice versa.

7.9 sumti and bridi questions: *ma* and *mo*

The following cmavo are discussed in this section:

ma	KOhA	sumti question
mo	GOhA	bridi question

Lojban questions are more fully explained in Section 19.5 (p. 451), but *ma* and *mo* are listed in this chapter for completeness. The cmavo *ma* asks for a sumti to make the bridi true:

Example 7.63

do	klama	ma
You	go-to	what?

> Where are you going?

The cmavo *mo*, on the other hand, asks for a selbri which makes the question bridi true. If the answer is a full bridi, then the arguments of the answer override the arguments in the question, in the same manner as the go'i-series cmavo. A simple example is:

Example 7.64

> do mo

> What predicate is true as applied to you?
> How are you?
> What are you doing?
> What are you?

Example 7.65 (p. 153) is a truly pregnant question that will have several meanings depending on context.

(One thing it probably does not mean is "Who are you?" in the sense "What is your name/identity?", which is better expressed by:

Example 7.65

ma	cmene	do
What-sumti	is-the-name-of	you?

> What is your name?

or even

Example 7.66

doi	*ma*
O	[what sumti?]

which uses the vocative *doi* to address someone, and simultaneously asks who the someone is.)

A further example of *mo*:

Example 7.67

lo	*mo*		*prenu*	*cu*	*darxi*	*do*	*.i*	*barda*
A	[what selbri?]	type-of	person		hit	you?		A big thing.

Which person hit you? The big one.

When *ma* or *mo* is repeated, multiple questions are being asked simultaneously:

Example 7.68

ma	*djuno*	*ma*
[What-sumti]	knows	[what-sumti]?

Who knows what?

7.10 Relativized pro-sumti: *ke'a*

The following cmavo are discussed in this section:

ke'a	KOhA	relativized sumti

This pro-sumti is used in relative clauses (explained in Chapter 8 (p. 161)) to indicate how the sumti being relativized fits within the clause. For example:

Example 7.69

mi	*catlu*	*lo*	*mlatu*	*poi*		*[zo'e]*
I	see	a	cat	such-that		something-unspecified

zbasu	*ke'a*			*lei*		*slasi*
makes	the-thing-being-relativized-[the-cat]		from	some-mass-of		plastic.

I see a cat made of plastic.

If *ke'a* were omitted from Example 7.69 (p. 154), it might be confused with:

Example 7.70

mi	*catlu*	*lo*	*mlatu*	*poi*
I	see	a	cat	such-that

[ke'a]		*zbasu*	*lei*	*slasi*
the-thing-being-relativized-[the-cat]		makes	a-mass-of	plastic

I see a cat that makes plastic.

The anaphora cmavo *ri* cannot be used in place of *ke'a* in Example 7.69 (p. 154) and Example 7.70 (p. 154), because the relativized sumti is not yet complete when the *ke'a* appears.

Note that *ke'a* is used only with relative clauses, and not with other embedded bridi such as abstract descriptions. In the case of relative clauses within relative clauses, *ke'a* may be subscripted to make the difference clear (see Section 8.10 (p. 176)).

7.11 Abstraction focus pro-sumti: *ce'u*

The following cmavo are discussed in this section:

ce'u	KOhA	abstraction focus

The cmavo *ce'u* is used within abstraction bridi, particularly property abstractions introduced by the cmavo *ka*. Abstractions, including the uses of *ce'u*, are discussed in full in Chapter 11 (p. 247).

In brief: Every property abstraction specifies a property of one of the sumti in it; that sumti place is filled by using *ce'u*. This convention enables us to distinguish clearly between:

Example 7.71

le	ka		ce'u	gleki
the	property-of		(X	being-happy)

the property of being happy
happiness

and

Example 7.72

le	ka		gleki		ce'u
the	property-of		(being-happy-about		X)

the property of being that which someone is happy about

7.12 Bound variable pro-sumti and pro-bridi: the da-series and the bu'a-series

The following cmavo are discussed in this section:

da	KOhA	da-series	something-1
de	KOhA	da-series	something-2
di	KOhA	da-series	something-3
bu'a	GOhA	bu'a-series	some-predicate-1
bu'e	GOhA	bu'a-series	some-predicate-2
bu'i	GOhA	bu'a-series	some-predicate-3

Bound variables belong to the predicate-logic part of Lojban, and are listed here for completeness only. Their semantics is explained in Chapter 16 (p. 375). It is worth mentioning that the Lojban translation of Example 7.2 (p. 139) is:

Example 7.73

la	djan.	cu	lafti	da		poi
That-named	John		raised	something-1		which

grana		ku'o	gi'e	desygau	da	
is-a-stick			and	shake-did	something-1.	

John picked up a stick and shook it.

7.13 Pro-sumti and pro-bridi cancelling

The following cmavo are discussed in this section:

da'o	DAhO	cancel all pro-sumti/pro-bridi

How long does a pro-sumti or pro-bridi remain stable? In other words, once we know the referent of a pro-sumti or pro-bridi, how long can we be sure that future uses of the same cmavo have the same referent? The answer to this question depends on which series the cmavo belongs to.

Personal pro-sumti are stable until there is a change of speaker or listener, possibly signaled by a vocative. Assignable pro-sumti and pro-bridi last indefinitely or until rebound with *goi* or *cei*. Bound variable pro-sumti and pro-bridi also generally last until re-bound; details are available in Section 16.14 (p. 395).

Utterance pro-sumti are stable only within the utterance in which they appear; similarly, reflexive pro-sumti are stable only within the bridi in which they appear; and *ke'a* is stable only within its relative clause. Anaphoric pro-sumti and pro-bridi are stable only within narrow limits depending on the rules for the particular cmavo.

Demonstrative pro-sumti, indefinite pro-sumti and pro-bridi, and sumti and bridi questions potentially change referents every time they are used.

However, there are ways to cancel all pro-sumti and pro-bridi, so that none of them have known referents. (Some, such as *mi*, will acquire the same referent as soon as they are used again after the cancellation.) The simplest way to cancel everything is with the cmavo *da'o* of selma'o DAhO, which is used solely for this purpose; it may appear anywhere, and has no effect on the grammar of texts containing it. One use of *da'o* is when entering a conversation, to indicate that one's pro-sumti assignments have nothing to do with any assignments already made by other participants in the conversation.

In addition, the cmavo *ni'o* and *no'i* of selma'o NIhO, which are used primarily to indicate shifts in topic, may also have the effect of canceling pro-sumti and pro-bridi assignments, or of reinstating ones formerly in effect. More explanations of NIhO can be found in Section 19.3 (p. 448).

7.14 The identity predicate: du

The following cmavo is discussed in this section:

> du | GOhA | identity

The cmavo *du* has the place structure:

x1 is identical with x2, x3, ...

and appears in selma'o GOhA for reasons of convenience: it is not a pro-bridi. *du* serves as mathematical "=", and outside mathematical contexts is used for defining or identifying. Mathematical examples may be found in Chapter 18 (p. 413).

The main difference between

Example 7.74

ko'a	du	le	nanmu
It-1	is-identical-to	the	man

and

Example 7.75

ko'a	mintu	le	nanmu
It-1	is-the-same-as	the	man

is this defining nature. Example 7.74 (p. 156) presumes that the speaker is responding to a request for information about what *ko'a* refers to, or that the speaker in some way feels the need to define *ko'a* for later reference. A bridi with *du* is an identity sentence, somewhat metalinguistically saying that all attached sumti are representations for the same referent. There may be any number of sumti associated with *du*, and all are said to be identical.

Example 7.75 (p. 156), however, predicates; it is used to make a claim about the identity of *ko'a*, which presumably has been defined previously.

Note: *du* historically is derived from *dunli*, but *dunli* has a third place which *du* lacks: the standard of equality.

7.15 lujvo based on pro-sumti

There exist rafsi allocated to a few cmavo of selma'o KOhA, but they are rarely used. (See Section 7.16 (p. 157) for a complete list.) The obvious way to use them is as internal sumti, filling in an appropriate place of the gismu or lujvo to which they are attached; as such, they usually stand as the first rafsi in their lujvo.

Thus *donta'a*, meaning "you-talk", would be interpreted as *tavla be do*, and would have the place structure

Example 7.76

> t1 talks to you about subject t3 in language t4

since **t2** (the addressee) is already known to be *do*.

On the other hand, the lujvo *donma'o*, literally "you-cmavo", which means "a second person personal pronoun", would be interpreted as *cmavo be zo do*, and have the place structure:

Example 7.77

> c1 is a second person pronoun in language c4

since both the **c2** place (the grammatical class) and the **c3** place (the meaning) are obvious from the context *do*.

An anticipated use of rafsi for cmavo in the *fo'a* series is to express lujvo which can't be expressed in a convenient rafsi form, because they are too long to express, or are formally inconvenient (fu'ivla, cmene, and so forth.) An example would be:

Example 7.78

fo'a	goi	le	kulnrsu,omi	.i	lo	fo'arselsanga
x6	stands-for	the	Finnish-culture	.	An	x6-song.

Finally, lujvo involving *zi'o* are also possible, and are fully discussed in Chapter 12 (p. 263). In brief, the convention is to use the rafsi for *zi'o* as a prefix immediately followed by the rafsi for the number of the place to be deleted. Thus, if we consider a beverage (something drunk without considering who, if anyone, drinks it) as a *se pinxe be zi'o*, the lujvo corresponding to this is *zilrelselpinxe* (deleting the second place of *se pinxe*). Deleting the x1 place in this fashion would move all remaining places up by one. This would mean that *zilpavypinxe* has the same place structure as *zilrelselpinxe*, and *lo zilpavypinxe*, like *lo zilrelselpinxe*, refers to a beverage, and not to a non-existent drinker.

The pro-bridi *co'e*, *du*, and *bu'a* also have rafsi, which can be used just as if they were gismu. The resulting lujvo have (except for *du*-based lujvo) highly context-dependent meanings.

7.16 KOhA cmavo by series

mi-series

mi	I (rafsi: *mib*)
do	you (rafsi: *don* and *doi*)
mi'o	you and I
mi'a	I and others, we but not you
ma'a	you and I and others
do'o	you and others
ko	you-imperative

ti-series

ti	this here; something nearby (rafsi: *tif*)
ta	that there; something distant (rafsi: *taz*)
tu	that yonder; something far distant (rafsi: *tuf*)

di'u-series

di'u	the previous utterance
de'u	an earlier utterance
da'u	a much earlier utterance
di'e	the next utterance
de'e	a later utterance
da'e	a much later utterance
dei	this very utterance
do'i	some utterance

ko'a-series

ko'a	it-1; 1st assignable pro-sumti
ko'e	it-2; 2nd assignable pro-sumti
ko'i	it-3; 3rd assignable pro-sumti
ko'o	it-4; 4th assignable pro-sumti
ko'u	it-5; 5th assignable pro-sumti
fo'a	it-6; 6th assignable pro-sumti (rafsi: *fo'a*)
fo'e	it-7; 7th assignable pro-sumti (rafsi: *fo'e*)
fo'i	it-8; 8th assignable pro-sumti (rafsi: *fo'i*)
fo'o	it-9; 9th assignable pro-sumti
fo'u	it-10; 10th assignable pro-sumti

ri-series

ri	(repeats the last sumti)
ra	(repeats a previous sumti)
ru	(repeats a long-ago sumti)

zo'e-series

zo'e	the obvious value
zu'i	the typical value
zi'o	the nonexistent value (rafsi: *zil*)

vo'a-series

vo'a	x1 of this bridi
vo'e	x2 of this bridi
vo'i	x3 of this bridi
vo'o	x4 of this bridi
vo'u	x5 of this bridi

da-series

da	something-1 (rafsi: *dav/dza*)
de	something-2
di	something-3

others:

ke'a	relativized sumti
ma	sumti question
ce'u	abstraction focus

7.17 GOhA and other pro-bridi by series

broda-series (not GOhA):

broda	is-1; 1st assignable pro-bridi
brode	is-2; 2nd assignable pro-bridi
brodi	is-3; 3rd assignable pro-bridi
brodo	is-4; 4th assignable pro-bridi
brodu	is-5; 5th assignable pro-bridi

go'i-series

go'i	(repeats the last bridi)
go'a	(repeats a previous bridi)
go'u	(repeats a long-ago bridi)
go'e	(repeats the last-but-one bridi)
go'o	(repeats a future bridi)
nei	(repeats the current bridi)
no'a	(repeats the next outer bridi)

bu'a-series

bu'a	some-predicate-1 (rafsi: *bul*)
bu'e	some-predicate-2
bu'i	some-predicate-3

others:

co'e	has the obvious relationship (rafsi: *com/co'e*)		
mo	bridi question		
du	identity: x1 is identical to x2, x3 ...	dub	du'o

7.18 Other cmavo discussed in this chapter

goi	GOI	pro-sumti assignment (ko'a-series)
cei	CEI	pro-bridi assignment (broda-series)
ra'o	RAhO	pro-sumti/pro-bridi update
soi	SOI	reciprocity
se'u	SEhU	soi terminator
da'o	DAhO	cancel all pro-sumti/pro-bridi

Chapter 8
Relative Clauses, Which Make sumti Even More Complicated

ko viska re prenu
poi bruna la santas.

8.1 What are you pointing at?

The following cmavo are discussed in this section:

poi	NOI	restrictive relative clause introducer
ke'a	GOhA	relative pro-sumti
ku'o	KUhO	relative clause terminator

Let us think about the problem of communicating what it is that we are pointing at when we are pointing at something. In Lojban, we can refer to what we are pointing at by using the pro-sumti *ti* if it is nearby, or *ta* if it is somewhat further away, or *tu* if it is distant. (Pro-sumti are explained in full in Chapter 7 (p. 139).)

However, even with the assistance of a pointing finger, or pointing lips, or whatever may be appropriate in the local culture, it is often hard for a listener to tell just what is being pointed at. Suppose one is pointing at a person (in particular, in the direction of his or her face), and says:

Example 8.1

ti	*cu*	*barda*
This-one		**is-big.**

What is the referent of *ti*? Is it the person? Or perhaps it is the person's nose? Or even (for *ti* can be plural as well as singular, and mean "these ones" as well as "this one") the pores on the person's nose?

161

To help solve this problem, Lojban uses a construction called a "relative clause". Relative clauses are usually attached to the end of sumti, but there are other places where they can go as well, as explained later in this chapter. A relative clause begins with a word of selma'o NOI, and ends with the elidable terminator *ku'o* (of selma'o KUhO). As you might suppose, *noi* is a cmavo of selma'o NOI; however, first we will discuss the cmavo *poi*, which also belongs to selma'o NOI.

In between the *poi* and the *ku'o* appears a full bridi, with the same syntax as any other bridi. Anywhere within the bridi of a relative clause, the pro-sumti *ke'a* (of selma'o KOhA) may be used, and it stands for the sumti to which the relative clause is attached (called the "relativized sumti"). Here are some examples before we go any further:

Example 8.2

ti	poi	ke'a	prenu	ku'o	cu	barda
This-thing	such-that-(	IT	is-a-person	)		is-large.

This thing which is a person is big.
This person is big.

Example 8.3

ti	poi	ke'a	nazbi	ku'o	cu	barda
This-thing	such-that-(	IT	is-a-nose	)		is-large.

This thing which is a nose is big.
This nose is big.

Example 8.4

ti	poi	ke'a	nazbi		kapkevna	ku'o	cu	barda
This-thing	such-that-(	IT	is-a-nose	type-of	skin-hole	)		is-big.

These things which are nose-pores are big.
These nose-pores are big.

In the literal translations throughout this chapter, the word "IT", capitalized, is used to represent the cmavo *ke'a*. In each case, it serves to represent the sumti (in Example 8.2 (p. 162) through Example 8.4 (p. 162), the cmavo *ti*) to which the relative clause is attached.

Of course, there is no reason why *ke'a* needs to appear in the x1 place of a relative clause bridi; it can appear in any place, or indeed even in a sub-bridi within the relative clause bridi. Here are two more examples:

Example 8.5

tu	poi	le	mlatu	pu	lacpu	ke'a	ku'o	cu	ratcu
That-distant-thing	such-that-(	the	cat	[past]	drags	IT	)		is-a-rat.

That thing which the cat dragged is a rat.
What the cat dragged is a rat.

Example 8.6

ta	poi	mi	djica	le	nu
That-thing	such-that-(	I	desire	the	event-of(

mi	ponse	ke'a	[kei]	ku'o	cu	bloti
I	own	IT	)	)		is-a-boat.

That thing that I want to own is a boat.

In Example 8.6 (p. 162), *ke'a* appears in an abstraction clause (abstractions are explained in Chapter 11 (p. 247)) within a relative clause.

Like any sumti, *ke'a* can be omitted. The usual presumption in that case is that it then falls into the x1 place:

Example 8.7

ti	poi	nazbi	cu	barda
This-thing	**which**	**is-a-nose**		**is-big.**

almost certainly means the same thing as Example 8.3 (p. 162). However, *ke'a* can be omitted if it is clear to the listener that it belongs in some place other than x1:

Example 8.8

tu	poi	le	mlatu	pu	lacpu	cu	ratcu
That-distant-thing	**which**	**the**	**cat**	**[past]**	**drags**		**is-a-rat**

is equivalent to Example 8.4 (p. 162).

As stated before, *ku'o* is an elidable terminator, and in fact it is almost always elidable. Throughout the rest of this chapter, *ku'o* will not be written in any of the examples unless it is absolutely required: thus, Example 8.2 (p. 162) can be written:

Example 8.9

ti	poi	prenu	cu	barda
That	**which**	**is-a-person**		**is-big.**

That person is big.

without any change in meaning. Note that *poi* is translated "which" rather than "such-that" when *ke'a* has been omitted from the x1 place of the relative clause bridi. The word "which" is used in English to introduce English relative clauses: other words that can be used are "who" and "that", as in:

Example 8.10

I saw a man who was going to the store.

and

Example 8.11

The building that the school was located in is large.

In Example 8.10 (p. 163) the relative clause is "who was going to the store", and in Example 8.11 (p. 163) it is "that the school was located in". Sometimes "who", "which", and "that" are used in literal translations in this chapter in order to make them read more smoothly.

8.2 Incidental relative clauses

The following cmavo is discussed in this section:

noi	NOI	incidental relative clause introducer

There are two basic kinds of relative clauses: restrictive relative clauses introduced by *poi*, and incidental (sometimes called simply "non-restrictive") relative clauses introduced by *noi*. The difference between restrictive and incidental relative clauses is that restrictive clauses provide information that is essential to identifying the referent of the sumti to which they are attached, whereas incidental relative clauses provide additional information which is helpful to the listener but is not essential for identifying the referent of the sumti. All of the examples in Section 8.1 (p. 161) are restrictive relative clauses: the information in the relative clause is essential to identification. (The title of this chapter, though, uses an incidental relative clause.)

Consider the following examples:

Example 8.12

le	gerku	poi	blanu	cu	barda
The	**dog**	**which**	**is-blue**		**is-large.**

The dog which is blue is large.

163

Example 8.13

le	gerku	noi		blanu	cu	barda
The	dog	incidentally-which		is-blue		is-large.

The dog, which is blue, is large.

In Example 8.12 (p. 163), the information conveyed by *poi blanu* is essential to identifying the dog in question: it restricts the possible referents from dogs in general to dogs that are blue. This is why *poi* relative clauses are called restrictive. In Example 8.13 (p. 164), on the other hand, the dog which is referred to has presumably already been identified clearly, and the relative clause *noi blanu* just provides additional information about it. (If in fact the dog hasn't been identified clearly, then the relative clause does not help identify it further.)

In English, the distinction between restrictive and incidental relative clauses is expressed in writing by surrounding incidental, but not restrictive, clauses with commas. These commas are functioning as parentheses, because incidental relative clauses are essentially parenthetical. This distinction in punctuation is represented in speech by a difference in tone of voice. In addition, English restrictive relative clauses can be introduced by "that" as well as "which" and "who", whereas incidental relative clauses cannot begin with "that". Lojban, however, always uses the cmavo *poi* and *noi* rather than punctuation or intonation to make the distinction.

Here are more examples of incidental relative clauses:

Example 8.14

mi	noi		pajni		cu	zvati
I	who-incidentally		am-a-judge			am-at [some-place].

I, a judge, am present.

In this example, *mi* is already sufficiently restricted, and the additional information that I am a judge is being provided solely for the listener's edification.

Example 8.15

xu	do	viska	le	mi	karce	noi		blabi
[True?]	You	see		my	car	incidentally-which		is-white.

Do you see my car, which is white?

In Example 8.15 (p. 164), the speaker is presumed to have only one car, and is providing incidental information that it is white. (Alternatively, he or she might have more than one car, since *le karce* can be plural, in which case the incidental information is that each of them is white.) Contrast Example 8.16 (p. 164) with a restrictive relative clause:

Example 8.16

xu	do	viska	le	mi	karce	poi	blabi
[True?]	You	see		my	car	which	is-white.

Do you see my car that is white?
Do you see my white car?

Here the speaker probably has several cars, and is restricting the referent of the sumti *le mi karce* (and thereby the listener's attention) to the white one only. Example 8.16 (p. 164) means much the same as Example 8.17 (p. 164), which does not use a relative clause:

Example 8.17

xu	do	viska	le	mi	blabi	karce
[True?]	You	see		my	white	car.

Do you see my car, the white one?

So a restrictive relative clause attached to a description can often mean the same as a description involving a tanru. However, *blabi karce*, like all tanru, is somewhat vague: in principle, it might refer to a car which carries white things, or even express some more complicated concept involving whiteness and car-ness; the restrictive relative clause of Example 8.16 (p. 164) can only refer to a car which is white, not to any more complex or extended concept.

8.3 Relative phrases

The following cmavo are discussed in this section:

pe	GOI	restrictive association
po	GOI	restrictive possession
po'e	GOI	restrictive intrinsic possession
po'u	GOI	restrictive identification
ne	GOI	incidental association
no'u	GOI	incidental identification
ge'u	GEhU	relative phrase terminator

There are types of relative clauses (those which have a certain selbri) which are frequently wanted in Lojban, and can be expressed using a shortcut called a relative phrase. Relative phrases are introduced by cmavo of selma'o GOI, and consist of a GOI cmavo followed by a single sumti.

Here is an example of *pe*, plus an equivalent sentence using a relative clause:

Example 8.18

le	stizu	pe		mi	cu	blanu
The	chair	associated-with		me		is-blue.

My chair is blue.

Example 8.19

le	stizu	poi	ke'a	srana		mi	cu	blanu
The	chair	such-that-(	IT	is-associated-with		me	)	is-blue.

In Example 8.18 (p. 165) and Example 8.19 (p. 165), the link between the chair and the speaker is of the loosest kind.

Here is an example of *po*:

Example 8.20

le	stizu	po		mi	cu	xunre
The	chair	specific-to		me		is-red.

Example 8.21

le	stizu	poi	ke'a	se steci	srana		mi	cu	xunre
The	chair	such-that-(	IT	is-specifically	associated-with		me	)	is-red.

Example 8.20 (p. 165) and Example 8.21 (p. 165) contrast with Example 8.18 (p. 165) and Example 8.19 (p. 165): the chair is more permanently connected with the speaker. A plausible (though not the only possible) contrast between Example 8.18 (p. 165) and Example 8.20 (p. 165) is that *pe mi* would be appropriate for a chair the speaker is currently sitting on (whether or not the speaker owned that chair), and *po mi* for a chair owned by the speaker (whether or not he or she was currently occupying it).

As a result, the relationship expressed between two sumti by *po* is usually called "possession", although it does not necessarily imply ownership, legal or otherwise. The central concept is that of specificity (*steci* in Lojban).

Here is an example of *po'e*, as well as another example of *po*:

Example 8.22

le	birka	po'e		mi	cu	spofu
The	arm	intrinsically-possessed-by		me		is-broken

Example 8.23

le	birka	poi	jinzi		ke	se steci
The	arm	which	is-intrinsically	(		specifically

srana		mi	cu	spofu
associated-with)		me		is-broken.

Example 8.24

le	botpi	po		mi	cu	spofu
The	bottle	specific-to		me		is-broken

Example 8.22 (p. 165) and Example 8.23 (p. 166) on the one hand, and Example 8.24 (p. 166) on the other, illustrate the contrast between two types of possession called "intrinsic" and "extrinsic", or sometimes "inalienable" and "alienable", respectively. Something is intrinsically (or inalienably) possessed by someone if the possession is part of the possessor, and cannot be changed without changing the possessor. In the case of Example 8.22 (p. 165), people are usually taken to intrinsically possess their arms: even if an arm is cut off, it remains the arm of that person. (If the arm is transplanted to another person, however, it becomes intrinsically possessed by the new user, though, so intrinsic possession is a matter of degree.)

By contrast, the bottle of Example 8.24 (p. 166) can be given away, or thrown away, or lost, or stolen, so it is possessed extrinsically (alienably). The exact line between intrinsic and extrinsic possession is culturally dependent. The U.S. Declaration of Independence speaks of the "inalienable rights" of men, but just what those rights are, and even whether the concept makes sense at all, varies from culture to culture.

Note that Example 8.22 (p. 165) can also be expressed without a relative clause:

Example 8.25

le	birka	be		mi	cu	spofu
The	arm	of-body		me		is-broken

reflecting the fact that the gismu *birka* has an x2 place representing the body to which the arm belongs. Many, but not all, cases of intrinsic possession can be thus covered without using *po'e* by placing the possessor into the appropriate place of the description selbri.

Here is an example of *po'u*:

Example 8.26

le	gerku	po'u	le	mi	pendo	cu	cinba	mi
The	dog	which-is		my	friend		kisses	me.

Example 8.27

le	gerku	poi	du	le	mi	pendo	cu	cinba	mi
The	dog	which	=		my	friend		kisses	me.

The cmavo *po'u* does not represent possession at all, but rather identity. (Note that it means *poi du* and its form was chosen to suggest the relationship.)

In Example 8.26 (p. 166), the use of *po'u* tells us that *le gerku* and *le mi pendo* represent the same thing. Consider the contrast between Example 8.26 (p. 166) and:

Example 8.28

le	mi	pendo	po'u	le	gerku	cu	cinba	mi
	My	friend	which-is	the	dog		kisses	me.

The facts of the case are the same, but the listener's knowledge about the situation may not be. In Example 8.26 (p. 166), the listener is presumed not to understand which dog is meant by *le gerku*, so the speaker adds a relative phrase clarifying that it is the particular dog which is the speaker's friend.

Example 8.28 (p. 166), however, assumes that the listener does not know which of the speaker's friends is referred to, and specifies that it is the friend that is the dog (which dog is taken to be obvious). Here is another example of the same contrast:

8.3 Relative phrases

Example 8.29

le	*tcadu*	*po'u*	*la nu,iork*

The city of New--York [not another city]

Example 8.30

la nu,iork	*po'u*	*le*	*tcadu*

New--York -- the city (not the state or some other New York)

The principle that the possessor and the possessed may change places applies to all the GOI cmavo, and allows for the possibility of odd effects:

Example 8.31

le	*kabri*	*pe*	*le*	*mi*	*pendo*	*cu*	*cmalu*
The	cup	associated-with		my	friend		is-small.

My friend's cup is small

Example 8.32

le	*mi*	*pendo*	*pe*	*le*	*kabri*	*cu*	*cmalu*
My	friend	associated-with		the	cup		is-small.

My friend, the one with the cup, is small.

Example 8.31 (p. 167) is useful in a context which is about my friend, and states that his or her cup is small, whereas Example 8.32 (p. 167) is useful in a context that is primarily about a certain cup, and makes a claim about "my friend of the cup", as opposed to some other friend of mine. Here the cup appears to "possess" the person! English can't even express this relationship with a possessive – "the cup's friend of mine" looks like nonsense – but Lojban has no trouble doing so.

Finally, the cmavo *ne* and *no'u* stand to *pe* and *po'u*, respectively, as *noi* does to *poi*- they provide incidental information:

Example 8.33

le	*blabi*	*gerku*	*ne*	*mi*	*cu*	*batci*	*do*
The	white	dog,	incidentally-associated-with	me	,	bites	you.

The white dog, which is mine, bites you.

In Example 8.33 (p. 167), the white dog is already fully identified (after all, presumably the listener knows which dog bit him or her!). The fact that it is yours is merely incidental to the main bridi claim.

Distinguishing between *po'u* and *no'u* can be a little tricky. Consider a room with several men in it, one of whom is named Jim. If you don't know their names, I might say:

Example 8.34

le	*nanmu*	*no'u*	*la*	*djim.*	*cu*	*terpemci*
The	man,	incidentally-who-is	that-named	Jim	,	is-a-poet.

The man, Jim, is a poet.

Here I am saying that one of the men is a poet, and incidentally telling you that he is Jim. But if you do know the names, then

Example 8.35

le	*nanmu*	*po'u*	*la*	*djim.*	*cu*	*terpemci*
The	man	who-is	that-named	Jim		is-a-poet.

The man Jim is a poet.

is appropriate. Now I am using the fact that the man I am speaking of is Jim in order to pick out which man I mean.

It is worth mentioning that English sometimes over-specifies possession from the Lojban point of view (and the point of view of many other languages, including ones closely related to English). The idiomatic English sentence

Example 8.36

> The man put his hands in his pockets.

seems strange to a French- or German-speaking person: whose pockets would he put his hands into? and even odder, whose hands would he put into his pockets? In Lojban, the sentence

Example 8.37

le	nanmu	cu	punji	le	xance		le	daski
The	**man**		**puts**	**the**	**hand**	**at-locus**	**the**	**pocket.**

is very natural. Of course, if the man is in fact putting his hands into another's pockets, or another's hands into his pockets, the fact can be specified.

Finally, the elidable terminator for GOI cmavo is *ge'u* of selma'o GEhU; it is almost never required. However, if a logical connective immediately follows a sumti modified by a relative phrase, then an explicit *ge'u* is needed to allow the connective to affect the relativized sumti rather than the sumti of the relative phrase. (What about the cmavo after which selma'o GOI is named? It is discussed in Section 7.5 (p. 144), as it is not semantically akin to the other kinds of relative phrases, although the syntax is the same.)

8.4 Multiple relative clauses: *zi'e*

zi'e	ZIhE	relative clause joiner

Sometimes it is necessary or useful to attach more than one relative clause to a sumti. This is made possible in Lojban by the cmavo *zi'e* (of selma'o ZIhE), which is used to join one or more relative clauses together into a single unit, thus making them apply to the same sumti. For example:

Example 8.38

le	gerku	poi	blabi	zi'e	poi	batci	le	nanmu	cu	klama

> The dog which is white and which bites the man goes.

The most usual translation of *zi'e* in English is "and", but *zi'e* is not really a logical connective: unlike most of the true logical connectives (which are explained in Chapter 14 (p. 317)), it cannot be converted into a logical connection between sentences.

It is perfectly correct to use *zi'e* to connect relative clauses of different kinds:

Example 8.39

le	gerku	poi	blabi	zi'e	noi
The	**dog**	**that-is**	**(white)**	**and**	**incidentally-such-that**

le	mi	pendo	cu	ponse	ke'a	cu	klama
(-	**my**	**friend**		**owns**	**IT**	**)**	**goes.**

> The dog that is white, which my friend owns, is going.

In Example 8.39 (p. 168), the restrictive clause *poi blabi* specifies which dog is referred to, but the incidental clause *noi le mi pendo cu ponse* is mere incidental information: the listener is supposed to already have identified the dog from the *poi blabi*. Of course, the meaning (though not necessarily the emphasis) is the same if the incidental clause appears first.

It is also possible to connect relative phrases with *zi'e*, or a relative phrase with a relative clause:

Example 8.40

le	botpi	po	mi	zi'e	poi	blanu	cu	spofu
The	**bottle**	**specific-to**	**me**	**and**	**which-is**	**blue**		**is-broken.**

> My blue bottle is broken.

Note that if the colloquial translation of Example 8.40 (p. 168) were "My bottle, which is blue, is broken", then *noi* rather than *poi* would have been correct in the Lojban version, since that version of the English implies that you do not need to know the bottle is blue. As written, Example 8.40 (p. 168) suggests that I probably have more than one bottle, and the one in question needs to be picked out as the blue one.

Example 8.41

mi	ba	zutse	le	stizu	pe
I	**[future]**	**sit-in**	**the**	**chair**	**associated-with**

mi	zi'e	po	do	zi'e	poi	xunre
me	**and**	**specific-to**	**you**	**and**	**which**	**is-red.**

I will sit in my chair (really yours), the red one.

Example 8.41 (p. 169) illustrates that more than two relative phrases or clauses can be connected with *zi'e*. It almost defies colloquial translation because of the very un-English contrast between *pe mi*, implying that the chair is temporarily connected with me, and *po do*, implying that the chair has a more permanent association with you. (Perhaps I am a guest in your house, in which case the chair would naturally be your property.)

Here is another example, mixing a relative phrase and two relative clauses, a restrictive one and a non-restrictive one:

Example 8.42

mi	ba	citka	le	dembi	pe	mi	zi'e	poi	cpana
I	**[future]**	**eat**	**the**	**beans**	**associated-with**	**me**	**and**	**which**	**are-upon**

le	mi	palta	zi'e	noi	do	dunda	ke'a	mi
my	**plate**	**and**	**which-incidentally**	**you**	**gave**	**IT**	**to**	**me.**

I'll eat my beans that are on my plate, the ones you gave me.

8.5 Non-veridical relative clauses: *voi*

voi | NOI | non-veridical relative clause introducer

There is another member of selma'o NOI which serves to introduce a third kind of relative clause: *voi*. Relative clauses introduced by *voi* are restrictive, like those introduced by *poi*. However, there is a fundamental difference between *poi* and *voi* relative clauses. A *poi* relative clause is said to be veridical, in the same sense that a description using *lo* or *loi* is: it is essential to the interpretation that the bridi actually be true. For example:

Example 8.43

le	gerku	poi	blabi	cu	klama
The	**dog**	**which**	**is-white**		**goes.**

it must actually be true that the dog is white, or the sentence constitutes a miscommunication. If there is a white dog and a brown dog, and the speaker uses *le gerku poi blabi* to refer to the brown dog, then the listener will not understand correctly. However,

Example 8.44

le	gerku	voi	blabi	cu	klama
The	**dog**	**which-I-describe-as**	**white**		**goes.**

puts the listener on notice that the dog in question may not actually meet objective standards (whatever they are) for being white: only the speaker can say exactly what is meant by the term. In this way, *voi* is like *le*; the speaker's intention determines the meaning.

As a result, the following two sentences

Example 8.45

le	nanmu	cu	ninmu
That-which-I-describe-as	**a-man**		**is-a-woman.**

The "guy" is actually a gal.

Example 8.46

ti	voi	nanmu	cu	ninmu
This-thing	which-I-describe-as	a-man		is-a-woman.

mean essentially the same thing (except that Example 8.46 (p. 170) involves pointing thanks to the use of *ti*, whereas Example 8.45 (p. 169) doesn't), and neither one is self-contradictory: it is perfectly all right to describe something as a man (although perhaps confusing to the listener) even if it actually is a woman.

8.6 Relative clauses and descriptors

So far, this chapter has described the various kinds of relative clauses (including relative phrases). The list is now complete, and the rest of the chapter will be concerned with the syntax of sumti that include relative clauses. So far, all relative clauses have appeared directly after the sumti to which they are attached. This is the most common position (and originally the only one), but a variety of other placements are also possible which produce a variety of semantic effects.

There are actually three places where a relative clause can be attached to a description sumti: after the descriptor (*le*, *lo*, or whatever), after the embedded selbri but before the elidable terminator (which is *ku*), and after the *ku*. The relative clauses attached to descriptors that we have seen have occupied the second position. Thus Example 8.43 (p. 169), if written out with all elidable terminators, would appear as:

Example 8.47

le	gerku	poi	blabi	ku'o	ku	cu	klama	vau
The	(dog	which	(is-white	)	)		goes	.

The dog which is white is going.

Here *ku'o* is the terminator paired with *poi* and *ku* with *le*, and *vau* is the terminator of the whole bridi.

When a simple descriptor using *le*, like *le gerku*, has a relative clause attached, it is purely a matter of style and emphasis where the relative clause should go. Therefore, the following examples are all equivalent in meaning to Example 8.47 (p. 170):

Example 8.48

le	poi	blabi	ku'o	gerku	cu	klama
The	such-that-(	it-is-white	)	dog		goes.

Example 8.49

le	gerku	ku	poi	blabi		cu	klama
The	(dog	)	which	is-white			goes.

Example 8.47 (p. 170) will seem most natural to speakers of languages like English, which always puts relative clauses after the noun phrases they are attached to; Example 8.48 (p. 170), on the other hand, may seem more natural to Finnish or Chinese speakers, who put the relative clause first. Note that in Example 8.48 (p. 170), the elidable terminator *ku'o* must appear, or the selbri of the relative clause (*blabi*) will merge with the selbri of the description (*gerku*), resulting in an ungrammatical sentence. The purpose of the form appearing in Example 8.49 (p. 170) will be apparent shortly.

As is explained in detail in Section 6.7 (p. 124), two different numbers (known as the "inner quantifier" and the "outer quantifier") can be attached to a description. The inner quantifier specifies how many things the descriptor refers to: it appears between the descriptor and the description selbri. The outer quantifier appears before the descriptor, and specifies how many of the things referred to by the descriptor are involved in this particular bridi. In the following example,

Example 8.50

re	le	mu	prenu	cu	klama	le	zarci
Two	of the	five	persons		go-to	the	market.

Two of the five people [that I have in mind] are going to the market.

mu is the inner quantifier and *re* is the outer quantifier. Now what is meant by attaching a relative clause to the sumti *re le mu prenu*? Suppose the relative clause is *poi ninmu* (meaning "who are women"). Now the three possible attachment points discussed previously take on significance.

Example 8.51

re		*le*	*poi*		*ninmu*		*ku'o*
Two	of	the	such-that([they]		are-women	)	

mu	*prenu*		*cu*	*klama*	*le*	*zarci*
five	persons		go-to	the	market.	

Two women out of the five persons go to the market.

Example 8.52

re		*le*	*mu*	*prenu*	*poi*		*ninmu*		*[ku]*	*cu*	*klama*	*le*	*zarci*
Two	of	the	(five	persons	which-(		are-women)	)			go-to	the	market.

Two of the five women go to the market.

Example 8.53

re		*le*	*mu*	*prenu*	*ku*	*poi*		*ninmu*		*cu*	*klama*	*le*	*zarci*
(Two	of	the	five	persons	)	which-(		are-women	)	go-to	the	market.

Two women out of the five persons go to the market.

As the parentheses show, Example 8.52 (p. 171) means that all five of the persons are women, whereas Example 8.53 (p. 171) means that the two who are going to the market are women. How do we remember which is which? If the relative clause comes after the explicit *ku*, as in Example 8.53 (p. 171), then the sumti as a whole is qualified by the relative clause. If there is no *ku*, or if the relative clause comes before an explicit *ku*, then the relative clause is understood to apply to everything which the underlying selbri applies to.

What about Example 8.51 (p. 171)? By convention, it means the same as Example 8.53 (p. 171), and it requires no *ku*, but it does typically require a *ku'o* instead. Note that the relative clause comes before the inner quantifier.

When *le* is the descriptor being used, and the sumti has no explicit outer quantifier, then the outer quantifier is understood to be *ro* (meaning "all"), as is explained in Section 6.7 (p. 124). Thus *le gerku* is taken to mean "all of the things I refer to as dogs", possibly all one of them. In that case, there is no difference between a relative clause after the *ku* or before it. However, if the descriptor is *lo*, the difference is quite important:

Example 8.54

lo		*prenu*	*ku*	*noi*		*blabi*		*cu*	*klama*	*le*	*zarci*
(Some	persons	)	incidentally-which-(		are-white	)	go-to	the	market.	

Some people, who are white, go to the market.

Example 8.55

lo		*prenu*	*noi*		*blabi*	*[ku]*	*cu*	*klama*	*le*	*zarci*
Some	(persons	incidentally-which	are-white	)		go	to-the	market.	

Some of the people, who by the way are white, go to the market.

Both Example 8.54 (p. 171) and Example 8.55 (p. 171) tell us that one or more persons are going to the market. However, they make very different incidental claims. Now, what does *lo prenu noi blabi* mean? Well, the default inner quantifier is *ro* (meaning "all"), and the default outer quantifier is *su'o* (meaning "at least one"). Therefore, we must first take all persons, then choose at least one of them. That one or more people will be going.

In Example 8.54 (p. 171), the relative clause described the sumti once the outer quantifier was applied: one or more people, who are white, are going. But in Example 8.55 (p. 171), the relative clause actually describes the sumti before the outer quantification is applied, so that it ends up meaning "First take all persons – by the way, they're all white". But not all people are white, so the incidental claim being made here is false.

The safe strategy, therefore, is to always use *ku* when attaching a *noi* relative clause to a *lo* descriptor. Otherwise we may end up claiming far too much.

When the descriptor is *la*, indicating that what follows is a selbri used for naming, then the positioning of relative clauses has a different significance. A relative clause inside the *ku*, whether before or after the selbri, is reckoned part of the name; a relative clause outside the *ku* is not. Therefore,

Example 8.56

mi	viska	la		nanmu	poi		terpa	le	ke'a	xirma	[ku]
I	see	that-named-(	man	which	fears	the	of-IT	horse	).

I see Man Afraid Of His Horse.

says that the speaker sees a person with a particular name, who does not necessarily fear any horses, whereas

Example 8.57

mi	viska	la		nanmu	ku	poi		terpa	le	ke'a	xirma.
I	see	that-named-(	Man	)	which	fears	the	of-IT	horse.

I see the person named "Man" who is afraid of his horse.

refers to one (or more) of those named "Man", namely the one(s) who are afraid of their horses.

Finally, so-called indefinite sumti like *re karce*, which means almost the same as *re lo karce* (which in turn means the same as *re lo ro karce*), can have relative clauses attached; these are taken to be of the outside-the- *ku* variety. Here is an example:

Example 8.58

mi	ponse	re	karce	[ku]	poi		xekri
I	possess	two	cars		which-are	black.

The restrictive relative clause only affects the two cars being affected by the main bridi, not all cars that exist. It is ungrammatical to try to place a relative clause within an indefinite sumti (that is, before an explicitly expressed terminating *ku*.) Use an explicit *lo* instead.

8.7 Possessive sumti

In Example 8.15 (p. 164) through Example 8.17 (p. 164), the sumti *le mi karce* appears, glossed as "my car". Although it might not seem so, this sumti actually contains a relative phrase. When a sumti appears between a descriptor and its description selbri, it is actually a *pe* relative phrase. So

Example 8.59

le	mi	karce	cu	xunre
	My	car		is-red.

and

Example 8.60

le	pe		mi	karce	cu	xunre
The	(associated-with	me)	car		is-red.

mean exactly the same thing. Furthermore, since there are no special considerations of quantifiers here,

Example 8.61

le	karce	pe		mi	cu	xunre
The	car	associated-with	me		is-red.

means the same thing as well. A sumti like the one in Example 8.59 (p. 172) is called a "possessive sumti". Of course, it does not really indicate possession in the sense of ownership, but like *pe* relative phrases, indicates only weak association; you can say *le mi karce* even if you've only borrowed it for the night. (In English, "my car" usually means *le karce po mi*, but we do not have the same sense of possession in "my seat on the bus"; Lojban simply makes the weaker sense the standard one.) The inner sumti, *mi* in Example 8.59 (p. 172), is correspondingly called the "possessor sumti".

Historically, possessive sumti existed before any other kind of relative phrase or clause, and were retained when the machinery of relative phrases and clauses as detailed in this chapter so far was slowly built up. When preposed relative clauses of the Example 8.60 (p. 172) type were devised, possessive sumti were most easily viewed as a special case of them.

Although any sumti, however complex, can appear in a full-fledged relative phrase, only simple sumti can appear as possessor sumti, without a *pe*. Roughly speaking, the legal possessor sumti are: pro-sumti, quotations, names and descriptions, and numbers. In addition, the possessor sumti may not be preceded by a quantifier, as such a form would be interpreted as the unusual "descriptor + quantifier + sumti" type of description. All these sumti forms are explained in full in Chapter 6 (p. 115).

Here is an example of a description used in a possessive sumti:

Example 8.62

le			le	nanmu	ku	karce	cu	blanu
The	(associated-with	the	man	)	car		is-blue.

The man's car is blue.

Note the explicit *ku* at the end of the possessor sumti, which prevents the selbri of the possessor sumti from merging with the selbri of the main description sumti. Because of the need for this *ku*, the most common kind of possessor sumti are pro-sumti, especially personal pro-sumti, which require no elidable terminator. Descriptions are more likely to be attached with relative phrases.

And here is a number used as a possessor sumti:

Example 8.63

le	li		mu	jdice	se bende
The	of-the-number		five	judging	team-member

Juror number 5

which is not quite the same as "the fifth juror"; it simply indicates a weak association between the particular juror and the number 5.

A possessive sumti may also have regular relative clauses attached to it. This would need no comment if it were not for the following special rule: a relative clause immediately following the possessor sumti is understood to affect the possessor sumti, not the possessive. For example:

Example 8.64

le	mi	noi		sipna	vau	karce	cu	na	klama
The	of-me	incidentally-which-(		is-sleeping	)	car		isn't	going.

means that my car isn't going; the incidental claim of *noi sipna* applies to me, not my car, however. If I wanted to say that the car is sleeping (whatever that might mean) I would need:

Example 8.65

le	mi	karce	poi		sipna	cu	na	klama
The	of-me	car	which		sleeps		isn't	going.

Note that Example 8.64 (p. 173) uses *vau* rather than *ku'o* at the end of the relative clause: this terminator ends every simple bridi and is almost always elidable; in this case, though, it is a syllable shorter than the equally valid alternative, *ku'o*.

8.8 Relative clauses and complex sumti: *vu'o*

The following cmavo is discussed in this section:

| vu'o | VUhO | relative clause attacher |

Normally, relative clauses attach only to simple sumti or parts of sumti: pro-sumti, names and descriptions, pure numbers, and quotations. An example of a relative clause attached to a pure number is:

Example 8.66

li	pai	noi	na'e	frinu	namcu
The-number	pi,	incidentally-which	is-a-non-	fraction	number

The irrational number pi

And here is an incidental relative clause attached to a quotation:

Example 8.67

lu	mi	klama	le	zarci	li'u
[quote]	I	go-to	the	market	[unquote]

noi			mi	cusku	ke'a	cu	jufra
incidentally-which-(			I	express	IT	)	is-a-sentence.

"I'm going to the market", which I'd said, is a sentence.

which may serve to identify the author of the quotation or some other relevant, but subsidiary, fact about it. All such relative clauses appear only after the simple sumti, never before it.

In addition, sumti with attached sumti qualifiers of selma'o LAhE or NAhE+BO (which are explained in detail in Section 6.10 (p. 128)) can have a relative clause appearing after the qualifier and before the qualified sumti, as in:

Example 8.68

la'e		poi	tolcitno	vau	lu		le	xunre
A-referent-of		(which	is-old	)	[quote]		The	Red

cmaxirma	li'u		cu	zvati	le	vu		kumfa
Small-horse	[unquote]		is-at	the	[far-distance]			room.

An old "The Red Pony" is in the far room.

Example 8.68 (p. 174) is a bit complex, and may need some picking apart. The quotation *lu le xunre cmaxirma li'u* means the string of words "The Red Pony". If the *la'e* at the beginning of the sentence were omitted, Example 8.68 (p. 174) would claim that a certain string of words is in a room distant from the speaker. But obviously a string of words can't be in a room! The effect of the *la'e* is to modify the sumti so that it refers not to the words themselves, but to the referent of those words, a novel by John Steinbeck (presumably in Lojban translation). The particular copy of "The Red Pony" is identified by the restrictive relative clause. Example 8.68 (p. 174) means exactly the same as:

Example 8.69

la'e		lu		le	xunre	cmaxirma	li'u		lu'u
A-referent-of		([quote]		The	Red	Small-horse	[unquote]		)

poi		to'ercitno	cu	zvati	le	vu		kumfa
which		is-old	is-at	the	[far-distance]			room.

and the two sentences can be considered stylistic variants. Note the required *lu'u* terminator, which prevents the relative clause from attaching to the quotation itself: we do not wish to refer to an old quotation!

Sometimes, however, it is important to make a relative clause apply to the whole of a more complex sumti, one which involves logical or non-logical connection (explained in Chapter 14 (p. 317)). For example,

Example 8.70

la		frank.	.e	la		djordj.	noi
That-named		Frank	and	that-named		George	incidentally-who

nanmu		cu	klama	le	zdani	
is-a-man			go-to	the	house.	

Frank and George, who is a man, go to the house.

The incidental claim in Example 8.70 (p. 174) is not that Frank and George are men, but only that George is a man, because the incidental relative clause attaches only to *la djordj*, the immediately preceding simple sumti.

To make a relative clause attach to both parts of the logically connected sumti in Example 8.70 (p. 174), a new cmavo is needed, *vu'o* (of selma'o VUhO). It is placed between the sumti and the relative clause, and extends the sphere of influence of that relative clause to the entire preceding sumti, including however many logical or non-logical connectives there may be.

Example 8.71

la	*frank.*	*.e*	*la*	*djordj.*	*vu'o*
(That-named	Frank	and	that-named	George	)

noi	*nanmu*	*cu*	*klama*	*le*	*zdani*
incidentally-who	are-men		go	to-the	house.

Frank and George, who are men, go to the house.

The presence of *vu'o* here means that the relative clause *noi nanmu* extends to the entire logically connected sumti *la frank. .e la djordj.*; in other words, both Frank and George are claimed to be men, as the colloquial translation shows.

English is able to resolve the distinction correctly in the case of Example 8.70 (p. 174) and Example 8.71 (p. 175) by making use of number: "who is" rather than "who are". Lojban doesn't distinguish between singular and plural verbs: *nanmu* can mean "is a man" or "are men", so another means is required. Furthermore, Lojban's mechanism works correctly in general: if *nanmu* (meaning "is-a-man") were replaced with *pu bajra* ("ran"), English would have to make the distinction some other way:

Example 8.72

la	*frank.*	*.e*	*la*	*djordj.*	*noi*
That-named	Frank	and	(that-named	George	who

pu	*bajra*	*cu*	*klama*	*le*	*zdani*
[past]	runs)		go-to	the	house.

Frank and George, who ran, go to the house.

Example 8.73

la	*frank.*	*.e*	*la*	*djordj.*	*vu'o*
(That-named	Frank	and	that-named	George	)

noi	*pu*	*bajra*	*cu*	*klama*	*le*	*zdani*
who	[past]	run		go-to	the	house.

Frank and George, who ran, go to the house.

In spoken English, tone of voice would serve; in written English, one or both sentences would need rewriting.

8.9 Relative clauses in vocative phrases

Vocative phrases are explained in more detail in Section 6.11 (p. 130). Briefly, they are a method of indicating who a sentence or discourse is addressed to: of identifying the intended listener. They take three general forms, all beginning with cmavo from selma'o COI or DOI (called "vocative words"; there can be one or many), followed by either a name, a selbri, or a sumti. Here are three examples:

Example 8.74

coi. frank.

Hello, Frank.

Example 8.75

> *co'o xirma*

Goodbye, horse.

Example 8.76

> *fi'i la frank. .e la djordj.*

Welcome, Frank and George!

Note that Example 8.75 (p. 176) says farewell to something which doesn't really have to be a horse, something that the speaker simply thinks of as being a horse, or even might be something (a person, for example) who is named "Horse". In a sense, Example 8.75 (p. 176) is ambiguous between *co'o le xirma* and *co'o la xirma*, a relatively safe semantic ambiguity, since names are ambiguous in general: saying "George" doesn't distinguish between the possible Georges.

Similarly, Example 8.74 (p. 175) can be thought of as an abbreviation of:

Example 8.77

coi	*la*	*frank.*
Hello,	**the-one-named**	**"Frank"** .

Syntactically, vocative phrases are a kind of free modifier, and can appear in many places in Lojban text, generally at the beginning or end of some complete construct; or, as in Example 8.74 (p. 175) to Example 8.76 (p. 176), as sentences by themselves.

As can be seen, the form of vocative phrases is similar to that of sumti, and as you might expect, vocative phrases allow relative clauses in various places. In vocative phrases which are simple names (after the vocative words), any relative clauses must come just after the names:

Example 8.78

coi.	*frank.*	*poi*	*xunre*	*se bende*
Hello,	**Frank**	**who**	**is-a-red**	**team-member**

Hello, Frank from the Red Team!

The restrictive relative clause in Example 8.78 (p. 176) suggests that there is some other Frank (perhaps on the Green Team) from whom this Frank, the one the speaker is greeting, must be distinguished.

A vocative phrase containing a selbri can have relative clauses either before or after the selbri; both forms have the same meaning. Here are some examples:

Example 8.79

co'o	*poi*	*mi*	*zvati*	*ke'a*	*ku'o*	*xirma*
Goodbye,	**such-that-(**	**I**	**am-at**	**IT**	**)**	**horse**

Goodbye, horse where I am!

Example 8.80

co'o	*xirma*	*poi*	*mi*	*zvati*
Goodbye,	**horse**	**such-that-(**	**I**	**am-at-it).**

Example 8.79 (p. 176) and Example 8.80 (p. 176) mean the same thing. In fact, relative clauses can appear in both places.

8.10 Relative clauses within relative clauses

For the most part, these are straightforward and uncomplicated: a sumti that is part of a relative clause bridi may itself be modified by a relative clause:

Example 8.81

le	*prenu*	*poi*	*zvati*	*le*	*kumfa*	*poi*	*blanu*	*cu*	*masno*
The	**person**	**who**	**is-in**	**the**	**room**	**which**	**is-blue**		**is-slow.**

However, an ambiguity can exist if *ke'a* is used in a relative clause within a relative clause: does it refer to the outermost sumti, or to the sumti within the outer relative clause to which the inner relative clause is attached? The latter. To refer to the former, use a subscript on *ke'a*:

Example 8.82

le	prenu	poi	zvati	le	kumfa	poi	ke'axire	zbasu	ke'a	cu	masno
The	person	who	is-in	the	room	which	IT-sub-2	built	IT		is-slow.

The person who is in the room which he built is slow.

Here, the meaning of "IT-sub-2" is that sumti attached to the second relative clause, counting from the innermost, is used. Therefore, *ke'axipa* (IT-sub-1) means the same as plain *ke'a*.

Alternatively, you can use a prenex (explained in full in Chapter 16 (p. 375)), which is syntactically a series of sumti followed by the special cmavo *zo'u*, prefixed to the relative clause bridi:

Example 8.83

le	prenu	poi	ke'a	goi	ko'a	zo'u
The	man	who	(IT	=	it1	:

ko'a	zvati	le	kumfa	poi	ke'a	goi	ko'e	zo'u
it1	is-in	the	room	which	(IT	=	it2	:

ko'a	zbasu	ko'e	cu	masno
it1	built	it2)		is-slow.

Example 8.83 (p. 177) is more verbose than Example 8.82 (p. 177), but may be clearer, since it explicitly spells out the two *ke'a* cmavo, each on its own level, and assigns them to the assignable cmavo *ko'a* and *ko'e* (explained in Section 7.5 (p. 144)).

8.11 Index of relative clause cmavo

Relative clause introducers (selma'o NOI):

noi	incidental clauses
poi	restrictive clauses
voi	restrictive clauses (non-veridical)

Relative phrase introducers (selma'o GOI):

goi	pro-sumti assignment
pe	restrictive association
ne	incidental association
po	extrinsic (alienable) possession
po'e	intrinsic (inalienable) possession
po'u	restrictive identification
no'u	incidental identification

Relativizing pro-sumti (selma'o KOhA):

ke'a	pro-sumti for relativized sumti

Relative clause joiner (selma'o ZIhE):

zi'e	joins relative clauses applying to a single sumti

Relative clause associator (selma'o VUhO):

vu'o	causes relative clauses to apply to all of a complex sumti

Elidable terminators (each its own selma'o):

ku'o	relative clause elidable terminator
ge'u	relative phrase elidable terminator

Chapter 9
To Boston Via The Road Go I, With An Excursion Into The Land Of Modals

9.1 Introductory

The basic type of Lojban sentence is the bridi: a claim by the speaker that certain objects are related in a certain way. The objects are expressed by Lojban grammatical forms called *sumti*; the relationship is expressed by the Lojban grammatical form called a *selbri*.

The sumti are not randomly associated with the selbri, but according to a systematic pattern known as the "place structure" of the selbri. This chapter describes the various ways in which the place structure of Lojban bridi is expressed and by which it can be manipulated. The place structure of a selbri is a sequence of empty slots into which the sumti associated with that selbri are placed. The sumti are said to occupy the places of the selbri.

For our present purposes, every selbri is assumed to have a well-known place structure. If the selbri is a brivla, the place structure can be looked up in a dictionary (or, if the brivla is a lujvo not in any dictionary, inferred from the principles of lujvo construction as explained in Chapter 12 (p. 263)); if the selbri is a tanru, the place structure is the same as that of the final component in the tanru.

The stock example of a place structure is that of the gismu *klama*:

klama x1 comes/goes to destination x2 from origin x3 via route x4 employing means of transport x5.

The "x1 ... x5" indicates that *klama* is a five-place predicate, and show the natural order (as assigned by the language engineers) of those places: agent, destination, origin, route, means.

The place structures of brivla are not absolutely stable aspects of the language. The work done so far has attempted to establish a basic place structure on which all users can, at first, agree. In the light of actual experience with the individual selbri of the language, there will inevitably be some degree of change to the brivla place structures.

9.2 Standard bridi form: *cu*

The following cmavo is discussed in this section:

cu | CU | prefixed selbri separator

The most usual way of constructing a bridi from a selbri such as *klama* and an appropriate number of sumti is to place the sumti intended for the x1 place before the selbri, and all the other sumti in order after the selbri, thus:

Example 9.1

mi	*cu*	*klama*	*la*		*bastn.*	*la*		*.atlantas.*
I		go	to-that-named		Boston	from-that-named		Atlanta

le		*dargu*	*le*		*karce*
via-the		road	using-the		car.

Here the sumti are assigned to the places as follows:

x1	agent	*mi*
x2	destination	*la bastn.*
x3	origin	*la .atlantas.*
x4	route	*le dargu*
x5	means	*le karce*

(Note: Many of the examples in the rest of this chapter will turn out to have the same meaning as Example 9.1 (p. 180); this fact will not be reiterated.)

This ordering, with the x1 place before the selbri and all other places in natural order after the selbri, is called "standard bridi form", and is found in the bulk of Lojban bridi, whether used in main sentences or in subordinate clauses. However, many other forms are possible, such as:

Example 9.2

mi	*la*		*bastn.*	*la*		*.atlantas.*
I,	to-that-named		Boston	from-that-named		Atlanta

le		*dargu*	*le*		*karce*	*cu*	*klama*
via-the		road	using-the		car,		go.

Here the selbri is at the end; all the sumti are placed before it. However, the same order is maintained. Similarly, we may split up the sumti, putting some before the selbri and others after it:

Example 9.3

mi	*la*		*bastn.*	*cu*	*klama*	*la*		*.atlantas.*
I	to-that-named		Boston		go	from-that-named		Atlanta

le		*dargu*	*le*		*karce*
via-the		road	using-the		car.

All of the variant forms in this section and following sections can be used to place emphasis on the part or parts which have been moved out of their standard places. Thus, Example 9.2 (p. 180) places emphasis on the selbri (because it is at the end); Example 9.3 (p. 180) emphasizes *la bastn.*, because it has been moved before the selbri. Moving more than one component may dilute this emphasis. It is permitted, but no stylistic significance has yet been established for drastic reordering.

In all these examples, the cmavo *cu* (belonging to selma'o CU) is used to separate the selbri from any preceding sumti. It is never absolutely necessary to use *cu*. However, providing it helps the reader or listener to locate the selbri quickly, and may make it possible to place a complex sumti just before the selbri, allowing the speaker to omit elidable terminators, possibly a whole stream of them, that would otherwise be necessary.

The general rule, then, is that the selbri may occur anywhere in the bridi as long as the sumti maintain their order. The only exception (and it is an important one) is that if the selbri appears first, the x1 sumti is taken to have been omitted:

Example 9.4

klama	la	bastn.
A-goer	**to-that-named**	**Boston**
Goes		**to-Boston**

la	.atlantas.
from-that-named	**Atlanta**
	from-Atlanta

le	dargu
via-the	**road**
via-the	**road**

le	karce
using-the	**car.**
using-the	**car.**

Look: a goer to Boston from Atlanta via the road using the car!

Here the x1 place is empty: the listener must guess from context who is going to Boston. In Example 9.4 (p. 181), *klama* is glossed "a goer" rather than "go" because "Go" at the beginning of an English sentence would suggest a command: "Go to Boston!". Example 9.4 (p. 181) is not a command, simply a normal statement with the x1 place unspecified, causing the emphasis to fall on the selbri *klama*. Such a bridi, with empty x1, is called an "observative", because it usually calls on the listener to observe something in the environment which would belong in the x1 place. The third translation above shows this observative nature. Sometimes it is the relationship itself which the listener is asked to observe.

(There is a way to both provide a sumti for the x1 place and put the selbri first in the bridi: see Example 9.14 (p. 183).)

Suppose the speaker desires to omit a place other than the x1 place? (Presumably it is obvious or, for one reason or another, not worth saying.) Places at the end may simply be dropped:

Example 9.5

mi klama la bastn. la .atlantas.

I go to-Boston from-Atlanta (via an unspecified route, using an unspecified means).

Example 9.5 (p. 181) has empty x4 and x5 places: the speaker does not specify the route or the means of transport. However, simple omission will not work for a place when the places around it are to be specified: in

Example 9.6

mi	klama	la	bastn.	la	.atlantas.	le	karce
I	**go**	**to-that-named**	**Boston**	**from-that-named**	**Atlanta**	**via-the**	**car.**

le karce occupies the x4 place, and therefore Example 9.6 (p. 181) means:
I go to Boston from Atlanta, using the car as a route.

This is nonsense, since a car cannot be a route. What the speaker presumably meant is expressed by:

Example 9.7

mi	klama	la	bastn.	la	.atlantas.
I	**go**	**to-that-named**	**Boston**	**from-that-named**	**Atlanta**

zo'e	le	karce
via-something-unspecified	**using-the**	**car.**

Here the sumti cmavo *zo'e* is used to explicitly fill the x4 place; *zo'e* means "the unspecified thing" and has the same meaning as leaving the place empty: the listener must infer the correct meaning from context.

9.3 Tagging places: FA

The following cmavo are discussed in this section:

fa	FA	tags x1 place
fe	FA	tags x2 place
fi	FA	tags x3 place
fo	FA	tags x4 place
fu	FA	tags x5 place
fi'a	FA	place structure question

In sentences like Example 9.1 (p. 180), it is easy to get lost and forget which sumti falls in which place, especially if the sumti are more complicated than simple names or descriptions. The place structure tags of selma'o FA may be used to help clarify place structures. The five cmavo *fa*, *fe*, *fi*, *fo*, and *fu* may be inserted just before the sumti in the x1 to x5 places respectively:

Example 9.8

fa	mi	cu	klama	fe	la		bastn.	fi	la		.atlantas.
x1=	I		go	x2=	that-named		Boston	x3=	that-named		Atlanta

fo	le	dargu	fu	le	karce
x4=	the	road	x5=	the	car.

I go to Boston from Atlanta via the road using the car.

In Example 9.8 (p. 182), the tag *fu* before *le karce* clarifies that *le karce* occupies the x5 place of *klama*. The use of *fu* tells us nothing about the purpose or meaning of the x5 place; it simply says that *le karce* occupies it.

In Example 9.8 (p. 182), the tags are overkill; they serve only to make Example 9.1 (p. 180) even longer than it is. Here is a better illustration of the use of FA tags for clarification:

Example 9.9

fa	mi	klama	fe	le	zdani	be	mi	be'o	poi
x1=	I	go	x2=	(the	house	of	me)		which

nurma	vau	fi	la	nu,IORK.
is-rural		x3=	that-named	New-York.

In Example 9.9 (p. 182), the place structure of *klama* is as follows:

x1	agent	mi
x2	destination	le zdani be mi be'o poi nurma vau
x3	origin	la nu,IORK.
x4	route	(empty)
x5	means	(empty)

The *fi* tag serves to remind the hearer that what follows is in the x3 place of *klama*; after listening to the complex sumti occupying the x2 place, it's easy to get lost.

Of course, once the sumti have been tagged, the order in which they are specified no longer carries the burden of distinguishing the places. Therefore, it is perfectly all right to scramble them into any order desired, and to move the selbri to anywhere in the bridi, even the beginning:

Example 9.10

klama	fa	mi	fi	la	.atlantas.	fu	le	karce
go	x1= I	x3=	that-named	Atlanta	x5=	the	car

fe	la	bastn.	fo	le	dargu
x2=	that-named	Boston	x4=	the	road.

Go I from Atlanta using the car to Boston via the road.

Note that no *cu* is permitted before the selbri in Example 9.10 (p. 183), because *cu* separates the selbri from any preceding sumti, and Example 9.10 (p. 183) has no such sumti.

Example 9.11

fu	le	karce	fo	le	dargu	fi	la	.atlantas.
x5=	the	car	x4=	the	road	x3=	that-named	Atlanta

fe	la	bastn.	cu	klama	fa	mi
x2=	that-named	Boston		go	x1=	I

Using the car, via the road, from Atlanta to Boston go I.

Example 9.11 (p. 183) exhibits the reverse of the standard bridi form seen in Example 9.1 (p. 180) and Example 9.8 (p. 182), but still means exactly the same thing. If the FA tags were left out, however, producing:

Example 9.12

le	karce	le	dargu	la	.atlantas.
The	car	to-the	road	from-that-named	Atlanta

la	bastn.	cu	klama	mi
via-that-named	Boston		goes	using-me.

The car goes to the road from Atlanta, with Boston as the route, using me as a means of transport.

the meaning would be wholly changed, and in fact nonsensical.

Tagging places with FA cmavo makes it easy not only to reorder the places but also to omit undesirable ones, without any need for *zo'e* or special rules about the x1 place:

Example 9.13

klama	fi	la	.atlantas.	fe	la	bastn.
A-goer	x3=	that-named	Atlanta	x2=	that-named	Boston

fu	le	karce
x5=	the	car.

A goer from Atlanta to Boston using the car.

Here the x1 and x4 places are empty, and so no sumti are tagged with *fa* or *fo*; in addition, the x2 and x3 places appear in reverse order.

What if some sumti have FA tags and others do not? The rule is that after a FA-tagged sumti, any sumti following it occupy the places numerically succeeding it, subject to the proviso that an already-filled place is skipped:

Example 9.14

klama	fa	mi	la	bastn.	la	.atlantas.
Go	x1= I		x2=that-named	Boston	x3=that-named	Atlanta

le	dargu	le	karce
x4=the	road	x5=the	car.

Go I to Boston from Atlanta via the road using the car.

In Example 9.14 (p. 183), the *fa* causes *mi* to occupy the x1 place, and then the following untagged sumti occupy in order the x2 through x5 places. This is the mechanism by which Lojban allows placing the selbri first while specifying a sumti for the x1 place.

Here is a more complex (and more confusing) example:

Example 9.15

mi	klama	fi	la		.atlantas.	le	dargu
I	go	x3=	that-named	Atlanta,		the	road

fe	la		bastn.	le	karce
x2=	that-named	Boston,		the	car.

I go from Atlanta via the road to Boston using the car.

In Example 9.15 (p. 184), *mi* occupies the x1 place because it is the first sumti in the sentence (and is before the selbri). The second sumti, *la .atlantas.*, occupies the x3 place by virtue of the tag *fi*, and *le dargu* occupies the x4 place as a result of following *la .atlantas.*. Finally, *la bastn.* occupies the x2 place because of its tag *fe*, and *le karce* skips over the already-occupied x3 and x4 places to land in the x5 place.

Such a convoluted use of tags should probably be avoided except when trying for a literal translation of some English (or other natural-language) sentence; the rules stated here are merely given so that some standard interpretation is possible.

It is grammatically permitted to tag more than one sumti with the same FA cmavo. The effect is that of making more than one claim:

Example 9.16

[fa]	la		rik.	fa	la		djein.	klama
[x1=]	that-named	Rick	x1=	that-named	Jane	goes-to

[fe]	le	skina	fe	le	zdani	fe	le	zarci
[x2=]	the	movie	x2=	the	house	x2=	the	office

may be taken to say that both Rick and Jane go to the movie, the house, and the office, merging six claims into one. More likely, however, it will simply confuse the listener. There are better ways, involving logical connectives (explained in Chapter 14 (p. 317)), to say such things in Lojban. In fact, putting more than one sumti into a place is odd enough that it can only be done by explicit FA usage: this is the motivation for the proviso above, that already-occupied places are skipped. In this way, no sumti can be forced into a place already occupied unless it has an explicit FA cmavo tagging it.

The cmavo *fi'a* also belongs to selma'o FA, and allows Lojban users to ask questions about place structures. A bridi containing *fi'a* is a question, asking the listener to supply the appropriate other member of FA which will make the bridi a true statement:

Example 9.17

fi'a	do	dunda	[fe]	le	vi	rozgu
[what-place]?	you	give	x2=	the	nearby	rose

In what way are you involved in the giving of this rose?
Are you the giver or the receiver of this rose?

In Example 9.17 (p. 184), the speaker uses the selbri *dunda*, whose place structure is:

dunda x1 gives x2 to x3

The tagged sumti *fi'a do* indicates that the speaker wishes to know whether the sumti *do* falls in the x1 or the x3 place (the x2 place is already occupied by *le rozgu*). The listener can reply with a sentence consisting solely of a FA cmavo: *fa* if the listener is the giver, *fi* if he/she is the receiver.

I have inserted the tag *fe* in brackets into Example 9.17 (p. 184), but it is actually not necessary, because *fi'a* does not count as a numeric tag; therefore, *le vi rozgu* would necessarily be in the x2 place even if no tag were present, because it immediately follows the selbri.

There is also another member of FA, namely *fai*, which is discussed in Section 9.12 (p. 199).

9.4 Conversion: SE

The following cmavo are discussed in this section:

se	SE	2nd place conversion
te	SE	3rd place conversion
ve	SE	4th place conversion
xe	SE	5th place conversion

So far we have seen ways to move sumti around within a bridi, but the actual place structure of the selbri has always remained untouched. The conversion cmavo of selma'o SE are incorporated within the selbri itself, and produce a new selbri (called a converted selbri) with a different place structure. In particular, after the application of any SE cmavo, the number and purposes of the places remain the same, but two of them have been exchanged, the x1 place and another. Which place has been exchanged with x1 depends on the cmavo chosen. Thus, for example, when *se* is used, the x1 place is swapped with the x2 place.

Note that the cmavo of SE begin with consecutive consonants in alphabetical order. There is no "1st place conversion" cmavo, because exchanging the x1 place with itself is a pointless maneuver.

Here are the place structures of *se klama*:

x1 is the destination of x2's going from x3 via x4 using x5

and *te klama*:

x1 is the origin and x2 the destination of x3 going via x4 using x5

and *ve klama*:

x1 is the route to x2 from x3 used by x4 going via x5

and *xe klama*:

x1 is the means in going to x2 from x3 via x4 employed by x5

Note that the place structure numbers in each case continue to be listed in the usual order, x1 to x5.

Consider the following pair of examples:

Example 9.18

la	bastn.	cu	se klama	mi
That-named	**Boston**		**is-the-destination**	**of-me.**

Boston is my destination.
Boston is gone to by me.

Example 9.19

fe	la	bastn.	cu	klama	fa	mi
x2=	**that-named**	**Boston**		**go**	**x1=**	**I.**

To Boston go I.

Example 9.18 (p. 185) and Example 9.19 (p. 185) mean the same thing, in the sense that there is a relationship of going with the speaker as the agent and Boston as the destination (and with unspecified origin, route, and means). Structurally, however, they are quite different. Example 9.18 (p. 185) has *la bastn.* in the x1 place and *mi* in the x2 place of the selbri *se klama*, and uses standard bridi order; Example 9.19 (p. 185) has *mi* in the x1 place and *la bastn.* in the x2 place of the selbri *klama*, and uses a non-standard order.

The most important use of conversion is in the construction of descriptions. A description is a sumti which begins with a cmavo of selma'o LA or LE, called the descriptor, and contains (in the simplest case) a selbri. We have already seen the descriptions *le dargu* and *le karce*. To this we could add:

Example 9.20

le	klama

the go-er, the one who goes

In every case, the description is about something which fits into the x1 place of the selbri. In order to get a description of a destination (that is, something fitting the x2 place of *klama*), we must convert the selbri to *se klama*, whose x1 place is a destination. The result is

Example 9.21

> le ⋮ se ⋮ klama

the destination gone to by someone

Likewise, we can create three more converted descriptions:

Example 9.22

> le ⋮ te ⋮ klama

the origin of someone's going

Example 9.23

> le ⋮ ve ⋮ klama

the route of someone's going

Example 9.24

> le ⋮ xe ⋮ klama

the means by which someone goes

Example 9.23 (p. 186) does not mean "the route" plain and simple: that is *le pluta*, using a different selbri. It means a route that is used by someone for an act of *klama*; that is, a journey with origin and destination. A "road" on Mars, on which no one has traveled or is ever likely to, may be called *le pluta*, but it cannot be *le ve klama*, since there exists no one for whom it is *le ve klama be fo da* (the route taken in an actual journey by someone [da]).

When converting selbri that are more complex than a single brivla, it is important to realize that the scope of a SE cmavo is only the following brivla (or equivalent unit). In order to convert an entire tanru, it is necessary to enclose the tanru in *ke...ke'e* brackets:

Example 9.25

mi	se		ke	blanu	zdani	[ke'e]	ti
I	[2nd-conversion]		(	blue	house	)	this-thing

The place structure of *blanu zdani* (blue house) is the same as that of *zdani*, by the rule given in Section 9.1 (p. 179). The place structure of *zdani* is:

zdani x1 is a house/nest/lair/den for inhabitant x2

The place structure of *se ke blanu zdani [ke'e]* is therefore:

x1 is the inhabitant of the blue house (etc.) x2

Consequently, Example 9.25 (p. 186) means:

I am the inhabitant of the blue house which is this thing.

Conversion applied to only part of a tanru has subtler effects which are explained in Section 5.11 (p. 96).

It is grammatical to convert a selbri more than once with SE; later (inner) conversions are applied before earlier (outer) ones. For example, the place structure of *se te klama* is achieved by exchanging the x1 and x2 place of *te klama*, producing:

x1 is the destination and x2 is the origin of x3 going via x4 using x5

On the other hand, *te se klama* has a place structure derived from swapping the x1 and x3 places of *se klama*:

x1 is the origin of x2's going to x3 via x4 using x5

which is quite different. However, multiple conversions like this are never necessary. Arbitrary scrambling of places can be achieved more easily and far more intelligibly with FA tags, and only a single conversion is ever needed in a description.

(Although no one has made any real use of it, it is perhaps worth noting that compound conversions of the form *setese*, where the first and third cmavo are the same, effectively swap the two given places while leaving the others, including x1, alone: *setese* (or equivalently *tesete*) swap the x2 and x3 places, whereas *texete* (or *xetexe*) swap the x3 and x5 places.)

9.5 Modal places: FIhO, FEhU

The following cmavo are discussed in this section:

fi'o	FIhO	modal place prefix
fe'u	FEhU	modal terminator

Sometimes the place structures engineered into Lojban are inadequate to meet the needs of actual speech. Consider the gismu *viska*, whose place structure is:

viska x1 sees x2 under conditions x3

Seeing is a threefold relationship, involving an agent (le viska), an object of sight (le se viska), and an environment that makes seeing possible (le te viska). Seeing is done with one or more eyes, of course; in general, the eyes belong to the entity in the x1 place.

Suppose, however, that you are blind in one eye and are talking to someone who doesn't know that. You might want to say, "I see you with the left eye." There is no place in the place structure of *viska* such as "with eye x4" or the like. Lojban allows you to solve the problem by adding a new place, changing the relationship:

Example 9.26

mi	viska	do	fi'o		kanla	[fe'u]	le	zunle
I	see	you	[modal]		eye:		the	left-thing

I see you with the left eye.

The three-place relation *viska* has now acquired a fourth place specifying the eye used for seeing. The combination of the cmavo *fi'o* (of selma'o FIhO) followed by a selbri, in this case the gismu *kanla*, forms a tag which is prefixed to the sumti filling the new place, namely *le zunle*. The semantics of *fi'o kanla le zunle* is that *le zunle* fills the x1 place of *kanla*, whose place structure is

kanla x1 is an/the eye of body x2

Thus *le zunle* is an eye. The x2 place of *kanla* is unspecified and must be inferred from the context. It is important to remember that even though *le zunle* is placed following *fi'o kanla*, semantically it belongs in the x1 place of *kanla*. The selbri may be terminated with *fe'u* (of selma'o FEhU), an elidable terminator which is rarely required unless a non-logical connective follows the tag (omitting *fe'u* in that case would make the connective affect the selbri).

The term for such an added place is a "modal place", as distinguished from the regular numbered places. (This use of the word "modal" is specific to the Loglan Project, and does not agree with the standard uses in either logic or linguistics, but is now too entrenched to change easily.) The *fi'o* construction marking a modal place is called a "modal tag", and the sumti which follows it a "modal sumti"; the purely Lojban terms *sumti tcita* and *seltcita sumti*, respectively, are also commonly used. Modal sumti may be placed anywhere within the bridi, in any order; they have no effect whatever on the rules for assigning unmarked bridi to numbered places, and they may not be marked with FA cmavo.

Consider Example 9.26 (p. 187) again. Another way to view the situation is to consider the speaker's left eye as a tool, a tool for seeing. The relevant selbri then becomes *pilno*, whose place structure is

pilno x1 uses x2 as a tool for purpose x3

and we can rewrite Example 9.26 (p. 187) as

Example 9.27

mi	viska	do	fi'o	se		pilno	le	zunle	kanla
I	see	you	[modal]	[conversion]		use:	the	left	eye.

I see you using my left eye.

Here the selbri belonging to the modal is *se pilno*. The conversion of *pilno* is necessary in order to get the "tool" place into x1, since only x1 can be the modal sumti. The "tool user" place is the x2 of *se pilno* (because it is the x1 of *pilno*) and remains unspecified. The tag *fi'o pilno* would mean "with tool user", leaving the tool unspecified.

9.6 Modal tags: BAI

There are certain selbri which seem particularly useful in constructing modal tags. In particular, *pilno* is one of them. The place structure of *pilno* is:

pilno x1 uses x2 as a tool for purpose x3

and almost any selbri which represents an action may need to specify a tool. Having to say *fi'o se pilno* frequently would make many Lojban sentences unnecessarily verbose and clunky, so an abbreviation is provided in the language design: the compound cmavo *sepi'o*.

Here *se* is used before a cmavo, namely *pi'o*, rather than before a brivla. The meaning of this cmavo, which belongs to selma'o BAI, is exactly the same as that of *fi'o pilno fe'u*. Since what we want is a tag based on *se pilno* rather than *pilno*- the tool, not the tool user – the grammar allows a BAI cmavo to be converted using a SE cmavo. Example 9.27 (p. 187) may therefore be rewritten as:

Example 9.28

mi	viska	do	sepi'o	le	zunle	kanla
I	see	you	with-tool:	the	left	eye

I see you using my left eye.

The compound cmavo *sepi'o* is much shorter than *fi'o se pilno [fe'u]* and can be thought of as a single word meaning "with-tool". The modal tag *pi'o*, with no *se*, similarly means "with-tool-user", probably a less useful concept. Nevertheless, the parallelism with the place structure of *pilno* makes the additional syllable worthwhile.

Some BAI cmavo make sense with as well as without a SE cmavo; for example, *ka'a*, the BAI corresponding to the gismu *klama*, has five usable forms corresponding to the five places of *klama* respectively:

ka'a	with-goer
seka'a	with-destination
teka'a	with-origin
veka'a	with-route
xeka'a	with-means-of-transport

Any of these tags may be used to provide modal places for bridi, as in the following examples:

Example 9.29

la	.eivn.	cu	vecnu	loi	flira	cinta	ka'a	mi
That-named	Avon		sells	a-mass-of	face	paint	with-goer	me.

I am a traveling cosmetics salesperson for Avon.

(Example 9.29 (p. 188) may seem a bit strained, but it illustrates the way in which an existing selbri, *vecnu* in this case, may have a place added to it which might otherwise seem utterly unrelated.)

Example 9.30

mi	cadzu	seka'a	la	bratfyd.
I	walk	with-destination	that-named	Bradford.

I am walking to Bradford.

Example 9.31

bloti	teka'a	la	nu,IORK.
[Observative:]-is-a-boat	with-origin	that-named	New-York

A boat from New York!

Example 9.32

do	bajra	veka'a	lo	djine
You	**run**	**with-route**	**a**	**circle.**

You are running in circles.

Example 9.33

mi	citka	xeka'a	le	vinji
I	**eat**	**with-means-of-transport**	**the**	**airplane.**

I eat in the airplane.

There are sixty-odd cmavo of selma'o BAI, based on selected gismu that seemed useful in a variety of settings. The list is somewhat biased toward English, because many of the cmavo were selected on the basis of corresponding English prepositions and preposition compounds such as "with", "without", and "by means of". The BAI cmavo, however, are far more precise than English prepositions, because their meanings are fixed by the place structures of the corresponding gismu.

All BAI cmavo have the form CV'V or CVV. Most of them are CV'V, where the C is the first consonant of the corresponding gismu and the two Vs are the two vowels of the gismu. The table in Section 9.16 (p. 202) shows the exceptions.

There is one additional BAI cmavo that is not derived from a gismu: *do'e*. This cmavo is used when an extra place is needed, but it seems useful to be vague about the semantic implications of the extra place:

Example 9.34

lo	nanmu	be do'e	le	berti	cu	klama	le	tcadu
Some	**man**	**[related-to]**	**the**	**north**		**came**	**to-the**	**city.**

A man of the north came to the city.

Here *le berti* is provided as a modal place of the selbri *nanmu*, but its exact significance is vague, and is paralleled in the colloquial translation by the vague English preposition "of". Example 9.34 (p. 189) also illustrates a modal place bound into a selbri with *be*. This construction is useful when the selbri of a description requires a modal place; this and other uses of *be* are more fully explained in Section 5.7 (p. 88).

9.7 Modal sentence connection: the causals

The following cmavo are discussed in this section:

ri'a	BAI	rinka modal: physical cause
ki'u	BAI	krinu modal: justification
mu'i	BAI	mukti modal: motivation
ni'i	BAI	nibli modal: logical entailment

This section has two purposes. On the one hand, it explains the grammatical construct called "modal sentence connection". On the other, it exemplifies some of the more useful BAI cmavo: the causals. (There are other BAI cmavo which have causal implications: *ja'e* means "with result", and so *seja'e* means "with cause of unspecified nature"; likewise, *gau* means "with agent" and *tezu'e* means "with purpose". These other modal cmavo will not be further discussed here, as my purpose is to explain modal sentence connection rather than Lojbanic views of causation.)

There are four causal gismu in Lojban, distinguishing different versions of the relationships lumped in English as "causal":

rinka	event x1 physically causes event x2
krinu	event x1 is the justification for event x2
mukti	event x1 is the (human) motive for event x2
nibli	event x1 logically entails event x2

Each of these gismu has a related modal: *ri'a, ki'u, mu'i,* and *ni'i* respectively. Using these gismu and these modals, we can create various causal sentences with different implications:

Example 9.35

le	spati	cu	banro	ri'a		le	nu
The	plant		grows	with-physical-cause		the	event-of

do	djacu	dunda	fi	le	spati
you	water	give	to	the	plant.

The plant grows because you water it.

Example 9.36

la	djan.	cpacu	le	pamoi	se jinga
	John	gets	the	first	prize

ki'u		le	nu	la		djan.	jinga
with-justification		the	event-of	that-named		John	wins.

John got the first prize because he won.

Example 9.37

mi	lebna	le	cukta	mu'i
I	took	the	book	with-motivation

le	nu		mi	viska	le	cukta
the	event-of		I	saw	the	book.

I took the book because I saw it.

Example 9.38

la	sokrates.	morsi	binxo		ni'i
	Socrates	dead	became		with-logical-justification

le	nu		la		sokrates.	remna
the	event-of		that-named		Socrates	is-human.

Socrates died because Socrates is human.

In Example 9.35 (p. 190) through Example 9.38 (p. 190), the same English word "because" is used to translate all four modals, but the types of cause being expressed are quite different. Let us now focus on Example 9.35 (p. 190), and explore some variations on it.

As written, Example 9.35 (p. 190) claims that the plant grows, but only refers to the event of watering it in an abstraction bridi (abstractions are explained in Chapter 11 (p. 247)) without actually making a claim. If I express Example 9.35 (p. 190), I have said that the plant in fact grows, but I have not said that you actually water it, merely that there is a causal relationship between watering and growing. This is semantically asymmetrical. Suppose I wanted to claim that the plant was being watered, and only mention its growth as ancillary information? Then we could reverse the main bridi and the abstraction bridi, saying:

Example 9.39

do	djacu	dunda	fi	le	spati
You	water	give	to	the	plant

seri'a		le	nu		ri	banro
with-physical-effect		the	event-of		it	grows.

You water the plant; therefore, it grows.

with the *ri'a* changed to *seri'a*. In addition, there are also symmetrical forms:

Example 9.40

le	nu	do	djacu	dunda	fi	le	spati	cu
The	event-of	(you	water	give	to	the	plant)	

rinka	le	nu	le	spati	cu	banro
causes	the	event-of	(the	plant		grows).

Your watering the plant causes its growth.

If you water the plant, then it grows.

does not claim either event, but asserts only the causal relationship between them. So in Example 9.40 (p. 191), I am not saying that the plant grows nor that you have in fact watered it. The second colloquial translation shows a form of "if-then" in English quite distinct from the logical connective "if-then" explained in Chapter 14 (p. 317).

Suppose we wish to claim both events as well as their causal relationship? We can use one of two methods:

Example 9.41

le	spati	cu	banro	.iri'abo	do
The	plant		grows.	Because	you

djacu	dunda	fi	le	spati
water	give	to	the	plant.

The plant grows because you water it.

Example 9.42

do	djacu	dunda	fi	le	spati
You	water	give	to	the	plant.

.iseri'abo	le	spati	cu	banro
Therefore	the	plant		grows.

You water the plant; therefore, it grows.

The compound cmavo *.iri'abo* and *.iseri'abo* serve to connect two bridi, as the initial *i* indicates. The final *bo* is necessary to prevent the modal from "taking over" the following sumti. If the *bo* were omitted from Example 9.41 (p. 191) we would have:

Example 9.43

le	spati	cu	banro	.i	ri'a		do
The	plant		grows.		Because-of		you,

	djacu	dunda	fi	le	spati
[something]	water	gives	to	the	plant.

The plant grows. Because of you, water is given to the plant.

Because *ri'a do* is a modal sumti in Example 9.43 (p. 191), there is no longer an explicit sumti in the x1 place of *djacu dunda*, and the translation must be changed.

The effect of sentences like Example 9.41 (p. 191) and Example 9.42 (p. 191) is that the modal, *ri'a* in this example, no longer modifies an explicit sumti. Instead, the sumti is implicit, the event given by a full bridi. Furthermore, there is a second implication: that the first bridi fills the x2 place of the gismu *rinka*; it specifies an event which is the effect. I am therefore claiming three things: that the plant grows, that you have watered it, and that there is a cause-and-effect relationship between the two.

In principle, any modal tag can appear in a sentence connective of the type exemplified by Example 9.41 (p. 191) and Example 9.42 (p. 191). However, it makes little sense to use any modals which do not expect events or other abstractions to fill the places of the corresponding gismu. The sentence connective *.ibaubo* is perfectly grammatical, but it is hard to imagine any two sentences which could be connected by an "in-language" modal. This is because a sentence describes an event, and an event can be a cause or an effect, but not a language.

9.8 Other modal connections

Like many Lojban grammatical constructions, sentence modal connection has both forethought and afterthought forms. (See Chapter 14 (p. 317) for a more detailed discussion of Lojban connectives.) Section 9.7 (p. 189) exemplifies only afterthought modal connection, illustrated here by:

Example 9.44

mi	jgari	lei		djacu	
I	grasp	the-mass-of		water	

.iri'abo		mi	jgari	le	kabri
with-physical-cause		I	grasp	the	cup.

Causing the mass of water to be grasped by me, I grasped the cup.
I grasp the water because I grasp the cup.

An afterthought connection is one that is signaled only by a cmavo (or a compound cmavo, in this case) between the two constructs being connected. Forethought connection uses a signal both before the first construct and between the two: the use of "both" and "and" in the first half of this sentence represents a forethought connection (though not a modal one).

To make forethought modal sentence connections in Lojban, place the modal plus *gi* before the first bridi, and *gi* between the two. No *i* is used within the construct. The forethought equivalent of Example 9.44 (p. 192) is:

Example 9.45

ri'agi		mi	jgari	le	kabri	gi
With-physical-cause		I	grasp	the	cup	,

mi	jgari	lei		djacu	
I	grasp	the-mass-of		water.	

Because I grasp the cup, I grasp the water.

Note that the cause, the x1 of *rinka* is now placed first. To keep the two bridi in the original order of Example 9.44 (p. 192), we could say:

Example 9.46

seri'agi		mi	jgari	lei		djacu	gi
With-physical-effect		I	grasp	the-mass-of		water	,

mi	jgari	le	kabri
I	grasp	the	cup.

In English, the sentence "Therefore I grasp the water, I grasp the cup" is ungrammatical, because "therefore" is not grammatically equivalent to "because". In Lojban, *seri'agi* can be used just like *ri'agi*.

When the two bridi joined by a modal connection have one or more elements (selbri or sumti or both) in common, there are various condensed forms that can be used in place of full modal sentence connection with both bridi completely stated.

When the bridi are the same except for a single sumti, as in Examples 8.1 through 8.3, then a sumti modal connection may be employed:

Example 9.47

mi	jgari	ri'agi	le	kabri	gi	lei		djacu
I	grasp	because	the	cup	,	the-mass-of		water.

Example 9.47 (p. 192) means exactly the same as Example 9.44 (p. 192) through Example 9.46 (p. 192), but there is no idiomatic English translation that will distinguish it from them.

If the two connected bridi are different in more than one sumti, then a termset may be employed. Termsets are explained more fully in Section 14.11 (p. 332), but are essentially a mechanism for creating connections between multiple sumti simultaneously.

Example 9.48

mi	dunda	le	cukta	la		djan.
I	gave	the	book	to-that-named		John.

.imu'ibo	la		djan.	dunda	lei		jdini	mi
Motivated-by	that-named		John	gave	the-mass-of		money	to-me.

I gave the book to John, because John gave money to me.

means the same as:

Example 9.49

nu'i	mu'igi	la		djan.	lei		jdini	mi	gi
[start]	because	that-named		John,	the-mass-of		money,	me	;

mi	le	cukta	la		djan.	nu'u	dunda
I,	the	book,	that-named		John	[end]	gives.

Here there are three sumti in each half of the termset, because the two bridi share only their selbri.

There is no modal connection between selbri as such: bridi which differ only in the selbri can be modally connected using bridi-tail modal connection. The bridi-tail construct is more fully explained in Section 14.9 (p. 328), but essentially it consists of a selbri with optional sumti following it. Example 9.37 (p. 190) is suitable for bridi-tail connection, and could be shortened to:

Example 9.50

mi	mu'igi	viska	le	cukta	gi	lebna	le	cukta
I,	because	saw	the	book,		took	the	book.

Again, no straightforward English translation exists. It is even possible to shorten Example 9.50 (p. 193) further to:

Example 9.51

mi	mu'igi	viska	gi		lebna	vau	le	cukta
I	because	saw,	therefore		took,		the	book.

where *le cukta* is set off by the non-elidable *vau* and is made to belong to both bridi-tails – see Section 14.9 (p. 328) for more explanations.

Since this is a chapter on rearranging sumti, it is worth pointing out that Example 9.51 (p. 193) can be further rearranged to:

Example 9.52

mi	le	cukta	mu'igi	viska	gi		lebna
I,	the	book,	because	saw,	therefore		took.

which doesn't require the extra *vau*; all sumti before a conjunction of bridi-tails are shared.

Finally, mathematical operands can be modally connected.

Example 9.53

li		ny.	du	li		vo
the-number		n	=	the-number		4.

.ini'ibo	li		ny.	du	li		re	su'i	re
Entailed-by	the-number		n	=	the-number		2	+	2.

n = 4 because n = 2 + 2.

can be reduced to:

Example 9.54

li	ny.	du	li
the-number	n	=	the-number

ni'igi	vei	re	su'i	re	[ve'o]	gi	vo
because	(	2	+	2	)	therefore	4.

n is 2 + 2, and is thus 4.

The cmavo *vei* and *ve'o* represent mathematical parentheses, and are required so that *ni'igi* affects more than just the immediately following operand, namely the first *re*. (The right parenthesis, *ve'o*, is an elidable terminator.) As usual, no English translation does Example 9.54 (p. 194) justice.

Note: Due to restrictions on the Lojban parsing algorithm, it is not possible to form modal connectives using the *fi'o*-plus-selbri form of modal. Only the predefined modals of selma'o BAI can be compounded as shown in Section 9.7 (p. 189) and Section 9.8 (p. 192).

9.9 Modal selbri

Consider the example:

Example 9.55

mi	tavla	bau	la	lojban.
I	speak	in-language	that-named	Lojban

bai	tu'a	la	frank.
with-compeller	some-act-by	that-named	Frank.

I speak in Lojban, under compulsion by Frank.

Example 9.55 (p. 194) has two modal sumti, using the modals *bau* and *bai*. Suppose we wanted to specify the language explicitly but be vague about who's doing the compelling. We can simplify Example 9.55 (p. 194) to:

Example 9.56

mi	tavla	bau	la	lojban.	bai	[ku].
I	speak	in-language	that-named	Lojban	under-compulsion	

In Example 9.56 (p. 194), the elidable terminator *ku* has taken the place of the sumti which would normally follow *bai*. Alternatively, we could specify the one who compels but keep the language vague:

Example 9.57

mi	tavla	bau	[ku]
I	speak	in-some-language	

bai	tu'a	la	frank.
under-compulsion-by	some-act-by	that-named	Frank.

We are also free to move the modal-plus- *ku* around the bridi:

Example 9.58

bau	[ku]	bai	ku	mi	tavla
In-some-language		under-compulsion		I	speak.

An alternative to using *ku* is to place the modal cmavo right before the selbri, following the *cu* which often appears there. When a modal is present, the *cu* is almost never necessary.

Example 9.59

mi	bai	tavla	bau	la	lojban.
I	compelledly	speak	in-language	that-named	Lojban.

In this use, the modal is like a tanru modifier semantically, although grammatically it is quite distinct. Example 9.59 (p. 194) is very similar in meaning to:

Example 9.60

mi	se bapli	tavla	bau	la	lojban.
I	**compelledly**	**speak**	**in-language**	**that-named**	**Lojban.**

The *se* conversion is needed because *bapli tavla* would be a "compeller type of speaker" rather than a "compelled (by someone) type of speaker", which is what a *bai tavla* is.

If the modal preceding a selbri is constructed using *fi'o*, then *fe'u* is required to prevent the main selbri and the modal selbri from colliding:

Example 9.61

mi	fi'o	kanla	fe'u	viska	do
I	**with**	**eye**		**see**	**you.**

I see you with my eye(s).

There are two other uses of modals. A modal can be attached to a pair of bridi-tails that have already been connected by a logical, non-logical, or modal connection (see Chapter 14 (p. 317) for more on logical and non-logical connections):

Example 9.62

mi	bai		ke	ge	klama	le	zarci
I	**under-compulsion**		**(**	**both**	**go**	**to-the**	**market**

gi	cadzu	le	bisli	[ke'e]
and	**walk**	**on-the**	**ice**	**).**

Under compulsion, I both go to the market and walk on the ice.

Here the *bai* is spread over both *klama le zarci* and *cadzu le bisli*, and the *ge ... gi* represents the logical connection "both-and" between the two.

Similarly, a modal can be attached to multiple sentences that have been combined with *tu'e* and *tu'u*, which are explained in more detail in Section 19.2 (p. 447):

Example 9.63

bai		tu'e	mi	klama	le	zarci
Under-compulsion		**[start]**	**I**	**go**	**to-the**	**market.**

.i	mi	cadzu	le	bisli	[tu'u]
I	**walk**	**on-the**	**ice**	**[end].**	

means the same thing as Example 9.62 (p. 195).

Note: Either BAI modals or *fi'o*-plus-selbri modals may correctly be used in any of the constructions discussed in this section.

9.10 Modal relative phrases; Comparison

The following cmavo are discussed in this section:

pe	GOI	restrictive relative phrase
ne	GOI	incidental relative phrase
mau	BAI	zmadu modal
me'a	BAI	mleca modal

Relative phrases and clauses are explained in much more detail in Chapter 8 (p. 161). However, there is a construction which combines a modal with a relative phrase which is relevant to this chapter. Consider the following examples of relative clauses:

Example 9.64

la	.apasionatas.	poi	se cusku
The	**Appassionata**	**which**	**is-expressed-by**

la	.artr.	rubnstain.	cu	se nelci	mi
that-named	**Arthur**	**Rubinstein**		**is-liked-by**	**me.**

Example 9.65

la	.apasionatas.	noi	se finti
The	Appassionata,	which	is-created-by

la		betovn.		cu	se nelci	mi
that-named	Beethoven,				is-liked-by	me.

In Example 9.64 (p. 195), *la .apasionatas.* refers to a particular performance of the sonata, namely the one performed by Rubinstein. Therefore, the relative clause *poi se cusku* uses the cmavo *poi* (of selma'o NOI) to restrict the meaning of *la .apasionatas* to the performance in question.

In Example 9.65 (p. 196), however, *la .apasionatas.* refers to the sonata as a whole, and the information that it was composed by Beethoven is merely incidental. The cmavo *noi* (also of selma'o NOI) expresses the incidental nature of this relationship.

The cmavo *pe* and *ne* (of selma'o GOI) are roughly equivalent to *poi* and *noi* respectively, but are followed by sumti rather than full bridi. We can abbreviate Example 9.64 (p. 195) and Example 9.65 (p. 196) to:

Example 9.66

la	.apasionatas.	pe	la	.artr.	rubnstain.	se nelci	mi
The	Appassionata	of	that-named	Arthur	Rubinstein	is-liked-by	me.

Example 9.67

la	.apasionatas.	ne	la	betovn.	se nelci	mi
The	Appassionata,	which-is-of	that-named	Beethoven,	is-liked-by	me.

Here the precise selbri of the relative clauses is lost: all we can tell is that the Appassionata is connected in some way with Rubinstein (in Example 9.66 (p. 196)) and Beethoven (in Example 9.67 (p. 196)), and that the relationships are respectively restrictive and incidental.

It happens that both *cusku* and *finti* have BAI cmavo, namely *cu'u* and *fi'e*. We can recast Example 9.66 (p. 196) and Example 9.67 (p. 196) as:

Example 9.68

la	.apasionatas	pe cu'u
The	Appassionata	expressed-by

la	.artr.	rubnstain.	cu	se nelci	mi
that-named	Arthur	Rubinstein		is-liked-by	me.

Example 9.69

la	.apasionatas	ne fi'e
The	Appassionata,	invented-by

la	betovn.	cu	se nelci	mi
that-named	Beethoven,		is-liked-by	me.

Example 9.68 (p. 196) and Example 9.69 (p. 196) have the full semantic content of Example 9.64 (p. 195) and Example 9.65 (p. 196) respectively.

Modal relative phrases are often used with the BAI cmavo *mau* and *me'a*, which are based on the comparative gismu *zmadu* (more than) and *mleca* (less than) respectively. The place structures are:

zmadu	x1 is more than x2 in property/quantity x3 by amount x4
mleca	x1 is less than x2 in property/quantity x3 by amount x4

Here are some examples:

9.10 Modal relative phrases; Comparison

Example 9.70

la	frank.	nelci	la	betis.
That-named	Frank	likes	that-named	Betty,

ne	semau	la	meiris.
which-is	more-than	that-named	Mary.

Frank likes Betty more than (he likes) Mary.

Example 9.70 (p. 197) requires that Frank likes Betty, but adds the information that his liking for Betty exceeds his liking for Mary. The modal appears in the form *semau* because the x2 place of *zmadu* is the basis for comparison: in this case, Frank's liking for Mary.

Example 9.71

la	frank.	nelci	la	meiris.
That-named	Frank	likes	that-named	Mary,

ne	seme'a	la	betis.
which-is	less-than	that-named	Betty.

Frank likes Mary less than (he likes) Betty.

Here we are told that Frank likes Mary less than he likes Betty; the information about the comparison is the same. It would be possible to rephrase Example 9.70 (p. 197) using *me'a* rather than *semau*, and Example 9.71 (p. 197) using *mau* rather than *seme'a*, but such usage would be unnecessarily confusing. Like many BAI cmavo, *mau* and *me'a* are more useful when converted with *se*.

If the *ne* were omitted in Example 9.70 (p. 197) and Example 9.71 (p. 197), the modal sumti (*la meiris.* and *la betis.* respectively) would become attached to the bridi as a whole, producing a very different translation. Example 9.71 (p. 197) would become:

Example 9.72

la	frank.	nelci	la	meiris.	seme'a	la	betis.
That-named	Frank	likes	that-named	Mary	is-less-than	that-named	Betty.

Frank's liking Mary is less than Betty.

which compares a liking with a person, and is therefore nonsense.

Pure comparison, which states only the comparative information but says nothing about whether Frank actually likes either Mary or Betty (he may like neither, but dislike Betty less), would be expressed differently, as:

Example 9.73

le	ni	la	frank.
The	quantity-of	that-named	Frank's

nelci	la	betis.	cu
liking	that-named	Betty	

zmadu	le	ni	la	frank.
is-more-than	the	quantity-of	that-named	Frank's

nelci	la	meiris.
liking	that-named	Mary.

The mechanisms explained in this section are appropriate to many modals other than *semau* and *seme'a*. Some other modals that are often associated with relative phrases are: *seba'i* ("instead of"), *ci'u* ("on scale"), *de'i* ("dated"), *du'i* ("as much as"). Some BAI tags can be used equally well in relative phrases or attached to bridi; others seem useful only attached to bridi. But it is also possible that the usefulness of particular BAI modals is an English-speaker bias, and that speakers of other languages may find other BAIs useful in divergent ways.

Note: The uses of modals discussed in this section are applicable both to BAI modals and to *fi'o*-plus-selbri modals.

9.11 Mixed modal connection

It is possible to mix logical connection (explained in Chapter 14 (p. 317)) with modal connection, in a way that simultaneously asserts the logical connection and the modal relationship. Consider the sentences:

Example 9.74

mi	nelci	do	.ije	mi	nelci	la	djein.
I	like	you.	And	I	like	that-named	Jane.

which is a logical connection, and

Example 9.75

mi	nelci	do	.iki'ubo	mi	nelci	la	djein.
I	like	you.	Justified-by	I	like	that-named	Jane.

The meanings of Example 9.74 (p. 198) and Example 9.75 (p. 198) can be simultaneously expressed by combining the two compound cmavo, thus:

Example 9.76

mi	nelci	do	.ijeki'ubo	mi	nelci	la	djein.
I	like	you.	And-justified-by	I	like	that-named	Jane.

Here the two sentences *mi nelci do* and *mi nelci la djein.* are simultaneously asserted, their logical connection is asserted, and their causal relationship is asserted. The logical connective *je* comes before the modal *ki'u* in all such mixed connections.

Since *mi nelci do* and *mi nelci la djein.* differ only in the final sumti, we can transform Example 9.76 (p. 198) into a mixed sumti connection:

Example 9.77

mi	nelci	do	.eki'ubo	la	djein.
I	like	you	and/because	that-named	Jane.

Note that this connection is an afterthought one. Mixed connectives are always afterthought; forethought connectives must be either logical or modal.

There are numerous other afterthought logical and non-logical connectives that can have modal information planted within them. For example, a bridi-tail connected version of Example 9.77 (p. 198) would be:

Example 9.78

mi	nelci	do	gi'eki'ubo	nelci	la	djein.
I	like	you	and/because	like	that-named	Jane.

The following three complex examples all mean the same thing.

Example 9.79

mi	bevri	le	dakli
I	carry	the	sack.

.ijeseri'abo	tu'e	mi	bevri	le	gerku
And-[effect]	(	I	carry	the	dog.

.ijadu'ibo	mi	bevri	le	mlatu	[tu'u]
And/or-[equal]	I	carry	the	cat.	)

I carry the sack. As a result I carry the dog or I carry the cat, equally.

Example 9.80

mi	bevri	le	dakli
I	carry	the	sack

gi'eseri'ake	bevri	le	gerku
and-[effect]	(carry	the	dog

gi'adu'ibo	bevri	le	mlatu	[ke'e]
and/or-[equal]	carry	the	cat)	

I carry the sack and as a result carry the dog or carry the cat equally.

Example 9.81

mi	bevri	le	dakli
I	carry	the	sack

.eseri'ake	le	gerku
and-[effect]	(the	dog

.adu'ibo	le	mlatu	[ke'e]
and/or-[equal]	the	cat)	

I carry the sack, and as a result the cat or the dog equally.

In Example 9.79 (p. 198), the *tu'e...tu'u* brackets are the equivalent of the *ke...ke'e* brackets in Example 9.80 (p. 199) and Example 9.81 (p. 199), because *ke...ke'e* cannot extend across more than one sentence. It would also be possible to change the *.ijeseri'abo* to *.ije seri'a*, which would show that the *tu'e...tu'u* portion was an effect, but would not pin down the *mi bevri le dakli* portion as the cause. It is legal for a modal (or a tense; see Chapter 10 (p. 207)) to modify the whole of a *tu'e...tu'u* construct.

Note: The uses of modals discussed in this section are applicable both to BAI modals and to *fi'o*-plus-selbri modals.

9.12 Modal conversion: JAI

The following cmavo are discussed in this section:

jai	JAI	modal conversion
fai	FA	modal place structure tag

So far, conversion of numbered bridi places with SE and the addition of modal places with BAI have been two entirely separate operations. However, it is possible to convert a selbri in such a way that, rather than exchanging two numbered places, a modal place is made into a numbered place. For example,

Example 9.82

mi	cusku		bau	la	lojban.
I	express	[something]	in-language	that-named	Lojban.

has an explicit x1 place occupied by *mi* and an explicit *bau* place occupied by *la lojban*. To exchange these two, we use a modal conversion operator consisting of *jai* (of selma'o JAI) followed by the modal cmavo. Thus, the modal conversion of Example 9.82 (p. 199) is:

Example 9.83

la	lojban.	jai bau cusku	fai	mi
That-named	Lojban	is-the-language-of-expression	used-by	me.

In Example 9.83 (p. 199), the modal place *la lojban.* has become the x1 place of the new selbri *jai bau cusku*. What has happened to the old x1 place? There is no numbered place for it to move to, so it moves to a special "unnumbered place" marked by the tag *fai* of selma'o FA.

Note: For the purposes of place numbering, *fai* behaves like *fi'a*; it does not affect the numbering of the other places around it.

Like SE conversions, JAI conversions are especially convenient in descriptions. We may refer to "the language of an expression" as *le jai bau cusku*, for example.

In addition, it is grammatical to use *jai* without a following modal. This usage is not related to modals, but is explained here for completeness. The effect of *jai* by itself is to send the x1 place, which should be an abstraction, into the *fai* position, and to raise one of the sumti from the abstract sub-bridi into the x1 place of the main bridi. This feature is discussed in more detail in Section 11.10 (p. 259). The following two examples mean the same thing:

Example 9.84

le	nu	mi	lebna	le	cukta	cu	se krinu
The	event-of	(I	take	the	book)		is-justified-by

le	nu	mi	viska	le	cukta
the	event-of	(I	see	the	book).

My taking the book is justified by my seeing it.

Example 9.85

mi	jai se krinu	le	nu	mi	viska	le	cukta	kei
I	am-justified-by	the	event-of	(I	see	the	book)	

[fai	le	nu	mi	lebna	le	cukta]
[namely,	the	event-of	(I	take	the	book)]

I am justified in taking the book by seeing the book.

Example 9.85 (p. 200), with the bracketed part omitted, allows us to say that "I am justified" whereas in fact it is my action that is justified. This construction is vague, but useful in representing natural-language methods of expression.

Note: The uses of modals discussed in this section are applicable both to BAI modals and to *fi'o*-plus-selbri modals.

9.13 Modal negation

Negation is explained in detail in Chapter 15 (p. 353). There are two forms of negation in Lojban: contradictory and scalar negation. Contradictory negation expresses what is false, whereas scalar negation says that some alternative to what has been stated is true. A simple example is the difference between "John didn't go to Paris" (contradictory negation) and "John went to (somewhere) other than Paris" (scalar negation).

Contradictory negation involving BAI cmavo is performed by appending *-nai* (of selma'o NAI) to the BAI. A common use of modals with *-nai* is to deny a causal relationship:

Example 9.86

mi	nelci	do	mu'inai	le	nu	do	nelci	mi

I like you, but not because you like me.

Example 9.86 (p. 200) denies that the relationship between my liking you (which is asserted) and your liking me (which is not asserted) is one of motivation. Nothing is said about whether you like me or not, merely that that hypothetical liking is not the motivation for my liking you.

Scalar negation is achieved by prefixing *na'e* (of selma'o NAhE), or any of the other cmavo of NAhE, to the BAI cmavo.

Example 9.87

le	spati	cu	banro	na'emu'i	le	nu
The	plant		grows	other-than-motivated-by	the	event-of

do	djacu	dunda	fi	le	spati
you	water	give	to	the	plant.

Example 9.87 (p. 200) says that the relationship between the plant's growth and your watering it is not one of motivation: the plant is not motivated to grow, as plants are not something which can

have motivation as a rule. Implicitly, some other relationship between watering and growth exists, but Example 9.87 (p. 200) doesn't say what it is (presumably *ri'a*).

Note: Modals made with *fi'o* plus a selbri cannot be negated directly. The selbri can itself be negated either with contradictory or with scalar negation, however.

9.14 Sticky modals

The following cmavo is discussed in this section:

| ki | KI | stickiness flag |

Like tenses, modals can be made persistent from the bridi in which they appear to all following bridi. The effect of this "stickiness" is to make the modal, along with its following sumti, act as if it appeared in every successive bridi. Stickiness is put into effect by following the modal (but not any following sumti) with the cmavo *ki* of selma'o KI. For example,

Example 9.88

mi	tavla	bau	la	lojban.	bai
I	speak	in-language	that-named	Lojban	compelled-by

ki	tu'a	la	frank.
	some-property-of	that-named	Frank.

.ibabo	mi	tavla	bau	la	gliban.
Afterward,	I	speak	in-language	that-named	English.

means the same as:

Example 9.89

mi	tavla	bau	la	lojban.	bai
I	speak	in-language	that-named	Lojban	compelled-by

tu'a	la	frank.
some-property-of	that-named	Frank.

.ibabo	mi	tavla	bau	la	gliban.	bai
Afterward,	I	speak	in-language	that-named	English	compelled-by

tu'a	la	frank.
some-property-of	that-named	Frank.

In Example 9.88 (p. 201), *bai* is made sticky, and so Frank's compelling is made applicable to every following bridi. *bau* is not sticky, and so the language may vary from bridi to bridi, and if not specified in a particular bridi, no assumption can safely be made about its value.

To cancel stickiness, use the form *BAI ki ku*, which stops any modal value for the specified BAI from being passed to the next bridi. To cancel stickiness for all modals simultaneously, and also for any sticky tenses that exist (*ki* is used for both modals and tenses), use *ki* by itself, either before the selbri or (in the form *ki ku*) anywhere in the bridi:

Example 9.90

| mi | ki | tavla |

I speak (no implication about language or compulsion).

Note: Modals made with *fi'o*-plus-selbri cannot be made sticky. This is an unfortunate, but unavoidable, restriction.

9.15 Logical and non-logical connection of modals

Logical and non-logical connectives are explained in detail in Chapter 14 (p. 317). For the purposes of this chapter, it suffices to point out that a logical (or non-logical) connection between two bridi which differ only in a modal can be reduced to a single bridi with a connective between the modals. As a result, Example 9.91 (p. 202) and Example 9.92 (p. 202) mean the same thing:

Example 9.91

la	frank.	bajra	seka'a	le	zdani
That-named	Frank	runs	with-destination	the	house.

.ije	la	frank.	bajra	teka'a	le	zdani
And	that-named	Frank	runs	with-origin	the	house.

Frank runs to the house, and Frank runs from the house.

Example 9.92

la	frank.	bajra	seka'a
That-named	Frank	runs	with-destination

je	teka'a	le	zdani
and	with-origin	the	house.

Frank runs to and from the house.

Neither example implies whether a single act, or two acts, of running is referred to. To compel the sentence to refer to a single act of running, you can use the form:

Example 9.93

la	frank.	bajra	seka'a	le	zdani
That-named	Frank	runs	with-destination	the	house

ce'e	teka'a	le	zdani
[joined-to]	with-origin	the	house.

The cmavo *ce'e* creates a termset containing two terms (termsets are explained in Chapter 14 (p. 317) and Chapter 16 (p. 375)). When a termset contains more than one modal tag derived from a single BAI, the convention is that the two tags are derived from a common event.

9.16 CV'V cmavo of selma'o BAI with irregular forms

There are 65 cmavo of selma'o BAI, of which all but one (*do'e*, discussed in Section 9.6 (p. 188)), are derived directly from selected gismu. Of these 64 cmavo, 36 are entirely regular and have the form CV'V, where C is the first consonant of the corresponding gismu, and the Vs are the two vowels of the gismu. The remaining BAI cmavo, which are irregular in one way or another, are listed in the table below. The table is divided into sub-tables according to the nature of the exception; some cmavo appear in more than one sub-table, and are so noted.

Table 9.1. Monosyllables of the form CVV

cmavo	gismu	comments
bai	bapli	
bau	bangu	
cau	claxu	
fau	fasnu	
gau	gasnu	
kai	ckaji	uses 2nd consonant of gismu
mau	zmadu	uses 2nd consonant of gismu
koi	korbi	
rai	traji	uses 2nd consonant of gismu
sau	sarcu	
tai	tamsmi	based on lujvo, not gismu
zau	zanru	

Table 9.2. Second consonant of the gismu as the C: (the gismu is always of the form CCVCV)

ga'a	zgana	
kai	ckaji	has CVV form (monosyllable)
ki'i	ckini	
la'u	klani	has irregular 2nd V
le'a	klesi	has irregular 2nd V
mau	zmadu	has CVV form (monosyllable)
me'e	cmene	
ra'a	srana	
ra'i	krasi	
rai	traji	has CVV form (monosyllable)
ti'i	stidi	
tu'i	stuzi	

Table 9.3. Irregular 2nd V

fi'e	finti	
la'u	klani	uses 2nd consonant of gismu
le'a	klesi	uses 2nd consonant of gismu
ma'e	marji	
mu'u	mupli	
ti'u	tcika	
va'o	vanbi	

Table 9.4. Special cases

ri'i	lifri	uses 3rd consonant of gismu
tai	tamsmi	based on lujvo, not gismu
va'u	xamgu	CV'V cmavo can't begin with x

9.17 Complete table of BAI cmavo with rough English equivalents

The following table shows all the cmavo belonging to selma'o BAI, and has five columns. The first column is the cmavo itself; the second column is the gismu linked to it. The third column gives an English phrase which indicates the meaning of the cmavo; and the fourth column indicates its meaning when preceded by *se*.

For those cmavo with meaningful *te*, *ve*, and even *xe* conversions (depending on the number of places of the underlying gismu), the meanings of these are shown on one or two extra rows following the primary row for that cmavo.

It should be emphasized that the place structures of the gismu control the meanings of the BAI cmavo. The English phrases shown here are only suggestive, and are often too broad or too narrow to correctly specify what the acceptable range of uses for the modal tag are.

ba'i	basti	replaced by	instead of		
bai	bapli	compelled by	compelling		
bau	bangu	in language	in language of		
be'i	benji	sent by	transmitting	sent to	with transmit origin	transmitted via
ca'i	catni	by authority of	with authority over		
cau	claxu	lacked by	without		
ci'e	ciste	in system	with system function	of system components	
ci'o	cinmo	felt by	feeling emotion		

203

ci'u	ckilu	on the scale	on scale measuring		
cu'u	cusku	as said by	expressing	as told to	expressed in medium
de'i	detri	dated	on the same date as		
di'o	diklo	at the locus of	at specific locus		
do'e	-----	vaguely related to			
du'i	dunli	as much as	equal to		
du'o	djuno	according to	knowing facts	knowing about	under epistemology
fa'e	fatne	reverse of	in reversal of		
fau	*fasnu*	in the event of			
fi'e	finti	created by	creating work	created for purpose	
ga'a	zgana	to observer	observing	observed by means	observed under conditions
gau	gasnu	with agent	as agent in doing		
ja'e	jalge	resulting in	results because of		
ja'i	javni	by rule	by rule prescribing		
ji'e	jimte	up to limit	as a limit of		
ji'o	jitro	under direction	controlling		
ji'u	jicmu	based on	supporting		
ka'a	klama	gone to by	with destination	with origin	via route	by transport mode
ka'i	krati	represented by	on behalf of		
kai	ckaji	characterizing	with property		
ki'i	ckini	as relation of	related to	with relation	
ki'u	krinu	justified by	with justified result		
koi	korbi	bounded by	as boundary of	bordering	
ku'u	kulnu	in culture	in culture of		
la'u	klani	as quantity of	in quantity		
le'a	klesi	in category	as category of	defined by quality	
li'e	lidne	led by	leading		
ma'e	marji	of material	made from material	in material form of	
ma'i	manri	in reference frame	as a standard of		

9.17 Complete table of BAI cmavo with rough English equivalents

mau	zmadu	exceeded by	more than		
me'a	mleca	undercut by	less than		
me'e	cmene	with name	as a name for		
mu'i	mukti	motivated by	motive therefore		
mu'u	mupli	exemplified by	as an example of		
ni'i	nibli	entailed by	entails		
pa'a	panra	in addition to	similar to	similar in pattern	similar by standard
pa'u	pagbu	with component	as a part of		
pi'o	pilno	used by	using tool		
po'i	porsi	in the sequence	sequenced by rule		
pu'a	pluka	pleased by	in order to please		
pu'e	pruce	by process	processing from	processing into	passing through stages
ra'a	*srana*	pertained to by	concerning		
ra'i	*krasi*	from source	as an origin of		
rai	traji	with superlative	superlative in	at extreme	superlative among
ri'a	rinka	caused by	causing		
ri'i	lifri	experienced by	experiencing		
sau	sarcu	requiring	necessarily for	necessarily under conditions	
si'u	sidju	aided by	assisting in		
ta'i	tadji	by method	as a method for		
tai	tamsmi	as a form of	in form	in form similar to	
ti'i	stidi	suggested by	suggesting	suggested to	
ti'u	tcika	with time	at the time of		
tu'i	stuzi	with site	as location of		
va'o	vanbi	under conditions	as conditions for		
va'u	xamgu	benefiting from	with beneficiary		
zau	zanru	approved by	approving		
zu'e	zukte	with actor	with means to goal	with goal	

The lujvo *tamsmi* on which *tai* is based is derived from the tanru *tarmi simsa* and has the place structure:

tamsmi x1 has form x2, similar in form to x3 in property/quality x4

This lujvo is employed because *tarmi* does not have a place structure useful for the modal's purpose.

Chapter 10
Imaginary Journeys: The Lojban Space/Time Tense System

za'o klama

10.1 Introductory

This chapter attempts to document and explain the space/time tense system of Lojban. It does not attempt to answer all questions of the form "How do I say such-and-such (an English tense) in Lojban?" Instead, it explores the Lojban tense system from the inside, attempting to educate the reader into a Lojbanic viewpoint. Once the overall system is understood and the resources that it makes available are familiar, the reader should have some hope of using appropriate tense constructs and being correctly understood.

The system of Lojban tenses presented here may seem really complex because of all the pieces and all the options; indeed, this chapter is the longest one in this book. But tense is in fact complex in every language. In your native language, the subtleties of tense are intuitive. In foreign languages, you are seldom taught the entire system until you have reached an advanced level. Lojban tenses are extremely systematic and productive, allowing you to express subtleties based on what they mean rather than on how they act similarly to English tenses. This chapter concentrates on presenting an intuitive approach to the meaning of Lojban tense words and how they may be creatively and productively combined.

What is "tense"? Historically, "tense" is the attribute of verbs in English and related languages that expresses the time of the action. In English, three tenses are traditionally recognized, conventionally called the past, the present, and the future. There are also a variety of compound tenses used in English. However, there is no simple relationship between the form of an English tense and the time actually expressed:

I go to London tomorrow.
I will go to London tomorrow.
I am going to London tomorrow.

all mean the same thing, even though the first sentence uses the present tense; the second, the future tense; and the third, a compound tense usually called "present progressive". Likewise, a newspaper headline says "JONES DIES", although it is obvious that the time referred to must be in the past. Tense is a mandatory category of English: every sentence must be marked for tense, even if in a way contrary to logic, because every main verb has a tense marker built into to it. By contrast, Lojban brivla have no implicit tense marker attached to them.

In Lojban, the concept of tense extends to every selbri, not merely the verb-like ones. In addition, tense structures provide information about location in space as well as in time. All tense information is optional in Lojban: a sentence like:

Example 10.1

mi	klama	le	zarci
I	**go-to**	**the**	**market.**

can be understood as:

I went to the market.
I am going to the market.
I have gone to the market.
I will go to the market.
I continually go to the market.

as well as many other possibilities: context resolves which is correct.

The placement of a tense construct within a Lojban bridi is easy: right before the selbri. It goes immediately after the *cu*, and can in fact always replace the *cu* (although in very complex sentences the rules for eliding terminators may be changed as a result). In the following examples, *pu* is the tense marker for "past time":

Example 10.2

mi	cu	pu	klama	le	zarci
mi		pu	klama	le	zarci
I		**in-the-past**	**go-to**	**the**	**market.**

I went to the market.

It is also possible to put the tense somewhere else in the bridi by adding *ku* after it. This *ku* is an elidable terminator, but it's almost never possible to actually elide it except at the end of the bridi:

Example 10.3

puku	mi	klama	le	zarci
In-the-past	**I**	**go-to**	**the**	**market.**

Earlier, I went to the market.

Example 10.4

mi	klama	puku	le	zarci
I	**go-to**	**in-the-past**	**the**	**market.**

I went earlier to the market.

Example 10.5

mi	klama	le	zarci	pu	[ku]
I	**go-to**	**the**	**market**	**in-the-past.**	

I went to the market earlier.

208

Example 10.2 (p. 208) through Example 10.5 (p. 208) are different only in emphasis. Abnormal order, such as Example 10.3 (p. 208) through Example 10.5 (p. 208) exhibit, adds emphasis to the words that have been moved; in this case, the tense cmavo *pu*. Words at either end of the sentence tend to be more noticeable.

10.2 Spatial tenses: FAhA and VA

The following cmavo are discussed in this section:

vi	VA	short distance
va	VA	medium distance
vu	VA	long distance
zu'a	FAhA	left
ri'u	FAhA	right
ga'u	FAhA	up
ni'a	FAhA	down
ca'u	FAhA	front
ne'i	FAhA	within
be'a	FAhA	north of

(The complete list of FAhA cmavo can be found in Section 10.27 (p. 244).)

Why is this section about spatial tenses rather than the more familiar time tenses of Section 10.1 (p. 207), asks the reader? Because the model to be used in explaining both will be easier to grasp for space than for time. The explanation of time tenses will resume in Section 10.4 (p. 211).

English doesn't have mandatory spatial tenses. Although there are plenty of ways in English of showing where an event happens, there is absolutely no need to do so. Considering this fact may give the reader a feel for what the optional Lojban time tenses are like. From the Lojban point of view, space and time are interchangeable, although they are not treated identically.

Lojban specifies the spatial tense of a bridi (the place at which it occurs) by using words from selma'o FAhA and VA to describe an imaginary journey from the speaker to the place referred to. FAhA cmavo specify the direction taken in the journey, whereas VA cmavo specify the distance gone. For example:

Example 10.6

le	nanmu	va	batci	le	gerku
The	man	[medium-distance]	bites	the	dog.

Over there the man is biting the dog.

What is at a medium distance? The event referred to by the bridi: the man biting the dog. What is this event at a medium distance from? The speaker's location. We can understand the *va* as saying: "If you want to get from the speaker's location to the location of the bridi, journey for a medium distance (in some direction unspecified)." This "imaginary journey" can be used to understand not only Example 10.6 (p. 209), but also every other spatial tense construct.

Suppose you specify a direction with a FAhA cmavo, rather than a distance with a VA cmavo:

Example 10.7

le	nanmu	zu'a	batci	le	gerku
The	man	[left]	bites	the	dog.

Here the imaginary journey is again from the speaker's location to the location of the bridi, but it is now performed by going to the left (in the speaker's reference frame) for an unspecified distance. So a reasonable translation is:

To my left, the man bites the dog.

The "my" does not have an explicit equivalent in the Lojban, because the speaker's location is understood as the starting point.

(Etymologically, by the way, *zu'a* is derived from *zunle*, the gismu for "left", whereas *vi*, *va*, and *vu* are intended to be reminiscent of *ti*, *ta*, and *tu*, the demonstrative pronouns "this-here", "that-there", and "that-yonder".)

209

What about specifying both a direction and a distance? The rule here is that the direction must come before the distance:

Example 10.8

le	nanmu	zu'avi		batci	le	gerku
The	man	[left-short-distance]		bites	the	dog.

Slightly to my left, the man bites the dog.

As explained in Section 10.1 (p. 207), it would be perfectly correct to use *ku* to move this tense to the beginning or the end of the sentence to emphasize it:

Example 10.9

zu'aviku		le	nanmu	cu	batci	le	gerku
[Left-short-distance]		the	man		bites	the	dog.

Slightly to my left, the man bites the dog.

10.3 Compound spatial tenses

Humph, says the reader: this talk of "imaginary journeys" is all very well, but what's the point of it? – *zu'a* means "on the left" and *vi* means "nearby", and there's no more to be said. The imaginary-journey model becomes more useful when so-called compound tenses are involved. A compound tense is exactly like a simple tense, but has several FAhAs run together:

Example 10.10

le	nanmu	ga'u	zu'a	batci	le	gerku
The	man	[up]	[left]	bites	the	dog.

The proper interpretation of Example 10.10 (p. 210) is that the imaginary journey has two stages: first move from the speaker's location upward, and then to the left. A translation might read:

Left of a place above me, the man bites the dog.

(Perhaps the speaker is at the bottom of a manhole, and the dog-biting is going on at the edge of the street.)

In the English translation, the keywords "left" and "above" occur in reverse order to the Lojban order. This effect is typical of what happens when we "unfold" Lojban compound tenses into their English equivalents, and shows why it is not very useful to try to memorize a list of Lojban tense constructs and their colloquial English equivalents.

The opposite order also makes sense:

Example 10.11

le	nanmu	zu'a	ga'u	batci	le	gerku
The	man	[left]	[up]	bites	the	dog.

Above a place to the left of me, the man bites the dog.

In ordinary space, the result of going up and then to the left is the same as that of going left and then up, but such a simple relationship does not apply in all environments or to all directions: going south, then east, then north may return one to the starting point, if that point is the North Pole.

Each direction can have a distance following:

Example 10.12

le	nanmu	zu'avi		ga'u	vu		batci	le	gerku
The	man	[left-short-distance]		[up]	[long-distance]		bites	the	dog.

Far above a place slightly to the left of me, the man bites the dog.

A distance can also come at the beginning of the tense construct, without any specified direction. (Example 10.6 (p. 209), with VA alone, is really a special case of this rule when no directions at all follow.)

Example 10.13

le	nanmu	vi		zu'a	batci	le	gerku
The	man	[short-distance]		[left]	bites	the	dog.

Left of a place near me, the man bites the dog.

Any number of directions may be used in a compound tense, with or without specified distances for each:

Example 10.14

le	nanmu	ca'u	vi	ni'a	va	ri'u	vu
The	man	[front]	[short]	[down]	[medium]	[right]	[long]
ne'i	batci	le	gerku				
[within]	bites	the	dog.				

Within a place a long distance to the right of a place which is a medium distance downward from a place a short distance in front of me, the man bites the dog.

Whew! It's a good thing tense constructs are optional: having to say all that could certainly be painful. Note, however, how much shorter the Lojban version of Example 10.14 (p. 211) is than the English version.

10.4 Temporal tenses: PU and ZI

The following cmavo are discussed in this section:

pu	PU	past
ca	PU	present
ba	PU	future
zi	ZI	short time distance
za	ZI	medium time distance
zu	ZI	long time distance

Now that the reader understands spatial tenses, there are only two main facts to understand about temporal tenses: they work exactly like the spatial tenses, with selma'o PU and ZI standing in for FAhA and VA; and when both spatial and temporal tense cmavo are given in a single tense construct, the temporal tense is expressed first. (If space could be expressed before or after time at will, then certain constructions would be ambiguous.)

Example 10.15

le	nanmu	pu	batci	le	gerku
The	man	[past]	bites	the	dog.

The man bit the dog.

means that to reach the dog-biting, you must take an imaginary journey through time, moving towards the past an unspecified distance. (Of course, this journey is even more imaginary than the ones talked about in the previous sections, since time-travel is not an available option.)

Lojban recognizes three temporal directions: *pu* for the past, *ca* for the present, and *ba* for the future. (Etymologically, these derive from the corresponding gismu *purci*, *cabna*, and *balvi*. See Section 10.23 (p. 240) for an explanation of the exact relationship between the cmavo and the gismu.) There are many more spatial directions, since there are FAhA cmavo for both absolute and relative directions as well as "direction-like relationships" like "surrounding", "within", "touching", etc. (See Section 10.27 (p. 244) for a complete list.) But there are really only two directions in time: forward and backward, toward the future and toward the past. Why, then, are there three cmavo of selma'o PU?

The reason is that tense is subjective: human beings perceive space and time in a way that does not necessarily agree with objective measurements. We have a sense of "now" which includes part of the objective past and part of the objective future, and so we naturally segment the time line into three parts. The Lojban design recognizes this human reality by providing a separate time-direction cmavo for the "zero direction", Similarly, there is a FAhA cmavo for the zero space direction: *bu'u*, which means something like "coinciding".

(Technical note for readers conversant with relativity theory: The Lojban time tenses reflect time as seen by the speaker, who is assumed to be a "point-like observer" in the relativistic sense: they do not say anything about physical relationships of relativistic interval, still less about implicit causality. The nature of tense is not only subjective but also observer-based.)

Here are some examples of temporal tenses:

Example 10.16

le	nanmu	puzi		batci	le	gerku
The	man	[past-short-distance]		bites	the	dog.

A short time ago, the man bit the dog.

Example 10.17

le	nanmu	pu	pu	batci	le	gerku
The	man	[past]	[past]	bites	the	dog.

Earlier than an earlier time than now, the man bit the dog.
The man had bitten the dog.
The man had been biting the dog.

Example 10.18

le	nanmu	ba	puzi	batci	le	gerku
The	man	[future]	[past-short]	bites	the	dog.

Shortly earlier than some time later than now, the man will bite the dog.
Soon before then, the man will have bitten the dog.
The man will have just bitten the dog.
The man will just have been biting the dog.

What about the analogue of an initial VA without a direction? Lojban does allow an initial ZI with or without following PUs:

Example 10.19

le	nanmu	zi	pu	batci	le	gerku
The	man	[short]	[past]	bites	the	dog.

Before a short time from or before now, the man bit or will bite the dog.

Example 10.20

le	nanmu	zu		batci	le	gerku
The	man	[long]		bites	the	dog.

A long time from or before now, the man will bite or bit the dog.

Example 10.19 (p. 212) and Example 10.20 (p. 212) are perfectly legitimate, but may not be very much used: *zi* by itself signals an event that happens at a time close to the present, but without saying whether it is in the past or the future. A rough translation might be "about now, but not exactly now".

Because we can move in any direction in space, we are comfortable with the idea of events happening in an unspecified space direction ("nearby" or "far away"), but we live only from past to future, and the idea of an event which happens "nearby in time" is a peculiar one. Lojban provides lots of such possibilities that don't seem all that useful to English-speakers, even though you can put them together productively; this fact may be a limitation of English.

Finally, here are examples which combine temporal and spatial tense:

Example 10.21

le	nanmu	puzu	vu	batci	le	gerku
The	man	[past-long-time]	[long-space]	bites	the	dog.

Long ago and far away, the man bit the dog.

Alternatively,

Example 10.22

le	nanmu	cu	batci	le	gerku	puzuvuku
The	man		bites	the	dog	[past-long-time-long-space].

The man bit the dog long ago and far away.

10.5 Interval sizes: VEhA and ZEhA

The following cmavo are discussed in this section:

ve'i	VEhA	short space interval
ve'a	VEhA	medium space interval
ve'u	VEhA	long space interval
ze'i	ZEhA	short time interval
ze'a	ZEhA	medium time interval
ze'u	ZEhA	long time interval

So far, we have considered only events that are usually thought of as happening at a particular point in space and time: a man biting a dog at a specified place and time. But Lojbanic events may be much more "spread out" than that: *mi vasxu* (I breathe) is something which is true during the whole of my life from birth to death, and over the entire part of the earth where I spend my life. The cmavo of VEhA (for space) and ZEhA (for time) can be added to any of the tense constructs we have already studied to specify the size of the space or length of the time over which the bridi is claimed to be true.

Example 10.23

le	verba	ve'i		cadzu	le	bisli
The	child	[small-space-interval]		walks-on	the	ice.

In a small space, the child walks on the ice.
The child walks about a small area of the ice.

means that her walking was done in a small area. Like the distances, the interval sizes are classified only roughly as "small, medium, large", and are relative to the context: a small part of a room might be a large part of a table in that room.

Here is an example using a time interval:

Example 10.24

le	verba	ze'a		cadzu	le	bisli
The	child	[medium-time-interval]		walks-on	the	ice.

For a medium time, the child walks/walked/will walk on the ice.

Note that with no time direction word, Example 10.24 (p. 213) does not say when the walking happened: that would be determined by context. It is possible to specify both directions or distances and an interval, in which case the interval always comes afterward:

Example 10.25

le	verba	pu	ze'a		cadzu	le	bisli
The	child	[past]	[medium-time-interval]		walks-on	the	ice.

For a medium time, the child walked on the ice.
The child walked on the ice for a while.

In Example 10.25 (p. 213), the relationship of the interval to the specified point in time or space is indeterminate. Does the interval start at the point, end at the point, or is it centered on the point? By adding an additional direction cmavo after the interval, this question can be conclusively answered:

Example 10.26

mi	ca	ze'ica	cusku	dei
I	[present]	[short-time-interval-present]	express	this-utterance.

I am now saying this sentence.

means that for an interval starting a short time in the past and extending to a short time in the future, I am expressing the utterance which is Example 10.26 (p. 214). Of course, "short" is relative, as always in tenses. Even a long sentence takes up only a short part of a whole day; in a geological context, the era of *Homo sapiens* would only be a *ze'i* interval.

By contrast,

Example 10.27

mi	ca	ze'ipu	cusku	dei
I	[present]	[short-time-interval-past]	express	this-utterance.

I have just been saying this sentence.

means that for a short time interval extending from the past to the present I have been expressing Example 10.27 (p. 214). Here the imaginary journey starts at the present, lays down one end point of the interval, moves into the past, and lays down the other endpoint. Another example:

Example 10.28

mi	pu	ze'aba	citka	le	mi	sanmi
I	[past]	[medium-time-interval-future]	eat	the	of-me	meal.

For a medium time afterward, I ate my meal.
I ate my meal for a while.

With *ca* instead of *ba*, Example 10.28 (p. 214) becomes Example 10.29 (p. 214),

Example 10.29

mi	pu	ze'aca	citka	le	mi	sanmi
I	[past]	[medium-time-interval-present]	eat	the	of-me	meal.

For a medium time before and afterward, I ate my meal.
I ate my meal for a while.

because the interval would then be centered on the past moment rather than oriented toward the future of that moment. The colloquial English translations are the same – English is not well-suited to representing this distinction.

Here are some examples of the use of space intervals with and without specified directions:

Example 10.30

ta	ri'u	ve'i	finpe
That-there	[right]	[short-space-interval]	is-a-fish.

That thing on my right is a fish.

In Example 10.30 (p. 214), there is no equivalent in the colloquial English translation of the "small interval" which the fish occupies. Neither the Lojban nor the English expresses the orientation of the fish. Compare Example 10.31 (p. 214):

Example 10.31

ta	ri'u	ve'ica'u	finpe
That-there	[right]	[short-space-interval-front]	is-a-fish.

That thing on my right extending forwards is a fish.

Here the space interval occupied by the fish extends from a point on my right to another point in front of the first point.

10.6 Vague intervals and non-specific tenses

What is the significance of failing to specify an interval size of the type discussed in Section 10.5 (p. 213)? The Lojban rule is that if no interval size is given, the size of the space or time interval is left vague by the speaker. For example:

Example 10.32

mi	pu	klama	le	zarci
I	[past]	go-to	the	market.

really means:

At a moment in the past, and possibly other moments as well, the event "I went to the market" was in progress.

The vague or unspecified interval contains an instant in the speaker's past. However, there is no indication whether or not the whole interval is in the speaker's past! It is entirely possible that the interval during which the going-to-the-market is happening stretches into the speaker's present or even future.

Example 10.32 (p. 215) points up a fundamental difference between Lojban tenses and English tenses. An English past-tense sentence like "I went to the market" generally signifies that the going-to-the-market is entirely in the past; that is, that the event is complete at the time of speaking. Lojban *pu* has no such implication.

This property of a past tense is sometimes called "aorist", in reference to a similar concept in the tense system of Classical Greek. All of the Lojban tenses have the same property, however:

Example 10.33

le	tricu	ba	crino
The	tree	[future]	is-green.

The tree will be green.

does not imply (as the colloquial English translation does) that the tree is not green now. The vague interval throughout which the tree is, in fact, green may have already started.

This general principle does not mean that Lojban has no way of indicating that a tree will be green but is not yet green. Indeed, there are several ways of expressing that concept: see Section 10.10 (p. 219) (event contours) and Section 10.20 (p. 237) (logical connection between tenses).

10.7 Dimensionality: VIhA

The following cmavo are discussed in this section:

vi'i	VIhA	on a line
vi'a	VIhA	in an area
vi'u	VIhA	through a volume
vi'e	VIhA	throughout a space/time interval

The cmavo of ZEhA are sufficient to express time intervals. One fundamental difference between space and time, however, is that space is multi-dimensional. Sometimes we want to say not only that something moves over a small interval, but also perhaps that it moves in a line. Lojban allows for this. I can specify that a motion "in a small space" is more specifically "in a short line", "in a small area", or "through a small volume".

What about the child walking on the ice in Example 10.23 (p. 213) through Example 10.25 (p. 213)? Given the nature of ice, probably the area interpretation is most sensible. I can make this assumption explicit with the appropriate member of selma'o VIhA:

Example 10.34

le	verba	ve'a	vi'a	cadzu	le	bisli
The	child	[medium-space-interval]	[2-dimensional]	walks-on	the	ice.

In a medium-sized area, the child walks on the ice.

Space intervals can contain either VEhA or VIhA or both, but if both, VEhA must come first, as Example 10.34 (p. 215) shows.

The reader may wish to raise a philosophical point here. (Readers who don't wish to, should skip this paragraph.) The ice may be two-dimensional, or more accurately its surface may be, but since the child is three-dimensional, her walking must also be. The subjective nature of Lojban tense comes to the rescue here: the action is essentially planar, and the third dimension of height is simply irrelevant to walking. Even walking on a mountain could be called *vi'a*, because relatively speaking the mountain is associated with an essentially two-dimensional surface. Motion which is not confined to such a surface (e.g., flying, or walking through a three-dimensional network of tunnels, or climbing among mountains rather than on a single mountain) would be properly described with *vi'u*. So the cognitive, rather than the physical, dimensionality controls the choice of VIhA cmavo.

VIhA has a member *vi'e* which indicates a 4-dimensional interval, one that involves both space and time. This allows the spatial tenses to invade, to some degree, the temporal tenses; it is possible to make statements about space-time considered as an Einsteinian whole. (There are presently no cmavo of FAhA assigned to "pastward" and "futureward" considered as space rather than time directions – they could be added, though, if Lojbanists find space-time expression useful.) If a temporal tense cmavo is used in the same tense construct with a *vi'e* interval, the resulting tense may be self-contradictory.

10.8 Movement in space: MOhI

The following cmavo is discussed in this section:

| mo'i | MOhI | movement flag |

All the information carried by the tense constructs so far presented has been presumed to be static: the bridi is occurring somewhere or other in space and time, more or less remote from the speaker. Suppose the truth of the bridi itself depends on the result of a movement, or represents an action being done while the speaker is moving? This too can be represented by the tense system, using the cmavo *mo'i* (of selma'o MOhI) plus a spatial direction and optional distance; the direction now refers to a direction of motion rather than a static direction from the speaker.

Example 10.35

le	verba	mo'i	ri'u	cadzu	le	bisli
The	child	[movement]	[right]	walks-on	the	ice.

The child walks toward my right on the ice.

This is quite different from:

Example 10.36

le	verba	ri'u	cadzu	le	bisli
The	child	[right]	walks-on	the	ice.

To the right of me, the child walks on the ice.

In either case, however, the reference frame for defining "right" and "left" is the speaker's, not the child's. This can be changed thus:

Example 10.37

le	verba	mo'i	ri'u	cadzu	le	bisli
The	child	[movement]	[right]	walks-on	the	ice

ma'i		vo'a
in-reference-frame		the-x1-place.

The child walks toward her right on the ice.

Example 10.37 (p. 216) is analogous to Example 10.35 (p. 216). The cmavo *ma'i* belongs to selma'o BAI (explained in Section 9.6 (p. 188)), and allows specifying a reference frame.

Both a regular and a *mo'i*-flagged spatial tense can be combined, with the *mo'i* construct coming last:

Example 10.38

le	verba	zu'avu	mo'i	ri'uvi	cadzu	le	bisli
The	child	[left-long]	[movement]	[right-short]	walks-on	the	ice.

Far to the left of me, the child walks a short distance toward my right on the ice.

It is not grammatical to use multiple directions like *zu'a ca'u* after *mo'i*, but complex movements can be expressed in a separate bridi.

Here is an example of a movement tense on a bridi not inherently involving movement:

Example 10.39

mi	mo'i	ca'uvu	citka	le	mi	sanmi
I	[movement]	[front-long]	eat	the	associated-with-me	meal.

While moving a long way forward, I eat my meal.

(Perhaps I am eating in an airplane.)

There is no parallel facility in Lojban at present for expressing movement in time – time travel – but one could be added easily if it ever becomes useful.

10.9 Interval properties: TAhE and *roi*

The following cmavo are discussed in this section:

di'i	TAhE	regularly
na'o	TAhE	typically
ru'i	TAhE	continuously
ta'e	TAhE	habitually
di'inai	TAhE	irregularly
na'onai	TAhE	atypically
ru'inai	TAhE	intermittently
ta'enai	TAhE	contrary to habit
roi	ROI	"n" times
roinai	ROI	other than "n" times
ze'e	ZEhA	whole time interval
ve'e	VEhA	whole space interval

Consider Lojban bridi which express events taking place in time. Whether a very short interval (a point) or a long interval of time is involved, the event may not be spread consistently throughout that interval. Lojban can use the cmavo of selma'o TAhE to express the idea of continuous or non-continuous actions.

Example 10.40

mi	puzu	ze'u	velckule
I	[past-long-distance]	[long-interval]	am-a-school-attendee (pupil).

Long ago I attended school for a long time.

probably does not mean that I attended school continuously throughout the whole of that long-ago interval. Actually, I attended school every day, except for school holidays. More explicitly,

Example 10.41

mi	puzu	ze'u	di'i	velckule
I	[past-long-distance]	[long-interval]	[regularly]	am-a-pupil.

Long ago I regularly attended school for a long time.

The four TAhE cmavo are differentiated as follows: *ru'i* covers the entirety of the interval, *di'i* covers the parts of the interval which are systematically spaced subintervals; *na'o* covers part of the interval, but exactly which part is determined by context; *ta'e* covers part of the interval, selected with reference to the behavior of the actor (who often, but not always, appears in the x1 place of the bridi).

Using TAhE does not require being so specific. Either the time direction or the time interval or both may be omitted (in which case they are vague). For example:

Example 10.42

mi	ba	ta'e	klama	le	zarci
I	[future]	[habitually]	go-to	the	market.
I	will	habitually	go to	the	market.

I will make a habit of going to the market.

specifies the future, but the duration of the interval is indefinite. Similarly,

Example 10.43

mi	na'o	klama	le	zarci
I	[typically]	go-to	the	market.

I typically go/went/will go to the market.

illustrates an interval property in isolation. There are no distance or direction cmavo, so the point of time is vague; likewise, there is no interval cmavo, so the length of the interval during which these goings-to-the-market take place is also vague. As always, context will determine these vague values.

"Intermittently" is the polar opposite notion to "continuously", and is expressed not with its own cmavo, but by adding the negation suffix -nai (which belongs to selma'o NAI) to ru'i. For example:

Example 10.44

le	verba	ru'inai	cadzu	le	bisli
The	child	[continuously-not]	walks-on	the	ice.

The child intermittently walks on the ice.

As shown in the cmavo table above, all the cmavo of TAhE may be negated with -nai; ru'inai and di'inai are probably the most useful.

An intermittent event can also be specified by counting the number of times during the interval that it takes place. The cmavo roi (which belongs to selma'o ROI) can be appended to a number to make a quantified tense. Quantified tenses are common in English, but not so commonly named: they are exemplified by the adverbs "never", "once", "twice", "thrice", ... "always", and by the related phrases "many times", "a few times", "too many times", and so on. All of these are handled in Lojban by a number plus -roi:

Example 10.45

mi	paroi	klama	le	zarci
I	[one-time]	go-to	the	market.

I go to the market once.

Example 10.46

mi	du'eroi	klama	le	zarci
I	[too-many-times]	go-to	the	market.

I go to the market too often.

With the quantified tense alone, we don't know whether the past, the present, or the future is intended, but of course the quantified tense need not stand alone:

Example 10.47

mi	pu	reroi	klama	le	zarci
I	[past]	[two-times]	go-to	the	market.

I went to the market twice.

The English is slightly over-specific here: it entails that both goings-to-the-market were in the past, which may or may not be true in the Lojban sentence, since the implied interval is vague. Therefore, the interval may start in the past but extend into the present or even the future.

Adding *-nai* to *roi* is also permitted, and has the meaning "other than (the number specified)":

Example 10.48

le	ratcu	reroinai	citka	le	cirla
The	rat	**[twice-not]**	**eats**	**the**	**cheese.**

The rat eats the cheese other than twice.

This may mean that the rat eats the cheese fewer times, or more times, or not at all.

It is necessary to be careful with sentences like Example 10.45 (p. 218) and Example 10.47 (p. 218), where a quantified tense appears without an interval. What Example 10.47 (p. 218) really says is that during an interval of unspecified size, at least part of which was set in the past, the event of my going to the market happened twice. The example says nothing about what happened outside that vague time interval. This is often less than we mean. If we want to nail down that I went to the market once and only once, we can use the cmavo *ze'e* which represents the "whole time interval": conceptually, an interval which stretches from time's beginning to its end:

Example 10.49

mi	ze'e	paroi	klama	le	zarci
I	**[whole-interval]**	**[once]**	**go-to**	**the**	**market.**

Since specifying no ZEhA leaves the interval vague, Example 10.47 (p. 218) might in appropriate context mean the same as Example 10.49 (p. 219) after all – but Example 10.49 (p. 219) allows us to be specific when specificity is necessary.

A PU cmavo following *ze'e* has a slightly different meaning from one that follows another ZEhA cmavo. The compound cmavo *ze'epu* signifies the interval stretching from the infinite past to the reference point (wherever the imaginary journey has taken you); *ze'eba* is the interval stretching from the reference point to the infinite future. The remaining form, *ze'eca*, makes specific the "whole of time" interpretation just given. These compound forms make it possible to assert that something has never happened without asserting that it never will.

Example 10.50

mi	ze'epu	noroi	klama	le	zarci
I	**[whole-interval-past]**	**[never]**	**go-to**	**the**	**market.**

I have never gone to the market.

says nothing about whether I might go in future.

The space equivalent of *ze'e* is *ve'e*, and it can be used in the same way with a quantified space tense: see Section 10.11 (p. 222) for an explanation of space interval modifiers.

10.10 Event contours: ZAhO and *re'u*

The following cmavo are discussed in this section:

pu'o	ZAhO	inchoative
ca'o	ZAhO	continuitive
ba'o	ZAhO	perfective
co'a	ZAhO	initiative
co'u	ZAhO	cessitive
mo'u	ZAhO	completitive
za'o	ZAhO	superfective
co'i	ZAhO	achievative
de'a	ZAhO	pausative
di'a	ZAhO	resumptive
re'u	ROI	ordinal tense

The cmavo of selma'o ZAhO express the Lojban version of what is traditionally called "aspect". This is not a notion well expressed by English tenses, but many languages (including Chinese and

Russian among Lojban's six source languages) consider it more important than the specification of mere position in time.

The "event contours" of selma'o ZAhO, with their bizarre keywords, represent the natural portions of an event considered as a process, an occurrence with an internal structure including a beginning, a middle, and an end. Since the keywords are scarcely self-explanatory, each ZAhO will be explained in detail here. Note that from the viewpoint of Lojban syntax, ZAhOs are interval modifiers like TAhEs or ROI compounds; if both are found in a single tense, the TAhE/ROI comes first and the ZAhO afterward. The imaginary journey described by other tense cmavo moves us to the portion of the event-as-process which the ZAhO specifies.

It is important to understand that ZAhO cmavo, unlike the other tense cmavo, specify characteristic portions of the event, and are seen from an essentially timeless perspective. The "beginning" of an event is the same whether the event is in the speaker's present, past, or future. It is especially important not to confuse the speaker-relative viewpoint of the PU tenses with the event-relative viewpoint of the ZAhO tenses.

The cmavo *pu'o*, *ca'o*, and *ba'o* (etymologically derived from the PU cmavo) refer to an event that has not yet begun, that is in progress, or that has ended, respectively:

Example 10.51

mi	pu'o	damba
I	[inchoative]	fight.

I'm on the verge of fighting.

Example 10.52

la	stiv.	ca'o	bacru
That-named	Steve	[continuitive]	utters.

Steve continues to talk.

Example 10.53

le	verba	ba'o	cadzu	le	bisli
The	child	[perfective]	walks-on	the	ice.

The child is finished walking on the ice.

As discussed in Section 10.6 (p. 215), the simple PU cmavo make no assumptions about whether the scope of a past, present, or future event extends into one of the other tenses as well. Example 10.51 (p. 220) through Example 10.53 (p. 220) illustrate that these ZAhO cmavo do make such assumptions possible: the event in Example 10.51 (p. 220) has not yet begun, definitively; likewise, the event in Example 10.53 (p. 220) is definitely over.

Note that in Example 10.51 (p. 220) and Example 10.53 (p. 220), *pu'o* and *ba'o* may appear to be reversed: *pu'o*, although etymologically connected with *pu*, is referring to a future event; whereas *ba'o*, connected with *ba*, is referring to a past event. This is the natural result of the event-centered view of ZAhO cmavo. The inchoative, or *pu'o*, part of an event, is in the "pastward" portion of that event, when seen from the perspective of the event itself. It is only by inference that we suppose that Example 10.51 (p. 220) refers to the speaker's future: in fact, no PU tense is given, so the inchoative part of the event need not be coincident with the speaker's present: *pu'o* is not necessarily, though in fact often is, the same as *ca pu'o*.

The cmavo in Example 10.51 (p. 220) through Example 10.53 (p. 220) refer to spans of time. There are also two points of time that can be usefully associated with an event: the beginning, marked by *co'a*, and the end, marked by *co'u*. Specifically, *co'a* marks the boundary between the *pu'o* and *ca'o* parts of an event, and *co'u* marks the boundary between the *ca'o* and *ba'o* parts:

Example 10.54

mi	ba	co'a	citka	le	mi	sanmi
I	[future]	[initiative]	eat	the	associated-with-me	meal.

I will begin to eat my meal.

Example 10.55

mi	pu	co'u	citka	le	mi	sanmi
I	[past]	[cessitive]	eat	the	associated-with-me	meal.

I ceased eating my meal.

Compare Example 10.54 (p. 220) with:

Example 10.56

mi	ba	di'i	co'a	bajra
I	[future]	[regularly]	[initiative]	run.

I will regularly begin to run.

which illustrates the combination of a TAhE with a ZAhO.

A process can have two end points, one reflecting the "natural end" (when the process is complete) and the other reflecting the "actual stopping point" (whether complete or not). Example 10.55 (p. 221) may be contrasted with:

Example 10.57

mi	pu	mo'u	citka	le	mi	sanmi
I	[past]	[completitive]	eat	the	associated-with-me	meal.

I finished eating my meal.

In Example 10.57 (p. 221), the meal has reached its natural end; in Example 10.55 (p. 221), the meal has merely ceased, without necessarily reaching its natural end.

A process such as eating a meal does not necessarily proceed uninterrupted. If it is interrupted, there are two more relevant point events: the point just before the interruption, marked by *de'a*, and the point just after the interruption, marked by *di'a*. Some examples:

Example 10.58

mi	pu	de'a	citka	le	mi	sanmi
I	[past]	[pausative]	eat	the	associated-with-me	meal.

I stopped eating my meal (with the intention of resuming).

Example 10.59

mi	ba	di'a	citka	le	mi	sanmi
I	[future]	[resumptive]	eat	the	associated-with-me	meal.

I will resume eating my meal.

In addition, it is possible for a process to continue beyond its natural end. The span of time between the natural and the actual end points is represented by *za'o*:

Example 10.60

le	ctuca	pu	za'o	ciksi
The	teacher	[past]	[superfective]	explained

le	cmaci	seldanfu	le	tadgri
the	mathematics	problem	to-the	student-group.

The teacher kept on explaining the mathematics problem to the class too long.

That is, the teacher went on explaining after the class already understood the problem.

An entire event can be treated as a single moment using the cmavo *co'i*:

Example 10.61

la	djan.	pu	co'i	catra	la	djim
That-named	John	[past]	[achievative]	kills	that-named	Jim.

John was at the point in time where he killed Jim.

Finally, since an activity is cyclical, an individual cycle can be referred to using a number followed by *re'u*, which is the other cmavo of selma'o ROI:

Example 10.62

mi	pare'u	klama	le	zarci
I	[first-time]	go-to	the	store.

I go to the store for the first time (within a vague interval).

Note the difference between:

Example 10.63

mi	pare'u	paroi	klama	le	zarci
I	[first-time]	[one-time]	go-to	the	store.

For the first time, I go to the store once.

and

Example 10.64

mi	paroi	pare'u	klama	le	zarci
I	[one-time]	[first-time]	go-to	the	store.

There is one occasion on which I go to the store for the first time.

10.11 Space interval modifiers: FEhE

The following cmavo is discussed in this section:

| fe'e | FEhE | space interval modifier flag |

Like time intervals, space intervals can also be continuous, discontinuous, or repetitive. Rather than having a whole separate set of selma'o for space interval properties, we instead prefix the flag *fe'e* to the cmavo used for time interval properties. A space interval property would be placed just after the space interval size and/or dimensionality cmavo:

Example 10.65

ko	vi'i	fe'e	di'i	sombo	le	gurni
You-imperative	[1-dimensional]	[space:]	[regularly]	sow	the	grain.

Sow the grain in a line and evenly!

Example 10.66

mi	fe'e	ciroi	tervecnu	lo	selsalta
I	[space:]	[three-places]	buy	those-which-are	salad-ingredients.

I buy salad ingredients in three locations.

Example 10.67

ze'e	roroi	ve'e	fe'e	roroi	ku
[whole-time]	[all-times]	[whole-space]	[space:]	[all-places]	

li	re	su'i	re	du	li	vo
The-number	2	+	2	=	the-number	4.

Always and everywhere, two plus two is four.

As shown in Example 10.67 (p. 222), when a tense comes first in a bridi, rather than in its normal position before the selbri (in this case *du*), it is emphasized.

The *fe'e* marker can also be used for the same purpose before members of ZAhO. (The cmavo *be'a* belongs to selma'o FAhA; it is the space direction meaning "north of".)

Example 10.68

tu	ve'abe'a	fe'e	co'a	rokci
That-yonder	[medium-space-interval-north]	[space]	[initiative]	is-a-rock.

That is the beginning of a rock extending to my north.
That is the south face of a rock.

Here the notion of a "beginning point" represented by the cmavo *co'a* is transferred from "beginning in time" to "beginning in space" under the influence of the *fe'e* flag. Space is not inherently oriented, unlike time, which flows from past to future: therefore, some indication of orientation is necessary, and the *ve'abe'a* provides an orientation in which the south face is the "beginning" and the north face is the "end", since the rock extends from south (near me) to north (away from me).

Many natural languages represent time by a space-based metaphor: in English, what is past is said to be "behind us". In other languages, the metaphor is reversed. Here, Lojban is representing space (or space interval modifiers) by a time-based metaphor: the choice of a FAhA cmavo following a VEhA cmavo indicates which direction is mapped onto the future. (The choice of future rather than past is arbitrary, but convenient for English-speakers.)

If both a TAhE (or ROI) and a ZAhO are present as space interval modifiers, the *fe'e* flag must be prefixed to each.

10.12 Tenses as sumti tcita

So far, we have seen tenses only just before the selbri, or (equivalently in meaning) floating about the bridi with *ku*. There is another major use for tenses in Lojban: as sumti tcita, or argument tags. A tense may be used to add spatial or temporal information to a bridi as, in effect, an additional place:

Example 10.69

mi	klama	le	zarci	ca	le	nu	do	klama
I	go-to	the	market	[present]	the	event-of	you	go-to

le	zdani
the	house.

I go to the market when you go to the house.

Here *ca* does not appear before the selbri, nor with *ku*; instead, it governs the following sumti, the *le nu* construct. What Example 10.69 (p. 223) asserts is that the action of the main bridi is happening at the same time as the event mentioned by that sumti. So *ca*, which means "now" when used with a selbri, means "simultaneously-with" when used with a sumti. Consider another example:

Example 10.70

mi	klama	le	zarci	pu	le	nu	do	pu	klama
I	go-to	the	market	[past]	the	event-of	you	[past]	go-to

le	zdani
the	house.

The second *pu* is simply the past tense marker for the event of your going to the house, and says that this event is in the speaker's past. How are we to understand the first *pu*, the sumti tcita?

All of our imaginary journeys so far have started at the speaker's location in space and time. Now we are specifying an imaginary journey that starts at a different location, namely at the event of your going to the house. Example 10.70 (p. 223) then says that my going to the market is in the past, relative not to the speaker's present moment, but instead relative to the moment when you went to the house. Example 10.70 (p. 223) can therefore be translated:
I had gone to the market before you went to the house.

(Other translations are possible, depending on the ever-present context.) Spatial direction and distance sumti tcita are exactly analogous:

Example 10.71

le	ratcu	cu	citka	le	cirla	vi		le	panka
The	rat		eats	the	cheese	[short-time-distance]		the	park.

The rat eats the cheese near the park.

Example 10.72

le	ratcu	cu	citka	le	cirla	vi		le	vu		panka
The	rat		eats	the	cheese	[short-distance]		the	[long-distance]		park

The rat eats the cheese near the faraway park.

Example 10.73

le	ratcu	cu	citka	le	cirla	vu		le	vi		panka
The	rat		eats	the	cheese	[long-distance]		the	[short-distance]		park

The rat eats the cheese far away from the nearby park.

The event contours of selma'o ZAhO (and their space equivalents, prefixed with *fe'e*) are also useful as sumti tcita. The interpretation of ZAhO tcita differs from that of FAhA, VA, PU, and ZI tcita, however. The event described in the sumti is viewed as a process, and the action of the main bridi occurs at the phase of the process which the ZAhO specifies, or at least some part of that phase. The action of the main bridi itself is seen as a point event, so that there is no issue about which phase of the main bridi is intended. For example:

Example 10.74

mi	morsi	ba'o		le	nu		mi	jmive
I	am-dead	[perfective]		the	event-of		I	live.

I die in the aftermath of my living.

Here the (point-)event of my being dead is the portion of my living-process which occurs after the process is complete. Contrast Example 10.74 (p. 224) with:

Example 10.75

mi	morsi	ba		le	nu		mi	jmive
I	am-dead	[future]		the	event-of		I	live.

As explained in Section 10.6 (p. 215), Example 10.75 (p. 224) does not exclude the possibility that I died before I ceased to live!

Likewise, we might say:

Example 10.76

mi	klama	le	zarci	pu'o		le	nu		mi	citka
I	go-to	the	store	[inchoative]		the	event-of		I	eat

which indicates that before my eating begins, I go to the store, whereas

Example 10.77

mi	klama	le	zarci	ba'o		le	nu		mi	citka
I	go-to	the	store	[perfective]		the	event-of		I	eat

would indicate that I go to the store after I am finished eating.

Here is an example which mixes temporal ZAhO (as a tense) and spatial ZAhO (as a sumti tcita):

Example 10.78

le	bloti	pu	za'o		xelklama
The	boat	[past]	[superfective]		is-a-transport-mechanism

fe'e	ba'o		le	lalxu
[space]	[perfective]		the	lake.

The boat sailed for too long and beyond the lake.

Probably it sailed up onto the dock. One point of clarification: although *xelklama* appears to mean simply "is-a-mode-of-transport", it does not – the bridi of Example 10.78 (p. 224) has four omitted arguments, and thus has the (physical) journey which goes on too long as part of its meaning.

The remaining tense cmavo, which have to do with interval size, dimension, and continuousness (or lack thereof) are interpreted to let the sumti specify the particular interval over which the main bridi operates:

Example 10.79

mi	klama	le	zarci	reroi	le	ca	djedi
I	go-to	the	market	[twice]	the	[present]	day.

I go/went/will go to the market twice today.

Be careful not to confuse a tense used as a sumti tcita with a tense used within a seltcita sumti:

Example 10.80

loi		snime	cu	carvi
Some-of-the-mass-of		snow		rains

ze'u		le	ca	dunra
[long-time-interval]		the	[present]	winter.

Snow falls during this winter.

claims that the interval specified by "this winter" is long, as events of snowfall go, whereas

Example 10.81

loi		snime	cu	carvi	ca	le	ze'u	dunra
Some-of-the-mass-of		snow		rains	[present]	the	[long-time]	winter.

Snow falls in the long winter.

claims that during some part of the winter, which is long as winters go, snow falls.

10.13 Sticky and multiple tenses: KI

The following cmavo is discussed in this section:

ki	KI	sticky tense set/reset

So far we have only considered tenses in isolated bridi. Lojban provides several ways for a tense to continue in effect over more than a single bridi. This property is known as "stickiness": the tense gets "stuck" and remains in effect until explicitly "unstuck". In the metaphor of the imaginary journey, the place and time set by a sticky tense may be thought of as a campsite or way-station: it provides a permanent origin with respect to which other tenses are understood. Later imaginary journeys start from that point rather than from the speaker.

To make a tense sticky, suffix *ki* to it:

Example 10.82

mi	puki		klama	le	zarci
I	[past-sticky]		go-to	the	market.

.i	le	nanmu	cu	batci	le	gerku
	The	man		bites	the	dog.

I went to the market. The man bit the dog.

Here the use of *puki* rather than just *pu* ensures that the tense will affect the next sentence as well. Otherwise, since the second sentence is tenseless, there would be no way of determining its tense; the event of the second sentence might happen before, after, or simultaneously with that of the first sentence.

(The last statement does not apply when the two sentences form part of a narrative. See Section 10.14 (p. 227) for an explanation of "story time", which employs a different set of conventions.)

What if the second sentence has a tense anyway?

Example 10.83

mi	puki	klama	le	zarci
I	[past-sticky]	go-to	the	market.

.i	le	nanmu	pu	batci	le	gerku
	The	man	[past]	bites	the	dog.

Here the second *pu* does not replace the sticky tense, but adds to it, in the sense that the starting point of its imaginary journey is taken to be the previously set sticky time. So the translation of Example 10.83 (p. 226) is:

Example 10.84

I went to the market. The man had earlier bitten the dog.

and it is equivalent in meaning (when considered in isolation from any other sentences) to:

Example 10.85

mi	pu	klama	le	zarci
I	[past]	go-to	the	market.

.i	le	nanmu	pupu	batci	le	gerku
	The	man	[past-past]	bites	the	dog.

The point has not been discussed so far, but it is perfectly grammatical to have more than one tense construct in a sentence:

Example 10.86

puku	mi	ba	klama	le	zarci
[past]	I	[future]	go-to	the	market.

Earlier, I was going to go to the market.

Here there are two tenses in the same bridi, the first floating free and specified by *puku*, the second in the usual place and specified by *ba*. They are considered cumulative in the same way as the two tenses in separate sentences of Example 10.85 (p. 226). Example 10.86 (p. 226) is therefore equivalent in meaning, except for emphasis, to:

Example 10.87

mi	puba	klama	le	zarci
I	[past-future]	go-to	the	market.

I was going to go to the market.

Compare Example 10.88 (p. 226) and Example 10.89 (p. 226), which have a different meaning from Example 10.86 (p. 226) and Example 10.87 (p. 226):

Example 10.88

mi	ba	klama	le	zarci	puku
I	[future]	go-to	the	market	[past].

I will have gone to the market earlier.

Example 10.89

mi	bapu	klama	le	zarci
I	[future-past]	go-to	the	market.

I will have gone to the market.

So when multiple tense constructs in a single bridi are involved, order counts – the tenses cannot be shifted around as freely as if there were only one tense to worry about.

But why bother to allow multiple tense constructs at all? They specify separate portions of the imaginary journey, and can be useful in order to make part of a tense sticky. Consider Example 10.90 (p. 227), which adds a second bridi and a *ki* to Example 10.86 (p. 226):

Example 10.90

pu	ki		ku	mi	ba	klama	le	zarci
[past]	[sticky]			I	[future]	go-to	the	market.

.i	le	nanmu	cu	batci	le	gerku
	The	man		bites	the	dog.

What is the implied tense of the second sentence? Not *puba*, but only *pu*, since only *pu* was made sticky with *ki*. So the translation is:

I was going to go to the market. The man bit the dog.

Lojban has several ways of embedding a bridi within another bridi: descriptions, abstractors, relative clauses. (Technically, descriptions contain selbri rather than bridi.) Any of the selbri of these subordinate bridi may have tenses attached. These tenses are interpreted relative to the tense of the main bridi:

Example 10.91

mi	pu	klama	le	ba'o	zarci
I	[past]	go-to	the	[perfective]	market

I went to the former market.

The significance of the *ba'o* in Example 10.91 (p. 227) is that the speaker's destination is described as being "in the aftermath of being a market"; that is, it is a market no longer. In particular, the time at which it was no longer a market is in the speaker's past, because the *ba'o* is interpreted relative to the *pu* tense of the main bridi.

Here is an example involving an abstraction bridi:

Example 10.92

mi	ca	jinvi	le	du'u	mi	ba	morsi
I	now	opine	the	fact-that	I	will-be	dead.

I now believe that I will be dead.

Here the event of being dead is said to be in the future with respect to the opinion, which is in the present.

ki may also be used as a tense by itself. This cancels all stickiness and returns the bridi and all following bridi to the speaker's location in both space and time.

In complex descriptions, multiple tenses may be saved and then used by adding a subscript to *ki*. A time made sticky with *kixipa* (ki-sub-1) can be returned to by specifying *kixipa* as a tense by itself. In the case of written expression, the writer's here-and-now is often different from the reader's, and a pair of subscripted *ki* tenses could be used to distinguish the two.

10.14 Story time

Making strict use of the conventions explained in Section 10.13 (p. 225) would be intolerably awkward when a story is being told. The time at which a story is told by the narrator is usually unimportant to the story. What matters is the flow of time within the story itself. The term "story" in this section refers to any series of statements related in more-or-less time-sequential order, not just a fictional one.

Lojban speakers use a different set of conventions, commonly called "story time", for inferring tense within a story. It is presumed that the event described by each sentence takes place some time more or less after the previous ones. Therefore, tenseless sentences are implicitly tensed as "what happens next". In particular, any sticky time setting is advanced by each sentence.

The following mini-story illustrates the important features of story time. A sentence-by-sentence explication follows:

Example 10.93

pu	zu	ki	ku	ne'i	ki	le	kevna
[past]	[long]	[sticky]	[,]	[inside]	[sticky]	the	cave,

le	ninmu	goi	ko'a	zutse	le	rokci
the	woman	defined-as	she-1	sat-on	the	rock

Long ago, in a cave, a woman sat on a rock.

Example 10.94

.i	ko'a	citka	loi	kanba	rectu
	She-1	eat-(tenseless)	some-of-the-mass-of	goat	flesh.

She was eating goat's meat.

Example 10.95

.i	ko'a	pu	jukpa	ri	le	mudyfagri
	She	[past]	cook	the-last-mentioned	by-method-the	wood-fire.

She had cooked the meat over a wood fire.

Example 10.96

.i	lei	rectu	cu	zanglare
	The-mass-of	flesh		is-(favorable)-warm.

The meat was pleasantly warm.

Example 10.97

.i	le	labno	goi	ko'e
	The	wolf	defined-as	it-2

ba	za	ki	nenri	klama	le	kevna
[future]	[medium]	[sticky]	within	came	to-the	cave.

A while later, a wolf came into the cave.

Example 10.98

.i	ko'e	lebna	lei	rectu	ko'a
	It-2	takes-(tenseless)	the-mass-of	flesh	from-her-1.

It took the meat from her.

Example 10.99

.i	ko'e	bartu	klama
	It-2	out	ran

It ran out.

Example 10.93 (p. 228) sets both the time (long ago) and the place (in a cave) using *ki*, just like the sentence sequences in Section 10.13 (p. 225). No further space cmavo are used in the rest of the story, so the place is assumed to remain unchanged. The English translation of Example 10.93 (p. 228) is marked for past tense also, as the conventions of English storytelling require: consequently, all other English translation sentences are also in the past tense. (We don't notice how strange this is; even stories about the future are written in past tense!) This conventional use of past tense is not used in Lojban narratives.

Example 10.94 (p. 228) is tenseless. Outside story time, it would be assumed that its event happens simultaneously with that of Example 10.93 (p. 228), since a sticky tense is in effect; the rules of story time, however, imply that the event occurs afterwards, and that the story time has advanced (changing the sticky time set in Example 10.93 (p. 228)).

Example 10.95 (p. 228) has an explicit tense. This is taken relative to the latest setting of the sticky time; therefore, the event of Example 10.95 (p. 228) happens before that of Example 10.94 (p. 228). It cannot be determined if Example 10.95 (p. 228) happens before or after Example 10.93 (p. 228).

Example 10.96 (p. 228) is again tenseless. Story time was not changed by the flashback in Example 10.95 (p. 228), so Example 10.96 (p. 228) happens after Example 10.94 (p. 228).

Example 10.97 (p. 228) specifies the future (relative to Example 10.96 (p. 228)) and makes it sticky. So all further events happen after Example 10.97 (p. 228).

Example 10.98 (p. 228) and Example 10.99 (p. 228) are again tenseless, and so happen after Example 10.97 (p. 228). (Story time is changed.)

So the overall order is Example 10.93 (p. 228) - Example 10.95 (p. 228) - Example 10.94 (p. 228) - Example 10.96 (p. 228) - (medium interval) - Example 10.97 (p. 228) - Example 10.98 (p. 228) - Example 10.99 (p. 228). It is also possible that Example 10.95 (p. 228) happens before Example 10.93 (p. 228).

If no sticky time (or space) is set initially, the story is set at an unspecified time (or space): the effect is like that of choosing an arbitrary reference point and making it sticky. This style is common in stories that are jokes. The same convention may be used if the context specifies the sticky time sufficiently.

10.15 Tenses in subordinate bridi

English has a set of rules, formally known as "sequence of tense rules", for determining what tense should be used in a subordinate clause, depending on the tense used in the main sentence. Here are some examples:

Example 10.100

John says that George is going to the market.

Example 10.101

John says that George went to the market.

Example 10.102

John said that George went to the market.

Example 10.103

John said that George had gone to the market.

In Example 10.100 (p. 229) and Example 10.101 (p. 229), the tense of the main sentence is the present: "says". If George goes when John speaks, we get the present tense "is going" ("goes" would be unidiomatic); if George goes before John speaks, we get the past tense "went". But if the tense of the main sentence is the past, with "said", then the tense required in the subordinate clause is different. If George goes when John speaks, we get the past tense "went"; if George goes before John speaks, we get the past-perfect tense "had gone".

The rule of English, therefore, is that both the tense of the main sentence and the tense of the subordinate clause are understood relative to the speaker of the main sentence (not John, but the person who speaks Example 10.100 (p. 229) through Example 10.103 (p. 229)).

Lojban, like Russian and Esperanto, uses a different convention. A tense in a subordinate bridi is understood to be relative to the tense already set in the main bridi. Thus Example 10.100 (p. 229) through Example 10.103 (p. 229) can be expressed in Lojban respectively thus:

Example 10.104

la	djan.	ca		cusku	le	se	du'u
	John	[present]	says	the		statement-that

la		djordj.	ca		klama	le	zarci
That-named	George	[present]	goes-to	the	market.

Example 10.105

la		djan.	ca		cusku	le	se	du'u
That-named	John	[present]	says	the		statement-that

la		djordj.	pu	klama	le	zarci
That-named	George	[past]	goes-to	the	market.

Example 10.106

la	djan.	pu	cusku	le	se	du'u
That-named	John	[past]	says	the		statement-that
la	djordj.	ca	klama	le	zarci	
That-named	George	[present]	goes-to	the	market.	

Example 10.107

la	djan.	pu	cusku	le	se	du'u
That-named	John	[past]	says	the		statement-that
la	djordj.	pu	klama	le	zarci	
That-named	George	[past]	goes-to	the	market.	

Probably the most counterintuitive of the Lojban examples is Example 10.106 (p. 230). The *ca* looks quite odd, as if George were going to the market right now, rather than back when John spoke. But this *ca* is really a *ca* with respect to a reference point specified by the outer *pu*. This behavior is the same as the additive behavior of multiple tenses in the same bridi, as explained in Section 10.13 (p. 225).

There is a special cmavo *nau* (of selma'o CUhE) which can be used to override these rules and get to the speaker's current reference point. (Yes, it sounds like English "now".) It is not grammatical to combine *nau* with any other cmavo in a tense, except by way of a logical or non-logical connection (see Section 10.20 (p. 237)). Here is a convoluted sentence with several nested bridi which uses *nau* at the lowest level:

Example 10.108

la	djan.	pu	cusku	le	se	du'u
That-named	John	[past]	says	the		statement-that
la	.alis	pu	cusku	le	se	du'u
That-named	Alice	[past]	says	the		statement-that
la	djordj.	pu	cusku	le	se	du'u
That-named	George	[past]	says	the		statement-that
la	maris.	nau	klama	le	zarci	
That-named	Mary	[now]	goes-to	the	market.	

John said that Alice had said that George had earlier said that Mary is now going to the market.

The use of *nau* does not affect sticky tenses.

10.16 Tense relations between sentences

The sumti tcita method, explained in Section 10.12 (p. 223), of asserting a tense relationship between two events suffers from asymmetry. Specifically,

Example 10.109

le	verba	cu	cadzu	le	bisli
The	child		walks-on	the	ice
zu'a	le	nu	le	nanmu	cu	batci	le	gerku
[left]	the	event-of	the	man		bites	the	dog.

The child walks on the ice to the left of where the man bites the dog.

which specifies an imaginary journey leftward from the man biting the dog to the child walking on the ice, claims only that the child walks on the ice. By the nature of *le nu*, the man's biting the dog is merely referred to without being claimed. If it seems desirable to claim both, each event can be expressed as a main sentence bridi, with a special form of *i* connecting them:

Example 10.110

le	nanmu	cu	batci	le	gerku
The	man		bites	the	dog.

.izu'abo	le	verba	cu	cadzu		le	bisli
[Left]	the	child		walks-on		the	ice.

The man bites the dog. To the left, the child walks on the ice.

.izu'abo is a compound cmavo: the *i* separates the sentences and the *zu'a* is the tense. The *bo* is required to prevent the *zu'a* from gobbling up the following sumti, namely *le verba*.

Note that the bridi in Example 10.110 (p. 231) appear in the reverse order from their appearance in Example 10.109 (p. 230). With *.izu'abo* (and all other afterthought tense connectives) the sentence specifying the origin of the journey comes first. This is a natural order for sentences, but requires some care when converting between this form and the sumti tcita form.

Example 10.110 (p. 231) means the same thing as:

Example 10.111

le	nanmu	cu	batci	le	gerku	.i	zu'a	la'edi'u
The	man		bites	the	dog.		[Left]	the-referent-of-the-last-sentence

le	verba	cu	cadzu		le	bisli
the	child		walks-on		the	ice.

The man bites the dog. Left of what I just mentioned, the child walks on the ice.

If the *bo* is omitted in Example 10.110 (p. 231), the meaning changes:

Example 10.112

le	nanmu	cu	batci	le	gerku
The	man		bites	the	dog.

.i	zu'a	le	verba	cu		cadzu	le	bisli
	[Left]	the	child		[something]	walks-on	the	ice.

The man bites the dog. To the left of the child, something walks on the ice.

Here the first place of the second sentence is unspecified, because *zu'a* has absorbed the sumti *le verba*.

Do not confuse either Example 10.110 (p. 231) or Example 10.112 (p. 231) with the following:

Example 10.113

le	nanmu	cu	batci	le	gerku
The	man		bites	the	dog.

.i	zu'aku	le	verba	cu	cadzu	le	bisli
	[Left]	the	child		walks-on	the	ice.

The man bites the dog. Left of me, the child walks on the ice.

In Example 10.113 (p. 231), the origin point is the speaker, as is usual with *zu'aku*. Example 10.110 (p. 231) makes the origin point of the tense the event described by the first sentence.

Two sentences may also be connected in forethought by a tense relationship. Just like afterthought tense connection, forethought tense connection claims both sentences, and in addition claims that the time or space relationship specified by the tense holds between the events the two sentences describe.

The origin sentence is placed first, preceded by a tense plus *gi*. Another *gi* is used to separate the sentences:

Example 10.114

pugi	mi	klama	le	zarci	gi	mi	klama	le	zdani
[past]	I	go-to	the	market	[,]	I	go-to	the	house.

Before I go to the market, I go to the house.

A parallel construction can be used to express a tense relationship between sumti:

Example 10.115

mi	klama	pugi	le	zarci	gi	le	zdani
I	go-to	[past]	the	market	[,]	the	house.

Because English does not have any direct way of expressing a tense-like relationship between nouns, Example 10.115 (p. 232) cannot be expressed in English without paraphrasing it either into Example 10.114 (p. 231) or else into "I go to the house before the market", which is ambiguous – is the market going?

Finally, a third forethought construction expresses a tense relationship between bridi-tails rather than whole bridi. (The construct known as a "bridi-tail" is explained fully in Section 14.9 (p. 328); roughly speaking, it is a selbri, possibly with following sumti.) Example 10.116 (p. 232) is equivalent in meaning to Example 10.114 (p. 231) and Example 10.115 (p. 232):

Example 10.116

mi	pugi	klama	le	zarci	gi	klama	le	zdani
I	[past]	go-to	the	market	[,]	go-to	the	house.

I, before going to the market, go to the house.

In both Example 10.115 (p. 232) and Example 10.116 (p. 232), the underlying sentences *mi klama le zarci* and *mi klama le zdani* are not claimed; only the relationship in time between them is claimed.

Both the forethought and the afterthought forms are appropriate with PU, ZI, FAhA, VA, and ZAhO tenses. In all cases, the equivalent forms are (where X and Y stand for sentences, and TENSE for a tense cmavo):

subordinate	X TENSE le nu Y
afterthought coordinate	Y .i+TENSE+bo X
forethought coordinate	TENSE+gi X gi Y

10.17 Tensed logical connectives

The Lojban tense system interacts with the Lojban logical connective system. That system is a separate topic, explained in Chapter 14 (p. 317) and touched on only in summary here. By the rules of the logical connective system, Example 10.117 (p. 232) through Example 10.119 (p. 232) are equivalent in meaning:

Example 10.117

| la | teris. | satre | le | mlatu | .ije | la | teris. | satre | le | ractu |

Terry strokes the cat. And Terry strokes the rabbit.

Example 10.118

| la | teris. | satre | le | mlatu | gi'e | satre | le | ractu |

Terry strokes the cat and strokes the rabbit.

Example 10.119

| la | teris. | satre | le | mlatu | .e | le | ractu |

Terry strokes the cat and the rabbit.

Suppose we wish to add a tense relationship to the logical connective "and"? To say that Terry strokes the cat and later strokes the rabbit, we can combine a logical connective with a tense connective by placing the logical connective first, then the tense, and then the cmavo *bo*, thus:

Example 10.120

| la | teris. | satre | le | mlatu | .ijebabo | la | teris. | satre | le | ractu |

Terry strokes the cat. And then Terry strokes the rabbit.

Example 10.121

| la | teris. | satre | le | mlatu | gi'ebabo | satre | le | ractu |

Terry strokes the cat, and then strokes the rabbit.

Example 10.122

| la | teris. | satre | le | mlatu | .ebabo | le | ractu |

Terry strokes the cat and then the rabbit.

Example 10.120 (p. 232) through Example 10.122 (p. 233) are equivalent in meaning. They are also analogous to Example 10.117 (p. 232) through Example 10.119 (p. 232) respectively. The *bo* is required for the same reason as in Example 10.110 (p. 231): to prevent the *ba* from functioning as a sumti tcita for the following sumti (or, in Example 10.121 (p. 233), from being attached to the following selbri).

In addition to the *bo* construction of Example 10.120 (p. 232) through Example 10.122 (p. 233), there is also a form of tensed logical connective with *ke...ke'e* (*tu'e...tu'u* for sentences). The logical connective system makes Example 10.123 (p. 233) through Example 10.125 (p. 233) equivalent in meaning:

Example 10.123

mi	bevri	le	dakli	.ije	tu'e	mi	bevri	le	gerku
I	carry	the	sack.	And	(	I	carry	the	dog.

.ija		mi	bevri	le	mlatu	tu'u
And/or	I		carry	the	cat	).

I carry the sack. And I carry the dog, or I carry the cat, or I carry both.

Example 10.124

mi	bevri	le	dakli	gi'eke	bevri	le	gerku	gi'a	bevri
I	carry	the	sack	and	(carry	the	dog	and/or	carry

le	mlatu
the	cat).

I carry the sack, and also carry the dog or carry the cat or carry both.

Example 10.125

mi	bevri	le	dakli	.eke	le	gerku	.a	le	mlatu
I	carry	the	sack	and	(the	dog	or	the	cat).

I carry the sack and also the dog or the cat or both.

Note the uniformity of the Lojban, as contrasted with the variety of ways in which the English provides for the correct grouping. In all cases, the meaning is that I carry the sack in any case, and either the cat or the dog or both.

To express that I carry the sack first (earlier in time), and then the dog or the cat or both simultaneously, I can insert tenses to form Example 10.126 (p. 233) through Example 10.128 (p. 234):

Example 10.126

mi	bevri	le	dakli	.ije	ba		tu'e	mi	bevri	le	gerku
I	carry	the	sack.	And	[future]	(		I	carry	the	dog.

.ija		cabo		mi	bevri	le	mlatu	tu'u
And/or	[present]		I	carry	the	cat.	)

I carry the sack. And then I will carry the dog or I will carry the cat or I will carry both at once.

Example 10.127

mi	bevri	le	dakli	gi'e	bake		bevri	le	gerku
I	carry	the	sack	and	[future]	(carry	the	dog

gi'a		cabo		bevri	le	mlatu
and/or	[present]		carry	the	cat).

I carry the sack and then will carry the dog or carry the cat or carry both at once.

Example 10.128

mi	bevri	le	dakli	.e	bake	le	gerku
I	carry	the	sack	and	[future]	(the	dog

.a	cabo	le	mlatu
and/or	[present]	the	cat).

I carry the sack, and then the dog or the cat or both at once.

Example 10.126 (p. 233) through Example 10.128 (p. 234) are equivalent in meaning to each other, and correspond to the tenseless Example 10.123 (p. 233) through Example 10.125 (p. 233) respectively.

10.18 Tense negation

Any bridi which involves tenses of selma'o PU, FAhA, or ZAhO can be contradicted by a -nai suffixed to the tense cmavo. Some examples:

Example 10.129

mi	punai	klama	le	zarci
I	[past-not]	go-to	the	market.

I didn't go to the market.

As a contradictory negation, Example 10.129 (p. 234) implies that the bridi as a whole is false without saying anything about what is true. When the negated tense is a sumti tcita, -nai negation indicates that the stated relationship does not hold:

Example 10.130

mi	klama	le	zarci	ca	nai
I	go-to	the	market	[present]	[not]

le	nu	do	klama	le	zdani
the	event-of	you	go-to	the	house.

It is not true that I went to the market at the same time that you went to the house.

Example 10.131

le	nanmu	cu	batci	le	gerku	ne'inai	le	kumfa
The	man		bites	the	dog	[within-not]	the	room.

The man didn't bite the dog inside the room.

Example 10.132

mi	morsi	ca'onai	le	nu	mi	jmive
I	am-dead	[continuitive-negated]	the	event-of	I	live.

It is false that I am dead during my life.

It is also possible to perform scalar negation of whole tense constructs by placing a member of NAhE before them. Unlike contradictory negation, scalar negation asserts a truth: that the bridi is true with some tense other than that specified. The following examples are scalar negation analogues of Example 10.129 (p. 234) to Example 10.131 (p. 234):

Example 10.133

mi	na'e	pu	klama	le	zarci
I	[non-]	[past]	go-to	the	market.

I go to the market other than in the past.

Example 10.134

le	nanmu	cu	batci	le	gerku	to'e	ne'i	le	kumfa
The	man		bites	the	dog	[opposite-of]	[within]	the	room.

The man bites the dog outside the room.

Example 10.135

mi	klama	le	zarci	na'e	ca	le	nu
I	go-to	the	market	[non-]	[present]	the	event-of

do	klama	le	zdani
you	go-to	the	house.

I went to the market at a time other than the time at which you went to the house.

Example 10.136

mi	morsi	na'e	ca'o	le	nu	mi	jmive
I	am-dead	[non-]	[continuitive]	the	event-of	I	live.

I am dead other than during my life.

Unlike -nai contradictory negation, scalar negation of tenses is not limited to PU and FAhA:

Example 10.137

le	verba	na'e	ri'u	cadzu	le	bisli
The	child	[non-]	[right]	walks-on	the	ice

The child walks on the ice other than to my right.

The use of -nai on cmavo of TAhE and ROI has already been discussed in Section 10.9 (p. 217); this use is also a scalar negation.

10.19 Actuality, potentiality, capability: CAhA

The following cmavo are discussed in this section:

ca'a	CAhA	actually is
ka'e	CAhA	is innately capable of
nu'o	CAhA	can but has not
pu'i	CAhA	can and has

Lojban bridi without tense markers may not necessarily refer to actual events: they may also refer to capabilities or potential events. For example:

Example 10.138

ro	datka	cu	flulimna
All	ducks		are-float-swimmers.

All ducks swim by floating.

is a Lojban truth, even though the colloquial English translation is false or at best ambiguous. This is because the tenseless Lojban bridi doesn't necessarily claim that every duck is swimming or floating now or even at a specific time or place. Even if we add a tense marker to Example 10.138 (p. 235),

Example 10.139

ro	datka	ca	flulimna
All	ducks	[present]	are-float-swimmers.

All ducks are now swimming by floating.

the resulting Example 10.139 (p. 235) might still be considered a truth, even though the colloquial English seems even more likely to be false. All ducks have the potential of swimming even if they are not exercising that potential at present. To get the full flavor of "All ducks are now swimming", we must append a marker from selma'o CAhA to the tense, and say:

Example 10.140

ro	datka	ca	ca'a	flulimna
All	ducks	[present]	[actual]	are-float-swimmers.

All ducks are now actually swimming by floating.

A CAhA cmavo is always placed after any other tense cmavo, whether for time or for space. However, a CAhA cmavo comes before *ki*, so that a CAhA condition can be made sticky.

Example 10.140 (p. 235) is false in both Lojban and English, since it claims that the swimming is an actual, present fact, true of every duck that exists, whereas in fact there is at least one duck that is not swimming now.

Furthermore, some ducks are dead (and therefore sink); some ducks have just hatched (and do not know how to swim yet), and some ducks have been eaten by predators (and have ceased to exist as separate objects at all). Nevertheless, all these ducks have the innate capability of swimming – it is part of the nature of duckhood. The cmavo *ka'e* expresses this notion of innate capability:

Example 10.141

ro	datka	ka'e	flulimna
All	**ducks**	**[capable]**	**are-float-swimmers.**

All ducks are innately capable of swimming.

Under some epistemologies, innate capability can be extended in order to apply the innate properties of a mass to which certain individuals belong to the individuals themselves, even if those individuals are themselves not capable of fulfilling the claim of the bridi. For example:

Example 10.142

la	djan.	ka'e	viska
That-named	**John**	**[capable]**	**sees.**

John is innately capable of seeing.
John can see.

might be true about a human being named John, even though he has been blind since birth, because the ability to see is innately built into his nature as a human being. It is theoretically possible that conditions might occur that would enable John to see (a great medical discovery, for example). On the other hand,

Example 10.143

le	cukta	ka'e	viska
The	**book**	**[capable]**	**sees.**

The book can see.

is not true in most epistemologies, since the ability to see is not part of the innate nature of a book.

Consider once again the newly hatched ducks mentioned earlier. They have the potential of swimming, but have not yet demonstrated that potential. This may be expressed using *nu'o*, the cmavo of CAhA for undemonstrated potential:

Example 10.144

ro	cifydatka	nu'o	flulimna
All	**infant-ducks**	**[can-but-has-not]**	**are-float-swimmers.**

All infant ducks have an undemonstrated potential for swimming by floating.
Baby ducks can swim but haven't yet.

Contrariwise, if Frank is not blind from birth, then *pu'i* is appropriate:

Example 10.145

la	frank.	pu'i	viska
That-named	**Frank**	**[can-and-has]**	**sees.**

Frank has demonstrated a potential for seeing.
Frank can see and has seen.

Note that the glosses given at the beginning of this section for *ca'a*, *nu'o*, and *pu'i* incorporate *ca* into their meaning, and are really correct for *ca ca'a*, *ca nu'o*, and *ca pu'i*. However, the CAhA cmavo are perfectly meaningful with other tenses than the present:

Example 10.146

mi	pu	ca'a	klama	le	zarci
I	[past]	[actual]	go-to	the	store.

I actually went to the store.

Example 10.147

la	frank.	ba	nu'o	klama	le	zdani
That-named	Frank	[future]	[can-but-has-not]	goes-to	the	store.

Frank could have, but will not have, gone to the store (at some understood moment in the future).

As always in Lojban tenses, a missing CAhA can have an indeterminate meaning, or the context can be enough to disambiguate it. Saying

Example 10.148

ta	jelca
That	burns/is-burning/might-burn/will-burn.

with no CAhA specified can translate the two very different English sentences "That is on fire" and "That is inflammable." The first demands immediate action (usually), whereas the second merely demands caution. The two cases can be disambiguated with:

Example 10.149

ta	ca	ca'a	jelca
That	[present]	[actual]	burns.

That is on fire.

and

Example 10.150

ta	ka'e	jelca
That	[capable]	burns.

That is capable of burning.
That is inflammable.

When no indication is given, as in the simple observative

Example 10.151

jelca
It burns!

the prudent Lojbanist will assume the meaning "Fire!"

10.20 Logical and non-logical connections between tenses

Like many things in Lojban, tenses may be logically connected; logical connection is explained in more detail in Chapter 14 (p. 317). Some of the terminology in this section will be clear only if you already understand logical connectives.

The appropriate logical connectives belong to selma'o JA. A logical connective between tenses can always be expanded to one between sentences:

Example 10.152

mi	pu	je	ba	klama	le	zarci
I	[past]	and	[future]	go-to	the	market.

I went and will go to the market.

means the same as:

Example 10.153

mi	pu	klama	le	zarci
I	[past]	go-to	the	market.

.ije	mi	ba	klama	le	zarci
And	I	[future]	go-to	the	market.

I went to the market, and I will go to the market.

Tense connection and tense negation are combined in:

Example 10.154

mi	punai	je	canai	je	ba	klama	le	zarci
I	[past-not]	and	[present-not]	and	[future]	go-to	the	market.

I haven't yet gone to the market, but I will in future.

Example 10.154 (p. 238) is far more specific than

Example 10.155

mi	ba	klama	le	zarci
I	[future]	go-to	the	market.

which only says that I will go, without claiming anything about my past or present. *ba* does not imply *punai* or *canai*; to compel that interpretation, either a logical connection or a ZAhO is needed.

Tense negation can often be removed in favor of negation in the logical connective itself. The following examples are equivalent in meaning:

Example 10.156

mi	mo'izu'anai	je	mo'iri'u	cadzu
I	[motion-left-not]	and	[motion-right]	walk.

I walk not leftward but rightward.

Example 10.157

mi	mo'izu'a	naje	mo'iri'u	cadzu
I	[motion-left]	not-and	[motion-right]	walk.

I walk not leftward but rightward.

There are no forethought logical connections between tenses allowed by the grammar, to keep tenses simpler. Nor is there any way to override simple left-grouping of the connectives, the Lojban default.

The non-logical connectives of selma'o JOI, BIhI, and GAhO are also permitted between tenses. One application is to specify intervals not by size, but by their end-points (*bi'o* belongs to selma'o BIhI, and connects the end-points of an ordered interval, like English "from ... to"):

Example 10.158

mi	puza	bi'o	bazu	vasxu
I	[past-medium]	from...to	[future-long]	breathe.

I breathe from a medium time ago till a long time to come.

(It is to be hoped that I have a long life ahead of me.)

One additional use of non-logical connectives within tenses is discussed in Section 10.21 (p. 238). Other uses will probably be identified in future.

10.21 Sub-events

Another application of non-logical tense connection is to talk about sub-events of events. Consider a six-shooter: a gun which can fire six bullets in succession before reloading. If I fire off the entire magazine twice, I can express the fact in Lojban thus:

Example 10.159

mi	reroi	pi'u	xaroi	cecla
I	[twice]	[cross-product]	[six-times]	shoot

le	seldanti
the	projectile-launcher.

On two occasions, I fire the gun six times.

It would be confusing, though grammatical, to run the *reroi* and the *xaroi* directly together. However, the non-logical connective *pi'u* expresses a Cartesian product (also known as a cross product) of two sets. In this case, there is a set of two firings each of which is represented by a set of six shots, for twelve shots in all (hence the name "product": the product of 2 and 6 is 12). Its use specifies very precisely what occurs.

In fact, you can specify strings of interval properties and event contours within a single tense without the use of a logical or non-logical connective cmavo. This allows tenses of the type:

Example 10.160

la	djordj.	ca'o	co'a	ciska
That-named	George	[continuitive]	[initiative]	writes.

George continues to start to write.

Example 10.161

mi	reroi	ca'o	xaroi	darxi	le	damri
I	[twice]	[continuitive]	[six-times]	hit	the	drum.

On two occasions, I continue to beat the drum six times.

10.22 Conversion of sumti tcita: JAI

The following cmavo are discussed in this section:

jai	JAI	tense conversion
fai	FA	indefinite place

Conversion is the regular Lojban process of moving around the places of a place structure. The cmavo of selma'o SE serve this purpose, exchanging the first place with one of the others:

Example 10.162

mi	cu	klama	le	zarci
I		go-to	the	market.

Example 10.163

le	zarci	cu	se klama	mi
The	market		is-gone-to	by-me.

It is also possible to bring a place that is specified by a sumti tcita (for the purposes of this chapter, a tense sumti tcita) to the front, by using *jai* plus the tense as the grammatical equivalent of SE:

Example 10.164

le	ratcu	cu	citka	le	cirla	vi		le	panka
The	rat		eats	the	cheese	[short-distance]		the	park.

The rat eats the cheese in the park.

Example 10.165

le	panka	cu	jai vi	citka	le	cirla	fai	le	ratcu
The	park		is-the-place-of	eating	the	cheese	by	the	rat.

The park is where the rat eats the cheese.

In Example 10.165 (p. 239), the construction JAI+tense converts the location sumti into the first place. The previous first place has nowhere to go, since the location sumti is not a numbered place; however, it can be inserted back into the bridi with *fai*, the indefinite member of selma'o FA.

(The other members of FA are used to mark the first, second, etc. places of a bridi explicitly:

Example 10.166

    fa mi cu klama fe le zarci

means the same as

Example 10.167

    fe le zarci cu klama fa mi

as well as the simple

Example 10.168

    mi cu klama le zarci

in which the place structure is determined by position.)

Like SE conversion, JAI+tense conversion is especially useful in descriptions with LE selma'o:

Example 10.169

mi	viska	le	jai vi	citka	be	le	cirla
I	saw	the	place-of	eating		the	cheese.

Here the eater of the cheese is elided, so no *fai* appears.

Of course, temporal tenses are also usable with JAI:

Example 10.170

mi	djuno	fi	le	jai	ca	morsi	be	fai	la	djan.
I	know	about	the		[present]	is-dead	of		that-named	"John".

I know the time of John's death.
I know when John died.

10.23 Tenses versus modals

Grammatically, every use of tenses seen so far is exactly paralleled by some use of modals as explained in Chapter 9 (p. 179). Modals and tenses alike can be followed by sumti, can appear before the selbri, can be used in pure and mixed connections, can participate in JAI conversions. The parallelism is perfect. However, there is a deep difference in the semantics of tense constructs and modal constructs, grounded in historical differences between the two forms. Originally, modals and tenses were utterly different things in earlier versions of Loglan; only in Lojban have they become grammatically interchangeable. And even now, differences in semantics continue to be maintained.

The core distinction is that whereas the modal bridi

Example 10.171

mi	nelci	do	mu'i	le	nu	do	nelci	mi
I	like	you	with-motivation	the	event-of	you	like	me.

I like you because you like me.

places the *le nu* sumti in the x1 place of the gismu *mukti* (which underlies the modal *mu'i*), namely the motivating event, the tensed bridi

Example 10.172

mi	nelci	do	ba	le	nu	do	nelci	mi
I	like	you	after	the	event-of	you	like	me.

I like you after you like me.

places the *le nu* sumti in the x2 place of the gismu *balvi* (which underlies the tense *ba*), namely the point of reference for the future tense. Paraphrases of Example 10.171 (p. 240) and Example 10.172 (p. 240), employing the brivla *mukti* and *balvi* explicitly, would be:

Example 10.173

le	*nu*	*do*	*nelci*	*mi*	*cu*	*mukti*	*le*	*nu*
The	event-of	you	like	me		motivates	the	event-of

mi	*nelci*	*do*
I	like	you.

Your liking me is the motive for my liking you.

and

Example 10.174

le	*nu*	*mi*	*nelci*	*do*	*cu*	*balvi*	*le*	*nu*
The	event-of	I	like	you		is-after	the	event-of

do	*nelci*	*mi*
you	like	me.

My liking you follows (in time) your liking me.

(Note that the paraphrase is not perfect due to the difference in what is claimed; Example 10.173 (p. 241) and Example 10.174 (p. 241) claim only the causal and temporal relationships between the events, not the existence of the events themselves.)

As a result, the afterthought sentence-connective forms of Example 10.171 (p. 240) and Example 10.172 (p. 240) are, respectively:

Example 10.175

mi	*nelci*	*do*	*.imu'ibo*	*do*	*nelci*	*mi*
I	like	you.	[That-is] Because	you	like	me.

Example 10.176

do	*nelci*	*mi*	*.ibabo*	*mi*	*nelci*	*do*
You	like	me.	Afterward,	I	like	you.

In Example 10.175 (p. 241), the order of the two bridi *mi nelci do* and *do nelci mi* is the same as in Example 10.171 (p. 240). In Example 10.176 (p. 241), however, the order is reversed: the origin point *do nelci mi* physically appears before the future-time event *mi nelci do*. In both cases, the bridi characterizing the event in the x2 place appears before the bridi characterizing the event in the x1 place of *mukti* or *balvi*.

In forethought connections, however, the asymmetry between modals and tenses is not found. The forethought equivalents of Example 10.175 (p. 241) and Example 10.176 (p. 241) are

Example 10.177

mu'igi	*do*	*nelci*	*mi*	*gi*	*mi*	*nelci*	*do*
Because	you	like	me	,	I	like	you.

and

Example 10.178

bagi	*do*	*nelci*	*mi*	*gi*	*mi*	*nelci*	*do*
After	you	like	me	,	I	like	you.

respectively.

The following modal sentence schemata (where X and Y represent sentences) all have the same meaning:

    X .i BAI bo Y
    BAI gi Y gi X
    X BAI le nu Y

whereas the following tensed sentence schemata also have the same meaning:

X .i TENSE bo Y
TENSE gi X gi Y
Y TENSE le nu X

neglecting the question of what is claimed. In the modal sentence schemata, the modal tag is always followed by Y, the sentence representing the event in the x1 place of the gismu that underlies the BAI. In the tensed sentences, no such simple rule exists.

10.24 Tense questions: *cu'e*

The following cmavo is discussed in this section:

cu'e | CUhE | tense question

There are two main ways to ask questions about tense. The main English tense question words are "When?" and "Where?". These may be paraphrased respectively as "At what time?" and "At what place?" In these forms, their Lojban equivalents simply involve a tense plus *ma*, the Lojban sumti question:

Example 10.179

do	klama	le	zdani	ca		ma
You	go-to	the	house	[present]		[what-sumti?].
You	go-to	the	house	at		what-time?

When do you go to the house?

Example 10.180

le	verba	vi		ma		pu	cadzu	le	bisli
The	child	[short-space]		[what-sumti?]		[past]	walks-on	the	ice.
The	child	at/near		what-place			walked-on	the	ice?

Where did the child walk on the ice?

There is also a non-specific tense and modal question, *cu'e*, belonging to selma'o CUhE. This can be used wherever a tense or modal construct can be used.

Example 10.181

le	nanmu	cu'e		batci	le	gerku
The	man	[what-tense?]		bites	the	dog.

When/Where/How does the man bite the dog?

Possible answers to Example 10.181 (p. 242) might be:

Example 10.182

va
[medium-space].

Some ways from here.

Example 10.183

puzu
[past]-[long-time].

A long time ago.

Example 10.184

vi		le	lunra
[short-space]		The	moon.

On the moon.

Example 10.185

> *pu'o*
> **[inchoative]**

He hasn't yet done so.

or even the modal reply (from selma'o BAI; see Section 9.6 (p. 188)):

Example 10.186

seka'a	*le*	*briju*
With-destination	**the**	**office.**

The only way to combine *cu'e* with other tense cmavo is through logical connection, which makes a question that pre-specifies some information:

Example 10.187

do	*puzi*	*je*	*cu'e*	*sombo*	*le*	*gurni*
You	**[past-short]**	**and**	**[when?]**	**sow**	**the**	**grain?**

You sowed the grain a little while ago; when else do you sow it?

Additionally, the logical connective itself can be replaced by a question word:

Example 10.188

la	*.artr.*	*pu*	*je'i*	*ba*	*nolraitru*
That-named	**Arthur**	**[past]**	**[which?]**	**[future]**	**is-a-king**

Was Arthur a king or will he be?

Answers to Example 10.188 (p. 243) would be logical connectives such as *je*, meaning "both", *naje* meaning "the latter", or *jenai* meaning "the former".

10.25 Explicit magnitudes

It is a limitation of the VA and ZI system of specifying magnitudes that they can only prescribe vague magnitudes: small, medium, or large. In order to express both an origin point and an exact distance, the Lojban construction called a "termset" is employed. (Termsets are explained further in Section 14.11 (p. 332) and Section 16.7 (p. 382).) It is grammatical for a termset to be placed after a tense or modal tag rather than a sumti, which allows both the origin of the imaginary journey and its distance to be specified. Here is an example:

Example 10.189

la	*frank.*	*sanli*	*zu'a*	*nu'i*		*la*	*djordj.*
That-named	**Frank**	**stands**	**[left]**	**[start-termset]**		**George**	

la'u	*lo*	*mitre*		*be*	*li*		*mu*	*[nu'u]*
[quantity]	**a**	**thing-measuring-in-meters**		**the-number**			**5**	**[end-termset].**

Frank is standing five meters to the left of George.

Here the termset extends from the *nu'i* to the implicit *nu'u* at the end of the sentence, and includes the terms *la djordj.*, which is the unmarked origin point, and the tagged sumti *lo mitre be li mu*, which the cmavo *la'u* (of selma'o BAI, and meaning "with quantity"; see Section 9.6 (p. 188)) marks as a quantity. Both terms are governed by the tag *zu'a*

It is not necessary to have both an origin point and an explicit magnitude: a termset may have only a single term in it. A less precise version of Example 10.189 (p. 243) is:

Example 10.190

la	frank.	sanli	zu'a	nu'i	la'u
That-named	Frank	stands	[left]	[termset]	[quantity]

lo	mitre		be	li		mu
a	thing-measuring-in-meters			the-number		5.

Frank stands five meters to the left.

10.26 Finally (an exercise for the much-tried reader)

Example 10.191

.a'o do pu seju ba roroi ca'o fe'e su'oroi jimpe fi le lojbo temci selsku ciste

10.27 Summary of tense selma'o

PU

temporal direction

pu	past
ca	present
ba	future

ZI

temporal distance

zi	short
za	medium
zu	long

ZEhA

temporal interval

ze'i	short
ze'a	medium
ze'u	long
ze'e	infinite

ROI

objective quantified tense flag

noroi	never
paroi	once
[N]roi	[N] times
roroi	always
pare'u	the first time
rere'u	the second time
[N]re'u	the [N]th time

TAhE

subjective quantified tense

di'i	regularly
na'o	typically
ru'i	continuously
ta'e	habitually

ZAhO

event contours
see Section 10.10 (p. 219)

FAhA

spatial direction

see Section 10.28 (p. 245)

VA

spatial distance

vi	short
va	medium
vu	long

VEhA

spatial interval

ve'i	short
ve'a	medium
ve'u	long
ve'e	infinite

VIhA

spatial dimensionality

vi'i	line
vi'a	plane
vi'u	space
vi'e	space-time

FEhE

spatial interval modifier flag

fe'enoroi	nowhere
fe'eroroi	everywhere
fe'eba'o	beyond

etc.

MOhI

spatial movement flag

mo'i	motion

see Section 10.28 (p. 245)

KI

set or reset sticky tense

tense+*ki*	set
ki alone	reset

CUhE

tense question, reference point

cu'e	asks for a tense or aspect
nau	use speaker's reference point

JAI

tense conversion

jaica	the time of
jaivi	the place of

etc.

10.28 List of spatial directions and direction-like relations

The following list of FAhA cmavo gives rough English glosses for the cmavo, first when used without *mo'i* to express a direction, and then when used with *mo'i* to express movement in the direction. When possible, the gismu from which the cmavo is derived is also listed.

ca'u	crane	in front (of)	forward
ti'a	trixe	behind	backward
zu'a	zunle	on the left (of)	leftward
ga'u	gapru	above	upward(ly)
ni'a	cnita	below	downward(ly)
ne'i	nenri	within	into
ru'u	sruri	surrounding	orbiting
pa'o	pagre	transfixing	passing through
ne'a		next to	moving while next to
te'e		bordering	moving along the border (of)
re'o		adjacent (to)	along
fa'a	farna	towards	arriving at
to'o		away from	departing from
zo'i		inward (from)	approaching
ze'o		outward (from)	receding from
zo'a		tangential (to)	passing (by)
be'a	berti	north (of)	northward(ly)
ne'u	snanu	south (of)	southward(ly)
du'a	stuna	east (of)	eastward(ly)
vu'a		west (of)	westward(ly)

Special note on *fa'a*, *to'o*, *zo'i*, and *ze'o*:

zo'i and *ze'o* refer to direction towards or away from the speaker's location, or whatever the origin is. *fa'a* and *to'o* refer to direction towards or away from some other point.

Chapter 11
Events, Qualities, Quantities, And Other Vague Words: On Lojban Abstraction

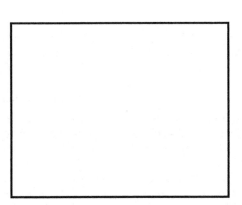

le si'o kunti

11.1 The syntax of abstraction

The purpose of the feature of Lojban known as "abstraction" is to provide a means for taking whole bridi and packaging them up, as it were, into simple selbri. Syntactically, abstractions are very simple and uniform; semantically, they are rich and complex, with few features in common between one variety of abstraction and another. We will begin by discussing syntax without regard to semantics; as a result, the notion of abstraction may seem unmotivated at first. Bear with this difficulty until Section 11.2 (p. 248).

An abstraction selbri is formed by taking a full bridi and preceding it by any cmavo of selma'o NU. There are twelve such cmavo; they are known as "abstractors". The bridi is closed by the elidable terminator *kei*, of selma'o KEI. Thus, to change the bridi

Example 11.1

mi	klama	le	zarci
I	go-to	the	store

into an abstraction using *nu*, one of the members of selma'o NU, we change it into

Example 11.2

nu	mi	klama	le	zarci	[kei]
an-event-of	my	going-to	the	store	

The bridi may be a simple selbri, or it may have associated sumti, as here. It is important to beware of eliding *kei* improperly, as many of the common uses of abstraction selbri involve following them with words that would appear to be part of the abstraction if *kei* had been elided.

(Technically, *kei* is never necessary, because the elidable terminator *vau* that closes every bridi can substitute for it; however, *kei* is specific to abstractions, and using it is almost always clearer.)

The grammatical uses of an abstraction selbri are exactly the same as those of a simple brivla. In particular, abstraction selbri may be used as observatives, as in Example 11.2 (p. 247), or used in tanru:

Example 11.3

la	*djan.*		*cu*	*nu*	*sonci*	*kei*		*djica*
That-named	**John**	**is-an**		**(event-of**	**being-a-soldier**	**)**	**type-of**	**desirer.**

John wants to be a soldier.

Abstraction selbri may also be used in descriptions, preceded by *le* (or any other member of selma'o LE):

Example 11.4

la	*djan.*	*cu*	*djica*	*le*	*nu*	*sonci*	*[kei]*
That-named	**John**		**desires**	**the**	**event-of**	**being-a-soldier.**	

We will most often use descriptions containing abstraction either at the end of a bridi, or just before the main selbri with its *cu*; in either of these circumstances, *kei* can normally be elided.

The place structure of an abstraction selbri depends on the particular abstractor, and will be explained individually in the following sections.

Note: In glosses of bridi within abstractions, the grammatical form used in the English changes. Thus, in the gloss of Example 11.2 (p. 247) we see "my going-to the store" rather than "I go-to the store"; likewise, in the glosses of Example 11.3 (p. 248) and Example 11.4 (p. 248) we see "being-a-soldier" rather than "is-a-soldier". This procedure reflects the desire for more understandable glosses, and does not indicate any change in the Lojban form. A bridi is a bridi, and undergoes no change when it is used as part of an abstraction selbri.

11.2 Event abstraction

The following cmavo is discussed in this section:

nu | NU | event abstractor

The examples in Section 11.1 (p. 247) made use of *nu* as the abstractor, and it is certainly the most common abstractor in Lojban text. Its purpose is to capture the event or state of the bridi considered as a whole. Do not confuse the *le* description built on a *nu* abstraction with ordinary descriptions based on *le* alone. The following sumti are quite distinct:

Example 11.5

le | klama

the comer, that which comes

Example 11.6

le | se | klama

the destination

Example 11.7

le | te | klama

the origin

Example 11.8

le | ve | klama

the route

Example 11.9

le ⦙ *xe* ⦙ *klama*

the means of transportation

Example 11.10

le ⦙ *nu* ⦙ *klama*

the event of someone coming to somewhere from somewhere by some route using some means

Example 11.5 (p. 248) through Example 11.9 (p. 249) are descriptions that isolate the five individual sumti places of the selbri *klama*. Example 11.10 (p. 249) describes something associated with the bridi as a whole: the event of it.

In Lojban, the term "event" is divorced from its ordinary English sense of something that happens over a short period of time. The description:

Example 11.11

le	*nu*	*mi*	*vasxu*
the	event-of	my	breathing

is an event which lasts for the whole of my life (under normal circumstances). On the other hand,

Example 11.12

le	*nu*	*la*	*djan.*	*cinba*	*la*	*djein.*
the	event-of	that-named	John	kissing	that-named	Jane

is relatively brief by comparison (again, under normal circumstances).

We can see from Example 11.10 (p. 249) through Example 11.12 (p. 249) that ellipsis of sumti is valid in the bridi of abstraction selbri, just as in the main bridi of a sentence. Any sumti may be ellipsized if the listener will be able to figure out from context what the proper value of it is, or else to recognize that the proper value is unimportant. It is extremely common for *nu* abstractions in descriptions to have the x1 place ellipsized:

Example 11.13

mi	*nelci*	*le*	*nu*	*limna*
I	like	the	event-of	swimming.

I like swimming.

is elliptical, and most probably means:

Example 11.14

mi	*nelci*	*le*	*nu*	*mi*	*limna*
I	like	the	event-of	I	swim.

In the proper context, of course, Example 11.13 (p. 249) could refer to the event of somebody else swimming. Its English equivalent, "I like swimming", can't be interpreted as "I like Frank's swimming"; this is a fundamental distinction between English and Lojban. In Lojban, an omitted sumti can mean whatever the context indicates that it should mean.

Note that the lack of an explicit NU cmavo in a sumti can sometimes hide an implicit abstraction. In the context of Example 11.14 (p. 249), the appearance of *le se nelci* ("that which is liked") is in effect an abstraction:

Example 11.15

le	*se nelci*	*cu*	*cafne*
The	liked-thing		is-frequent.

The thing which I like happens often.

which in this context means

My swimming happens often.

Event descriptions with *le nu* are commonly used to fill the "under conditions..." places, among others, of gismu and lujvo place structures:

Example 11.16

la	lojban.	cu	frili		mi
That-named	Lojban		is-easy-for	me	

	le	nu		mi	tadni	[kei]
under-conditions	the	event-of	I	study		

Lojban is easy for me when I study.

(The "when" of the English would also be appropriate for a construction involving a Lojban tense, but the Lojban sentence says more than that the studying is concurrent with the ease.)

The place structure of a *nu* abstraction selbri is simply:

x1 is an event of (the bridi)

11.3 Types of event abstractions

The following cmavo are discussed in this section:

mu'e	NU	point-event abstractor
pu'u	NU	process abstractor
zu'o	NU	activity abstractor
za'i	NU	state abstractor

Event abstractions with *nu* suffice to express all kinds of events, whether long, short, unique, repetitive, or whatever. Lojban also has more finely discriminating machinery for talking about events, however. There are four other abstractors of selma'o NU for talking about four specific types of events, or four ways of looking at the same event.

An event considered as a point in time is called a "point-event", or sometimes an "achievement". (This latter word should be divorced, in this context, from all connotations of success or triumph.) A point-event can be extended in duration, but it is still a point-event if it is thought of as unitary, having no internal structure. The abstractor *mu'e* means "point-event-of":

Example 11.17

le	mu'e	la	djan.	catra	la	djim.	cu	zekri
The	point-event-of	(that-named	John	kills	that-named	Jim)		is-a-crime.

John's killing Jim (considered as a point in time) is a crime.

An event considered as extended in time, and structured with a beginning, a middle containing one or more stages, and an end, is called a "process". The abstractor *pu'u* means "process-of":

Example 11.18

ca'o		le	pu'u		le	latmo	balje'a		cu	porpi		kei
[continuitive]	the	process-of(	the	Latin	great-state		breaking-up	)				

so'i	je'atru		cu	selcatra
many	state-rulers	were-killed		

During the fall of the Roman Empire, many Emperors were killed.

An event considered as extended in time and cyclic or repetitive is called an "activity". The abstractor *zu'o* means "activity-of":

Example 11.19

mi	tatpi	ri'a		le	zu'o		mi	plipe
I	am-tired	because-of	the	activity-of	(I	jump).		

I am tired because I jump.

An event considered as something that is either happening or not happening, with sharp boundaries, is called a "state". The abstractor *za'i* means "state-of":

Example 11.20

le	za'i	mi	jmive		cu	ckape	do
The	state-of	(I	am-alive)			is-dangerous-to	you.

My being alive is dangerous to you.

The abstractors in Example 11.17 (p. 250) through Example 11.20 (p. 251) could all have been replaced by *nu*, with some loss of precision. Note that Lojban allows every sort of event to be viewed in any of these four ways:

the "state of running" begins when the runner starts and ends when the runner stops;

the "activity of running" consists of the cycle "lift leg, step forward, drop leg, lift other leg..." (each such cycle is a process, but the activity consists in the repetition of the cycle);

the "process of running" puts emphasis on the initial sprint, the steady speed, and the final slowdown;

the "achievement of running" is most alien to English, but sees the event of running as a single indivisible thing, like "Pheidippides' run from Marathon to Athens" (the original marathon).

Further information on types of events can be found in Section 11.12 (p. 261).

The four event type abstractors have the following place structures:

mu'e: x1 is a point event of (the bridi)
pu'u: x1 is a process of (the bridi) with stages x2
za'i: x1 is a continuous state of (the bridi) being true
zu'o: x1 is an activity of (the bridi) consisting of repeated actions x2

11.4 Property abstractions

The following cmavo are discussed in this section:

ka	NU	property abstractor
ce'u	KOhA	abstraction focus

The things described by *le nu* descriptions (or, to put it another way, the things of which *nu* selbri may correctly be predicated) are only moderately "abstract". They are still closely tied to happenings in space and time. Properties, however, are much more ethereal. What is "the property of being blue", or "the property of being a go-er"? They are what logicians call "intensions". If John has a heart, then "the property of having a heart" is an abstract object which, when applied to John, is true. In fact,

Example 11.21

la	djan.	cu	se risna	zo'e
That-named	John		has-as-heart	something-unspecified.

John has a heart.

has the same truth conditions as

Example 11.22

la	djan.	cu	ckaji
That-named	John		has-the-property

le	ka	se risna	[zo'e]	[kei]
the	property-of	having-as-heart	something.	

John has the property of having a heart.

(The English word "have" frequently appears in any discussion of Lojban properties: things are said to "have" properties, but this is not the same sense of "have" as in "I have money", which is possession.)

Property descriptions, like event descriptions, are often wanted to fill places in brivla place structures:

Example 11.23

do	cnino	mi	le		ka	xunre		[kei]
You	are-new	to-me	in-the-quality-of-the		property-of	being-red.		

You are new to me in redness.

(The English suffix "-ness" often signals a property abstraction, as does the suffix "-ity".)

We can also move the property description to the x1 place of Example 11.23 (p. 252), producing:

Example 11.24

le	ka		do	xunre		[kei]	cu	cnino	mi
The	property-of		your	being-red				is-new	to me.

Your redness is new to me.

It would be suitable to use Example 11.23 (p. 252) and Example 11.24 (p. 252) to someone who has returned from the beach with a sunburn.

There are several different properties that can be extracted from a bridi, depending on which place of the bridi is "understood" as being specified externally. Thus:

Example 11.25

ka		mi	prami	[zo'e]		[kei]
a-property-of		me	loving	something-unspecified		

is quite different from

Example 11.26

ka		[zo'e]		prami	mi	[kei]
a-property-of		something-unspecified		loving	me	

In particular, sentences like Example 11.27 (p. 252) and Example 11.28 (p. 252) are quite different in meaning:

Example 11.27

la		djan.	cu	zmadu	la		djordj.
That-named		John		exceeds	that-named		George

le	ka		mi	prami	
in-the	property-of		(I	love	X)

I love John more than I love George.

Example 11.28

la		djan.	cu	zmadu	la		djordj.
That-named		John		exceeds	that-named		George

le	ka		prami	mi	
in-the	property of		(X	loves	me).

John loves me more than George loves me.

The "X" used in the glosses of Example 11.27 (p. 252) through Example 11.28 (p. 252) as a place-holder cannot be represented only by ellipsis in Lojban, because ellipsis means that there must be a specific value that can fill the ellipsis, as mentioned in Section 11.2 (p. 248). Instead, the cmavo *ce'u* of selma'o KOhA is employed when an explicit sumti is wanted. (The form "X" will be used in literal translations.)

Therefore, an explicit equivalent of Example 11.27 (p. 252), with no ellipsis, is:

Example 11.29

la		djan.	cu	zmadu	la		djordj.
That-named		John		exceeds	that-named		George

le	ka		mi	prami	ce'u
in-the	property-of		(I	love	X).

and of Example 11.28 (p. 252) is:

Example 11.30

la	djan.	cu	zmadu	la		djordj.
That-named	John		exceeds	that-named		George

le	ka		ce'u	prami	mi
in-the	property-of		(X	loves	me).

This convention allows disambiguation of cases like:

Example 11.31

le	ka		[zo'e]	dunda	le	xirma	[zo'e]	[kei]
the	property-of			giving	the	horse		

into

Example 11.32

le	ka		ce'u	dunda	le	xirma		[zo'e]		[kei]
the	property-of		(X	is-a-giver-of	the	horse	to	someone-unspecified		)

the property of being a giver of the horse

which is the most natural interpretation of Example 11.31 (p. 253), versus

Example 11.33

le	ka		[zo'e]		dunda	le	xirma		ce'u	[kei]
the	property-of		(someone-unspecified	is-a-giver-of	the	horse	to	X		)

the property of being one to whom the horse is given

which is also a possible interpretation.

It is also possible to have more than one *ce'u* in a *ka* abstraction, which transforms it from a property abstraction into a relationship abstraction. Relationship abstractions "package up" a complex relationship for future use; such an abstraction can be translated back into a selbri by placing it in the x2 place of the selbri *bridi*, whose place structure is:

bridi x1 is a predicate relationship with relation x2 (abstraction) among arguments (sequence/set) x3

The place structure of *ka* abstraction selbri is simply:

ka x1 is a property of (the bridi)

11.5 Amount abstractions

The following cmavo is discussed in this section:

ni	NU	amount abstraction

Amount abstractions are far more limited than event or property abstractions. They really make sense only if the selbri of the abstracted bridi is subject to measurement of some sort. Thus we can speak of:

Example 11.34

le	ni		le	pixra	cu	blanu		[kei]
the	amount-of		(the	picture		being-blue		)

the amount of blueness in the picture

because "blueness" could be measured with a colorimeter or a similar device. However,

Example 11.35

le	ni		la		djein.	cu	mamta		[kei]
the	amount-of		(that-named	Jane			being-a-mother		)

the amount of Jane's mother-ness (?)
the amount of mother-ness in Jane (?)

makes very little sense in either Lojban or English. We simply do not have any sort of measurement scale for being a mother.

Semantically, a sumti with *le ni* is a number; however, it cannot be treated grammatically as a quantifier in Lojban unless prefixed by the mathematical cmavo *mo'e*:

Example 11.36

li	*pa*	*vu'u*	*mo'e*	*le*	*ni*
the-number	1	minus	the-operand	the	amount-of (

le	*pixra*	*cu*	*blanu*	*[kei]*
the	picture		being-blue	)

1 - B, where **B** = blueness of the picture

Mathematical Lojban is beyond the scope of this chapter, and is explained more fully in Chapter 18 (p. 413).

There are contexts where either property or amount abstractions make sense, and in such constructions, amount abstractions can make use of *ce'u* just like property abstractors. Thus,

Example 11.37

le	*pixra*	*cu*	*cenba*	*le*	*ka*	*ce'u*	*blanu*	*[kei]*
The	picture		varies	in-the	property-of	(X	is blue	).

The picture varies in being blue.
The picture varies in blueness.

is not the same as

Example 11.38

le	*pixra*	*cu*	*cenba*	*le*	*ni*	*ce'u*	*blanu*	*[kei]*
The	picture		varies	in-the	amount-of	(X	is blue	).

The picture varies in how blue it is.
The picture varies in blueness.

Example 11.37 (p. 254) conveys that the blueness comes and goes, whereas Example 11.38 (p. 254) conveys that its quantity changes over time.

Whenever we talk of measurement of an amount, there is some sort of scale, and so the place structure of *ni* abstraction selbri is:

ni x1 is the amount of (the bridi) on scale x2

Note: the best way to express the x2 places of abstract sumti is to use something like *le ni ... kei be*. See Example 11.62 (p. 258) for the use of this construction.

11.6 Truth-value abstraction: *jei*

The "blueness of the picture" discussed in Section 11.5 (p. 253) refers to the measurable amount of blue pigment (or other source of blueness), not to the degree of truth of the claim that blueness is present. That abstraction is expressed in Lojban using *jei*, which is closely related semantically to *ni*. In the simplest cases, *le jei* produces not a number but a truth value:

Example 11.39

le	*jei*	*li*	*re*	*su'i*	*re*	*du*	*li*	*vo*	*[kei]*
the	truth-value-of	the-number	2	+	2	=	the-number	4	

the truth of 2 + 2 being 4

is equivalent to "truth", and

Example 11.40

le	*jei*	*li*	*re*	*su'i*	*re*	*du*	*li*	*mu*	*[kei]*
the	truth-value-of	the-number	2	+	2	=	the-number	5	

the truth of 2 + 2 being 5

is equivalent to "falsehood".

However, not everything in life (or even in Lojban) is simply true or false. There are shades of gray even in truth value, and *jei* is Lojban's mechanism for indicating the shade of grey intended:

Example 11.41

mi	ba	jdice	le	jei		la		djordj.
I	**[future]**	**decide**	**the**	**(truth-value of**		**that-named**		**George**

cu	zekri		gasnu	[kei]
	being-a-(crime		**doer)**	**).**

I will decide whether George is a criminal.

Example 11.41 (p. 255) does not imply that George is, or is not, definitely a criminal. Depending on the legal system I am using, I may make some intermediate decision. As a result, *jei* requires an x2 place analogous to that of *ni*:

jei x1 is the truth value of (the bridi) under epistemology x2

Abstractions using *jei* are the mechanism for fuzzy logic in Lojban; the *jei* abstraction refers to a number between 0 and 1 inclusive (as distinct from *ni* abstractions, which are often on open-ended scales). The detailed conventions for using *jei* in fuzzy-logic contexts have not yet been established.

11.7 Predication/sentence abstraction

The following cmavo is discussed in this section:

du'u	NU	predication abstraction

There are some selbri which demand an entire predication as a sumti; they make claims about some predication considered as a whole. Logicians call these the "propositional attitudes", and they include (in English) things like knowing, believing, learning, seeing, hearing, and the like. Consider the English sentence:

Example 11.42

I know that Frank is a fool.

How's that in Lojban? Let us try:

Example 11.43

mi	djuno	le	nu	la	frank.	cu	bebna	[kei]

I know the event of Frank being a fool.

Not quite right. Events are actually or potentially physical, and can't be contained inside one's mind, except for events of thinking, feeling, and the like; Example 11.43 (p. 255) comes close to claiming that Frank's being-a-fool is purely a mental activity on the part of the speaker. (In fact, Example 11.43 (p. 255) is an instance of improperly marked "sumti raising", a concept discussed further in Section 11.10 (p. 259)).

Try again:

Example 11.44

mi	djuno	le	jei	la	frank.	cu	bebna	[kei]

I know the truth-value of Frank being a fool.

Closer. Example 11.44 (p. 255) says that I know whether or not Frank is a fool, but doesn't say that he is one, as Example 11.42 (p. 255) does. To catch that nuance, we must say:

Example 11.45

mi	djuno	le	du'u	la	frank.	cu	bebna	[kei]

I know the predication that Frank is a fool.

Now we have it. Note that the implied assertion "Frank is a fool" is not a property of *le du'u* abstraction, but of *djuno*; we can only know what is in fact true. (As a result, *djuno* like *jei* has a place for epistemology, which specifies how we know.) Example 11.46 (p. 256) has no such implied assertion:

Example 11.46

| mi | kucli | le | du'u | la | frank. | cu | bebna | [kei] |

I am curious about whether Frank is a fool.

and here *du'u* could probably be replaced by *jei* without much change in meaning:

Example 11.47

| mi | kucli | le | jei | la | frank. | cu | bebna | [kei] |

I am curious about how true it is that Frank is a fool.

As a matter of convenience rather than logical necessity, *du'u* has been given an x2 place, which is a sentence (piece of language) expressing the bridi:

du'u x1 is the predication (the bridi), expressed in sentence x2

and *le se du'u ...* is very useful in filling places of selbri which refer to speaking, writing, or other linguistic behavior regarding bridi:

Example 11.48

la	djan.	cusku	le	se du'u
That-named	**John**	**expresses**	**the**	**(sentence-expressing-that**

la	djordj.	klama	le	zarci	[kei]
that-named	**George**	**goes-to**	**the**	**store**	**)**

John says that George goes to the store.

Example 11.48 (p. 256) differs from

Example 11.49

la	djan	cusku	lu
That-named	**John**	**expresses,**	**quote,**

la	djordj.	klama	le	zarci	li'u
that-named	**George**	**goes**	**to-the**	**store,**	**unquote.**

John says "George goes to the store".

because Example 11.49 (p. 256) claims that John actually said the quoted words, whereas Example 11.48 (p. 256) claims only that he said some words or other which were to the same purpose.

le se du'u is much the same as *lu'e le du'u*, a symbol for the predication, but *se du'u* can be used as a selbri, whereas *lu'e* is ungrammatical in a selbri. (See Section 6.10 (p. 128) for a discussion of *lu'e*.)

11.8 Indirect questions

The following cmavo is discussed in this section:

| kau | UI | indirect question marker |

There is an alternative type of sentence involving *du'u* and a selbri expressing a propositional attitude. In addition to sentences like

Example 11.50

I know that John went to the store.

we can also say things like

Example 11.51

I know who went to the store.

This form is called an "indirect question" in English because the embedded English sentence is a question: "Who went to the store?" A person who says Example 11.51 (p. 256) is claiming to know the answer to this question. Indirect questions can occur with many other English verbs as well: I can wonder, or doubt, or see, or hear, as well as know who went to the store.

To express indirect questions in Lojban, we use a *le du'u* abstraction, but rather than using a question word like "who" (*ma* in Lojban), we use any word that will fit grammatically and mark it with the suffix particle *kau*. This cmavo belongs to selma'o UI, so grammatically it can appear anywhere. The simplest Lojban translation of Example 11.51 (p. 256) is therefore:

Example 11.52

mi	djuno	le	du'u
I	know	the	predication-of

ma	kau		pu	klama	le	zarci
X	[indirect-question]		[past]	going-to	the	store.

In Example 11.52 (p. 257), we have chosen to use *ma* as the word marked by *kau*. In fact, any other sumti would have done as well: *zo'e* or *da* or even *la djan.*. Using *la djan.* would suggest that it was John who I knew had gone to the store, however:

Example 11.53

mi	djuno	le	du'u
I	know	the	predication-of/fact-that

la	djan.	kau		pu	klama	le	zarci
that-named	John	[indirect-question]		[past]	going-to	the	store.

I know who went to the store, namely John.
I know that it was John who went to the store.

Using one of the indefinite pro-sumti such as *ma*, *zo'e*, or *da* does not suggest any particular value.

Why does Lojban require the *kau* marker, rather than using *ma* as English and Chinese and many other languages do? Because *ma* always signals a direct question, and so

Example 11.54

mi	djuno	le	du'u	ma	pu	klama	le	zarci
I	know	the	predication-of	[what sumti?]	[past]	goes-to	the	store

means

Example 11.55

Who is it that I know goes to the store?

It is actually not necessary to use *le du'u* and *kau* at all if the indirect question involves a sumti; there is generally a paraphrase of the type:

Example 11.56

mi	djuno	fi	le	pu	klama	be	le	zarci
I	know	about	the	[past]	goer	to	the	store.

I know something about the one who went to the store (namely, his identity).

because the x3 place of *djuno* is the subject of knowledge, as opposed to the fact that is known. But when the questioned point is not a sumti, but (say) a logical connection, then there is no good alternative to *kau*:

Example 11.57

mi	ba	zgana	le	du'u		la	djan.
I	[future]	observe	the	predication-of/fact-that		that-named	John

jikau		la	djordj.	cu	zvati	le	panka
[connective-indirect-question]		that-named	George		is-at	the	park.

I will see whether John or George (or both) is at the park.

In addition, Example 11.56 (p. 257) is only a loose paraphrase of Example 11.52 (p. 257), because it is left to the listener's insight to realize that what is known about the goer-to-the-store is his identity rather than some other of his attributes.

11.9 Minor abstraction types

The following cmavo are discussed in this section:

li'i	NU	experience abstractor
si'o	NU	concept abstractor
su'u	NU	general abstractor

There are three more abstractors in Lojban, all of them little used so far. The abstractor *li'i* expresses experience:

Example 11.58

mi	morji	le	li'i	mi	verba
I	remember	the	experience-of	(my	being-a-child)

The abstractor *si'o* expresses a mental image, a concept, an idea:

Example 11.59

mi	nelci	le	si'o	la	lojban.	cu	mulno
I	enjoy	the	concept-of	that-named	Lojban		being-complete.

Finally, the abstractor *su'u* is a vague abstractor, whose meaning must be grasped from context:

Example 11.60

ko	zgana	le	su'u	le	ci	smacu	cu	bajra
you [imperative]	observe	the	abstract-nature-of	the	three	mice		running

See how the three mice run!

All three of these abstractors have an x2 place. An experience requires an experiencer, so the place structure of *li'i* is:

li'i x1 is the experience of (the bridi) as experienced by x2

Similarly, an idea requires a mind to hold it, so the place structure of *si'o* is:

si'o x1 is the idea/concept of (the bridi) in the mind of x2

Finally, there needs to be some way of specifying just what sort of abstraction *su'u* is representing, so its place structure is:

su'u x1 is an abstract nature of (the bridi) of type x2

The x2 place of *su'u* allows it to serve as a substitute for any of the other abstractors, or as a template for creating new ones. For example,

Example 11.61

le	nu	mi	klama
the	event-of	my	going

can be paraphrased as

Example 11.62

le	su'u	mi	klama	kei	be	lo	fasnu
the	abstract-nature-of	(my	going)		of-type	an	event

and there is a book whose title might be rendered in Lojban as:

Example 11.63

le	su'u	la	.iecuas.
the	**abstract-nature-of**	**(that-named**	**Jesus**

kuctai	selcatra	kei
is-an-intersect-shape	**type-of-killed-one**	**)**

be	lo	sa'ordzifa'a
of-type	**a**	**slope-low-direction**

ke	nalmatma'e	sutyterjvi
type-of	**non-motor-vehicle**	**speed-competition**

The Crucifixion of Jesus Considered As A Downhill Bicycle Race

Note the importance of using *kei* after *su'u* when the x2 of *su'u* (or any other abstractor) is being specified; otherwise, the *be lo* ends up inside the abstraction bridi.

11.10 Lojban sumti raising

The following cmavo are discussed in this section:

tu'a	LAhE	an abstraction involving
jai	JAI	abstraction conversion

It is sometimes inconvenient, in a situation where an abstract description is logically required, to express the abstraction. In English we can say:

Example 11.64

I try to open the door.

which in Lojban is:

Example 11.65

mi	troci	le	nu	[mi]	gasnu
I	**try**	**the**	**event-of**	**(I**	**am-agent-in**

le	nu	le	vorme	cu	karbi'o
the	**event-of**	**(the**	**door**		**open-becomes)).**

which has an abstract description within an abstract description, quite a complex structure. In English (but not in all other languages), we may also say:

Example 11.66

I try the door.

where it is understood that what I try is actually not the door itself, but the act of opening it. The same simplification can be done in Lojban, but it must be marked explicitly using a cmavo. The relevant cmavo is *tu'a*, which belongs to selma'o LAhE. The Lojban equivalent of Example 11.66 (p. 259) is:

Example 11.67

mi	troci	tu'a	le	vorme
I	**try**	**some-action-to-do-with**	**the**	**door.**

The term "sumti-raising", as in the title of this section, signifies that a sumti which logically belongs within an abstraction (or even within an abstraction which is itself inside an intermediate abstraction) is "raised" to the main bridi level. This transformation from Example 11.65 (p. 259) to Example 11.67 (p. 259) loses information: nothing except convention tells us what the abstraction was.

Using *tu'a* is a kind of laziness: it makes speaking easier at the possible expense of clarity for the listener. The speaker must be prepared for the listener to respond something like:

Example 11.68

tu'a	le	vorme	lu'u	ki'a
something-to-do-with	**the**	**door**	**[terminator]**	**[confusion!]**

which indicates that *tu'a le vorme* cannot be understood. (The terminator for *tu'a* is *lu'u*, and is used in Example 11.68 (p. 259) to make clear just what is being questioned: the sumti-raising, rather than the word *vorme* as such.) An example of a confusing raised sumti might be:

Example 11.69

tu'a	la	djan.	cu	cafne
something-to-do-with	that-named	John		frequently-occurs

This must mean that something which John does, or which happens to John, occurs frequently: but without more context there is no way to figure out what. Note that without the *tu'a*, Example 11.69 (p. 260) would mean that John considered as an event frequently occurs – in other words, that John has some sort of on-and-off existence! Normally we do not think of people as events in English, but the x1 place of *cafne* is an event, and if something that does not seem to be an event is put there, the Lojbanic listener will attempt to construe it as one. (Of course, this analysis assumes that *djan.* is the name of a person, and not the name of some event.)

Logically, a counterpart of some sort is needed to *tu'a* which transposes an abstract sumti into a concrete one. This is achieved at the selbri level by the cmavo *jai* (of selma'o JAI). This cmavo has more than one function, discussed in Section 9.12 (p. 199) and Section 10.22 (p. 239); for the purposes of this chapter, it operates as a conversion of selbri, similarly to the cmavo of selma'o SE. This conversion changes

Example 11.70

tu'a	mi	rinka	le	nu	do	morsi
something-to-do-with	me	causes	the	event-of	you	are-dead

My action causes your death.

into

Example 11.71

mi	jai	rinka	le	nu	do	morsi
I	am-associated-with	causing	the	event-of	your	death.

I cause your death.

In English, the subject of "cause" can either be the actual cause (an event), or else the agent of the cause (a person, typically); not so in Lojban, where the x1 of *rinka* is always an event. Example 11.70 (p. 260) and Example 11.71 (p. 260) look equally convenient (or inconvenient), but in making descriptions, Example 11.71 (p. 260) can be altered to:

Example 11.72

le	jai	rinka	be	le	nu	do	morsi
that-which-is	associated-with	causing	(	the	event-of	your	death)

the one who caused your death

because *jai* modifies the selbri and can be incorporated into the description – not so for *tu'a*.

The weakness of *jai* used in descriptions in this way is that it does not specify which argument of the implicit abstraction is being raised into the x1 place of the description selbri. One can be more specific by using the modal form of *jai* explained in Section 9.12 (p. 199):

Example 11.73

le	jai gau	rinka	be	le	nu	do	morsi
that-which-is	agent-in	causing	(	the	event-of	your	death)

11.11 Event-type abstractors and event contour tenses

This section is a logical continuation of Section 11.3 (p. 250).

There exists a relationship between the four types of events explained in Section 11.3 (p. 250) and the event contour tense cmavo of selma'o ZAhO. The specific cmavo of NU and of ZAhO are mutually interdefining; the ZAhO contours were chosen to fit the needs of the NU event types and vice versa. Event contours are explained in full in Section 10.10 (p. 219), and only summarized here.

The purpose of ZAhO cmavo is to represent the natural portions of an event, such as the beginning, the middle, and the end. They fall into several groups:

The cmavo *pu'o*, *ca'o*, and *ba'o* represent spans of time: before an event begins, while it is going on, and after it is over, respectively.

The cmavo *co'a*, *de'a*, *di'a*, and *co'u* represent points of time: the start of an event, the temporary stopping of an event, the resumption of an event after a stop, and the end of an event, respectively. Not all events can have breaks in them, in which case *de'a* and *di'a* do not apply.

The cmavo *mo'u* and *za'o* correspond to *co'u* and *ba'o* respectively, in the case of those events which have a natural ending point that may not be the same as the actual ending point: *mo'u* refers to the natural ending point, and *za'o* to the time between the natural ending point and the actual ending point (the "excessive" or "superfective" part of the event).

The cmavo *co'i* represents an entire event considered as a point-event or achievement.

All these cmavo are applicable to events seen as processes and abstracted with *pu'u*. Only processes have enough internal structure to make all these points and spans of time meaningful.

For events seen as states and abstracted with *za'i*, the meaningful event contours are the spans *pu'o*, *ca'o*, and *ba'o*; the starting and ending points *co'a* and *co'u*, and the achievement contour *co'i*. States do not have natural endings distinct from their actual endings. (It is an open question whether states can be stopped and resumed.)

For events seen as activities and abstracted with *zu'o*, the meaningful event contours are the spans *pu'o*, *ca'o*, and *ba'o*, and the achievement contour *co'i*. Because activities are inherently cyclic and repetitive, the beginning and ending points are not well-defined: you do not know whether an activity has truly begun until it begins to repeat.

For events seen as point-events and abstracted with *mu'e*, the meaningful event contours are the spans *pu'o* and *ba'o* but not *ca'o* (a point-event has no duration), and the achievement contour *co'i*.

Note that the parts of events are themselves events, and may be treated as such. The points in time may be seen as *mu'e* point-events; the spans of time may constitute processes or activities. Therefore, Lojban allows us to refer to processes within processes, activities within states, and many other complicated abstract things.

11.12 Abstractor connection

An abstractor may be replaced by two or more abstractors joined by logical or non-logical connectives. Connectives are explained in detail in Chapter 14 (p. 317). The connection can be expanded to one between two bridi which differ only in abstraction marker. Example 11.74 (p. 261) and Example 11.75 (p. 261) are equivalent in meaning:

Example 11.74

le	ka	la	frank.	ciska	cu	xlali
The	quality-of	that-named	Frank	writing		is-bad,

.ije	le	ni	la	frank.	ciska	cu	xlali
and	the	quantity-of	that-named	Frank	writing		is-bad.

Example 11.75

| le | ka | je | ni | la | frank. | ciska | cu | xlali |

The quality and quantity of Frank's writing is bad.

This feature of Lojban has hardly ever been used, and nobody knows what uses it may eventually have.

11.13 Table of abstractors

The following table gives each abstractor, an English gloss for it, a Lojban gismu which is connected with it (more or less remotely: the associations between abstractors and gismu are meant more as memory hooks than for any kind of inference), the rafsi associated with it, and (on the following line) its place structure.

nu	event of	fasnu	nun	x1 is an event of (the bridi)
ka	property of	ckaji	kam	x1 is a property of (the bridi)
ni	amount of	klani	nil	x1 is an amount of (the bridi) measured on scale x2
jei	truth-value of	jetnu	jez	x1 is a truth-value of (the bridi) under epistemology x2
li'i	experience of	lifri	liz	x1 is an experience of (the bridi) to experiencer x2
si'o	idea of	sidbo	siz	x1 is an idea/concept of (the bridi) in the mind of x2
du'u	predication of	-----	dum	x1 is the bridi (the bridi) expressed by sentence x2
su'u	abstraction of	sucta	sus	x1 is an abstract nature of (the bridi)
za'i	state of	zasti	zam	x1 is a state of (the bridi)
zu'o	activity of	zukte	zum	x1 is an activity of (the bridi)
pu'u	process of	pruce	pup	x1 is a process of (the bridi)
mu'e	point-event of	mulno	mub	x1 is a point-event/achievement of (the bridi)

Chapter 12
Dog House And White House: Determining lujvo Place Structures

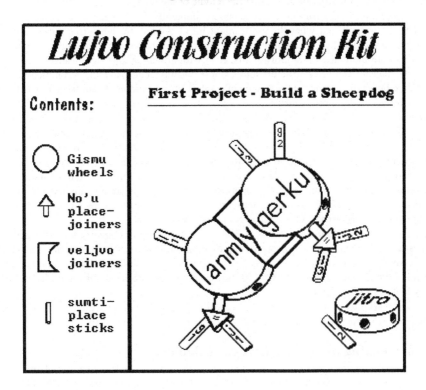

12.1 Why have lujvo?

The Lojban vocabulary is founded on its list of 1350-plus gismu, made up by combining word lists from various sources. These gismu are not intended to be either a complete vocabulary for the language nor a minimal list of semantic primitives. Instead, the gismu list serves as a basis for the creation of compound words, or lujvo. The intention is that (except in certain semantically broad but shallow fields such as cultures, nations, foods, plants, and animals) suitable lujvo can be devised to cover the ten million or so concepts expressible in all the world's languages taken together. Grammatically, lujvo behave just like gismu: they have place structures and function as selbri.

There is a close relationship between lujvo and tanru. In fact, lujvo are condensed forms of tanru:

Example 12.1

ti		fagri	festi
That	is	fire	waste.

contains a tanru which can be reduced to the lujvo in:

Example 12.2

ti	fagyfesti
That	is-fire-waste.
That	is-ashes.

Although the lujvo *fagyfesti* is derived from the tanru *fagri festi*, it is not equivalent in meaning to it. In particular, *fagyfesti* has a distinct place structure of its own, not the same as that of *festi*. (In contrast, the tanru does have the same place structure as *festi*.) The lujvo needs to take account of the places of *fagri* as well. When a tanru is made into a lujvo, there is no equivalent of *be...bei...be'o* (described in Section 5.7 (p. 88)) to incorporate sumti into the middle of the lujvo.

So why have lujvo? Primarily to reduce semantic ambiguity. On hearing a tanru, there is a burden on the listener to figure out what the tanru might mean. Adding further terms to the tanru reduces ambiguity in one sense, by providing more information; but it increases ambiguity in another sense, because there are more and more tanru joints, each with an ambiguous significance. Since lujvo, like other brivla, have a fixed place structure and a single meaning, encapsulating a commonly-used tanru into a lujvo relieves the listener of the burden of creative understanding. In addition, lujvo are typically shorter than the corresponding tanru.

There are no absolute laws fixing the place structure of a newly created lujvo. The maker must consider the place structures of all the components of the tanru and then decide which are still relevant and which can be removed. What is said in this chapter represents guidelines, presented as one possible standard, not necessarily complete, and not the only possible standard. There may well be lujvo that are built without regard for these guidelines, or in accordance with entirely different guidelines, should such alternative guidelines someday be developed. The reason for presenting any guidelines at all is so that Lojbanists have a starting point for deciding on a likely place structure – one that others seeing the same word can also arrive at by similar consideration.

If the tanru includes connective cmavo such as *bo*, *ke*, *ke'e*, or *je*, or conversion or abstraction cmavo such as *se* or *nu*, there are ways of incorporating them into the lujvo as well. Sometimes this makes the lujvo excessively long; if so, the cmavo may be dropped. This leads to the possibility that more than one tanru could produce the same lujvo. Typically, however, only one of the possible tanru is useful enough to justify making a lujvo for it.

The exact workings of the lujvo-making algorithm, which takes a tanru built from gismu (and possibly cmavo) and produces a lujvo from it, are described in Section 4.11 (p. 68).

12.2 The meaning of tanru: a necessary detour

The meaning of a lujvo is controlled by – but is not the same as – the meaning of the tanru from which the lujvo was constructed. The tanru corresponding to a lujvo is called its *veljvo* in Lojban, and since there is no concise English equivalent, that term will be used in this chapter. Furthermore, the left (modifier) part of a tanru will be called the *seltau*, and the right (modified) part the *tertau*, following the usage of Chapter 5 (p. 79). For brevity, we will speak of the seltau or tertau of a lujvo, meaning of course the seltau or tertau of the veljvo of that lujvo. (If this terminology is confusing, substituting "modifier" for *seltau* and "modified" for *tertau* may help.)

The place structure of a tanru is always the same as the place structure of its tertau. As a result, the meaning of the tanru is a modified version of the meaning of the tertau; the tanru will typically, but not always, refer to a subset of the things referred to by the tertau.

The purpose of a tanru is to join concepts together without necessarily focusing on the exact meaning of the seltau. For example, in the *Iliad*, the poet talks about "the wine-dark sea", in which "wine" is a seltau relative to "dark", and the pair of words is a seltau relative to "sea". We're talking about the sea, not about wine or color. The other words are there to paint a scene in the listener's mind, in which the real action will occur, and to evoke relations to other sagas of the time similarly describing the sea. Logical inferences about wine or color will be rejected as irrelevant.

As a simple example, consider the rather non-obvious tanru *klama zdani*, or "goer-house". The gismu *zdani* has two places:

Example 12.3
> x1 is a nest/house/lair/den for inhabitant x2

(but in this chapter we will use simply "house", for brevity), and the gismu *klama* has five:

Example 12.4

x1 goes to destination x2 from origin point x3 via route x4 using means x5

The tanru *klama zdani* will also have two places, namely those of *zdani*. Since a *klama zdani* is a type of *zdani*, we can assume that all goer-houses – whatever they may be – are also houses.

But is knowing the places of the tertau everything that is needed to understand the meaning of a tanru? No. To see why, let us switch to a less unlikely tanru: *gerku zdani*, literally "dog house". A tanru expresses a very loose relation: a *gerku zdani* is a house that has something to do with some dog or dogs. What the precise relation might be is left unstated. Thus, the meaning of *lo gerku zdani* can include all of the following: houses occupied by dogs, houses shaped by dogs, dogs which are also houses (e.g. houses for fleas), houses named after dogs, and so on. All that is essential is that the place structure of *zdani* continues to apply.

For something (call it z1) to qualify as a *gerku zdani* in Lojban, it's got to be a house, first of all. For it to be a house, it's got to house someone (call that z2). Furthermore, there's got to be a dog somewhere (called g1). For g1 to count as a dog in Lojban, it's got to belong to some breed as well (called g2). And finally, for z1 to be in the first place of *gerku zdani*, as opposed to just *zdani*, there's got to be some relationship (called r) between some place of *zdani* and some place of *gerku*. It doesn't matter which places, because if there's a relationship between some place of *zdani* and any place of *gerku*, then that relationship can be compounded with the relationship between the places of *gerku*- namely, *gerku* itself – to reach any of the other *gerku* places. Thus, if the relationship turns out to be between z2 and g2, we can still state r in terms of z1 and g1: "the relationship involves the dog g1, whose breed has to do with the occupant of the house z1".

Doubtless to the relief of the reader, here's an illustration. We want to find out whether the White House (the one in which the U. S. President lives, that is) counts as a *gerku zdani*. We go through the five variables. The White House is the z1. It houses Bill Clinton as z2, as of this writing, so it counts as a *zdani*. Let's take a dog – say, Spot (g1). Spot has to have a breed; let's say it's a Saint Bernard (g2). Now, the White House counts as a *gerku zdani* if there is any relationship (r) at all between the White House and Spot. (We'll choose the g1 and z1 places to relate by r; we could have chosen any other pair of places, and simply gotten a different relationship.)

The sky is the limit for r; it can be as complicated as "The other day, g1 (Spot) chased Socks, who is owned by Chelsea Clinton, who is the daughter of Bill Clinton, who lives in z1 (the White House)" or even worse. If no such r can be found, well, you take another dog, and keep going until no more dogs can be found. Only then can we say that the White House cannot fit into the first place of *gerku zdani*.

As we have seen, no less than five elements are involved in the definition of *gerku zdani*: the house, the house dweller, the dog, the dog breed (everywhere a dog goes in Lojban, a dog breed follows), and the relationship between the house and the dog. Since tanru are explicitly ambiguous in Lojban, the relationship r cannot be expressed within a tanru (if it could, it wouldn't be a tanru any more!) All the other places, however, can be expressed – thus:

Example 12.5

la	*blabi*	*zdani*	*cu*	*gerku*	*be*	*fa*	*la*	*spot.*
That-named	White	House		is-a-dog	(	namely	that-named	Spot

bei	*la*	*sankt.*	*berNARD.*	*be'o*
of-breed	that-named	Saint	Bernard	)

zdani	*la*	*bil.*	*klinton.*
type-of-house-for	that-named	Bill	Clinton.

Not the most elegant sentence ever written in either Lojban or English. Yet if there is any relation at all between Spot and the White House, Example 12.5 (p. 265) is arguably true. If we concentrate on just one type of relation in interpreting the tanru *gerku zdani*, then the meaning of *gerku zdani* changes. So if we understand *gerku zdani* as having the same meaning as the English word "doghouse", the White House would no longer be a *gerku zdani* with respect to Spot, because as far as we know Spot does not actually live in the White House, and the White House is not a doghouse (derogatory terms for incumbents notwithstanding).

12.3 The meaning of lujvo

This is a fairly long way to go to try and work out how to say "doghouse"! The reader can take heart; we're nearly there. Recall that one of the components involved in fixing the meaning of a tanru – the one left deliberately vague – is the precise relation between the tertau and the seltau. Indeed, fixing this relation is tantamount to giving an interpretation to the ambiguous tanru.

A lujvo is defined by a single disambiguated instance of a tanru. That is to say, when we try to design the place structure of a lujvo, we don't need to try to discover the relation between the tertau and the seltau. We already know what kind of relation we're looking for; it's given by the specific need we wish to express, and it determines the place structure of the lujvo itself.

Therefore, it is generally not appropriate to simply devise lujvo and decide on place structures for them without considering one or more specific usages for the coinage. If one does not consider specifics, one will be likely to make erroneous generalizations on the relationship r.

The insight driving the rest of this chapter is this: while the relation expressed by a tanru can be very distant (e.g. Spot chasing Socks, above), the relationship singled out for disambiguation in a lujvo should be quite close. This is because lujvo-making, paralleling natural language compounding, picks out the most salient relationship r between a tertau place and a seltau place to be expressed in a single word. The relationship "dog chases cat owned by daughter of person living in house" is too distant, and too incidental, to be likely to need expression as a single short word; the relationship "dog lives in house" is not. From all the various interpretations of *gerku zdani*, the person creating *gerzda* should pick the most useful value of r. The most useful one is usually going to be the most obvious one, and the most obvious one is usually the closest one.

In fact, the relationship will almost always be so close that the predicate expressing r will be either the seltau or the tertau predicate itself. This should come as no surprise, given that a word like *zdani* in Lojban is a predicate. Predicates express relations; so when you're looking for a relation to tie together *le zdani* and *le gerku*, the most obvious relation to pick is the very relation named by the tertau, *zdani*: the relation between a home and its dweller. As a result, the object which fills the first place of *gerku* (the dog) also fills the second place of *zdani* (the house-dweller).

The seltau-tertau relationship in the veljvo is expressed by the seltau or tertau predicate itself. Therefore, at least one of the seltau places is going to be equivalent to a tertau place. This place is thus redundant, and can be dropped from the place structure of the lujvo. As a corollary, the precise relationship between the veljvo components can be implicitly determined by finding one or more places to overlap in this way.

So what is the place structure of *gerzda*? We're left with three places, since the dweller, the *se zdani*, turned out to be identical to the dog, the *gerku*. We can proceed as follows:

(The notation introduced casually in Section 12.2 (p. 264) will be useful in the rest of this chapter. Rather than using the regular x1, x2, etc. to represent places, we'll use the first letter of the relevant gismu in place of the "x", or more than one letter where necessary to resolve ambiguities. Thus, $z1$ is the first place of *zdani*, and $g2$ is the second place of *gerku*.)

The place structure of *zdani* is given as Example 12.3 (p. 264), but is repeated here using the new notation:

Example 12.6

> $z1$ is a nest/house/lair/den of $z2$

The place structure of *gerku* is:

Example 12.7

> $g1$ is a dog of breed $g2$

But $z2$ is the same as $g1$; therefore, the tentative place structure for *gerzda* now becomes:

Example 12.8

> $z1$ is a house for dweller $z2$ of breed $g2$

which can also be written

Example 12.9

    z_1 is a house for dog g_1 of breed g_2

or more comprehensively

Example 12.10

    z_1 is a house for dweller/dog $z_2=g_1$ of breed g_2

Despite the apparently conclusive nature of Example 12.10 (p. 267), our task is not yet done: we still need to decide whether any of the remaining places should also be eliminated, and what order the lujvo places should appear in. These concerns will be addressed in the remainder of the chapter; but we are now equipped with the terminology needed for those discussions.

12.4 Selecting places

The set of places of an ordinary lujvo are selected from the places of its component gismu. More precisely, the places of such a lujvo are derived from the set of places of the component gismu by eliminating unnecessary places, until just enough places remain to give an appropriate meaning to the lujvo. In general, including a place makes the concept expressed by a lujvo more general; excluding a place makes the concept more specific, because omitting the place requires assuming a standard value or range of values for it.

It would be possible to design the place structure of a lujvo from scratch, treating it as if it were a gismu, and working out what arguments contribute to the notion to be expressed by the lujvo. There are two reasons arguing against doing so and in favor of the procedure detailed in this chapter.

The first is that it might be very difficult for a hearer or reader, who has no preconceived idea of what concept the lujvo is intended to convey, to work out what the place structure actually is. Instead, he or she would have to make use of a lujvo dictionary every time a lujvo is encountered in order to work out what a *se jbopli* or a *te klagau* is. But this would mean that, rather than having to learn just the 1300-odd gismu place structures, a Lojbanist would also have to learn myriads of lujvo place structures with little or no apparent pattern or regularity to them. The purpose of the guidelines documented in this chapter is to apply regularity and to make it conventional wherever possible.

The second reason is related to the first: if the veljvo of the lujvo has not been properly selected, and the places for the lujvo are formulated from scratch, then there is a risk that some of the places formulated may not correspond to any of the places of the gismu used in the veljvo of the lujvo. If that is the case – that is to say, if the lujvo places are not a subset of the veljvo gismu places – then it will be very difficult for the hearer or reader to understand what a particular place means, and what it is doing in that particular lujvo. This is a topic that will be further discussed in Section 12.14 (p. 279).

However, second-guessing the place structure of the lujvo is useful in guiding the process of subsequently eliminating places from the veljvo. If the Lojbanist has an idea of what the final place structure should look like, he or she should be able to pick an appropriate veljvo to begin with, in order to express the idea, and then to decide which places are relevant or not relevant to expressing that idea.

12.5 Symmetrical and asymmetrical lujvo

A common pattern, perhaps the most common pattern, of lujvo-making creates what is called a "symmetrical lujvo". A symmetrical lujvo is one based on a tanru interpretation such that the first place of the seltau is equivalent to the first place of the tertau: each component of the tanru characterizes the same object. As an illustration of this, consider the lujvo *balsoi*: it is intended to mean "both great and a soldier"- that is, "great soldier", which is the interpretation we would tend to give its veljvo, *banli sonci*. The underlying gismu place structures are:

Example 12.11

    banli b_1 is great in property b_2 by standard b_3
    sonci s_1 is a soldier of army s_2

In this case the s1 place of *sonci* is redundant, since it is equivalent to the b1 place of *banli*. Therefore the place structure of *balsoi* need not include places for both s1 and b1, as they refer to the same thing. So the place structure of *balsoi* is at most

Example 12.12

b1=s1 is a great soldier of army s2 in property b2 by standard b3

Some symmetrical veljvo have further equivalent places in addition to the respective first places. Consider the lujvo *tinju'i*, "to listen" ("to hear attentively, to hear and pay attention"). The place structures of the gismu *tirna* and *jundi* are:

Example 12.13

tirna t1 hears sound t2 against background noise t3
jundi j1 pays attention to j2

and the place structure of the lujvo is:

Example 12.14

j1=t1 listens to j2=t2 against background noise t3

Why so? Because not only is the j1 place (the one who pays attention) equivalent to the t1 place (the hearer), but the j2 place (the thing paid attention to) is equivalent to the t2 place (the thing heard).

A substantial minority of lujvo have the property that the first place of the seltau (*gerku* in this case) is equivalent to a place other than the first place of the tertau; such lujvo are said to be "asymmetrical". (There is a deliberate parallel here with the terms "asymmetrical tanru" and "symmetrical tanru" used in Chapter 5 (p. 79).)

In principle any asymmetrical lujvo could be expressed as a symmetrical lujvo. Consider *gerzda*, discussed in Section 12.3 (p. 266), where we learned that the g1 place was equivalent to the z2 place. In order to get the places aligned, we could convert *zdani* to *se zdani* (or *selzda* when expressed as a lujvo). The place structure of *selzda* is

Example 12.15

s1 is housed by nest s2

and so the three-part lujvo *gerselzda* would have the place structure

Example 12.16

s1=g1 is a dog housed in nest s2 of dog breed g2

However, although *gerselzda* is a valid lujvo, it doesn't translate "doghouse"; its first place is the dog, not the doghouse. Furthermore, it is more complicated than necessary; *gerzda* is simpler than *gerselzda*.

From the reader's or listener's point of view, it may not always be obvious whether a newly met lujvo is symmetrical or asymmetrical, and if the latter, what kind of asymmetrical lujvo. If the place structure of the lujvo isn't given in a dictionary or elsewhere, then plausibility must be applied, just as in interpreting tanru.

The lujvo *karcykla*, for example, is based on *karce klama*, or "car goer". The place structure of *karce* is:

Example 12.17

karce: ka1 is a car carrying ka2 propelled by ka3

A asymmetrical interpretation of *karcykla* that is strictly analogous to the place structure of *gerzda*, equating the kl2 (destination) and ka1 (car) places, would lead to the place structure

Example 12.18

kl1 goes to car kl2=ka1 which carries ka2 propelled by ka3 from origin kl3 via route kl4 by means of kl5

But in general we go about in cars, rather than going to cars, so a far more likely place structure treats the ka1 place as equivalent to the kl5 place, leading to

Example 12.19

> kl1 goes to destination kl2 from origin kl3 via route kl4 by means of car kl5=ka1 carrying ka2 propelled by ka3.

instead.

12.6 Dependent places

In order to understand which places, if any, should be completely removed from a lujvo place structure, we need to understand the concept of dependent places. One place of a brivla is said to be dependent on another if its value can be predicted from the values of one or more of the other places. For example, the g2 place of *gerku* is dependent on the g1 place. Why? Because when we know what fits in the g1 place (Spot, let us say, a well-known dog), then we know what fits in the g2 place ("St. Bernard", let us say). In other words, when the value of the g1 place has been specified, the value of the g2 place is determined by it. Conversely, since each dog has only one breed, but each breed contains many dogs, the g1 place is not dependent on the g2 place; if we know only that some dog is a St. Bernard, we cannot tell by that fact alone which dog is meant.

For *zdani*, on the other hand, there is no dependency between the places. When we know the identity of a house-dweller, we have not determined the house, because a dweller may dwell in more than one house. By the same token, when we know the identity of a house, we do not know the identity of its dweller, for a house may contain more than one dweller.

The rule for eliminating places from a lujvo is that dependent places provided by the seltau are eliminated. Therefore, in *gerzda* the dependent g2 place is removed from the tentative place structure given in Example 12.10 (p. 267), leaving the place structure:

Example 12.20

> z1 is the house dwelt in by dog z2=g1

Informally put, the reason this has happened – and it happens a lot with seltau places – is that the third place was describing not the doghouse, but the dog who lives in it. The sentence

Example 12.21

la	*mon.*	*rePOS.*	*gerzda*	*la*	*spat.*
That-named	**Mon**	**Repos**	**is-a-doghouse-of**	**that-named**	**Spot.**

really means

Example 12.22

la	*mon.*	*rePOS.*	*zdani*	*la*	*spat.*	*noi*	*gerku*
That-named	**Mon**	**Repos**	**is-a-house-of**	**that-named**	**Spot,**	**who**	**is-a-dog.**

since that is the interpretation we have given *gerzda*. But that in turn means

Example 12.23

la	*mon.*	*rePOS.*	*zdani*	*la*	*spat*
That-named	**Mon**	**Repos**	**is-a-house-of**	**that-named**	**Spot,**

noi ke'a	*gerku*	*zo'e*
who	**is-a-dog**	**of-unspecified-breed.**

Specifically,

Example 12.24

la	*mon.*	*rePOS.*	*zdani*	*la*	*spat.*
That-named	**Mon**	**Repos**	**is-a-house-of**	**that-named**	**Spot,**

noi ke'a	*gerku*	*la*	*sankt.*	*berNARD.*
who	**is-a-dog-of-breed**	**that-named**	**St.**	**Bernard.**

and in that case, it makes little sense to say

Example 12.25

la	mon.	rePOS.	gerzda	la	spat.	noi ke'a	gerku
That-named	Mon	Repos	is-a-doghouse-of	that-named	Spot,	who	is-a-dog

	la		sankt.	berNARD.	ku'o		
of-breed	that-named		St.	Bernard,			

	la		sankt.	berNARD.			
of-breed	that-named		St.	Bernard.			

employing the over-ample place structure of Example 12.10 (p. 267). The dog breed is redundantly given both in the main selbri and in the relative clause, and (intuitively speaking) is repeated in the wrong place, since the dog breed is supplementary information about the dog, and not about the doghouse.

As a further example, take *cakcinki*, the lujvo for "beetle", based on the tanru *calku cinki*, or "shell-insect". The gismu place structures are:

Example 12.26

calku: ca_1 is a shell/husk around ca_2 made of ca_3

cinki: ci_1 is an insect/arthropod of species ci_2

This example illustrates a cross-dependency between a place of one gismu and a place of the other. The ca_3 place is dependent on ci_1, because all insects (which fit into ci_1) have shells made of chitin (which fits into ca_3). Furthermore, ca_1 is dependent on ci_1 as well, because each insect has only a single shell. And since ca_2 (the thing with the shell) is equivalent to ci_1 (the insect), the place structure is

Example 12.27

$ci_1=ca_2$ is a beetle of species ci_2

with not a single place of *calku* surviving independently!

(Note that there is nothing in this explanation that tells us just why *cakcinki* means "beetle" (member of Coleoptera), since all insects in their adult forms have chitin shells of some sort. The answer, which is in no way predictable, is that the shell is a prominent, highly noticeable feature of beetles in particular.)

What about the dependency of ci_2 on ci_1? After all, no beetle belongs to more than one species, so it would seem that the ci_2 place of *cakcinki* could be eliminated on the same reasoning that allowed us to eliminate the g_2 place of *gerzda* above. However, it is a rule that dependent places are not eliminated from a lujvo when they are derived from the tertau of its veljvo. This rule is imposed to keep the place structures of lujvo from drifting too far from the tertau place structure; if a place is necessary in the tertau, it's treated as necessary in the lujvo as well.

In general, the desire to remove places coming from the tertau is a sign that the veljvo selected is simply wrong. Different place structures imply different concepts, and the lujvo maker may be trying to shoehorn the wrong concept into the place structure of his or her choosing. This is obvious when someone tries to shoehorn a *klama* tertau into a *litru* or *cliva* concept, for example: these gismu differ in their number of arguments, and suppressing places of *klama* in a lujvo doesn't make any sense if the resulting modified place structure is that of *litru* or *cliva*.

Sometimes the dependency is between a single place of the tertau and the whole event described by the seltau. Such cases are discussed further in Section 12.13 (p. 277).

Unfortunately, not all dependent places in the seltau can be safely removed: some of them are necessary to interpreting the lujvo's meaning in context. It doesn't matter much to a doghouse what breed of dog inhabits it, but it can make quite a lot of difference to the construction of a school building what kind of school is in it! Music schools need auditoriums and recital rooms, elementary schools need playgrounds, and so on: therefore, the place structure of *kuldi'u* (from *ckule dinju*, and meaning "school building") needs to be

Example 12.28

d_1 is a building housing school c_1 teaching subject c_3 to audience c_4

even though c_3 and c_4 are plainly dependent on c_1. The other places of *ckule*, the location (c_2) and operators (c_5), don't seem to be necessary to the concept "school building", and are dependent on c1 to boot, so they are omitted. Again, the need for case-by-case consideration of place structures is demonstrated.

12.7 Ordering lujvo places.

So far, we have concentrated on selecting the places to go into the place structure of a lujvo. However, this is only half the story. In using selbri in Lojban, it is important to remember the right order of the sumti. With lujvo, the need to attend to the order of sumti becomes critical: the set of places selected should be ordered in such a way that a reader unfamiliar with the lujvo should be able to tell which place is which.

If we aim to make understandable lujvo, then, we should make the order of places in the place structure follow some conventions. If this does not occur, very real ambiguities can turn up. Take for example the lujvo *jdaselsku*, meaning "prayer". In the sentence

Example 12.29

di'e	*jdaselsku*		*la*	*dong.*
This-utterance	**is-a-prayer**	**somehow-related-to**	**that-named**	**Dong.**

we must be able to know if Dong is the person making the prayer, giving the meaning

Example 12.30

> This is a prayer by Dong

or is the entity being prayed to, resulting in

Example 12.31

> This is a prayer to Dong

We could resolve such problems on a case-by-case basis for each lujvo (Section 12.14 (p. 279) discusses when this is actually necessary), but case-by-case resolution for run-of-the-mill lujvo makes the task of learning lujvo place structures unmanageable. People need consistent patterns to make sense of what they learn. Such patterns can be found across gismu place structures (see Section 12.16 (p. 283)), and are even more necessary in lujvo place structures. Case-by-case consideration is still necessary; lujvo creation is a subtle art, after all. But it is helpful to take advantage of any available regularities.

We use two different ordering rules: one for symmetrical lujvo and one for asymmetrical ones. A symmetrical lujvo like *balsoi* (from Section 12.5 (p. 267)) has the places of its tertau followed by whatever places of the seltau survive the elimination process. For *balsoi*, the surviving places of *banli* are b2 and b3, leading to the place structure:

Example 12.32

> b1=s1 is a great soldier of army s2 in property b2 by standard b3

just what appears in Example 12.11 (p. 267). In fact, all place structures shown until now have been in the correct order by the conventions of this section, though the fact has been left tacit until now.

The motivation for this rule is the parallelism between the lujvo bridi-schema

Example 12.33

b1	*balsoi*	*s2*	*b2*	*b3*
b1	**is-a-great-soldier**	**of-army-s2**	**in-property-b2**	**by-standard-b3**

and the more or less equivalent bridi-schema

Example 12.34

b1	*sonci*	*s2*	*gi'e*	*banli*	*b2*	*b3*
b1	**is-a-soldier**	**of-army-s2**	**and**	**is-great**	**in-property-b2**	**by-standard-b3**

where *gi'e* is the Lojban word for "and" when placed between two partial bridi, as explained in Section 14.9 (p. 328).

Asymmetrical lujvo like *gerzda*, on the other hand, employ a different rule. The seltau places are inserted not at the end of the place structure, but rather immediately after the tertau place which is equivalent to the first place of the seltau. Consider *dalmikce*, meaning "veterinarian": its veljvo is *danlu mikce*, or "animal doctor". The place structures for those gismu are:

Example 12.35

> *danlu*: d1 is an animal of species d2
>
> *mikce*: m1 is a doctor to patient m2 for ailment m3 using treatment m4

and the lujvo place structure is:

Example 12.36

> m1 is a doctor for animal m2=d1 of species d2 for ailment m3 using treatment m4

Since the shared place is m2=d1, the animal patient, the remaining seltau place d2 is inserted immediately after the shared place; then the remaining tertau places form the last two places of the lujvo.

12.8 lujvo with more than two parts.

The theory we have outlined so far is an account of lujvo with two parts. But often lujvo are made containing more than two parts. An example is *bavlamdei*, "tomorrow": it is composed of the rafsi for "future", "adjacent", and "day". How does the account we have given apply to lujvo like this?

The best way to approach such lujvo is to continue to classify them as based on binary tanru, the only difference being that the seltau or the tertau or both is itself a lujvo. So it is easiest to make sense of *bavlamdei* as having two components: *bavla'i*, "next", and *djedi*. If we know or invent the lujvo place structure for the components, we can compose the new lujvo place structure in the usual way.

In this case, *bavla'i* is given the place structure

Example 12.37

> b1=l1 is next after b2=l2

making it a symmetrical lujvo. We combine this with *djedi*, which has the place structure:

Example 12.38

> duration d1 is d2 days long (default 1) by standard d3

While symmetrical lujvo normally put any trailing tertau places before any seltau places, the day standard is a much less important concept than the day the tomorrow follows, in the definition of *bavlamdei*. This is an example of how the guidelines presented for selecting and ordering lujvo places are just that, not laws that must be rigidly adhered to. In this case, we choose to rank places in order of relative importance. The resulting place structure is:

Example 12.39

> d1=b1=l1 is a day following b2=l2, d2 days later (default 1) by standard d3

Here is another example of a multi-part lujvo: *cladakyxa'i*, meaning "long-sword", a specific type of medieval weapon. The gismu place structures are:

Example 12.40

> *clani*: c1 is long in direction c2 by standard c3
>
> *dakfu*: d1 is a knife for cutting d2 with blade made of d3
>
> *xarci*: xa1 is a weapon for use against xa2 by wielder xa3

Since *cladakyxa'i* is a symmetrical lujvo based on *cladakfu xarci*, and *cladakfu* is itself a symmetrical lujvo, we can do the necessary analyses all at once. Plainly c1 (the long thing), d1 (the knife), and xa1 (the weapon) are all the same. Likewise, the d2 place (the thing cut) is the same as the xa2 place (the target of the weapon), given that swords are used to cut victims. Finally, the c2 place (direction of length) is always along the sword blade in a longsword, by definition, and so is dependent on c1=d1=xa1. Adding on the places of the remaining gismu in right-to-left order we get:

Example 12.41

> xa1=d1=c1 is a long-sword for use against xa2=d2 by wielder xa3, with a blade made of d3, length measured by standard c3.

If the last place sounds unimportant to you, notice that what counts legally as a "sword", rather than just a "knife", depends on the length of the blade (the legal limit varies in different jurisdictions). This fifth place of *cladakyxa'i* may not often be explicitly filled, but it is still useful on occasion. Because it is so seldom important, it is best that it be last.

12.9 Eliding SE rafsi from seltau

It is common to form lujvo that omit the rafsi based on cmavo of selma'o SE, as well as other cmavo rafsi. Doing so makes lujvo construction for common or useful constructions shorter. Since it puts more strain on the listener who has not heard the lujvo before, the shortness of the word should not necessarily outweigh ease in understanding, especially if the lujvo refers to a rare or unusual concept.

Consider as an example the lujvo *ti'ifla*, from the veljvo *stidi flalu*, and meaning "bill, proposed law". The gismu place structures are:

Example 12.42

> *stidi*: agent st1 suggests idea/action st2 to audience st3
> *flalu*: f1 is a law specifying f2 for community f3 under conditions f4
> by lawgiver f5

This lujvo does not fit any of our existing molds: it is the second seltau place, st2, that is equivalent to one of the tertau places, namely f1. However, if we understand *ti'ifla* as an abbreviation for the lujvo *selti'ifla*, then we get the first places of seltau and tertau lined up. The place structure of *selti'i* is:

Example 12.43

> *selti'i*: idea/action se1 is suggested by agent se2 to audience se3

Here we can see that se1 (what is suggested) is equivalent to f1 (the law), and we get a normal symmetrical lujvo. The final place structure is:

Example 12.44

> f1=se1 is a bill specifying f2 for community f3 under conditions f4 by suggester se2 to audience/ lawgivers f5=se3

or, relabeling the places,

Example 12.45

> f1=st2 is a bill specifying f2 for community f3 under conditions f4 by suggester st1 to audience/ lawgivers f5=st3

where the last place (st3) is probably some sort of legislature.

Abbreviated lujvo like *ti'ifla* are more intuitive (for the lujvo-maker) than their more explicit counterparts like *selti'ifla* (as well as shorter). They don't require the coiner to sit down and work out the precise relation between the seltau and the tertau: he or she can just rattle off a rafsi pair. But should the lujvo get to the stage where a place structure needs to be worked out, then the precise relation does need to be specified. And in that case, such abbreviated lujvo form a trap in lujvo place ordering, since they obscure the most straightforward relation between the seltau and tertau. To give our lujvo-making guidelines as wide an application as possible, and to encourage analyzing the seltau-tertau relation in lujvo, lujvo like *ti'ifla* are given the place structure they would have with the appropriate SE added to the seltau.

Note that, with these lujvo, an interpretation requiring SE insertion is safe only if the alternatives are either implausible or unlikely to be needed as a lujvo. This may not always be the case, and Lojbanists should be aware of the risk of ambiguity.

12.10 Eliding SE rafsi from tertau

Eliding SE rafsi from tertau gets us into much more trouble. To understand why, recall that lujvo, following their veljvo, describe some type of whatever their tertau describe. Thus, *posydji* describes a type of *djica*, *gerzda* describes a type of *zdani*, and so on. What is certain is that *gerzda* does not describe a *se zdani*- it is not a word that could be used to describe an inhabitant such as a dog.

Now consider how we would translate the word "blue-eyed". Let's tentatively translate this word as *blakanla* (from *blanu kanla*, meaning "blue eye"). But immediately we are in trouble: we cannot say

Example 12.46

la	djak.	cu blakanla
That-named	**Jack**	**is-a-blue-eye**

because Jack is not an eye, *kanla*, but someone with an eye, *se kanla*. At best we can say

Example 12.47

la	djak.	cu	se blakanla
That-named	**Jack**		**is-the-bearer-of-blue-eyes**

But look now at the place structure of *blakanla*: it is a symmetrical lujvo, so the place structure is:

Example 12.48

bl1=k1 is a blue eye of bl2=k2

We end up being most interested in talking about the second place, not the first (we talk much more of people than of their eyes), so *se* would almost always be required.

What is happening here is that we are translating the tertau wrongly, under the influence of English. The English suffix "-eyed" does not mean "eye", but someone with an eye, which is *selkanla*.

Because we've got the wrong tertau (eliding a *se* that really should be there), any attempt to accommodate the resulting lujvo into our guidelines for place structure is fitting a square peg in a round hole. Since they can be so misleading, lujvo with SE rafsi elided from the tertau should be avoided in favor of their more explicit counterparts: in this case, *blaselkanla*.

12.11 Eliding KE and KEhE rafsi from lujvo

People constructing lujvo usually want them to be as short as possible. To that end, they will discard any cmavo they regard as niceties. The first such cmavo to get thrown out are usually *ke* and *ke'e*, the cmavo used to structure and group tanru. We can usually get away with this, because the interpretation of the tertau with *ke* and *ke'e* missing is less plausible than that with the cmavo inserted, or because the distinction isn't really important.

For example, in *bakrecpa'o*, meaning "beefsteak", the veljvo is

Example 12.49

[ke]	bakni	rectu	[ke'e]	panlo
(	**bovine**	**meat**	)	**slice**

because of the usual Lojban left-grouping rule. But there doesn't seem to be much difference between that veljvo and

Example 12.50

bakni	ke	rectu	panlo	[ke'e]
bovine	(	**meat**	**slice**	)

On the other hand, the lujvo *zernerkla*, meaning "to sneak in", almost certainly was formed from the veljvo

Example 12.51

zekri	ke	nenri	klama	[ke'e]
crime	(	**inside**	**go**	)

to go within, criminally

because the alternative,

Example 12.52

[ke]	*zekri*	*nenri*	*[ke'e]*	*klama*
(	crime	inside	)	go

doesn't make much sense. (To go to the inside of a crime? To go into a place where it is criminal to be inside – an interpretation almost identical with Example 12.51 (p. 274) anyway?)

There are cases, however, where omitting a KE or KEhE rafsi can produce another lujvo, equally useful. For example, *xaskemcakcurnu* means "oceanic shellfish", and has the veljvo

Example 12.53

xamsi			*ke*	*calku*	*curnu*
ocean	type-of	(	shell	worm	)

("worm" in Lojban refers to any invertebrate), but *xasycakcurnu* has the veljvo

Example 12.54

[ke]	*xamsi*	*calku*	*[ke'e]*		*curnu*
(	ocean	shell	)	type-of	worm

and might refer to the parasitic worms that infest clamshells.

Such misinterpretation is more likely than not in a lujvo starting with *sel-* (from *se*), *nal-* (from *na'e*) or *tol-* (from *to'e*): the scope of the rafsi will likeliest be presumed to be as narrow as possible, since all of these cmavo normally bind only to the following brivla or *ke...ke'e* group. For that reason, if we want to modify an entire lujvo by putting *se*, *na'e* or *to'e* before it, it's better to leave the result as two words, or else to insert *ke*, than to just stick the SE or NAhE rafsi on.

It is all right to replace the phrase *se klama* with *selkla*, and the places of *selkla* are exactly those of *se klama*. But consider the related lujvo *dzukla*, meaning "to walk to somewhere". It is a symmmetrical lujvo, derived from the veljvo *cadzu klama* as follows:

Example 12.55

> *cadzu*: c1 walks on surface c2 using limbs c3
> *klama*: k1 goes to k2 from k3 via route k4 using k5
> *dzukla*: c1=k1 walks to k2 from k3 via route k4 using limbs k5=c3 on surface c2

We can swap the k1 and k2 places using *se dzukla*, but we cannot directly make *se dzukla* into *seldzukla*, which would represent the veljvo *selcadzu klama* and plausibly mean something like "to go to a walking surface". Instead, we would need *selkemdzukla*, with an explicit rafsi for *ke*. Similarly, *nalbrablo* (from *na'e barda bloti*) means "non-big boat", whereas *na'e brablo* means "other than a big boat".

If the lujvo we want to modify with SE has a seltau already starting with a SE rafsi, we can take a shortcut. For instance, *gekmau* means "happier than", while *selgekmau* means "making people happier than, more enjoyable than, more of a 'se gleki' than". If something is less enjoyable than something else, we can say it is *se selgekmau*.

But we can also say it is *selselgekmau*. Two *se* cmavo in a row cancel each other (*se se gleki* means the same as just *gleki*), so there would be no good reason to have *selsel* in a lujvo with that meaning. Instead, we can feel free to interpret *selsel-* as *selkemsel-*. The rafsi combinations *terter-*, *velvel-* and *xelxel-* work in the same way.

Other SE combinations like *selter-*, although they might conceivably mean *se te*, more than likely should be interpreted in the same way, namely as *se ke te*, since there is no need to re-order places in the way that *se te* provides. (See Section 9.4 (p. 185).)

12.12 Abstract lujvo

The cmavo of NU can participate in the construction of lujvo of a particularly simple and well-patterned kind. Consider that old standard example, *klama*:

Example 12.56

k1 comes/goes to k2 from k3 via route k4 by means k5.

The selbri *nu klama [kei]* has only one place, the event-of-going, but the full five places exist implicitly between *nu* and *kei*, since a full bridi with all sumti may be placed there. In a lujvo, there is no room for such inside places, and consequently the lujvo *nunkla* (*nun-* is the rafsi for *nu*), needs to have six places:

Example 12.57

nu1 is the event of k1's coming/going to k2 from k3 via route k4 by means k5.

Here the first place of *nunklama* is the first and only place of *nu*, and the other five places have been pushed down by one to occupy the second through the sixth places. Full information on *nu*, as well as the other abstractors mentioned in this section, is given in Chapter 11 (p. 247).

For those abstractors which have a second place as well, the standard convention is to place this place after, rather than before, the places of the brivla being abstracted. The place structure of *nilkla*, the lujvo derived from *ni klama*, is the imposing:

Example 12.58

ni1 is the amount of k1's coming/going to k2 from k3 via route k4 by means k5, measured on scale ni2.

It is not uncommon for abstractors to participate in the making of more complex lujvo as well. For example, *nunsoidji*, from the veljvo

Example 12.59

nu	sonci	kei	djica
event-of	**being-a-soldier**		**desirer**

has the place structure

Example 12.60

d1 desires the event of (s1 being a soldier of army s2) for purpose d3

where the d2 place has disappeared altogether, being replaced by the places of the seltau. As shown in Example 12.60 (p. 276), the ordering follows this idea of replacement: the seltau places are inserted at the point where the omitted abstraction place exists in the tertau.

The lujvo *nunsoidji* is quite different from the ordinary asymmetric lujvo *soidji*, a "soldier desirer", whose place structure is just

Example 12.61

d1 desires (a soldier of army s2) for purpose d3

A *nunsoidji* might be someone who is about to enlist, whereas a *soidji* might be a camp-follower.

One use of abstract lujvo is to eliminate the need for explicit *kei* in tanru: *nunkalri gasnu* means much the same as *nu kalri kei gasnu*, but is shorter. In addition, many English words ending in *-hood* are represented with *nun-* lujvo, and other words ending in "-ness" or "-dom" are often representable with *kam-* lujvo (*kam-* is the rafsi for *ka*); *kambla* is "blueness".

Even though the cmavo of NU are long-scope in nature, governing the whole following bridi, the NU rafsi should generally be used as short-scope modifiers, like the SE and NAhE rafsi discussed in Section 12.9 (p. 273).

There is also a rafsi for the cmavo *jai*, namely *jax*, which allows sentences like

Example 12.62

mi	jai	rinka	le	nu	do	morsi
I	**am-associated-with**	**causing**	**the**	**event-of**	**your**	**death.**

I cause your death.

explained in Section 11.10 (p. 259), to be rendered with lujvo:

Example 12.63

mi	jaxri'a	le	nu	do	morsi
I	am-part-of-the-cause-of	the	event-of	your	dying.

In making a lujvo that contains *jax-* for a selbri that contains *jai*, the rule is to leave the *fai* place as a *fai* place of the lujvo; it does not participate in the regular lujvo place structure. (The use of *fai* is explained in Section 9.12 (p. 199) and Section 10.22 (p. 239).)

12.13 Implicit-abstraction lujvo

Eliding NU rafsi involves the same restrictions as eliding SE rafsi, plus additional ones. In general, NU rafsi should not be elided from the tertau, since that changes the kind of thing the lujvo is talking about from an abstraction to a concrete sumti. However, they may be elided from the seltau if no reasonable ambiguity would result.

A major difference, however, between SE elision and NU elision is that the former is a rather sparse process, providing a few convenient shortenings. Eliding *nu*, however, is extremely important in producing a class of lujvo called "implicit-abstraction lujvo".

Let us make a detailed analysis of the lujvo *nunctikezgau*, meaning "to feed". (If you think this lujvo is excessively longwinded, be patient.) The veljvo of *nunctikezgau* is *nu citka kei gasnu*. The relevant place structures are:

Example 12.64

> *nu*: n1 is an event
> *citka*: c1 eats c2
> *gasnu*: g1 does action/is the agent of event g2

In accordance with the procedure for analyzing three-part lujvo given in Section 12.8 (p. 272), we will first create an intermediate lujvo, *nuncti*, whose veljvo is *nu citka [kei]*. By the rules given in Section 12.12 (p. 275), *nuncti* has the place structure

Example 12.65

> n1 is the event of c1 eating c2

Now we can transform the veljvo of *nunctikezgau* into *nuncti gasnu*. The g2 place (what is brought about by the actor g1) obviously denotes the same thing as n1 (the event of eating). So we can eliminate g2 as redundant, leaving us with a tentative place structure of

Example 12.66

> g1 is the actor in the event n1=g2 of c1 eating c2

But it is also possible to omit the n1 place itself! The n1 place describes the event brought about; an event in Lojban is described as a bridi, by a selbri and its sumti; the selbri is already known (it's the seltau), and the sumti are also already known (they're in the lujvo place structure). So n1 would not give us any information we didn't already know. In fact, the n1=g2 place is dependent on c1 and c2 jointly – it does not depend on either c1 or c2 by itself. Being dependent and derived from the seltau, it is omissible. So the final place structure of *nunctikezgau* is:

Example 12.67

> g1 is the actor in the event of c1 eating c2

There is one further step that can be taken. As we have already seen with *balsoi* in Section 12.5 (p. 267), the interpretation of lujvo is constrained by the semantics of gismu and of their sumti places. Now, any asymmetrical lujvo with *gasnu* as its tertau will involve an event abstraction either implicitly or explicitly, since that is how the g2 place of *gasnu* is defined.

Therefore, if we assume that *nu* is the type of abstraction one would expect to be a *se gasnu*, then the rafsi *nun* and *kez* in *nunctikezgau* are only telling us what we would already have guessed – that the seltau of a *gasnu* lujvo is an event. If we drop these rafsi out, and use instead the shorter lujvo *ctigau*, rejecting its symmetrical interpretation ("someone who both does and eats"; "an eating doer"), we can still deduce that the seltau refers to an event.

(You can't "do an eater"/ *gasnu lo citka,* with the meaning of *do* as "bring about an event"; so the seltau must refer to an event, *nu citka.* The English slang meanings of "do someone", namely "socialize with someone" and "have sex with someone", are not relevant to *gasnu.*)

So we can simply use *ctigau* with the same place structure as *nunctikezgau:*

Example 12.68

> agent g1 causes c1 to eat c2
> g1 feeds c2 to c1

This particular kind of asymmetrical lujvo, in which the seltau serves as the selbri of an abstraction which is a place of the tertau, is called an implicit-abstraction lujvo, because one deduces the presence of an abstraction which is unexpressed (implicit).

To give another example: the gismu *basti,* whose place structure is

Example 12.69

> b1 replaces b2 in circumstances b3

can form the lujvo *basygau,* with the place structure:

Example 12.70

> g1 (agent) replaces b1 with b2 in circumstances b3

where both *basti* and *basygau* are translated "replace" in English, but represent different relations: *basti* may be used with no mention of any agent doing the replacing.

In addition, *gasnu*-based lujvo can be built from what we would consider nouns or adjectives in English. In Lojban, everything is a predicate, so adjectives, nouns and verbs are all treated in the same way. This is consistent with the use of similar causative affixes in other languages. For example, the gismu *litki,* meaning "liquid", with the place structure

Example 12.71

> l1 is a quantity of liquid of composition l2 under conditions l3

can give *likygau,* meaning "to liquefy":

Example 12.72

> g1 (agent) causes l1 to be a quantity of liquid of composition l2 under conditions l3.

While *likygau* correctly represents "causes to be a liquid", a different lujvo based on *galfi* (meaning "modify") may be more appropriate for "causes to become a liquid". On the other hand, *fetsygau* is potentially confusing, because it could mean "agent in the event of something becoming female" (the implicit-abstraction interpretation) or simply "female agent" (the parallel interpretation), so using implicit-abstraction lujvo is always accompanied with some risk of being misunderstood.

Many other Lojban gismu have places for event abstractions, and therefore are good candidates for the tertau of an implicit-abstraction lujvo. For example, lujvo based on *rinka,* with its place structure

Example 12.73

> event r1 causes event r2 to occur

are closely related to those based on *gasnu.* However, *rinka* is less generally useful than *gasnu,* because its r1 place is another event rather than a person: *lo rinka* is a cause, not a causer. Thus the place structure of *likyri'a,* a lujvo analogous to *likygau,* is

Example 12.74

> event r1 causes l1 to be a quantity of liquid of composition l2 under conditions l3

and would be useful in translating sentences like "The heat of the sun liquefied the block of ice."

Implicit-abstraction lujvo are a powerful means in the language of rendering quite verbose bridi into succinct and manageable concepts, and increasing the expressive power of the language.

12.14 Anomalous lujvo

Some lujvo that have been coined and actually employed in Lojban writing do not follow the guidelines expressed above, either because the places that are equivalent in the seltau and the tertau are in an unusual position, or because the seltau and tertau are related in a complex way, or both. An example of the first kind is *jdaselsku*, meaning "prayer", which was mentioned in Section 12.7 (p. 271). The gismu places are:

Example 12.75

> *lijda*: l1 is a religion with believers l2 and beliefs l3
> *cusku*: c1 expresses text c2 to audience c3 in medium c4

and *selsku*, the tertau of *jdaselsku*, has the place structure

Example 12.76

> s1 is a text expressed by s2 to audience s3 in medium s4

Now it is easy to see that the l2 and s2 places are equivalent: the believer in the religion (l2) is the one who expresses the prayer (s2). This is not one of the cases for which a place ordering rule has been given in Section 12.7 (p. 271) or Section 12.13 (p. 277); therefore, for lack of a better rule, we put the tertau places first and the remaining seltau places after them, leading to the place structure:

Example 12.77

> s1 is a prayer expressed by s2=l2 to audience s3 in medium s4 pertaining to religion l1

The l3 place (the beliefs of the religion) is dependent on the l1 place (the religion) and so is omitted.

We could make this lujvo less messy by replacing it with *se seljdasku*, where *seljdasku* is a normal symmetrical lujvo with place structure:

Example 12.78

> c1=l2 religiously expresses prayer c2 to audience c3 in medium s4 pertaining to religion l1

which, according to the rule expressed in Section 12.9 (p. 273), can be further expressed as *selseljdasku*. However, there is no need for the ugly *selsel-* prefix just to get the rules right: *jdaselsku* is a reasonable, if anomalous, lujvo.

However, there is a further problem with *jdaselsku*, not resolvable by using *seljdasku*. No veljvo involving just the two gismu *lijda* and *cusku* can fully express the relationship implicit in prayer. A prayer is not just anything said by the adherents of a religion; nor is it even anything said by them acting as adherents of that religion. Rather, it is what they say under the authority of that religion, or using the religion as a medium, or following the rules associated with the religion, or something of the kind. So the veljvo is somewhat elliptical.

As a result, both *seljdasku* and *jdaselsku* belong to the second class of anomalous lujvo: the veljvo doesn't really supply all that the lujvo requires.

Another example of this kind of anomalous lujvo, drawn from the tanru lists in Section 5.14 (p. 101), is *lange'u*, meaning "sheepdog". Clearly a sheepdog is not a dog which is a sheep (the symmetrical interpretation is wrong), nor a dog of the sheep breed (the asymmetrical interpretation is wrong). Indeed, there is simply no overlap in the places of *lanme* and *gerku* at all. Rather, the lujvo refers to a dog which controls sheep flocks, a *terlanme jitro gerku*, the lujvo from which is *terlantroge'u* with place structure:

Example 12.79

> g1=j1 is a dog that controls sheep flock l3=j2 made up of sheep l1 in activity j3 of dog breed g2

based on the gismu place structures

Example 12.80

> *lanme*: l1 is a sheep of breed l2 belonging to flock l3
> *gerku*: g1 is a dog of breed g2
> *jitro*: j1 controls j2 in activity j3

Note that this lujvo is symmetrical between *lantro* (sheep-controller) and *gerku*, but *lantro* is itself an asymmetrical lujvo. The l2 place, the breed of sheep, is removed as dependent on l1. However, the lujvo *lange'u* is both shorter than *terlantroge'u* and sufficiently clear to warrant its use: its place structure, however, should be the same as that of the longer lujvo, for which *lange'u* can be understood as an abbreviation.

Another example is *xanmi'e*, "to command by hand, to beckon". The component place structures are:

Example 12.81

> *xance*: xa1 is the hand of xa2
>
> *minde*: m1 gives commands to m2 to cause m3 to happen

The relation between the seltau and tertau is close enough for there to be an overlap: xa2 (the person with the hand) is the same as m1 (the one who commands). But interpreting *xanmi'e* as a symmetrical lujvo with an elided *sel-* in the seltau, as if from *se xance minde*, misses the point: the real relation expressed by the lujvo is not just "one who commands and has a hand", but "to command using the hand". The concept of "using" suggests the gismu *pilno*, with place structure

Example 12.82

> p1 uses tool p2 for purpose p3

Some possible three-part veljvo are (depending on how strictly you want to constrain the veljvo)

Example 12.83

[ke]	xance	pilno	[ke'e]		minde
(	hand	user	)	type-of	commander

Example 12.84

[ke]	minde	xance	[ke'e]		pilno
(	commander	hand	)	type-of	user

or even

Example 12.85

minde		ke	xance	pilno	[ke'e]
commander	type-of	(	hand	user	)

which lead to the three different lujvo *xanplimi'e*, *mi'erxanpli*, and *minkemxanpli* respectively.

Does this make *xanmi'e* wrong? By no means. But it does mean that there is a latent component to the meaning of *xanmi'e*, the gismu *pilno*, which is not explicit in the veljvo. And it also means that, for a place structure derivation that actually makes sense, rather than being ad-hoc, the Lojbanist should probably go through a derivation for *xancypliminde* or one of the other possibilities that is analogous to the analysis of *terlantroge'u* above, even if he or she decides to stick with a shorter, more convenient form like *xanmi'e*. In addition, of course, the possibilities of elliptical lujvo increase their potential ambiguity enormously – an unavoidable fact which should be borne in mind.

12.15 Comparatives and superlatives

English has the concepts of "comparative adjectives" and "superlative adjectives" which can be formed from other adjectives, either by adding the suffixes "-er" and "-est" or by using the words "more" and "most", respectively. The Lojbanic equivalents, which can be made from any brivla, are lujvo with the tertau *zmadu*, *mleca*, *zenba*, *jdika*, and *traji*. In order to make these lujvo regular and easy to make, certain special guidelines are imposed.

We will begin with lujvo based on *zmadu* and *mleca*, whose place structures are:

Example 12.86

> *zmadu*: z1 is more than z2 in property z3 in quantity z4
>
> *mleca*: m1 is less than m2 in property m3 in quantity m4

For example, the concept "young" is expressed by the gismu *citno*, with place structure

12.15 Comparatives and superlatives

Example 12.87

> *citno*: c1 is young

The comparative concept "younger" can be expressed by the lujvo *citmau* (based on the veljvo *citno zmadu*, meaning "young more-than").

Example 12.88

mi	citmau	do	lo	nanca	be	li	xa
I	am-younger-than	you	by	one-year	multiplied-by	the-number	six.

I am six years younger than you.

The place structure for *citmau* is

Example 12.89

> z1=c1 is younger than z2=c1 by amount z4

Similarly, in Lojban you can say:

Example 12.90

do	citme'a	mi	lo	nanca	be	li	xa
You	are-less-young-than	me	by	one-year	multiplied-by	the-number	six.

You are six years less young than me.

In English, "more" comparatives are easier to make and use than "less" comparatives, but in Lojban the two forms are equally easy.

Because of their much simpler place structure, lujvo ending in *-mau* and *-me'a* are in fact used much more frequently than *zmadu* and *mleca* themselves as selbri. It is highly unlikely for such lujvo to be construed as anything other than implicit-abstraction lujvo. But there is another type of ambiguity relevant to these lujvo, and which has to do with what is being compared.

For example, does *nelcymau* mean "X likes Y more than X likes Z", or "X likes Y more than Z likes Y"? Does *klamau* mean: "X goes to Y more than to Z", "X goes to Y more than Z does", "X goes to Y from Z more than from W", or what?

We answer this concern by putting regularity above any considerations of concept usefulness: by convention, the two things being compared always fit into the first place of the seltau. In that way, each of the different possible interpretations can be expressed by SE-converting the seltau, and making the required place the new first place. As a result, we get the following comparative lujvo place structures:

Example 12.91

> *nelcymau*: z1, more than z2, likes n2 by amount z4
>
> *selnelcymau*: z1, more than z2, is liked by n1 in amount z4
>
> *klamau*: z1, more than z2, goes to k2 from k3 via k4 by means of k5
>
> *selklamau*: z1, more than z2, is gone to by k1 from k3 via k4 by means of k5
>
> *terklamau*: z1, more than z2, is an origin point from destination k2 for k1's going via k4 by means of k5

(See Chapter 11 (p. 247) for the way in which this problem is resolved when lujvo aren't used.)

The ordering rule places the things being compared first, and the other seltau places following. Unfortunately the z4 place, which expresses by how much one entity exceeds the other, is displaced into a lujvo place whose number is different for each lujvo. For example, while *nelcymau* has z4 as its fourth place, *klamau* has it as its sixth place. In any sentence where a difficulty arises, this amount-place can be redundantly tagged with *vemau* (for *zmadu*) or *veme'a* (for *mleca*) to help make the speaker's intention clear.

It is important to realize that such comparative lujvo do not presuppose their seltau. Just as in English, saying someone is younger than someone else doesn't imply that they're young in the first place: an octogenarian, after all, is still younger than a nonagenarian. Rather, the 80-year-old has a greater *ni citno* than the 90-year-old. Similarly, a 5-year-old is older than a 1-year-old, but is not considered "old" by most standards.

There are some comparative concepts which are in which the *se zmadu* is difficult to specify. Typically, these involve comparisons implicitly made with a former state of affairs, where stating a z2 place explicitly would be problematic.

In such cases, it is best not to use *zmadu* and leave the comparison hanging, but to use instead the gismu *zenba*, meaning "increase" (and *jdika*, meaning "decrease", in place of *mleca*). The gismu *zenba* was included in the language precisely in order to capture those notions of increase which *zmadu* can't quite cope with; in addition, we don't have to waste a place in lujvo or tanru on something that we'd never fill in with a value anyway. So we can translate "I'm stronger now" not as

Example 12.92

mi	ca	tsamau
I	now	am-stronger.

which implies that I'm currently stronger than somebody else (the elided occupant of the second or z2 place), but as

Example 12.93

mi	ca	tsaze'a

I increase in strength.

Finally, lujvo with a tertau of *traji* are used to build superlatives. The place structure of *traji* is

Example 12.94

t1 is superlative in property t2, being the t3 extremum (largest by default) of set t4

Consider the gismu *xamgu*, whose place structure is:

Example 12.95

xa1 is good for xa2 by standard xa3

The comparative form is *xagmau*, corresponding to English "better", with a place structure (by the rules given above) of

Example 12.96

z1 is better than z2 for xa2 by standard xa3 in amount z4

We would expect the place structure of *xagrai*, the superlative form, to somehow mirror that, given that comparatives and superlatives are comparable concepts, resulting in:

Example 12.97

xa1=t1 is the best of the set t4 for xa2 by standard xa3.

The t2 place in *traji*, normally filled by a property abstraction, is replaced by the seltau places, and the t3 place specifying the extremum of *traji* (whether the most or the least, that is) is presumed by default to be "the most".

But the set against which the t1 place of *traji* is compared is not the t2 place (which would make the place structure of *traji* fully parallel to that of *zmadu*), but rather the t4 place. Nevertheless, by a special exception to the rules of place ordering, the t4 place of *traji*-based lujvo becomes the second place of the lujvo. Some examples:

Example 12.98

la	djudis.	cu	citrai	lo'i	lobypli

Judy is the youngest of all Lojbanists.

Example 12.99

la	.ainctain.	cu	balrai	lo'i	skegunka

Einstein was the greatest of all scientists.

12.16 Notes on gismu place structures

Unlike the place structures of lujvo, the place structures of gismu were assigned in a far less systematic way through a detailed case-by-case analysis and repeated reviews with associated changes. (The gismu list is now baselined, so no further changes are contemplated.) Nevertheless, certain regularities were imposed both in the choice of places and in the ordering of places which may be helpful to the learner and the lujvo-maker, and which are therefore discussed here.

The choice of gismu places results from the varying outcome of four different pressures: brevity, convenience, metaphysical necessity, and regularity. (These are also to some extent the underlying factors in the lujvo place structures generated by the methods of this chapter.) The implications of each are roughly as follows:

Brevity tends to remove places: the fewer places a gismu has, the easier it is to learn, and the less specific it is. As mentioned in Section 12.4 (p. 267), a brivla with fewer place structures is less specific, and generality is a virtue in gismu, because they must thoroughly blanket all of semantic space.

Convenience tends to increase the number of places: if a concept can be expressed as a place of some existing gismu, there is no need to make another gismu, a lujvo or a fu'ivla for it.

Metaphysical necessity can either increase or decrease places: it is a pressure tending to provide the "right number" of places. If something is part of the essential nature of a concept, then a place must be made for it; on the other hand, if instances of the concept need not have some property, then this pressure will tend to remove the place.

Regularity is a pressure which can also either increase or decrease places. If a gismu has a given place, then gismu which are semantically related to it are likely to have the place also.

Here are some examples of gismu place structures, with a discussion of the pressures operating on them:

Example 12.100

xekri: xe1 is black

Brevity was the most important goal here, reinforced by one interpretation of metaphysical necessity. There is no mention of color standards here, as many people have pointed out; like all color gismu, *xekri* is explicitly subjective. Objective color standards can be brought in by an appropriate BAI tag such as *ci'u* ("in system"; see Section 9.6 (p. 188)) or by making a lujvo.

Example 12.101

jbena: j1 is born to j2 at time j3 and location j4

The gismu *jbena* contains places for time and location, which few other gismu have: normally, the time and place at which something is done is supplied by a tense tag (see Chapter 10 (p. 207)). However, providing these places makes *le te jbena* a simple term for "birthday" and *le ve jbena* for "birthplace", so these places were provided despite their lack of metaphysical necessity.

Example 12.102

rinka: event r1 is the cause of event r2

The place structure of *rinka* does not have a place for the agent, the one who causes, as a result of the pressure toward metaphysical necessity. A cause-effect relationship does not have to include an agent: an event (such as snow melting in the mountains) may cause another event (such as the flooding of the Nile) without any human intervention or even knowledge.

Indeed, there is a general tendency to omit agent places from most gismu except for a few such as *gasnu* and *zukte* which are then used as tertau in order to restore the agent place when needed: see Section 12.13 (p. 277).

Example 12.103

cinfo c1 is a lion of species/breed c2

The c2 place of *cinfo* is provided as a result of the pressure toward regularity. All animal and plant gismu have such an x2 place; although there is in fact only one species of lion, and breeds of lion, though they exist, aren't all that important in talking about lions. The species/breed place must exist for such diversified species as dogs, and for general terms like *cinki* (insect), and are provided for all other animals and plants as a matter of regularity.

Less can be said about gismu place structure ordering, but some regularities are apparent. The places tend to appear in decreasing order of psychological saliency or importance. There is an implication within the place structure of *klama*, for example, that *lo klama* (the one going) will be talked about more often, and is thus more important, than *lo se klama* (the destination), which is in turn more important than *lo xe klama* (the means of transport).

Some specific tendencies (not really rules) can also be observed. For example, when there is an agent place, it tends to be the first place. Similarly, when a destination and an origin point are mentioned, the destination is always placed just before the origin point. Places such as "under conditions" and "by standard", which often go unfilled, are moved to near the end of the place structure.

Chapter 13
Oooh! Arrgh! Ugh! Yecch! Attitudinal and Emotional Indicators

.oi ro'i ro'a ro'e

13.1 What are attitudinal indicators?

This chapter explains the various words that Lojban provides for expressing attitude and related notions. In natural languages, attitudes are usually expressed by the tone of voice when speaking, and (very imperfectly) by punctuation when writing. For example, the bare words

Example 13.1

    John is coming.

can be made, through tone of voice, to express the speaker's feeling of happiness, pity, hope, surprise, or disbelief. These fine points of tone cannot be expressed in writing. Attitudes are also expressed with various sounds which show up in print as oddly spelled words, such as the "Oooh!", "Arrgh!", "Ugh!", and "Yecch!" in the title. These are part of the English language; people born to other languages use a different set; yet you won't find any of these words in a dictionary.

In Lojban, everything that can be spoken can also be written. Therefore, these tones of voice must be represented by explicit words known as "attitudinal indicators", or just "attitudinals". This rule seems awkward and clunky to English-speakers at first, but is an essential part of the Lojbanic way of doing things.

The simplest way to use attitudinal indicators is to place them at the beginning of a text. In that case, they express the speaker's prevailing attitude. Here are some examples, correlated with the attitudes mentioned following Example 13.1 (p. 285):

285

Example 13.2

.ui	la	djan	klama
[Whee!]	that-named	John	is-coming!

Example 13.3

.uu	la	djan	klama
[Alas!]	that-named	John	is-coming.

Example 13.4

.a'o	la	djan	klama
[Hopefully]	that-named	John	is-coming.

Example 13.5

.ue	la	djan	klama
[Wow!]	that-named	John	is-coming!

Example 13.6

.ianai	la	djan	klama
[Nonsense!]	that-named	John	is-coming.

The primary Lojban attitudinals are all the cmavo of the form VV or V'V: one of the few cases where cmavo have been classified solely by their form. There are 39 of these cmavo: all 25 possible vowel pairs of the form V'V, the four standard diphthongs (.ai, .au, .ei, and .oi), and the ten more diphthongs that are permitted only in these attitudinal indicators and in names and borrowings (.ia, .ie, .ii, .io, .iu, .ua, .ue, .ui, .uo, and .uu). Note that each of these cmavo has a period before it, marking the pause that is mandatory before every word beginning with a vowel. Attitudinals, like most of the other kinds of indicators described in this chapter, belong to selma'o UI.

Attitudinals can also be compound cmavo, of the types explained in Sections 4-8; Example 13.6 (p. 286) illustrates one such possibility, the compound attitudinal .ianai. In attitudinals, -nai indicates polar negation: the opposite of the simple attitudinal without the -nai. Thus, as you might suppose, .ia expresses belief, since .ianai expresses disbelief.

In addition to the attitudinals, there are other classes of indicators: intensity markers, emotion categories, attitudinal modifiers, observationals, and discursives. All of them are grammatically equivalent, which is why they are treated together in this chapter.

Every indicator behaves in more or less the same way with respect to the grammar of the rest of the language. In general, one or more indicators can be inserted at the beginning of an utterance or after any word. Indicators at the beginning apply to the whole utterance; otherwise, they apply to the word that they follow. More details can be found in Section 13.9 (p. 299).

Throughout this chapter, tables of indicators will be written in four columns. The first column is the cmavo itself. The second column is a corresponding English word, not necessarily a literal translation. The fourth column represents the opposite of the second column, and shows the approximate meaning of the attitudinal when suffixed with -nai. The third column, which is sometimes omitted, indicates a neutral point between the second and fourth columns, and shows the approximate meaning of the attitudinal when it is suffixed with -cu'i. The cmavo cu'i belongs to selma'o CAI, and is explained more fully in Section 13.4 (p. 292).

One flaw that the English glosses are particularly subject to is that in English it is often difficult to distinguish between expressing your feelings and talking about them, particularly with the limited resource of the written word. So the gloss for .ui should not really be "happiness" but some sound or tone that expresses happiness. However, there aren't nearly enough of those that have unambiguous or obvious meanings in English to go around for all the many, many different emotions Lojban speakers can readily express.

Many indicators of CV'V form are loosely derived from specific gismu. The gismu should be thought of as a memory hook, not an equivalent of the cmavo. Such gismu are shown in this chapter between square brackets, thus: [gismu].

13.2 Pure emotion indicators

Attitudinals make no claim: they are expressions of attitude, not of facts or alleged facts. As a result, attitudinals themselves have no truth value, nor do they directly affect the truth value of a bridi that they modify. However, since emotional attitudes are carried in your mind, they reflect reactions to that version of the world that the mind is thinking about; this is seldom identical with the real world. At times, we are thinking about our idealized version of the real world; at other times we are thinking about a potential world that might or might not ever exist.

Therefore, there are two groups of attitudinals in Lojban. The "pure emotion indicators" express the way the speaker is feeling, without direct reference to what else is said. These indicators comprise the attitudinals which begin with *u* or *o* and many of those beginning with *i*.

The cmavo beginning with *u* are simple emotions, which represent the speaker's reaction to the world as it is, or as it is perceived to be.

.ua	discovery		confusion
.u'a	gain		loss
.ue	surprise	no surprise	expectation
.u'e	wonder		commonplace
.ui	happiness		unhappiness
.u'i	amusement		weariness
.uo	completion		incompleteness
.u'o	courage	timidity	cowardice
.uu	pity		cruelty
.u'u	repentance	lack of regret	innocence

Here are some typical uses of the *u* attitudinals:

Example 13.7

.ua	mi	facki	fi	le	mi	mapku
[Eureka!]	I	found-out	about	the	of-me	hat.

[Eureka!] I found my hat! [emphasizes the discovery of the hat]

Example 13.8

.u'a	mi	facki	fi	le	mi	mapku
[Gain!]	I	found-out	about	the	of-me	hat.

[Gain!] I found my hat! [emphasizes the obtaining of the hat]

Example 13.9

.ui	mi	facki	fi	le	mi	mapku
[Yay!]	I	found-out	about	the	of-me	hat.

[Yay!] I found my hat! [emphasizes the feeling of happiness]

Example 13.10

.uo	mi	facki	fi	le	mi	mapku
[At-last!]	I	found-out	about	the	of-me	hat.

[At last!] I found my hat! [emphasizes that the finding is complete]

Example 13.11

.uu	do	cortu
[Pity!]	you	feel-pain.

[Pity!] you feel pain. [expresses speaker's sympathy]

Example 13.12

.u'u	do	cortu
[Repentance!]	you	feel-pain.

[Repentance!] you feel pain. [expresses that speaker feels guilty]

In Example 13.10 (p. 287), note that the attitudinal *.uo* is translated by an English non-attitudinal phrase: "At last!" It is common for the English equivalents of Lojban attitudinals to be short phrases of this sort, with more or less normal grammar, but actually expressions of emotion.

In particular, both *.uu* and *.u'u* can be translated into English as "I'm sorry"; the difference between these two attitudes frequently causes confusion among English-speakers who use this phrase, leading to responses like "Why are you sorry? It's not your fault!"

It is important to realize that *.uu*, and indeed all attitudinals, are meant to be used sincerely, not ironically. In English, the exclamation "Pity!" is just as likely to be ironically intended, but this usage does not extend to Lojban. Lying with attitudinals is (normally) as inappropriate to Lojban discourse as any other kind of lying: perhaps worse, because misunderstood emotions can cause even greater problems than misunderstood statements.

The following examples display the effects of *nai* and *cu'i* when suffixed to an attitudinal:

Example 13.13

.ue	la	djan.	klama
[Surprise!]	that-named	John	comes.

Example 13.14

.uecu'i	la	djan.	klama
[Ho-hum.]	that-named	John	comes.

Example 13.15

.uenai	la	djan.	klama
[Expected!]	that-named	John	comes.

In Example 13.15 (p. 288), John's coming has been anticipated by the speaker. In Example 13.13 (p. 288) and Example 13.14 (p. 288), no such anticipation has been made, but in Example 13.14 (p. 288) the lack-of-anticipation goes no further – in Example 13.13 (p. 288), it amounts to actual surprise.

It is not possible to firmly distinguish the pure emotion words beginning with *o* or *i* from those beginning with *u*, but in general they represent more complex, more ambivalent, or more difficult emotions.

.o'a	pride	modesty	shame
.o'e	closeness	detachment	distance
.oi	complaint/pain	doing OK	pleasure
.o'i	caution	boldness	rashness
.o'o	patience	mere tolerance	anger
.o'u	relaxation	composure	stress

Here are some examples:

Example 13.16

.oi	la	djan.	klama
[Complaint!]	that-named	John	is-coming.

Here the speaker is distressed or discomfited over John's coming. The word *.oi* is derived from the Yiddish word "oy" of similar meaning. It is the only cmavo with a Yiddish origin.

Example 13.17

.o'onai	la	djan.	klama
[Anger!]	that-named	John	is-coming!

Here the speaker feels anger over John's coming.

Example 13.18

.o'i	la	djan.	klama
[Beware!]	that-named	John	is-coming.

Here there is a sense of danger in John's arrival.

Example 13.19

.o'ecu'i	la	djan.	klama
[Detachment!]	that-named	John	is-coming.

Example 13.20

.o'u	la	djan.	klama
[Phew!]	that-named	John	is-coming.

In Example 13.19 (p. 289) and Example 13.20 (p. 289), John's arrival is no problem: in the former example, the speaker feels emotional distance from the situation; in the latter example, John's coming is actually a relief of some kind.

The pure emotion indicators beginning with *i* are those which could not be fitted into the *u* or *o* groups because there was a lack of room, so they are a mixed lot. *.ia, i'a, .ie,* and *i'e* do not appear here, as they belong in Section 13.3 (p. 289) instead.

.ii	fear	nervousness	security
.i'i	togetherness		privacy
.io	respect		disrespect
.i'o	appreciation		envy
.iu	love	no love lost	hatred
.i'u	familiarity		mystery

Here are some examples:

Example 13.21

.ii	smacu
[Fear!]	[Observative:]-a-mouse!

Eek! A mouse!

Example 13.22

la	djan.	.iu	klama
That-named	John	[love!]	is-coming.

Example 13.23

la	djan.	.ionai	klama
That-named	John	[disrespect!]	is-coming.

Example 13.21 (p. 289) shows an attitude-colored observative; the attitudinal modifies the situation described by the observative, namely the mouse that is causing the emotion. Lojban-speaking toddlers, if there ever are any, will probably use sentences like Example 13.21 (p. 289) a lot.

Example 13.22 (p. 289) and Example 13.23 (p. 289) use attitudinals that follow *la djan.* rather than being at the beginning of the sentence. This form means that the attitude is attached to John rather than the event of his coming; the speaker loves or disrespects John specifically. Compare:

Example 13.24

la	djan.	klama	.iu
That-named	John	is-coming	[love!]

where it is specifically the coming of John that inspires the feeling.

Example 13.23 (p. 289) is a compact way of swearing at John: you could translate it as "That good-for-nothing John is coming."

13.3 Propositional attitude indicators

As mentioned at the beginning of Section 13.2 (p. 287), attitudinals may be divided into two groups, the pure emotion indicators explained in that section, and a contrasting group which may be called the "propositional attitude indicators". These indicators establish an internal, hypothetical world which the speaker is reacting to, distinct from the world as it really is. Thus we may be expressing our attitude towards "what the world would be like if …", or more directly stating our attitude towards making the potential world a reality.

In general, the bridi paraphrases of pure emotions look (in English) something like "I'm going to the market, and I'm happy about it". The emotion is present with the subject of the primary claim, but is logically independent of it. Propositional attitudes, though, look more like "I intend to go to the market", where the main claim is logically subordinate to the intention: I am not claiming that I am actually going to the market, but merely that I intend to.

There is no sharp distinction between attitudinals beginning with *a* and those beginning with *e*; however, the original intent (not entirely realized due to the need to cram too many attitudes into too little space) was to make the members of the *a*-series the purer, more attitudinal realizers of a potential world, while the members of the *e*-series were more ambivalent or complex about the speaker's intention with regard to the predication. The relationship between the *a*-series and the *e*-series is similar to that between the *u*-series and the *o*-series, respectively. A few propositional attitude indicators overflowed into the *i*-series as well.

In fact, the entire distinction between pure emotions and propositional attitudes is itself a bit shaky: *u'u* can be seen as a propositional attitude indicator meaning "I regret that …", and *a'e* (discussed below) can be seen as a pure emotion meaning "I'm awake/aware". The division of the attitudinals into pure-emotion and propositional-attitude classes in this chapter is mostly by way of explanation; it is not intended to permit firm rulings on specific points. Attitudinals are the part of Lojban most distant from the "logical language" aspect.

Here is the list of propositional attitude indicators grouped by initial letter, starting with those beginning with *a*:

.a'a	attentive	inattentive	avoiding
.a'e	alertness		exhaustion
.ai	intent	indecision	refusal
.a'i	effort	no real effort	repose
.a'o	hope		despair
.au	desire	indifference	reluctance
.a'u	interest	no interest	repulsion

Some examples (of a parental kind):

Example 13.25

.a'a	do	zgana	le	veltivni
[attentive]	you	observe	the	television-receiver.

I'm noticing that you are watching the TV.

Example 13.26

.a'enai	do	ranji	bacru
[exhaustion]	you	continuously	utter.

I'm worn out by your continuous talking.

Example 13.27

.ai	mi	benji	do	le	ckana
[intent]	I	transfer	you	to-the	bed.

I'm putting you to bed.

Example 13.28

.a'i	mi	ba	gasnu	le	nu	do	cikna	binxo
[effort]	I	[future]	am-the-actor-in	the	event-of	you	awake-ly	become.

It'll be hard for me to wake you up.

Example 13.29

.a'o	*mi*	*kanryze'a*	*ca*	*le*	*bavlamdei*
[hope]	I	am-health-increased	at-time	the	future-adjacent-day.

I hope I feel better tomorrow!

Example 13.30

.au	*mi*	*sipna*
[desire]	I	sleep.

I want to sleep.

Example 13.31

.a'ucu'i	*do*	*pante*
[no-interest]	you	complain.

I have no interest in your complaints.

(In a real-life situation, Examples 3.1-3.7 would also be decorated by various pure emotion indicators, certainly including *.oicai*, but probably also *.iucai*.)

Splitting off the attitude into an indicator allows the regular bridi grammar to do what it does best: express the relationships between concepts that are intended, desired, hoped for, or whatever. Rephrasing these examples to express the attitude as the main selbri would make for unacceptably heavyweight grammar.

Here are the propositional attitude indicators beginning with *e*, which stand roughly in the relation to those beginning with *a* as the pure-emotion indicators beginning with *o* do to those beginning with *u*- they are more complex or difficult:

.e'a	permission		prohibition
.e'e	competence		incompetence
.ei	obligation		freedom
.e'i	constraint	independence	resistance to constraint
.e'o	request		negative request
.e'u	suggestion	no suggestion	warning

More examples (after a good night's sleep):

Example 13.32

.e'a	*do*	*sazri*	*le*	*karce*
[permission]	you	drive	the	car.

Sure, you can drive the car.

Example 13.33

.e'e	*mi*	*lifri*	*tu'a*	*do*
[competence]	I	experience	something-related-to	you.

I feel up to dealing with you.

Example 13.34

.ei	*mi*	*tisygau*	*le*	*karce*	*ctilyvau*
[obligation]	I	fill	the	car-type-of	petroleum-container.

I should fill the car's gas tank.

Example 13.35

.e'o	*ko*	*ko*	*kurji*
[request]	you-imperative	of-you-imperative	take-care.

Please take care of yourself!

Example 13.36

.e'u	do	klama	le	panka
[suggestion]	**you**	**go**	**to-the**	**park.**

I suggest going to the park.

Finally, the propositional attitude indicators beginning with *i*, which are the overflow from the other sets:

.ia	belief	skepticism	disbelief
.i'a	acceptance		blame
.ie	agreement		disagreement
.i'e	approval	non-approval	disapproval

Still more examples (much, much later):

Example 13.37

.ianai	do	pu	pensi	le	nu	tcica	mi
[disbelief]	**you**	**[past]**	**think**	**the**	**event-of**	**deceiving**	**me.**

I can't believe you thought you could fool me.

Example 13.38

do	.i'anai	na	xruti	do	le	zdani
You	**[blame]**	**did-not**	**return**	**you**	**to-the**	**house.**

I blame you for not coming home.

Example 13.39

.ie	mi	na	cusku	lu'e
[agreement]	**I**	**did-not**	**express**	**a-symbol-for**

le	tcika	be	le	nu	xruti
the	**time-of-day**	**of**	**the**	**event-of**	**return.**

It's true I didn't tell you when to come back.

Example 13.40

.i'enai	do	.i'e	zukte
[disapproval]	**you**	**[approval]**	**act.**

I don't approve of what you did, but I approve of you.

Example 13.40 (p. 292) illustrates the use of a propositional attitude indicator, *i'e*, in both the usual sense (at the beginning of the bridi) and as a pure emotion (attached to *do*). The event expressed by the main bridi is disapproved of by the speaker, but the referent of the sumti in the x1 place (namely the listener) is approved of.

To indicate that an attitudinal discussed in this section is not meant to indicate a propositional attitude, the simplest expedient is to split the attitudinal off into a separate sentence. Thus, a version of Example 13.32 (p. 291) which actually claimed that the listener was or would be driving the car might be:

Example 13.41

do	sazri	le	karce	.i	.e'a
You	**drive**	**the**	**car.**		**[Permission].**

You're driving (or will drive) the car, and that's fine.

13.4 Attitudes as scales

In Lojban, all emotions and attitudes are scales. These scales run from some extreme value (which we'll call "positive") to an opposite extreme (which we'll call "negative"). In the tables above, we have seen three points on the scale: "positive", neutral, and "negative". The terms "positive" and "negative" are put into quotation marks because they are loaded words when applied to emotions, and the attitudinal system reflects this loading, which is a known cultural bias. Only two of the "positive" words, namely *.ii* (fear) and *.oi* (pain/complaint), represent emotions commonly thought of as less "virtuous" in most cases than their negative counterparts. But these two were felt to be instinctive, distinct, and very powerful emotions that needed to be expressible in a monosyllable when necessary, while their counterparts are less commonly expressed.

(Why the overt bias? Because there are a lot of attitudinals and they will be difficult to learn as an entire set. By aligning our scales arbitrarily, we give the monosyllable *nai* a useful meaning and make it easier for a novice to recognize at least the positive or negative alignment of an indicator, if not the specific word. Other choices considered were "random" orientation, which would have unknown biases and be difficult to learn, and orientation based on our guesses as to which scale orientations made the most frequent usages shorter, which would be biased in favor of American perceptions of "usefulness". If bias must exist in our indicator set, it might as well be a known bias that eases learning, and in addition might as well favor a harmonious and positive world-view.)

In fact, though, each emotional scale has seven positions defined, three "positive" ones (shown below on the left), three "negative" ones (shown below on the right), and a neutral one indicating that no particular attitude on this scale is felt. The following chart indicates the seven positions of the scale and the associated cmavo. All of these cmavo, except *nai*, are in selma'o CAI.

cai	sai	ru'e	cu'i	nairu'e	naisai	naicai
carmi	*tsali*	*ruble*	*cumki*	-	-	-

A scalar attitude is expressed by using the attitudinal word, and then following it by the desired scalar intensity. The bias creeps in because the "negative" emotions take the extra syllable *nai* to indicate their negative position on the axis, and thus require a bit more effort to express.

Much of this system is optional. You can express an attitude without a scale indicator, if you don't want to stop and think about how strongly you feel. Indeed, for most attitudinals, we've found that either no scalar value is used, or *cai* is used to indicate especially high intensity. Less often, *ru'e* is used for a recognizably weak intensity, and *cu'i* is used in response to the attitudinal question *pei* (see Section 13.10 (p. 300)) to indicate that the emotion is not felt.

The following shows the variations resulting from intensity variation:

Example 13.42

.ei

[obligation]

I ought to
(a non-specific obligation)

Example 13.43

.eicai
[obligation-maximal]

I shall/must
(an intense obligation or requirement, possibly a formal one)

Example 13.44

.eisai
[obligation-strong]

I should
(a strong obligation or necessity, possibly an implied but not formal requirement)

Example 13.45

.eiru'e
[obligation-weak]

I might
(a weak obligation in English often mixed with permission and desire)

Example 13.46

.eicu'i
[obligation-neutral]

No matter
(no particular obligation)

Example 13.47

.einai
[obligation-not]

I need not
(a non-obligation)

You can also utter a scale indicator without a specific emotion. This is often used in the language: in order to emphasize a point about which you feel strongly, you mark what you are saying with the scale indicator *cai*. You could also indicate that you don't care using *cu'i* by itself.

13.5 The space of emotions

Each of the attitude scales constitutes an axis in a multi-dimensional space. In effect, given our total so far of 39 scales, we have a 39-dimensional space. At any given time, our emotions and attitudes are represented by a point in this 39-dimensional space, with the intensity indicators serving as coordinates along each dimension. A complete attitudinal inventory, should one decide to express it, would consist of reading off each of the scale values for each of the emotions, with the vector sum serving as a distinct single point, which is our attitude.

Now no one is going to ever utter a string of 100-odd attitudinals to express their emotions. If asked, we normally do not recognize more than one or two emotions at a time – usually the ones that are strongest or which most recently changed in some significant way. But the scale system provides some useful insights into a possible theory of emotion (which might be testable using Lojban), and incidentally explains how Lojbanists express compound emotions when they do recognize them.

The existence of 39 scales highlights the complexity of emotion. We also aren't bound to the 39. There are modifiers described in Section 13.6 (p. 294) that multiply the set of scales by an order of magnitude. You can also have mixed feelings on a scale, which might be expressed by *cu'i*, but could also be expressed by using both the "positive" and "negative" scale emotions at once. One expression of "fortitude" might be *.ii.iinai-* fear coupled with security.

Uttering one or more attitudinals to express an emotion reflects several things. We will tend to utter emotions in their immediate order of importance to us. We feel several emotions at once, and our expression reflects these emotions simultaneously, although their order of importance to us is also revealing – of our attitude towards our attitude, so to speak. There is little analysis necessary; for those emotions you feel, you express them; the "vector sum" naturally expresses the result. This is vital to their nature as attitudinals – if you had to stop and think about them, or to worry about grammar, they wouldn't be emotions but rationalizations.

People have proposed that attitudinals be expressed as bridi just like everything else; but emotions aren't logical or analytical – saying "I'm awed" is not the same as saying "Wow!!!". The Lojban system is intended to give the effects of an analytical system without the thought involved. Thus, you can simply feel in Lojban.

A nice feature of this design is that you can be simple or complex, and the system works the same way. The most immediate benefit is in learning. You only need to learn a couple of the scale words and a couple of attitude words, and you're ready to express your emotions Lojbanically. As you learn more, you can express your emotions more thoroughly and more precisely, but even a limited vocabulary offers a broad range of expression.

13.6 Emotional categories

The Lojban attitudinal system was designed by starting with a long list of English emotion words, far too many to fit into the 39 available VV-form cmavo. To keep the number of cmavo limited, the emotion words in the list were grouped together by common features: each group was then assigned a separate cmavo. This was like making tanru in reverse, and the result is a collection of indicators that can be combined, like tanru, to express very complex emotions. Some examples in a moment.

The most significant "common feature" we identified was that the emotional words on the list could easily be broken down into six major groups, each of which was assigned its own cmavo:

ro'a	social	asocial	antisocial
ro'e	mental		mindless
ro'i	emotional		denying emotion
ro'o	physical		denying physical
ro'u	sexual		sexual abstinence
re'e	spiritual	secular	sacrilegious

Using these, we were able to assign *o'u* to mark a scale of what we might call "generalized comfort". When you are comfortable, relaxed, satisfied, you express comfort with *o'u*, possibly followed by a scale indicator to indicate how comfortable you are. The six cmavo given above allow you to turn this scale into six separate ones, should you wish.

For example, embarrassment is a social discomfort, expressible as *.o'unairo'a*. Some emotions that we label "stress" in English are expressed in Lojban with *.o'unairo'i*. Physical distress can be expressed with *.o'unairo'o*, which makes a nice groan if you say it with feeling. Mental discomfort might be what you feel when you don't know the answer to the test question, but feel that you should. Most adults can recall some instance where we felt sexual discomfort, *o'unairo'u*. Spiritual discomfort, *o'unaire'e*, might be felt by a church-goer who has wandered into the wrong kind of religious building.

Most of the time when expressing an emotion, you won't categorize it with these words. Emotional expressions should be quickly expressible without having to think about them. However, we sometimes have mixed emotions within this set, as for example emotional discomfort coupled with physical comfort or vice versa.

Coupling these six words with our 39 attitude scales, each of which has a positive and negative side, already gives you far more emotional expression words than we have emotional labels in English. Thus, you'll never see a Lojban-English emotional dictionary that covers all the Lojban possibilities. Some may be useless, but others convey emotions that probably never had a word for them before, though many have felt them (*.eiro'u*, for example – look it up).

You can use scale markers and *nai* on these six category words, and you can also use category words without specifying the emotion. Thus, "I'm trying to concentrate" could be expressed simply as *ro'e*, and if you are feeling anti-social in some non-specific way, *ro'anai* will express it.

There is a mnemonic device for the six emotion categories, based on moving your arms about. In the following table, your hands begin above your head and move down your body in sequence.

ro'a	hands above head	social
ro'e	hands on head	intellectual
ro'i	hands on heart	emotional
ro'o	hands on belly	physical
ro'u	hands on groin	sexual
re'e	hands moving around	spiritual

The implicit metaphors "heart" for emotional and "belly" for physical are not really Lojbanic, but they work fine for English-speakers.

13.7 Attitudinal modifiers

The following cmavo are discussed in this section:

ga'i	[galtu]	hauteur; rank	equal rank	meekness; lack of rank
le'o		aggressive	passive	defensive
vu'e	[vrude]	virtue (*zabna*)		sin (*mabla*)
se'i	[sevzi]	self-orientation		other-orientation
ri'e	[zifre]	release	restraint	control

fu'i	[frili]	with help; easily	without help	with opposition; with difficulty
be'u		lack/need	presence/satisfaction	satiation
se'a	[sevzi]	self-sufficiency		dependency

It turned out that, once we had devised the six emotion categories, we also recognized some other commonalities among emotions. These tended to fit nicely on scales of their own, but generally tend not to be thought of as separate emotions. Some of these are self-explanatory, some need to be placed in context. Some of these tend to go well with only a few of the attitudinals, others go with nearly all of them. To really understand these modifiers, try to use them in combination with one or two of the attitudinals found in Section 13.2 (p. 287) and Section 13.3 (p. 289), and see what emotional pictures you can build:

The cmavo *ga'i* expresses the scale used to indicate condescension or polite deference; it is not respect in general, which is *.io*. Whatever it is attached to is marked as being below (for *ga'i*) or above (for *ga'inai*) the speaker's rank or social position. Note that it is always the referent, not the speaker or listener, who is so marked: in order to mark the listener, the listener must appear in the sentence, as with *doi ga'inai*, which can be appended to a statement addressed to a social superior.

Example 13.48

ko	ga'inai	nenri	klama	le	mi	zdani
You-imperative	**[low-rank!]**	**enter-type-of**	**come-to**	**the**	**of-me**	**house.**

I would be honored if you would enter my residence.

Note that imperatives in Lojban need not be imperious! Corresponding examples with *ga'icu'i* and *ga'i*:

Example 13.49

ko	ga'icu'i	nenri	klama	le	mi	zdani
You-imperative	**[equal-rank!]**	**enter-type-of**	**come-to**	**the**	**of-me**	**house.**

Come on in to my place.

Example 13.50

ko	ga'i	nenri	klama	le	mi	zdani
You-imperative	**[high-rank!]**	**enter-type-of**	**come-to**	**the**	**of-me**	**house.**

You! Get inside!

Since *ga'i* expresses the relative rank of the speaker and the referent, it does not make much sense to attach it to *mi*, unless the speaker is using *mi* to refer to a group (as in English "we"), or a past or future version of himself with a different rank.

It is also possible to attach *ga'i* to a whole bridi, in which case it expresses the speaker's superiority to the event the bridi refers to:

Example 13.51

ga'i	le	xarju	pu	citka
[High-rank!]	**the**	**pig**	**[past]**	**eats.**

The pig ate (which is an event beneath my notice).

When used without being attached to any bridi, *ga'i* expresses the speaker's superiority to things in general, which may represent an absolute social rank: *ga'icai* is an appropriate opening word for an emperor's address from the throne.

The cmavo *le'o* represents the scale of aggressiveness. We seldom overtly recognize that we are feeling aggressive or defensive, but perhaps in counseling sessions, a psychologist might encourage someone to express these feelings on this scale. And football teams could be urged on by their coach using *ro'ole'o*. *le'o* is also useful in threats as an alternative to *o'onai*, which expresses anger.

The cmavo *vu'e* represents ethical virtue or its absence. An excess of almost any emotion is usually somewhat "sinful" in the eyes of most ethical systems. On the other hand, we often feel virtuous about our feelings – what we call righteous indignation might be *o'onaivu'e*. Note that this is distinct from lack of guilt: *.u'unai*.

The cmavo *se'i* expresses the difference between selfishness and generosity, for example (in combination with *.au*):

Example 13.52

> *.ause'i*
> **[desire-self]**

> I want it!

Example 13.53

> *.ause'inai*
> **[desire-other]**

> I want you to have it!

In both cases, the English "it" is vague, reflecting the absence of a bridi. Example 13.52 (p. 297) and Example 13.53 (p. 297) are pure expressions of attitude. Analogously, *.uuse'i* is self-pity, whereas *.uuse'inai* is pity for someone else.

The modifier *ri'e* indicates emotional release versus emotional control. "I will not let him know how angry I am", you say to yourself before entering the room. The Lojban is much shorter:

Example 13.54

.o'onai	*ri'enai*
[anger]	**[control]**

On the other hand, *ri'e* can be used by itself to signal an emotional outburst.

The cmavo *fu'i* may express a reason for feeling the way we do, as opposed to a feeling in itself; but it is a reason that is more emotionally determined than most. For example, it could show the difference between the mental discomfort mentioned in Section 13.6 (p. 294) when it is felt on an easy test, as opposed to on a hard test. When someone gives you a back massage, you could use *.o'ufu'i* to show appreciation for the assistance in your comfort.

The cmavo *be'u* expresses, roughly speaking, whether the emotion it modifies is in response to something you don't have enough of, something you have enough of, or something you have too much of. It is more or less the attitudinal equivalent of the subjective quantifier cmavo *mo'a*, *rau*, and *du'e* (these belong to selma'o PA, and are discussed in Section 18.8 (p. 422)). For example,

Example 13.55

> *.uiro'obe'unai*
> **[Yay-physical-enough!]**

might be something you say after a large meal which you enjoyed.

Like all modifiers, *be'u* can be used alone:

Example 13.56

le	cukta	be'u	cu	zvati	ma
The	**book**	**[Needed!]**		**is-at-location**	**[what-sumti?]**

Where's the book? I need it!

Lastly, the modifier *se'a* shows whether the feeling is associated with self-sufficiency or with dependence on others.

Example 13.57

> *.e'ese'a*
> **[I-can-self-sufficient!]**

> I can do it all by myself!

is something a Lojban-speaking child might say. On the other hand,

Example 13.58

> .e'ese'anai
> **[I-can-dependent]**

> I can do it if you help me.

from the same child would indicate a (hopefully temporary) loss of self-confidence. It is also possible to negate the *e'e* in Example 13.54 (p. 297) and Example 13.55 (p. 297), leading to:

Example 13.59

> .e'enaise'a
> **[I-can't-self-sufficient]**

> I can't do it if you insist on "helping" me!

and

Example 13.60

> .e'enaise'anai
> **[I-can't-dependent]**

> I can't do it by myself!

Some of the emotional expressions may seem too complicated to use. They might be for most circumstances. It is likely that most combinations will never get used. But if one person uses one of these expressions, another person can understand (as unambiguously as the expresser intends) what emotion is being expressed. Most probably as the system becomes well-known and internalized by Lojban-speakers, particular attitudinal combinations will come to be standard expressions (if not cliches) of emotion.

13.8 Compound indicators

The grammar of indicators is quite simple; almost all facets are optional. You can combine indicators in any order, and they are still grammatical. The presumed denotation is additive; thus the whole is the sum of the parts regardless of the order expressed, although the first expressed is presumed most important to the speaker. Every possible string of UI cmavo has some meaning.

Within a string of indicators, there will be conventions of interpretation which amount to a kind of second-order grammar. Each of the modifier words is presumed to modify an indicator to the left, if there is one. (There is an "unspecified emotion" word, *ge'e*, reserved to ensure that if you want to express a modifier without a root emotion, it doesn't attach to and modify a previous but distinct emotional expression.)

For example, *.ieru'e* expresses a weak positive value on the scale of agreement: the speaker agrees (presumably with the listener or with something else just stated), but with the least possible degree of intensity. But *.ie ge'eru'e* expresses agreement (at an unspecified level), followed by some other unstated emotion which is felt at a weak level. A rough English equivalent of *.ie ge'eru'e* might be "I agree, but ..." where the "but" is left hanging. (Again, attitudes aren't always expressed in English by English attitudinals.)

A scale variable similarly modifies the previous emotion word. You put the scale word for a root emotion word before a modifier, since the latter can have its own scale word. This merely maximizes the amount of information expressible. For example, *.oinaicu'i ro'ucai* expresses a feeling midway between pain (*.oi*) and pleasure (*.oinai*) which is intensely sexual (*ro'u*) in nature.

The cmavo *nai* is the most tightly bound modifier in the language: it always negates exactly one word – the preceding one. Of all the words used in indicator constructs, *nai* is the only one with any meaning outside the indicator system. If you try to put an indicator between a non-indicator cmavo and its *nai* negator, the *nai* will end up negating the last word of the indicator. The result, though unambiguous, is not what you want. For example,

Example 13.61

mi	.e	.ui	nai	do
I	and	[Yay!]	[Not!]	you.

means "I and (unfortunately) you", whereas

Example 13.62

mi	.e	nai	.ui	do
I	and	[Not!]	[Yay!]	you.

means "I but (fortunately) not you". Attitudinal *nai* expresses a "scalar negation", a concept explained in Section 15.3 (p. 357); since every attitudinal word implies exactly one scale, the effect of *nai* on each should be obvious.

Thus, the complete internal grammar of UI is as follows, with each listed part optionally present or absent without affecting grammaticality, though it obviously would affect meaning.

attitudinal	nai	intensity-word	nai	modifier	nai	intensity-word	nai	(possiblyrepeated)

ge'e, the non-specific emotion word, functions as an attitudinal. If multiple attitudes are being expressed at once, then in the 2nd or greater position, either *ge'e* or a VV word must be used to prevent any modifiers from modifying the previous attitudinal.

13.9 The uses of indicators

The behavior of indicators in the "outside grammar" is nearly as simple as their internal structure. Indicator groupings are identified immediately after the metalinguistic erasers *si*, *sa*, and *su* and some, though not all, kinds of quotations. The details of such interactions are discussed in Section 19.16 (p. 466).

A group of indicators may appear anywhere that a single indicator may, except in those few situations (as in *zo* quotation, explained in Section 19.10 (p. 458)) where compound cmavo may not be used.

At the beginning of a text, indicators modify everything following them indefinitely: such a usage is taken as a raw emotional expression, and we normally don't turn off our emotions when we start and stop sentences. In every other place in an utterance, the indicator (or group) attaches to the word immediately to its left, and indicates that the attitude is being expressed concerning the object or concept to which the word refers.

If the word that an indicator (or group) attaches to is itself a cmavo which governs a grammatical structure, then the indicator construct pertains to the referent of the entire structure. There is also a mechanism, discussed in Section 19.8 (p. 456), for explicitly marking the range of words to which an indicator applies.

More details about the uses of indicators, and the way they interact with other specialized cmavo, are given in Chapter 19 (p. 447). It is worth mentioning that real-world interpretation is not necessarily consistent with the formal scope rules. People generally express emotions when they feel them, with only a minimum of grammatical constraint on that expression; complexities of emotional expression are seldom logically analyzable. Lojban attempts to provide a systematic reference that could possibly be ingrained to an instinctive level. However, it should always be assumed that the referent of an indicator has some uncertainty.

For example, in cases of multiple indicators expressed together, the combined form has some ambiguity of interpretation. It is possible to interpret the second indicator as expressing an attitude about the first, or to interpret both as expressing attitudes about the common referent. For example, in

Example 13.63

mi	pu	tavla	do	.o'onai	.oi
I	[past]	talk-to	you	[Grrr!]	[Oy!]

can be interpreted as expressing complaint about the anger, in which case it means "Damn, I snapped at you"; or as expressing both anger and complaint about the listener, in which case it means "I told you, you pest!"

Similarly, an indicator after the final brivla of a tanru may be taken to express an attitude about the particular brivla placed there – as the rules have it – or about the entire bridi which hinges on that brivla. Remembering that indicators are supposedly direct expressions of emotion, this ambiguity is acceptable.

Even if the scope rules given for indicators turn out to be impractical or unintuitive for use in conversation, they are still useful in written expression. There, where you can go back and put in markers or move words around, the scope rules can be used in lieu of elaborate nuances of body language and intonation to convey the writer's intent.

13.10 Attitude questions; empathy; attitude contours

The following cmavo are discussed in this section:

pei	attitude question		
dai	empathy		
bu'o	start emotion	continue emotion	end emotion

You can ask someone how they are feeling with a normal bridi sentence, but you will get a normal bridi answer in response, one which may be true or false. Since the response to a question about emotions is no more logical than the emotion itself, this isn't appropriate.

The word *pei* is therefore reserved for attitude questions. Asked by itself, it captures all of the denotation of English "How are you?" coupled with "How do you feel?" (which has a slightly different range of usage).

When asked in the context of discourse, *pei* acts like other Lojban question words – it requests the respondent to "fill in the blank", in this case with an appropriate attitudinal describing the respondent's feeling about the referent expression. As with other questions, plausibility is polite; if you answer with an irrelevant UI cmavo, such as a discursive, you are probably making fun of the questioner. (A *ge'e*, however, is always in order – you are not required to answer emotionally. This is not the same as *.i'inai*, which is privacy as the reverse of conviviality.)

Most often, however, the asker will use *pei* as a place holder for an intensity marker. (As a result, *pei* is placed in selma'o CAI, although selma'o UI would have been almost as appropriate. Grammatically, there is no difference between UI and CAI.) Such usage corresponds to a whole range of idiomatic usages in natural languages:

Example 13.64
> *.iepei*
> **[agreement-question]**

> Do you agree?

Example 13.65
> *.iare'epei*
> **[belief-spiritual-question]**

> Are you a Believer?

Example 13.66
> *.aipei*
> **[intention-question]**

> Are you going to do it?

Example 13.66 (p. 300) might appear at the end of a command, to which the response

Example 13.67
> *.aicai*
> **[intention-maximal]**

corresponds to "Aye! Aye!" (hence the choice of cmavo).

Example 13.68

>.e'apei
>**[permission-question]**

Please, Mommy! Can I??

Additionally, when *pei* is used at the beginning of an indicator construct, it asks specifically if that construct reflects the attitude of the respondent, as in (asked of someone who has been ill or in pain):

Example 13.69

>*pei.o'u*
>**[question-comfort]**

Are you comfortable?

Example 13.70

>*pei.o'ucu'i*
>**[question-comfort-neutral]**

Are you no longer in pain?

Example 13.71

>*pei.o'usai*
>**[question-comfort-strong]**

Are you again healthy?

Empathy, which is not really an emotion, is expressed by the indicator *dai*. (Don't confuse empathy with sympathy, which is *.uuse'inai*.) Sometimes, as when telling a story, you want to attribute emotion to someone else. You can of course make a bridi claim that so-and-so felt such-and-such an emotion, but you can also make use of the attitudinal system by adding the indicator *dai*, which attributes the preceding attitudinal to someone else – exactly whom, must be determined from context. You can also use *dai* conversationally when you empathize, or feel someone else's emotion as if it were your own:

Example 13.72

>.oiro'odai
>**[Pain-physical-empathy]**

Ouch, that must have hurt!

It is even possible to "empathize" with a non-living object:

Example 13.73

le	bloti	.iidai	.uu	pu	klama	le	xasloi
The	ship	[fear-empathy]	[pity!]	[past]	goes-to	the	ocean-floor.

Fearfully the ship, poor thing, sank.

suggesting that the ship felt fear at its impending destruction, and simultaneously reporting the speaker's pity for it.

Both *pei* and *dai* represent exceptions to the normal rule that attitudinals reflect the speaker's attitude.

Finally, we often want to report how our attitudes are changing. If our attitude has not changed, we can just repeat the attitudinal. (Therefore, *.ui .ui .ui* is not the same as *.uicai*, but simply means that we are continuing to be happy.) If we want to report that we are beginning to feel, continuing to feel, or ceasing to feel an emotion, we can use the attitudinal contour cmavo *bu'o*.

When attached to an attitudinal, *bu'o* means that you are starting to have that attitude, *bu'ocu'i* that you are continuing to have it, and *bu'onai* that you are ceasing to have it. Some examples:

Example 13.74

.o'onai	bu'o
[Anger!]	[start-emotion]

I'm getting angry!

Example 13.75

.iu	bu'onai	.uinai
[Love!]	[end-emotion]	[unhappiness!]

I don't love you any more; I'm sad.

Note the difference in effect between Example 13.75 (p. 302) and:

Example 13.76

mi	ca	ba'o	prami	do	ja'e	le	nu	mi	badri
I	[present]	[cessitive]	love	you	with-result	the	event-of	(I	am-sad).

I no longer love you; therefore, I am sad.

which is a straightforward bridi claim. Example 13.76 (p. 302) states that you have (or have had) certain emotions; Example 13.75 (p. 302) expresses those emotions directly.

13.11 Evidentials

The following cmavo are discussed in this section:

ja'o	[jalge]	I conclude		
ca'e		I define		
ba'a	[balvi]	I expect	I experience	I remember
su'a	[sucta]	I generalize		I particularize
ti'e	[tirna]	I hear (hearsay)		
ka'u	[kulnu]	I know by cultural means		
se'o	[senva]	I know by internal experience		
za'a	[zgana]	I observe		
pe'i	[pensi]	I opine		
ru'a	[sruma]	I postulate		
ju'a	[jufra]	I state		

Now we proceed from the attitudinal indicators and their relatives to the other, semantically unrelated, categories of indicators. The indicators known as "evidentials" show how the speaker came to say the utterance; i.e. the source of the information or the idea. Lojban's list of evidentials was derived from lists describing several American Indian languages. Evidentials are also essential to the constructed language Láadan, designed by the linguist and novelist Suzette Haden Elgin. Láadan's set of indicators was drawn on extensively in developing the Lojban indicator system.

It is important to realize, however, that evidentials are not some odd system used by some strange people who live at the other end of nowhere: although their English equivalents aren't single words, English-speakers have vivid notions of what constitutes evidence, and of the different kinds of evidence.

Like the attitudinal indicators, the evidentials belong to selma'o UI, and may be treated identically for grammatical purposes. Most of them are not usually considered scalar in nature, but a few have associated scales.

A bridi with an evidential in it becomes "indisputable", in the sense that the speaker is saying "how it is with him or her", which is beyond argument. Claims about one's own mental states may be true or false, but are hardly subject to other people's examination. If you say that you think, or perceive, or postulate such-and-such a predication, who can contradict you? Discourse that uses evidentials has therefore a different rhetorical flavor than discourse that does not; arguments tend to become what can be called dialogues or alternating monologues, depending on your prejudices.

Evidentials are most often placed at the beginning of sentences, and are often attached to the *i* that separates sentences in connected discourse. It is in the nature of an evidential to affect the entire bridi in which it is placed: like the propositional attitude indicators, they strongly affect the claim made by the main bridi.

A bridi marked by *ja'o* is a conclusion by the speaker based on other (stated or unstated) information or ideas. Rough English equivalents of *ja'o* are "thus" and "therefore".

A bridi marked by *ca'e* is true because the speaker says so. In addition to definitions of words, *ca'e* is also appropriate in what are called performatives, where the very act of speaking the words makes them true. An English example is "I now pronounce you husband and wife", where the very act of uttering the words makes the listeners into husband and wife. A Lojban translation might be:

Example 13.77

ca'e	*le*	*re*	*do*		*cu*	*simxu*		*speni*
[I-define!]	**the**	**two**	**of-you**			**are-mutual**		**spouses.**

The three scale positions of *ba'a*, when attached to a bridi, indicate that it is based on the speaker's view of the real world. Thus *ba'a* means that the statement represents a future event as anticipated by the speaker; *ba'acu'i*, a present event as experienced by the speaker; *ba'anai*, a past event as remembered by the speaker. It is accidental that this scale runs from future to past instead of past to future.

Example 13.78

ba'acu'i		*le*	*tuple*	*be*	*mi*	*cu*	*se cortu*
[I-experience!]		**the**	**leg**	**of**	**me**		**is-the-locus-of-pain.**

My leg hurts.

A bridi marked by *su'a* is a generalization by the speaker based on other (stated or unstated) information or ideas. The difference between *su'a* and *ja'o* is that *ja'o* suggests some sort of reasoning or deduction (not necessarily rigorous), whereas *su'a* suggests some sort of induction or pattern recognition from existing examples (not necessarily rigorous).

The opposite point of the scale, *su'anai*, indicates abduction, or drawing specific conclusions from general premises or patterns.

This cmavo can also function as a discursive (see Section 13.12 (p. 304)), in which case *su'a* means "abstractly" or "in general", and *su'anai* means "concretely" or "in particular".

A bridi marked by *ti'e* is relayed information from some source other than the speaker. There is no necessary implication that the information was relayed via the speaker's ears; what we read in a newspaper is an equally good example of *ti'e*, unless we have personal knowledge of the content.

Example 13.79

ti'e		*la*		*.uengas*	*cu*		*zergau*
[I-hear!]		**Wenga**					**is-a-criminal-doer.**

I hear that Wenga is a crook.

A bridi marked by *ka'u* is one held to be true in the speaker's cultural context, as a matter of myth or custom, for example. Such statements should be agreed on by a community of people – you cannot just make up your own cultural context – although "objectivity" in the sense of actual correspondence with the facts is certainly not required.

On the other hand, *se'o* marks a bridi whose truth is asserted by the speaker as a result of an internal experience not directly available to others, such as a dream, vision, or personal revelation. In some cultures, the line between *ka'u* and *se'o* is fuzzy or even nonexistent.

A bridi marked by *za'a* is based on perception or direct observation by the speaker. This use of "observe" is not connected with the Lojban "observative", or bridi with the first sumti omitted. The latter has no explicit aspect, and could be a direct observation, a conclusion, an opinion, or other aspectual point of view.

Example 13.80

za'a	do	tatpi
[I-observe!]	you	are-tired.

I see you are tired.

A bridi marked by *pe'i* is the opinion of the speaker. The form *pe'ipei* is common, meaning "Is this your opinion?". (Strictly, this should be *peipe'i*, in accordance with the distinction explained in Examples 10.6-10.8, but since *pe'i* is not really a scale, there is no real difference between the two orders.)

Example 13.81

pe'i	la	kartagos.	.ei	se daspo
[I-opine!]	that-named	Carthage	[obligation]	is-destroyed.

In my opinion, Carthage should be destroyed.

A bridi marked by *ru'a* is an assumption made by the speaker. This is similar to one possible use of *e'u*.

Example 13.82

ru'a	doi	livinston.
[I-presume]	o	Livingstone.

Dr. Livingstone, I presume? (A rhetorical question: Stanley knew who he was.)

Finally, the evidential *ju'a* is used to avoid stating a specific basis for a statement. It can also be used when the basis for the speaker's statement is not covered by any other evidential. For the most part, using *ju'a* is equivalent to using no evidential at all, but in question form it can be useful: *ju'apei* means "What is the basis for your statement?" and serves as an evidential, as distinct from emotional, question.

13.12 Discursives

The term "discursive" is used for those members of selma'o UI that provide structure to the discourse, and which show how a given word or utterance relates to the whole discourse. To express these concepts in regular bridi would involve extra layers of nesting: rather than asserting that "I also came", we would have to say "I came; furthermore, the event of my coming is an additional instance of the relationship expressed by the previous sentence", which is intolerably clumsy. Typical English equivalents of discursives are words or phrases like "however", "summarizing", "in conclusion", and "for example".

Discursives are not attitudinals: they express no particular emotion. Rather, they are abbreviations for metalinguistic claims that reference the sentence or text they are found in.

Discursives are most often used at the beginning of sentences, often attached to the *i* that separates sentences in running discourse, but can (like all other indicators) be attached to single words when it seems necessary or useful.

The discursives discussed in this section are given in groups, roughly organized by function. First, the "consecutive discourse" group:

ku'i	[karbi]	however/but/in contrast
ji'a	[jmina]	additionally
si'a	[simsa]	similarly
mi'u	[mintu]	ditto
po'o		the only relevant case

These five discursives are mutually exclusive, and therefore they are not usually considered as scales. The first four are used in consecutive discourse. The first, *ku'i*, makes an exception to the previous argument. The second, *ji'a*, adds weight to the previous argument. The third, *si'a*, adds quantity to the previous argument, enumerating an additional example. The fourth, *mi'u*, adds a parallel case to the previous argument, and can also be used in tables or the like to show that something is being repeated from the previous column. It is distinct from *go'i* (of selma'o GOhA, discussed in Section 7.6 (p. 146)), which is a non-discursive version of "ditto" that explicitly repeats the claim of the previous bridi.

Lastly, *po'o* is used when there is no other comparable case, and thus corresponds to some of the uses of "only", a word difficult to express in pure bridi form:

Example 13.83

mi	po'o	darxi	le	mi	tamne	fo	le	nazbi
I	[only]	hit	the	of-me	cousin	at-locus	the	nose.

Only I (nobody else) hit my cousin on his nose.

Example 13.84

mi	darxi	po'o	le	mi	tamne	fo	le	nazbi
I	hit	[only]	the	of-me	cousin	at-locus	the	nose.

I only hit my cousin on his nose (I did nothing else to him).

Example 13.85

mi	darxi	le	mi	tamne	po'o	fo	le	nazbi
I	hit	the	of-me	cousin	[only]	at-locus	the	nose.

I hit only my cousin on his nose (no one else).

Example 13.86

mi	darxi	le	mi	tamne	fo	le	nazbi	po'o
I	hit	the	of-me	cousin	at-locus	the	nose	[only].

I hit my cousin only on his nose (nowhere else).

Note that "only" can go before or after what it modifies in English, but *po'o*, as an indicator, always comes afterward.

Next, the "commentary on words" group:

va'i	[valsi]	in other words	in the same words
ta'u	[tanru]	expanding a tanru	making a tanru

The discursives *va'i* and *ta'u* operate at the level of words, rather than discourse proper, or if you like, they deal with how things are said. An alternative English expression for *va'i* is "rephrasing"; for *va'inai*, "repeating". Also compare *va'i* with *ke'u*, discussed below.

The cmavo *ta'u* is a discursive unique to Lojban; it expresses the particularly Lojbanic device of tanru. Since tanru are semantically ambiguous, they are subject to misunderstanding. This ambiguity can be removed by expanding the tanru into some semantically unambiguous structure, often involving relative clauses or the introduction of additional brivla. The discursive *ta'u* marks the transition from the use of a brief but possibly confusing tanru to its fuller, clearer expansion; the discursive *ta'unai* marks a transition in the reverse direction.

Next, the "commentary on discourse" group:

li'a	[klina]	clearly; obviously		obscurely
ba'u	[banli]	exaggeration	accuracy	understatement
zo'o		humorously	dully	seriously
sa'e	[satci]	precisely speaking		loosely speaking
to'u	[tordu]	in brief		in detail
do'a	[dunda]	generously		parsimoniously
sa'u	[sampu]	simply		elaborating
pa'e	[pajni]	justice		prejudice
je'u	[jetnu]	truly		falsely

This group is used by the speaker to characterize the nature of the discourse, so as to prevent misunderstanding. It is well-known that listeners often fail to recognize a humorous statement and take it seriously, or miss an exaggeration, or try to read more into a statement than the speaker intends to put there. In speech, the tone of voice often provides the necessary cue, but the reader of ironic or understated or imprecise discourse is often simply clueless. As with the attitudinals, the use of these cmavo may seem fussy to new Lojbanists, but it is important to remember that *zo'o*, for example, is the equivalent of smiling while you speak, not the equivalent of a flat declaration like "What I'm about to say is supposed to be funny."

A few additional English equivalents: for *sa'enai*, "roughly speaking" or "approximately speaking"; for *sa'unai*, "furthermore"; for *to'u*, "in short" or "skipping details"; for *do'a*, "broadly construed"; for *do'anai* (as you might expect), "narrowly construed".

The cmavo *pa'e* is used to claim (truly or falsely) that one is being fair or just to all parties mentioned, whereas *pa'enai* admits (or proclaims) a bias in favor of one party.

The scale of *je'u* and *je'unai* is a little different from the others in the group. By default, we assume that people speak the truth – or at least, that if they are lying, they will do their best to conceal it from us. So under what circumstances would *je'unai* be used, or *je'u* be useful? For one thing, *je'u* can be used to mark a tautology: a sentence that is a truth of logic, like "All cats are cats." Its counterpart *je'unai* then serves to mark a logical contradiction. In addition, *je'unai* can be used to express one kind of sarcasm or irony, where the speaker pretends to believe what he/she says, but actually wishes the listener to infer a contrary opinion. Other forms of irony can be marked with *zo'o* (humor) or *.ianai* (disbelief).

When used as a discursive, *su'a* (see Section 13.11 (p. 302)) belongs to this group.

Next, the "knowledge" group:

ju'o	[djuno]	certainly	uncertain	certainly not
la'a	[lakne]	probably		improbably

These two discursives describe the speaker's state of knowledge about the claim of the associated bridi. They are similar to the propositional attitudes of Section 13.3 (p. 289), as they create a hypothetical world. We may be quite certain that something is true, and label our bridi with *ju'o*; but it may be false all the same.

Next, the "discourse management" group:

ta'o	[tanjo]	by the way		returning to point
ra'u	[ralju]	chiefly	equally	incidentally
mu'a	[mupli]	for example	omitting examples	end examples
zu'u		on the one hand		on the other hand
ke'u	[krefu]	repeating		continuing
da'i		supposing		in fact

This final group is used to perform what may be called "managing the discourse": providing reference points to help the listener understand the flow from one sentence to the next.

Other English equivalents of *ta'onai* are "anyway", "anyhow", "in any case", "in any event", "as I was saying", and "continuing".

The scale of *ra'u* has to do with the importance of the point being, or about to be, expressed: *ra'u* is the most important point, *ra'ucu'i* is a point of equal importance, and *ra'unai* is a lesser point. Other English equivalents of *ra'u* are "above all" and "primarily".

The cmavo *ke'u* is very similar to *va'i*, although *ke'unai* and *va'inai* are quite different. Both *ke'u* and *va'i* indicate that the same idea is going to be expressed using different words, but the two cmavo differ in emphasis. Using *ke'u* emphasizes that the content is the same; using *va'i* emphasizes that the words are different. Therefore, *ke'unai* shows that the content is new (and therefore the words are also); *va'inai* shows that the words are the same (and therefore so is the content). One English equivalent of *ke'unai* is "furthermore".

The discursive *da'i* marks the discourse as possibly taking a non-real-world viewpoint ("Supposing that", "By hypothesis"), whereas *da'inai* insists on the real-world point of view ("In fact", "In truth", "According to the facts"). A common use of *da'i* is to distinguish between:

Example 13.87

ganai	da'i	do	viska	le	mi	citno	mensi
If	**[hypothetical]**	**you**	**see**	**the**	**of-me**	**young**	**sister,**

gi	ju'o	do	djuno	le	du'u		ri	pazvau
then	**[certain]**	**you**	**know**	**the**	**predication-of**		**she**	**is-pregnant.**

If you were to see my younger sister, you would certainly know she is pregnant.

and:

Example 13.88

ganai	da'inai	do	viska	le	mi	citno	mensi
If	**[factual]**	**you**	**see**	**the**	**of-me**	**young**	**sister,**

gi	ju'o	do	djuno	le	du'u		ri	pazvau
then	**[certainty]**	**you**	**know**	**the**	**predication-of**		**she**	**is-pregnant.**

If you saw my younger sister, you would certainly know she is pregnant.

It is also perfectly correct to omit the discursive altogether, and leave the context to indicate which significance is meant. (Chinese always leaves this distinction to the context: the Chinese sentence

Example 13.89

ru^2guo^3 ni^3 kan^4dao^4 wo^3 mei^4mei, ni^3 yi^2ding^4 zhi^1dao^4 ta^1 $huai^2yun^4$ le

if you see-arrive my younger-sister, you certainly know she pregnant

is the equivalent of either Example 13.87 (p. 307) or Example 13.88 (p. 307).)

13.13 Miscellaneous indicators

Some indicators do not fall neatly into the categories of attitudinal, evidential, or discursive. This section discusses the following miscellaneous indicators:

ki'a	metalinguistic confusion		
na'i	metalinguistic negator		
jo'a	metalinguistic affirmer		
li'o	omitted text (quoted material)		
sa'a	material inserted by editor/narrator		
xu	true-false question		
pau	question premarker		rhetorical question
pe'a	figurative language		literal language
bi'u	new information		old information
ge'e	non-specific indicator		

The cmavo *ki'a* is one of the most common of the miscellaneous indicators. It expresses metalinguistic confusion; i.e. confusion about what has been said, as opposed to confusion not tied to the discourse (which is *.uanai*). The confusion may be about the meaning of a word or of a grammatical construct, or about the referent of a sumti. One of the uses of English "which" corresponds to *ki'a*:

Example 13.90

mi	nelci	le	ctuca
I	**like**	**the**	**teacher.**

.i	le	ki'a	ctuca
	The	**which**	**teacher?**

Which teacher?

Here, the second speaker does not understand the referent of the sumti *le ctuca*, and so echoes back the sumti with the confusion marker.

The metalinguistic negation cmavo *na'i* and its opposite *jo'a* are explained in full in Chapter 15 (p. 353). In general, *na'i* indicates that there is something wrong with a piece of discourse: either an error, or a false underlying assumption, or something else of the sort. The discourse is invalid or inappropriate due to the marked word or construct.

Similarly, *jo'a* marks something which looks wrong but is in fact correct. These two cmavo constitute a scale, but are kept apart for two reasons: *na'inai* means the same as *jo'a*, but would be too confusing as an affirmation; *jo'anai* means the same as *na'i*, but is too long to serve as a convenient metalinguistic negator.

The next two cmavo are used to assist in quoting texts written or spoken by others. It is often the case that we wish to quote only part of a text, or to supply additional material either by way of commentary or to make a fragmentary text grammatical. The cmavo *li'o* serves the former function. It indicates that words were omitted from the quotation. What remains of the quotation must be grammatical, however, as *li'o* does not serve any grammatical function. It cannot, for example, take the place of a missing selbri in a bridi, or supply the missing tail of a description sumti: *le li'o* in isolation is not grammatical.

The cmavo *sa'a* indicates in a quotation that the marked word or construct was not actually expressed, but is inserted for editorial, narrative, or grammatical purposes. Strictly, even a *li'o* should appear in the form *li'osa'a*, since the *li'o* was not part of the original quotation. In practice, this and other forms which are already associated with metalinguistic expressions, such as *sei* (of selma'o SEI) or *to'i* (of selma'o TO) need not be marked except where confusion might result.

In the rare case that the quoted material already contains one or more instances of *sa'a*, they can be changed to *sa'asa'a*.

The cmavo *xu* marks truth questions, which are discussed in detail in Section 15.8 (p. 367). In general, *xu* may be translated "Is it true that ... ?" and questions whether the attached bridi is true. When *xu* is attached to a specific word or construct, it directs the focus of the question to that word or construct.

Lojban question words, unlike those of English, frequently do not stand at the beginning of the question. Placing the cmavo *pau* at the beginning of a bridi helps the listener realize that the bridi is a question, like the symbol at the beginning of written Spanish questions that looks like an upside-down question mark. The listener is then warned to watch for the actual question word.

Although *pau* is grammatical in any location (like all indicators), it is not really useful except at or near the beginning of a bridi. Its scalar opposite, *paunai*, signals that a bridi is not really a question despite its form. This is what we call in English a rhetorical question: an example appears in the English text near the beginning of Section 13.11 (p. 302).

The cmavo *pe'a* is the indicator of figurative speech, indicating that the previous word should be taken figuratively rather than literally:

Example 13.91

mi	viska	le	blanu	pe'a	zdani
I	see	the	blue	[figurative]	house.

I see the "blue" house.

Here the house is not blue in the sense of color, but in some other sense, whose meaning is entirely culturally dependent. The use of *pe'a* unambiguously marks a cultural reference: *blanu* in Example 13.91 (p. 308) could mean "sad" (as in English) or something completely different.

The negated form, *pe'anai*, indicates that what has been said is to be interpreted literally, in the usual way for Lojban; natural-language intuition is to be ignored.

Alone among the cmavo of selma'o UI, *pe'a* has a rafsi, namely *pev*. This rafsi is used in forming figurative (culturally dependent) lujvo, whose place structure need have nothing to do with the place structure of the components. Thus *risnyjelca* (heart burn) might have a place structure like:

x1 is the heart of x2, burning in atmosphere x3 at temperature x4

whereas *pevrisnyjelca*, explicitly marked as figurative, might have the place structure:

x1 is indigestion/heartburn suffered by x2

which obviously has nothing to do with the places of either *risna* or *jelca*.

The uses of *bi'u* and *bi'unai* correspond to one of the uses of the English articles "the" and "a/an". An English-speaker telling a story may begin with "I saw a man who ...". Later in the story, the same man will be referred to with the phrase "the man". Lojban does not use its articles in the same way: both "a man" and "the man" would be translated *le nanmu*, since the speaker has in mind a specific man. However, the first use might be marked *le bi'u nanmu*, to indicate that this is a new man, not mentioned before. Later uses could correspondingly be tagged *le bi'unai nanmu*.

Most of the time, the distinction between *bi'u* and *bi'unai* need not be made, as the listener can infer the right referent. However, if a different man were referred to still later in the story, *le bi'u nanmu* would clearly show that this man was different from the previous one.

Finally, the indicator *ge'e* has been discussed in Section 13.8 (p. 298) and Section 13.10 (p. 300). It is used to express an attitude which is not covered by the existing set, or to avoid expressing any attitude.

Another use for *ge'e* is to explicitly avoid expressing one's feeling on a given scale; in this use, it functions like a member of selma'o CAI: *.iige'e* means roughly "I'm not telling whether I'm afraid or not."

kau	indirect question

This cmavo is explained in detail in Section 11.8 (p. 256). It marks the word it is attached to as the focus of an indirect question:

Example 13.92

mi	djuno	le	du'u	dakau	klama	le	zarci
I	know	the	predication-of	somebody-[indirect?]	goes	to-the	store.

I know who goes to the store.

13.14 Vocative scales

"Vocatives" are words used to address someone directly; they precede and mark a name used in direct address, just as *la* (and the other members of selma'o LA) mark a name used to refer to someone. The vocatives actually are indicators – in fact, discursives – but the need to tie them to names and other descriptions of listeners requires them to be separated from selma'o UI. But like the cmavo of UI, the members of selma'o COI can be "negated" with *nai* to get the opposite part of the scale.

Because of the need for redundancy in noisy environments, the Lojban design does not compress the vocatives into a minimum number of scales. Doing so would make a non-redundant *nai* too often vital to interpretation of a protocol signal, as explained later in this section.

The grammar of vocatives is explained in Section 6.11 (p. 130); but in brief, a vocative may be followed by a name (without *la*), a description (without *le* or its relatives), a complete sumti, or nothing at all (if the addressee is obvious from the context). There is an elidable terminator, *do'u* (of selma'o DOhU) which is almost never required unless no name (or other indication of the addressee) follows the vocative.

Using any vocative except *mi'e* (explained below) implicitly defines the meaning of the pro-sumti *do*, as the whole point of vocatives is to specify the listener, or at any rate the desired listener – even if the desired listener isn't listening! We will use the terms "speaker" and "listener" for clarity, although in written Lojban the appropriate terms would be "writer" and "reader".

In the following list of vocatives, the translations include the symbol X. This represents the name (or identifying description, or whatever) of the listener.

The cmavo *doi* is the general-purpose vocative. Unlike the cmavo of selma'o COI, explained below, *doi* can precede a name directly without an intervening pause. It is not considered a scale, and *doinai* is not grammatical. In general, *doi* needs no translation in English (we just use names by themselves without any preceding word, although in poetic styles we sometimes say "Oh X", which is equivalent to *doi*). One may attach an attitudinal to *doi* to express various English vocatives. For example, *doi .io* means "Sir/Madam!", whereas *doi .ionai* means "You there!".

All members of selma'o COI require a pause when used immediately before a name, in order to prevent the name from absorbing the COI word. This is unlike selma'o DOI and LA, which do not require pauses because the syllables of these cmavo are not permitted to be embedded in a Lojban name. When calling out to someone, this is fairly natural, anyway. "Hey! John!" is thus a better translation of *ju'i .djan.* than "Hey John!". No pause is needed if the vocative reference is something other than a name, as in the title of the Lojban journal, *ju'i lobypli*.

(Alternatively, *doi* can be inserted between the COI cmavo and the name, making a pause unnecessary: *coi doi djan.*)

coi ┆ greetings

"Hello, X"; "Greetings, X"; indicates a greeting to the listener.

co'o ┆ partings

"Good-bye, X"; indicates parting from immediate company by either the speaker or the listener. *coico'o* means "greeting in passing".

ju'i ┆ [jundi] ┆ attention ┆ at ease ┆ ignore me/us

"Attention/Lo/Hark/Behold/Hey!/Listen, X"; indicates an important communication that the listener should listen to.

nu'e ┆ [nupre] ┆ promise ┆ release promise ┆ non-promise

"I promise, X"; indicates a promise to the listener. In some contexts, *nu'e* may be prefixed to an oath or other formal declaration.

ta'a ┆ [tavla] ┆ interruption

"I interrupt, X", "I desire the floor, X"; a vocative expression to (possibly) interrupt and claim the floor to make a statement or expression. This can be used for both rude and polite interruptions, although rude interruptions will probably tend not to use a vocative at all. An appropriate response to an interruption might be *re'i* (or *re'inai* to ignore the interruption).

pe'u ┆ [cpedu] ┆ request

"Please, X"; indicates a request to the listener. It is a formal, non-attitudinal, equivalent of *e'o* with a specific recipient being addressed. On the other hand, *e'o* may be used when there is no specific listener, but merely a "sense of petition floating in the air", as it were.

ki'e ┆ [ckire] ┆ appreciation; gratitude ┆ disappreciation; ingratitude

"Thank you, X"; indicates appreciation or gratitude toward the listener. The usual response is *je'e*, but *fi'i* is appropriate on rare occasions: see the explanation of *fi'i*.

fi'i ┆ [friti] ┆ welcome; offering ┆ unwelcome; inhospitality

"At your service, X"; "Make yourself at home, X"; offers hospitality (possibly in response to thanks, but not necessarily) to the listener. Note that *fi'i* is *not* the equivalent of American English "You're welcome" as a mechanical response to "Thank you"; that is *je'e*, as noted below.

be'e ┆ [benji] ┆ request to send

"Request to send to X"; indicates that the speaker wishes to express something, and wishes to ensure that the listener is listening. In a telephone conversation, can be used to request the desired conversant(s). A more colloquial equivalent is "Hello? Can I speak to X?".

re'i ┆ [bredi] ┆ ready to receive ┆ not ready

"Ready to receive, X"; indicates that the speaker is attentive and awaiting communication from the listener. It can be used instead of *mi'e* to respond when called to the telephone. The negative form can be used to prevent the listener from continuing to talk when the speaker is unable to pay attention: it can be translated "Hold on!" or "Just a minute".

mu'o ┆ [mulno] ┆ completion of utterance ┆ more to follow

"Over, X"; indicates that the speaker has completed the current utterance and is ready to hear a response from the listener. The negative form signals that the pause or non-linguistic sound which follows does not represent the end of the current utterance: more colloquially, "I'm not done talking!"

je'e ┆ [jimpe] ┆ successful receipt ┆ unsuccessful receipt

"Roger, X!", "I understand"; acknowledges the successful receipt of a communication from the listener. The negative form indicates failure to receive correctly, and is usually followed by *ke'o*. The colloquial English equivalents of *je'e* and *je'enai* are the grunt typically written "uh-huh" and "What?/Excuse me?". *je'e* is also used to mean "You're welcome" when that is a response to "Thank you".

vi'o ⋮ will comply ⋮ will not comply

"Wilco, X", "I understand and will comply". Similar to *je'e* but signals an intention (similar to *.ai*) to comply with the other speaker's request. This cmavo is the main way of saying "OK" in Lojban, in the usual sense of "Agreed!", although *.ie* carries some of the same meaning. The negative form indicates that the message was received but that you will not comply: a very colloquial version is "No way!".

ke'o ⋮ [krefu] ⋮ please repeat ⋮ no repeat needed

"What did you say, X?"; a request for repetition or clarification due to unsuccessful receipt or understanding. This is the vocative equivalent of *ki'a*, and is related to *je'enai*. The negative form may be rendered "Okay, already; I get the point!"

fe'o ⋮ [fanmo] ⋮ end of communication ⋮ not done

"Over and out, X"; indicates completion of statement(s) and communication directed at the identified person(s). Used to terminate a letter if a signature is not required because the sender has already been identified (as in memos). The negative form means "Wait, hold it, we're not done!" and differs from *mu'onai* in that it means more exchanges are to follow, rather than that the current exchange is incomplete. Do not confuse *fe'o* with *fa'o* (selma'o FAhO) which is a mechanical, extra-grammatical signal that a text is complete. One may say *fe'o* to one participant of a multi-way conversation and then go on speaking to the others.

mi'e ⋮ [cmavo: mi] ⋮ self-identification ⋮ non-identification

"And I am X"; a generalized self-vocative. Although grammatically just like the other members of selma'o COI, *mi'e* is quite different semantically. In particular, rather than specifying the listener, the person whose name (or description) follows *mi'e* is taken to be the speaker. Therefore, using *mi'e* specifies the meaning of the pro-sumti *mi*. It can be used to introduce oneself, to close letters, or to identify oneself on the telephone.

This cmavo is often combined with other members of COI: *fe'omi'e* would be an appropriate closing at the end of a letter; *re'imi'e* would be a self-vocative used in delayed responses, as when called to the phone, or possibly in a roll-call. As long as the *mi'e* comes last, the following name is that of the speaker; if another COI cmavo is last, the following name is that of the listener. It is not possible to name both speaker and listener in a single vocative expression, but this fact is of no importance, because wherever one vocative expression is grammatical, any number of consecutive ones may appear.

The negative form denies an identity which someone else has attributed to you; *mi'enai .djan.* means that you are saying you are not John.

Many of the vocatives have been listed with translations which are drawn from radio use: "roger", "wilco", "over and out". This form of translation does not mean that Lojban is a language of CB enthusiasts, but rather that in most natural languages these forms are so well handled by the context that only in specific domains (like speaking on the radio) do they need special words. In Lojban, dependence on the context can be dangerous, as speaker and listener may not share the right context, and so the vocatives provide a formal protocol for use when it is appropriate. Other appropriate contexts include computer communications and parliamentary procedure: in the latter context, the protocol question *ta'apei* would mean "Will the speaker yield?"

13.15 A sample dialogue

The following dialogue in Lojban illustrates the uses of attitudinals and protocol vocatives in conversation. The phrases enclosed in *sei ... se'u* indicate the speaker of each sentence.

la	rik.	.e	la		.alis.	nerkla	le	kafybarja
That-name	Rick	and	that-named		Alice	in-go	to-the	coffee-bar.

Rick and Alice go into the coffee bar.

.i	sei		la		rik.	cusku	se'u
	[Comment]		that-named		Rick	says,	[end-comment]

ta'a		ro	zvati	be	ti
[Interrupt]		all	at		this-place,

mi	ba		za		speni		ti		.iu
I	[future]		[medium]		am-spouse-to		this-one		[love].

Rick said, "Sorry to break in, everybody. Pretty soon I'm getting married to my love here."

.i	sei		la		djordj.	cusku	se'u
	[Comment]		that-named		George	says,	[end-comment]

.a'o		ko		gleki		doi	ma
[Hope]		[You-imperative]		are-happy,		O	[who?]

George said, "I hope you'll be happy, um, ...?"

.i	sei		la		pam.	cusku	se'u		pe'u	.alis.
	[Comment]		that-named		Pam	says,	[end-comment]		[Please]	Alice,

xu		mi	ba		terfriti		le	nunspenybi'o
[Is-it-true?]		I	[future]		receive-offer-of		the	event-of-spouse-becoming?

Pam said, "Please, Alice, am I going to be invited to the wedding?"

.i	sei		la		mark.	cusku	se'u
	[Comment]		that-named		Mark	says,	[end-comment]

coi		ba		za		speni
[Greetings]		[future]		[medium]		spouse(s),

a'o	le	re	do		lifri		le	ka		gleki
[Hope]	the	two	of-you		experience		the	property-of		being-happy.

Mark said, "Hello, spouses-to-be. I hope both of you will be very happy."

.i	sei		la		rik.	cusku	se'u
	[Comment]		that-named		Rick	says,	[end-comment]

mi'e		.rik.		doi	terpreti
[I-am]		Rick,		O	questioners.

Rick said, "My name is Rick, for those of you who want to know."

.i	sei		la		.alis.	cusku	se'u
	[Comment]		that-named		Alice	says,	[end-comment]

nu'e		.pam.	.o'e		ro'i		do	ba		zvati
[Promise-to]		Pam,	[closeness]		[emotional]		you	[future]		are-at.

Alice said, "I promise you'll be there, Pam honey."

.i	sei		la		fred.	cusku	se'u
	[Comment]		that-named		Fred	says,	[end-comment]

.ui		nai	cai		ro'i		mi	ji'a
[Happy]		[not]	[maximal]		[emotional]		I	[additionally]

prami	la		.alis.	fe'o		.rik.
love	that-named		Alice.	[Over-and-out-to]		Rick.

"I love Alice too," said Fred miserably. "Have a nice life, Rick."

.i	la	fred.	cliva
	that-named	Fred	leaves.

And he left.

.i	sei	la	rik.	cusku	se'u
	[Comment]	that-named	Rick	says,	[end-comment]

fi'i	ro	zvati
[Welcome-to]	all	at-place,

ko	pinxe	pa	ckafi	fi'o	pleji	mi
[You-imperative]	drink	one	coffee	with	payer	me.

Rick said, raising his voice, "A cup of coffee for the house, on me."

.i	sei	la	pam.	cusku	se'u
	[Comment]	that-named	Pam	says,	[end-comment]

be'e	selfu
[Request-to-speak-to]	server.

Pam said, "Waiter!"

.i	sei	le	selfu	cu	cusku	se'u	re'i
	[Comment]	the	server		says,	[end-comment]	[Ready-to-receive].

The waiter replied, "May I help you?"

.i	sei	la	pam.	cusku	se'u
	[Comment]	that-named	Pam	says,	[end-comment]

.e'o	ko		selfu	le	traji		xamgu	ckafi
[Petition]	[You-imperative]		serve	the	(superlatively		good)	coffee

le	ba	za	speni	fi'o	pleji	mi
to-the	[future]	[medium]	spouse	with	payer	me.

Pam said, "One Jamaica Blue for the lovebirds here, on my tab."

.i	sei	le	selfu	cu	cusku	se'u	vi'o
	[Comment]	the	server		says,	[end-comment]	[Will-comply]

"Gotcha", said the waiter.

.i	sei	la	rik.	cusku	se'u	ki'e	.pam.
	[Comment]	that-named	Rick	says,	[end-comment]	[Thanks]	Pam.

"Thanks, Pam", said Rick.

.i	sei	la	pam.	cusku	se'u	je'e
	[Comment]	that-named	Pam	says,	[end-comment]	[Acknowledge].

"Sure", said Pam.

.i	sei	la	djan.	cusku	se'u
	[Comment]	that-named	John	says,	[end-comment]

.y.	mi	.y.	mutce	spopa		.y.	le	nu	le	speni
[Uh]	I	[uh]	very	[nonexistent-gismu]		[uh]	the	event-of	the	spouse

si	.y.	ba	speni	.y.	.y.	su	.yyyyyy.	mu'o
[erase]	[uh]	[future]	spouse	[uh]	[uh]	[erase-all]	[uh]	[over]

John said, "I, er, a lotta, uh, marriage, upcoming marriage, ... Oh, forget it. Er, later."

.i	sei	la	djordj.	cusku	se'u
	[Comment]	that-named	George	says,	[end-comment]

ke'o	.djan.	zo'o
[Repeat-O]	John	[humor].

"How's that again, John?" said George.

.i	sei		la		pam.	cusku	se'u
	[Comment]		that-named		Pam	says,	[end-comment]

ju'i		.djordj.	.e'unai		le	kabri	ba		zi	farlu
[Attention]		George,	[Warning]		the	cup	[future]		[short]	falls.

"George, watch out!" said Pam. "The cup's falling!"

.i	le	kabri	cu	je'a		farlu
	The	cup		indeed		falls.

The cup fell.

.i	sei		la		djan.	cusku	se'u
	[Comment]		that-named		John	says,	[end-comment]

e'o		doi	djordj.	zo'o		rapygau
[Petition]		o	George	[humor]		repeat-cause.

John said, "Try that again, George!"

.i	sei		la		djordj.	cusku	se'u
	[Comment]		that-named		George	says,	[end-comment]

co'o		ro	zvati	pe		secau	la		djan.	ga'i
[Partings]		all	at-place	which-are		without	that-named		John	[superiority]

"Goodbye to all of you," said George sneeringly, "except John."

.i	la		djordj.	cliva
	that-named		George	leaves.

George left.

13.16 Tentative conclusion

The exact ramifications of the indicator system in actual usage are unknown. There has never been anything like it in natural language before. The system provides great potential for emotional expression and transcription, from which significant Sapir-Whorf effects can be anticipated. When communicating across cultural boundaries, where different indicators are often used for the same emotion, accidental offense can be avoided. If we ever ran into an alien race, a culturally neutral language of emotion could be vital. (A classic example, taken from the science fiction of Larry Niven, is to imagine speaking Lojban to the carnivorous warriors called Kzinti, noting that a human smile bares the teeth, and could be seen as an intent to attack.) And for communicating emotions to computers, when we cannot identify all of the signals involved in subliminal human communication (things like body language are also cultural), a system like this is needed.

We have tried to err on the side of overkill. There are distinctions possible in this system that no one may care to make in any culture. But it was deemed more neutral to overspecify and let usage decide, than to choose a limited set and constrain emotional expression. For circumstances in which even the current indicator set is not enough, it is possible using the cmavo *sei*, explained in Section 19.12 (p. 461), to create metalinguistic comments that act like indicators.

We envision an evolutionary development. At this point, the system is little more than a mental toy. Many of you who read this will try playing around with various combinations of indicators, trying to figure out what emotions they express and when the expressions might be useful. You may even find an expression for which there currently is no good English word and start using it. Why not, if it helps you express your feelings?

There will be a couple dozen of these used pretty much universally – mostly just simple attitudinals with, at most, intensity markers. These are the ones that will quickly be expressed at the subconscious level. But every Lojbanist who plays with the list will bring in a couple of new words. Poets will paint emotional pictures, and people who identify with those pictures will use the words so created for their own experiences.

13.16 Tentative conclusion

Just as a library of tanru is built up, so will a library of attitudes be built. Unlike the tanru, though, the emotional expressions are built on some fairly nebulous root emotions – words that cannot be defined with the precision of the gismu. The emotion words of Lojban will very quickly take on a life of their own, and the outline given here will evolve into a true system of emotions.

There are several theories as to the nature of emotion, and they change from year to year as we learn more about ourselves. Whether or not Lojban's additive/scalar emotional model is an accurate model for human emotions, it does support the linguistic needs for expressing those emotions. Researchers may learn more about the nature of human emotions by exploring the use of the system by Lojban speakers. They also may be able to use the Lojban system as a means for more clearly recording emotions.

The full list of scales and attitudes will probably not be used until someone speaks the language from birth. Until then, people will use the attitudes that are important to them. In this way, we counter cultural bias – if a culture is prone to recognizing and/or expressing certain emotions more than others, its members will use only those out of the enormous set available. If a culture hides certain emotions, its members simply won't express them.

Perhaps native Lojban speakers will be more expressively clear about their emotions than others. Perhaps they will feel some emotions more strongly than others in ways that can be correlated with the word choices; any difference from the norms of other cultures could be significant. Psychologists have devised elaborate tests for measuring attitudes and personality; this may be the easiest area in which to detect any systematic cultural effect of the type sought to confirm Sapir-Whorf, simply because we already have tools in existence to test it. Because Lojban is unique among languages in having such extensive and expressive indicators, it is likely that a Sapir-Whorf effect will occur and will be recognized.

It is unlikely that we will know the true potential of a system like this one until and unless we have children raised entirely in a multi-cultural Lojban-speaking environment. We learn too many cultural habits in the realm of emotional communication "at our mother's knee". Such children will have a Lojban system that has stronger reinforcement than any typical culture system. The second generation of such children, then, could be said to be the start of a true Lojbanic culture.

We shouldn't need to wait that long to detect significant effects. Emotion is so basic to our lives that even a small change or improvement in emotional communication would have immediately noticeable effects. Perhaps it will be the case that the most important contribution of our "logical language" will be in the non-logical realm of emotion!

Chapter 14
If Wishes Were Horses: The Lojban Connective System

14.1 Logical connection and truth tables

Lojban is a logical language: the name of the language itself means "logical language". The fundamentals of ordinary logic (there are variant logics, which aren't addressed in this book) include the notions of a "sentence" (sometimes called a "statement" or "proposition"), which asserts a truth or falsehood, and a small set of "truth functions", which combine two sentences to create a new sentence. The truth functions have the special characteristic that the truth value (that is, the truth or falsehood) of the results depends only on the truth value of the component sentences. For example,

Example 14.1

  John is a man or James is a woman.

is true if "John is a man" is true, or if "James is a woman" is true. If we know whether John is a man, and we know whether James is a woman, we know whether "John is a man or James is a woman" is true, provided we know the meaning of "or". Here "John is a man" and "James is a woman" are the component sentences.

  We will use the phrase "negating a sentence" to mean changing its truth value. An English sentence may always be negated by prefixing "It is false that ...", or more idiomatically by inserting "not" at the right point, generally before the verb. "James is not a woman" is the negation of "James is a woman", and vice versa. Recent slang can also negate a sentence by following it with the exclamation "Not!"

  Words like "or" are called "logical connectives", and Lojban has many of them, as befits a logical language. This chapter is mostly concerned with explaining the forms and uses of the Lojban logical connectives. There are a number of other logical connectives in English such as "and", "and/or", "if", "only if", "whether or not", and others; however, not every use of these English words corresponds to a logical connective. This point will be made clear in particular cases as needed. The other English meanings are supported by different Lojban connective constructs.

The Lojban connectives form a system (as the title of this chapter suggests), regular and predictable, whereas natural-language connectives are rather less systematic and therefore less predictable.

There exist 16 possible different truth functions. A truth table is a graphical device for specifying a truth function, making it clear what the value of the truth function is for every possible value of the component sentences. Here is a truth table for "or":

first	second	result
True	True	True
True	False	True
False	True	True
False	False	False

This table means that if the first sentence stated is true, and the second sentence stated is true, then the result of the truth function is also true. The same is true for every other possible combination of truth values except the one where both the first and the second sentences are false, in which case the truth value of the result is also false.

Suppose that "John is a man" is true (and "John is not a man" is false), and that "James is a woman" is false (and "James is not a woman" is true). Then the truth table tells us that

"John is a man, or James is not a woman" (true true) is true

"John is a man, or James is a woman" (true , false) is true

"John is not a man, or James is not a woman" (false, true) is true

"John is not a man, or James is a woman" (false, false) is false

Note that the kind of "or" used in this example can also be expressed (in formal English) with "and/or". There is a different truth table for the kind of "or" that means "either ... or ... but not both".

To save space, we will write truth tables in a shorter format henceforth. Let the letters T and F stand for True and False. The rows will always be given in the order shown above: TT, TF, FT, FF for the two sentences. Then it is only necessary to give the four letters from the result column, which can be written TTTF, as can be seen by reading down the third column of the table above. So TTTF is the abbreviated truth table for the "or" truth function. Here are the 16 possible truth functions, with an English version of what it means to assert that each function is, in fact, true ("first" refers to the first sentence, and "second" to the second sentence):

TTTT	(always true)
TTTF	first is true and/or second is true.
TTFT	first is true if second is true.
TTFF	first is true whether or not second is true.
TFTT	first is true only if second is true.
TFTF	whether or not first is true, second is true.
TFFT	first is true if and only if second is true.
TFFF	first is true and second is true
FTTT	first and second are not both true.
FTTF	first or second is true, but not both.
FTFT	whether or not first is true, second is false.
FTFF	first is true, but second is false.
FFTT	first is false whether or not second is true.
FFTF	first is false, but second is true.
FFFT	neither first nor second is true.
FFFF	(always false)

Skeptics may work out the detailed truth tables for themselves.

14.2 The Four basic vowels

Lojban regards four of these 16 truth functions as fundamental, and assigns them the four vowels **A**, **E**, **O**, and **U**. These letters do not represent actual cmavo or selma'o, but rather a component vowel from which actual logical-connective cmavo are built up, as explained in the next section. Here are the four vowels, their truth tables, and rough English equivalents:

A	TTTF	or, and/or
E	TFFF	and
O	TFFT	if and only if
U	TTFF	whether or not

More precisely:

    A is true if either or both sentences are true

    E is true if both sentences are true, but not otherwise

    O is true if the sentences are both true or both false

    U is true if the first sentence is true, regardless of the truth value of the second sentence

With the four vowels, the ability to negate either sentence, and the ability to exchange the sentences, as if their order had been reversed, we can create all of the 16 possible truth functions except TTTT and FFFF, which are fairly useless anyway. The following table illustrates how to create each of the 14 remaining truth functions:

TTTF	**A**
TTFT	**A** with second sentence negated
TTFF	**U**
TFTT	**A** with first sentence negated
TFTF	**U** with sentences exchanged
TFFT	**O**
TFFF	**E**
FTTT	**A** with both sentences negated
FTTF	**O** with either first or second negated (not both)
FTFT	**U** with sentences exchanged and then second negated
FTFF	**E** with second sentence negated
FFTT	**U** with first sentence negated
FFTF	**E** with first sentence negated
FFFT	**E** with both sentences negated

Note that exchanging the sentences is only necessary with **U**. The three other basic truth functions are commutative; that is, they mean the same thing regardless of the order of the component sentences. There are other ways of getting some of these truth tables; these just happen to be the methods usually employed.

14.3 The six types of logical connectives

In order to remain unambiguous, Lojban cannot have only a single logical connective for each truth function. There are many places in the grammar of the language where logical connection is permitted, and each must have its appropriate set of connectives. If the connective suitable for sumti were used to connect selbri, ambiguity would result.

Consider the English sentence:

Example 14.2

    Mary went to the window and ...

where the last word could be followed by "the door", a noun phrase, or by "saw the horses", a sentence with subject omitted, or by "John went to the door", a full sentence, or by one of a variety of other English grammatical constructions. Lojban cannot tolerate such grammatical looseness.

Instead, there are a total of five different selma'o used for logical connection: A, GA, GIhA, GUhA, and JA. Each of these includes four cmavo, one based on each of the four vowels, which is always the last vowel in the cmavo. In selma'o A, the vowel is the entire cmavo.

Thus, in selma'o A, the cmavo for the function **A** is *a*. (Do not confuse A, which is a selma'o, with **A**, which is a truth function, or *a*, which is a cmavo.) Likewise, the cmavo for **E** in selma'o GIhA is *gi'e*, and the cmavo for **U** in selma'o GA is *gu*. This systematic regularity makes the cmavo easier to learn.

Obviously, four cmavo are not enough to express the 14 truth functions explained in Section 14.1 (p. 317). Therefore, compound cmavo must be used. These compound cmavo follow a systematic pattern: each has one cmavo from the five logical connection selma'o at its heart, and may also contain one or more of the auxiliary cmavo *se*, *na*, or *nai*. Which auxiliaries are used with which logical connection cmavo, and with what grammar and meaning, will be explained in the following sections. The uses of each of these auxiliary cmavo relates to its other uses in other parts of Lojban grammar.

For convenience, each of the types of compound cmavo used for logical connection is designated by a Lojban name. The name is derived by changing the final "-A" of the selma'o name to "-ek"; the reasons for using "-ek" are buried deep in the history of the Loglan Project. Thus, compound cmavo based on selma'o A are known as eks, and those based on selma'o JA are known as jeks. (When writing in English, it is conventional to use "eks" as the plural of "ek".) When the term "logical connective" is used in this chapter, it refers to one or more of these kinds of compound cmavo.

Why does the title of this section refer to "six types" when there are only five selma'o? A jek may be preceded by *i*, the usual Lojban cmavo for connecting two sentences. The compound produced by *i* followed by a jek is known as an ijek. It is useful to think of ijeks as a sixth kind of logical connective, parallel to eks, jeks, geks, giheks, and guheks.

There also exist giks, joiks, ijoiks, and joigiks, which are not logical connectives, but are other kinds of compound cmavo which will be introduced later.

14.4 Logical connection of bridi

Now we are ready to express Example 14.1 (p. 317) in Lojban! The kind of logical connective which is placed between two Lojban bridi to connect them logically is an ijek:

Example 14.3

la	djan.	nanmu	.ija	la		djeimyz.	ninmu
That-named	John	is-a-man	or	that-named		James	is-a-woman.

Here we have two separate Lojban bridi, *la djan. nanmu* and *la djeimyz. ninmu*. These bridi are connected by *.ija*, the ijek for the truth function **A**. The *i* portion of the ijek tells us that we are dealing with separate sentences here. Similarly, we can now say:

Example 14.4

la	djan.	nanmu	.ije	la		djeimyz.	ninmu
That-named	John	is-a-man	and	that-named		James	is-a-woman.

Example 14.5

la	djan.	nanmu	.ijo	la		djeimyz.	ninmu
That-named	John	is-a-man	if-and-only-if	that-named		James	is-a-woman.

Example 14.6

la	djan.	nanmu	.iju	la		djeimyz.	ninmu
That-named	John	is-a-man	whether-or-not	that-named		James	is-a-woman.

To obtain the other truth tables listed in Section 14.2 (p. 319), we need to know how to negate the two bridi which represent the component sentences. We could negate them directly by inserting *na* before the selbri, but Lojban also allows us to place the negation within the connective itself.

14.4 Logical connection of bridi

To negate the first or left-hand bridi, prefix na to the JA cmavo but after the i. To negate the second or right-hand bridi, suffix -nai to the JA cmavo. In either case, the negating word is placed on the side of the connective that is closest to the bridi being negated.

So to express the truth table FTTF, which requires **O** with either of the two bridi negated (not both), we can say either:

Example 14.7

la	djan.	nanmu	.inajo	la	djeimyz.	ninmu
That-named	John	is-not-a-man	if-and-only-if	that-named	James	is-a-woman.

Example 14.8

la	djan.	nanmu	.ijonai	la	djeimyz.	ninmu
That-named	John	is-a-man	if-and-only-if	that-named	James	is-not-a-woman.

The meaning of both Example 14.7 (p. 321) and Example 14.8 (p. 321) is the same as that of:

Example 14.9

John is a man or James is a woman, but not both.

Here is another example:

Example 14.10

la	djan.	nanmu	.ijanai	la	djeimyz.	ninmu
That-named	John	is-a-man	or	that-named	James	is-not-a-woman.

John is a man if James is a woman.

How's that again? Are those two English sentences in Example 14.10 (p. 321) really equivalent? In English, no. The Lojban TTFT truth function can be glossed "A if B", but the "if" does not quite have its English sense. Example 14.10 (p. 321) is true so long as John is a man, even if James is not a woman; likewise, it is true just because James is not a woman, regardless of John's gender. This kind of "if-then" is technically known as a "material conditional".

Since James is not a woman (by our assertions in Section 14.1 (p. 317)), the English sentence "John is a man if James is a woman" seems to be neither true nor false, since it assumes something which is not true. It turns out to be most convenient to treat this "if" as TTFT, which on investigation means that Example 14.10 (p. 321) is true. Example 14.11 (p. 321), however, is equally true:

Example 14.11

la	djan.	ninmu	.ijanai	la	djeimyz.	ninmu
That-named	John	is-a-woman	if	that-named	James	is-a-woman.

This can be thought of as a principle of consistency, and may be paraphrased as follows: "If a false statement is true, any statement follows from it." All uses of English "if" must be considered very carefully when translating into Lojban to see if they really fit this Lojban mold.

Example 14.12 (p. 321), which uses the TFTT truth function, is subject to the same rules: the stated gloss of TFTT as "only if" works naturally only when the right-hand bridi is false; if it is true, the left-hand bridi may be either true or false. The last gloss of Example 14.12 (p. 321) illustrates the use of "if ... then" as a more natural substitute for "only if".

Example 14.12

la	djan.	nanmu	.inaja	la	djeimyz.	ninmu
That-named	John	is-not-a-man	or	that-named	James	is-a-woman.

John is a man only if James is a woman.
If John is a man, then James is a woman.

The following example illustrates the use of se to, in effect, exchange the two sentences. The normal use of se is to (in effect) transpose places of a bridi, as explained in Section 5.11 (p. 96).

Example 14.13

> *la* ⋮ *djan.* ⋮ *nanmu* ⋮ *.iseju* ⋮ *la* ⋮ *djeimyz.* ⋮ *ninmu*
>
> Whether or not John is a man, James is a woman.

If both *na* and *se* are present, which is legal but never necessary, *na* would come before *se*. The full syntax of ijeks, therefore, is:

.i [na] [se] JA [nai]

> where the cmavo in brackets are optional.

14.5 Forethought bridi connection

Many concepts in Lojban are expressible in two different ways, generally referred to as "afterthought" and "forethought". Section 14.4 (p. 320) discussed what is called "afterthought bridi logical connection". The word "afterthought" is used because the connective cmavo and the second bridi were added, as it were, afterwards and without changing the form of the first bridi. This form might be used by someone who makes a statement and then wishes to add or qualify that statement after it has been completed. Thus,

Example 14.14

> *la djan. nanmu*

is a complete bridi, and adding an afterthought connection to make

Example 14.15

> *la* ⋮ *djan.* ⋮ *nanmu* ⋮ *.ija* ⋮ *la* ⋮ *djeimyz.* ⋮ *ninmu*
>
> John is a man or James is a woman (or both)

provides additional information without requiring any change in the form of what has come before; changes which may not be possible or practical, especially in speaking. (The meaning, however, may be changed by the use of a negating connective.) Afterthought connectives make it possible to construct all the important truth-functional relationships in a variety of ways.

In forethought style the speaker decides in advance, before expressing the first bridi, that a logical connection will be expressed. Forethought and afterthought connectives are expressed with separate selma'o. The forethought logical connectives corresponding to afterthought ijeks are geks:

Example 14.16

> *ga* ⋮ *la* ⋮ *djan.* ⋮ *nanmu* ⋮ *gi* ⋮ *la* ⋮ *djeimyz.* ⋮ *ninmu*
>
> Either John is a man or James is a woman (or both).

ga is the cmavo which represents the **A** truth function in selma'o GA. The word *gi* does not belong to GA at all, but constitutes its own selma'o: it serves only to separate the two bridi without having any content of its own. The English translation of *ga...gi* is "either ... or", but in the English form the truth function is specified both by the word "either" and by the word "or": not so in Lojban.

Even though two bridi are being connected, geks and giks do not have any *i* in them. The forethought construct binds up the two bridi into a single sentence as far as the grammar is concerned.

Some more examples of forethought bridi connection are:

Example 14.17

> *ge* ⋮ *la* ⋮ *djan.* ⋮ *nanmu* ⋮ *gi* ⋮ *la* ⋮ *djeimyz.* ⋮ *ninmu*
>
> (It is true that) both John is a man and James is a woman.

Example 14.18

> *gu* ⋮ *la* ⋮ *djan.* ⋮ *nanmu* ⋮ *gi* ⋮ *la* ⋮ *djeimyz.* ⋮ *ninmu*
>
> It is true that John is a man, whether or not James is a woman.

14.5 Forethought bridi connection

It is worth emphasizing that Example 14.18 (p. 322) does not assert that James is (or is not) a woman. The *gu* which indicates that *la djeimyz. ninmu* may be true or false is unfortunately rather remote from the bridi thus affected.

Perhaps the most important of the truth functions commonly expressed in forethought is TFTT, which can be paraphrased as "if ... then ...":

Example 14.19

ganai	la	djan.	nanmu	gi	la	djeimyz.	ninmu
Either	that-named	John	is-not-a-man,	or	that-named	James	is-a-woman.

If John is a man, then James is a woman.

Note the placement of the *nai* in Example 14.19 (p. 323). When added to afterthought selma'o such as JA, a following *nai* negates the second bridi, to which it is adjacent. Since GA cmavo precede the first bridi, a following *nai* negates the first bridi instead.

Why does English insist on forethought in the translation of Example 14.19 (p. 323)? Possibly because it would be confusing to seemingly assert a sentence and then make it conditional (which, as the Lojban form shows, involves a negation). Truth functions which involve negating the first sentence may be confusing, even to the Lojbanic understanding, when expressed using afterthought.

It must be reiterated here that not every use of English "if ... then" is properly translated by *.inaja* or *ganai...gi*; anything with implications of time needs a somewhat different Lojban translation, which will be discussed in Section 14.18 (p. 347). Causal sentences like "If you feed the pig, then it will grow" are not logical connectives of any type, but rather need a translation using *rinka* as the selbri joining two event abstractions, thus:

Example 14.20

le	nu	do	cidja	dunda	fi	le	xarju
The	event-of	(you	food	give	to	the	pig)

cu	rinka	le	nu	ri	ba	banro
causes	the	event-of	(it	will	grow).

Causality is discussed in far more detail in Section 9.7 (p. 189).

Example 14.21 (p. 323) and Example 14.22 (p. 323) illustrates a truth function, FTTF, which needs to negate either the first or the second bridi. We already understand how to negate the first bridi:

Example 14.21

gonai	la	djan.	nanmu	gi	la	djeimyz.	ninmu

John is not a man if and only if James is a woman.
Either John is a man or James is a woman but not both.

How can the second bridi be negated? By adding *-nai* to the *gi*.

Example 14.22

go	la	djan.	nanmu	ginai	la	djeimyz.	ninmu

John is a man if and only if James is not a woman.
Either John is a man or James is a woman but not both.

A compound cmavo based on *gi* is called a gik; the only giks are *gi* itself and *ginai*.
Further examples:

Example 14.23

ge	la	djan.	nanmu	ginai	la	djeimyz.	ninmu

John is a man and James is not a woman.

Example 14.24

ganai	la	djan.	nanmu	ginai	la	djeimyz.	ninmu

John is not a man or James is not a woman.

The syntax of geks is:

[se] GA [nai]

and of giks (which are not themselves connectives, but part of the machinery of forethought connection) is:

gi [nai]

14.6 sumti connection

Geks and ijeks are sufficient to state every possible logical connection between two bridi. However, it is often the case that two bridi to be logically connected have one or more portions in common:

Example 14.25

| la | djan. | klama | le | zarci | .ije | la | .alis. | klama | le | zarci |

John goes to the market, and Alice goes to the market.

Here only a single sumti differs between the two bridi. Lojban does not require that both bridi be expressed in full. Instead, a single bridi can be given which contains both of the different sumti and uses a logical connective from a different selma'o to combine the two sumti:

Example 14.26

| la | | djan | .e | la | | .alis. | klama | le | zarci |
| That-named | John | and | that-named | Alice | go-to | the | market. |

Example 14.26 (p. 324) means exactly the same thing as Example 14.25 (p. 324): one may be rigorously transformed into the other without any change of logical meaning. This rule is true in general for every different kind of logical connection in Lojban; all of them, with one exception (see Section 14.12 (p. 333)), can always be transformed into a logical connection between sentences that expresses the same truth function.

The afterthought logical connectives between sumti are eks, which contain a connective cmavo of selma'o A. If ijeks were used in Example 14.26 (p. 324), the meaning would be changed:

Example 14.27

| la | | djan. | | | .ije |
| That-named | John | [is/does-something]. | And |

| la | | .alis. | klama | le | zarci |
| that-named | Alices | goes-to | the | market. |

leaving the reader uncertain why John is mentioned at all.

Any ek may be used between sumti, even if there is no direct English equivalent:

Example 14.28

| la | | djan. | .o | | la | | .alis. | klama | le | zarci |
| That-named | John | if-and-only-if | that-named | Alice | goes-to | the | market. |

John goes to the market if, and only if, Alice does.

The second line of Example 14.27 (p. 324) is highly stilted English, but the first line (of which it is a literal translation) is excellent Lojban.

What about forethought sumti connection? As is the case for bridi connection, geks are appropriate. They are not the only selma'o of forethought logical-connectives, but are the most commonly used ones.

Example 14.29

| ga | la | djan. | gi | la | .alis. | klama | le | zarci |

Either John or Alice (or both) goes to the market.

Of course, eks include all the same patterns of compound cmavo that ijeks do. When na or se is part of an ek, a special writing convention is invoked, as in the following example:

Example 14.30

la	djan.	na.a	la	.alis.	klama	le	zarci
That-named	**John**	**only-if**	**that-named**	**Alice**	**goes-to**	**the**	**market.**

John goes to the market only if Alice does.

Note the period in *na.a*. The cmavo of A begin with vowels, and therefore must always be preceded by a pause. It is conventional to write all connective compounds as single words (with no spaces), but this pause must still be marked in writing as in speech; otherwise, the *na* and *a* would tend to run together.

14.7 More than two propositions

So far we have seen logical connectives used to connect exactly two sentences. How about connecting three or more? Is this possible in Lojban? The answer is yes, subject to some warnings and some restrictions.

Of the four primitive truth functions **A**, **E**, **O**, and **U**, all but **O** have the same truth values no matter how their component sentences are associated in pairs. Therefore,

Example 14.31

mi	dotco	.ije	mi	ricfu	.ije	mi	nanmu
I	**am-German.**	**And**	**I**	**am-rich.**	**And**	**I**	**am-a-man.**

means that all three component sentences are true. Likewise,

Example 14.32

mi	dotco	.ija	mi	ricfu	.ija	mi	nanmu
I	**am-German.**	**Or**	**I**	**am-rich.**	**Or**	**I**	**am-a-man.**

means that one or more of the component sentences is true.

O, however, is different. Working out the truth table for

Example 14.33

mi	dotco	.ijo	mi	ricfu	.ijo	mi	nanmu
I	**am-German.**	**If-and-only-if**	**I**	**am-rich.**	**If-and-only-if**	**I**	**am-a-man.**

shows that Example 14.33 (p. 325) does not mean that either I am all three of these things or none of them; instead, an accurate translation would be:

Of the three properties – German-ness, wealth, and manhood – I possess either exactly one or else all three.

Because of the counterintuitiveness of this outcome, it is safest to avoid **O** with more than two sentences. Likewise, the connectives which involve negation also have unexpected truth values when used with more than two sentences.

In fact, no combination of logical connectives can produce the "all or none" interpretation intended (but not achieved) by Example 14.33 (p. 325) without repeating one of the bridi. See Example 14.48 (p. 328).

There is an additional difficulty with the use of more than two sentences. What is the meaning of:

Example 14.34

mi	nelci	la	djan.	.ije	mi	nelci	la	martas.
I	**like**	**that-named**	**John.**	**And**	**I**	**like**	**that-named**	**Martha.**

.ija	mi	nelci	la	meris.
Or	**I**	**like**	**that-named**	**Mary.**

Does this mean:

Example 14.35

I like John, and I like either Martha or Mary or both.

Or is the correct translation:

Example 14.36

Either I like John and I like Martha, or I like Mary, or both.

Example 14.36 (p. 326) is the correct translation of Example 14.34 (p. 325). The reason is that Lojban logical connectives pair off from the left, like many constructs in the language. This rule, called the left-grouping rule, is easy to forget, especially when intuition pulls the other way. Forethought connectives are not subject to this problem:

Example 14.37

ga	ge	mi	nelci	la		djan.
Either	(Both	I	like	that-named		John

gi	mi	nelci	la		martas.
and	I	like	that-named		Martha)

gi	mi	nelci	la		meris.
or	I	like	that-named		Mary.

is equivalent in meaning to Example 14.34 (p. 325), whereas

Example 14.38

ge	mi	nelci	la		djan.
Both	I	like	that-named		John

gi	ga	mi	nelci	la		martas.
and	(Either	I	like	that-named		Martha

gi	mi	nelci	la		meris.
or	I	like	that-named		Mary).

is not equivalent to Example 14.34 (p. 325), but is instead a valid translation into Lojban, using forethought, of Example 14.35 (p. 325).

14.8 Grouping of afterthought connectives

There are several ways in Lojban to render Example 14.35 (p. 325) using afterthought only. The simplest method is to make use of the cmavo *bo* (of selma'o BO). This cmavo has several functions in Lojban, but is always associated with high precedence and short scope. In particular, if *bo* is placed after an ijek, the result is a grammatically distinct kind of ijek which overrides the regular left-grouping rule. Connections marked with *bo* are interpreted before connections not so marked. Example 14.39 (p. 326) is equivalent in meaning to Example 14.38 (p. 326):

Example 14.39

mi	nelci	la		djan.	.ije	mi	nelci	la		martas.
I	like	that-named		John,	and	I	like	that-named		Martha

.ijabo	mi	nelci	la		meris.
or	I	like	that-named		Mary.

The English translation feebly indicates with a comma what the Lojban marks far more clearly: the "I like Martha" and "I like Mary" sentences are joined by *.ija* first, before the result is joined to "I like John" by *.ije*.

Eks can have *bo* attached in exactly the same way, so that Example 14.40 (p. 326) is equivalent in meaning to Example 14.39 (p. 326):

Example 14.40

mi nelci la djan. .e la martas. .abo la meris.

Forethought connectives, however, never can be suffixed with *bo*, for every use of forethought connectives clearly indicates the intended pattern of grouping.

14.8 Grouping of afterthought connectives

What happens if *bo* is used on both connectives, giving them the same high precedence, as in Example 14.41 (p. 327)?

Example 14.41

> *mi nelci la djan. .ebo la martas. .abo la meris.*

Does this wind up meaning the same as Example 14.34 (p. 325) and Example 14.36 (p. 326)? Not at all. A second rule relating to *bo* is that where several *bo*-marked connectives are used in succession, the normal Lojban left-grouping rule is replaced by a right-grouping rule. As a result, Example 14.41 (p. 327) in fact means the same as Example 14.39 (p. 326) and Example 14.40 (p. 326). This rule may be occasionally exploited for special effects, but is tricky to keep straight; in writing intended to be easy to understand, multiple consecutive connectives marked with *bo* should be avoided.

The use of *bo*, therefore, gets tricky in complex connections of more than three sentences. Looking back at the English translations of Example 14.37 (p. 326) and Example 14.38 (p. 326), parentheses were used to clarify the grouping. These parentheses have their Lojban equivalents, two sets of them actually. *tu'e* and *tu'u* are used with ijeks, and *ke* and *ke'e* with eks and other connectives to be discussed later. (*ke* and *ke'e* are also used in other roles in the language, but always as grouping markers). Consider the English sentence:

Example 14.42

> I kiss you and you kiss me, if I love you and you love me.

where the semantics tells us that the instances of "and" are meant to have higher precedence than that of "if". If we wish to express Example 14.42 (p. 327) in afterthought, we can say:

Example 14.43

mi	*cinba*	*do*	*.ije[bo]*	*do*	*cinba*	*mi*
I	kiss	you	and	you	kiss	me,

.ijanai	*mi*	*prami*	*do*	*.ijebo*	*do*	*prami*	*mi*
if	I	love	you	and	you	love	me.

marking two of the ijeks with *bo* for high precedence. (The first *bo* is not strictly necessary, because of the left-grouping rule, and is shown here in brackets.)

But it may be clearer to use explicit parenthesis words and say:

Example 14.44

tu'e	*mi*	*cinba*	*do*	*.ije*	*do*	*cinba*	*mi*	*tu'u*
(	I	kiss	you	and	you	kiss	me	)

.ijanai	*tu'e*	*mi*	*prami*	*do*	*.ije*	*do*	*prami*	*mi*	*[tu'u]*
if	(	I	love	you	and	you	love	me	).

where the *tu'e...tu'u* pairs set off the structure. The cmavo *tu'u* is an elidable terminator, and its second occurrence in Example 14.44 (p. 327) is bracketed, because all terminators may be elided at the end of a text.

In addition, parentheses are a general solution: multiple parentheses may be nested inside one another, and additional afterthought material may be added without upsetting the existing structure. Neither of these two advantages apply to *bo* grouping. In general, afterthought constructions trade generality for simplicity.

Because of the left-grouping rule, the first set of *tu'e...tu'u* parentheses may actually be left off altogether, producing:

Example 14.45

mi	*cinba*	*do*	*.ije*	*do*	*cinba*	*mi*
I	kiss	you	and	you	kiss	me

.ijanai	*tu'e*	*mi*	*prami*	*do*	*.ije*	*do*	*prami*	*mi*	*[tu'u]*
if	(	I	love	you	and	you	love	me	).

What about parenthesized sumti connection? Consider

Example 14.46

I walk to either the market and the house, or the school and the office.

Two pairs of parentheses, analogous to Example 14.44 (p. 327), would seem to be the right approach. However, it is a rule of Lojban grammar that a sumti may not begin with *ke*, so the first set of parentheses must be omitted, producing Example 14.47 (p. 328), which is instead parallel to Example 14.45 (p. 327):

Example 14.47

mi	dzukla	le	zarci	.e	le	zdani
I	walk-to	the	market	and	the	house

.a	ke	le	ckule	.e	le	briju	[ke'e]
or	(	the	school	and	the	office	).

If sumti were allowed to begin with *ke*, unavoidable ambiguities would result, so *ke* grouping of sumti is allowed only just after a logical connective. This rule does not apply to *tu'e* grouping of bridi, as Example 14.44 (p. 327) shows.

Now we have enough facilities to handle the problem of Example 14.33 (p. 325): "I am German, rich, and a man – or else none of these." The following paraphrase has the correct meaning:

Example 14.48

[tu'e]	mi	dotco	.ijo	mi	ricfu	[tu'u]
(	I	am-German	if-and-only-if	I	am-rich	)

.ije	tu'e	mi	dotco	.ijo	mi	nanmu	[tu'u]
and	(	I	am-German	if-and-only-if	I	am-a-man	).

The truth table, when worked out, produces T if and only if all three component sentences are true or all three are false.

14.9 Compound bridi

So far we have seen how to handle two sentences that need have no similarity at all (bridi connection) and sentences that are identical except for a difference in one sumti (sumti connection). It would seem natural to ask how to logically connect sentences that are identical except for having different selbri.

Surprise! Lojban provides no logical connective that is designed to handle selbri and nothing else. Instead, selbri connection is provided as part of a more general-purpose mechanism called "compound bridi". Compound bridi result from logically connecting sentences that differ in their selbri and possibly some of their sumti.

The simplest cases result when the x1 sumti is the only common point:

Example 14.49

mi	klama	le	zarci	.ije	mi	nelci	la	djan.
I	go-to	the	market,	and	I	like	that-named	John.

is equivalent in meaning to the compound bridi:

Example 14.50

mi	klama	le	zarci	gi'e	nelci	la	djan.
I	go-to	the	market	and	like	that-named	John.

As Example 14.50 (p. 328) indicates, giheks are used in afterthought to create compound bridi; *gi'e* is the gihek corresponding to "and". The actual phrases *klama le zarci* and *nelci la djan.* that the gihek connects are known as "bridi-tails", because they represent (in this use) the "tail end" of a bridi, including the selbri and any following sumti, but excluding any sumti that precede the selbri:

Example 14.51

mi	ricfu	gi'e	klama	le	zarci
I	am-rich	and	go-to	the	market.

14.9 Compound bridi

In Example 14.51 (p. 328), the first bridi-tail is *ricfu*, a simple selbri, and the second bridi-tail is *klama le zarci*, a selbri with one following sumti.

Suppose that more than a single sumti is identical between the two sentences:

Example 14.52

mi	dunda	le	cukta	do	.ije	mi	lebna	lo	rupnu	do
I	give	the	book	to-you,	and	I	take	some	currency-units	from-you.

In Example 14.52 (p. 329), the first and last sumti of each bridi are identical; the selbri and the second sumti are different. By moving the final sumti to the beginning, a form analogous to Example 14.50 (p. 328) can be achieved:

Example 14.53

fi	do	fa	mi	dunda	le	cukta
to/from	you		I	give	the	book

gi'e	lebna	lo	rupnu
and	take	some	currency-units.

where the *fi* does not have an exact English translation because it merely places *do* in the third place of both *lebna* and *dunda*. However, a form that preserves natural sumti order also exists in Lojban. Giheks connect two bridi-tails, but also allow sumti to be added following the bridi-tail. These sumti are known as tail-terms, and apply to both bridi. The straightforward gihek version of Example 14.52 (p. 329) therefore is:

Example 14.54

mi	dunda	le	cukta	gi'e	lebna	lo	rupnu	vau	do
I	(give	the	book)	and	(take	some	currency-units)		to/from-you.

The *vau* (of selma'o VAU) serves to separate the bridi-tail from the tail-terms. Every bridi-tail is terminated by an elidable *vau*, but only in connection with compound bridi is it ever necessary to express this *vau*. Thus:

Example 14.55

mi	klama	le	zarci	[vau]
I	go-to	the	market.	

has a single elided *vau*, and Example 14.50 (p. 328) is equivalent to:

Example 14.56

mi klama le zarci [vau] gi'e nelci la djan. [vau] [vau]

where the double *vau* at the end of Example 14.56 (p. 329) terminates both the right-hand bridi-tail and the unexpressed tail-terms.

A final use of giheks is to combine bridi-tails used as complete sentences, the Lojban observative:

Example 14.57

klama	le	zarci	gi'e	dzukla	le	briju
A-goer	to-the	market	and	a-walker	to-the	office.

Since x1 is omitted in both of the bridi underlying Example 14.57 (p. 329), this compound bridi does not necessarily imply that the goer and the walker are the same. Only the presence of an explicit x1 (other than *zo'e*, which is equivalent to omission) can force the goer and the walker to be identical.

A strong argument for this convention is provided by analysis of the following example:

Example 14.58

klama	la	nu,IORK.
A-goer	to-that-named	New-York

la	finyks.
from-that-named	Phoenix

gi'e	klama	la	nu,IORK.
and	a-goer	to-that-named	New-York

la	rom.
from-that-named	Rome.

If the rule were that the x1 places of the two underlying bridi were considered identical, then (since there is nothing special about x1), the unspecified x4 (route) and x5 (means) places would also have to be the same, leading to the absurd result that the route from Phoenix to New York is the same as the route from Rome to New York. Inserting *da*, meaning roughly "something", into the x1 place cures the problem:

Example 14.59

da	klama	la	nu,IORK.	la	finyks.
Something	is-a-goer	to-that-named	New-York	from-that-named	Phoenix

gi'e	klama	la	nu,IORK.	la	rom.
and	is-a-goer	to-that-named	New-York	from-that-named	Rome.

The syntax of giheks is:

[na] [se] GIhA [nai]

which is exactly parallel to the syntax of eks.

14.10 Multiple compound bridi

Giheks can be combined with *bo* in the same way as eks:

Example 14.60

mi	nelci	la	djan.	gi'e	nelci	la	martas.	gi'abo	nelci	la	meris.

I like John and (like Martha or like Mary).

is equivalent in meaning to Example 14.39 (p. 326) and Example 14.40 (p. 326). Likewise, *ke...ke'e* grouping can be used after giheks:

Example 14.61

mi	dzukla	le	zarci
I	walk-to	the	market

gi'e	dzukla	le	zdani
and	walk-to	the	house,

gi'a	ke	dzukla	le	ckule
or	(	walk-to	the	school

gi'e	dzukla	le	briju	[ke'e]
and	walk-to	the	office.	)

is the gihek version of Example 14.47 (p. 328). The same rule about using *ke...ke'e* bracketing only just after a connective applies to bridi-tails as to sumti, so the first two bridi-tails in Example 14.61 (p. 330) cannot be explicitly grouped; implicit left-grouping suffices to associate them.

Each of the pairs of bridi-tails joined by multiple giheks can have its own set of tail-terms:

Example 14.62

	mi	dejni	lo	rupnu		la	djan.
[If]	I	owe	some	currency-units		to-that-named	John,

.inaja	mi	dunda	le	cukta	la		djan.
then	I	give	the	book	to-that-named		John

.ijabo	mi	lebna	le	cukta	la		djan.
or	I	take	the	book	from-that-named		John.

is equivalent in meaning to:

Example 14.63

	mi	dejni	lo	rupnu		nagi'a	dunda
[If]	I	owe	some	currency-units		then	(give

gi'abo	lebna	vau	le	cukta	vau	la		djan.
or	take)		a	book		to/from-that-named		John.

The literal English translation in Example 14.63 (p. 331) is almost unintelligible, but the Lojban is perfectly grammatical. *mi* fills the x1 place of all three selbri; *lo rupnu* is the x2 of *dejni*, whereas *le cukta* is a tail-term shared between *dunda* and *lebna*; *la djan.* is a tail-term shared by *dejni* and by *dunda gi'abo lebna*. In this case, greater clarity is probably achieved by moving *la djan.* to the beginning of the sentence, as in Example 14.53 (p. 329):

Example 14.64

fi		la		djan.		fa	mi	dejni	lo		rupnu
To/from		that-named		John,	[if]		I	owe	some		currency-units

nagi'a			dunda	gi'abo	lebna	vau	le		cukta
then		[I]	give	or	take		the		book.

Finally, what about forethought logical connection of bridi-tails? There is no direct mechanism for the purpose. Instead, Lojban grammar allows a pair of forethought-connected sentences to function as a single bridi-tail, and of course the sentences need not have terms before their selbri. For example:

Example 14.65

mi	ge	klama	le	zarci	gi	nelci	la		djan.
I	both	go-to	the	market	and	like	that-named		John.

is equivalent in meaning to Example 14.50 (p. 328).

Of course, either of the connected sentences may contain giheks:

Example 14.66

mi	ge	klama	le	zarci	gi'e	dzukla	le		zdani
I	both	(go	to-the	market	and	walk	to-the		house)

gi	nelci	la		djan.
and	like	that-named		John.

The entire gek-connected sentence pair may be negated as a whole by prefixing *na*:

Example 14.67

	mi	na	ge	klama	le	zarci	gi	dzukla	le		zdani
[False!]	I		both	go-to	the	market	and	walk-to	the		house.

Since a pair of sentences joined by geks is the equivalent of a bridi-tail, it may be followed by tail terms. The forethought equivalent of Example 14.54 (p. 329) is:

Example 14.68

mi	ge	dunda	le	cukta
I	both	(give	the	book)

gi	lebna	lo	rupnu	vau	do
and	(take	some	currency-units	)	to/from-you.

Here is a pair of gek-connected observatives, a forethought equivalent of Example 14.57 (p. 329):

Example 14.69

ge	klama	le	zarci	gi	dzukla	le	briju
Both	a-goer	to-the	market	and	a-walker	to-the	office.

Finally, here is an example of gek-connected sentences with both shared and unshared terms before their selbri:

Example 14.70

mi	gonai	le	zarci	cu	klama	gi	le	bisli	cu	dansu
I	either-but-not-both	to-the	office		go	or	on-the	ice		dance.

I either go to the office or dance on the ice (but not both).

14.11 Termset logical connection

So far we have seen sentences that differ in all components, and require bridi connection; sentences that differ in one sumti only, and permit sumti connection; and sentences that differ in the selbri and possibly one or more sumti, and permit bridi-tail connection. Termset logical connectives are employed for sentences that differ in more than one sumti but not in the selbri, such as:

Example 14.71

I go to the market from the office and to the house from the school.

The Lojban version of Example 14.71 (p. 332) requires two termsets joined by a logical connective. A "term" is either a sumti or a sumti preceded by a tense or modal tag such as *pu* or *bai*. Afterthought termsets are formed by linking terms together by inserting the cmavo *ce'e* (of selma'o CEhE) between each of them. Furthermore, the logical connective (which is a jek) must be prefixed by the cmavo *pe'e* (of selma'o PEhE). (We could refer to the combination of *pe'e* and a jek as a "pehejek", I suppose.)

Example 14.72

mi	klama	le	zarci	ce'e	le	briju
I	go	to-the	market	[plus]	from-the	office

pe'e	je	le	zdani	ce'e	le	ckule
[joint]	and	to-the	house	[plus]	from-the	school.

The literal translation uses "[plus]" to indicate the termset connective, and "[joint]" to indicate the position of the logical connective joint. As usual, there is an equivalent bridi-connection form:

Example 14.73

mi	klama	le	zarci	le	briju
I	go	to-the	market	from-the	office,

.ije	mi	klama	le	zdani	le	ckule
and	I	go	to-the	house	from-the	school.

which illustrates that the two bridi differ in the x2 and x3 places only.

What happens if the two joined sets of terms are of unequal length? Expanding to bridi connection will always make clear which term goes in which place of which bridi. It can happen that a sumti may fall in the x2 place of one bridi and the x3 place of another:

Example 14.74

mi	pe'e	ja	do	ce'e	le	zarci	cu	klama	le	briju
I	[joint]	or	you	[plus]	to-the	market		go	to/from-the	office.

can be clearly understood by expansion to:

Example 14.75

mi	klama	le	briju	.ija	do	le	zarci	cu	klama
I	go	to-the	office,	or	you	to-the	market		go

le	briju
from-the	office.

So *le briju* is your origin but my destination, and thus falls in the x2 and x3 places of *klama* simultaneously! This is legal because even though there is only one selbri, *klama*, there are two distinct bridi expressed here. In addition, *mi* in Example 14.74 (p. 332) is serving as a termset containing only one term. An analogous paradox applies to compound bridi with tail-terms and unequal numbers of sumti within the connected bridi-tails:

Example 14.76

mi		klama	le	zarci	gi'e	dzukla	vau	le	briju
I	(	go	to-the	market	and	walk	)	to/from-the	office.

means that I go to the market from the office, and I walk to the office; *le briju* is the x3 place of *klama* and the x2 place of *dzukla*.

Forethought termsets also exist, and use *nu'i* of selma'o NUhI to signal the beginning and *nu'u* of selma'o NUhU (an elidable terminator) to signal the end. Nothing is inserted between the individual terms: they simply sit side-by-side. To make a logical connection in a forethought termset, use a gek, with the gek just after the *nu'i*, and an extra *nu'u* just before the gik:

Example 14.77

mi	klama	nu'i		ge	le	zarci	le	briju
I	go	[start-termset]		both	to-the	market	from-the	office

nu'u	gi	le	zdani	le	ckule	[nu'u]
[joint]	and	to-the	house	from-the	school	[end-termset].

Note that even though two termsets are being connected, only one *nu'i* is used.

The grammatical uses of termsets that do not contain logical connectives are explained in Section 9.8 (p. 192), Section 10.25 (p. 243), and Section 16.7 (p. 382).

14.12 Logical connection within tanru

As noted at the beginning of Section 14.9 (p. 328), there is no logical connective in Lojban that joins selbri and nothing but selbri. However, it is possible to have logical connectives within a selbri, forming a kind of tanru that involves a logical connection. Consider the simple tanru *blanu zdani*, blue house. Now anything that is a blue ball, in the most ordinary understanding of the phrase at least, is both blue and a ball. And indeed, instead of *blanu bolci*, Lojbanists can say *blanu je bolci*, using a jek connective within the tanru. (We saw jeks used in Section 14.11 (p. 332) also, but there they were always prefixed by *pe'e*; in this section they are used alone.) Here is a pair of examples:

Example 14.78

ti	blanu	zdani
This	is-a-blue-type-of	house.

Example 14.79

ti	blanu	je	zdani
This	is-blue	and	is-a-house.

But of course Example 14.78 (p. 333) and Example 14.79 (p. 333) are not necessarily equivalent in meaning! It is the most elementary point about Lojban tanru that Example 14.78 (p. 333) might just as well mean

Example 14.80

This is a house for blue inhabitants.

and Example 14.79 (p. 333) certainly is not equivalent in meaning to Example 14.80 (p. 333).

A full explanation of logical connection within tanru belongs rather to a discussion of selbri structure than to logical connectives in general. Why? Because although Example 14.79 (p. 333) happens to mean the same as

Example 14.81

  ti blanu gi'e zdani

and therefore as

Example 14.82

  ti blanu .ije ti zdani

the rule of expansion into separate bridi simply does not always work for tanru connection. Supposing Alice to be a person who lives in blue houses, then

Example 14.83

la	*.alis.*	*cu*	*blanu*	*je*	*zdani*	*prenu*
That-named	Alice	is-a-(	blue	and	house)	type-of-person.

would be true, because tanru grouping with a jek has higher precedence than unmarked tanru grouping, but:

Example 14.84

la	*.alis.*	*cu*	*blanu*	*prenu*
That-named	Alice	is-a	blue	person,

.ije	*la*	*.alis.*	*cu*	*zdani*	*prenu*
and	that-named	Alice	is-a	house	person.

is probably false, because the blueness is associated with the house, not with Alice, even leaving aside the question of what it means to say "Alice is a blue person". (Perhaps she belongs to the Blue team, or is wearing blue clothes.) The semantic ambiguity of tanru make such logical manipulations impossible.

It suffices to note here, then, a few purely grammatical points about tanru logical connection. *bo* may be appended to jeks as to eks, with the same rules:

Example 14.85

la	*teris.*	*cu*	*ricfu*	*je*	*nakni*	*jabo*	*fetsi*
That-named	Terry		is-rich	and	(male	or	female).

The components of tanru may be grouped with *ke* both before and after a logical connective:

Example 14.86

la	*.teris.*	*cu*	*[ke]*	*ricfu*	*ja*	*pindi*	*[ke'e]*
That-named	Terry		(	is-rich	or	is-poor	)

je	*ke*	*nakni*	*ja*	*fetsi*	*[ke'e]*
and	(	male	or	female	).

where the first *ke...ke'e* pair may be omitted altogether by the rule of left-grouping, but is optionally permitted. In any case, the last instance of *ke'e* may be elided.

The syntax of jeks is:

[na] [se] JA [nai]

  parallel to eks and giheks.

Forethought tanru connection does not use geks, but uses guheks instead. Guheks have exactly the same form as geks:

[se] GUhA [nai]

Using guheks in tanru connection (rather than geks) resolves what would otherwise be an unacceptable ambiguity between bridi-tail and tanru connection:

Example 14.87

la	.alis.	gu'e	ricfu	gi	fetsi
That-named	Alice	is-both	rich	and	female.

Note that giks are used with guheks in exactly the same way they are used with geks. Like jeks, guheks bind more closely than unmarked tanru grouping does:

Example 14.88

la	.alis.	gu'e	blanu	gi	zdani	prenu
That-named	Alice	is-a-(both	blue	and	a-house)	type-of-person.

is the forethought version of Example 14.83 (p. 334).

A word of caution about the use of logically connected tanru within descriptions. English-based intuition can lead the speaker astray. In correctly reducing

Example 14.89

mi	viska	pa	nanmu	.ije	mi	viska	pa	ninmu
I	see	a	man,	and	I	see	a	woman.

to

Example 14.90

mi	viska	pa	nanmu	.e	pa	ninmu
I	see	a	man	and	a	woman.

there is a great temptation to reduce further to:

Example 14.91

mi	viska	pa	nanmu	je	ninmu
I	see	a	man	and	woman.

But Example 14.91 (p. 335) means that you see one thing which is both a man and a woman simultaneously! A *nanmu je ninmu* is a manwoman, a presumably non-existent creature who is both a *nanmu* and a *ninmu*.

14.13 Truth questions and connective questions

So far we have addressed only sentences which are statements. Lojban, like all human languages, needs also to deal with sentences which are questions. There are many ways of asking questions in Lojban, but some of these (like questions about quantity, tense, and emotion) are discussed in other chapters.

The simplest kind of question is of the type "Is it true that ..." where some statement follows. This type is called a "truth question", and can be represented in English by Example 14.92 (p. 335):

Example 14.92

Is it true that Fido is a dog?
Is Fido a dog?

Note the two formulations. English truth questions can always be formed by prefixing "Is is true that" to the beginning of a statement; there is also usually a more idiomatic way involving putting the verb before its subject. "Is Fido a dog?" is the truth question corresponding to "Fido is a dog". In Lojban, the equivalent mechanism is to prefix the cmavo *xu* (of selma'o UI) to the statement:

Example 14.93

xu	la	faidon.	gerku
Is-it-true-that	that-named	Fido	is-a-dog?

Example 14.92 (p. 335) and Example 14.93 (p. 335) are equivalent in meaning.

A truth question can be answered "yes" or "no", depending on the truth or falsity, respectively, of the underlying statement. The standard way of saying "yes" in Lojban is *go'i* and of saying "no" is *nago'i*. (The reasons for this rule are explained in Section 7.6 (p. 146).) In answer to Example 14.93 (p. 335), the possible answers are:

Example 14.94

> *go'i*

> Fido is a dog.

and

Example 14.95

> *nago'i*

> Fido is not a dog.

Some English questions seemingly have the same form as the truth questions so far discussed. Consider

Example 14.96

> Is Fido a dog or a cat?

Superficially, Example 14.96 (p. 336) seems like a truth question with the underlying statement:

Example 14.97

> Fido is a dog or a cat.

By translating Example 14.97 (p. 336) into Lojban and prefixing *xu* to signal a truth question, we get:

Example 14.98

xu	*la*	*faidon.*	*gerku*	*gi'onai*	*mlatu*	
Is-it-true-that	**that-named**	**Fido**	**is-a-dog**	**or**	**is-a-cat**	**(but not both)?**

Given that Fido really is either a dog or a cat, the appropriate answer would be *go'i*; if Fido were a fish, the appropriate answer would be *nago'i*.

But that is not what an English-speaker who utters Example 14.96 (p. 336) is asking! The true significance of Example 14.96 (p. 336) is that the speaker desires to know the truth value of either of the two underlying bridi (it is presupposed that only one is true).

Lojban has an elegant mechanism for rendering this kind of question which is very unlike that used in English. Instead of asking about the truth value of the connected bridi, Lojban users ask about the truth function which connects them. This is done by using a special question cmavo: there is one of these for each of the logical connective selma'o, as shown by the following table:

ge'i	GA	forethought connective question
gi'i	GIhA	bridi-tail connective question
gu'i	GUhA	tanru forethought connective question
je'i	JA	tanru connective question
ji	A	sumti connective question

(This list unfortunately departs from the pretty regularity of the other cmavo for logical connection. The two-syllable selma'o, GIhA and GUhA, make use of the cmavo ending in "-i" which is not used for a truth function, but *gi* and *i* were not available, and different cmavo had to be chosen. This table must simply be memorized, like most other non-connective cmavo assignments.)

One correct translation of Example 14.96 (p. 336) employs a question gihek:

Example 14.99

la	*.alis.*	*gerku*	*gi'i*	*mlatu*
That-named	**Alice**	**is-a-dog**	**[truth-function?]**	**is-a-cat?**

Here are some plausible answers:

Example 14.100

> *nagi'e*

> Alice is not a dog and is a cat.

Example 14.101

> *gi'enai*

Alice is a dog and is not a cat.

Example 14.102

> *nagi'enai*

Alice is not a dog and is not a cat.

Example 14.103

> *nagi'o*
> *gi'onai*

Alice is a dog or is a cat but not both (I'm not saying which).

Example 14.103 (p. 337) is correct but uncooperative.

As usual, Lojban questions are answered by filling in the blank left by the question. Here the blank is a logical connective, and therefore it is grammatical in Lojban to utter a bare logical connective without anything for it to connect.

The answer *gi'e*, meaning that Alice is a dog and is a cat, is impossible in the real world, but for:

Example 14.104

do	*djica*	*tu'a*	*loi*	*ckafi*
You	desire	something-about	a-mass-of	coffee

ji	*loi*	*tcati*
[truth-function?]	a-mass-of	tea?

Do you want coffee or tea?

the answer *e*, meaning that I want both, is perfectly plausible, if not necessarily polite.

The forethought questions *ge'i* and *gu'i* are used like the others, but ambiguity forbids the use of isolated forethought connectives as answers – they sound like the start of forethought-connected bridi. So although Example 14.105 (p. 337) is the forethought version of Example 14.104 (p. 337):

Example 14.105

do	*djica*	*tu'a*	*ge'i*	*loi*	*ckafi*
You	desire	something-about	[truth-function?]	a-mass-of	coffee

gi	*loi*	*tcati*
[or]	a-mass-of	tea?

the answer must be in afterthought form.

There are natural languages, notably Chinese, which employ the Lojbanic form of connective question. The Chinese sentence

Example 14.106

> ni^3 zou^3 hai^2shi pao^3
> You walk [or?] run?

means "Do you walk or run?", and is exactly parallel to the Lojban:

Example 14.107

do	*cadzu*	*gi'i*	*bajra*
You	walk	[or?]	run?

However, Chinese does not use logical connectives in the reply to such a question, so the resemblance, though striking, is superficial.

Truth questions may be used in bridi connection. This form of sentence is perfectly legitimate, and can be interpreted by using the convention that a truth question is true if the answer is "yes" and false if the answer is *no*. Analogously, an imperative sentence (involving the special pro-sumti *ko*, which means "you" but marks the sentence as a command) is true if the command is obeyed, and false otherwise. A request of Abraham Lincoln's may be translated thus:

Example 14.108

ganai	ti	ckafi	gi	ko	bevri	loi		tcati	mi
If	this	is-coffee	then	[you!]	bring	a-mass-of	tea	to-me,	

.ije	ganai	ti	tcati	gi	ko	bevri	loi		ckafi	mi
and	if	this	is-tea	then	[you!]	bring	a-mass-of	coffee	to-me.	

If this is coffee, bring me tea; but if this is tea, bring me coffee.

In logical terms, however, "but" is the same as "and"; the difference is that the sentence after a "but" is felt to be in tension or opposition to the sentence before it. Lojban represents this distinction by adding the discursive cmavo *ku'i* (of selma'o UI), which is explained in Section 13.12 (p. 304), to the logical *.ije*.)

14.14 Non-logical connectives

Way back in Section 14.1 (p. 317), the point was made that not every use of English "and", "if ... then", and so on represents a Lojban logical connective. In particular, consider the "and" of:

Example 14.109

John and Alice carried the piano.

Given the nature of pianos, this probably means that John carried one end and Alice the other. So it is not true that:

Example 14.110

John carried the piano, and Alice carried the piano.

which would mean that each of them carried the piano by himself/herself. Lojban deals with this particular linguistic phenomenon as a "mass". John and Alice are joined together into a mass, John-and-Alice, and it is this mass which carried the piano, not either of them separately. The cmavo *joi* (of selma'o JOI) is used to join two or more components into a mass:

Example 14.111

la	djan.	joi	la	.alis.	cu	bevri	le	pipno
That-named	John	massed-with	that-named	Alice		carry	the	piano.

Example 14.111 (p. 338) covers the case mentioned, where John and Alice divide the labor; it also could mean that John did all the hauling and Alice did the supervising. This possibility arises because the properties of a mass are the properties of its components, which can lead to apparent contradictions: if John is small and Alice is large, then John-and-Alice is both small and large. Masses are also discussed in Section 6.3 (p. 119).

Grammatically, *joi* can appear between two sumti (like an ek) or between two tanru components (like a jek). This flexibility must be paid for in the form of occasional terminators that cannot be elided:

Example 14.112

le	nanmu	ku	joi	le	ninmu	[ku]	cu	klama	le	zarci
The	man		massed-with	the	woman			go-to	the	market.

The cmavo *ku* is the elidable terminator for *le*, which can almost always be elided, but not in this case. If the first *ku* were elided here, Lojban's parsing rules would see *le nanmu joi* and assume that another tanru component is to follow; since the second *le* cannot be part of a tanru, a parsing error results. No such problem can occur with logical connectives, because an ek signals a following sumti and a jek a following tanru component unambiguously.

Single or compound cmavo involving members of selma'o JOI are called joiks, by analogy with the names for logical connectives. It is not grammatical to use joiks to connect bridi-tails.

In tanru, *joi* has the connotation "mixed with", as in the following example:

Example 14.113

ti	blanu	joi	xunre	bolci
This	is-a-(blue	mixed-with	red)	ball.

This is a blue and red ball.

Here the ball is neither wholly blue nor wholly red, but partly blue and partly red. Its blue/redness is a mass property. (Just how blue something has to be to count as "wholly blue" is an unsettled question, though. A *blanu zdani* may be so even though not every part of it is blue.)

There are several other cmavo in selma'o JOI which can be used in the same grammatical constructions. Not all of them are well-defined as yet in all contexts. All have clear definitions as sumti connectives; those definitions are shown in the following table:

A *joi* B	the mass with components A and B
A *ce* B	the set with elements A and B
A *ce'o* B	the sequence with elements A and B in order
A *sece'o* B	the sequence with elements B and A in order
A *jo'u* B	A and B considered jointly
A *fa'u* B	A and B respectively
A *sefa'u* B	B and A respectively
A *jo'e* B	the union of sets A and B
A *ku'a* B	the intersection of sets A and B
A *pi'u* B	the cross product of sets A and B
A *sepi'u* B	the cross product of sets B and A

The cmavo *se* is grammatical before any JOI cmavo, but only useful with those that have inherent order. Here are some examples of joiks:

Example 14.114

mi	cuxna	la	.alis.	la	frank.
I	choose	that-named	Alice	from-that-named	Frank

ce		la	.alis.	ce	la	djeimyz.
and-member		that-named	Alice	and-member	that-named	James.

I choose Alice from among Frank, Alice, and James.

The x3 place of *cuxna* is a set from which the choice is being made. A set is an abstract object which is determined by specifying its members. Unlike those of a mass, the properties of a set are unrelated to its members' properties: the set of all rats is large (since many rats exist), but the rats themselves are small. This chapter does not attempt to explain set theory (the mathematical study of sets) in detail: explaining propositional logic is quite enough for one chapter!

In Example 14.114 (p. 339) we specify that set by listing the members with *ce* joining them.

Example 14.115

ti	liste	mi	ce'o	do	ce'o	la	djan.
This	is-a-list-of	me	and-sequence	you	and-sequence	that-named	John.

This is a list of you, me, and John.

The x2 place of *liste* is a sequence of the things which are mentioned in the list. (It is worth pointing out that *lo liste* means a physical object such as a grocery list: a purely abstract list is *lo porsi*, a sequence.) Here the three sumti connected by *ce'o* are in a definite order, not just lumped together in a set or a mass.

So *joi*, *ce*, and *ce'o* are parallel, in that the sumti connected are taken to be individuals, and the result is something else: a mass, a set, or a sequence respectively. The cmavo *jo'u* serves as a fourth element in this pattern: the sumti connected are individuals, and the result is still individuals – but inseparably so. The normal Lojban way of saying that James and George are brothers is:

Example 14.116

la	djeimyz.	bruna	la	djordj.
That-named	James	is-the-brother-of	that-named	George.

possibly adding a discursive element meaning "and vice versa". However, "James and George are brothers" cannot be correctly translated as:

Example 14.117

la	djeimyz.	.e	la	djordj.	bruna
That-named	James	and	that-named	George	is-a-brother.

since that expands to two bridi and means that James is a brother and so is George, but not necessarily of each other. If the *e* is changed to *jo'u*, however, the meaning of Example 14.116 (p. 340) is preserved:

Example 14.118

la	djeimyz.	jo'u	that-named
That-named	James	in-common-with	that-named

la	djordj.	cu	remei	bruna
George		are-a-twosome	type-of-brothers.	

The tanru *remei bruna* is not strictly necessary in this sentence, but is used to make clear that we are not saying that James and George are both brothers of some third person not specified. Alternatively, we could turn the tanru around: the x1 place of *remei* is a mass with two components, leading to:

Example 14.119

la	djeimyz.	joi	
That-named	James	massed-with	

la	djordj.	cu	bruna	remei
that-named	George		are-a-brother	type-of-twosome.

where *joi* is used to create the necessary mass.

Likewise, *fa'u* can be used to put two individuals together where order matters. Typically, there will be another *fa'u* somewhere else in the same bridi:

Example 14.120

la	djeimyz.	fa'u	la	djordj.
That-named	James	jointly-in-order-with	that-named	George

prami	la	meris.	fa'u	la	martas.
loves	that-named	Mary	jointly-in-order-with	that-named	Martha.

James and George love Mary and Martha, respectively.

Here the information carried by the English adverb "respectively", namely that James loves Mary and George loves Martha, is divided between the two occurrences of *fa'u*. If both uses of *fa'u* were to be changed to *e*, we would get:

Example 14.121

la	djeimyz.	.e	la	djordj.	prami
That-named	James	and	that-named	George	love

la	meris.	.e	la	martas.
that-named	Mary	and	that-named	Martha.

which can be transformed to four bridi:

Example 14.122

la	djeimyz.	prami	la	meris.	.ije	la	djordj.	prami
That-named	James	loves	that-named	Mary,	and	that-named	George	loves

la	meris.	.ije	la	djeimyz.	prami	la	martas.
that-named	Mary,	and	that-named	James	loves	that-named	Martha,

.ije	la	djordj.	prami	la	martas.
and	that-named	George	loves	that-named	Martha.

which represents quite a different state of affairs from Example 14.120 (p. 340). The meaning of Example 14.120 (p. 340) can also be conveyed by a termset:

Example 14.123

la	djeimyz.	ce'e	la	meris.	pe'e
That-named	James	[plus]	that-named	Mary	[joint]

.e	la	djordj.	ce'e	la	martas.	prami
and	that-named	George	[plus]	that-named	Martha	loves.

at the expense of re-ordering the list of names so as to make the pairs explicit. This option is not available when one of the lists is only described rather than enumerated:

Example 14.124

la	djeimyz.	fa'u	la	djordj.	prami	re	mensi
That-named	James	and-respectively	that-named	George	love	two	sisters.

which conveys that James loves one sister and George the other, though we are not able to tell which of the sisters is which.

14.15 More about non-logical connectives

The final three JOI cmavo, *jo'e*, *ku'a*, and *pi'u*, are probably only useful when talking explicitly about sets. They represent three standard set operators usually called "union", "intersection", and "cross product" (also known as "Cartesian product"). The union of two sets is a set containing all the members that are in either set; the intersection of two sets is a set containing all the members that are in both sets. The cross product of two sets is the set of all possible ordered pairs, where each ordered pair contains a single element from the first set followed by a single element from the second. This may seem very abstract; hopefully, the following examples will help:

Example 14.125

lo'i	ricfu	ku	jo'e	lo'i	dotco	cu	barda
The-set-of	rich-things		union	the-set-of	German-things		is-large.

Example 14.126

lo'i	ricfu	ku	ku'a	lo'i	dotco	cu	cmalu
The-set-of	rich-things		intersection	the-set-of	German-things		is-small.

There is a parallelism between logic and set theory that makes Example 14.125 (p. 341) and Example 14.126 (p. 341) equivalent respectively to:

Example 14.127

lo'i	ricfu	ja	dotco	cu	barda
The-set-of	(rich-things	or	German-things)		is-large.

and

Example 14.128

lo'i	ricfu	je	dotco	cu	cmalu
The-set-of	(rich-things	and	German-things)		is-small.

The following example uses *se remei*, which is a set (not a mass) of two elements:

Example 14.129

la	djeimyz.	ce[bo]	la	djordj.	pi'u
That-named	James	and-set	that-named	George	cross-product

la	meris.	cebo	la	martas.	cu	prami	se	remei
that-named	Mary	and-set	that-named	Martha		are-lover		type-of-pairs.

means that each of the pairs James/Mary, George/Mary, James/Martha, and George/Martha love each other. Therefore it is similar in meaning to Example 14.121 (p. 340); however, that example speaks only of the men loving the women, not vice versa.

Joiks may be combined with *bo* or with *ke* in the same way as eks and jeks; this allows grouping of non-logical connections between sumti and tanru units, in complete parallelism with logical connections:

Example 14.130

mi	joibo	do	ce	la	djan.	joibo	la	djein.
(I	massed-with	you)	and	(that-named	John	massed-with	that-named	Jane)

cu	gunma	se	remei
	are-a-mass		type-of-two-set

asserts that there is a set of two items each of which is a mass.

Non-logical connection is permitted at the joint of a termset; this is useful for associating more than one sumti or tagged sumti with each side of the non-logical connection. The place structure of *casnu* is:

casnu the mass x1 discusses/talks about x2

so the x1 place must be occupied by a mass (for reasons not explained here); however, different components of the mass may discuss in different languages. To associate each participant with his or her language, we can say:

Example 14.131

mi	ce'e	bau	la	lojban.	pe'e	joi
(I	[plus]	in-language	that-named	Lojban	[joint]	massed-with

do	ce'e	bau	la	gliban.	nu'u	casnu
you	[plus]	in-language	that-named	English	)	discuss.

Like all non-logical connectives, the usage shown in Example 14.131 (p. 342) cannot be mechanically converted into a non-logical connective placed at another location in the bridi. The forethought equivalent of Example 14.131 (p. 342) is:

Example 14.132

nu'i joigi mi bau la lojban gi do bau la gliban. nu'u casnu

Non-logical forethought termsets are also useful when the things to be non-logically connected are sumti preceded with tense or modal (BAI) tags:

Example 14.133

la	djan.	fa'u	la	frank.	cusku
That-named	John	respectively-with	that-named	Frank	express

nu'i	bau	la	lojban.
[start-termset]	in-language	that-named	Lojban

nu'u	fa'u	bai
[joint]	respectively-with	under-compulsion-by

tu'a	la	djordj.	[nu'u]
something-about	that-named	George.	

John and Frank speak in Lojban and under George's compulsion, respectively.

Example 14.133 (p. 342) associates speaking in Lojban with John, and speaking under George's compulsion with Frank. We do not know what language Frank uses, or whether John speaks under anyone's compulsion.

Joiks may be prefixed with *i* to produce ijoiks, which serve to non-logically connect sentences. The ijoik *.ice'o* indicates that the event of the second bridi follows that of the first bridi in some way other than a time relationship (which is handled with a tense):

Example 14.134

mi	ba	gasnu	la'e		di'e		.i
I	[future]	do	the-referent-of		the-following:		

tu'e	kanji		lo	ni		cteki	.ice'o		lumci	le	karce
(	Compute		the	quantity-of		taxes.	And-then		wash	the	car.

.ice'o		dzukansa			le	gerku	tu'u
And-then		walkingly-accompany			the	dog.	)

List of things to do: Figure taxes. Wash car. Walk dog.

Example 14.134 (p. 343) represents a list of things to be done in priority order. The order is important, hence the need for a sequence connective, but does not necessarily represent a time order (the dog may end up getting walked first). Note the use of *tu'e* and *tu'u* as general brackets around the whole list. This is related to, but distinct from, their use in Section 14.8 (p. 326), because there is no logical connective between the introductory phrase *mi ba gasnu la'edi'e* and the rest. The brackets effectively show how large an utterance the word *di'e*, which means "the following utterance", refers to.

Similarly, *.ijoi* is used to connect sentences that represent the components of a joint event such as a joint cause: the Lojban equivalent of "Fran hit her head and fell out of the boat, so that she drowned" would join the events "Fran hit her head" and "Fran fell out of the boat" with *.ijoi*.

The following *nai*, if present, does not negate either of the things to be connected, but instead specifies that some other connection (logical or non-logical) is applicable: it is a scalar negation:

Example 14.135

mi	jo'u		nai	do	cu	remei
I	in-common-with		[not!]	you		are-a-twosome

The result of *mi jo'u do* would be two individuals, not a mass, therefore *jo'u* is not applicable; *joi* would be the correct connective.

There is no joik question cmavo as such; however, joiks and ijoiks may be uttered in isolation in response to a logical connective question, as in the following exchange:

Example 14.136

do	djica	tu'a		loi		ckafi
You	desire	something-about		a-mass-of		coffee

ji		loi	tcati
[what-connective?]		a-mass-of	tea?

Do you want coffee or tea?

Example 14.137

joi
Mixed-mass-and.

Both as a mass (i.e, mixed together).

Ugh. (Or in Lojban: *.a'unaisairo'o.*)

14.16 Interval connectives and forethought non-logical connection

In addition to the non-logical connectives of selma'o JOI explained in Section 14.14 (p. 338) and Section 14.15 (p. 341), there are three other connectives which can appear in joiks: *bi'i*, *bi'o*, and *mi'i*, all of selma'o BIhI. The first two cmavo are used to specify intervals: abstract objects defined by two endpoints. The cmavo *bi'i* is correct if the endpoints are independent of order, whereas *bi'o* or *sebi'o* are used when order matters.

An example of *bi'i* in sumti connection:

Example 14.138

mi	ca		sanli		
I	[present]		stand-on-surface		

la		drezdn.	bi'i	la		frankfurt.
that-named		Dresden	[interval]	that-named		Frankfurt.

I am standing between Dresden and Frankfurt.

In Example 14.138 (p. 344), it is all the same whether I am standing between Dresden and Frankfurt or between Frankfurt and Dresden, so *bi'i* is the appropriate interval connective. The sumti *la drezdn. bi'i la frankfurt.* falls into the x2 place of *sanli*, which is the surface I stand on; the interval specifies that surface by its limits. (Obviously, I am not standing on the whole of the interval; the x2 place of *sanli* specifies a surface which is typically larger in extent than just the size of the stander's feet.)

Example 14.139

mi	cadzu	ca		la	pacac.
I	walk	simultaneous-with		First-hour

bi'o		la	recac.
[ordered-interval]		Second-hour.

I walk from one o'clock to two o'clock.

In Example 14.139 (p. 344), on the other hand, it is essential that *la pacac.* comes before *la recac.*; otherwise we have an 11-hour (or 23-hour) interval rather than a one-hour interval. In this use of an interval, the whole interval is probably intended, or at least most of it.

Example 14.139 (p. 344) is equivalent to:

Example 14.140

mi	cadzu	ca		la	recac.
I	walk	simultaneous-with		Second-hour

se		bi'o		la	pacac.
[reverse]		[ordered]		First-hour.

English cannot readily express *sebi'o*, but its meaning can be understood by reversing the two sumti.

The third cmavo of selma'o BIhI, namely *mi'i*, expresses an interval seen from a different viewpoint: not a pair of endpoints, but a center point and a distance. For example:

Example 14.141

le	jbama	pu	daspo	la	.uacintyn.
The	bomb	[past]	destroys		Washington

mi'i	lo	minli		be	li	muno
[center]	what-is	measured-in-miles		by	li	50.

The bomb destroyed Washington and fifty miles around.

Here we have an interval whose center is Washington and whose distance, or radius, is fifty miles.

In Example 14.138 (p. 344), is it possible that I am standing in Dresden (or Frankfurt) itself? Yes. The connectives of selma'o BIhI are ambiguous about whether the endpoints themselves are included in or excluded from the interval. Two auxiliary cmavo *ga'o* and *ke'i* (of cmavo GAhO) are used to indicate the status of the endpoints: *ga'o* means that the endpoint is included, *ke'i* that it is excluded:

Example 14.142

mi	ca	sanli	la	drezdn.	ga'o
I	[present]	stand	that-named	Dresden	[inclusive]

bi'i	ga'o	la	frankfurt.
[interval]	[inclusive]	that-named	Frankfurt.

I am standing between Dresden and Frankfurt, inclusive of both.

Example 14.143

mi	ca	sanli	la	drezdn.	ga'o
I	[present]	stand	that-named	Dresden	[inclusive]

bi'i	ke'i	la	frankfurt.
[interval]	[exclusive]	that-named	Frankfurt.

I am standing between Dresden (inclusive) and Frankfurt (exclusive).

Example 14.144

mi	ca	sanli	la	drezdn.	ke'i
I	[present]	stand	that-named	Dresden	[exclusive]

bi'i	ga'o	la	frankfurt.
[interval]	[inclusive]	that-named	Frankfurt.

I am standing between Dresden (exclusive) and Frankfurt (inclusive).

Example 14.145

mi	ca	sanli	la	drezdn.	ke'i
I	[present]	stand	that-named	Dresden	[exclusive]

bi'i	ke'i	la	frankfurt.
[interval]	[exclusive]	that-named	Frankfurt.

I am standing between Dresden and Frankfurt, exclusive of both.

As these examples should make clear, the GAhO cmavo that applies to a given endpoint is the one that stands physically adjacent to it: the left-hand endpoint is referred to by the first GAhO, and the right-hand endpoint by the second GAhO. It is ungrammatical to have just one GAhO.

(Etymologically, *ga'o* is derived from *ganlo*, which means "closed", and *ke'i* from *kalri*, which means "open". In mathematics, inclusive intervals are referred to as closed intervals, and exclusive intervals as open ones.)

BIhI joiks are grammatical anywhere that other joiks are, including in tanru connection and (as ijoiks) between sentences. No meanings have been found for these uses.

Negated intervals, marked with a *-nai* following the BIhI cmavo, indicate an interval that includes everything but what is between the endpoints (with respect to some understood scale):

Example 14.146

do	dicra	.e'a	mi	ca	la	daucac.
You	disturb	(allowed)	me	at	that-named	10

bi'onai	la	gaicac.
not-from-...-to	that-named	12

You can contact me except from 10 to 12.

The complete syntax of joiks is:

[se] JOI [nai]
[se] BIhI [nai]
GAhO [se] BIhI [nai] GAhO

Notice that the colloquial English translations of *bi'i* and *bi'o* have forethought form: "between ... and" for *bi'i*, and "from ... to" for *bi'o*. In Lojban too, non-logical connectives can be expressed in forethought. Rather than using a separate selma'o, the forethought logical connectives are constructed from the afterthought ones by suffixing *gi*. Such a compound cmavo is not unnaturally called a "joigik"; the syntax of joigiks is any of:

[se] JOI [nai] GI
[se] BIhI [nai] GI
GAhO [se] BIhI [nai] GAhO GI

Joigiks may be used to non-logically connect bridi, sumti, and bridi-tails; and also in termsets. Example 14.111 (p. 338) in forethought becomes:

Example 14.147

joigi	*la*	*djan.*	*gi*	*la*	*.alis.*	*bevri*	*le*	*pipno*
[Together]	that-named	John	and	that-named	Alice	carry	the	piano.

The first *gi* is part of the joigik; the second *gi* is the regular gik that separates the two things being connected in all forethought forms.

Example 14.143 (p. 345) can be expressed in forethought as:

Example 14.148

mi	*ca*	*sanli*	*ke'i*	*bi'i*
I	[present]	stand	[exclusive]	between

ga'o	*gi*	*la*	*drezdn.*	*gi*	*la*	*frankfurt.*
[inclusive]	and	that-named	Dresden	and	that-named	Frankfurt.

I am standing between Dresden (exclusive) and Frankfurt (inclusive).

In forethought, unfortunately, the GAhOs become physically separated from the endpoints, but the same rule applies: the first GAhO refers to the first endpoint.

14.17 Logical and non-logical connectives within mekso

Lojban has a separate grammar embedded within the main grammar for representing mathematical expressions (or mekso in Lojban) such as "2 + 2". Mathematical expressions are explained fully in Chapter 18 (p. 413). The basic components of mekso are operands, like "2", and operators, like "+". Both of these may be either logically or non-logically connected.

Operands are connected in afterthought with eks and in forethought with geks, just like sumti. Operators, on the other hand, are connected in afterthought with jeks and in forethought with guheks, just like tanru components. (However, jeks and joiks with *bo* are not allowed for operators.) This parallelism is no accident.

In addition, eks with *bo* and with *ke...ke'e* are allowed for grouping logically connected operands, and *ke...ke'e* is allowed for grouping logically connected operators, although there is no analogue of tanru among the operators.

Only a few examples of each kind of mekso connection will be given. Despite the large number of rules required to support this feature, it is of relatively minor importance in either the mekso or the logical-connective scheme of things. These examples are drawn from Section 18.17 (p. 435), and contain many mekso features not explained in this chapter.

Example 14.149 (p. 346) exhibits afterthought logical connection between operands:

Example 14.149

vei	*ci*	*.a*	*vo*	*[ve'o]*	*prenu*	*cu*	*klama*	*le*	*zarci*
(	Three	or	four	)	people		go-to	the	market.

Example 14.150 (p. 347) is equivalent in meaning, but uses forethought connection:

Example 14.150

vei	ga	ci	gi	vo	[ve'o]	prenu	cu	klama	le	zarci
(	Either	3	or	4	)	people		go-to	the	market.

Note that the mekso in Example 14.149 (p. 346) and Example 14.150 (p. 347) are being used as quantifiers. Lojban requires that any mekso other than a simple number be enclosed in *vei* and *ve'o* parentheses when used as a quantifier. The right parenthesis mark, *ve'o*, is an elidable terminator.

Simple examples of logical connection between operators are hard to come by. A contrived example is:

Example 14.151

li	re	su'i	je	pi'i	re	du	li	vo
The-number	2	plus	and	times	2	equals	the-number	4.

2 + 2 = 4 and 2 x 2 = 4.

The forethought form of Example 14.151 (p. 347) is:

Example 14.152

li	re	ge	su'i	gi	pi'i	re	du	li	vo
The-number	two	both	plus	and	times	two	equals	the-number	four.

Both 2 + 2 = 4 and 2 x 2 = 4.

Non-logical connection with joiks or joigiks is also permitted between operands and between operators. One use for this construct is to connect operands with *bi'i* to create mathematical intervals:

Example 14.153

li	no	ga'o	bi'i	ke'i	pa
the-number	zero	(inclusive)	from-to	(exclusive)	one

[0,1)

the numbers from zero to one, including zero but not including one

You can also combine two operands with *ce'o*, the sequence connective of selma'o JOI, to make a compound subscript:

Example 14.154

xy.	boi	xi	vei	by.	ce'o	dy.	[ve'o]
"x"		sub	(	"b"	sequence	"d"	)

$x_{b,d}$

Note that the *boi* in Example 14.154 (p. 347) is not elidable, because the *xi* subscript needs something to attach to.

14.18 Tenses, modals, and logical connection

The tense and modal systems of Lojban interact with the logical connective system. No one chapter can explain all of these simultaneously, so each chapter must present its own view of the area of interaction with emphasis on its own concepts and terminology. In the examples of this chapter, the many tenses of various selma'o as well as the modals of selma'o BAI are represented by the simple time cmavo *pu*, *ca*, and *ba* (of selma'o PU) representing the past, the present, and the future respectively. Preceding a selbri, these cmavo state the time when the bridi was, is, or will be true (analogous to English verb tenses); preceding a sumti, they state that the event of the main bridi is before, simultaneous with, or after the event given by the sumti (which is generally a *le nu* abstraction; see Section 11.2 (p. 248)).

The two types of interaction between tenses and logical connectives are logically connected tenses and tensed logical connections. The former are fairly simple. Jeks may be used between tense cmavo to specify two connected bridi that differ only in tense:

Example 14.155

la	.artr.	pu	nolraitru
That-named	**Arthur**	**[past]**	**is-a-noblest-governor.**

.ije	la	.artr.	ba	nolraitru
And	**that-named**	**Arthur**	**[future]**	**is-a-noblest-governor.**

Arthur was a king, and Arthur will be a king.

can be reduced to:

Example 14.156

la	.artr.	pu	je	ba	nolraitru
That-named	**Arthur**	**[past]**	**and**	**[future]**	**is-a-noblest-governor.**

Arthur was and will be king.

Example 14.155 (p. 348) and Example 14.156 (p. 348) are equivalent in meaning; neither says anything about whether Arthur is king now.

Non-logical connection with joiks is also possible between tenses:

Example 14.157

mi	pu	bi'o	ba	vasxu
I	**[past]**	**from-...-to**	**[future]**	**breathe.**

I breathe from a past time until a future time.

The full tense system makes more interesting tense intervals expressible, such as "from a medium time ago until a long time from now".

No forethought connections between tenses are permitted by the grammar, nor is there any way to override the default left-grouping rule; these limitations are imposed to keep the tense grammar simpler. Whatever can be said with tenses or modals can be said with subordinate bridi stating the time, place, or mode explicitly, so it is reasonable to try to remove at least some complications.

Tensed logical connections are both more complex and more important than logical connections between tenses. Consider the English sentence:

Example 14.158

I went to the market, and I bought food.

The verbatim translation of Example 14.158 (p. 348), namely:

Example 14.159

mi	pu	klama	le	zarci	.ije	mi	pu	tervecnu	lo	cidja
I	**[past]**	**go-to**	**the**	**market.**	**And**	**I**	**[past]**	**buy**	**items-of**	**food.**

fails to fully represent a feature of the English, namely that the buying came after the going. (It also fails to represent that the buying was a consequence of the going, which can be expressed by a modal that is discussed in Chapter 9 (p. 179).) However, the tense information – that the event of my going to the market preceded the event of my buying food – can be added to the logical connective as follows. The .ije is replaced by .ijebo, and the tense cmavo ba is inserted between .ije and bo:

Example 14.160

mi	pu	klama	le	zarci
I	**[past]**	**go-to**	**the**	**market.**

.ije	babo	mi	pu	tervecnu	lo	cidja
And	**[later]**	**I**	**[past]**	**buy**	**items-of**	**food.**

Here the pu cmavo in the two bridi-tails express the time of both actions with respect to the speaker: in the past. The ba relates the two items to one another: the second item is later than the first item. The grammar does not permit omitting the bo; if it were omitted, the ba and the second pu would run together to form a compound tense bapu applying to the second bridi-tail only.

14.18 Tenses, modals, and logical connection

Adding tense or modal information to a logical connective is permitted only in the following situations:

Between an ek (or joik) and *bo*, as in:

Example 14.161

la	*.djan*	*.e*	*cabo*	*la*	*.alis.*	*klama*	*le*	*zarci*
That-named	John	and	[simultaneous]	that-named	Alice	go-to	the	market.

John and Alice go to the market simultaneously.

Between an ek (or joik) and *ke*, as in:

Example 14.162

mi	*dzukla*	*le*	*zarci*	*.e*	*pu*
I	walk-to	the	market	and	[earlier]

ke	*le*	*zdani*	*.a*	*le*	*ckule*	*[ke'e]*
(	the	house	or	the	school	).

I walk to the market and, before that, to the house or the school.

Between a gihek and *bo*, as in:

Example 14.163

mi	*dunda*	*le*	*cukta*	*gi'e*	*babo*
I	give	the	book	and	[later]

lebna	*lo*	*rupnu*		*vau*	*do*
take	some	currency-units			from/to-you.

I give you the book and then take some dollars (pounds, yen) from you.

Between a gihek and *ke*, as in:

Example 14.164

mi	*dzukla*	*le*	*zarci*	*gi'e*	*ca*
I	walk-to	the	market	and	[simultaneous]

ke	*cusku*	*zo'e*	*la*		*djan.*	*[ke'e]*
(	express	something	to-that-named		John.	)

I walk to the market and at the same time talk to John.

Between an ijek (or ijoik) and *bo*, as in:

Example 14.165

mi	*viska*	*pa*	*nanmu*	*.ije*	*babo*	*mi*	*viska*	*pa*	*ninmu*
I	see	a	man.	And	[later]	I	see	a	woman.

I see a man, and then I see a woman.

Between an ijek (or ijoik) and *tu'e*, as in:

Example 14.166

mi	*viska*	*pa*	*nanmu*	*.ije*	*batu'e*	*mi*	*viska*	*pa*	*ninmu*	*[tu'u]*
I	see	a	man.	And	[later]	I	see	a	woman.	

I see a man, and then I see a woman.

And finally, between a jek (or joik) and *bo*, as in:

Example 14.167

mi	*mikce*	*jebabo*	*ricfu*
I	am-a-doctor	and-[later]	rich

I am a doctor and future rich person.

As can be seen from Example 14.165 (p. 349) and Example 14.166 (p. 349), the choice between *bo* and *ke* (or *tu'e*) is arbitrary when there are only two things to be connected. If there were no tense information to include, of course neither would be required; it is only the rule that tense information must always be sandwiched between the logical connective and a following *bo*, *ke*, or *tu'e* that requires the use of one of these grouping cmavo in Example 14.161 (p. 349) and Example 14.163 (p. 349) through Example 14.167 (p. 349).

Non-logical connectives with *bo* and *ke* can include tense information in exactly the same way as logical connectives. Forethought connectives, however (except as noted below) are unable to do so, as are termsets or tense connectives. Mathematical operands and operators can also include tense information in their logical connectives as a result of their close parallelism with sumti and tanru components respectively:

Example 14.168

vei	ci	.ebabo	vo	[ve'o]	tadni	cu	zvati	le	kumfa
(	3	and-[future]	4	)	students		are-at	the	room.

Three and, later, four students were in the room.

is a simple example. There is a special grammatical rule for use when a tense applies to both of the selbri in a forethought bridi-tail connection: the entire forethought construction can just be preceded by a tense. For example:

Example 14.169

mi	pu	ge	klama	le	zarci	gi	tervecnu	lo	cidja
I	[past]	both	go-to	the	market	and	buy	some	food

I went to the market and bought some food.

Example 14.169 (p. 350) is similar to Example 14.159 (p. 348). There is no time relationship specified between the going and the buying; both are simply set in the past.

14.19 Abstractor connection and connection within abstractions

Last and (as a matter of fact) least: a logical connective is allowed between abstraction markers of selma'o NU. As usual, the connection can be expanded to a bridi connection between two bridi which differ only in abstraction marker. Jeks are the appropriate connective. Example 14.170 (p. 350) and Example 14.171 (p. 350) are equivalent in meaning:

Example 14.170

le	ka	la	frank.	ciska	cu	xlali
The	quality-of	that-named	Frank's	writing		is-bad,

.ije	le	ni	la	frank.	ciska	cu	xlali
and	the	quantity-of	that-named	Frank's	writing		is-bad.

Example 14.171

le	ka	je	ni	la	frank.	ciska	cu	xlali
The	quality	and	quantity	of	that-named	Frank's	writing		is-bad.

As with tenses and modals, there is no forethought and no way to override the left-grouping rule.

Logical connectives and abstraction are related in another way as well, though. Since an abstraction contains a bridi, the bridi may have a logical connection inside it. Is it legitimate to split the outer bridi into two, joined by the logical connection? Absolutely not. For example:

Example 14.172

mi	jinvi	le	du'u	loi	jmive
I	opine	the	fact-that	a-mass-of	living-things

cu	zvati	gi'onai	na	zvati	vau	la	.iupiter.
	(is-at	or-else	is-not	at)		that-named	Jupiter.

I believe there either is or isn't life on Jupiter.

is true, since the embedded sentence is a tautology, but:

Example 14.173

mi	jinvi	le	du'u	loi	jmive	cu	zvati	la	.iupiter.
I	opine	the	fact-that	a-mass-of	living-things		is-at	that-named	Jupiter

.ijonai	mi	jinvi	le	du'u	loi	jmive
or-else	I	opine	the	fact-that	a-mass-of	living-things

cu	zvati	la	.iupiter.
	isn't-at	that-named	Jupiter

is false, since I have no evidence one way or the other (*jinvi* requires some sort of evidence, real or fancied, unlike *krici*).

14.20 Constructs and appropriate connectives

The following table specifies, for each kind of construct that can be logically or non-logically connected in Lojban, what kind of connective is required for both afterthought and (when possible) forethought modes. An asterisk (*) indicates that tensed connection is permitted.

A dash indicates that connection of the specified type is not possible.

construct	afterthought logical	forethought logical	afterthought non-logical	forethought non-logical
bridi	ijek*	gek	ijoik*	joigik
sumti	ek*	gek	joik*	joigik
bridi-tails	gihek*	gek	-	joigik
termsets	ek*	gek	joik*	joigik
tanru parts	jek	guhek	joik*	-
operands	ek*	gek	joik*	joigik
operators	jek	guhek	joik	-
tenses/ modals	jek	-	joik	-
abstractors	jek	-	joik	-

14.21 Truth functions and corresponding logical connectives

The following table specifies, for each truth function, the most-often used cmavo or compound cmavo which expresses it for each of the six types of logical connective. (Other compound cmavo are often possible: for example, *se.a* means the same as *a*, and could be used instead.)

truth	ek	jek	gihek	gek-gik	guhek-gik
TTTF	a	ja	gi'a	ga-gi	gu'a-gi
TTFT	.a nai	ja nai	gi'a nai	ga-ginai	gu'a-ginai
TTFF	u	ju	gi'u	gu-gi	gu'u-gi
TFTT	na .a	na ja	na gi'a	ganai-gi	gu'anai-gi
TFTF	se .u	se ju	se gi'u	segu-gi	segu'u-gi
TFFT	o	jo	gi'o	go-gi	gu'o-gi
TFFF	e	je	gi'e	ge-gi	gu'e-gi
FTTT	na .a nai	na ja nai	na gi'a nai	ganai-ginai	gu'anai-ginai
FTTF	.o nai	jo nai	gi'o nai	go-ginai	gu'o-ginai
FTFT	se .u nai	se ju nai	se gi'u nai	segu-ginai	segu'u-ginai
FTFF	.e nai	je nai	gi'e nai	ge-ginai	gu'e-ginai
FFTT	na .u	na ju	na gi'u	gunai-gi	gu'unai-gi
FFTF	na .e	na je	na gi'e	genai-gi	gu'enai-gi
FFFT	na .e nai	na je nai	na gi'e nai	genai-ginai	gu'enai-ginai

Note: ijeks are exactly the same as the corresponding jeks, except for the prefixed *i*.

14.22 Rules for making logical and non-logical connectives

The full set of rules for inserting *na*, *se*, and *nai* into any connective is:
Afterthought logical connectives (eks, jeks, giheks, ijeks):

Negate first construct: Place *na* before the connective cmavo (but after the *i* of an ijek).
Negate second construct: Place *nai* after the connective cmavo.
Exchange constructs: Place *se* before the connective cmavo (after *na* if any).

Forethought logical connectives (geks, guheks):

Negate first construct: Place *nai* after the connective cmavo.
Negate second construct: Place *nai* after the *gi.*
Exchange constructs: Place *se* before the connective cmavo.

Non-logical connectives (joiks, joigiks):

Negate connection: Place *nai* after the connective cmavo (but before the *gi* of a joigik).
Exchange constructs: Place *se* before the connective cmavo.

14.23 Locations of other tables

Section 14.1 (p. 317): a table explaining the meaning of each truth function in English.
Section 14.2 (p. 319): a table relating the truth functions to the four basic vowels.
Section 14.13 (p. 335): a table of the connective question cmavo.
Section 14.14 (p. 338): a table of the meanings of JOI cmavo when used to connect sumti.

Chapter 15
"No" Problems: On Lojban Negation

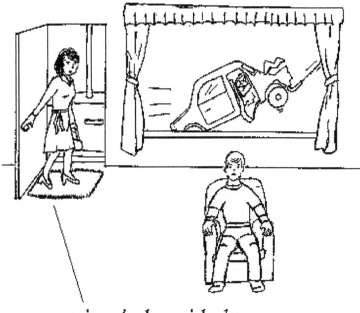

mi na'e lumci le karce

15.1 Introductory

The grammatical expression of negation is a critical part of Lojban's claim to being logical. The problem of negation, simply put, is to come up with a complete definition of the word "not". For Lojban's unambiguous grammar, this means further that meanings of "not" with different grammatical effect must be different words, and even different grammatical structures.

Logical assertions are implicitly required in a logical language; thus, an apparatus for expressing them is built into Lojban's logical connectives and other structures.

In natural languages, especially those of Indo-European grammar, we have sentences composed of two parts which are typically called "subject" and "predicate". In the statement

Example 15.1

> John goes to the store

"John" is the subject, and "goes to the store" is the predicate. Negating Example 15.1 (p. 353) to produce

Example 15.2

> John doesn't go to the store.

has the effect of declaring that the predicate does not hold for the subject. Example 15.2 (p. 353) says nothing about whether John goes somewhere else, or whether someone else besides John goes to the store.

We will call this kind of negation "natural language negation". This kind of negation is difficult to manipulate by the tools of logic, because it doesn't always follow the rules of logic. Logical negation is bi-polar: either a statement is true, or it is false. If a statement is false, then its negation must be true. Such negation is termed contradictory negation.

Let's look at some examples of how natural language negation can violate the rules of contradictory negation.

Example 15.3

    Some animals are not white.

Example 15.4

    Some animals are white.

Both of these statements are true; yet one is apparently the negation of the other. Another example:

Example 15.5

    I mustn't go to the dance.

Example 15.6

    I must go to the dance.

At first thought, Example 15.5 (p. 354) negates Example 15.6 (p. 354). Thinking further, we realize that there is an intermediate state wherein I am permitted to go to the dance, but not obligated to do so. Thus, it is possible that both statements are false.

Sometimes order is significant:

Example 15.7

    The falling rock didn't kill Sam.

Example 15.8

    Sam wasn't killed by the falling rock.

Our minds play tricks on us with this one. Because Example 15.7 (p. 354) is written in what is called the "active voice", we immediately get confused about whether "the falling rock" is a suitable subject for the predicate "did kill Sam". "Kill" implies volition to us, and rocks do not have volition. This confusion is employed by opponents of gun control who use the argument "Guns don't kill people; people kill people."

Somehow, we don't have the same problem with Example 15.8 (p. 354). The subject is Sam, and we determine the truth or falsity of the statement by whether he was or wasn't killed by the falling rock.

Example 15.8 (p. 354) also helps us focus on the fact that there are at least two questionable facts implicit in this sentence: whether Sam was killed, and if so, whether the falling rock killed him. If Sam wasn't killed, the question of what killed him is moot.

This type of problem becomes more evident when the subject of the sentence turns out not to exist:

Example 15.9

    The King of Mexico didn't come to dinner.

Example 15.10

    The King of Mexico did come to dinner.

In the natural languages, we would be inclined to say that both of these statements are false, since there is no King of Mexico.

The rest of this chapter is designed to explain the Lojban model of negation.

15.2 bridi negation

In discussing Lojban negation, we will call the form of logical negation that simply denies the truth of a statement "bridi negation". Using bridi negation, we can say the equivalent of "I haven't stopped beating my wife" without implying that I ever started, nor even that I have a wife, meaning simply

15.2 bridi negation

"It isn't true that I have stopped beating my wife." Since Lojban uses bridi as smaller components of complex sentences, bridi negation is permitted in these components as well at the sentence level.

For the bridi negation of a sentence to be true, the sentence being negated must be false. A major use of bridi negation is in making a negative response to a yes/no question; such responses are usually contradictory, denying the truth of the entire sentence. A negative answer to

Example 15.11

> Did you go to the store?

is taken as a negation of the entire sentence, equivalent to

Example 15.12

> No, I didn't go to the store.

The most important rule about bridi negation is that if a bridi is true, its negation is false, and vice versa.

The simplest way to express a bridi negation is to use the cmavo *na* of selma'o NA before the selbri of the affirmative form of the bridi (but after the *cu*, if there is one):

Example 15.13

mi	klama	le	zarci
I	go-to	the	store.

when negated becomes:

Example 15.14

mi	na	klama	le	zarci
I	[false]	go-to	the	store.

Note that we have used a special convention to show in the English that a bridi negation is present. We would like to use the word "not", because this highlights the naturalness of putting the negation marker just before the selbri, and makes the form easier to learn. But there is a major difference between Lojban's bridi negation with *na* and natural language negation with "not". In English, the word "not" can apply to a single word, to a phrase, to an English predicate, or to the entire sentence. In addition, "not" may indicate either contradictory negation or another form of negation, depending on the sentence. Lojban's internal bridi negation, on the other hand, always applies to an entire bridi, and is always a contradictory negation; that is, it contradicts the claim of the whole bridi.

Because of the ambiguity of English "not", we will use "[false]" in the translation of Lojban examples to remind the reader that we are expressing a contradictory negation. Here are more examples of bridi negation:

Example 15.15

mi	[cu]	na	ca	klama	le	zarci
I		[false]	now	am-a-go-er-to	the	market.

I am not going to the market now.

Example 15.16

lo	ca	nolraitru	be
The-actual	present	noblest-governor	of

le	fasygu'e	cu	na	krecau
the	French-country		[false]	is-hair-without.

The current king of France isn't bald.

Example 15.17

ti	na	barda	prenu	co	melbi	mi
This	[false]	is-a-big	person	of-type	(beautiful-to	me).

This isn't a big person who is beautiful to me.

Although there is this fundamental difference between Lojban's internal bridi negation and English negation, we note that in many cases, especially when there are no existential or quantified variables (the cmavo *da*, *de*, and *di* of selma'o KOhA, explained in Chapter 16 (p. 375)) in the bridi, you can indeed translate Lojban *na* as "not" (or "isn't" or "doesn't", as appropriate).

The most important rule about bridi negation is that if a bridi is true, its negation is false, and vice versa.

In Lojban, there are several structures that implicitly contain bridi, so that Lojban sentences may contain more than one occurrence of *na*. For example:

Example 15.18

mi	na	gleki		le	nu
I	[false]	am-happy-about		the	event-of

na		klama		le	nu		dansu
([false]		going-to		the	event-of		dancing).

It is not the case that I am happy about it not being the case that I am going to the dance.
I am not happy about not going to the dance.

In the previous example, we used internal negations in abstraction bridi; bridi negation may also be found in descriptions within sumti. For example:

Example 15.19

mi	nelci	le		na	melbi
I	am-fond-of	the-one-described-as		([false]	beautiful).

I am fond of the one who isn't beautiful.

A more extreme (and more indefinite) example is:

Example 15.20

mi	nelci	lo		na
I	am-fond-of	one-who-is		([false]

ca		nolraitru	be	le	frasygu'e
the-current		king	of	the	French-country).

I am fond of one who isn't the current king of France.

The claim of Example 15.20 (p. 356) could apply to anyone except a person who is fond of no one at all, since the relation within the description is false for everyone. You cannot readily express these situations in colloquial English.

Negation with *na* applies to an entire bridi, and not to just part of a selbri. Therefore, you won't likely have reason to put *na* inside a tanru. In fact, the grammar currently does not allow you to do so (except in a lujvo and in elaborate constructs involving GUhA, the forethought connector for selbri). Any situation where you might want to do so can be expressed in a less-compressed non-tanru form. This grammatical restriction helps ensure that bridi negation is kept separate from other forms of negation.

The grammar of *na* allows multiple adjacent negations, which cancel out, as in normal logic:

Example 15.21

ti	na	na	barda	prenu	co	melbi		mi
This	[false]	[false]	is-a-big	person	that	is-(beautiful-to		me).

which is the same as:

Example 15.22

ti	barda	prenu	co	melbi		mi
This	is-a-big	person	that	is-(beautiful-to		me).

When a selbri is tagged with a tense or a modal, negation with *na* is permitted in two positions: before or after the tag. No semantic difference between these forms has yet been defined, but this is not finally determined, since the interactions between tenses/modals and bridi negation have not been fully explored. In particular, it remains to be seen whether sentences using less familiar tenses, such as:

Example 15.23

mi	[cu]	ta'e	klama	le	zarci
I		habitually	go-to	the	market.

mean the same thing with *na* before the *ta'e*, as when the negation occurs afterwards; we'll let future, Lojban-speaking, logicians decide on how they relate to each other.

A final caution on translating English negations into Lojban: if you translate the English literally, you'll get the wrong one. With English causal statements, and other statements with auxiliary clauses, this problem is more likely.

Thus, if you translate the English:

Example 15.24

I do not go to the market because the car is broken.

as:

Example 15.25

mi	na	klama	le	zarci	ki'u
I	[false]	go-to	the	market	because-of

lenu		le	karce	cu	spofu
the-event-of		the	car		is-broken.

It is false that: I go to the market because the car is broken.

you end up negating too much.

Such mistranslations result from the ambiguity of English compounded by the messiness of natural language negation. A correct translation of the normal interpretation of Example 15.24 (p. 357) is:

Example 15.26

le	nu	mi	na	klama	le	zarci	cu	se	krinu
The	event-of	(my	[false]	going-to	the	market)			is-justified-by

le	nu	le	karce	cu	spofu
the	event-of	(the	car		being-broken).

My not going to the market is because the car is broken.

In Example 15.26 (p. 357), the negation is clearly confined to the event abstraction in the x1 sumti, and does not extend to the whole sentence. The English could also have been expressed by two separate sentences joined by a causal connective (which we'll not go into here).

The problem is not confined to obvious causals. In the English:

Example 15.27

I was not conscripted into the Army with the help of my uncle the Senator.

we do not intend the uncle's help to be part of the negation. We must thus move the negation into an event clause or use two separate sentences. The event-clause version would look like:

Example 15.28

The event-of (my [false] being-conscripted-into the Army) was aided by my uncle the Senator.

It is possible that someone will want to incorporate bridi negations into lujvo. For this reason, the rafsi -nar- has been reserved for *na*. However, before using this rafsi, make sure that you intend the contradictory bridi negation, and not the scalar negation described in Section 15.3 (p. 357), which will be much more common in tanru and lujvo.

15.3 Scalar Negation

Let us now consider some other types of negation. For example, when we say:

Example 15.29

> The chair is not brown.

we make a positive inference – that the chair is some other color. Thus, it is legitimate to respond:

Example 15.30

> It is green.

Whether we agree that the chair is brown or not, the fact that the statement refers to color has significant effect on how we interpret some responses. If we hear the following exchange:

Example 15.31

> The chair is not brown.
> Correct. The chair is wooden.

we immediately start to wonder about the unusual wood that isn't brown. If we hear the exchange:

Example 15.32

> Is the chair green?
> No, it is in the kitchen.

we are unsettled because the response seems to be a non-sequitur. But since it might be true and it is a statement about the chair, one can't say it is entirely irrelevant!

What is going on in these statements is something called "scalar negation". As the name suggests, scalar negation presumes an implied scale. A negation of this type not only states that one scalar value is false, but implies that another value on the scale must be true. This can easily lead to complications. The following exchange seems reasonably natural (a little suspension of disbelief in such inane conversation will help):

Example 15.33

> That isn't a blue house.
> Right! That is a green house.

We have acknowledged a scalar negation by providing a correct value which is another color in the set of colors permissible for houses. While a little less likely, the following exchange is also natural:

Example 15.34

> That isn't a blue house.
> Right! That is a blue car.

Again, we have acknowledged a scalar negation, and substituted a different object in the universe of discourse of things that can be blue.

Now, if the following exchange occurs:

Example 15.35

> That isn't a blue house.
> Right! That is a green car.

we find the result unsettling. This is because it seems that two corrections have been applied when there is only one negation. Yet out of context, "blue house" and "green car" seem to be reasonably equivalent units that should be mutually replaceable in a sentence. It's just that we don't have a clear way in English to say:

Example 15.36

> That isn't a "blue-house".

aloud so as to clearly imply that the scalar negation is affecting the pair of words as a single unit.

Another even more confusing example of scalar negation is to the sentence:

Example 15.37

> John didn't go to Paris from Rome.

Might Example 15.37 (p. 358) imply that John went to Paris from somewhere else? Or did he go somewhere else from Rome? Or perhaps he didn't go anywhere at all: maybe someone else did, or maybe there was no event of going whatsoever. One can devise circumstances where any one, two or all three of these statements might be inferred by a listener.

In English, we have a clear way of distinguishing scalar negation from predicate negation that can be used in many situations. We can use the partial word "non-" as a prefix. But this is not always considered good usage, even though it would render many statements much clearer. For example, we can clearly distinguish

Example 15.38

> That is a non-blue house.

from the related sentence

Example 15.39

> That is a blue non-house.

Example 15.38 (p. 359) and Example 15.39 (p. 359) have the advantage that, while they contain a negative indication, they are in fact positive assertions. They say what is true by excluding the false; they do not say what is false.

We can't always use "non-" though, because of the peculiarities of English's grammar. It would sound strange to say:

Example 15.40

> John went to non-Paris from Rome.

or

Example 15.41

> John went to Paris from non-Rome.

although these would clarify the vague negation. Another circumlocution for English scalar negation is "other than", which works where "non-" does not, but is wordier.

Finally, we have natural language negations that are called polar negations, or opposites:

Example 15.42

> John is moral

Example 15.43

> John is immoral

To be immoral is much more than to just be not moral: it implies the opposite condition. Statements like Example 15.43 (p. 359) are strong negations which not only deny the truth of a statement, but assert its opposite. Since, "opposite" implies a scale, polar negations are a special variety of scalar negations.

To examine this concept more closely, let us draw a linear scale, showing two examples of how the scale is used:

```
Affirmations (positive)    Negations (negative)
|-----------|-----------|-----------|-----------|
All       Most        Some        Few        None
Excellent Good        Fair        Poor       Awful
```

Some scales are more binary than the examples we diagrammed. Thus we have "not necessary" or "unnecessary" being the polar opposite of necessary. Another scale, especially relevant to Lojban, is interpreted based on situations modified by one's philosophy: "not true" may be equated with "false" in a bi-valued truth-functional logic, while in tri-valued logic an intermediate between "true" and "false" is permitted, and in fuzzy logic a continuous scale exists from true to false. The meaning of "not true" requires a knowledge of which variety of truth scale is being considered.

We will define the most general form of scalar negation as indicating only that the particular point or value in the scale or range is not valid and that some other (unspecified) point on the scale is correct. This is the intent expressed in most contexts by "not mild", for example.

Using this paradigm, contradictory negation is less restrictive than scalar negation – it says that the point or value stated is incorrect (false), and makes no statement about the truth of any other point or value, whether or not on the scale.

In English, scalar negation semantically includes phrases such as "other than", "reverse of", or "opposite from" expressions and their equivalents. More commonly, scalar negation is expressed in English by the prefixes "non-", "un-", "il-", and "im-". Just which form and permissible values are implied by a scalar negation is dependent on the semantics of the word or concept which is being negated, and on the context. Much confusion in English results from the uncontrolled variations in meaning of these phrases and prefixes.

In the examples of Section 15.4 (p. 360), we will translate the general case of scalar negation using the general formula "other than" when a phrase is scalar-negated, and "non-" when a single word is scalar-negated.

15.4 selbri and tanru negation

All the scalar negations illustrated in Section 15.3 (p. 357) are expressed in Lojban using the cmavo *na'e* (of selma'o NAhE). The most common use of *na'e* is as a prefix to the selbri:

Example 15.44

mi	klama	le	zarci
I	go-to	the	market.

Example 15.45

mi	na'e	klama	le	zarci
I	(other-than	go-to)	the	market.

Comparing these two, we see that the negation operator being used in Example 15.45 (p. 360) is *na'e*. But what exactly does *na'e* negate? Does the negation include only the gismu *klama*, which is the entire selbri in this case, or does it include the *le zarci* as well? In Lojban, the answer is unambiguously "only the gismu". The cmavo *na'e* always applies only to what follows it.

Example 15.45 (p. 360) looks as if it were parallel to:

Example 15.46

mi	na	klama	le	zarci
I	[false]	go-to	the	market.

but in fact there is no real parallelism at all. A negation using *na* denies the truth of a relationship, but a selbri negation with *na'e* asserts that a relationship exists other than that stated, one which specifically involves the sumti identified in the statement. The grammar allotted to *na'e* allows us to unambiguously express scalar negations in terms of scope, scale, and range within the scale. Before we explain the scalar aspects, let us show how the scope of *na'e* is determined.

In tanru, we may wish to negate an individual element before combining it with another to form the tanru. We in effect need a shorter-than-selbri-scope negation, for which we can use *na'e* as well. The positive sentence

Example 15.47

mi	cadzu	klama	le	zarci
I	walking-ly	go-to	the	market.

can be subjected to selbri negation in several ways. Two are:

Example 15.48

mi	na'e	cadzu	klama	le	zarci
I	(other-than	walkingly)	go-to	the	market.

Example 15.49

mi	cadzu	na'e	klama	le	zarci
I	walkingly	(other-than	go-to)	the	market.

These negations show the default scope of *na'e* is close-binding on an individual brivla in a tanru. Example 15.48 (p. 360) says that I am going to the market, but in some kind of a non-walking manner. (As with most tanru, there are a few other possible interpretations, but we'll assume this one – see Chapter 5 (p. 79) for a discussion of tanru meaning).

In neither Example 15.48 (p. 360) nor Example 15.49 (p. 361) does the *na'e* negate the entire selbri. While both sentences contain negations that deny a particular relationship between the sumti, they also have a component which makes a positive claim about such a relationship. This is clearer in Example 15.48 (p. 360), which says that I am going, but in a non-walking manner. In Example 15.49 (p. 361), we have claimed that the relationship between me and the market in some way involves walking, but is not one of "going to" (perhaps we are walking around the market, or walking-in-place while at the market).

The "scale", or actually the "set", implied in Lojban tanru negations is anything which plausibly can be substituted into the tanru. (Plausibility here is interpreted in the same way that answers to a *mo* question must be plausible – the result must not only have the right number of places and have sumti values appropriate to the place structure, it must also be appropriate or relevant to the context.) This minimal condition allows a speaker to be intentionally vague, while still communicating meaningful information. The speaker who uses selbri negation is denying one relationship, while minimally asserting a different relationship.

We also need a scalar negation form that has a scope longer than a single brivla. There exists such a longer-scope selbri negation form, as exemplified by (each Lojban sentence in the next several examples is given twice, with parentheses in the second copy showing the scope of the *na'e*):

Example 15.50

mi	na'e	ke	cadzu	klama	[ke'e]	le	zarci
mi	na'e	(ke	cadzu	klama	[ke'e])	le	zarci
I	other-than	(	walkingly	go-to	)	the	market.

This negation uses the same *ke* and *ke'e* delimiters (the *ke'e* is always elidable at the end of a selbri) that are used in tanru. The sentence clearly negates the entire selbri. The *ke'e*, whether elided or not, reminds us that the negation does not include the trailing sumti. While the trailing-sumti place-structure is defined as that of the final brivla, the trailing sumti themselves are not part of the selbri and are thus not negated by *na'e*.

Negations of just part of the selbri are also permitted:

Example 15.51

mi	na'e	ke	sutra	cadzu	ke'e	klama	le	zarci
mi	na'e	(ke	sutra	cadzu	ke'e)	klama	le	zarci
I	other-than	(	quickly	walkingly	)	go-to	the	market.

In Example 15.51 (p. 361), only the *sutra cadzu* tanru is negated, so the speaker is indeed going to the market, but not by walking quickly.

Negations made with *na'e* or *na'eke* also include within their scope any sumti attached to the brivla or tanru with *be* or *bei*. Such attached sumti are considered part of the brivla or tanru:

Example 15.52

mi	na'e	ke	sutra	cadzu	be	le	mi	birka
I	other-than	(	quickly	walking	on	the	of-me	arms-ly

ke'e	klama	le	zarci
)	go-to	the	market.

Note that Example 15.53 (p. 362) and Example 15.54 (p. 362) do not express the same thing:

Example 15.53

mi	na'e	ke	sutra	cadzu	[ke'e]	lemi	birka
mi	na'e	(ke	sutra	cadzu	[ke'e])	lemi	birka
I	other-than	(	quickly	walk-on	)	my	arms.

Example 15.54

mi	na'e	ke	sutra	cadzu	be	lemi	birka	[ke'e]
mi	na'e	(ke	sutra	cadzu	be	lemi	birka	[ke'e])
I	other-than	(	quickly	walk	on	my	arms	).

The translations show that the negation in Example 15.53 (p. 362) is more restricted in scope; i.e. less of the sentence is negated with respect to x1 (*mi*).

Logical scope being an important factor in Lojban's claims to be unambiguous, let us indicate the relative precedence of *na'e* as an operator. Grouping with *ke* and *ke'e*, of course, has an overt scope, which is its advantage. *na'e* is very close binding to its brivla. Internal binding of tanru, with *bo*, is not as tightly bound as *na'e*. *co*, the tanru inversion operator has a scope that is longer than all other tanru constructs.

In short, *na'e* and *na'eke* define a type of negation, which is shorter in scope than bridi negation, and which affects all or part of a selbri. The result of *na'e* negation remains an assertion of some specific truth and not merely a denial of another claim.

The similarity becomes striking when it is noticed that the rafsi *-nal-*, representing *na'e* when a tanru is condensed into a lujvo, forms an exact parallel to the English usage of *non-*. Turning a series of related negations into lujvo gives:

Example 15.55

na'e klama becomes nalkla

na'e cadzu klama becomes naldzukla

na'e sutra cadzu klama becomes nalsu'adzukla

nake sutra cadzu ke'e klama becomes nalsu'adzuke'ekla

Note: *-kem-* is the rafsi for *ke*, but it is omitted in the final lujvo as superfluous – *ke'e* is its own rafsi, and its inclusion in the lujvo implies a *ke* after the *-nal-*, since it needs to close something; only a *ke* immediately after the negation would make the *ke'e* meaningful in the tanru expressed in this lujvo.

In a lujvo, it is probably clearest to translate *-nal-* as "non-", to match the English combining forms, except when the *na'e* has single word scope and English uses "un-" or "im-" to negate that single word. Translation style should determine the use of "other than", "non-", or another negator for *na'e* in tanru; the translator must render the Lojban into English so it is clear in context. Let's go back to our simplest example:

Example 15.56

mi	na'e	klama	le	zarci
I	other-than	(go-to)	the	market.
I	not	go-to	the	market.

Example 15.57

mi	nalkla	le	zarci
I	am-a-non-go-er-to	the	market.

Note that to compare with the English translation form using "non-", we've translated the Lojban as if the selbri were a noun. Since Lojban *klama* is indifferently a noun, verb, or adjective, the difference is purely a translation change, not a true change in meaning. The English difference seems significant, though, due to the strongly different English grammatical forms and the ambiguity of English negation.

Consider the following highly problematic sentence:

Example 15.58

lo	ca	nolraitru
An-actual	**currently**	**noblest-governor**

be	le	fasygu'e		cu	krecau
of	**the**	**French-country**			**is-hair-without.**

The current King of France is bald.

The selbri *krecau* negates with *na'e* as:

Example 15.59

lo	ca	nolraitru
An-actual	**currently**	**noblest-governor**

be	le	fasygu'e		cu	na'e	krecau
of	**the**	**French-country**			**is-other-than**	**hair-without.**

The current King of France is other-than-bald.

or, as a lujvo:

Example 15.60

lo	ca	nolraitru
An-actual	**currently**	**noblest-governor**

be	le	fasygu'e		cu	nalkrecau
of	**the**	**French-country**			**is-non-hair-without.**

The current King of France is a non-bald-one.

Example 15.59 (p. 363) and Example 15.60 (p. 363) express the predicate negation forms using a negation word (*na'e*) or rafsi (*-nal-*); yet they make positive assertions about the current King of France; ie., that he is other-than-bald or non-bald. This follows from the close binding of *na'e* to the brivla. The lujvo form makes this overt by absorbing the negative marker into the word.

Since there is no current King of France, it is false to say that he is bald, or non-bald, or to make any other affirmative claim about him. Any sentence about the current King of France containing only a selbri negation is as false as the sentence without the negation. No amount of selbri negations have any effect on the truth value of the sentence, which is invariably "false", since no affirmative statement about the current King of France can be true. On the other hand, bridi negation does produce a truth:

Example 15.61

lo	ca	nolraitru
An-actual	**current**	**noblest-governor**

be	le	fasygu'e		cu	na	krecau
of	**the**	**French-country**			**[false]**	**is-hair-without.**

It is false that the current King of France is bald.

Note: *lo* is used in these sentences because negation relates to truth conditions. To meaningfully talk about truth conditions in sentences carrying a description, it must be clear that the description actually applies to the referent. A sentence using *le* instead of *lo* can be true even if there is no current king of France, as long as the speaker and the listener agree to describe something as the current king of France. (See the explanations of *le* in Section 6.2 (p. 116).)

15.5 Expressing scales in selbri negation

In expressing a scalar negation, we can provide some indication of the scale, range, frame-of-reference, or universe of discourse that is being dealt with in an assertion. As stated in Section 15.4 (p. 360), the default is the set of plausible alternatives. Thus if we say:

Example 15.62

le	stizu	cu	na'e	xunre
The	chair		is-a-non-	(red-thing).

the pragmatic interpretation is that we mean a different color and not

Example 15.63

le	stizu	cu	dzukla	be	le	zarci
The	chair		walkingly-goes	to	the	market.

However, if we have reason to be more explicit (an obtuse or contrary listener, or simply an overt logical analysis), we can clarify that we are referring to a color by saying:

Example 15.64

le	stizu	cu	na'e	xunre	skari
The	chair		(is-of-a-non	red)	color.

We might also have reduced the pragmatic ambiguity by making the two trailing sumti values explicit (the "as perceived by" and "under conditions" places have been added to the place structure of *xunre*). But assume we have a really stubborn listener (an artificially semi-intelligent computer?) who will find a way to misinterpret Example 15.64 (p. 364) even with three specific sumti provided.

In this case, we use a sumti tagged with the sumti tcita *ci'u*, which translates roughly as "on a scale of X", where **X** is the sumti. For maximal clarity, the tagged sumti can be bound into the negated selbri with *be*. To clarify Example 15.64 (p. 364), we might say:

Example 15.65

le	stizu	cu	na'e	xunre	be	ci'u	loka	skari
The	chair		is-non	(red	on	a-scale-of	a-property	color-ness).

We can alternately use the sumti tcita *teci'e*, based on *ciste*, which translates roughly as "of a system of components X", for universes of discourse; in this case, we would express Example 15.64 (p. 364) as:

Example 15.66

le	stizu	cu	na'e	xunre
The	chair		is-a-non	(red

be	teci'e	le	skari
of	a-system	with-components-the	colors)-thing.

Other places of *ciste* can be brought out using the grammar of selma'o BAI modals, allowing slightly different forms of expression, thus:

Example 15.67

le	stizu	cu	na'e	xunre
The	chair		is-a-non	(red

be	ci'e	lo'i	skari
of	a-system	which-is-the-set-of	colors)-thing.

The cmavo *le'a*, also in selma'o BAI, can be used to specify a category:

Example 15.68

le	stizu	cu	na'e	xunre
The	chair		is-a-non	(red

be	le'a	lo'i	skari
of	a-category	which-is-the-set-of	colors)-thing.

which is minimally different in meaning from Example 15.67 (p. 364).

The cmavo *na'e* is not the only member of selma'o NAhE. If we want to express a scalar negation which is a polar opposite, we use the cmavo *to'e*, which is grammatically equivalent to *na'e*:

Example 15.69

le	stizu	cu	to'e		xunre	be	ci'u	loka		skari
The	chair		is-a-(opposite-of	red)		on	scale	a-property-of		color-ness.

Likewise, the midpoint of a scale can be expressed with the cmavo *no'e*, also grammatically equivalent to *na'e*. Here are some parallel examples of *na'e*, *no'e*, and *to'e*:

Example 15.70

ta	melbi
That	is-beautiful.

Example 15.71

ta	na'e	melbi
That	is-other-than	beautiful.

That is ugly [in one sense].

Example 15.72

ta	no'e	melbi
That	is-neutrally	beautiful.

That is plain/ordinary-looking (neither ugly nor beautiful).

Example 15.73

ta	to'e	melbi
That	is-opposite-of	beautiful.

That is ugly/very ugly/repulsive.

The cmavo *to'e* has the assigned rafsi *-tol-* and *-to'e-*; the cmavo *no'e* has the assigned rafsi *-nor-* and *-no'e-*. The selbri in Example 15.71 (p. 365) through Example 15.73 (p. 365) could be replaced by the lujvo *nalmle*, *normle*, and *tolmle* respectively.

This large variety of scalar negations is provided because different scales have different properties. Some scales are open-ended in both directions: there is no "ultimately ugly" or "ultimately beautiful". Other scales, like temperature, are open at one end and closed at the other: there is a minimum temperature (so-called "absolute zero") but no maximum temperature. Still other scales are closed at both ends.

Correspondingly, some selbri have no obvious *to'e*- what is the opposite of a dog? – while others have more than one, and need *ci'u* to specify which opposite is meant.

15.6 sumti negation

There are two ways of negating sumti in Lojban. We have the choice of quantifying the sumti with zero, or of applying the sumti-negator *na'ebo* before the sumti. It turns out that a zero quantification serves for contradictory negation. As the cmavo we use implies, *na'ebo* forms a scalar negation.

Let us show examples of each.

Example 15.74

no	lo		ca		nolraitru		be
Zero	of-those-who-are		currently		noblest-governors		of

le	fasygu'e		cu	krecau
the	French-country			are-hair-without.

No current king of France is bald.

Is Example 15.74 (p. 365) true? Yes, because it merely claims that of the current Kings of France, however many there may be, none are bald, which is plainly true, since there are no such current Kings of France.

Now let us look at the same sentence using *na'ebo* negation:

Example 15.75

na'ebo		lo	ca	nolraitru
Something-other-than	(the	current	noblest-governor

be	le	fasygu'e		cu	krecau
of	the	French-country)		is-hair-without.

Something other than the current King of France is bald.

Example 15.75 (p. 366) is true provided that something reasonably describable as "other than a current King of France", such as the King of Saudi Arabia, or a former King of France, is in fact bald.

In place of *na'ebo*, you may also use *no'ebo* and *to'ebo*, to be more specific about the sumti which would be appropriate in place of the stated sumti. Good examples are hard to come by, but here's a valiant try:

Example 15.76

mi	klama	to'ebo	la	bastn.
I	go-to	the-opposite-of	that-named	Boston.

I go to Perth.

(Boston and Perth are nearly, but not quite, antipodal cities. In a purely United States context, San Francisco might be a better "opposite".) Coming up with good examples is difficult, because attaching *to'ebo* to a description sumti is usually the same as attaching *to'e* to the selbri of the description.

It is not possible to transform sumti negations of either type into bridi negations or scalar selbri negations. Negations of sumti will be used in Lojban conversation. The inability to manipulate these negations logically will, it is hoped, prevent the logical errors that result when natural languages attempt corresponding manipulations.

15.7 Negation of minor grammatical constructs

We have a few other constructs that can be negated, all of them based on negating individual words. For such negation, we use the suffix-combining negator, which is *nai*. *nai*, by the way, is almost always written as a compound into the previous word that it is negating, although it is a regular separate-word cmavo and the sole member of selma'o NAI.

Most of these negation forms are straightforward, and should be discussed and interpreted in connection with an analysis of the particular construct being negated. Thus, we will not go into much detail here.

The following are places where *nai* is used:

When attached to tenses and modals (see Section 9.13 (p. 200), Section 10.9 (p. 217), Section 10.18 (p. 234) and Section 10.20 (p. 237)), the *nai* suffix usually indicates a contradictory negation of the tagged bridi. Thus *punai* as a tense inflection means "not-in-the-past", or "not-previously", without making any implication about any other time period unless explicitly stated. As a result,

Example 15.77

mi	na	pu	klama	le	zarci
I	[false]	[past]	go-to	the	store.

I didn't go to the store.

and

Example 15.78

mi	punai	klama	le	zarci
I	[past-not]	go-to	the	store.

I didn't go to the store.

mean exactly the same thing, although there may be a difference of emphasis.

Tenses and modals can be logically connected, with the logical connectives containing contradictory negations; this allows negated tenses and modals to be expressed positively using logical connectives. Thus *punai je ca* means the same thing as *pu naje ca*.

As a special case, a *-nai* attached to the interval modifiers of selma'o TAhE, ROI, or ZAhO (explained in Chapter 10 (p. 207)) signals a scalar negation:

Example 15.79

mi	paroinai	dansu	le	bisli
I	[once]-[not]	dance-on	the	ice

means that I dance on the ice either zero or else two or more times within the relevant time interval described by the bridi. Example 15.79 (p. 367) is very different from the English use of "not once", which is an emphatic way of saying "never" – that is, exactly zero times.

In indicators and attitudinals of selma'o UI or CAI, *nai* denotes a polar negation. As discussed in Section 13.4 (p. 292), most indicators have an implicit scale, and *nai* changes the indicator to refer to the opposite end of the scale. Thus *.uinai* expresses unhappiness, and *.ienai* expresses disagreement (not ambivalence, which is expressed with the neutral or undecided intensity as *.iecu'i*).

Vocative cmavo of selma'o COI are considered a kind of indicator, but one which identifies the listener. Semantically, we could dispense with about half of the COI selma'o words based on the scalar paradigm. For example, *co'o* could be expressed as *coinai*. However, this is not generally done.

Most of the COI cmavo are used in what are commonly called protocol situations. These protocols are used, for example, in radio conversations, which often take place in a noisy environment. The negatives of protocol words tend to convey diametrically opposite communications situations (as might be expected). Therefore, only one protocol vocative is dependent on *nai*: negative acknowledgement, which is *je'enai* ("I didn't get that").

Unlike the attitudinal indicators, which tend to be unimportant in noisy situations, the protocol vocatives become more important. So if, in a noisy environment, a protocol listener makes out only *nai*, he or she can presume it is a negative acknowledgement and repeat transmission or otherwise respond accordingly. Section 13.14 (p. 309) provides more detail on this topic.

The abstractors of selma'o NU follow the pattern of the tenses and modals. NU allows negative abstractions, especially in compound abstractions connected by logical connectives: *su'ujeninai*, which corresponds to *su'u jenai ni* just as *punai je ca* corresponds to *pu naje ca*. It is not clear how much use logically connected abstractors will be: see Section 11.12 (p. 261).

A *nai* attached to a non-logical connective (of selma'o JOI or BIhI) is a scalar negation, and says that the bridi is false under the specified mixture, but that another connective is applicable. Non-logical connectives are discussed in Section 14.14 (p. 338).

15.8 Truth questions

One application of negation is in answer to truth questions (those which expect the answers "Yes" or "No"). The truth question cmavo *xu* is in selma'o UI; placed at the beginning of a sentence, it asks whether the sentence as a whole is true or false.

Example 15.80

xu	la	djan.	pu	klama
Is-it-true-that:	(that-named	John	previously	went-to

la	paris.	.e	la	rom.
that-named	Paris	and	that-named	Rome.)

You can now use each of the several kinds of negation we've discussed in answer to this (presuming the same question and context for each answer).

The straightforward negative answer is grammatically equivalent to the expanded sentence with the *na* immediately after the *cu* (and before any tense/modal):

Example 15.81

na	go'i
[false]	[repeat-previous]

No.

which means

Example 15.82

la	djan.	[cu]	na	pu	klama
That-named	John	[false]	previously	went-to	

la	paris.	.e	la	rom.
that-named	Paris	and	that-named	Rome.

It's not true that John went to Paris and Rome.

The respondent can change the tense, putting the *na* in either before or after the new tense:

Example 15.83

na	ba	go'i
[false]	[future]	[repeat-previous]

meaning

Example 15.84

la	djan.	[cu]	na	ba	klama
That-named	John		[false]	later	will-go-to

la	paris.	.e	la	rom.
that-named	Paris	and	that-named	Rome.

It is false that John will go to Paris and Rome.

or alternatively

Example 15.85

ba	na	go'i
[future]	[false]	[repeat-previous]

meaning

Example 15.86

la	djan.	[cu]	ba	na
that-named	John		later-will	[false]

klama	la	paris.	.e	la	rom.
go-to	that-named	Paris	and	that-named	Rome.

We stated in Section 15.3 (p. 357) that sentences like Example 15.84 (p. 368) and Example 15.86 (p. 368) appear to be semantically identical, but that subtle semantic distinctions may eventually be found.

You can also use a scalar negation with *na'e*, in which case, it is equivalent to putting a *na'eke* immediately after any tense:

Example 15.87

na'e	go'i
other-than	[repeat-previous]

which means

Example 15.88

la	djan.	[cu]	pu	na'eke	klama	[ke'e]
that-named	John		previously	other-than(	went-to	)

la	paris.	.e	la	rom.
that-named	Paris	and	that-named	Rome.

He might have telephoned the two cities instead of going there. The unnecessary *ke* and *ke'e* would have been essential if the selbri had been a tanru.

15.9 Affirmations

There is an explicit positive form for both selma'o NA (*ja'a*) and selma'o NAhE (*je'a*), each of which would supplant the corresponding negator in the grammatical position used, allowing one to assert the positive in response to a negative question or statement without confusion. Assuming the same context as in Section 15.8 (p. 367):

Example 15.89

xu	*na*	*go'i*
Is-it-true-that	**[false]**	**[repeat-previous]?**

or equivalently

Example 15.90

xu	*la*	*djan.*	*[cu]*	*na*	*pu*
Is-it-true-that:	**that-named**	**John**		**[false]**	**previously**

klama	*la*	*paris.*	*.e*	*la*	*rom.*
went-to	**that-name**	**Paris**	**and**	**that-named**	**Rome.**

The obvious, but incorrect, positive response to this negative question is:

Example 15.91

go'i

[repeat-previous]

A plain *go'i* does not mean "Yes it is"; it merely abbreviates repeating the previous statement unmodified, including any negators present; and Example 15.91 (p. 369) actually states that it is false that John went to both Paris and Rome.

When considering:

Example 15.92

na	*go'i*
[false]	**[repeat-previous]**

as a response to a negative question like Example 15.90 (p. 369), Lojban designers had to choose between two equally plausible interpretations with opposite effects. Does Example 15.92 (p. 369) create a double negative in the sentence by adding a new *na* to the one already there (forming a double negative and hence a positive statement), or does the *na* replace the previous one, leaving the sentence unchanged?

It was decided that substitution, the latter alternative, is the preferable choice, since it is then clear whether we intend a positive or a negative sentence without performing any manipulations. This is the way English usually works, but not all languages work this way – Russian, Japanese, and Navajo all interpret a negative reply to a negative question as positive.

The positive assertion cmavo of selma'o NA, which is "ja'a", can also replace the *na* in the context, giving:

Example 15.93

ja'a	*go'i*
[true]	**[repeat-previous]**

John did go to Paris and Rome.

ja'a can replace *na* in a similar manner wherever the latter is used:

Example 15.94

mi	ja'a	klama	le	zarci
I	[true]	go-to	the	store

I indeed go to the store.

je'a can replace *na'e* in exactly the same way, stating that scalar negation does not apply, and that the relation indeed holds as stated. In the absence of a negation context, it emphasizes the positive:

Example 15.95

ta	je'a	melbi
that	is-indeed	beautiful.

15.10 Metalinguistic negation forms

The question of truth or falsity is not entirely synonymous with negation. Consider the English sentence

Example 15.96

I have not stopped beating my wife.

If I never started such a heinous activity, then this sentence is neither true nor false. Such a negation simply says that something is wrong with the non-negated statement. Generally, we then use either tone of voice or else a correction to express a preferred true claim: "I never have beaten my wife."

Negations which follow such a pattern are called "metalinguistic negations". In natural languages, the mark of metalinguistic negation is that an indication of a correct statement always, or almost always, follows the negation. Tone of voice or emphasis may be further used to clarify the error.

Negations of every sort must be expressible in Lojban; errors are inherent to human thought, and are not excluded from the language. When such negations are metalinguistic, we must separate them from logical claims about the truth or falsity of the statement, as well as from scalar negations which may not easily express (or imply) the preferred claim. Because Lojban allows concepts to be so freely combined in tanru, limits on what is plausible or not plausible tend to be harder to determine.

Mimicking the muddled nature of natural language negation would destroy this separation. Since Lojban does not use tone of voice, we need other means to metalinguistically indicate what is wrong with a statement. When the statement is entirely inappropriate, we need to be able to express metalinguistic negation in a more non-specific fashion.

Here is a list of some different kinds of metalinguistic negation with English-language examples:

Example 15.97

I have not *stopped* beating my wife

(I never started – failure of presupposition).

Example 15.98

5 is not blue

(color does not apply to abstract concepts – failure of category).

Example 15.99

The current King of France is not bald.

(there is no current King of France – existential failure)

Example 15.100

I do not have THREE children.

(I have two – simple undue quantity)

Example 15.101

I have not held THREE jobs previously, but four.

(inaccurate quantity; the difference from the previous example is that someone who has held four jobs has also held three jobs)

Example 15.102

> It is not good, but bad.
>
> (undue quantity negation indicating that the value on a scale for measuring the predicate is incorrect)

Example 15.103

> She is not PRETTY; she is beautiful.
>
> (undue quantity transferred to a non-numeric scale)

Example 15.104

> The house is not blue, but green.
>
> (the scale/category being used is incorrect, but a related category applies)

Example 15.105

> The house is not blue, but is colored.
>
> (the scale/category being used is incorrect, but a broader category applies)

Example 15.106

> The cat is not blue, but long-haired.
>
> (the scale/category being used is incorrect, but an unrelated category applies)

Example 15.107

> A: He ain't coming today.
>
> B: "Ain't" ain't a word.
>
> (solecism, or improper grammatical action)

Example 15.108

> I haven't STOOPED beating my wife; I've STOPPED.
>
> (spelling or mispronunciation error)

Example 15.109

> Not only was it a sheep, it was a black sheep.
>
> (non-contradictory correction)

The set of possible metalinguistic errors is open-ended.

Many of these forms have a counterpart in the various examples that we've discussed under logical negation. Metalinguistic negation doesn't claim that the sentence is false or true, though. Rather, it claims that, due to some error in the statement, "true" and "false" don't really apply.

Because one can metalinguistically negate a true statement intending a non-contradictory correction (say, a spelling error); we need a way (or ways) to metalinguistically negate a statement which is independent of our logical negation schemes using *na*, *na'e* and kin. The cmavo *na'i* is assigned this function. If it is present in a statement, it indicates metalinguistically that something in the statement is incorrect. This metalinguistic negation must override any evaluation of the logic of the statement. It is equally allowed in both positive and negative statements.

Since *na'i* is not a logical operator, multiple occurrences of *na'i* need not be assumed to cancel each other. Indeed, we can use the position of *na'i* to indicate metalinguistically what is incorrect, preparatory to correcting it in a later sentence; for this reason, we give *na'i* the grammar of UI. The inclusion of *na'i* anywhere in a sentence makes it a non-assertion, and suggests one or more pitfalls in assigning a truth value.

Let us briefly indicate how the above-mentioned metalinguistic errors can be identified. Other metalinguistic problems can then be marked by devising analogies to these examples:

Existential failure can be marked by attaching *na'i* to the descriptor *lo* or the *poi* in a *da poi*-form sumti. (See Section 6.2 (p. 116) and Section 16.4 (p. 379) for details on these constructions.) Remember that if a *le* sumti seems to refer to a non-existent referent, you may not understand what the speaker has in mind – the appropriate response is then *ki'a*, asking for clarification.

Presupposition failure can be marked directly if the presupposition is overt; if not, one can insert a "mock presupposition" to question with the sumti tcita (selma'o BAI) word *ji'u*; *ji'uku* thus explicitly refers to an unexpressed assumption, and *ji'una'iku* metalinguistically says that something is wrong with that assumption. (See Chapter 9 (p. 179).)

Scale errors and category errors can be similarly expressed with selma'o BAI. *le'a* has meaning "of category/class/type X", *ci'u* has meaning "on scale X", and *ci'e*, based on *ciste*, can be used to talk about universes of discourse defined either as systems or sets of components, as shown in Section 15.8 (p. 367). *kai* and *la'u* also exist in BAI for discussing other quality and quantity errors.

We have to make particular note of potential problems in the areas of undue quantity and incorrect scale/category. Assertions about the relationships between gismu are among the basic substance of the language. It is thus invalid to logically require that if something is blue, that it is colored, or if it is not-blue, then it is some other color. In Lojban, *blanu* ("blue") is not explicitly defined as a *skari* ("color"). Similarly, it is not implicit that the opposite of "good" is "bad".

This mutual independence of gismu is only an ideal. Pragmatically, people will categorize things based on their world-views. We will write dictionary definitions that will relate gismu, unfortunately including some of these world-view assumptions. Lojbanists should try to minimize these assumptions, but this seems a likely area where logical rules will break down (or where Sapir-Whorf effects will be made evident). In terms of negation, however, it is vital that we clearly preserve the capability of denying a presumably obvious scale or category assumption.

Solecisms, grammatical and spelling errors will be marked by marking the offending word or phrase with *na'i* (in the manner of any selma'o UI cmavo). In this sense, *na'i* becomes equivalent to the English metalinguistic marker "[sic]". Purists may choose to use ZOI or LOhU/LEhU quotes or *sa'a*-marked corrections to avoid repeating a truly unparsable passage, especially if a computer is to analyze the speech/text. See Section 19.12 (p. 461) for explanations of these usages.

In summary, metalinguistic negation will typically take the form of referring to a previous statement and marking it with one or more *na'i* to indicate what metalinguistic errors have been made, and then repeating the statement with corrections. References to previous statements may be full repetitions, or may use members of selma'o GOhA. *na'i* at the beginning of a statement merely says that something is inappropriate about the statement, without specificity.

In normal use, metalinguistic negation requires that a corrected statement follow the negated statement. In Lojban, however, it is possible to completely and unambiguously specify metalinguistic errors without correcting them. It will eventually be seen whether an uncorrected metalinguistic negation remains an acceptable form in Lojban. In such a statement, metalinguistic expression would involve an ellipsis not unlike that of tenseless expression.

Note that metalinguistic negation gives us another kind of legitimate negative answer to a *xu* question (see Section 15.8 (p. 367)). *na'i* will be used when something about the questioned statement is inappropriate, such as in questions like "Have you stopped beating your wife?":

Example 15.110

xu	do	sisti	lezu'o
is-it-true-that:	you	cease	the-activity-of

do	rapydarxi	ledo	fetspe
you	repeat-hitting	your	female-spouse?

Have you stopped beating your wife?

Responses could include:

Example 15.111

na'i	go'i
[metalinguistic-negation]	[repeat-previous]

The bridi as a whole is inappropriate in some way.

Example 15.112

go'i	na'i
[repeat-previous]	**[metalinguistic-negation]**

The selbri (*sisti*) is inappropriate in some way.

One can also specifically qualify the metalinguistic negation, by explicitly repeating the erroneous portion of the bridi to be metalinguistically negated, or adding on of the selma'o BAI qualifiers mentioned above:

Example 15.113

go'i	ji'una'iku
[repeat-previous]	**[presupposition-wrong]**

Some presupposition is wrong with the previous bridi.

Finally, one may metalinguistically affirm a bridi with *jo'a*, another cmavo of selma'o UI. A common use for *jo'a* might be to affirm that a particular construction, though unusual or counterintuitive, is in fact correct; another usage would be to disagree with – by overriding – a respondent's metalinguistic negation.

15.11 Summary – Are All Possible Questions About Negation Now Answered?

Example 15.114

na go'i .ije na'e go'i .ije na'i go'i

Chapter 16
"Who Did You Pass On The Road? Nobody": Lojban And Logic

drata mupli pe'u djan.

16.1 What's wrong with this picture?

The following brief dialogue is from *Chapter 7* of *Through The Looking Glass* by Lewis Carroll.

Example 16.1

"Who did you pass on the road?" the King went on, holding out his hand to the Messenger for some more hay.

Example 16.2

"Nobody," said the Messenger.

Example 16.3

"Quite right," said the King: "this young lady saw him too. So of course Nobody walks slower than you."

Example 16.4

"I do my best," the Messenger said in a sulky tone. "I'm sure nobody walks much faster than I do!"

Example 16.5

"He can't do that," said the King, "or else he'd have been here first."

This nonsensical conversation results because the King insists on treating the word "nobody" as a name, a name of somebody. However, the essential nature of the English word "nobody" is that it doesn't refer to somebody; or to put the matter another way, there isn't anybody to which it refers.

The central point of contradiction in the dialogue arises in Example 16.3 (p. 375), when the King says "... Nobody walks slower than you". This claim would be plausible if "Nobody" were really a name, since the Messenger could only pass someone who does walk more slowly than he. But the Messenger interprets the word "nobody" in the ordinary English way, and says (in Example 16.4 (p. 375)) "... nobody walks much faster than I do" (i.e., I walk faster, or as fast as, almost everyone), which the King then again misunderstands. Both the King and the Messenger are correct according to their respective understandings of the ambiguous word "nobody/Nobody".

There are Lojban words or phrases corresponding to the problematic English words "somebody", "nobody", "anybody", "everybody" (and their counterparts "some/no/any/everyone" and "some/no/any/everything"), but they obey rules which can often be surprising to English-speakers. The dialogue above simply cannot be translated into Lojban without distortion: the name "Nobody" would have to be represented by a Lojban name, which would spoil the perfection of the wordplay. As a matter of fact, this is the desired result: a logical language should not allow two conversationalists to affirm "Nobody walks slower than the Messenger" and "Nobody walks faster than the Messenger" and both be telling the truth. (Unless, of course, nobody but the Messenger walks at all, or everyone walks at exactly the same speed.)

This chapter will explore the Lojban mechanisms that allow the correct and consistent construction of sentences like those in the dialogue. There are no new grammatical constructs explained in this chapter; instead, it discusses the way in which existing facilities that allow Lojban-speakers to resolve problems like the above, using the concepts of modern logic. However, we will not approach the matter from the viewpoint of logicians, although readers who know something of logic will discover familiar notions in Lojban guise.

Although Lojban is called a logical language, not every feature of it is "logical". In particular, the use of *le* is incompatible with logical reasoning based on the description selbri, because that selbri may not truthfully apply: you cannot conclude from my statement that

Example 16.6

mi	viska	le		nanmu
I	**see**	**the-one-I-refer-to-as-the**		**man.**

I see the man/men.

that there really is a man; the only thing you can conclude is that there is one thing (or more) that I choose to refer to as a man. You cannot even tell which man is meant for sure without asking me (although communication is served if you already know from the context).

In addition, the use of attitudinals (see Chapter 13 (p. 285)) often reduces or removes the ability to make deductions about the bridi to which those attitudinals are applied. From the fact that I hope George will win the election, you can conclude nothing about George's actual victory or defeat.

16.2 Existential claims, prenexes, and variables

Let us consider, to begin with, a sentence that is not in the dialogue:

Example 16.7

Something sees me.

There are two plausible Lojban translations of Example 16.7 (p. 376). The simpler one is:

Example 16.8

[zo'e]		viska	mi
Something-unspecified		**sees**	**me.**

The cmavo *zo'e* indicates that a sumti has been omitted (indeed, even *zo'e* itself can be omitted in this case, as explained in Section 7.7 (p. 150)) and the listener must fill in the correct value from context. In other words, Example 16.8 (p. 376) means "'You-know-what' sees me."

However, Example 16.7 (p. 376) is just as likely to assert simply that there is someone who sees me, in which case a correct translation is:

Example 16.9

da	zo'u	da	viska	mi
There-is-an-X	such-that	X	sees	me.

Example 16.9 (p. 377) does not presuppose that the listener knows who sees the speaker, but simply tells the listener that there is someone who sees the speaker. Statements of this kind are called "existential claims". (Formally, the one doing the seeing is not restricted to being a person; it could be an animal or – in principle – an inanimate object. We will see in Section 16.4 (p. 379) how to represent such restrictions.)

Example 16.9 (p. 377) has a two-part structure: there is the part *da zo'u*, called the prenex, and the part *da viska mi*, the main bridi. Almost any Lojban bridi can be preceded by a prenex, which syntactically is any number of sumti followed by the cmavo *zo'u* (of selma'o ZOhU). For the moment, the sumti will consist of one or more of the cmavo *da*, *de*, and *di* (of selma'o KOhA), glossed in the literal translations as "X", "Y", and "Z" respectively. By analogy to the terminology of symbolic logic, these cmavo are called "variables".

Here is an example of a prenex with two variables:

Example 16.10

da	de	zo'u	da	prami	de
There-is-an-X	there-is-a-Y	such	that	X	loves	Y.

Somebody loves somebody.

In Example 16.10 (p. 377), the literal interpretation of the two variables *da* and *de* as "there-is-an-X" and "there-is-a-Y" tells us that there are two things which stand in the relationship that one loves the other. It might be the case that the supposed two things are really just a single thing that loves itself; nothing in the Lojban version of Example 16.10 (p. 377) rules out that interpretation, which is why the colloquial translation does not say "Somebody loves somebody else." The things referred to by different variables may be different or the same. (We use "somebody" here rather than "something" for naturalness; lovers and beloveds are usually persons, though the Lojban does not say so.)

It is perfectly all right for the variables to appear more than once in the main bridi:

Example 16.11

da	zo'u	da	prami	da
There-is-an-X	such-that	X	loves	X

Somebody loves himself/herself.

What Example 16.11 (p. 377) claims is fundamentally different from what Example 16.10 (p. 377) claims, because *da prami da* is not structurally the same as *da prami de*. However,

Example 16.12

de	zo'u	de	prami	de
There-is-a-Y	such-that	Y	loves	Y

means exactly the same thing as Example 16.11 (p. 377); it does not matter which variable is used as long as they are used consistently.

It is not necessary for a variable to be a sumti of the main bridi directly:

Example 16.13

da	zo'u	le	da	gerku	cu	viska	mi
There-is-an-X	such-that	the	of-X	dog		sees	me

Somebody's dog sees me

is perfectly correct even though the *da* is used only in a possessive construction. (Possessives are explained in Section 8.7 (p. 172).)

It is very peculiar, however, even if technically grammatical, for the variable not to appear in the main bridi at all:

Example 16.14

da	zo'u	la	ralf.	gerku
There-is-an-X	such-that	that-named	Ralph	is-a-dog

There is something such that Ralph is a dog.

has a variable bound in a prenex whose relevance to the claim of the following bridi is completely unspecified.

16.3 Universal claims

What happens if we substitute "everything" for "something" in Example 16.7 (p. 376)? We get:

Example 16.15

Everything sees me.

Of course, this example is false, because there are many things which do not see the speaker. It is not easy to find simple truthful examples of so-called universal claims (those which are about everything), so bear with us for a while. (Indeed, some Lojbanists tend to avoid universal claims even in other languages, since they are so rarely true in Lojban.)

The Lojban translation of Example 16.15 (p. 378) is

Example 16.16

ro	da	zo'u	da	viska	mi
For-every	X	:	X	sees	me.

When the variable cmavo *da* is preceded by *ro*, the combination means "For every X" rather than "There is an X". Superficially, these English formulations look totally unrelated: Section 16.6 (p. 381) will bring them within a common viewpoint. For the moment, accept the use of *ro da* for "everything" on faith.

Here is a universal claim with two variables:

Example 16.17

ro	da	ro	de	zo'u	da	prami	de
For-every	X,	for-every	Y	:	X	loves	Y.

Everything loves everything.

Again, X and Y can represent the same thing, so Example 16.17 (p. 378) does not mean "Everything loves everything else." Furthermore, because the claim is universal, it is about every thing, not merely every person, so we cannot use "everyone" or "everybody" in the translation.

Note that *ro* appears before both *da* and *de*. If *ro* is omitted before either variable, we get a mixed claim, partly existential like those of Section 16.2 (p. 376), partly universal.

Example 16.18

ro	da	de	zo'u	da	viska	de
For-every	X,	there-is-a-Y	:	X	sees	Y.

Everything sees something.

Example 16.19

da	ro	de	zo'u	da	viska	de
There-is-an-X	such-that-for-every	Y	:	X	sees	Y.

Something sees everything.

Example 16.18 (p. 378) and Example 16.19 (p. 378) mean completely different things. Example 16.18 (p. 378) says that for everything, there is something which it sees, not necessarily the same thing seen for every seer. Example 16.19 (p. 378), on the other hand, says that there is a particular thing which can see everything that there is (including itself). Both of these are fairly silly, but they are different kinds of silliness.

There are various possible translations of universal claims in English: sometimes we use "anybody/anything" rather than "everybody/everything". Often it makes no difference which of these is used: when it does make a difference, it is a rather subtle one which is explained in Section 16.8 (p. 384).

16.4 Restricted claims: *da poi*

The universal claims of Section 16.3 (p. 378) are not only false but absurd: there is really very little to be said that is both true and non-trivial about every object whatsoever. Furthermore, we have been glossing over the distinction between "everything" and "everybody" and the other pairs ending in "-thing" and "-body". It is time to bring up the most useful feature of Lojban variables: the ability to restrict their ranges.

In Lojban, a variable *da, de,* or *di* may be followed by a *poi* relative clause in order to restrict the range of things that the variable describes. Relative clauses are described in detail in Chapter 8 (p. 161), but the kind we will need at present consist of *poi* followed by a bridi (often just a selbri) terminated with *ku'o* or *vau* (which can usually be elided). Consider the difference between

Example 16.20

da		*zo'u*	*da*	*viska*	*la*		*djim.*
There-is-an-X	**:**		**X**	**sees**	**that-named**		**Jim.**

Something sees Jim.

and

Example 16.21

da		*poi*		*prenu*		*zo'u*	*da*	*viska*	*la*		*djim.*
There-is-an-X	**which**		**is-a-person**		**:**		**X**	**sees**	**that-named**		**Jim.**

Someone sees Jim.

In Example 16.20 (p. 379), the variable *da* can refer to any object whatever; there are no restrictions on it. In Example 16.21 (p. 379), *da* is restricted by the *poi prenu* relative clause to persons only, and so *da poi prenu* translates as "someone." (The difference between "someone" and "somebody" is a matter of English style, with no real counterpart in Lojban.) If Example 16.21 (p. 379) is true, then Example 16.20 (p. 379) must be true, but not necessarily vice versa.

Universal claims benefit even more from the existence of relative clauses. Consider

Example 16.22

ro		*da*	*zo'u*	*da*	*vasxu*
For-every	**X**		**:**	**X**	**breathes**

Everything breathes

and

Example 16.23

ro		*da*	*poi*		*gerku*		*zo'u*	*da*	*vasxu*
For-every	**X**		**which**		**is-a-dog**		**:**	**X**	**breathes.**

Every dog breathes.
Each dog breathes.
All dogs breathe.

Example 16.22 (p. 379) is a silly falsehood, but Example 16.23 (p. 379) is an important truth (at least if applied in a timeless or potential sense: see Section 10.19 (p. 235)). Note the various colloquial translations "every dog", "each dog", and "all dogs". They all come to the same thing in Lojban, since what is true of every dog is true of all dogs. "All dogs" is treated as an English plural and the others as singular, but Lojban makes no distinction.

If we make an existential claim about dogs rather than a universal one, we get:

Example 16.24

da	poi	gerku	zo'u	da	vasxu
There-is-an-X	which	is-a-dog	:	X	breathes.

Some dog breathes.

16.5 Dropping the prenex

It isn't really necessary for every Lojban bridi involving variables to have a prenex on the front. In fact, none of the examples we've seen so far required prenexes at all! The rule for dropping the prenex is simple: if the variables appear in the same order within the bridi as they did in the prenex, then the prenex is superfluous. However, any *ro* or *poi* appearing in the prenex must be transferred to the first occurrence of the variable in the main part of the bridi. Thus, Example 16.9 (p. 377) becomes just:

Example 16.25

da	viska	mi
There-is-an-X-which	sees	me.

Something sees me.

and Example 16.23 (p. 379) becomes:

Example 16.26

ro	da	poi	gerku	cu	vasxu
For-every	X	which	is-a-dog,		it-breathes.

Every dog breathes.

You might well suppose, then, that the purpose of the prenex is to allow the variables in it to appear in a different order than the bridi order, and that would be correct. Consider

Example 16.27

ro	da	poi	prenu	ku'o	de
For-every	X	which	is-a-person,		there-is-a-Y

poi	gerku	ku'o	zo'u	de	batci	da
which	is-a-dog		:	Y	bites	X.

The prenex of Example 16.27 (p. 380) is like that of Example 16.18 (p. 378) (but with relative clauses): it notes that the following bridi is true of every person with respect to some dog, not necessarily the same dog for each. But in the main bridi part, the *de* appears before the *da*. Therefore, the true translation is

Example 16.28

Every person is bitten by some dog (or other).

If we tried to omit the prenex and move the *ro* and the relative clauses into the main bridi, we would get:

Example 16.29

de	poi	gerku	cu	batci	ro	da	poi	prenu
There-is-a-Y	which	is-a-dog		which-bites	every	X	which	is-a-person

Some dog bites everyone.

which has the structure of Example 16.19 (p. 378): it says that there is a dog (call him Fido) who bites, has bitten, or will bite every person that has ever existed! We can safely rule out Fido's existence, and say that Example 16.29 (p. 380) is false, while agreeing to Example 16.27 (p. 380).

Even so, Example 16.27 (p. 380) is most probably false, since some people never experience dogbite. Examples like 5.3 and 4.4 (might there be some dogs which never have breathed, because they died as embryos?) indicate the danger in Lojban of universal claims even when restricted. In English we are prone to say that "Everyone says" or that "Everybody does" or that "Everything is" when in fact there are obvious counterexamples which we are ignoring for the sake of making a rhetorical point. Such statements are plain falsehoods in Lojban, unless saved by a context (such as tense) which implicitly restricts them.

How can we express Example 16.27 (p. 380) in Lojban without a prenex? Since it is the order in which variables appear that matters, we can say:

Example 16.30

ro	da	poi	prenu		cu	se	batci		de		poi	gerku
Every	X	which	is-a-person				is-bitten-by		some-Y		which	is-a-dog.

using the conversion operator *se* (explained in Section 5.11 (p. 96)) to change the selbri *batci* ("bites") into *se batci* ("is bitten by"). The translation given in Example 16.28 (p. 380) uses the corresponding strategy in English, since English does not have prenexes (except in strained "logician's English"). This implies that a sentence with both a universal and an existential variable can't be freely converted with *se*; one must be careful to preserve the order of the variables.

If a variable occurs more than once, then any *ro* or *poi* decorations are moved only to the first occurrence of the variable when the prenex is dropped. For example,

Example 16.31

di		poi	prenu	zo'u
There-is-a-Z		which	is-a-person	:

ti		xarci		di		di
this-thing		is-a-weapon		for-use-against-Z		by-Z

This is a weapon for someone to use against himself/herself.

(in which *di* is used rather than *da* just for variety) loses its prenex as follows:

Example 16.32

ti		xarci		di	poi	prenu		ku'o	di
This-thing		is-a-weapon-for-use-against		some-Z	which	is-a-person			by-Z.

As the examples in this section show, dropping the prenex makes for terseness of expression often even greater than that of English (Lojban is meant to be an unambiguous language, not necessarily a terse or verbose one), provided the rules are observed.

16.6 Variables with generalized quantifiers

So far, we have seen variables with either nothing in front, or with the cmavo *ro* in front. Now *ro* is a Lojban number, and means "all"; thus *ro prenu* means "all persons", just as *re prenu* means "two persons". In fact, unadorned *da* is also taken to have an implicit number in front of it, namely *su'o*, which means "at least one". Why is this? Consider Example 16.9 (p. 377) again, this time with an explicit *su'o*:

Example 16.33

su'o		da	zo'u	da	viska	mi
For-at-least-one		X	:	X	sees	me.

Something sees me.

From this version of Example 16.9 (p. 377), we understand the speaker's claim to be that of all the things that there are, at least one of them sees him or her. The corresponding universal claim, Example 16.16 (p. 378), says that of all the things that exist, every one of them can see the speaker.

Any other number can be used instead of *ro* or *su'o* to precede a variable. Then we get claims like:

Example 16.34

re		da	zo'u	da	viska	mi
For-two		Xes	:	X	sees	me.

Two things see me.

This means that exactly two things, no more or less, saw the speaker on the relevant occasion. In English, we might take "Two things see me" to mean that at least two things see the speaker, but there might be more; in Lojban, though, that claim would have to be made as:

Example 16.35

su'ore	*da*	*zo'u*	*da*	*viska*	*mi*
For-at-least-two	**Xes**	**:**	**X**	**sees**	**me.**

which would be false if nothing, or only one thing, saw the speaker, but not otherwise. We note the *su'o* here meaning "at least"; *su'o* by itself is short for *su'opa* where *pa* means "one", as is explained in Section 18.9 (p. 424).

The prenex may be removed from Example 16.34 (p. 381) and Example 16.35 (p. 382) as from the others, leading to:

Example 16.36

re	*da*	*viska*	*mi*
Two	**Xes**	**see**	**me.**

and

Example 16.37

su'ore	*da*	*viska*	*mi*
At-least-two	**Xes**	**see**	**me.**

respectively, subject to the rules prescribed in Section 16.5 (p. 380).

Now we can explain the constructions *ro prenu* for "all persons" and *re prenu* for "two persons" which were casually mentioned at the beginning of this Section. In fact, *ro prenu*, a so-called "indefinite description", is shorthand for *ro DA poi prenu*, where "DA" represents a fictitious variable that hasn't been used yet and will not be used in future. (Even if all three of *da*, *de*, and *di* have been used up, it does not matter, for there are ways of getting more variables, discussed in Section 16.14 (p. 395).) So in fact

Example 16.38

re	*prenu*	*cu*	*viska*	*mi*
Two	**persons**		**see**	**me.**

is short for

Example 16.39

re	*da*	*poi*	*prenu*	*cu*	*viska*	*mi*
Two	**Xes**	**which**	**are-persons**		**see**	**me.**

which in turn is short for:

Example 16.40

re	*da*	*poi*	*prenu*	*zo'u*	*da*	*viska*	*mi*
For-two	**Xes**	**which**	**are-persons**	**:**	**X**	**sees**	**me.**

Note that when we move more than one variable to the prenex (along with its attached relative clause), we must make sure that the variables are in the same order in the prenex as in the bridi proper.

16.7 Grouping of quantifiers

Let us consider a sentence containing two quantifier expressions neither of which is *ro* or *su'o* (remembering that *su'o* is implicit where no explicit quantifier is given):

Example 16.41

ci	*gerku*	*cu*	*batci*	*re*	*nanmu*
Three	**dogs**		**bite**	**two**	**men.**

The question raised by Example 16.41 (p. 382) is, does each of the dogs bite the same two men, or is it possible that there are two different men per dog, for six men altogether? If the former interpretation is taken, the number of men involved is fixed at two; but if the latter, then the speaker has to be taken as saying that there might be any number of men between two and six inclusive. Let us transform Example 16.41 (p. 382) step by step as we did with Example 16.38 (p. 382):

Example 16.42

ci	da	poi	gerku	cu	batci	re	de	poi	nanmu
Three	Xes	which	are-dogs		bite	two	Ys	which	are-men.

(Note that we need separate variables *da* and *de*, because of the rule that says each indefinite description gets a variable never used before or since.)

Example 16.43

ci	da	poi	gerku	ku'o	re		de	poi	nanmu	zo'u
For-three	Xes	which	are-dogs	-,	for-two		Ys	which	are-men	:

da	batci	de
X	bites	Y.

Here we see that indeed each of the dogs is said to bite two men, and it might be different men each time; a total of six biting events altogether.

How then are we to express the other interpretation, in which just two men are involved? We cannot just reverse the order of variables in the prenex to

Example 16.44

re	de	poi	nanmu	ku'o	ci		da	poi	gerku	zo'u
For-two	Ys	which	are-men	-,	for-three		Xes	which	are-dogs,	:

da	batci	de
X	bites	Y.

for although we have now limited the number of men to exactly two, we end up with an indeterminate number of dogs, from three to six. The distinction is called a "scope distinction": in Example 16.42 (p. 383), *ci gerku* is said to have wider scope than *re nanmu*, and therefore precedes it in the prenex. In Example 16.44 (p. 383) the reverse is true.

The solution is to use a termset, which is a group of terms either joined by *ce'e* (of selma'o CEhE) between each term, or else surrounded by *nu'i* (of selma'o NUhI) on the front and *nu'u* (of selma'o NUhU) on the rear. Terms (which are either sumti or sumti prefixed by tense or modal tags) that are grouped into a termset are understood to have equal scope:

Example 16.45

	ci	gerku	ce'e	re	nanmu		cu	batci
nu'i	ci	gerku		re	nanmu	[nu'u]	cu	batci
	Three	dogs	[plus]	two	men,			bite.

which picks out two groups, one of three dogs and the other of two men, and says that every one of the dogs bites each of the men. The second Lojban version uses forethought; note that *nu'u* is an elidable terminator, and in this case can be freely elided.

What about descriptors, like *ci lo gerku*, *le nanmu* or *re le ci mlatu*? They too can be grouped in termsets, but usually need not be, except for the *lo* case which functions like the case without a descriptor. Unless an actual quantifier precedes it, *le nanmu* means *ro le nanmu*, as is explained in Section 6.7 (p. 124). Two sumti with *ro* quantifiers are independent of order, so:

Example 16.46

[ro]	le	ci	gerku	cu	batci	[ro]	le	re	nanmu
[All-of]	the	three	dogs		bite	[all-of]	the	two	men.

means that each of the dogs specified bites each of the men specified, for six acts of biting altogether. However, if there is an explicit quantifier before *le* other than *ro*, the problems of this section reappear.

16.8 The problem of "any"

Consider the English sentence

Example 16.47

Anyone who goes to the store, walks across the field.

Using the facilities already discussed, a plausible translation might be

Example 16.48

ro	da	poi	klama	le	zarci	cu	cadzu	le	foldi
All	X	such-that-it	goes-to	the	store		walks-on	the	field.

Everyone who goes to the store walks across the field.

But there is a subtle difference between Example 16.47 (p. 384) and Example 16.48 (p. 384). Example 16.48 (p. 384) tells us that, in fact, there are people who go to the store, and that they walk across the field. A sumti of the type *ro da poi klama* requires that there are things which *klama*: Lojban universal claims always imply the corresponding existential claims as well. Example 16.47 (p. 384), on the other hand, does not require that there are any people who go to the store: it simply states, conditionally, that if there is anyone who goes to the store, he or she walks across the field as well. This conditional form mirrors the true Lojban translation of Example 16.47 (p. 384):

Example 16.49

ro		da	zo'u	da	go		klama		le	zarci
For-every	X	:		X	if-and-only-if		it-is-a-goer-to		the	store

gi	cadzu		le	foldi
	is-a-walker-on		the	field.

Although Example 16.49 (p. 384) is a universal claim as well, its universality only implies that there are objects of some sort or another in the universe of discourse. Because the claim is conditional, nothing is implied about the existence of goers-to-the-store or of walkers-on-the-field, merely that any entity which is one is also the other.

There is another use of "any" in English that is not universal but existential. Consider

Example 16.50

I need any box that is bigger than this one.

Example 16.50 (p. 384) does not at all mean that I need every box bigger than this one, for indeed I do not; I require only one box. But the naive translation

Example 16.51

mi	nitcu	da		poi	tanxe		gi'e	bramau		ti
I	need	some-X		which	is-a-box		and	is-bigger-than		this-one

does not work either, because it asserts that there really is such a box, as the prenex paraphrase demonstrates:

Example 16.52

da		poi	tanxe		gi'e	bramau		ti	zo'u	mi	nitcu	da
There-is-an-X		which	is-a-box		and	is-bigger-than		this	:	I	need	X.

What to do? Well, the x2 place of *nitcu* can be filled with an event as well as an object, and in fact Example 16.51 (p. 384) can also be paraphrased as:

Example 16.53

mi	nitcu	lo	nu		mi	ponse	lo	tanxe
I	need	an	event-of		I	possess	some	box(es)

poi		bramau		ti
which-are		bigger-than		this-one.

Rewritten using variables, Example 16.53 (p. 384) becomes

Example 16.54

mi	nitcu	lo	nu	da		zo'u
I	need	an	event-of	there-being-an-X		such-that:

da	se	ponse		mi
X		is-possessed-by		me

gi'e	tanxe	gi'e	bramau	ti
and	is-a-box	and	is-bigger-than	this-thing.

So we see that a prenex can be attached to a bridi that is within a sentence. By default, a variable always behaves as if it is bound in the prenex which (notionally) is attached to the smallest enclosing bridi, and its scope does not extend beyond that bridi. However, the variable may be placed in an outer prenex explicitly:

Example 16.55

da		poi	tanxe	gi'e	bramau	ti	zo'u
There-is-an-X		which	is-a-box	and	is-bigger-than	this-one	such-that:

mi	nitcu	le	nu	mi	ponse	da
I	need	the	event-of	my	possessing	X.

But what are the implications of Example 16.53 (p. 384) and Example 16.55 (p. 385)? The main difference is that in Example 16.55 (p. 385), the *da* is said to exist in the real world of the outer bridi; but in Example 16.53 (p. 384), the existence is only within the inner bridi, which is a mere event that need not necessarily come to pass. So Example 16.55 (p. 385) means

Example 16.56

There's a box, bigger than this one, that I need

which is what Example 16.52 (p. 384) says, whereas Example 16.53 (p. 384) turns out to be an effective translation of our original Example 16.47 (p. 384). So uses of "any" that aren't universal end up being reflected by variables bound in the prenex of a subordinate bridi.

16.9 Negation boundaries

This section, as well as Section 16.10 (p. 388) through Section 16.12 (p. 392), are in effect a continuation of Chapter 15 (p. 353), introducing features of Lojban negation that require an understanding of prenexes and variables. In the examples below, "there is a Y" and the like must be understood as "there is at least one Y, possibly more".

As explained in Section 15.2 (p. 354), the negation of a bridi is usually accomplished by inserting *na* at the beginning of the selbri:

Example 16.57

mi	na	klama	le	zarci
I	[false]	go-to	the	store.

It is false that I go to the store.
I don't go to the store.

The other form of bridi negation is expressed by using the compound cmavo *naku* in the prenex, which is identified and compounded by the lexer before looking at the sentence grammar. In Lojban grammar, *naku* is then treated like a sumti. In a prenex, *naku* means precisely the same thing as the logician's "it is not the case that" in a similar English context. (Outside of a prenex, *naku* is also grammatically treated as a single entity – the equivalent of a sumti – but does not have this exact meaning; we'll discuss these other situations in Section 16.11 (p. 389).)

To represent a bridi negation using a prenex, remove the *na* from before the selbri and place *naku* at the left end of the prenex. This form is called "external bridi negation", as opposed to "internal bridi negation" using *na*. The prenex version of Example 16.57 (p. 385) is

Example 16.58

naku		zo'u	la	djan.	klama
It-is-not-the-case-that	**:**		**that-named**	**John**	**comes.**

It is false that: John comes.

However, *naku* can appear at other points in the prenex as well. Compare

Example 16.59

naku		de		zo'u	de	zutse
It-is-not-the-case-that:		**for-some-Y**		**:**	**Y**	**sits.**
It-is-false-that:		**for-at-least-one-Y**		**:**	**Y**	**sits.**

It is false that something sits.
Nothing sits.

with

Example 16.60

su'ode		naku		zo'u	de	zutse
For-at-least-one-Y,		**it-is-false-that**	**:**		**Y**	**sits.**

There is something that doesn't sit.

The relative position of negation and quantification terms within a prenex has a drastic effect on meaning. Starting without a negation, we can have:

Example 16.61

roda		su'ode		zo'u		da	prami	de
For-every-X,		**there-is-a-Y,**		**such-that**		**X**	**loves**	**Y.**

Everybody loves at least one thing (each, not necessarily the same thing).

or:

Example 16.62

su'ode		roda		zo'u	da	prami	de
There-is-a-Y,		**such-that-for-each-X**	**:**		**X**	**loves**	**Y.**

There is at least one particular thing that is loved by everybody.

The simplest form of bridi negation to interpret is one where the negation term is at the beginning of the prenex:

Example 16.63

naku		roda		su'ode		zo'u		da	prami	de
It-is-false-that:		**for-every-X,**		**there-is-a-Y,**		**such-that:**		**X**	**loves**	**Y.**

It is false that: everybody loves at least one thing.
(At least) someone doesn't love anything.

the negation of Example 16.61 (p. 386), and

Example 16.64

naku		su'ode		roda		zo'u		da	prami	de
It-is-false-that:		**there-is-a-Y**		**such-that**		**for-each-X**	**:**	**X**		**loves**	**Y.**

It is false that: there is at least one thing that is loved by everybody.
There isn't any one thing that everybody loves.

the negation of Example 16.62 (p. 386).

The rules of formal logic require that, to move a negation boundary within a prenex, you must "invert any quantifier" that the negation boundary passes across. Inverting a quantifier means that any *ro* (all) is changed to *su'o* (at least one) and vice versa. Thus, Example 16.63 (p. 386) and Example 16.64 (p. 386) can be restated as, respectively:

Example 16.65

su'oda	naku	su'ode	zo'u	da	prami	de
For-some-X,	it-is-false-that:	there-is-a-Y	such-that:	X	loves	Y.

There is somebody who doesn't love anything.

and:

Example 16.66

rode	naku	roda	zo'u	da	prami	de
For-every-Y,	it-is-false-that:	for-every-X	:	X	loves	Y.

For each thing, it is not true that everybody loves it.

Another movement of the negation boundary produces:

Example 16.67

su'oda	rode	naku	zo'u	da	prami	de
There-is-an-X	such-that-for-every-Y,	it-is-false-that	:	X	loves	Y.

There is someone who, for each thing, doesn't love that thing.

and

Example 16.68

rode	su'oda	naku	zo'u	da	prami	de
For-every-Y,	there-is-an-X,	such-that-it-is-false-that	:	X	loves	Y.

For each thing there is someone who doesn't love it.

Investigation will show that, indeed, each transformation preserves the meanings of Example 16.63 (p. 386) and Example 16.64 (p. 386).

The quantifier *no* (meaning "zero of") also involves a negation boundary. To transform a bridi containing a variable quantified with *no*, we must first expand it. Consider

Example 16.69

noda	rode	zo'u	da	prami	de
There-is-no-X,	for-every-Y,	such-that	X	loves	Y.

Nobody loves everything.

which is negated by:

Example 16.70

naku	noda	rode	zo'u	da	prami	de
It-is-false-that:	there-is-no-X-that,	for-every-Y	:	X	loves	Y.

It is false that there is nobody who loves everything.

We can simplify Example 16.70 (p. 387) by transforming the prenex. To move the negation phrase within the prenex, we must first expand the *no* quantifier. Thus "for no x" means the same thing as "it is false for some x", and the corresponding Lojban *noda* can be replaced by *naku su'oda*. Making this substitution, we get:

Example 16.71

naku	naku	su'oda
It-is-false-that	it-is-false-that	there-is-some-X-such-that

...rode	zo'u	da	prami	de
for-every-X	:	X	loves	Y

It is false that it is false that: for an X, for every Y: X loves Y.

Adjacent pairs of negation boundaries in the prenex can be dropped, so this means the same as:

Example 16.72

su'oda	rode	zo'u	da	prami	de
There-is-an-X-such-that,	for-every-Y	:	X	loves	Y.

At least one person loves everything.

which is clearly the desired contradiction of Example 16.69 (p. 387).

The interactions between quantifiers and negation mean that you cannot eliminate double negatives that are not adjacent. You must first move the negation phrases so that they are adjacent, inverting any quantifiers they cross, and then the double negative can be eliminated.

16.10 bridi negation and logical connectives

A complete discussion of logical connectives appears in Chapter 14 (p. 317). What is said here is intentionally quite incomplete and makes several oversimplifications.

A logical connective is a cmavo or compound cmavo. In this chapter, we will make use of the logical connectives "and" and "or" (where "or" really means "and/or", "either or both"). The following simplified recipes explain how to make some logical connectives:

To logically connect two Lojban sumti with "and", put them both in the bridi and separate them with the cmavo *e*.

To logically connect two Lojban bridi with "and", replace the regular separator cmavo *i* with the compound cmavo *.ije*.

To logically connect two Lojban sumti with "or", put them both in the bridi and separate them with the cmavo *a*.

To logically connect two Lojban bridi with "or", replace the regular separator cmavo *i* with the compound cmavo *.ija*.

More complex logical connectives also exist; in particular, one may place *na* before *e* or *a*, or between *i* and *je* or *ja*; likewise, one may place *nai* at the end of a connective. Both *na* and *nai* have negative effects on the sumti or bridi being connected. Specifically, *na* negates the first or left-hand sumti or bridi, and *nai* negates the second or right-hand one.

Whenever a logical connective occurs in a sentence, that sentence can be expanded into two sentences by repeating the common terms and joining the sentences by a logical connective beginning with *i*. Thus the following sentence:

Example 16.73

mi	.e	do	klama	ti
I	and	you	come-to	this-here

I and you come here.

can be expanded to:

Example 16.74

mi	klama	ti	.ije	do	klama	ti
I	come-to	this-here	and	you	come-to	this-here

I come here, and, you come here.

The same type of expansion can be performed for any logical connective, with any valid combination of *na* or *nai* attached. No change in meaning occurs under such a transformation.

Clearly, if we know what negation means in the expanded sentence forms, then we know what it means in all of the other forms. But what does negation mean between sentences?

The mystery is easily solved. A negation in a logical expression is identical to the corresponding bridi negation, with the negator placed at the beginning of the prenex. Thus:

Example 16.75

mi	.enai	do	prami	roda
I	**and-not**	**you**	**love**	**everything**

I, and not you, love everything.

expands to:

Example 16.76

mi	prami	roda	.ijenai	do	prami	roda
I	**love**	**everything,**	**and-not,**	**you**	**love**	**everything.**

and then into prenex form as:

Example 16.77

roda	zo'u	mi	prami	da	.ije
For-each-thing	**:**	**I**	**love**	**it,**	**and**

naku	zo'u	do	prami	da
it-is-false-that	**:**	**you**	**love**	**(the-same)-it.**

For each thing: I love it, and it is false that you love (the same) it.

By the rules of predicate logic, the *ro* quantifier on *da* has scope over both sentences. That is, once you've picked a value for *da* for the first sentence, it stays the same for both sentences. (The *da* continues with the same fixed value until a new paragraph or a new prenex resets the meaning.)

Thus the following example has the indicated translation:

Example 16.78

su'oda	zo'u	mi	prami	da
For-at-least-one-thing	**:**	**I**	**love**	**that-thing.**

.ije	naku	zo'u	do	prami	da
And	**it-is-false-that**	**:**	**you**	**love**	**that-(same)-thing.**

There is something that I love that you don't.

If you remember only two rules for prenex manipulation of negations, you won't go wrong:

Within a prenex, whenever you move *naku* past a bound variable (da, de, di, etc.), you must invert the quantifier.

A *na* before the selbri is always transformed into a *naku* at the left-hand end of the prenex, and vice versa.

16.11 Using *naku* outside a prenex

Let us consider the English sentence

Example 16.79

Some children do not go to school.

We cannot express this directly with *na*; the apparently obvious translation

Example 16.80

su'oda	poi	verba
At-least-one-X	**which-are**	**child(ren)**

na	klama	su'ode	poi	ckule
[false]	**go-to**	**at-least-one-Y**	**which-are**	**school(s).**

when converted to the external negation form produces:

Example 16.81

naku	zo'u	su'oda	poi	verba	cu
It-is-false	that	some-which	are	children	

klama	su'ode	poi	ckule
go-to	some-which	are	schools.

All children don't go to some school (not just some children).

Lojban provides a negation form which more closely emulates natural language negation. This involves putting *naku* before the selbri, instead of a *na*. *naku* is clearly a contradictory negation, given its parallel with prenex bridi negation. Using *naku*, Example 16.79 (p. 389) can be expressed as:

Example 16.82

su'oda	poi	verba	naku	klama	su'ode	poi	ckule
Some	which-are	children	don't	go-to	some	which-are	schools.

Some children don't go to a school.

Although it is not technically a sumti, *naku* can be used in most of the places where a sumti may appear. We'll see what this means in a moment.

When you use *naku* within a bridi, you are explicitly creating a negation boundary. As explained in Section 16.9 (p. 385), when a prenex negation boundary expressed by *naku* moves past a quantifier, the quantifier has to be inverted. The same is true for *naku* in the bridi proper. We can move *naku* to any place in the sentence where a sumti can go, inverting any quantifiers that the negation boundary crosses. Thus, the following are equivalent to Example 16.82 (p. 390) (no good English translations exist):

Example 16.83

su'oda	poi	verba	cu	klama	rode	poi	ckule	naku

For some children, for every school, they don't go to it.

Example 16.84

su'oda	poi	verba	cu	klama	naku	su'ode	poi	ckule

Some children don't go to (some) school(s).

Example 16.85

naku	roda	poi	verba	cu	klama	su'ode	poi	ckule

It is false that all children go to some school(s).

In Example 16.83 (p. 390), we moved the negation boundary rightward across the quantifier of *de*, forcing us to invert it. In Example 16.85 (p. 390) we moved the negation boundary across the quantifier of *da*, forcing us to invert it instead. Example 16.84 (p. 390) merely switched the selbri and the negation boundary, with no effect on the quantifiers.

The same rules apply if you rearrange the sentence so that the quantifier crosses an otherwise fixed negation. You can't just convert the selbri of Example 16.82 (p. 390) and rearrange the sumti to produce

Example 16.86

su'ode	poi	ckule	ku'o	naku	se	klama	roda	poi	verba

Some schools aren't gone-to-by every child.

or rather, Example 16.86 (p. 390) means something completely different from Example 16.82 (p. 390). Conversion with *se* under *naku* negation is not symmetric; not all sumti are treated identically, and some sumti are not invariant under conversion. Thus, internal negation with *naku* is considered an advanced technique, used to achieve stylistic compatibility with natural languages.

It isn't always easy to see which quantifiers have to be inverted in a sentence. Example 16.82 (p. 390) is identical in meaning to:

16.11 Using naku outside a prenex

Example 16.87

su'o	verba	naku	klama	su'o	ckule
Some	**children**	**don't**	**go-to**	**some**	**school.**

but in Example 16.87 (p. 391), the bound variables *da* and *de* have been hidden.

It is trivial to export an internal bridi negation expressed with *na* to the prenex, as we saw in Section 16.9 (p. 385); you just move it to the left end of the prenex. In comparison, it is non-trivial to export a *naku* to the prenex because of the quantifiers. The rules for exporting *naku* require that you export all of the quantified variables (implicit or explicit) along with *naku*, and you must export them from left to right, in the same order that they appear in the sentence. Thus Example 16.82 (p. 390) goes into prenex form as:

Example 16.88

su'oda	poi	verba	ku'o	naku		
For-some-X	**which**	**is-a-child,**		**it-is-not-the-case-that**		

su'ode	poi	ckule	zo'u	da	klama	de
there-is-a-Y	**which**	**is-a-school**	**such-that:**	**X**	**goes**	**to** Y.

We can now move the *naku* to the left end of the prenex, getting a contradictory negation that can be expressed with *na*:

Example 16.89

naku	roda	poi	verba		
It-is-not-the-case-that	**for-all-X's**	**which-are**	**children,**		

su'ode	poi	ckule	zo'u	da	klama	de
there-is-a-Y	**which-is**	**a-school**	**such-that:**	**X**	**goes-to**	Y.

from which we can restore the quantified variables to the sentence, giving:

Example 16.90

naku	zo'u	roda	poi	verba	cu	klama	su'ode	poi	ckule

It is not the case that all children go to some school.

or more briefly

Example 16.91

ro	verba	cu	na	klama	su'o	ckule
All	**children**		**[false]**	**go-to**	**some**	**school(s).**

As noted in Section 16.5 (p. 380), a sentence with two different quantified variables, such as Example 16.91 (p. 391), cannot always be converted with *se* without first exporting the quantified variables. When the variables have been exported, the sentence proper can be converted, but the quantifier order in the prenex must remain unchanged:

Example 16.92

roda	poi	verba	su'ode			
for-all-X's	**which-are**	**children,**	**there-is-a-Y**			

poi	ckule	zo'u	de	na	se	klama	da
which	**is-a-school**	**such-that:**	**Y**			**is-gone-to-by**	X.

While you can't freely convert with *se* when you have two quantified variables in a sentence, you can still freely move sumti to either side of the selbri, as long as the order isn't changed. If you use *na* negation in such a sentence, nothing special need be done. If you use *naku* negation, then quantified variables that cross the negation boundary must be inverted.

Clearly, if all of Lojban negation was built on *naku* negation instead of *na* negation, logical manipulation in Lojban would be as difficult as in natural languages. In Section 16.12 (p. 392), for example, we'll discuss DeMorgan's Law, which must be used whenever a sumti with a logical connection is moved across a negation boundary.

Since *naku* has the grammar of a sumti, it can be placed almost anywhere a sumti can go, including *be* and *bei* clauses; it isn't clear what these mean, and we recommend avoiding such constructs.

You can put multiple *naku* compounds in a sentence, each forming a separate negation boundary. Two adjacent *naku* compounds in a bridi are a double negative and cancel out:

Example 16.93

> *mi naku naku le zarci cu klama*

Other expressions using two *naku* compounds may or may not cancel out. If there is no quantified variable between them, then the *naku* compounds cancel.

Negation with internal *naku* is clumsy and non-intuitive for logical manipulations, but then, so are the natural language features it is emulating.

16.12 Logical Connectives and DeMorgan's Law

DeMorgan's Law states that when a logical connective between terms falls within a negation, then expanding the negation requires a change in the connective. Thus (where "p" and "q" stand for terms or sentences) "not (p or q)" is identical to "not p and not q", and "not (p and q)" is identical to "not p or not q". The corresponding changes for the other two basic Lojban connectives are: "not (p equivalent to q)" is identical to "not p exclusive-or not q", and "not (p whether-or-not q)" is identical to both "not p whether-or-not q" and "not p whether-or-not not q". In any Lojban sentence having one of the basic connectives, you can substitute in either direction from these identities. (These basic connectives are explained in Chapter 14 (p. 317).)

The effects of DeMorgan's Law on the logical connectives made by modifying the basic connectives with *nai, na* and *se* can be derived directly from these rules; modify the basic connective for DeMorgan's Law by substituting from the above identities, and then, apply each *nai, na* and *se* modifier of the original connectives. Cancel any double negatives that result.

When do we apply DeMorgan's Law? Whenever we wish to "distribute" a negation over a logical connective; and, for internal *naku* negation, whenever a logical connective moves in to, or out of, the scope of a negation – when it crosses a negation boundary.

Let us apply DeMorgan's Law to some sample sentences. These sentences make use of forethought logical connectives, which are explained in Section 14.5 (p. 322). It suffices to know that *ga* and *gi*, used before each of a pair of sumti or bridi, mean "either" and "or" respectively, and that *ge* and *gi* used similarly mean "both" and "and". Furthermore, *ga, ge,* and *gi* can all be suffixed with *nai* to negate the bridi or sumti that follows.

We have defined *na* and *naku zo'u* as, respectively, internal and external bridi negation. These forms being identical, the negation boundary always remains at the left end of the prenex. Thus, exporting or importing negation between external and internal bridi negation forms never requires DeMorgan's Law to be applied. Example 16.94 (p. 392) and Example 16.95 (p. 392) are exactly equivalent:

Example 16.94

la	*djan.*	*na*	*klama*	*ga*
that-named	**John**	**[false]**	**goes-to**	**either**

la	*paris.*	*gi*	*la*	*rom.*
that-named	**Paris**	**or**	**that-named**	**Rome.**

Example 16.95

naku	*zo'u*	*la*	*djan.*	*klama*
It-is-false	**that:**	**that-named**	**John**	**goes-to**

ga	*la*	*paris.*	*gi*	*la*	*rom.*
either	**that-named**	**Paris**	**or**	**that-named**	**Rome.**

It is not an acceptable logical manipulation to move a negator from the bridi level to one or more sumti. However, Example 16.94 (p. 392) and related examples are not sumti negations, but rather expand to form two logically connected sentences. In such a situation, DeMorgan's Law must be applied. For instance, Example 16.95 (p. 392) expands to:

Example 16.96

	ge	la	djan.	la	paris.	na	klama
[It-is-true-that]	both	that-named	John,	to-that-named	Paris,	[false]	goes,

gi	la	djan.	la	rom.	na	klama
and	that-named	John,	to-that-named	Rome,	[false]	goes.

The *ga* and *gi*, meaning "either-or", have become *ge* and *gi*, meaning "both-and", as a consequence of moving the negators into the individual bridi.

Here is another example of DeMorgan's Law in action, involving bridi-tail logical connection (explained in Section 14.9 (p. 328)):

Example 16.97

la	djein.	le	zarci	na	ge	dzukla	gi	bajrykla
that-named	Jane	to-the	market	[false]	both	walks	and	runs.

Example 16.98

la	djein.	le	zarci	ganai		dzukla	ginai		bajrykla
that-named	Jane	to-the	market	either-([false]		walks)	or-([false]		runs.
that-named	Jane	to-the	market	if		walks	then-([false]		runs).

(Placing *le zarci* before the selbri makes sure that it is properly associated with both parts of the logical connection. Otherwise, it is easy to erroneously leave it off one of the two sentences.)

It is wise, before freely doing transformations such as the one from Example 16.97 (p. 393) to Example 16.98 (p. 393), that you become familiar with expanding logical connectives to separate sentences, transforming the sentences, and then recondensing. Thus, you would prove the transformation correct by the following steps. By moving its *na* to the beginning of the prenex as a *naku*, Example 16.97 (p. 393) becomes:

Example 16.99

naku	zo'u	la	djein.	le	zarci
It-is-false-that	:	that-named	Jane	to-the	market

ge	dzukla	gi	bajrykla
(both	walks	and	runs).

And by dividing the bridi with logically connected selbri into two bridi,

Example 16.100

naku	zo'u	ge	la	djein.	le	zarci	cu	dzukla
It-is-false	that:	both	(that-named	Jane	to-the	market	cu	walks)

gi	la	djein.	le	zarci	cu	bajrykla
and	(that-named	Jane	to-the	market		runs).

is the result.

At this expanded level, we apply DeMorgan's Law to distribute the negation in the prenex across both sentences, to get

Example 16.101

ga	la	djein.	le	zarci	na	dzukla
Either	that-named	Jane	to-the	market	[false]	walks,

gi	la	djein.	le	zarci	na	bajrykla
or	that-named	Jane	to-the	market	[false]	runs.

which is the same as

Example 16.102

ganai	*la*	*djein.*	*le*	*zarci*	*cu*	*dzukla*
If	that-named	Jane	to-the	market		walks,

ginai		*la*		*djein.*	*le*	*zarci*	*cu*	*bajrykla*
then-([false]		that-named		Jane	to-the	market		runs).

If Jane walks to the market, then she doesn't run.

which then condenses down to Example 16.98 (p. 393).

DeMorgan's Law must also be applied to internal *naku* negations:

Example 16.103

ga	*la*	*paris.*	*gi*	*la*	*rom.*
(Either	that-named	Paris	or	that-named	Rome)

naku	*se*	*klama*	*la*	*djan.*
is-not	gone-to-by	that-named	John.	

Example 16.104

la	*djan.*	*naku*	*klama*	*ge*
that-named	John	doesn't	go-to	both

la	*paris.*	*gi*	*la*	*rom.*
that-named	Paris	and	that-named	Rome.

That Example 16.103 (p. 394) and Example 16.104 (p. 394) mean the same should become evident by studying the English. It is a good exercise to work through the Lojban and prove that they are the same.

16.13 selbri variables

In addition to the variables *da*, *de*, and *di* that we have seen so far, which function as sumti and belong to selma'o KOhA, there are three corresponding variables *bu'a*, *bu'e*, and *bu'i* which function as selbri and belong to selma'o GOhA. These new variables allow existential or universal claims which are about the relationships between objects rather than the objects themselves. We will start with the usual silly examples; the literal translation will represent *bu'a*, *bu'e* and *bu'i* with F, G, and H respectively.

Example 16.105

su'o	*bu'a*	*zo'u*	*la*	*djim.*
For-at-least-one	relationship-F	:	that-named	Jim

bu'a	*la*	*djan.*
stands-in-relationship-F	to-that-named	John.

There's some relationship between Jim and John.

The translations of Example 16.105 (p. 394) show how unidiomatic selbri variables are in English; Lojban sentences like Example 16.105 (p. 394) need to be totally reworded in English. Furthermore, when a selbri variable appears in the prenex, it is necessary to precede it with a quantifier such as *su'o*; it is ungrammatical to just say *bu'a zo'u*. This rule is necessary because only sumti can appear in the prenex, and *su'o bu'a* is technically a sumti – in fact, it is an indefinite description like *re nanmu*, since *bu'a* is grammatically equivalent to a brivla like *nanmu*. However, indefinite descriptions involving the bu'a-series cannot be imported from the prenex.

When the prenex is omitted, the preceding number has to be omitted too:

Example 16.106

la	*djim.*	*bu'a*	*la*	*djan.*
that-named	Jim	stands-in-at-least-one-relationship	to-that-named	John.

As a result, if the number before the variable is anything but *su'o*, the prenex is required:

Example 16.107

ro	bu'a	zo'u	la	djim.
For-every	relationship-F	:	that-named	Jim

bu'a		la	djan.
stands-in-relationship-F		to-that-named	John.

Every relationship exists between Jim and John.

Example 16.105 (p. 394) and Example 16.106 (p. 394) are almost certainly true: Jim and John might be brothers, or might live in the same city, or at least have the property of being jointly human. Example 16.107 (p. 395) is palpably false, however; if Jim and John were related by every possible relationship, then they would have to be both brothers and father-and-son, which is impossible.

16.14 A few notes on variables

A variable may have a quantifier placed in front of it even though it has already been quantified explicitly or implicitly by a previous appearance, as in:

Example 16.108

ci	da	poi	mlatu	cu	blabi	.ije	re	da	cu	barda
Three	Xs	which-are	cats		are-white,	and	two	Xs		are-big.

What does Example 16.108 (p. 395) mean? The appearance of *ci da* quantifies *da* as referring to three things, which are restricted by the relative clause to be cats. When *re da* appears later, it refers to two of those three things – there is no saying which ones. Further uses of *da* alone, if there were any, would refer once more to the three cats, so the requantification of *da* is purely local.

In general, the scope of a prenex that precedes a sentence extends to following sentences that are joined by ijeks (explained in Section 14.4 (p. 320)) such as the *.ije* in Example 16.108 (p. 395). Theoretically, a bare *i* terminates the scope of the prenex. Informally, however, variables may persist for a while even after an *i*, as if it were an *.ije*. Prenexes that precede embedded bridi such as relative clauses and abstractions extend only to the end of the clause, as explained in Section 16.8 (p. 384). A prenex preceding *tu'e...tu'u* long-scope brackets persists until the *tu'u*, which may be many sentences or even paragraphs later.

If the variables *da*, *de*, and *di* (or the selbri variables *bu'a*, *bu'e*, and *bu'i*) are insufficient in number for handling a particular problem, the Lojban approach is to add a subscript to any of them. Each possible different combination of a subscript and a variable cmavo counts as a distinct variable in Lojban. Subscripts are explained in full in Section 19.6 (p. 453), but in general consist of the cmavo *xi* (of selma'o XI) followed by a number, one or more lerfu words forming a single string, or a general mathematical expression enclosed in parentheses.

A quantifier can be prefixed to a variable that has already been bound either in a prenex or earlier in the bridi, thus:

Example 16.109

ci	da	poi	prenu	cu	se ralju	pa	da
Three	Xs	which	are-persons		are-led-by	one-of	X

Three people are led by one of them.

The *pa da* in Example 16.109 (p. 395) does not specify the number of things to which *da* refers, as the preceding *ci da* does. Instead, it selects one of them for use in this sumti only. The number of referents of *da* remains three, but a single one (there is no way of knowing which one) is selected to be the leader.

16.15 Conclusion

This chapter is incomplete. There are many more aspects of logic that I neither fully understand nor feel competent to explain, neither in abstract nor in their Lojban realization. Lojban was designed to be a language that makes predicate logic speakable, and achieving that goal completely will need to wait for someone who understands both logic and Lojban better than I do. I can only hope to have pointed out the areas that are well-understood (and by implication, those that are not).

Chapter 17
As Easy As A-B-C? The Lojban Letteral System And Its Uses

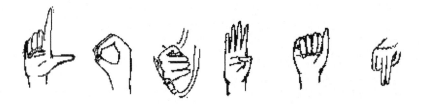

zai xanlerfu bu ly .obu jy by .abu ny.

17.1 What's a letteral, anyway?

James Cooke Brown, the founder of the Loglan Project, coined the word "letteral" (by analogy with "numeral") to mean a letter of the alphabet, such as "f" or "z". A typical example of its use might be

Example 17.1
> There are fourteen occurrences of the letteral "e" in this sentence.

(Don't forget the one within quotation marks.) Using the word "letteral" avoids confusion with "letter", the kind you write to someone. Not surprisingly, there is a Lojban gismu for "letteral", namely _lerfu_, and this word will be used in the rest of this chapter.

Lojban uses the Latin alphabet, just as English does, right? Then why is there a need for a chapter like this? After all, everyone who can read it already knows the alphabet. The answer is twofold:

First, in English there are a set of words that correspond to and represent the English lerfu. These words are rarely written down in English and have no standard spellings, but if you pronounce the English alphabet to yourself you will hear them: ay, bee, cee, dee ... . They are used in spelling out words and in pronouncing most acronyms. The Lojban equivalents of these words are standardized and must be documented somehow.

Second, English has names only for the lerfu used in writing English. (There are also English names for Greek and Hebrew lerfu: English-speakers usually refer to the Greek lerfu conventionally spelled "phi" as "fye", whereas "fee" would more nearly represent the name used by Greek-speakers. Still, not all English-speakers know these English names.) Lojban, in order to be culturally neutral, needs a

397

more comprehensive system that can handle, at least potentially, all of the world's alphabets and other writing systems.

Letterals have several uses in Lojban: in forming acronyms and abbreviations, as mathematical symbols, and as pro-sumti – the equivalent of English pronouns.

In earlier writings about Lojban, there has been a tendency to use the word *lerfu* for both the letterals themselves and for the Lojban words which represent them. In this chapter, that tendency will be ruthlessly suppressed, and the term "lerfu word" will invariably be used for the latter. The Lojban equivalent would be *lerfu valsi* or *lervla*.

17.2 A to Z in Lojban, plus one

The first requirement of a system of lerfu words for any language is that they must represent the lerfu used to write the language. The lerfu words for English are a motley crew: the relationship between "doubleyou" and "w" is strictly historical in nature; "aitch" represents "h" but has no clear relationship to it at all; and "z" has two distinct lerfu words, "zee" and "zed", depending on the dialect of English in question.

All of Lojban's basic lerfu words are made by one of three rules:

- to get a lerfu word for a vowel, add *bu*;
- to get a lerfu word for a consonant, add *y*;
- the lerfu word for ' is *.y'y*.

Therefore, the following table represents the basic Lojban alphabet:

'	a	b	c	d	e
.y'y.	.abu	by.	cy.	dy.	.ebu
f	g	i	j	k	l
fy.	gy.	.ibu	jy.	ky.	ly.
m	n	o	p	r	s
my.	ny.	.obu	py.	ry.	sy.
t	u	v	x	y	z
ty.	.ubu	vy.	xy.	.ybu	zy.

There are several things to note about this table. The consonant lerfu words are a single syllable, whereas the vowel and ' lerfu words are two syllables and must be preceded by pause (since they all begin with a vowel). Another fact, not evident from the table but important nonetheless, is that *by* and its like are single cmavo of selma'o BY, as is *.y'y*. The vowel lerfu words, on the other hand, are compound cmavo, made from a single vowel cmavo plus the cmavo *bu* (which belongs to its own selma'o, BU). All of the vowel cmavo have other meanings in Lojban (logical connectives, sentence separator, hesitation noise), but those meanings are irrelevant when *bu* follows.

Here are some illustrations of common Lojban words spelled out using the alphabet above:

Example 17.2

ty.	.abu	ny.	ry.	.ubu
t	a	n	r	u

Example 17.3

ky.	.obu	.y'y.	.abu
k	o	'	a

Spelling out words is less useful in Lojban than in English, for two reasons: Lojban spelling is phonemic, so there can be no real dispute about how a word is spelled; and the Lojban lerfu words sound more alike than the English ones do, since they are made up systematically. The English words "fail" and "vale" sound similar, but just hearing the first lerfu word of either, namely "eff" or "vee", is enough to discriminate easily between them – and even if the first lerfu word were somehow confused, neither "vail" nor "fale" is a word of ordinary English, so the rest of the spelling determines which word is meant. Still, the capability of spelling out words does exist in Lojban.

Note that the lerfu words ending in *y* were written (in Example 17.2 (p. 398) and Example 17.3 (p. 398)) with pauses after them. It is not strictly necessary to pause after such lerfu words, but failure to do so can in some cases lead to ambiguities:

Example 17.4

mi	*cy.*	*claxu*
I	lerfu-"c"	without

I am without (whatever is referred to by) the letter "c".

without a pause after *cy* would be interpreted as:

Example 17.5

micyclaxu
(Observative:)-doctor-without

Something unspecified is without a doctor.

A safe guideline is to pause after any cmavo ending in *y* unless the next word is also a cmavo ending in *y*. The safest and easiest guideline is to pause after all of them.

17.3 Upper and lower cases

Lojban doesn't use lower-case (small) letters and upper-case (capital) letters in the same way that English does; sentences do not begin with an upper-case letter, nor do names. However, upper-case letters are used in Lojban to mark irregular stress within names, thus:

Example 17.6

.iVAN.

the name "Ivan" in Russian/Slavic pronunciation.

It would require far too many cmavo to assign one for each upper-case and one for each lower-case lerfu, so instead we have two special cmavo *ga'e* and *to'a* representing upper case and lower case respectively. They belong to the same selma'o as the basic lerfu words, namely BY, and they may be freely interspersed with them.

The effect of *ga'e* is to change the interpretation of all lerfu words following it to be the upper-case version of the lerfu. An occurrence of *to'a* causes the interpretation to revert to lower case. Thus, *ga'e* *.abu* means not "a" but "A", and Ivan's name may be spelled out thus:

Example 17.7

.ibu	*ga'e*	*vy.*	*.abu*	*ny.*	*to'a*
i	[upper]	V	A	N	[lower]

The cmavo and compound cmavo of this type will be called "shift words".

How long does a shift word last? Theoretically, until the next shift word that contradicts it or until the end of text. In practice, it is common to presume that a shift word is only in effect until the next word other than a lerfu word is found.

It is often convenient to shift just a single letter to upper case. The cmavo *tau*, of selma'o LAU, is useful for the purpose. A LAU cmavo must always be immediately followed by a BY cmavo or its equivalent: the combination is grammatically equivalent to a single BY. (See Section 17.14 (p. 409) for details.)

A likely use of *tau* is in the internationally standardized symbols for the chemical elements. Each element is represented using either a single upper-case lerfu or one upper-case lerfu followed by one lower-case lerfu:

Example 17.8

tau	*sy.*
[single-shift]	S

S (chemical symbol for sulfur)

Example 17.9

tau	sy.	.ibu
[single-shift]	S	i

Si (chemical symbol for silicon)

If a shift to upper-case is in effect when *tau* appears, it shifts the next lerfu word only to lower case, reversing its usual effect.

17.4 The universal *bu*

So far we have seen *bu* only as a suffix to vowel cmavo to produce vowel lerfu words. Originally, this was the only use of *bu*. In developing the lerfu word system, however, it proved to be useful to allow *bu* to be attached to any word whatsoever, in order to allow arbitrary extensions of the basic lerfu word set.

Formally, *bu* may be attached to any single Lojban word. Compound cmavo do not count as words for this purpose. The special cmavo *ba'e*, *za'e*, *zei*, *zo*, *zoi*, *la'o*, *lo'u*, *si*, *sa*, *su*, and *fa'o* may not have *bu* attached, because they are interpreted before *bu* detection is done; in particular,

Example 17.10

zo	bu
the-word	"bu"

the word "bu"

is needed when discussing *bu* in Lojban. It is also illegal to attach *bu* to itself, but more than one *bu* may be attached to a word; thus *.abubu* is legal, if ugly. (Its meaning is not defined, but it is presumably different from *.abu*.) It does not matter if the word is a cmavo, a cmene, or a brivla. All such words suffixed by *bu* are treated grammatically as if they were cmavo belonging to selma'o BY. However, if the word is a cmene it is always necessary to precede and follow it by a pause, because otherwise the cmene may absorb preceding or following words.

The ability to attach *bu* to words has been used primarily to make names for various logograms and other unusual characters. For example, the Lojban name for the "happy face" is *.uibu*, based on the attitudinal *.ui* that means "happiness". Likewise, the "smiley face", written ":-)" and used on computer networks to indicate humor, is called *zo'obu* The existence of these names does not mean that you should insert *.uibu* into running Lojban text to indicate that you are happy, or *zo'obu* when something is funny; instead, use the appropriate attitudinal directly.

Likewise, *joibu* represents the ampersand character, "&", based on the cmavo *joi* meaning "mixed and". Many more such lerfu words will probably be invented in future.

The . and , characters used in Lojbanic writing to represent pause and syllable break respectively have been assigned the lerfu words *denpa bu* (literally, "pause bu") and *slaka bu* (literally, "syllable bu"). The written space is mandatory here, because *denpa* and *slaka* are normal gismu with normal stress: *denpabu* would be a fu'ivla (word borrowed from another language into Lojban) stressed *denPAbu*. No pause is required between *denpa* (or *slaka*) and *bu*, though.

17.5 Alien alphabets

As stated in Section 17.1 (p. 397), Lojban's goal of cultural neutrality demands a standard set of lerfu words for the lerfu of as many other writing systems as possible. When we meet these lerfu in written text (particularly, though not exclusively, mathematical text), we need a standard Lojbanic way to pronounce them.

There are certainly hundreds of alphabets and other writing systems in use around the world, and it is probably an unachievable goal to create a single system which can express all of them, but if perfection is not demanded, a usable system can be created from the raw material which Lojban provides.

One possibility would be to use the lerfu word associated with the language itself, Lojbanized and with *bu* added. Indeed, an isolated Greek "alpha" in running Lojban text is most easily handled by calling it *.alfas. bu*. Here the Greek lerfu word has been made into a Lojbanized name by adding *s* and then into a Lojban lerfu word by adding *bu*. Note that the pause after *.alfas.* is still needed.

Likewise, the easiest way to handle the Latin letters "h", "q", and "w" that are not used in Lojban is by a consonant lerfu word with *bu* attached. The following assignments have been made:

.y'y.bu	h
ky.bu	q
vy.bu	w

As an example, the English word "quack" would be spelled in Lojban thus:

Example 17.11

ky.bu	*.ubu*	*.abu*	*cy.*	*ky.*
q	**u**	**a**	**c**	**k**

Note that the fact that the letter "c" in this word has nothing to do with the sound of the Lojban letter *c* is irrelevant; we are spelling an English word and English rules control the choice of letters, but we are speaking Lojban and Lojban rules control the pronunciations of those letters.

A few more possibilities for Latin-alphabet letters used in languages other than English:

ty.bu	þ (thorn)
dy.bu	ð (edh)

However, this system is not ideal for all purposes. For one thing, it is verbose. The native lerfu words are often quite long, and with *bu* added they become even longer: the worst-case Greek lerfu word would be *.Omikron. bu*, with four syllables and two mandatory pauses. In addition, alphabets that are used by many languages have separate sets of lerfu words for each language, and which set is Lojban to choose?

The alternative plan, therefore, is to use a shift word similar to those introduced in Section 17.3 (p. 399). After the appearance of such a shift word, the regular lerfu words are re-interpreted to represent the lerfu of the alphabet now in use. After a shift to the Greek alphabet, for example, the lerfu word *ty* would represent not Latin "t" but Greek "tau". Why "tau"? Because it is, in some sense, the closest counterpart of "t" within the Greek lerfu system. In principle it would be all right to map *ty.* to "phi" or even "omega", but such an arbitrary relationship would be extremely hard to remember.

Where no obvious closest counterpart exists, some more or less arbitrary choice must be made. Some alien lerfu may simply not have any shifted equivalent, forcing the speaker to fall back on a *bu* form. Since a *bu* form may mean different things in different alphabets, it is safest to employ a shift word even when *bu* forms are in use.

Shifts for several alphabets have been assigned cmavo of selma'o BY:

lo'a	Latin/Roman/Lojban alphabet
ge'o	Greek alphabet
je'o	Hebrew alphabet
jo'o	Arabic alphabet
ru'o	Cyrillic alphabet

The cmavo *zai* (of selma'o LAU) is used to create shift words to still other alphabets. The BY word which must follow any LAU cmavo would typically be a name representing the alphabet with *bu* suffixed:

Example 17.12

> *zai .devanagar. bu*

> Devanagari (Hindi) alphabet

Example 17.13

> *zai .katakan. bu*

> Japanese katakana syllabary

Example 17.14

  zai .xiragan. bu

  Japanese hiragana syllabary

Unlike the cmavo above, these shift words have not been standardized and probably will not be until someone actually has a need for them. (Note the . characters marking leading and following pauses.)

In addition, there may be multiple visible representations within a single alphabet for a given letter: roman vs. italics, handwriting vs. print, Bodoni vs. Helvetica. These traditional "font and face" distinctions are also represented by shift words, indicated with the cmavo *ce'a* (of selma'o LAU) and a following BY word:

Example 17.15

  ce'a .xelveticas. bu

  Helvetica font

Example 17.16

  ce'a .xancisk. bu

  handwriting

Example 17.17

  ce'a .pavrel. bu

  12-point font size

The cmavo *na'a* (of selma'o BY) is a universal shift-word cancel: it returns the interpretation of lerfu words to the default of lower-case Lojban with no specific font. It is more general than *lo'a*, which changes the alphabet only, potentially leaving font and case shifts in place.

Several sections at the end of this chapter contain tables of proposed lerfu word assignments for various languages.

17.6 Accent marks and compound lerfu words

Many languages that make use of the Latin alphabet add special marks to some of the lerfu they use. French, for example, uses three accent marks above vowels, called (in English) "acute", "grave", and "circumflex". Likewise, German uses a mark called "umlaut"; a mark which looks the same is also used in French, but with a different name and meaning.

These marks may be considered lerfu, and each has a corresponding lerfu word in Lojban. So far, no problem. But the marks appear over lerfu, whereas the words must be spoken (or written) either before or after the lerfu word representing the basic lerfu. Typewriters (for mechanical reasons) and the computer programs that emulate them usually require their users to type the accent mark before the basic lerfu, whereas in speech the accent mark is often pronounced afterwards (for example, in German "a umlaut" is preferred to "umlaut a").

Lojban cannot settle this question by fiat. Either it must be left up to default interpretation depending on the language in question, or the lerfu-word compounding cmavo *tei* (of selma'o TEI) and *foi* (of selma'o FOI) must be used. These cmavo are always used in pairs; any number of lerfu words may appear between them, and the whole is treated as a single compound lerfu word. The French word "été", with acute accent marks on both "e" lerfu, could be spelled as:

Example 17.18

tei	*.ebu*	*.akut.bu*	*foi*	ty.	*tei*	*.akut.bu*	*.ebu*	*foi*
(	e	acute	)	t	(	acute	e	)

and it does not matter whether *akut. bu* appears before or after *.ebu*; the *tei...foi* grouping guarantees that the acute accent is associated with the correct lerfu. Of course, the level of precision represented by Example 17.18 (p. 402) would rarely be required: it might be needed by a Lojban-speaker when spelling out a French word for exact transcription by another Lojban-speaker who did not know French.

This system breaks down in languages which use more than one accent mark on a single lerfu; some other convention must be used for showing which accent marks are written where in that case. The obvious convention is to represent the mark nearest the basic lerfu by the lerfu word closest to the word representing the basic lerfu. Any remaining ambiguities must be resolved by further conventions not yet established.

Some languages, like Swedish and Finnish, consider certain accented lerfu to be completely distinct from their unaccented equivalents, but Lojban does not make a formal distinction, since the printed characters look the same whether they are reckoned as separate letters or not. In addition, some languages consider certain 2-letter combinations (like "ll" and "ch" in Spanish) to be letters; this may be represented by enclosing the combination in *tei...foi*.

In addition, when discussing a specific language, it is permissible to make up new lerfu words, as long as they are either explained locally or well understood from context: thus Spanish "ll" or Croatian "lj" could be called *.ibu*, but that usage would not necessarily be universally understood.

Section 17.19 (p. 411) contains a table of proposed lerfu words for some common accent marks.

17.7 Punctuation marks

Lojban does not have punctuation marks as such: the denpa bu and the slaka bu are really a part of the alphabet. Other languages, however, use punctuation marks extensively. As yet, Lojban does not have any words for these punctuation marks, but a mechanism exists for devising them: the cmavo *lau* of selma'o LAU. *lau* must always be followed by a BY word; the interpretation of the BY word is changed from a lerfu to a punctuation mark. Typically, this BY word would be a name or brivla with a *bu* suffix.

Why is *lau* necessary at all? Why not just use a *bu*-marked word and announce that it is always to be interpreted as a punctuation mark? Primarily to avoid ambiguity. The *bu* mechanism is extremely open-ended, and it is easy for Lojban users to make up *bu* words without bothering to explain what they mean. Using the *lau* cmavo flags at least the most important of such nonce lerfu words as having a special function: punctuation. (Exactly the same argument applies to the use of *zai* to signal an alphabet shift or *ce'a* to signal a font shift.)

Since different alphabets require different punctuation marks, the interpretation of a *lau*-marked lerfu word is affected by the current alphabet shift and the current font shift.

17.8 What about Chinese characters?

Chinese characters ("han [4] zi [4]" in Chinese, *kanji* in Japanese) represent an entirely different approach to writing from alphabets or syllabaries. (A syllabary, such as Japanese hiragana or Amharic writing, has one lerfu for each syllable of the spoken language.) Very roughly, Chinese characters represent single elements of meaning; also very roughly, they represent single syllables of spoken Chinese. There is in principle no limit to the number of Chinese characters that can exist, and many thousands are in regular use.

It is hopeless for Lojban, with its limited lerfu and shift words, to create an alphabet which will match this diversity. However, there are various possible ways around the problem.

First, both Chinese and Japanese have standard Latin-alphabet representations, known as "pinyin" for Chinese and "romaji" for Japanese, and these can be used. Thus, the word "han[4]zi[4]" is conventionally written with two characters, but it may be spelled out as:

Example 17.19

.y'y.bu	.abu	ny.	vo	zy.	.ibu	vo
h	a	n	4	z	i	4

The cmavo *vo* is the Lojban digit "4". It is grammatical to intersperse digits (of selma'o PA) into a string of lerfu words; as long as the first cmavo is a lerfu word, the whole will be interpreted as a string of lerfu words. In Chinese, the digits can be used to represent tones. Pinyin is more usually written using accent marks, the mechanism for which was explained in Section 17.6 (p. 402).

The Japanese company named "Mitsubishi" in English is spelled the same way in romaji, and could be spelled out in Lojban thus:

Example 17.20

my.	.ibu	ty.	sy.	.ubu	by.	.ibu	sy.	.y'y.bu	.ibu
m	**i**	**t**	**s**	**u**	**b**	**i**	**s**	**h**	**i**

Alternatively, a really ambitious Lojbanist could assign lerfu words to the individual strokes used to write Chinese characters (there are about seven or eight of them if you are a flexible human being, or about 40 if you are a rigid computer program), and then represent each character with a *tei*, the stroke lerfu words in the order of writing (which is standardized for each character), and a *foi*. No one has as yet attempted this project.

17.9 lerfu words as pro-sumti

So far, lerfu words have only appeared in Lojban text when spelling out words. There are several other grammatical uses of lerfu words within Lojban. In each case, a single lerfu word or more than one may be used. Therefore, the term "lerfu string" is introduced: it is short for "sequence of one or more lerfu words".

A lerfu string may be used as a pro-sumti (a sumti which refers to some previous sumti), just like the pro-sumti *ko'a*, *ko'e*, and so on:

Example 17.21

.abu prami by.

A loves B

In Example 17.21 (p. 404), *.abu* and *by.* represent specific sumti, but which sumti they represent must be inferred from context.

Alternatively, lerfu strings may be assigned by *goi*, the regular pro-sumti assignment cmavo:

Example 17.22

le gerku goi gy. cu xekri .i gy. klama le zdani

The dog, or G, is black. G goes to the house.

There is a special rule that sometimes makes lerfu strings more advantageous than the regular pro-sumti cmavo. If no assignment can be found for a lerfu string (especially a single lerfu word), it can be assumed to refer to the most recent sumti whose name or description begins in Lojban with that lerfu. So Example 17.22 (p. 404) can be rephrased:

Example 17.23

le gerku cu xekri. .i gy. klama le zdani

The dog is black. G goes to the house.

(A less literal English translation would use "D" for "dog" instead.)

Here is an example using two names and longer lerfu strings:

Example 17.24

la	stivn.	mark.	djonz.	merko
	Steven	**Mark**	**Jones**	**is-American.**

.i	la	.aleksandr.	paliitc.	kuzNIETsyf.	rusko
		Alexander	**Pavlovitch**	**Kuznetsov**	**is-Russian.**

.i	symyjy.	tavla	.abupyky.	bau	la	lojban.
	SMJ	**talks-to**	**APK**	**in**		**Lojban.**

Perhaps Alexander's name should be given as *ru'o.abupyky* instead.

What about

Example 17.25

.abu	dunda	by.	cy.
A	**gives**	**B**	**C**

Does this mean that A gives B to C? No. *by. cy.* is a single lerfu string, although written as two words, and represents a single pro-sumti. The true interpretation is that A gives BC to someone unspecified. To solve this problem, we need to introduce the elidable terminator *boi* (of selma'o BOI). This cmavo is used to terminate lerfu strings and also strings of numerals; it is required when two of these appear in a row, as here. (The other reason to use *boi* is to attach a free modifier – subscript, parenthesis, or what have you – to a lerfu string.) The correct version is:

Example 17.26

> *.abu [boi] dunda by. boi cy. [boi]*
>
> A gives B to C

where the two occurrences of *boi* in brackets are elidable, but the remaining occurrence is not. Likewise:

Example 17.27

xy.	*boi*	*ro*	*[boi]*	*prenu*	*cu*	*prami*
X		**all**		**persons**		**loves.**

> X loves everybody.

requires the first *boi* to separate the lerfu string *xy.* from the digit string *ro*.

17.10 References to lerfu

The rules of Section 17.9 (p. 404) make it impossible to use unmarked lerfu words to refer to lerfu themselves. In the sentence:

Example 17.28

.abu	*cu*	*lerfu*
A		**is-a-letteral.**

the hearer would try to find what previous sumti *.abu* refers to. The solution to this problem makes use of the cmavo *me'o* of selma'o LI, which makes a lerfu string into a sumti representing that very string of lerfu. This use of *me'o* is a special case of its mathematical use, which is to introduce a mathematical expression used literally rather than for its value.

Example 17.29

me'o	*.abu*	*cu*	*lerfu*

> The-expression "a" is-a-letteral.

Now we can translate Example 17.1 (p. 397) into Lojban:

Example 17.30

dei	*vasru*	*vo*	*lerfu*	*po'u*	*me'o*	*.ebu*
this-sentence	**contains**	**four**	**letterals**	**which-are**	**the-expression**	**"e"**

> This sentence contains four "e" s.

Since the Lojban sentence has only four *e* lerfu rather than fourteen, the translation is not a literal one – but Example 17.31 (p. 405) is a Lojban truth just as Example 17.1 (p. 397) is an English truth. Coincidentally, the colloquial English translation of Example 17.31 (p. 405) is also true!

The reader might be tempted to use quotation with *lu...li'u* instead of *me'o*, producing:

Example 17.31

lu	*.abu*	*li'u*	*cu*	*lerfu*
[quote]	**.abu**	**[unquote]**		**is-a-letteral.**

(The single-word quote *zo* cannot be used, because *.abu* is a compound cmavo.) But Example 17.31 (p. 405) is false, because it says:

Example 17.32

> The word *.abu* is a letteral

which is not the case; rather, the thing symbolized by the word *.abu* is a letteral. In Lojban, that would be:

Example 17.33

la'e	*lu*	*.abu*	*li'u*		*cu*	*lerfu*
The-referent-of	[quote]	.abu	[unquote]			is-a-letteral.

which is correct.

17.11 Mathematical uses of lerfu strings

This chapter is not about Lojban mathematics, which is explained in Chapter 18 (p. 413), so the mathematical uses of lerfu strings will be listed and exemplified but not explained.

A lerfu string as mathematical variable:

Example 17.34

li	*.abu*	*du*	*li*		*by.*	*su'i*	*cy.*
the-number	a	equals	the-number		b	plus	c

$a = b + c$

A lerfu string as function name (preceded by *ma'o* of selma'o MAhO):

Example 17.35

li	*.y.bu*	*du*	*li*		*ma'o*		*fy.*	*boi*	*xy.*
the-number	y	equals	the-number		the-function		f	of	x

$y = f(x)$

Note the *boi* here to separate the lerfu strings *fy* and *xy*.

A lerfu string as selbri (followed by a cmavo of selma'o MOI):

Example 17.36

le	*vi*	*ratcu*	*ny.moi*	*le'i*		*mi*	*ratcu*
the	here	rat	is-nth-of	the-set-of		my	rats

This rat is my Nth rat.

A lerfu string as utterance ordinal (followed by a cmavo of selma'o MAI):

Example 17.37

ny.mai

Nthly

A lerfu string as subscript (preceded by *xi* of selma'o XI):

Example 17.38

xy.	*xi*	*ky.*
x	sub	k

A lerfu string as quantifier (enclosed in *vei...ve'o* parentheses):

Example 17.39

vei	*ny.*	*[ve'o]*		*lo prenu*
(	"n"	)		persons

The parentheses are required because *ny. lo prenu* would be two separate sumti, *ny.* and *lo prenu*. In general, any mathematical expression other than a simple number must be in parentheses when used as a quantifier; the right parenthesis mark, the cmavo *ve'o*, can usually be elided.

All the examples above have exhibited single lerfu words rather than lerfu strings, in accordance with the conventions of ordinary mathematics. A longer lerfu string would still be treated as a single variable or function name: in Lojban, *.abu by. cy.* is not the multiplication "a × b × c" but is the variable **abc**. (Of course, a local convention could be employed that made the value of a variable like **abc**, with a multi-lerfu-word name, equal to the values of the variables **a**, **b**, and **c** multiplied together.)

There is a special rule about shift words in mathematical text: shifts within mathematical expressions do not affect lerfu words appearing outside mathematical expressions, and vice versa.

17.12 Acronyms

An acronym is a name constructed of lerfu. English examples are "DNA", "NATO", "CIA". In English, some of these are spelled out (like "DNA" and "CIA") and others are pronounced more or less as if they were ordinary English words (like "NATO"). Some acronyms fluctuate between the two pronunciations: "SQL" may be "ess cue ell" or "sequel".

In Lojban, a name can be almost any sequence of sounds that ends in a consonant and is followed by a pause. The easiest way to Lojbanize acronym names is to glue the lerfu words together, using ' wherever two vowels would come together (pauses are illegal in names) and adding a final consonant:

Example 17.40

> *la dyny'abub. .i la ny'abuty'obub. .i la cy'ibu'abub.*

> DNA. NATO. CIA.

> *... .i la sykybulyl. .i la .ibubymym. .i la ny'ybucyc.*

> ... SQL. IBM. NYC.

There is no fixed convention for assigning the final consonant. In Example 17.40 (p. 407), the last consonant of the lerfu string has been replicated into final position.

Some compression can be done by leaving out *bu* after vowel lerfu words (except for *.y.bu*, wherein the *bu* cannot be omitted without ambiguity). Compression is moderately important because it's hard to say long names without introducing an involuntary (and illegal) pause:

Example 17.41

> *la dyny'am. .i la ny'aty'om. .i la cy'i'am.*

> DNA. NATO. CIA.

> *... .i la sykybulym. .i la .ibymym. .i la ny'ybucym.*

> ... SQL. IBM. NYC.

In Example 17.41 (p. 407), the final consonant *m* stands for *merko*, indicating the source culture of these acronyms.

Another approach, which some may find easier to say and which is compatible with older versions of the language that did not have a ' character, is to use the consonant *z* instead of ':

Example 17.42

> *la dynyzaz. .i la nyzatyzoz. .i la cyzizaz.*

> DNA. NATO. CIA.

> *... .i la sykybulyz. .i la .ibymyz. .i la nyzybucyz.*

> ... SQL. IBM. NYC.

One more alternative to these lengthy names is to use the lerfu string itself prefixed with *me*, the cmavo that makes sumti into selbri:

Example 17.43

la	me	dy	ny.	.abu
that-named	what-pertains-to	"d"	"n"	"a"

This works because *la*, the cmavo that normally introduces names used as sumti, may also be used before a predicate to indicate that the predicate is a (meaningful) name:

Example 17.44

la	cribe	cu	ciska
That-named	"Bear"		writes.

Bear is a writer.

Example 17.44 (p. 408) does not of course refer to a bear (*le cribe* or *lo cribe*) but to something else, probably a person, named "Bear". Similarly, *me dy ny. .abu* is a predicate which can be used as a name, producing a kind of acronym which can have pauses between the individual lerfu words.

17.13 Computerized character codes

Since the first application of computers to non-numerical information, character sets have existed, mapping numbers (called "character codes") into selected lerfu, digits, and punctuation marks (collectively called "characters"). Historically, these character sets have only covered the English alphabet and a few selected punctuation marks. International efforts have now created Unicode, a unified character set that can represent essentially all the characters in essentially all the world's writing systems. Lojban can take advantage of these encoding schemes by using the cmavo *se'e* (of selma'o BY). This cmavo is conventionally followed by digit cmavo of selma'o PA representing the character code, and the whole string indicates a single character in some computerized character set:

Example 17.45

me'o	se'e	cixa	cu	lerfu	la	.asycy'i'is.
The-expression	[code]	36		is-a-letteral-in-set		ASCII

loi	merko	rupnu
for-the-mass-of	American	currency-units.

The character code 36 in ASCII represents American dollars.
"$" represents American dollars.

Understanding Example 17.45 (p. 408) depends on knowing the value in the ASCII character set (one of the simplest and oldest) of the "$" character. Therefore, the *se'e* convention is only intelligible to those who know the underlying character set. For precisely specifying a particular character, however, it has the advantages of unambiguity and (relative) cultural neutrality, and therefore Lojban provides a means for those with access to descriptions of such character sets to take advantage of them.

As another example, the Unicode character set (also known as ISO 10646) represents the international symbol of peace, an inverted trident in a circle, using the base-16 value 262E. In a suitable context, a Lojbanist may say:

Example 17.46

me'o	se'e	rexarerei	sinxa	le	ka	panpi
the-expression	[code]	262E	is-a-sign-of	the	quality-of	being-at-peace

When a *se'e* string appears in running discourse, some metalinguistic convention must specify whether the number is base 10 or some other base, and which character set is in use.

17.14 List of all auxiliary lerfu-word cmavo

bu	BU	makes previous word into a lerfu word
ga'e	BY	upper case shift
to'a	BY	lower case shift
tau	LAU	case-shift next lerfu word only
lo'a	BY	Latin/Lojban alphabet shift
ge'o	BY	Greek alphabet shift
je'o	BY	Hebrew alphabet shift
jo'o	BY	Arabic alphabet shift
ru'o	BY	Cyrillic alphabet shift
se'e	BY	following digits are a character code
na'a	BY	cancel all shifts
zai	LAU	following lerfu word specifies alphabet
ce'a	LAU	following lerfu word specifies font
lau	LAU	following lerfu word is punctuation
tei	TEI	start compound lerfu word
foi	FOI	end compound lerfu word

Note that LAU cmavo must be followed by a BY cmavo or the equivalent, where "equivalent" means: either any Lojban word followed by *bu*, another LAU cmavo (and its required sequel), or a *tei...foi* compound cmavo.

17.15 Proposed lerfu words – introduction

The following sections contain tables of proposed lerfu words for some of the standard alphabets supported by the Lojban lerfu system. The first column of each list is the lerfu (actually, a Latin-alphabet name sufficient to identify it). The second column is the proposed name-based lerfu word, and the third column is the proposed lerfu word in the system based on using the cmavo of selma'o BY with a shift word.

These tables are not meant to be authoritative (several authorities within the Lojban community have niggled over them extensively, disagreeing with each other and sometimes with themselves). They provide a working basis until actual usage is available, rather than a final resolution of lerfu word problems. Probably the system presented here will evolve somewhat before settling down into a final, conventional form.

For Latin-alphabet lerfu words, see Section 17.2 (p. 398) (for Lojban) and Section 17.5 (p. 400) (for non-Lojban Latin-alphabet lerfu).

17.16 Proposed lerfu words for the Greek alphabet

alpha	.alfas. bu	.abu
beta	.betas. bu	by
gamma	.gamas. bu	gy
delta	.deltas. bu	dy
epsilon	.Epsilon. bu	.ebu
zeta	.zetas. bu	zy
eta	.etas. bu	.e'ebu
theta	.tetas. bu	ty. bu
iota	.iotas. bu	.ibu
kappa	.kapas. bu	ky
lambda	.lymdas. bu	ly
mu	.mus. bu	my
nu	.nus. bu	ny
xi	.ksis. bu	ksis. bu
omicron	.Omikron. bu	.obu
pi	.pis. bu	py

rho	.ros. bu	ry
sigma	.sigmas. bu	sy
tau	.taus. bu	ty
upsilon	.Upsilon. bu	.ubu
phi	.fis. bu	py. bu
chi	.xis. bu	ky. bu
psi	.psis. bu	psis. bu
omega	.omegas. bu	.o'obu
rough	.dasei,as. bu	.y'y
smooth	.psiles. bu	xutla bu

17.17 Proposed lerfu words for the Cyrillic alphabet

The second column in this listing is based on the historical names of the letters in Old Church Slavonic. Only those letters used in Russian are shown; other languages require more letters which can be devised as needed.

a	.azys. bu	.abu
b	.bukys. bu	by
v	.vedis. bu	vy
g	.glagolis. bu	gy
d	.dobros. bu	dy
e	.iestys. bu	.ebu
zh	.jivet. bu	jy
z	.zemlias. bu	zy
i	.ije,is. bu	.ibu
short i	.itord. bu	.itord. bu
k	.kakos. bu	ky
l	.liudi,ies. bu	ly
m	.myslites. bu	my
n	.naciys. bu	ny
o	.onys. bu	.obu
p	.pokois. bu	py
r	.riytsis. bu	ry
s	.slovos. bu	sy
t	.tyvriydos. bu	ty
u	.ukys. bu	.ubu
f	.friytys. bu	fy
kh	.xerys. bu	xy
ts	.tsis. bu	tsys. bu
ch	.tcriyviys. bu	tcys. bu
sh	.cas. bu	cy
shch	.ctas. bu	ctcys. bu
hard sign	.ier. bu	jdari bu
yeri	.ierys. bu	.y.bu
soft sign	.ieriys. bu	ranti bu
reversed e	.ecarn. bu	.ecarn. bu
yu	.ius. bu	.iubu
ya	.ias. bu	.iabu

17.18 Proposed lerfu words for the Hebrew alphabet

aleph	.alef. bu	.alef. bu
bet	.bet. bu	by
gimel	.gimel. bu	gy
daled	.daled. bu	dy

he	.xex. bu	.y'y
vav	.vav. bu	vy
zayin	.zai,in. bu	zy
khet	.xet. bu	xy. bu
tet	.tet. bu	ty. bu
yud	.iud. bu	.iud. bu
kaf	.kaf. bu	ky
lamed	.LYmed. bu	ly
mem	.mem. bu	my
nun	.nun. bu	ny
samekh	.samex. bu	samex. bu
ayin	.ai,in. bu	.ai,in bu
pe	.pex. bu	py
tzadi	.tsadik. bu	tsadik. bu
quf	.kuf. bu	ky. bu
resh	.rec. bu	ry
shin	.cin. bu	cy
sin	.sin. bu	sy
taf	.taf. bu	ty.
dagesh	.daGEC. bu	daGEC. bu
hiriq	.xirik. bu	.ibu
tzeirekh	.tseirex. bu	.eibu
segol	.seGOL. bu	.ebu
qubbutz	.kubuts. bu	.ubu
qamatz	.kamats. bu	.abu
patach	.patax. bu	.a'abu
sheva	.cyVAS. bu	.y.bu
kholem	.xolem. bu	.obu
shuruq	.curuk. bu	.u'ubu

17.19 Proposed lerfu words for some accent marks and multiple letters

This list is intended to be suggestive, not complete: there are lerfu such as Polish "dark" l and Maltese h-bar that do not yet have symbols.

acute	.akut. bu or .pritygal. bu [pritu galtu]
grave	.grav. bu or .zulgal. bu [zunle galtu]
circumflex	.cirkumfleks. bu or .midgal. bu [midju galtu]
tilde	.tildes. bu
macron	.makron. bu
breve	.brevis. bu
over-dot	.gapmoc. bu [gapru mokca]
umlaut/trema	.relmoc. bu [re mokca]
over-ring	.gapyjin. bu [gapru djine]
cedilla	.seDIlys. bu
double-acute	.re'akut. bu [re akut.]
ogonek	.ogoniek. bu
hacek	.xatcek. bu
ligatured fi	tei fy. ibu foi
Danish/Latin ae ae	tei .abu .ebu foi
Dutch ij	tei .ibu jy. foi
German es-zed	tei sy. zy. foi

17.20 Proposed lerfu words for radio communication

There is a set of English words which are used, by international agreement, as lerfu words (for the English alphabet) over the radio, or in noisy situations where the utmost clarity is required. Formally they are known as the "ICAO Phonetic Alphabet", and are used even in non-English-speaking countries.

This table presents the standard English spellings and proposed Lojban versions. The Lojbanizations are not straightforward renderings of the English sounds, but make some concessions both to the English spellings of the words and to the Lojban pronunciations of the lerfu (thus *carlis. bu*, not *tcarlis. bu*).

Alfa	.alfas. bu
Bravo	.bravos. bu
Charlie	.carlis. bu
Delta	.deltas. bu
Echo	.ekos. bu
Foxtrot	.fokstrot. bu
Golf	.golf. bu
Hotel	.xoTEL. bu
India	.indias. bu
Juliet	.juliet. bu
Kilo	.kilos. bu
Lima	.limas. bu
Mike	.maik. bu
November	.novembr. bu
Oscar	.oskar. bu
Papa	.paPAS. bu
Quebec	.keBEK. bu
Romeo	.romios. bu
Sierra	.sieras. bu
Tango	.tangos. bu
Uniform	.Uniform. bu
Victor	.viktas. bu
Whiskey	.uiskis. bu
X-ray	.eksreis. bu
Yankee	.iankis. bu
Zulu	.zulus. bu

Chapter 18
lojbau mekso: Mathematical Expressions in Lojban

NO NO

18.1 Introductory

lojbau mekso ("Lojbanic mathematical-expression") is the part of the Lojban language that is tailored for expressing statements of a mathematical character, or for adding numerical information to non-mathematical statements. Its formal design goals include:

1. representing all the different forms of expression used by mathematicians in their normal modes of writing, so that a reader can unambiguously read off mathematical text as written with minimal effort and expect a listener to understand it;
2. providing a vocabulary of commonly used mathematical terms which can readily be expanded to include newly coined words using the full resources of Lojban;
3. permitting the formulation, both in writing and in speech, of unambiguous mathematical text;
4. encompassing all forms of quantified expression found in natural languages, as well as encouraging greater precision in ordinary language situations than natural languages allow.

Goal 1 requires that mekso not be constrained to a single notation such as Polish notation or reverse Polish notation, but make provision for all forms, with the most commonly used forms the most easily used.

Goal 2 requires the provision of several conversion mechanisms, so that the boundary between mekso and full Lojban can be crossed from either side at many points.

Goal 3 is the most subtle. Written mathematical expression is culturally unambiguous, in the sense that mathematicians in all parts of the world understand the same written texts to have the

413

same meanings. However, international mathematical notation does not prescribe unique forms. For example, the expression

Example 18.1

   $3x + 2y$

contains omitted multiplication operators, but there are other possible interpretations for the strings $3x$ and $2y$ than as mathematical multiplication. Therefore, the Lojban verbal (spoken and written) form of Example 18.1 (p. 414) must not omit the multiplication operators.

The remainder of this chapter explains (in as much detail as is currently possible) the mekso system. This chapter is by intention complete as regards mekso components, but only suggestive about uses of those components – as of now, there has been no really comprehensive use made of mekso facilities, and many matters must await the test of usage to be fully clarified.

18.2 Lojban numbers

The following cmavo are discussed in this section:

pa	PA	1	xa	PA	6
re	PA	2	ze	PA	7
ci	PA	3	bi	PA	8
vo	PA	4	so	PA	9
mu	PA	5	no	PA	0

The simplest kind of mekso are numbers, which are cmavo or compound cmavo. There are cmavo for each of the 10 decimal digits, and numbers greater than 9 are made by stringing together the cmavo. Some examples:

Example 18.2

pa	re	ci
one	**two**	**three**
123		

one hundred and twenty three

Example 18.3

pa	no
one	**zero**
10	

ten

Example 18.4

pa	re	ci	vo	mu	xa	ze	bi	so	no
one	**two**	**three**	**four**	**five**	**six**	**seven**	**eight**	**nine**	**zero**
1234567890

one billion, two hundred and thirty-four million, five hundred and sixty-seven thousand, eight hundred and ninety.

Therefore, there are no separate cmavo for "ten", "hundred", etc.

There is a pattern to the digit cmavo (except for *no*, 0) which is worth explaining. The cmavo from 1 to 5 end in the vowels *a*, *e*, *i*, *o*, *u* respectively; and the cmavo from 6 to 9 likewise end in the vowels *a*, *e*, *i*, and *o* respectively. None of the digit cmavo begin with the same consonant, to make them easy to tell apart in noisy environments.

18.3 Signs and numerical punctuation

The following cmavo are discussed in this section:

ma'u	PA	positive sign
ni'u	PA	negative sign
pi	PA	decimal point
fi'u	PA	fraction slash
ra'e	PA	repeating decimal
ce'i	PA	percent sign
ki'o	PA	comma between digits

A number can be given an explicit sign by the use of *ma'u* and *ni'u*, which are the positive and negative signs as distinct from the addition, subtraction, and negation operators. For example:

Example 18.5

ni'u	*pa*
negative-sign	**1**

-1

Grammatically, the signs are part of the number to which they are attached. It is also possible to use *ma'u* and *ni'u* by themselves as numbers; the meaning of these numbers is explained in Section 18.8 (p. 422).

Various numerical punctuation marks are likewise expressed by cmavo, as illustrated in the following examples:

Example 18.6

ci	*pi*	*pa*	*vo*	*pa*	*mu*
three	**point**	**one**	**four**	**one**	**five**

3.1415

(In some cultures, a comma is used instead of a period in the symbolic version of Example 18.6 (p. 415); *pi* is still the Lojban representation for the decimal point.)

Example 18.7

re	*fi'u*	*ze*
two	**fraction**	**seven**

$\frac{2}{7}$

Example 18.7 (p. 415) is the name of the number two-sevenths; it is not the same as "the result of 2 divided by 7" in Lojban, although numerically these two are equal. If the denominator of the fraction is present but the numerator is not, the numerator is taken to be 1, thus expressing the reciprocal of the following number:

Example 18.8

fi'u	*ze*
fraction	**seven**

$\frac{1}{7}$

Example 18.9

pi	*ci*	*mu*	*ra'e*	*pa*	*vo*	*re*	*bi*	*mu*	*ze*
point	**three**	**five**	**repeating**	**one**	**four**	**two**	**eight**	**five**	**seven**

.35142857142857...

Note that the *ra'e* marks unambiguously where the repeating portion "142857" begins.

Example 18.10

ci	*mu*	*ce'i*
three	**five**	**percent**

35%

Example 18.11

pa	ki'o	re	ci	vo	ki'o	mu	xa	ze
one	comma	two	three	four	comma	five	six	seven

1,234,567

(In some cultures, spaces are used in the symbolic representation of Example 18.11 (p. 416); *ki'o* is still the Lojban representation.)

It is also possible to have less than three digits between successive *ki'o* s, in which case zeros are assumed to have been elided:

Example 18.12

pa	ki'o	re	ci	ki'o	vo
one	comma	two	three	comma	four

1,023,004

In the same way, *ki'o* can be used after *pi* to divide fractions into groups of three:

Example 18.13

pi	ki'o	re	re
point	comma	two	two

.022

Example 18.14

pi	pa	ki'o	pa	re	ki'o	pa
point	one	comma	one	two	comma	one

.001012001

18.4 Special numbers

The following cmavo are discussed in this section:

ci'i	PA	infinity
ka'o	PA	imaginary i, sqrt(-1)
pai	PA	π, pi (approx 3.14159...)
te'o	PA	exponential e (approx 2.71828...)
fi'u	PA	golden ratio, Φ, phi, (1 + sqrt(5))/2 (approx. 1.61803...)

The last cmavo is the same as the fraction sign cmavo: a fraction sign with neither numerator nor denominator represents the golden ratio.

Numbers can have any of these digit, punctuation, and special-number cmavo of Sections 2, 3, and 4 in any combination:

Example 18.15

ma'u	ci'i

+∞

Example 18.16

ci	ka'o	re

3i2 (a complex number equivalent to 3 + 2i)

Note that *ka'o* is both a special number (meaning "i") and a number punctuation mark (separating the real and the imaginary parts of a complex number).

Example 18.17

ci'i	no

infinity zero

$\aleph_0$ (a transfinite cardinal)

The special numbers *pai* and *te'o* are mathematically important, which is why they are given their own cmavo:

Example 18.18

> *pai*
>
> pi, π

Example 18.19

> *te'o*
>
> e

However, many combinations are as yet undefined:

Example 18.20

> *pa* | *pi* | *re* | *pi* | *ci*
>
> 1.2.3

Example 18.21

pa	*ni'u*		*re*
1	negative-sign		2

Example 18.21 (p. 417) is not "1 minus 2", which is represented by a different cmavo sequence altogether. It is a single number which has not been assigned a meaning. There are many such numbers which have no well-defined meaning; they may be used for experimental purposes or for future expansion of the Lojban number system.

It is possible, of course, that some of these "oddities" do have a meaningful use in some restricted area of mathematics. A mathematician appropriating these structures for specialized use needs to consider whether some other branch of mathematics would use the structure differently.

More information on numbers may be found in Section 18.8 (p. 422) to Section 18.12 (p. 431).

18.5 Simple infix expressions and equations

The following cmavo are discussed in this section:

du	GOhA	equals
su'i	VUhU	plus
vu'u	VUhU	minus
pi'i	VUhU	times
te'a	VUhU	raised to the power
ny.	BY	letter "n"
vei	VEI	left parenthesis
ve'o	VEhO	right parenthesis

Let us begin at the beginning: one plus one equals two. In Lojban, that sentence translates to:

Example 18.22

li		*pa*	*su'i*	*pa*	*du*	*li*		*re*
The-number		one	plus	one	equals	the-number		two.
1 + 1 = 2								

Example 18.22 (p. 417), a mekso sentence, is a regular Lojban bridi that exploits mekso features. *du* is the predicate meaning "x1 is mathematically equal to x2". It is a cmavo for conciseness, but it has the same grammatical uses as any brivla. Outside mathematical contexts, *du* means "x1 is identical with x2" or "x1 is the same object as x2".

The cmavo *li* is the number article. It is required whenever a sentence talks about numbers as numbers, as opposed to using numbers to quantify things. For example:

Example 18.23

> *le* | *ci* | *prenu*
>
> the three persons

requires no *li* article, because the *ci* is being used to specify the number of *prenu*. However, the sentence

Example 18.24

levi	sfani	cu	grake	li	ci
This	fly		masses-in-grams	the-number	three.

This fly has a mass of 3 grams.

requires *li* because *ci* is being used as a sumti. Note that this is the way in which measurements are stated in Lojban: all the predicates for units of length, mass, temperature, and so on have the measured object as the first place and a number as the second place. Using *li* for *le* in Example 18.23 (p. 417) would produce

Example 18.25

li	ci	prenu
The-number	3	is-a-person.

which is grammatical but nonsensical: numbers are not persons.

The cmavo *su'i* belongs to selma'o VUhU, which is composed of mathematical operators, and means "addition". As mentioned before, it is distinct from *ma'u* which means the positive sign as an indication of a positive number:

Example 18.26

li	ma'u	pa	su'i
The-number	positive-sign	one	plus

ni'u	pa	du	li	no
negative-sign	one	equals	the-number	zero.

$+1 + -1 = 0$

Of course, it is legal to have complex mekso on both sides of *du*:

Example 18.27

li	mu	su'i	pa	du	li	ci	su'i	ci
The-number	five	plus	one	equals	the-number	three	plus	three.

$5 + 1 = 3 + 3$

Why don't we say *li mu su'i li pa* rather than just *li mu su'i pa*? The answer is that VUhU operators connect mekso operands (numbers, in Example 18.27 (p. 418)), not general sumti. *li* is used to make the entire mekso into a sumti, which then plays the roles applicable to other sumti: in Example 18.27 (p. 418), filling the places of a bridi

By default, Lojban mathematics is like simple calculator mathematics: there is no notion of "operator precedence". Consider the following example, where *pi'i* means "times", the multiplication operator:

Example 18.28

li	ci	su'i	vo	pi'i	mu	du	li	reci
The-number	three	plus	four	times	five	equals	the-number	two-three.

$3 + 4 \times 5 = 23$

Is the Lojban version of Example 18.28 (p. 418) true? No! "3 + 4 × 5" is indeed 23, because the usual conventions of mathematics state that multiplication takes precedence over addition; that is, the multiplication "4 × 5" is done first, giving 20, and only then the addition "3 + 20". But VUhU operators by default are done left to right, like other Lojban grouping, and so a truthful bridi would be:

Example 18.29

li	ci	su'i	vo	pi'i	mu	du	li	cimu
The-number	three	plus	four	times	five	equals	the-number	three-five.

$3 + 4 \times 5 = 35$

Here we calculate 3 + 4 first, giving 7, and then calculate 7 × 5 second, leading to the result 35. While possessing the advantage of simplicity, this result violates the design goal of matching the standards of mathematics. What can be done?

There are three solutions, all of which will probably be used to some degree. The first solution is to ignore the problem. People will say *li ci su'i vo pi'i mu* and mean 23 by it, because the notion that multiplication takes precedence over addition is too deeply ingrained to be eradicated by Lojban parsing, which totally ignores semantics. This convention essentially allows semantics to dominate syntax in this one area.

(Why not hard-wire the precedences into the grammar, as is done in computer programming languages? Essentially because there are too many operators, known and unknown, with levels of precedence that vary according to usage. The programming language 'C' has 13 levels of precedence, and its list of operators is not even extensible. For Lojban this approach is just not practical. In addition, hard-wired precedence could not be overridden in mathematical systems such as spreadsheets where the conventions are different.)

The second solution is to use explicit means to specify the precedence of operators. This approach is fully general, but clumsy, and will be explained in Section 18.20 (p. 440).

The third solution is simple but not very general. When an operator is prefixed with the cmavo *bi'e* (of selma'o BIhE), it becomes automatically of higher precedence than other operators not so prefixed. Thus,

Example 18.30

li	ci	su'i	vo	bi'e	pi'i	mu	du	li	reci
The-number	three	plus	four	times	five	equals	the-number	two-three.	

$3 + 4 \times 5 = 23$

is a truthful Lojban bridi. If more than one operator has a *bi'e* prefix, grouping is from the right; multiple *bi'e* prefixes on a single operator are not allowed.

In addition, of course, Lojban has the mathematical parentheses *vei* and *ve'o*, which can be used just like their written equivalents "(" and ")" to group expressions in any way desired:

Example 18.31

li	vei	ny.	su'i	pa	ve'o	pi'i	vei	ny.	su'i	pa	[ve'o]
The-number	(	n	plus	one	)	times	(	n	plus	one	)

du	li	ny.	[bi'e]	te'a	re
equals	the-number	n		to-the-power	two

su'i	re	bi'e	pi'i	ny.	su'i	pa
plus	two		times	n	plus	1.

$(n+1)(n+1) = n^2 + 2n + 1$

There are several new usages in Example 18.31 (p. 419): *te'a* means "raised to the power", and we also see the use of the lerfu word *ny*, representing the letter "n". In mekso, letters stand for just what they do in ordinary mathematics: variables. The parser will accept a string of lerfu words (called a "lerfu string") as the equivalent of a single lerfu word, in agreement with computer-science conventions; "abc" is a single variable, not the equivalent of "a × b × c". (Of course, a local convention could state that the value of a variable like "abc", with a multi-lerfu name, was equal to the values of the variables "a", "b", and "c" multiplied together.)

The explicit operator *pi'i* is required in the Lojban verbal form whereas multiplication is implicit in the symbolic form. Note that *ve'o* (the right parenthesis) is an elidable terminator: the first use of it in Example 18.31 (p. 419) is required, but the second use (marked by square brackets) could be elided. Additionally, the first *bi'e* (also marked by square brackets) is not necessary to get the proper grouping, but it is included here for symmetry with the other one.

18.6 Forethought operators (Polish notation, functions)

The following cmavo are discussed in this section:

boi	BOI	numeral/lerfu string terminator
va'a	VUhU	negation/additive inverse
pe'o	PEhO	forethought flag
ku'e	KUhE	forethought terminator
ma'o	MAhO	convert operand to operator
py.	BY	letter "p"
xy.	BY	letter "x"
zy.	BY	letter "z"
fy.	BY	letter "f"

The infix form explained so far is reasonable for many purposes, but it is limited and rigid. It works smoothly only where all operators have exactly two operands, and where precedences can either be assumed from context or are limited to just two levels, with some help from parentheses.

But there are many operators which do not have two operands, or which have a variable number of operands. The preferred form of expression in such cases is the use of "forethought operators", also known as Polish notation. In this style of writing mathematics, the operator comes first and the operands afterwards:

Example 18.32

li	su'i	paboi	reboi	ci[boi]	du	li	xa
The-number	the-sum-of	one	two	three	equals	the-number	six.

sum(1,2,3) = 6

Note that the normally elidable number terminator *boi* is required after *pa* and *re* because otherwise the reading would be *pareci*= 123. It is not required after *ci* but is inserted here in brackets for the sake of symmetry. The only time *boi* is required is, as in Example 18.32 (p. 420), when there are two consecutive numbers or lerfu strings.

Forethought mekso can use any number of operands, in Example 18.32 (p. 420), three. How do we know how many operands there are in ambiguous circumstances? The usual Lojban solution is employed: an elidable terminator, namely *ku'e*. Here is an example:

Example 18.33

li	py.	su'i	va'a	ny.	ku'e	su'i	zy	du
The-number	"p"	plus	negative-of(	"n"	)	plus	"z"	equals

li	xy.
the-number	"x" .

p + -n + z = x

where we know that *va'a* is a forethought operator because there is no operand preceding it.

va'a is the numerical negation operator, of selma'o VUhU. In contrast, *vu'u* is not used for numerical negation, but only for subtraction, as it always has two or more operands. Do not confuse *va'a* and *vu'u*, which are operators, with *ni'u*, which is part of a number.

In Example 18.33 (p. 420), the operator *va'a* and the terminator *ku'e* serve in effect as parentheses. (The regular parentheses *vei* and *ve'o* are NOT used for this purpose.) If the *ku'e* were omitted, the *su'i zy* would be swallowed up by the *va'a* forethought operator, which would then appear to have two operands, *ny* and *su'i zy.*, where the latter is also a forethought expression.

Forethought mekso is also useful for matching standard functional notation. How do we represent "z = f(x)"? The answer is:

Example 18.34

li	zy	du	li	ma'o	fy.boi	xy.
The-number	z	equals	the-number	the-operator	f	x.

z = f(x)

Again, no parentheses are used. The construct *ma'o fy.boi* is the equivalent of an operator, and appears in forethought here (although it could also be used as a regular infix operator). In mathematics, letters sometimes mean functions and sometimes mean variables, with only the context to tell which.

Lojban chooses to accept the variable interpretation as the default, and uses the special flag *ma'o* to mark a lerfu string as an operator. The cmavo *xy.* and *zy.* are variables, but *fy.* is an operator (a function) because *ma'o* marks it as such. The *boi* is required because otherwise the *xy.* would look like part of the operator name. (The use of *ma'o* can be generalized from lerfu strings to any mekso operand: see Section 18.21 (p. 440).)

When using forethought mekso, the optional marker *pe'o* may be placed in front of the operator. This usage can help avoid confusion by providing clearly marked *pe'o* and *ku'e* pairs to delimit the operand list. Example 18.32 (p. 420) to Example 18.34 (p. 420), respectively, with explicit *pe'o* and *ku'e*:

Example 18.35

  li pe'o su'i paboi reboi ciboi ku'e du li xa

Example 18.36

  li py. su'i pe'o va'a ny. ku'e su'i zy du li xy.

Example 18.37

  li zy du li pe'o ma'o fy.boi xy. ku'e

Note: When using forethought mekso, be sure that the operands really are operands: they cannot contain regular infix expressions unless parenthesized with *vei* and *ve'o*. An earlier version of the complex Example 18.119 (p. 436) came to grief because I forgot this rule.

18.7 Other useful selbri for mekso bridi

So far our examples have been isolated mekso (it is legal to have a bare mekso as a sentence in Lojban) and equation bridi involving *du*. What about inequalities such as "x < 5"? The answer is to use a bridi with an appropriate selbri, thus:

Example 18.38

li	xy.	mleca	li	mu
The-number	x	is-less-than	the-number	5.

Here is a partial list of selbri useful in mathematical bridi:

du	x1 is identical to x2, x3, x4, ...
dunli	x1 is equal/congruent to x2 in/on property/quality/dimension/quantity x3
mleca	x1 is less than x2
zmadu	x1 is greater than x2
dubjavme'a	x1 is less than or equal to x2 [*du ja mleca*, equal or less]
dubjavmau	x1 is greater than or equal to x2 [*du ja zmadu*, equal or greater]
tamdu'i	x1 is similar to x2 [*tarmi dunli*, shape-equal]
turdu'i	x1 is isomorphic to x2 [*stura dunli*, structure-equal]
cmima	x1 is a member of set x2
gripau	x1 is a subset of set x2 [*girzu pagbu*, set-part]
na'ujbi	x1 is approximately equal to x2 [*namcu jibni*, number-near]
terci'e	x1 is a component with function x2 of system x3

Note the difference between *dunli* and *du*; *dunli* has a third place that specifies the kind of equality that is meant. *du* refers to actual identity, and can have any number of places:

Example 18.39

py.	du	xy.boi	zy.
"p"	is-identical-to	"x"	"z"

p = x = z

Lojban bridi can have only one predicate, so the *du* is not repeated.

Any of these selbri may usefully be prefixed with *na*, the contradictory negation cmavo, to indicate that the relation is false:

Example 18.40

li	re	su'i	re	na	du	li	mu
the-number	2	+	2	is-not	equal-to	the-number	5.

$2 + 2 \neq 5$

As usual in Lojban, negated bridi say what is false, and do not say anything about what might be true.

18.8 Indefinite numbers

The following cmavo are discussed in this section:

ro	PA	all
so'a	PA	almost all
so'e	PA	most
so'i	PA	many
so'o	PA	several
so'u	PA	a few
no'o	PA	the typical number of
da'a	PA	all but (one) of
piro	PA+PA	the whole of/all of
piso'a	PA+PA	almost the whole of
piso'e	PA+PA	most of
piso'i	PA+PA	much of
piso'o	PA+PA	a small part of
piso'u	PA+PA	a tiny part of
pino'o	PA+PA	the typical portion of
rau	PA	enough
du'e	PA	too many
mo'a	PA	too few
pirau	PA+PA	enough of
pidu'e	PA+PA	too much of
pimo'a	PA+PA	too little of

Not all the cmavo of PA represent numbers in the usual mathematical sense. For example, the cmavo *ro* means "all" or "each". This number does not have a definite value in the abstract: *li ro* is undefined. But when used to count or quantify something, the parallel between *ro* and *pa* is clearer:

Example 18.41

mi	catlu	pa	prenu
I	look-at	one	person

Example 18.42

mi	catlu	ro	prenu
I	look-at	all	persons

Example 18.41 (p. 422) might be true, whereas Example 18.42 (p. 422) is almost certainly false.

The cmavo *so'a*, *so'e*, *so'i*, *so'o*, and *so'u* represent a set of indefinite numbers less than *ro*. As you go down an alphabetical list, the magnitude decreases:

Example 18.43

mi	catlu	so'a	prenu
I	look-at	almost-all	persons

Example 18.44

mi	catlu	so'e	prenu
I	look-at	most	persons

Example 18.45

mi	catlu	so'i	prenu
I	**look-at**	**many**	**persons**

Example 18.46

mi	catlu	so'o	prenu
I	**look-at**	**several**	**persons**

Example 18.47

mi	catlu	so'u	prenu
I	**look-at**	**a-few**	**persons**

The English equivalents are only rough: the cmavo provide space for up to five indefinite numbers between *ro* and *no*, with a built-in ordering. In particular, *so'e* does not mean "most" in the sense of "a majority" or "more than half".

Each of these numbers, plus *ro*, may be prefixed with *pi* (the decimal point) in order to make a fractional form which represents part of a whole rather than some elements of a totality. *piro* therefore means "the whole of":

Example 18.48

mi	citka	piro	lei	nanba
I	**eat**	**the-whole-of**	**the-mass-of**	**bread**

Similarly, *piso'a* means "almost the whole of"; and so on down to *piso'u*, "a tiny part of". These numbers are particularly appropriate with masses, which are usually measured rather than counted, as Example 18.48 (p. 423) shows.

In addition to these cmavo, there is *no'o*, meaning "the typical value", and *pino'o*, meaning "the typical portion": Sometimes *no'o* can be translated "the average value", but the average in question is not, in general, a mathematical mean, median, or mode; these would be more appropriately represented by operators.

Example 18.49

mi	catlu	no'o	prenu
I	**look-at**	**a-typical-number-of**	**persons**

Example 18.50

mi	citka	pino'o	lei	nanba
I	**eat**	**a-typical-amount-of**	**the-mass-of**	**bread.**

da'a is a related cmavo meaning "all but":

Example 18.51

mi	catlu	da'a	re	prenu
I	**look-at**	**all-but**	**two**	**persons**

Example 18.52

mi	catlu	da'a	so'u	prenu
I	**look-at**	**all-but**	**a-few**	**persons**

Example 18.52 (p. 423) is similar in meaning to Example 18.43 (p. 422).

If no number follows *da'a*, then *pa* is assumed; *da'a* by itself means "all but one", or in ordinal contexts "all but the last":

Example 18.53

ro	ratcu	ka'e	citka	da'a	ratcu
All	**rats**	**can**	**eat**	**all-but-one**	**rats.**

All rats can eat all other rats.

(The use of *da'a* means that Example 18.53 (p. 423) does not require that all rats can eat themselves, but does allow it. Each rat has one rat it cannot eat, but that one might be some rat other than itself. Context often dictates that "itself" is, indeed, the "other" rat.)

As mentioned in Section 18.3 (p. 414), *ma'u* and *ni'u* are also legal numbers, and they mean "some positive number" and "some negative number" respectively.

Example 18.54

li	ci	vu'u	re	du	li	ma'u
the-number	3	–	2	=		some-positive-number

Example 18.55

li	ci	vu'u	vo	du	li	ni'u
the-number	3	–	4	=		some-negative-number

Example 18.56

mi	ponse	ma'u	rupnu
I	possess	a-positive-number-of	currency-units.

All of the numbers discussed so far are objective, even if indefinite. If there are exactly six superpowers (*rairgugde*, "superlative-states") in the world, then *ro rairgugde* means the same as *xa rairgugde*. It is often useful, however, to express subjective indefinite values. The cmavo *rau* (enough), *du'e* (too many), and *mo'a* (too few) are then appropriate:

Example 18.57

mi	ponse	rau	rupnu
I	possess	enough	currency-units.

Like the *so'a*-series, *rau*, *du'e*, and *mo'a* can be preceded by *pi*; for example, *pirau* means "a sufficient part of."

Another possibility is that of combining definite and indefinite numbers into a single number. This usage implies that the two kinds of numbers have the same value in the given context:

Example 18.58

mi	viska	le	rore	gerku
I	saw	the	all-of/two	dogs.

I saw both dogs.

Example 18.59

mi	speni	so'ici	prenu
I	am-married-to	many/three	persons.

I am married to three persons (which is "many" in the circumstances).

Example 18.59 (p. 424) assumes a mostly monogamous culture by stating that three is "many".

18.9 Approximation and inexact numbers

The following cmavo are discussed in this section:

ji'i	PA	approximately
su'e	PA	at most
su'o	PA	at least
me'i	PA	less than
za'u	PA	more than

The cmavo *ji'i* (of selma'o PA) is used in several ways to indicate approximate or rounded numbers. If it appears at the beginning of a number, the whole number is approximate:

Example 18.60

ji'i	vo	no
approximation	**four**	**zero**

approximately 40

If *ji'i* appears in the middle of a number, all the digits following it are approximate:

Example 18.61

vo	no	ji'i	mu	no
four	**zero**	**approximation**	**five**	**zero**

roughly 4050 (where the "four thousand" is exact, but the "fifty" is approximate)

If *ji'i* appears at the end of a number, it indicates that the number has been rounded. In addition, it can then be followed by a sign cmavo (*ma'u* or *ni'u*), which indicate truncation towards positive or negative infinity respectively.

Example 18.62

re	pi	ze	re	ji'i
two	**point**	**seven**	**two**	**approximation**

2.72 (rounded)

Example 18.63

re	pi	ze	re	ji'i	ma'u
two	**point**	**seven**	**two**	**approximation**	**positive-sign**

2.72 (rounded up)

Example 18.64

re	pi	ze	pa	ji'i	ni'u
two	**point**	**seven**	**one**	**approximation**	**negative-sign**

2.71 (rounded down)

Example 18.62 (p. 425) through Example 18.64 (p. 425) are all approximations to *te'o* (exponential e). *ji'i* can also appear by itself, in which case it means "approximately the typical value in this context".

The four cmavo *su'e*, *su'o*, *me'i*, and *za'u*, also of selma'o PA, express inexact numbers with upper or lower bounds:

Example 18.65

mi	catlu	su'e	re	prenu
I	**look-at**	**at-most**	**two**	**persons**

Example 18.66

mi	catlu	su'o	re	prenu
I	**look-at**	**at-least**	**two**	**persons**

Example 18.67

mi	catlu	me'i	re	prenu
I	**look-at**	**less-than**	**two**	**persons**

Example 18.68

mi	catlu	za'u	re	prenu
I	**look-at**	**more-than**	**two**	**persons**

Each of these is a subtly different claim: Example 18.66 (p. 425) is true of two or any greater number, whereas Example 18.68 (p. 425) requires three persons or more. Likewise, Example 18.65 (p. 425) refers to zero, one, or two; Example 18.67 (p. 425) to zero or one. (Of course, when the context allows numbers other than non-negative integers, *me'i re* can be any number less than 2, and likewise with the other cases.) The exact quantifier, "exactly 2, neither more nor less" is just *re*. Note that *su'ore* is the exact Lojban equivalent of English plurals.

If no number follows one of these cmavo, *pa* is understood: therefore,

Example 18.69

mi	catlu	su'o	prenu
I	look-at	at-least-[one]	person

is a meaningful claim.

Like the numbers in Section 18.8 (p. 422), all of these cmavo may be preceded by *pi* to make the corresponding quantifiers for part of a whole. For example, *pisu'o* means "at least some part of". The quantifiers *ro*, *su'o*, *piro*, and *pisu'o* are particularly important in Lojban, as they are implicitly used in the descriptions introduced by the cmavo of selma'o LA and LE, as explained in Section 6.7 (p. 124). Descriptions in general are outside the scope of this chapter.

18.10 Non-decimal and compound bases

The following cmavo are discussed in this section:

ju'u	VUhU	to the base
dau	PA	hex digit A = 10
fei	PA	hex digit B = 11
gai	PA	hex digit C = 12
jau	PA	hex digit D = 13
rei	PA	hex digit E = 14
vai	PA	hex digit F = 15
pi'e	PA	compound base point

In normal contexts, Lojban assumes that all numbers are expressed in the decimal (base 10) system. However, other bases are possible, and may be appropriate in particular circumstances.

To specify a number in a particular base, the VUhU operator *ju'u* is suitable:

Example 18.70

li	panopano	ju'u	re	du	li	pano	
The-number	1010	base	2	equals	the-number	1	0.

Here, the final *pa no* is assumed to be base 10, as usual; so is the base specification. (The base may also be changed permanently by a metalinguistic specification; no standard way of doing so has as yet been worked out.)

Lojban has digits for representing bases up to 16, because 16 is a base often used in computer applications. In English, it is customary to use the letters A-F as the base 16 digits equivalent to the numbers ten through fifteen. In Lojban, this ambiguity is avoided:

Example 18.71

li	daufeigai	ju'u	paxa	du	li	rezevobi
The-number	ABC	base	16	equals	the-number	2748.

Example 18.72

li	jaureivai	ju'u	paxa	du	li	cimuxaze
The-number	DEF	base	16	equals	the-number	3567.

Note the pattern in the cmavo: the diphthongs *au*, *ei*, *ai* are used twice in the same order. The digits for A to D use consonants different from those used in the decimal digit cmavo; E and F unfortunately overlap 2 and 4 – there was simply not enough available cmavo space to make a full differentiation possible. The cmavo are also in alphabetical order.

The base point *pi* is used in non-decimal bases just as in base 10:

Example 18.73

li	vai	pi	bi	ju'u	paxa	du	li	pamu	pi	mu
The-number	F	.	8	base	16	equals	the-number	15	.	5.

Since *ju'u* is an operator of selma'o VUhU, it is grammatical to use any operand as the left argument. Semantically, however, it is undefined to use anything but a numeral string on the left. The reason for making *ju'u* an operator is to allow reference to a base which is not a constant.

There are some numerical values that require a "base" that varies from digit to digit. For example, times represented in hours, minutes, and seconds have, in effect, three "digits": the first is base 24, the second and third are base 60. To express such numbers, the compound base separator *pi'e* is used:

Example 18.74

ci	*pi'e*	*rere*	*pi'e*	*vono*

3:22:40

Each digit sequence separated by instances of *pi'e* is expressed in decimal notation, but the number as a whole is not decimal and can only be added and subtracted by special rules:

Example 18.75

li		*ci*	*pi'e*	*rere*	*pi'e*	*vono*	*su'i*		*pi'e*	*ci*	*pi'e*	*cici*
The-number		**3**	:	**22**	:	**40**	**plus**		:	**3**	:	**33**

du	*li*		*ci*	*pi'e*	*rexa*	*pi'e*	*paci*
equals	**the-number**		**3**	:	**26**	:	**13.**

3:22:40 + 0:3:33 = 3:26:13

Of course, only context tells you that the first part of the numbers in Example 18.74 (p. 427) and Example 18.75 (p. 427) is hours, the second minutes, and the third seconds.

The same mechanism using *pi'e* can be used to express numbers which have a base larger than 16. For example, base-20 Mayan mathematics might use digits from *no* to *paso*, each separated by *pi'e*:

Example 18.76

li		*pa*	*pi'e*	*re*	*pi'e*	*ci*	*ju'u*	*reno*	*du*		*li*		*vovoci*
the-number		**1**	;	**2**	;	**3**	**base**	**20**	**equals**		**the-number**		**443**

Carefully note the difference between:

Example 18.77

pano		*ju'u*	*reno*
the-digit-10		**base**	**20**

which is equal to ten, and:

Example 18.78

pa	*pi'e*	*no*	*ju'u*	*reno*
1;0		**base**	**20**

which is equal to twenty.

Both *pi* and *pi'e* can be used to express large-base fractions:

Example 18.79

li		*pa*	*pi'e*	*vo*	*pi*	*ze*	*ju'u*	*reno*
The-number		**1**	;	**4**	.	**7**	**base**	**20**

du	*li*		*revo*	*pi*	*cimu*
equals	**the-number**		**24**	.	**35**

pi'e is also used where the base of each digit is vague, as in the numbering of the examples in this chapter:

Example 18.80

dei		*jufra*		*panopi'epapamoi*
This-utterance		**is-a-sentence-type-of**		**10;11th-thing.**

This is Sentence 10.11.

18.11 Special mekso selbri

The following cmavo are discussed in this section:

mei	MOI	cardinal selbri
moi	MOI	ordinal selbri
si'e	MOI	portion selbri
cu'o	MOI	probability selbri
va'e	MOI	scale selbri
me	ME	make sumti into selbri
me'u	MEhU	terminator for ME

Lojban possesses a special category of selbri which are based on mekso. The simplest kind of such selbri are made by suffixing a member of selma'o MOI to a number. There are five members of MOI, each of which serves to create number-based selbri with specific place structures.

The cmavo *mei* creates cardinal selbri. The basic place structure is:

x1 is a mass formed from the set x2 of n members, one or more of which is/are x3

A cardinal selbri interrelates a set with a given number of members, the mass formed from that set, and the individuals which make the set up. The mass argument is placed first as a matter of convenience, not logical necessity.

Some examples:

Example 18.81

lei		*mi*	*ratcu*	*cu*	*cimei*
Those-I-describe-as-the-mass-of		**my**	**rats**		**are-a-threesome.**

My rats are three.
I have three rats.

Here, the mass of my rats is said to have three components; that is, I have three rats.

Another example, with one element this time:

Example 18.82

mi	*poi*	*pamei*		*cu*	*cusku*	*dei*
I	**who**	**am-an-individual**			**express**	**this-sentence.**

In Example 18.82 (p. 428), *mi* refers to a mass, "the mass consisting of me". Personal pronouns are vague between masses, sets, and individuals.

However, when the number expressed before *-mei* is an objective indefinite number of the kind explained in Section 18.8 (p. 422), a slightly different place structure is required:

x1 is a mass formed from a set x2 of n members, one or more of which is/are x3, measured relative to the set x4.

An example:

Example 18.83

lei		*ratcu*	*poi*	*zvati*	*le*	*panka*
The-mass-of		**rats**	**which**	**are-in**	**the**	**park**

cu	*so'umei*		*lo'i*		*ratcu*
	are-a-fewsome-with-respect-to		**the-set-of**		**rats.**

The rats in the park are a small number of all the rats there are.

In Example 18.83 (p. 428), the x2 and x3 places are vacant, and the x4 place is filled by *lo'i ratcu*, which (because no quantifiers are explicitly given) means "the whole of the set of all those things which are rats", or simply "the set of all rats."

Example 18.84

le'i	ratcu	poi	zvati	le	panka	cu	se	so'imei
The-set-of	rats	which-are	in	the	park		is-a	manysome.

There are many rats in the park.

In Example 18.84 (p. 429), the conversion cmavo *se* swaps the x1 and the x2 places, so that the new x1 is the set. The x4 set is unspecified, so the implication is that the rats are "many" with respect to some unspecified comparison set.

More explanations about the interrelationship of sets, masses, and individuals can be found in Section 6.3 (p. 119).

The cmavo *moi* creates ordinal selbri. The place structure is:

x1 is the (n)th member of set x2 when ordered by rule x3

Some examples:

Example 18.85

ti	pamoi	le'i	mi	ratcu
This-one	is-the-first-of	the	associated-with-me	rats.

This is my first rat.

Example 18.86

ta	romoi	le'i	mi	ratcu
That	is-the-allth-of	the	associated-with-me	rats.

That is my last rat.

Example 18.87

mi	raumoi	le	velskina	porsi
I	am-enough-th-in	the	movie-audience	sequence

I am enough-th in the movie line.

Example 18.87 (p. 429) means, in the appropriate context, that my position in line is sufficiently far to the front that I will get a seat for the movie.

The cmavo *si'e* creates portion selbri. The place structure is:

x1 is an (n)th portion of mass x2

Some examples:

Example 18.88

levi	sanmi	cu	fi'ucisi'e	lei	mi	djedi	cidja
This-here	meal		is-a-slash-three-portion-of		my	day	food.

This meal is one-third of my daily food.

The cmavo *cu'o* creates probability selbri. The place structure is:

event x1 has probability (n) of occurring under conditions x2

The number must be between 0 and 1 inclusive. For example:

Example 18.89

le	nu	lo	sicni	cu	sedja'o	cu	pimucu'o
The	event	of-a	coin		being-a-head-displayer		has-probability-.5.

The cmavo *va'e* creates a scale selbri. The place structure is:

x1 is at scale position (n) on the scale x2

If the scale is granular rather than continuous, a form like *cifi'uxa* (3/6) may be used; in this case, 3/6 is not the same as 1/2, because the third position on a scale of six positions is not the same as the first position on a scale of two positions. Here is an example:

Example 18.90

levi	rozgu	cu	sofi'upanova'e	xunre
This-here	**rose**		**is-8/10-scale**	**red.**

This rose is 8 out of 10 on the scale of redness.
This rose is very red.

When the quantifier preceding any MOI cmavo includes the subjective numbers *rau*, *du'e*, or *mo'a* (enough, too many, too few) then an additional place is added for "by standard". For example:

Example 18.91

lei		ratcu	poi		zvati	le
The-mass-of		**rats**	**which-are**		**in**	**the**

panka	cu	du'emei		fo		mi
park		**are-too-many**		**by-standard**		**me.**

There are too many rats in the park for me.

The extra place (which for -*mei* is the x4 place labeled by *fo*) is provided rather than using a BAI tag such as *ma'i* because a specification of the standard for judgment is essential to the meaning of subjective words like "enough".

This place is not normally explicit when using one of the subjective numbers directly as a number. Therefore, *du'e ratcu* means "too many rats" without specifying any standard.

It is also grammatical to substitute a lerfu string for a number:

Example 18.92

ta	ny.moi	le'i	mi	ratcu
That	**is-nth-of**	**the-set-of**	**associated-with-me**	**rats.**

That is my nth rat.

More complex mekso cannot be placed directly in front of MOI, due to the resulting grammatical ambiguities. Instead, a somewhat artificial form of expression is required.

The cmavo *me* (of selma'o ME) has the function of making a sumti into a selbri. A whole *me* construction can have a member of MOI added to the end to create a complex mekso selbri:

Example 18.93

ta	me	li		ny.	su'i	pa	me'u	moi
That	**is**	**the-number**		**n**	**plus**	**one**		**-th-of**

le'i	mi	ratcu
the-set-of	**associated-with-me**	**rats.**

That is my (n+1)-th rat.

Here the mekso *ny. su'i pa* is made into a sumti (with *li*) and then changed into a mekso selbri with *me* and *me'u moi*. The elidable terminator *me'u* is required here in order to keep the *pa* and the *moi* separate; otherwise, the parser will combine them into the compound *pamoi* and reject the sentence as ungrammatical.

It is perfectly possible to use non-numerical sumti after *me* and before a member of MOI, producing strange results indeed:

Example 18.94

le	nu	mi	nolraitru		cu	me
The	**event-of**	**me**	**being-a-nobly-superlative-ruler**			

le'e		snime	bolci	be	vi	la	xel.	cu'o
has-the-stereotypical		**snow**	**type-of-ball**	**at**		**Hell**	**probability.**

I have a snowball's chance in Hell of being king.

Note: the elidable terminator *boi* is not used between a number and a member of MOI. As a result, the *me'u* in Example 18.93 (p. 430) could also be replaced by a *boi*, which would serve the same function of preventing the *pa* and *moi* from joining into a compound.

18.12 Number questions

The following cmavo is discussed in this section:

xo	PA	number question

The cmavo *xo*, a member of selma'o PA, is used to ask questions whose answers are numbers. Like most Lojban question words, it fills the blank where the answer should go. (See Section 19.5 (p. 451) for more on Lojban questions.)

Example 18.95

li	re	su'i	re	du	li	xo
The-number	2	plus	2	equals	the-number	what?

What is 2 + 2?

Example 18.96

le	xomoi	prenu	cu	darxi	do
The	what-number-th	person		hit	you?

Which person [as in a police lineup] hit you?

xo can also be combined with other digits to ask questions whose answers are already partly specified. This ability could be very useful in writing tests of elementary arithmetical knowledge:

Example 18.97

li	remu	pi'i	xa	du	li	paxono
The-number	25	times	6	equals	the-number	1?0

to which the correct reply would be *mu*, or 5. The ability to utter bare numbers as grammatical Lojban sentences is primarily intended for giving answers to *xo* questions. (Another use, obviously, is for counting off physical objects one by one.)

18.13 Subscripts

The following cmavo is discussed in this section:

xi	XI	subscript

Subscripting is a general Lojban feature, not used only in mekso; there are many things that can logically be subscripted, and grammatically a subscript is a free modifier, usable almost anywhere. In particular, of course, mekso variables (lerfu strings) can be subscripted:

Example 18.98

li	xy.boixici	du	li	xy.boixipa	su'i	xy.boixire
The-number	x-sub-3	equals	the-number	x-sub-1	plus	x-sub-2.

$x_3 = x_1 + x_2$

Subscripts always begin with the flag *xi* (of selma'o XI). *xi* may be followed by a number, a lerfu string, or a general mekso expression in parentheses:

Example 18.99

xy.boixino

x_0

Example 18.100

xy.boixiny.

x_n

Example 18.101

> xy.boixi ⁞ vei ⁞ ny. ⁞ su'i ⁞ pa ⁞ [ve'o]
> $X_{(n+1)}$

Note that subscripts attached directly to lerfu words (variables) generally need a *boi* terminating the variable. Free modifiers, of which subscripts are one variety, generally require the explicit presence of an otherwise elidable terminator.

There is no standard way of handling superscripts (other than those used as exponents) or for subscripts or superscripts that come before the main expression. If necessary, further cmavo could be assigned to selma'o XI for these purposes.

The elidable terminator for a subscript is that for a general number or lerfu string, namely *boi*. By convention, a subscript following another subscript is taken to be a sub-subscript:

Example 18.102

> xy.boi ⁞ xi ⁞ by.boi ⁞ xi ⁞ vo
> X_{b_4}

See Example 18.123 (p. 437) for the standard method of specifying multiple subscripts on a single object.

More information on the uses of subscripts may be found in Section 19.6 (p. 453).

18.14 Infix operators revisited

The following cmavo are discussed in this section:

tu'o	PA	null operand
ge'a	VUhU	null operator
gei	VUhU	exponential notation

The infix operators presented so far have always had exactly two operands, and for more or fewer operands forethought notation has been required. However, it is possible to use an operator in infix style even though it has more or fewer than two operands, through the use of a pair of tricks: the null operand *tu'o* and the null operator *ge'a*. The first is suitable when there are too few operands, the second when there are too many. For example, suppose we wanted to express the numerical negation operator *va'a* in infix form. We would use:

Example 18.103

li	tu'o	va'a	ny.	du	li	no	vu'u	ny.
The-number	(null)	additive-inverse	n	equals	the-number	zero	minus	n.

$-n = 0 - n$

The *tu'o* fulfills the grammatical requirement for a left operand for the infix use of *va'a*, even though semantically none is needed or wanted.

Finding a suitable example of *ge'a* requires exhibiting a ternary operator, and ternary operators are not common. The operator *gei*, however, has both a binary and a ternary use. As a binary operator, it provides a terse representation of scientific (also called "exponential") notation. The first operand of *gei* is the exponent, and the second operand is the mantissa or fraction:

Example 18.104

li	cinonoki'oki'o	du
The-number	three-zero-zero-comma-comma	equals

li	bi	gei	ci
the-number	eight	scientific	three.

$300{,}000{,}000 = 3 \times 10^8$

Why are the arguments to *gei* in reverse order from the conventional symbolic notation? So that *gei* can be used in forethought to allow easy specification of a large (or small) imprecise number:

Example 18.105

gei	reno
(scientific)	**two-zero**

10^{20}

Note, however, that although 10 is far and away the most common exponent base, it is not the only possible one. The third operand of *gei*, therefore, is the base, with 10 as the default value. Most computers internally store so-called "floating-point" numbers using 2 as the exponent base. (This has nothing to do with the fact that computers also represent all integers in base 2; the IBM 360 series used an exponent base of 16 for floating point, although each component of the number was expressed in base 2.) Here is a computer floating-point number with a value of 40:

Example 18.106

papano	bi'eju'u	re	gei
(one-one-zero	**base**	**2)**	**scientific**

pipanopano		bi'eju'u	re	ge'a		re
(point-one-zero-one-zero	**base**	**2)**	**with-base**	**2**		

$.1010_2 \times 2^{110_2}$

18.15 Vectors and matrices

The following cmavo are discussed in this section:

jo'i	JOhI	start vector
te'u	TEhU	end vector
pi'a	VUhU	matrix row combiner
sa'i	VUhU	matrix column combiner

A mathematical vector is a list of numbers, and a mathematical matrix is a table of numbers. Lojban considers matrices to be built up out of vectors, which are in turn built up out of operands.

jo'i, the only cmavo of selma'o JOhI, is the vector indicator: it has a syntax reminiscent of a forethought operator, but has very high precedence. The components must be simple operands rather than full expressions (unless parenthesized). A vector can have any number of components; *te'u* is the elidable terminator. An example:

Example 18.107

li	jo'i	paboi	reboi	te'u	su'i	jo'i	ciboi	voboi
The-number	**array**	**(one,**	**two**	**)**	**plus**	**array**	**(three,**	**four)**

du	li	jo'i	voboi	xaboi
equals	**the-number**	**array**	**(four,**	**six).**

$(1,2) + (3,4) = (4,6)$

Vectors can be combined into matrices using either *pi'a*, the matrix row operator, or *sa'i*, the matrix column operator. The first combines vectors representing rows of the matrix, and the second combines vectors representing columns of the matrix. Both of them allow any number of arguments: additional arguments are tacked on with the null operator *ge'a*.

Therefore, the "magic square" matrix

8	1	6
3	5	7
4	9	2

can be represented either as:

Example 18.108

jo'i		biboi	paboi	xa	pi'a		jo'i		ciboi	muboi	ze
the-vector	(8	1		6)	matrix-row	the-vector	(3	5		7),

ge'a	jo'i		voboi	soboi	re
	the-vector	(4	9		2)

or as

Example 18.109

jo'i		biboi	ciboi	vo	sa'i		jo'i		paboi	muboi	so
the-vector	(8	3		4)	matrix-column	the-vector	(1	5		9),

ge'a	jo'i		xaboi	zeboi	re
	the-vector	(6	7		2)

The regular mekso operators can be applied to vectors and to matrices, since grammatically both of these are expressions. It is usually necessary to parenthesize matrices when used with operators in order to avoid incorrect groupings. There are no VUhU operators for the matrix operators of inner or outer products, but appropriate operators can be created using a suitable symbolic lerfu word or string prefixed by *ma'o*.

Matrices of more than two dimensions can be built up using either *pi'a* or *sa'i* with an appropriate subscript numbering the dimension. When subscripted, there is no difference between *pi'a* and *sa'i*.

18.16 Reverse Polish notation

The following cmavo is discussed in this section:

fu'a | FUhA | reverse Polish flag

So far, the Lojban notational conventions have mapped fairly familiar kinds of mathematical discourse. The use of forethought operators may have seemed odd when applied to "+", but when applied to "f" they appear as the usual functional notation. Now comes a sharp break. Reverse Polish (RP) notation represents something completely different; even mathematicians don't use it much. (The only common uses of RP, in fact, are in some kinds of calculators and in the implementation of some programming languages.)

In RP notation, the operator follows the operands. (Polish notation, where the operator precedes its operands, is another name for forethought mekso of the kind explained in Section 18.6 (p. 419).) The number of operands per operator is always fixed. No parentheses are required or permitted. In Lojban, RP notation is always explicitly marked by a *fu'a* at the beginning of the expression; there is no terminator. Here is a simple example:

Example 18.110

li		fu'a	reboi	ci		su'i	du	li		mu
the-number	(RP!)	two,	three,	plus	equals	the-number	five.

The operands are *re* and *ci*; the operator is *su'i*.

Here is a more complex example:

Example 18.111

li		fu'a	reboi	ci		pi'i	voboi	mu	pi'i		su'i
the-number	(RP!)	(two,	three,	times),	(four,	five,	times),	plus

du		li		rexa
equals	the-number	two-six

Here the operands of the first *pi'i* are *re* and *ci*; the operands of the second *pi'i* are *vo* and *mu* (with *boi* inserted where needed), and the operands of the *su'i* are *reboi ci pi'i*, or 6, and *voboi mu pi'i*, or 20. As you can see, it is easy to get lost in the world of reverse Polish notation; on the other hand, it is especially easy for a mechanical listener (who has a deep mental stack and doesn't get lost) to comprehend.

The operands of an RP operator can be any legal mekso operand, including parenthesized mekso that can contain any valid syntax, whether more RP or something more conventional.

In Lojban, RP operators are always parsed with exactly two operands. What about operators which require only one operand, or more than two operands? The null operand *tu'o* and the null operator *ge'a* provide a simple solution. A one-operand operator like *va'a* always appears in a reverse Polish context as *tu'o va'a*. The *tu'o* provides the second operand, which is semantically ignored but grammatically necessary. Likewise, the three-operand version of *gei* appears in reverse Polish as *ge'a gei*, where the *ge'a* effectively merges the 2nd and 3rd operands into a single operand. Here are some examples:

Example 18.112

li	fu'a	ciboi	muboi	vu'u
The-number	**(RP!)**	**(three,**	**five,**	**minus)**

du	li		fu'a	reboi	tu'o	va'a
equals	**the-number**		**(RP!)**	**two,**	**null,**	**negative-of.**

3 − 5 = -2

Example 18.113

li	cinoki'oki'o		du
The-number	**30-comma-comma**		**equals**

li	fu'a	biboi	ciboi	panoboi	ge'a	gei
the-number	**(RP!)**	**8,**	**(3,**	**10,**	**null-op),**	**exponential-notation.**

$30{,}000{,}000 = 3 \times 10 \wedge 8$

18.17 Logical and non-logical connectives within mekso

The following cmavo are discussed in this section:

.abu	BY	letter "a"
by	BY	letter "b"
cy	BY	letter "c"
fe'a	VUhU	nth root of (default square root)
lo'o	LOhO	terminator for LI

As befits a logical language, Lojban has extensive provision for logical connectives within both operators and operands. Full details on logical and non-logical connectives are provided in Chapter 14 (p. 317). Operands are connected in afterthought with selma'o A and in forethought with selma'o GA, just like sumti. Operators are connected in afterthought with selma'o JA and in forethought with selma'o GUhA, just like tanru components. This parallelism is no accident.

In addition, A+BO and A+KE constructs are allowed for grouping logically connected operands, and *ke...ke'e* is allowed for grouping logically connected operators, although there are no analogues of tanru among the operators.

Despite the large number of rules required to support this feature, it is of relatively minor importance in the mekso scheme of things. Example 18.114 (p. 435) exhibits afterthought logical connection between operands:

Example 18.114

vei	ci	.a	vo	ve'o	prenu	cu	klama	le	zarci
(	**Three**	**or**	**four**	**)**	**people**		**go**	**to-the**	**market.**

Example 18.115 (p. 435) is equivalent in meaning, but uses forethought connection:

Example 18.115

vei	ga	ci	gi	vo	ve'o	prenu	cu	klama	le	zarci
(	**Either**	**3**	**or**	**4**	**)**	**people**		**go**	**to-the**	**market.**

Note that the mekso here are being used as quantifiers. Lojban requires that any mekso other than a simple number be enclosed in parentheses when used as a quantifier. This rule prevents ambiguities that do not exist when using *li*.

By the way, *li* has an elidable terminator, *lo'o*, which is needed when a *li* sumti is followed by a logical connective that could seem to be within the mekso. For example:

Example 18.116

	li	*re*	*su'i*	*re*	*du*
	The-number	two	plus	two	equals

li	*vo*	*lo'o*	*.onai*	*lo*	*nalseldjuno*	*namcu*
the-number	four		or-else	a	non-known	number.

Omitting the *lo'o* would cause the parser to assume that another operand followed the *.onai* and reject *lo* as an invalid operand.

Simple examples of logical connection between operators are hard to come by. A contrived example is:

Example 18.117

	li	*re*	*su'i*	*je*	*pi'i*	*re*	*du*	*li*	*vo*
	The-number	two	plus	and	times	two	equals	the-number	four.

2 + 2 = 4 and 2 × 2 = 4.

The forethought-connection form of Example 18.117 (p. 436) is:

Example 18.118

	li	*re*	*ge*	*su'i*	*gi*	*pi'i*	*re*	*du*	*li*	*vo*
	the-number	two	both	plus	and	times	two	equals	the-number	four.

Both 2 + 2 = 4 and 2 × 2 = 4.

Here is a classic example of operand logical connection:

Example 18.119

go		*li*		*.abu*	*bi'epi'i*	*vei*	*xy.*	*te'a*	*re*	*ve'o*	*su'i*
If-and-only-if		the-number		"a"	times	(	"x"	power	two	)	plus

by.	*bi'epi'i*	*xy.*	*su'i*	*cy.*	*du*	*li*		*no*
"b"	times	"x"	plus	"c"	equals	the-number		zero

gi	*li*		*xy.*	*du*	*li*		*vei*	*va'a*		*by.*	*ku'e*
then	the-number		x	equals	the-number	[	the-negation-of(	b	)

su'i	*ja*	*vu'u*	*fe'a*
plus	or	minus	the-root-of

vei	*by.*	*bi'ete'a*	*re*	*vu'u*	*vo*	*bi'epi'i*	*.abu*	*bi'epi'i*	*cy.*
(	"b"	power	2	minus	four	times	"a"	times	"c"

ve'o	*[ku'e]*	*ve'o*	*fe'i*		*re*	*bi'epi'i*	*.abu*
)	]	]	divided-by	two	times	"a"

Iff $ax^2 + bx + c = 0$, then $x = \dfrac{-b \pm \sqrt{b^2 - 4ac}}{2a}$

Note the mixture of styles in Example 18.119 (p. 436): the negation of b and the square root are represented by forethought and most of the operator precedence by prefixed *bi'e*, but explicit parentheses had to be added to group the numerator properly. In addition, the square root parentheses cannot be removed here in favor of simple *fe'a* and *ku'e* bracketing, because infix operators are present in the operand. Getting Example 18.119 (p. 436) to parse perfectly using the current parser took several tries: a more relaxed style would dispense with most of the *bi'e* cmavo and just let the standard precedence rules be understood.

Non-logical connection with JOI and BIhI is also permitted between operands and between operators. One use for this construct is to connect operands with *bi'o* to create intervals:

Example 18.120

li	no	ga'o	bi'o	ke'i	pa
the-number	zero	(inclusive)	from-to	(exclusive)	one

[0,1)

the numbers from zero to one, including zero but not including one

Intervals defined by a midpoint and range rather than beginning and end points can be expressed by *mi'i*:

Example 18.121

li	pimu	ga'o	mi'i	ke'i	pimu
the-number	0.5	(inclusive)	centered-with-range	(exclusive)	0.5

which expresses the same interval as Example 18.120 (p. 437). Note that the *ga'o* and *ke'i* still refer to the endpoints, although these are now implied rather than expressed. Another way of expressing the same thing:

Example 18.122

li	pimu	su'i	ni'upimu	bi'o	ke'i	ma'upimu
the-number	0.5	plus	[-0.5	from-to	(exclusive)	+0.5]

Here we have the sum of a number and an interval, which produces another interval centered on the number. As Example 18.122 (p. 437) shows, non-logical (or logical) connection of operands has higher precedence than any mekso operator.

You can also combine two operands with *ce'o*, the sequence connective of selma'o JOI, to make a compound subscript:

Example 18.123

xy.	xi	vei	by.	ce'o	dy.	[ve'o]
"x"	sub	(	"b"	sequence	"d"	)

$x_{b,d}$

18.18 Using Lojban resources within mekso

The following cmavo are discussed in this section:

na'u	NAhU	selbri to operator
ni'e	NIhE	selbri to operand
mo'e	MOhE	sumti to operand
te'u	TEhU	terminator for all three

One of the mekso design goals requires the ability to make use of Lojban's vocabulary resources within mekso to extend the built-in cmavo for operands and operators. There are three relevant constructs: all three share the elidable terminator *te'u* (which is also used to terminate vectors marked with *jo'i*)

The cmavo *na'u* makes a selbri into an operator. In general, the first place of the selbri specifies the result of the operator, and the other unfilled places specify the operands:

Example 18.124

li	na'u	tanjo	te'u
The-number	the-operator	tangent	[end-operator]

vei	pai	fe'i	re	[ve'o]	du	li	ci'i
(	π	/	2	)	=	the-number	infinity.

$\tan(\pi/2) = \infty$

tanjo is the gismu for "x1 is the tangent of x2", and the *na'u* here makes it into an operator which is then used in forethought

The cmavo *ni'e* makes a selbri into an operand. The x1 place of the selbri generally represents a number, and therefore is often a *ni* abstraction, since *ni* abstractions represent numbers. The *ni'e* makes that number available as a mekso operand. A common application is to make equations relating pure dimensions:

Example 18.125

li		ni'e	ni		clani	[te'u]
The-number			**quantity-of**		**length**	

pi'i	ni'e	ni		ganra	[te'u]
times		**quantity-of**		**width**	

pi'i	ni'e	ni		condi	te'u
times		**quantity-of**		**depth**	

du	li		ni'e	ni		canlu
equals	**the-number**			**quantity-of**		**volume.**

Length × Width × Depth = Volume

The cmavo *mo'e* operates similarly to *ni'e*, but makes a sumti (rather than a selbri) into an operand. This construction is useful in stating equations involving dimensioned numbers:

Example 18.126

li		mo'e	re	ratcu	su'i		mo'e	re	ractu
The-number			**two**	**rats**	**plus**			**two**	**rabbits**

du	li		mo'e	vo	danlu
equals	**the-number**			**four**	**animals.**

2 rats + 2 rabbits = 4 animals.

Another use is in constructing Lojbanic versions of so-called "folk quantifiers", such as "a pride of lions":

Example 18.127

mi	viska	vei	mo'e	lo'e		lanzu	ve'o		cinfo
I	**see**	**(**			**the-typical**	**family**	**)-number-of**		**lions.**

I see a pride of lions.

18.19 Other uses of mekso

The following cmavo are discussed in this section:

me'o	LI	the mekso
nu'a	NUhA	operator to selbri
mai	MAI	utterance ordinal
mo'o	MAI	higher order utterance ordinal
roi	ROI	quantified tense

So far we have seen mekso used as sumti (with *li*), as quantifiers (often parenthesized), and in MOI and ME-MOI selbri. There are a few other minor uses of mekso within Lojban.

The cmavo *me'o* has the same grammatical use as *li* but slightly different semantics. *li* means "the number which is the value of the mekso ...", whereas *me'o* just means "the mekso ..." So it is true that:

Example 18.128

li		re	su'i	re	du		li		vo
The-number		**two**	**plus**	**two**	**equals**		**the-number**		**four.**

2 + 2 = 4

but false that:

Example 18.129

me'o		re	su'i	re	du		me'o		vo
The-mekso		**two**	**plus**	**two**	**equals**		**the-mekso**		**four.**

"2 + 2" = "4"

438

since the expressions "2 + 2" and "4" are not the same. The relationship between *li* and *me'o* is related to that between *la djan.*, the person named John, and *zo .djan.*, the name "John"

The cmavo *nu'a* is the inverse of *na'u*, and allows a mekso operator to be used as a normal selbri, with the place structure:

x1 is the result of applying (operator) to x2, x3, ...

for as many places as may be required. For example:

Example 18.130

li	*ni'umu*	*cu*	*nu'a*	*va'a*	*li*	*ma'umu*
The-number	**-5**		**is-the-operator**	**negation-of**	**the-number**	**+5.**

uses *nu'a* to make the operator *va'a* into a two-place bridi

Used together, *nu'a* and *na'u* make it possible to ask questions about mekso operators, even though there is no specific cmavo for an operator question, nor is it grammatical to utter an operator in isolation. Consider Example 18.131 (p. 439), to which Example 18.132 (p. 439) is one correct answer:

Example 18.131

li	*re*	*na'u*
The-number	**two**	**applied-to-selbri**

mo	*re*	*du*	*li*	*vo*
which-selbri?	**two**	**equals**	**the-number**	**four.**

2 ? 2 = 4

Example 18.132

nu'a	*su'i*
plus	

In Example 18.131 (p. 439), *na'u mo* is an operator question, because *mo* is the selbri question cmavo and *na'u* makes the selbri into an operator. Example 18.132 (p. 439) makes the true answer *su'i* into a selbri (which is a legal utterance) with the inverse cmavo *nu'a*. Mechanically speaking, inserting Example 18.132 (p. 439) into Example 18.131 (p. 439) produces:

Example 18.133

li	*re*	*na'u*	*nu'a*
The-number	**two**	**(the-operator**	**the-selbri**

su'i	*re*	*du*	*li*	*vo*
plus)	**two**	**equals**	**the-number**	**four.**

where the *na'u nu'a* cancels out, leaving a truthful bridi

Numerical free modifiers, corresponding to English "firstly", "secondly", and so on, can be created by suffixing a member of selma'o MAI to a digit string or a lerfu string. (Digit strings are compound cmavo beginning with a cmavo of selma'o PA, and containing only cmavo of PA or BY; lerfu strings begin with a cmavo of selma'o BY, and likewise contain only PA or BY cmavo.) Here are some examples:

Example 18.134

pamai

firstly

Example 18.135

remai

secondly

Example 18.136

romai

all-ly

lastly

Example 18.137

> *ny.mai*
>
> nth-ly

Example 18.138

> *pasomo'o*
>
> nineteenthly (higher order)
> Section 19

The difference between *mai* and *mo'o* is that *mo'o* enumerates larger subdivisions of a text. Each *mo'o* subdivision can then be divided into pieces and internally numbered with *mai*. If this chapter were translated into Lojban, each section would be numbered with *mo'o*. (See Section 19.7 (p. 455) for more on these words.)

A numerical tense can be created by suffixing a digit string with *roi*. This usage generates tenses corresponding to English "once", "twice", and so on. This topic belongs to a detailed discussion of Lojban tenses, and is explained further in Section 10.9 (p. 217).

Note: the elidable terminator *boi* is not used between a number and a member of MAI or ROI.

18.20 Explicit operator precedence

As mentioned earlier, Lojban does provide a way for the precedences of operators to be explicitly declared, although current parsers do not understand these declarations.

The declaration is made in the form of a metalinguistic comment using *ti'o*, a member of selma'o SEI. *sei*, the other member of SEI, is used to insert metalinguistic comments on a bridi which give information about the discourse which the bridi comprises. The format of a *ti'o* declaration has not been formally established, but presumably would take the form of mentioning a mekso operator and then giving it either an absolute numerical precedence on some pre-established scale, or else specifying relative precedences between new operators and existing operators.

In future, we hope to create an improved machine parser that can understand declarations of the precedences of simple operators belonging to selma'o VUhU. Originally, all operators would have the same precedence. Declarations would have the effect of raising the specified cmavo of VUhU to higher precedence levels. Complex operators formed with *na'u*, *ni'e*, or *ma'o* would remain at the standard low precedence; declarations with respect to them are for future implementation efforts. It is probable that such a parser would have a set of "commonly assumed precedences" built into it (selectable by a special *ti'o* declaration) that would match mathematical intuition: times higher than plus, and so on.

18.21 Miscellany

A few other points:

se can be used to convert an operator as if it were a selbri, so that its arguments are exchanged. For example:

Example 18.139

li	*ci*	*se*	*vu'u*	*vo*	*du*	*li*	*pa*
The-number	three	(inverse)	minus	four	equals	the-number	one.

3 subtracted from 4 equals 1.

The other converters of selma'o SE can also be used on operators with more than two operands, and they can be compounded to create (probably unintelligible) operators as needed.

Members of selma'o NAhE are also legal on an operator to produce a scalar negation of it. The implication is that some other operator would apply to make the bridi true:

Example 18.140

li	*ci*	*na'e*	*su'i*	*vo*	*du*	*li*	*pare*
The-number	3	non-	plus	4	equals	the-number	12.

Example 18.141

li	ci	to'e	vu'u	re	du	li	mu
The-number	3	opposite-of-	minus	2	equals	the-number	5.

The sense in which "plus" is the opposite of "minus" is not a mathematical but rather a linguistic one; negated operators are defined only loosely.

la'e and *lu'e* can be used on operands with the usual semantics to get the referent of or a symbol for an operand. Likewise, a member of selma'o NAhE followed by *bo* serves to scalar-negate an operand, implying that some other operand would make the bridi true:

Example 18.142

li	re	su'i	re	du	li	na'ebo	mu
The-number	2	plus	2	equals	the-number	non-	5.

2 + 2 = something other than 5.

The digits 0-9 have rafsi, and therefore can be used in making lujvo. Additionally, all the rafsi have CVC form and can stand alone or together as names:

Example 18.143

la	zel.	poi	gunta	la	tebes.	pu	nanmu
Those-named	"Seven"	who	attack	that-named	"Thebes"	[past]	are-men.

The Seven Against Thebes were men.

Of course, there is no guarantee that the name *zel.* is connected with the number rafsi: an alternative which cannot be misconstrued is:

Example 18.144

la	zemei	poi	gunta
Those-named-the	Sevensome	who	attack

la	tebes.	pu	nanmu
that-named	Thebes	[past]	are-men.

Certain other members of PA also have assigned rafsi: *so'a, so'e, so'i, so'o, so'u, da'a, ro, su'e, su'o, pi,* and *ce'i*. Furthermore, although the cmavo *fi'u* does not have a rafsi as such, it is closely related to the gismu *frinu*, meaning "fraction"; therefore, in a context of numeric rafsi, you can use any of the rafsi for *frinu* to indicate a fraction slash.

A similar convention is used for the cmavo *cu'o* of selma'o MOI, which is closely related to *cunso* (probability); use a rafsi for *cunso* in order to create lujvo based on *cu'o*. The cmavo *mei* and *moi* of MOI have their own rafsi, two each in fact: *mem/ mei* and *mom/ moi* respectively.

The grammar of mekso as described so far imposes a rigid distinction between operators and operands. Some flavors of mathematics (lambda calculus, algebra of functions) blur this distinction, and Lojban must have a method of doing the same. An operator can be changed into an operand with *ni'enu'a*, which transforms the operator into a matching selbri and then the selbri into an operand.

To change an operand into an operator, we use the cmavo *ma'o*, already introduced as a means of changing a lerfu string such as *fy.* into an operator. In fact, *ma'o* can be followed by any mekso operand, using the elidable terminator *te'u* if necessary.

There is a potential semantic ambiguity in *ma'o fy. [te'u]* if *fy.* is already in use as a variable: it comes to mean "the function whose value is always **f**". However, mathematicians do not normally use the same lerfu words or strings as both functions and variables, so this case should not arise in practice.

18.22 Four score and seven: a mekso problem

Abraham Lincoln's Gettysburg Address begins with the words "Four score and seven years ago". This section exhibits several different ways of saying the number "four score and seven". (A "score", for those not familiar with the term, is 20; it is analogous to a "dozen" for 12.) The trivial way:

Example 18.145

li	bize
eight	**seven**

87

Example 18.145 (p. 442) is mathematically correct, but sacrifices the spirit of the English words, which are intended to be complex and formal.

Example 18.146

li	vo	pi'i	reno	su'i	ze
the-number	**four**	**times**	**twenty**	**plus**	**seven**

$4 \times 20 + 7$

Example 18.146 (p. 442) is also mathematically correct, but still misses something. "Score" is not a word for 20 in the same way that "ten" is a word for 10: it contains the implication of 20 objects. The original may be taken as short for "Four score years and seven years ago". Thinking of a score as a twentysome rather than as 20 leads to:

Example 18.147

li	mo'e	voboi	renomei
the-number	**[sumti-to-mex]**	**four**	**twentysomes**

te'u	su'i	ze
[end-sumti-to-mex]	**plus**	**seven**

In Example 18.147 (p. 442), *voboi renomei* is a sumti signifying four things each of which are groups of twenty; the *mo'e* and *te'u* then make this sumti into a number in order to allow it to be the operand of *su'i*.

Another approach is to think of "score" as setting a representation base. There are remnants of base-20 arithmetic in some languages, notably French, in which 87 is "quatre-vingt-sept", literally "four-twenties-seven". (This fact makes the Gettysburg Address hard to translate into French!) If "score" is the representation base, then we have:

Example 18.148

li	vo	pi'e	ze	ju'u	reno
the-number	**four**	**;**	**seven**	**base**	**20**

47_{20}

Overall, Example 18.147 (p. 442) probably captures the flavor of the English best. Example 18.145 (p. 442) and Example 18.146 (p. 442) are too simple, and Example 18.148 (p. 442) is too tricky. Nevertheless, all four examples are good Lojban. Pedagogically, these examples illustrate the richness of lojbau mekso: anything that can be said at all, can probably be said in more than one way.

18.23 mekso selma'o summary

Except as noted, each selma'o has only one cmavo.

BOI	elidable terminator for numerals and lerfu strings
BY	lerfu for variables and functions (see Section 17.11 (p. 406))
FUhA	reverse-Polish flag
GOhA	includes *du* (mathematical equality) and other non-mekso cmavo
JOhI	array flag
KUhE	elidable terminator for forethought mekso
LI	mekso articles (*li* and *me'o*)
MAhO	make operand into operator
MOI	creates mekso selbri (*moi*, *mei*, *si'e*, and *cu'o*, see Section 18.11 (p. 428))
MOhE	make sumti into operand
NAhU	make selbri into operator
NIhE	make selbri into operand

NUhA	make operator into selbri
PA	numbers (see Section 18.25 (p. 443))
PEhO	optional forethought mekso marker
TEhU	elidable terminator for NAhU, NIhE, MOhE, MAhO, and JOhI
VEI	left parenthesis
VEhO	right parenthesis
VUhU	operators (see Section 18.24 (p. 443))
XI	subscript flag

18.24 Complete table of VUhU cmavo, with operand structures

The operand structures specify what various operands (labeled a, b, c, ...) mean. The implied context is forethought, since only forethought operators can have a variable number of operands; however, the same rules apply to infix and RP uses of VUhU.

su'i	plus	$(((a + b) + c) + ...)$
pi'i	times	$(((a \times b) \times c) \times ...)$
vu'u	minus	$(((a - b) - c) - ...)$
fe'i	divided by	$(((a / b) / c) / ...)$
ju'u	number base	numeral string **a** interpreted in the base **b**
pa'i	ratio	the ratio of **a** to **b** a:b
fa'i	reciprocal of/multiplicative inverse	$1 / a$
gei	scientific notation	b × (c [default 10] to the **a** power)
ge'a	null operator	(no operands)
de'o	logarithm	log **a** to base **b** (default 10 or **e** as appropriate)
te'a	to the power/exponential	**a** to the **b** power
fe'a	nth root of/inverse power	b^{th} root of a (default square root: b = 2)
cu'a	absolute value/norm	$\|a\|$
ne'o	factorial	a!
pi'a	matrix row vector combiner	(all operands are row vectors)
sa'i	matrix column vector combiner	(all operands are column vectors)
ri'o	integral	integral of a with respect to b over range c
sa'o	derivative	derivative of a with respect to b of degree c (default 1)
fu'u	non-specific operator	(variable)
si'i	sigma (Σ) summation	summation of a using variable b over range c
va'a	negation of/additive inverse	-a
re'a	matrix transpose/dual	a^*

18.25 Complete table of PA cmavo: digits, punctuation, and other numbers.

Table 18.1. Decimal digits

no	non	0
pa	pav	1
re	rel	2
ci	cib	3
vo	von	4
mu	mum	5
xa	xav	6
ze	zel	7
bi	biv	8
so	soz	9

Table 18.2. Hexadecimal digits

dau	A/10
fei	B/11
gai	C/12
jau	D/13
rei	E/14
vai	F/15

Table 18.3. Special numbers

pai	π
ka'o	imaginary i
te'o	exponential e
ci'i	infinity (∞)

Table 18.4. Number punctuation

pi	piz	decimal point
ce'i	cez	percentage
fi'u	fi'u (from frinu; see Section 18.20 (p. 440))	fraction (not division)
pi'e	mixed-base point	
ma'u	plus sign (not addition)	
ni'u	minus sign (not subtraction)	
ki'o	thousands comma	
ra'e	repeating-decimal indicator	
ji'i	approximation sign	
ka'o	complex number separator	

Table 18.5. Indefinite numbers

ro	all	rol	
so'a	soj	almost all	
so'e	sop	most	
so'i	many	sor	so'i
so'o	sos	several	
so'u	sot	few	
da'a	daz	all but	

Table 18.6. Subjective numbers

rau	enough
du'e	too few
mo'a	too many

Table 18.7. Miscellaneous

xo	number question
tu'o	null operand

18.26 Table of MOI cmavo, with associated rafsi and place structures

mei	mem	mei

x1 is a mass formed from a set x2 of n members, one or more of which is/are x3, [measured relative to the set x4/by standard x4]

moi	mom	moi

x1 is the (n)th member of set x2 when ordered by rule x3 [by standard x4]

si'e	

18.26 Table of MOI cmavo, with associated rafsi and place structures

x1 is an (n)th portion of mass x2 [by standard x3]

cu'o ⋮ cu'o (borrowed from *cunso*; see Section 18.20 (p. 440))

event x1 has probability (n) of occurring under conditions x2 [by standard x3]

va'e ⋮

x1 is at scale position (n) on the scale x2 [by standard x3]

Chapter 19
Putting It All Together: Notes on the Structure of Lojban Texts

19.1 Introductory

This chapter is incurably miscellaneous. It describes the cmavo that specify the structure of Lojban texts, from the largest scale (paragraphs) to the smallest (single words). There are fewer examples than are found in other chapters of this book, since the linguistic mechanisms described are generally made use of in conversation or else in long documents.

This chapter is also not very self-contained. It makes passing reference to a great many concepts which are explained in full only in other chapters. The alternative would be a chapter on text structure which was as complex as all the other chapters put together. Lojban is a unified language, and it is not possible to understand any part of it (in full) before understanding every part of it (to some degree).

19.2 Sentences: I

The following cmavo is discussed in this section:

.i I sentence separator

Since Lojban is audio-visually isomorphic, there needs to be a spoken and written way of signaling the end of a sentence and the start of the following one. In written English, a period serves this purpose; in spoken English, a tone contour (rising or falling) usually does the job, or sometimes a long pause. Lojban uses a single separator: the cmavo *i* (of selma'o I):

447

Example 19.1

mi	klama	le	zarci	.i	do	cadzu	le	bisli
I	go-to	the	store.		You	walk-on	the	ice.

The word "separator" should be noted. *i* is not normally used after the last sentence nor before the first one, although both positions are technically grammatical. *i* signals a new sentence on the same topic, not necessarily by the same speaker. The relationship between the sentences is left vague, except in stories, where the relationship usually is temporal, and the following sentence states something that happened after the previous sentence.

Note that although the first letter of an English sentence is capitalized, the cmavo *i* is never capitalized. In writing, it is appropriate to place extra space before *i* to make it stand out better for the reader. In some styles of Lojban writing, every *i* is placed at the beginning of a line, possibly leaving space at the end of the previous line.

An *i* cmavo may or may not be used when the speaker of the following sentence is different from the speaker of the preceding sentence, depending on whether the sentences are felt to be connected or not.

An *i* cmavo can be compounded with a logical or non-logical connective (a jek or joik), a modal or tense connective, or both: these constructs are explained in Section 9.8 (p. 192), Section 10.16 (p. 230), and Section 14.4 (p. 320). In all cases, the *i* comes first in the compound. Attitudinals can also be attached to an *i* if they are meant to apply to the whole sentence: see Section 13.9 (p. 299).

There exist a pair of mechanisms for binding a sequence of sentences closely together. If the *i* (with or without connectives) is followed by *bo* (of selma'o BO), then the two sentences being separated are understood to be more closely grouped than sentences connected by *i* alone.

Similarly, a group of sentences can be preceded by *tu'e* (of selma'o TUhE) and followed by *tu'u* (of selma'o TUhU) to fuse them into a single unit. A common use of *tu'e...tu'u* is to group the sentences which compose a poem: the title sentence would precede the group, separated from it by *i*. Another use might be a set of directions, where each numbered direction might be surrounded by *tu'e...tu'u* and contain one or more sentences separated by *i*. Grouping with *tu'e* and *tu'u* is analogous to grouping with *ke* and *ke'e* to establish the scope of logical or non-logical connectives (see Section 14.8 (p. 326)).

19.3 Paragraphs: NIhO

The following cmavo are discussed in this section:

ni'o	NIhO	new topic
no'i	NIhO	old topic
da'o	DAhO	cancel cmavo assignments

The paragraph is a concept used in writing systems for two purposes: to indicate changes of topic, and to break up the hard-to-read appearance of large blocks of text on the page. The former function is represented in both spoken and written Lojban by the cmavo *ni'o* and *no'i*, both of selma'o NIhO. Of these two, *ni'o* is the more common. By convention, written Lojban is broken into paragraphs just before any *ni'o* or *no'i*, but a very long passage on a single topic might be paragraphed before an *i*. On the other hand, it is conventional in English to start a new paragraph in dialogue when a new speaker starts, but this convention is not commonly observed in Lojban dialogues. Of course, none of these conventions affect meaning in any way.

A *ni'o* can take the place of an *i* as a sentence separator, and in addition signals a new topic or paragraph. Grammatically, any number of *ni'o* cmavo can appear consecutively and are equivalent to a single one; semantically, a greater number of *ni'o* cmavo indicates a larger-scale change of topic. This feature allows complexly structured text, with topics, subtopics, and sub-subtopics, to be represented clearly and unambiguously in both spoken and written Lojban. However, some conventional differences do exist between *ni'o* in writing and in conversation.

In written text, a single *ni'o* is a mere discursive indicator of a new subject, whereas *ni'oni'o* marks a change in the context. In this situation, *ni'oni'o* implicitly cancels the definitions of all pro-sumti of selma'o KOhA as well as pro-bridi of selma'o GOhA. (Explicit cancelling is expressed by the cmavo *da'o* of selma'o DAhO, which has the free grammar of an indicator – it can appear almost anywhere.) The use of *ni'oni'o* does not affect indicators (of selma'o UI) or tense references, but *ni'oni'oni'o*, indicating a drastic change of topic, would serve to reset both indicators and tenses. (See Section 19.8 (p. 456) for a discussion of indicator scope.)

In spoken text, which is inherently less structured, these levels are reduced by one, with *ni'o* indicating a change in context sufficient to cancel pro-sumti and pro-bridi assignment. On the other hand, in a book, or in stories within stories such as "The Arabian Nights", further levels may be expressed by extending the *ni'o* string as needed. Normally, a written text will begin with the number of *ni'o* cmavo needed to signal the largest scale division which the text contains. *ni'o* strings may be subscripted to label each context of discourse: see Section 19.6 (p. 453).

no'i is similar in effect to *ni'o*, but indicates the resumption of a previous topic. In speech, it is analogous to (but much shorter than) such English discursive phrases as "But getting back to the point ...". By default, the topic resumed is that in effect before the last *ni'o*. When subtopics are nested within topics, then *no'i* would resume the previous subtopic and *no'ino'i* the previous topic. Note that *no'i* also resumes tense and pro-sumti assignments dropped at the previous *ni'o*.

If a *ni'o* is subscripted, then a *no'i* with the same subscript is assumed to be a continuation of it. A *no'i* may also have a negative subscript, which would specify counting backwards a number of paragraphs and resuming the topic found thereby.

19.4 Topic-comment sentences: ZOhU

The following cmavo is discussed in this section:

zo'u : ZOhU : topic/comment separator

The normal Lojban sentence is just a bridi, parallel to the normal English sentence which has a subject and a predicate:

Example 19.2

mi : klama : le : zarci

I went-to the market

In Chinese, the normal sentence form is different: a topic is stated, and a comment about it is made. (Japanese also has the concept of a topic, but indicates it by attaching a suffix; other languages also distinguish topics in various ways.) The topic says what the sentence is about:

Example 19.3

zhe^4 xiao^{1}xi^2 : wo^3 zhi^{1}dao le

this news : I know [perfective]

As for this news, I knew it.

I've heard this news already.

The colon in the first two versions of Example 19.3 (p. 449) separate the topic ("this news") from the comment ("I know already").

Lojban uses the cmavo *zo'u* (of selma'o ZOhU) to separate topic (a sumti) from comment (a bridi):

Example 19.4

le	nuzba	zo'u	mi	ba'o	djuno
The	news	:	I	[perfective]	know.

Example 19.4 (p. 449) is the literal Lojban translation of Example 19.3 (p. 449). Of course, the topic-comment structure can be changed to a straightforward bridi structure:

Example 19.5

mi	ba'o	djuno	le	nuzba
I	[perfective]	know	the	news.

Example 19.5 (p. 449) means the same as Example 19.4 (p. 449), and it is simpler. However, often the position of the topic in the place structure of the selbri within the comment is vague:

Example 19.6

le	finpe	zo'u	citka
the	**fish**	**:**	**eat**

Is the fish eating or being eaten? The sentence doesn't say. The Chinese equivalent of Example 19.6 (p. 450) is:

Example 19.7

yu[2]: chi[1]

fish: eat

which is vague in exactly the same way.

Grammatically, it is possible to have more than one sumti before *zo'u*. This is not normally useful in topic-comment sentences, but is necessary in the other use of *zo'u*: to separate a quantifying section from a bridi containing quantified variables. This usage belongs to a discussion of quantifier logic in Lojban (see Section 16.2 (p. 376)), but an example would be:

Example 19.8

ro	da	poi	prenu	ku'o
For-all	**X**	**which**	**are-persons,**	

su'o	de	zo'u	de	patfu	da
there-exists-a	**Y**	**such-that**	**Y**	**is-the-father-of**	**X.**

Every person has a father.

The string of sumti before *zo'u* (called the "prenex": see Section 16.2 (p. 376)) may contain both a topic and bound variables:

Example 19.9

loi	patfu	ro	da	poi	prenu	ku'o
For-the-mass-of	**fathers**	**for-all**	**X**	**which**	**are-persons,**	

su'o	de	zo'u	de	patfu	da
there-exists-a	**Y**	**such-that**	**Y**	**is-the-father-of**	**X.**

As for fathers, every person has one.

To specify a topic which affects more than one sentence, wrap the sentences in *tu'e...tu'u* brackets and place the topic and the *zo'u* directly in front. This is the exception to the rule that a topic attaches directly to a sentence:

Example 19.10

loi	jdini	zo'u	tu'e		do	ponse	.inaja	do	djica	[tu'u]
The-mass-of	**money**	**:**	**(**	**[if]**	**you**	**possess,**	**then**	**you**	**want**	**)**

Money: if you have it, you want it.

Note: In Lojban, you do not "want money"; you "want to have money" or something of the sort, as the x2 place of *djica* demands an event. As a result, the straightforward rendering of Example 19.9 (p. 450) without a topic is not:

Example 19.11

do	ponse	loi jdini	.inaja	do	djica	ri
You	**possess**	**money**	**only-if**	**you**	**desire**	**its-mere-existence.**

where *ri* means *loi jdini* and is interpreted as "the mere existence of money", but rather:

Example 19.12

do	ponse	loi jdini	.inaja	do	djica	tu'a	ri
You	**possess**	**money**	**only-if**	**you**	**desire**	**something-about**	**it.**

namely, the possession of money. But topic-comment sentences like Example 19.10 (p. 450) are inherently vague, and this difference between *ponse* (which expects a physical object in x2) and *djica* is ignored. See Example 19.45 (p. 458) for another topic/comment sentence.

The subject of an English sentence is often the topic as well, but in Lojban the sumti in the x1 place is not necessarily the topic, especially if it is the normal (unconverted) x1 for the selbri. Thus Lojban sentences don't necessarily have a "subject" in the English sense.

19.5 Questions and answers

The following cmavo are discussed in this section:

xu	UI	truth question
ma	KOhA	sumti question
mo	GOhA	bridi question
xo	PA	number question
ji	A	sumti connective question
ge'i	GA	forethought connective question
gi'i	GIhA	bridi-tail connective question
gu'i	GUhA	tanru forethought connective question
je'i	JA	tanru connective question
pei	UI	attitude question
fi'a	FA	place structure question
cu'e	CUhE	tense/modal question
pau	UI	question premarker

Lojban questions are not at all like English questions. There are two basic types: truth questions, of the form "Is it true that ...", and fill-in-the-blank questions. Truth questions are marked by preceding the bridi, or following any part of it specifically questioned, with the cmavo *xu* (of selma'o UI):

Example 19.13

xu	do	klama	le	zarci
[True-or-false?]	You	go-to	the	store

Are you going to the store/Did you go to the store?

(Since the Lojban is tenseless, either colloquial translation might be correct.) Truth questions are further discussed in Section 15.8 (p. 367).

Fill-in-the-blank questions have a cmavo representing some Lojban word or phrase which is not known to the questioner, and which the answerer is to supply. There are a variety of cmavo belonging to different selma'o which provide different kinds of blanks.

Where a sumti is not known, a question may be formed with *ma* (of selma'o KOhA), which is a kind of pro-sumti:

Example 19.14

ma	klama	le	zarci
[What-sumti?]	goes-to	the	store

Who is going to the store?

Of course, the *ma* need not be in the x1 place:

Example 19.15

do	klama	ma
You	go-to	[what-sumti?]

Where are you going?

The answer is a simple sumti:

Example 19.16

> *le zarci*
>
> The store.

A sumti, then, is a legal utterance, although it does not by itself constitute a bridi – it does not claim anything, but merely completes the open-ended claim of the previous bridi.

There can be two *ma* cmavo in a single question:

Example 19.17

> *ma klama ma*
>
> Who goes where?

and the answer would be two sumti, which are meant to fill in the two *ma* cmavo in order:

Example 19.18

mi	*le*	*zarci*
I,	[to]-the	store.

An even more complex example, depending on the non-logical connective *fa'u* (of selma'o JOI), which is like the English "and ... respectively":

Example 19.19

ma	*fa'u*	*ma*	*klama*	*ma*	*fa'u*	*ma*

Who and who goes where and where, -respectively?

An answer might be

Example 19.20

la	*djan.*	*la*	*marcas.*	*le*	*zarci*	*le*	*briju*
	John,		Marsha,	the	store,	the	office.

John and Marsha go to the store and the office, respectively.

(Note: A mechanical substitution of Example 19.20 (p. 452) into Example 19.19 (p. 452) produces an ungrammatical result, because * *... le zarci fa'u le briju* is ungrammatical Lojban: the first *le zarci* has to be closed with its proper terminator *ku*, for reasons explained in Section 14.14 (p. 338). This effect is not important: Lojban behaves as if all elided terminators have been supplied in both question and answer before inserting the latter into the former. The exchange is grammatical if question and answer are each separately grammatical.)

Questions to be answered with a selbri are expressed with *mo* of selma'o GOhA, which is a kind of pro-bridi:

Example 19.21

la	*lojban.*	*mo*
	Lojban	[what-selbri?]

What is Lojban?

Here the answerer is to supply some predicate which is true of Lojban. Such questions are extremely open-ended, due to the enormous range of possible predicate answers. The answer might be just a selbri, or might be a full bridi, in which case the sumti in the answer override those provided by the questioner. To limit the range of a *mo* question, make it part of a tanru.

Questions about numbers are expressed with *xo* of selma'o PA:

Example 19.22

do	*viska*	*xo*	*prenu*
You	saw	[what-number?]	persons.

How many people did you see?

The answer would be a simple number, another kind of non-bridi utterance:

Example 19.23

> *vomu*
>
> **Forty-five.**

Fill-in-the-blank questions may also be asked about: logical connectives (using cmavo *ji* of A, *ge'i* of GA, *gi'i* of GIhA, *gu'i* of GUhA, or *je'i* of JA, and receiving an ek, gihek, ijek, or ijoik as an answer) – see Section 14.13 (p. 335); attitudes (using *pei* of UI, and receiving an attitudinal as an answer) – see Section 13.10 (p. 300); place structures (using *fi'a* of FA, and receiving a cmavo of FA as an answer) – see Section 9.3 (p. 182); tenses and modals (using *cu'e* of CUhE, and receiving any tense or BAI cmavo as an answer) – see Section 9.6 (p. 188) and Chapter 10 (p. 207).

Questions can be marked by placing *pau* (of selma'o UI) before the question bridi. See Section 13.13 (p. 307) for details.

The full list of non-bridi utterances suitable as answers to questions is:

- any number of sumti (with elidable terminator *vau*, see Chapter 6 (p. 115))
- an ek or gihek (logical connectives, see Chapter 14 (p. 317))
- a number, or any mathematical expression placed in parentheses (see Chapter 18 (p. 413))
- a bare *na* negator (to negate some previously expressed bridi), or corresponding *ja'a* affirmer (see Chapter 15 (p. 353))
- a relative clause (to modify some previously expressed sumti, see Chapter 8 (p. 161))
- a prenex/topic (to modify some previously expressed bridi, see Chapter 16 (p. 375))
- linked arguments (beginning with *be* or *bei* and attached to some previously expressed selbri, often in a description, see Section 5.7 (p. 88))

At the beginning of a text, the following non-bridi are also permitted:

- one or more names (to indicate direct address without *doi*, see Chapter 6 (p. 115))
- indicators (to express a prevailing attitude, see Chapter 13 (p. 285))
- *nai* (to vaguely negate something or other, see Section 15.7 (p. 366))

Where not needed for the expression of answers, most of these are made grammatical for pragmatic reasons: people will say them in conversation, and there is no reason to rule them out as ungrammatical merely because most of them are vague.

19.6 Subscripts: XI

The following cmavo is discussed in this section:

> xi ┊ XI ┊ subscript

The cmavo *xi* (of selma'o XI) indicates that a subscript (a number, a lerfu string, or a parenthesized mekso) follows. Subscripts can be attached to almost any construction and are placed following the construction (or its terminator word, which is generally required). They are useful either to extend the finite cmavo list to infinite length, or to make more refined distinctions than the standard cmavo list permits. The remainder of this section mentions some places where subscripts might naturally be used.

Lojban gismu have at most five places:

Example 19.24

mi	*cu*	*klama*	*le*	*zarci*	*le*	*zdani*	*le*	*dargu*	*le*	*karce*
I		go	to the	market	from the	house	via the	road	using the	car.

Consequently, selma'o SE (which operates on a selbri to change the order of its places) and selma'o FA (which provides place number tags for individual sumti) have only enough members to handle up to five places. Conversion of Example 19.24 (p. 453), using *xe* to swap the x1 and x5 places, would produce:

Example 19.25

le	karce	cu	xe-klama		le	zarci
The	car		is-a-transportation-means	to	the	market

	le	zdani		le	dargu		mi
from	the	house	via	the	road	for	me.

And reordering of the place structures might produce:

Example 19.26

fo	le	dargu	fi	le	zdani	fa	mi
Via	the	road,	from	the	house,		I,

fe	le	zarci		fu	le	karce	cu	klama
to	the	market,	using	the	car,		go.

Example 19.24 (p. 453) to Example 19.26 (p. 454) all mean the same thing. But consider the lujvo *nunkla*, formed by applying the abstraction operator *nu* to *klama*:

Example 19.27

la'e		di'u		cu	nunkla		mi
The-referent-of	the-previous-sentence			is-an-event-of-going	by	me

	le	zarci		le	zdani		le	dargu		le	karce
to	the	market	from	the	house	via	the	road	using	the	car.

Example 19.27 (p. 454) shows that *nunkla* has six places: the five places of *klama* plus a new one (placed first) for the event itself. Performing transformations similar to that of Example 19.25 (p. 454) requires an additional conversion cmavo that exchanges the x1 and x6 places. The solution is to use any cmavo of SE with a subscript "6" (Section 19.6 (p. 453)):

Example 19.28

le	karce	cu	sexixa nunkla		mi
The	car		is-a-transportation-means-in-the-event-of-going	by	me

	le	zarci		le	zdani
to	the	market	from	the	house

	le	dargu	la'edi'u
via	the	road	is-an-event-which-is-referred-to-by-the-last-sentence.

Likewise, a sixth place tag can be created by using any cmavo of FA with a subscript:

Example 19.29

fu	le	dargu	fo	le	zdani	fe	mi
Via	the	road,	from	the	house,	by	me,

fa	la'edi'u
	is-an-event-which	is-referred-to-by-the-last-sentence,

fi	le	zarci		faxixa	le	karce	cu	nunkla
to	the	market,	using	the	car,		is-an-event-of-going.

Example 19.27 (p. 454) to Example 19.29 (p. 454) also all mean the same thing, and each is derived straightforwardly from any of the others, despite the tortured nature of the English glosses. In addition, any other member of SE or FA could be substituted into *sexixa* and *faxixa* without change of meaning: *vexixa* means the same thing as *sexixa*.

Lojban provides two groups of pro-sumti, both belonging to selma'o KOhA. The ko'a-series cmavo are used to refer to explicitly specified sumti to which they have been bound using *goi*. The da-series, on the other hand, are existentially or universally quantified variables. (These concepts are explained more fully in Chapter 16 (p. 375).) There are ten ko'a-series cmavo and 3 da-series cmavo available.

If more are required, any cmavo of the ko'a-series or the da-series can be subscripted:

Example 19.30

da	xi	vo
X	sub	4

is the 4th bound variable of the 1st sequence of the da-series, and

Example 19.31

ko'i	xi	paso
something-3	sub	18

is the 18th free variable of the 3rd sequence of the ko'a-series. This convention allows 10 sequences of ko'a-type pro-sumti and 3 sequences of da-type pro-sumti, each with as many members as needed. Note that *daxivo* and *dexivo* are considered to be distinct pro-sumti, unlike the situation with *sexixa* and *vexixa* above. Exactly similar treatment can be given to the bu'a-series of selma'o GOhA and to the gismu pro-bridi *broda, brode, brodi, brodo,* and *brodu.*

Subscripts on lerfu words are used in the standard mathematical way to extend the number of variables:

Example 19.32

li	xy.boixipa	du	li	xy.boixire	su'i	xy.boixici
The-number	x-sub-1	equals	the-number	x-sub-2	plus	x-sub-3

$x_1 = x_2 + x_3$

and can be used to extend the number of pro-sumti as well, since lerfu strings outside mathematical contexts are grammatically and semantically equivalent to pro-sumti of the ko'a-series. (In Example 19.32 (p. 455), note the required terminator *boi* after each *xy.* cmavo; this terminator allows the subscript to be attached without ambiguity.)

Names, which are similar to pro-sumti, can also be subscripted to distinguish two individuals with the same name:

Example 19.33

la	djan.	xipa	cusku	lu	mi'enai	do	li'u	la	djan.	xire
	John	1	expresses	[quote]	I-am-not	you	[unquote]	to		John	2	.

Subscripts on tenses allow talking about more than one time or place that is described by the same general cmavo. For example, *puxipa* could refer to one point in the past, and *puxire* a second point (earlier or later).

You can place a subscript on the word *ja'a*, the bridi affirmative of selma'o NA, to express so-called fuzzy truths. The usual machinery for fuzzy logic (statements whose truth value is not merely "true" or "false", but is expressed by a number in the range 0 to 1) in Lojban is the abstractor *jei*:

Example 19.34

li	pimu	jei	mi	ganra
The-number	.5	is-the-truth-value-of	my	being-broad.

However, by convention we can attach a subscript to *ja'a* to indicate fuzzy truth (or to *na* if we change the amount):

Example 19.35

mi	ja'a	xipimu	ganra
I	truly	sub-.5	am-broad

Finally, as mentioned in Section 19.2 (p. 447), *ni'o* and *no'i* cmavo with matching subscripts mark the start and the continuation of a given topic respectively. Different topics can be assigned to different subscripts.

Other uses of subscripts will doubtless be devised in future.

19.7 Utterance ordinals: MAI

The following cmavo are discussed in this section:

mai	MAI	utterance ordinal, -thly
mo'o	MAI	higher order utterance ordinal

Numerical free modifiers, corresponding to English "firstly", "secondly", and so on, can be created by suffixing *mai* or *mo'o* of selma'o MAI to a number or a lerfu string. Here are some examples:

Example 19.36

mi	klama	pamai	le	zarci	.e	remai	le	zdani
I	go-to	(firstly)	the	store	and	(secondly)	the	house.

This does not imply that I go to the store before I go to the house: that meaning requires a tense. The sumti are simply numbered for convenience of reference. Like other free modifiers, the utterance ordinals can be inserted almost anywhere in a sentence without affecting its grammar or its meaning.

Any of the Lojban numbers can be used with MAI: *romai*, for example, means "all-thly" or "lastly". Likewise, if you are enumerating a long list and have forgotten which number is wanted next, you can say *ny.mai*, or "Nthly".

The difference between *mai* and *mo'o* is that *mo'o* enumerates larger subdivisions of a text; *mai* was designed for lists of numbered items, whereas *mo'o* was intended to subdivide structured works. If this chapter were translated into Lojban, it might number each section with *mo'o*: this section would then be introduced with *zemo'o*, or "Section 7."

19.8 Attitude scope markers: FUhE/FUhO

The following cmavo are discussed in this section:

fu'e	FUhE	open attitudinal scope
fu'o	FUhO	close attitudinal scope

Lojban has a complex system of "attitudinals", words which indicate the speaker's attitude to what is being said. The attitudinals include indicators of emotion, intensity markers, discursives (which show the structure of discourse), and evidentials (which indicate "how the speaker knows"). Most of these words belong to selma'o UI; the intensity markers belong to selma'o CAI for historical reasons, but the two selma'o are grammatically identical. The individual cmavo of UI and CAI are discussed in Chapter 13 (p. 285); only the rules for applying them in discourse are presented here.

Normally, an attitudinal applies to the preceding word only. However, if the preceding word is a structural cmavo which begins or ends a whole construction, then that whole construction is affected by the attitudinal:

Example 19.37

mi	viska	le	blanu	.ia	zdani	[ku]
I	see	the	blue	[belief]	house.	

I see the house, which I believe to be blue.

Example 19.38

mi	viska	le	blanu	zdani	.ia	[ku]
I	see	the	blue	house	[belief].	

I see the blue thing, which I believe to be a house.

Example 19.39

mi	viska	le	.ia	blanu	zdani	[ku]
I	see	the	[belief]	blue	house	

I see what I believe to be a blue house.

Example 19.40

mi	viska	le	blanu	zdani	ku	.ia
I	see	(the	blue	house)		[belief]

I see what I believe to be a blue house.

An attitudinal meant to cover a whole sentence can be attached to the preceding *i*, expressed or understood:

Example 19.41

[.i]	.ia	mi	viska	le	blanu	zdani
[belief]	I	see	the	blue	house.

I believe I see a blue house.

or to an explicit *vau* placed at the end of a bridi.

Likewise, an attitudinal meant to cover a whole paragraph can be attached to *ni'o* or *no'i*. An attitudinal at the beginning of a text applies to the whole text.

However, sometimes it is necessary to be more specific about the range of one or more attitudinals, particularly if the range crosses the boundaries of standard Lojban syntactic constructions. The cmavo *fu'e* (of selma'o FUhE) and *fu'o* (of selma'o FUhO) provide explicit scope markers. Placing *fu'e* in front of an attitudinal disconnects it from what precedes it, and instead says that it applies to all following words until further notice. The notice is given by *fu'o*, which can appear anywhere and cancels all in-force attitudinals. For example:

Example 19.42

mi	viska	le	fu'e	.ia	blanu	zdani	fu'o	ponse
I	see	the	[start]	[belief]	blue	house	[end]	possessor

I see the owner of what I believe to be a blue house.

Here, only the *blanu zdani* portion of the three-part tanru *blanu zdani ponse* is marked as a belief of the speaker. Naturally, the attitudinal scope markers do not affect the rules for interpreting multi-part tanru: *blanu zdani* groups first because tanru group from left to right unless overridden with *ke* or *bo*.

Other attitudinals of more local scope can appear after attitudinals marked by FUhE; these attitudinals are added to the globally active attitudinals rather than superseding them.

19.9 Quotations: LU, LIhU, LOhU, LEhU

The following cmavo are discussed in this section:

lu	LU	begin quotation
li'u	LIhU	end quotation
lo'u	LOhU	begin error quotation
le'u	LEhU	end error quotation

Grammatically, quotations are very simple in Lojban: all of them are sumti, and they all mean something like "the piece of text here quoted":

Example 19.43

mi	pu	cusku	lu	mi'e	.djan.	[li'u]
I	[past]	express	[quote]	I-am	John	[unquote]

I said, "I'm John".

But in fact there are four different flavors of quotation in the language, involving six cmavo of six different selma'o. This being the case, quotation deserves some elaboration.

The simplest kind of quotation, exhibited in Example 19.43 (p. 457), uses the cmavo *lu* (of selma'o LU) as the opening quotation mark, and the cmavo *li'u* (of selma'o LIhU) as the closing quotation mark. The text between *lu* and *li'u* must be a valid, parseable Lojban text. If the quotation is ungrammatical, so is the surrounding expression. The cmavo *li'u* is technically an elidable terminator, but it's almost never possible to elide it except at the end of text.

The cmavo *lo'u* (of selma'o LOhU) and *le'u* (of selma'o LEhU) are used to surround a quotation that is not necessarily grammatical Lojban. However, the text must consist of morphologically correct Lojban words (as defined in Chapter 4 (p. 49)), so that the *le'u* can be picked out reliably. The words need not be meaningful, but they must be recognizable as cmavo, brivla, or cmene. Quotation with *lo'u* is essential to quoting ungrammatical Lojban for teaching in the language, the equivalent of the * that is used in English to mark such errors:

Example 19.44

lo'u	mi du do du la djan.	le'u
[quote]	mi du do du la djan.	[unquote]

na	tergerna	la	lojban.
is-not	a-grammatical-structure	in	Lojban.

Example 19.44 (p. 458) is grammatical even though the embedded quotation is not. Similarly, *lo'u* quotation can quote fragments of a text which themselves do not constitute grammatical utterances:

Example 19.45

lu	le mlatu cu viska le finpe	li'u	zo'u
[quote]	le mlatu cu viska le finpe	[unquote]	:

lo'u	viska le	le'u	cu	selbasti
[quote]	viska le	[unquote]		is-replaced-by

.ei	lo'u	viska lo	le'u
[obligation!]	[quote]	viska lo	[unquote].

In the sentence *le mlatu viska le finpe*, *viska le* should be replaced by *viska lo*.

Note the topic-comment formulation (Section 19.4 (p. 449)) and the indicator applying to the selbri only (Section 19.8 (p. 456)). Neither *viska le* nor *viska lo* is a valid Lojban utterance, and both require *lo'u* quotation.

Additionally, pro-sumti or pro-bridi in the quoting sentence can refer to words appearing in the quoted sentence when *lu...li'u* is used, but not when *lo'u ... le'u* is used:

Example 19.46

la	tcarlis.	cusku	lu	le	ninmu	cu	morsi	li'u
	Charlie	says	[quote]	the	woman		is-dead	[unquote].

.iku'i	ri	jmive
However,	the-last-mentioned	is-alive.

Charlie says "The woman is dead", but she is alive.

In Example 19.46 (p. 458), *ri* is a pro-sumti which refers to the most recent previous sumti, namely *le ninmu*. Compare:

Example 19.47

la	tcarlis.	cusku	lo'u	le	ninmu	cu	morsi	le'u
	Charlie	says	[quote]	le	ninmu	cu	morsi	[unquote].

.iku'i	ri	jmive
However,	the-last-mentioned	is-alive.

Charlie says *le ninmu cu morsi*, but he is alive.

In Example 19.47 (p. 458), *ri* cannot refer to the referent of the alleged sumti *le ninmu*, because *le ninmu cu morsi* is a mere uninterpreted sequence of Lojban words. Instead, *ri* ends up referring to the referent of the sumti *la tcarlis.*, and so it is Charlie who is alive.

The metalinguistic erasers *si*, *sa*, and *su*, discussed in Section 19.13 (p. 463), do not operate in text between *lo'u* and *le'u*. Since the first *le'u* terminates a *lo'u* quotation, it is not directly possible to have a *lo'u* quotation within another *lo'u* quotation. However, it is possible for a *le'u* to occur within a *lo'u* ... *le'u* quotation by preceding it with the cmavo *zo*, discussed in Section 19.10 (p. 458). Note that *le'u* is not an elidable terminator; it is required.

19.10 More on quotations: ZO, ZOI

The following cmavo are discussed in this section:

zo	ZO	quote single word
zoi	ZOI	non-Lojban quotation
la'o	ZOI	non-Lojban name

The cmavo *zo* (of selma'o ZO) is a strong quotation mark for the single following word, which can be any Lojban word whatsoever. Among other uses, *zo* allows a metalinguistic word to be referenced without having it act on the surrounding text. The word must be a morphologically legal (but not necessarily meaningful) single Lojban word; compound cmavo are not permitted. For example:

Example 19.48

> *zo si cu lojbo valsi*

> *si* is a Lojbanic word.

Since *zo* acts on a single word only, there is no corresponding terminator. Brevity, then, is a great advantage of *zo*, since the terminators for other kinds of quotation are rarely or never elidable.

The cmavo *zoi* (of selma'o ZOI) is a quotation mark for quoting non-Lojban text. Its syntax is *zoi X. text .X*, where X is a Lojban word (called the delimiting word) which is separated from the quoted text by pauses, and which is not found in the written text or spoken phoneme stream. It is common, but not required, to use the lerfu word (of selma'o BY) which corresponds to the Lojban name of the language being quoted:

Example 19.49

> *zoi gy. John is a man .gy. cu glico jufra*

> "John is a man" is an English sentence.

where *gy* stands for *glico*. Other popular choices of delimiting words are *.kuot.*, a Lojban name which sounds like the English word "quote", and the word *zoi* itself. Another possibility is a Lojban word suggesting the topic of the quotation.

Within written text, the Lojban written word used as a delimiting word may not appear, whereas within spoken text, the sound of the delimiting word may not be uttered. This leads to occasional breakdowns of audio-visual isomorphism: Example 19.50 (p. 459) is fine in speech but ungrammatical as written, whereas Example 19.51 (p. 459) is correct when written but ungrammatical in speech.

Example 19.50

> *mi djuno fi le valsi po'u zoi gy. gyrations .gy.*

> I know about the word which-is "gyrations".

Example 19.51

> *mi djuno fi le valsi po'u zoi jai. gyrations .jai*

> I know about the word which-is "gyrations".

The text *gy* appears in the written word "gyrations", whereas the sound represented in Lojban by *jai* appears in the spoken word "gyrations". Such borderline cases should be avoided as a matter of good style.

It should be noted particularly that *zoi* quotation is the only way to quote rafsi, specifically CCV rafsi, because they are not Lojban words, and *zoi* quotation is the only way to quote things which are not Lojban words. (CVC and CVV rafsi look like names and cmavo respectively, and so can be quoted using other methods.) For example:

Example 19.52

> *zoi ry. sku .ry. cu rafsi zo cusku*

> "*sku*" is a rafsi of "*cusku*".

(A minor note on interaction between *lo'u ... le'u* and *zoi*: The text between *lo'u* and *le'u* should consist of Lojban words only. In fact, non-Lojban material in the form of a *zoi* quotation may also appear. However, if the word *le'u* is used either as the delimiting word for the *zoi* quotation, or within the quotation itself, the outer *lo'u* quotation will be prematurely terminated. Therefore, *le'u* should be avoided as the delimiting word in any *zoi* quotation.)

Lojban strictly avoids any confusion between things and the names of things:

Example 19.53

zo	.bab.	cmene	la	bab.
The-word	**"Bob"**	**is-the-name-of**	**the-one-named**	**Bob.**

In Example 19.53 (p. 460), *zo .bab.* is the word, whereas *la bab.* is the thing named by the word. The cmavo *la'e* and *lu'e* (of selma'o LAhE) convert back and forth between references and their referents:

Example 19.54

zo	.bab.	cmene	la'e	zo	.bab.
The-word	**"Bob"**	**is-the-name-of**	**the-referent-of**	**the-word**	**"Bob"** .

Example 19.55

lu'e	la	bab.	cmene	la	bab.
A-symbol-for		**Bob**	**is-the-name-of**		**Bob.**

Example 19.53 (p. 460) through Example 19.55 (p. 460) all mean approximately the same thing, except for differences in emphasis. Example 19.56 (p. 460) is different:

Example 19.56

la bab. cmene la bab.

Bob is the name of Bob.

and says that Bob is both the name and the thing named, an unlikely situation. People are not names.

(In Example 19.53 (p. 460) through Example 19.54 (p. 460), the name *bab.* was separated from a preceding *zo* by a pause, thus: *zo .bab..* The reason for this extra pause is that all Lojban names must be separated by pause from any preceding word other than *la, lai, la'i* (all of selma'o LA) and *doi* (of selma'o DOI). There are numerous other cmavo that may precede a name: of these, *zo* is one of the most common.)

The cmavo *la'o* also belongs to selma'o ZOI, and is mentioned here for completeness, although it does not signal the beginning of a quotation. Instead, *la'o* serves to mark non-Lojban names, especially the Linnaean binomial names (such as "Homo sapiens") which are the internationally standardized names for species of animals and plants. Internationally known names which can more easily be recognized by spelling rather than pronunciation, such as "Goethe", can also appear in Lojban text with *la'o*:

Example 19.57

la'o dy. Goethe .dy. cu me la'o ly. Homo sapiens .ly.

Goethe is a Homo sapiens.

Using *la'o* for all names rather than Lojbanizing, however, makes for very cumbersome text. A rough equivalent of *la'o* might be *la me zoi.*

19.11 Contrastive emphasis: BAhE

The following cmavo are discussed in this section:

ba'e	BAhE	emphasize next word
za'e	BAhE	next word is nonce

English often uses strong stress on a word to single it out for contrastive emphasis, thus

Example 19.58

I saw George.

is quite different from

Example 19.59

I saw *George.*

The heavy stress on "*George*" (represented in writing by *italics*) indicates that I saw George rather than someone else. Lojban does not use stress in this way: stress is used only to help separate words (because every brivla is stressed on the penultimate syllable) and in names to match other languages' stress patterns. Note that many other languages do not use stress in this way either; typically word order is rearranged, producing something like

Example 19.60

> It was George whom I saw.

In Lojban, the cmavo *ba'e* (of selma'o BAhE) precedes a single word which is to be emphasized:

Example 19.61

mi	viska	la	ba'e	.djordj.
I	saw	the-one-named	[emphasis]	"George"	.

> I saw *George*.

Note the pause before the name *djordj.*, which serves to separate it unambiguously from the *ba'e*. Alternatively, the *ba'e* can be moved to a position before the *la*, which in effect emphasizes the whole construct *la djordj.*:

Example 19.62

mi	viska	ba'e	la	djordj.
I	saw	[emphasis]	the-one-named	"George"	.

> I saw *George*.

Marking a word with a cmavo of BAhE does not change the word's grammar in any way. Any word in a bridi can receive contrastive emphasis marking:

Example 19.63

> *ba'e mi viska la djordj.*

> I, no one else, saw George.

Example 19.64

> *mi ba'e viska la djordj.*

> I saw (not heard or smelled) George.

Emphasis on one of the structural components of a Lojban bridi can also be achieved by rearranging it into an order that is not the speaker's or writer's usual order. Any sumti moved out of place, or the selbri when moved out of place, is emphatic to some degree.

For completeness, the cmavo *za'e* should be mentioned, also of selma'o BAhE. It marks a word as possibly irregular, non-standard, or nonce (created for the occasion):

Example 19.65

mi	klama	la	za'e	.albeinias.
I	go-to		so-called	Albania

marks a Lojbanization of an English name, where a more appropriate standard form might be something like *la ckiipyris.*, reflecting the country's name in Albanian.

Before a lujvo or fu'ivla, *za'e* indicates that the word has been made up on the spot and may be used in a sense that is not found in the unabridged dictionary (when we have an unabridged dictionary!).

19.12 Parenthesis and metalinguistic commentary: TO, TOI, SEI

The following cmavo are discussed in this section:

to	TO	open parenthesis
to'i	TO	open editorial parenthesis
toi	TOI	close parenthesis
sei	SEI	metalinguistic bridi marker

The cmavo *to* and *toi* are discursive (non-mathematical) parentheses, for inserting parenthetical remarks. Any text whatsoever can go within the parentheses, and it is completely invisible to its context. It can, however, refer to the context by the use of pro-sumti and pro-bridi: any that have been assigned in the context are still assigned in the parenthetical remarks, but the reverse is not true.

Example 19.66

doi	lisas.	mi	djica	le	nu		to	doi	frank.
O	Lisa,	I	desire	the	event-of	(	O		Frank,

ko		sisti	toi	do	viska	le	mlatu
[imperative]		stop!	)	you	see	the	cat.

Lisa, I want you to (Frank! Stop!) see the cat.

Example 19.66 (p. 462) implicitly redefines *do* within the parentheses: the listener is changed by *doi frank*. When the context sentence resumes, however, the old listener, Lisa, is automatically restored.

There is another cmavo of selma'o TO: *to'i*. The difference between *to* and *to'i* is the difference between parentheses and square brackets in English prose. Remarks within *to* ... *toi* cmavo are implicitly by the same speaker, whereas remarks within *to'i* ... *toi* are implicitly by someone else, perhaps an editor:

Example 19.67

la frank. cusku lu mi prami do to'isa'a do du la djein. toi li'u

Frank expresses "I love you [you = Jane]"

The *sa'a* suffix is a discursive cmavo (of selma'o UI) meaning "editorial insertion", and indicating that the marked word or construct (in this case, the entire bracketed remark) is not part of the quotation. It is required whenever the *to'i* ... *toi* remark is physically within quotation marks, at least when speaking to literal-minded listeners; the convention may be relaxed if no actual confusion results.

Note: The parser believes that parentheses are attached to the previous word or construct, because it treats them as syntactic equivalents of subscripts and other such so-called "free modifiers". Semantically, however, parenthetical remarks are not necessarily attached either to what precedes them or what follows them.

The cmavo *sei* (of selma'o SEI) begins an embedded discursive bridi. Comments added with *sei* are called "metalinguistic", because they are comments about the discourse itself rather than about the subject matter of the discourse. This sense of the term "metalinguistic" is used throughout this chapter, and is not to be confused with the sense "language for expressing other languages".

When marked with *sei*, a metalinguistic utterance can be embedded in another utterance as a discursive. In this way, discursives which do not have cmavo assigned in selma'o UI can be expressed:

Example 19.68

la frank. prami sei la frank. gleki la djein.

Frank loves (Frank is happy) Jane.

Using the happiness attitudinal, *.ui*, would imply that the speaker was happy. Instead, the speaker attributes happiness to Frank. It would probably be safe to elide the one who is happy, and say:

Example 19.69

la frank. prami sei gleki la djein.

Frank loves (he is happy) Jane.

The grammar of the bridi following *sei* has an unusual limitation: the sumti must either precede the selbri, or must be glued into the selbri with *be* and *bei*:

Example 19.70

la frank. prami sei gleki be fa la suzn. la djein.

Frank loves (Susan is happy) Jane.

This restriction allows the terminator cmavo *se'u* to almost always be elided.

Since a discursive utterance is working at a "higher" level of abstraction than a non-discursive utterance, a non-discursive utterance cannot refer to a discursive utterance. Specifically, the various back-counting, reciprocal, and reflexive constructs in selma'o KOhA ignore the utterances at "higher" metalinguistic levels in determining their referent. It is possible, and sometimes necessary, to refer to lower metalinguistic levels. For example, the English "he said" in a conversation is metalinguistic. For this purpose, quotations are considered to be at a lower metalinguistic level than the surrounding context (a quoted text cannot refer to the statements of the one who quotes it), whereas parenthetical remarks are considered to be at a higher level than the context.

Lojban works differently from English in that the "he said" can be marked instead of the quotation. In Lojban, you can say:

Example 19.71

la	djan.	cusku	lu	mi	klama	le	zarci	li'u
John	expresses	[quote]	I	go-to	the	store	[unquote].

which literally claims that John uttered the quoted text. If the central claim is that John made the utterance, as is likely in conversation, this style is the most sensible. However, in written text which quotes a conversation, you don't want the "he said" or "she said" to be considered part of the conversation. If unmarked, it could mess up the anaphora counting. Instead, you can use:

Example 19.72

lu	mi	klama	le	zarci	seisa'a
[quote]	I	go-to	the	store	(

la	djan.	cusku	be	dei	li'u
John	expresses		this-sentence	)[unquote]

"I go to the store", said John.

And of course other orders are possible:

Example 19.73

lu seisa'a la djan. cusku be dei mi klama le zarci

John said, "I go to the store".

Example 19.74

lu mi klama seisa'a la djan cusku le zarci

"I go", John said, "to the store".

Note the *sa'a* following each *sei*, marking the *sei* and its attached bridi as an editorial insert, not part of the quotation. In a more relaxed style, these *sa'a* cmavo would probably be dropped.

The elidable terminator for *sei* is *se'u* (of selma'o SEhU); it is rarely needed, except to separate a selbri within the *sei* comment from an immediately following selbri (or component) outside the comment.

19.13 Erasure: SI, SA, SU

The following cmavo are discussed in this section:

si	SI	erase word
sa	SA	erase phrase
su	SU	erase discourse

The cmavo *si* (of selma'o SI) is a metalinguistic operator that erases the preceding word, as if it had never been spoken:

Example 19.75

ti	gerku	si	mlatu
This	is-a-dog,	er,	is-a-cat.

means the same thing as *ti mlatu*. Multiple *si* cmavo in succession erase the appropriate number of words:

Example 19.76

ta	blanu	zdani	si	si	xekri	zdani
That	is-a-blue	house,	er,	er,	is-a-black	house.

In order to erase the word *zo*, it is necessary to use three *si* cmavo in a row:

Example 19.77

zo	.bab.	se	cmene	zo	si	si	si	la	bab.
The-word	"Bob"	is-the-name-of	the	word	si	,	er,	er,	Bob.

The first use of *si* does not erase anything, but completes the *zo* quotation. Two more *si* cmavo are then necessary to erase the first *si* and the *zo*.

Incorrect names can likewise cause trouble with *si*:

Example 19.78

mi	tavla	fo	la	.esperanto
I	talk	in-language	that-named	and-speranto,

si	si	.esperanton.
er,	er,	Esperanto.

The Lojbanized spelling *.esperanto* breaks up, as a consequence of the Lojban morphology rules (see Chapter 4 (p. 49)) into two Lojban words, the cmavo *e* and the undefined lujvo *speranto*. Therefore, two *si* cmavo are needed to erase them. Of course, *.e speranto* is not grammatical after *la*, but recognition of *si* is done before grammatical analysis.

Even more messy is the result of an incorrect *zoi*:

Example 19.79

mi	cusku	zoi	fy.	gy.	fy.	si	si	si	si	zo .djan
I	express	[foreign]	[quote]	gy	[unquote],	er,	er,	er,	er,	"John" .

In Example 19.79 (p. 464), the first *fy* is taken to be the delimiting word. The next word must be different from the delimiting word, and *gy.*, the Lojban name for the letter *g*, was chosen arbitrarily. Then the delimiting word must be repeated. For purposes of *si* erasure, the entire quoted text is taken to be a word, so four words have been uttered, and four more *si* cmavo are needed to erase them altogether. Similarly, a stray *lo'u* quotation mark must be erased with *fy. le'u si si si*, by completing the quotation and then erasing it all with three *si* cmavo.

What if less than the entire *zo* or *zoi* construct is erased? The result is something which has a loose *zo* or *zoi* in it, without its expected sequels, and which is incurably ungrammatical. Thus, to erase just the word quoted by *zo*, it turns out to be necessary to erase the *zo* as well:

Example 19.80

mi	se	cmene	zo	.djan.	si	si	zo	.djordj.
I		am-named-by	the-word	"John,"	er,	er,	the-word	"George."

The parser will reject *zo .djan. si .djordj.*, because in that context *djordj.* is a name (of selma'o CMENE) rather than a quoted word.

Note: The current machine parser does not implement *si* erasure.

As the above examples plainly show, precise erasures with *si* can be extremely hard to get right. Therefore, the cmavo *sa* (of selma'o SA) is provided for erasing more than one word. The cmavo following *sa* should be the starting marker of some grammatical construct. The effect of the *sa* is to erase back to and including the last starting marker of the same kind. For example:

Example 19.81

mi	viska	le	sa	.i	mi	cusku	zo	.djan.
I	see	the	...		I	say	the-word	"John" .

Since the word following *sa* is *i*, the sentence separator, its effect is to erase the preceding sentence. So Example 19.81 (p. 464) is equivalent to:

Example 19.82

> *mi cusku zo .djan.*

Another example, erasing a partial description rather than a partial sentence:

Example 19.83

mi	viska	le	blanu	.zdan.	sa	le	xekri	zdani
I	see	the	blue	hou	...	the	black	house.

In Example 19.83 (p. 465), *le blanu .zdan.* is ungrammatical, but clearly reflects the speaker's original intention to say *le blanu zdani*. However, the *zdani* was cut off before the end and changed into a name. The entire ungrammatical *le* construct is erased and replaced by *le xekri zdani*.

Note: The current machine parser does not implement *sa* erasure. Getting *sa* right is even more difficult (for a computer) than getting *si* right, as the behavior of *si* is defined in terms of words rather than in terms of grammatical constructs (possibly incorrect ones) and words are conceptually simpler entities. On the other hand, *sa* is generally easier for human beings, because the rules for using it correctly are less finicky.

The cmavo *su* (of selma'o SU) is yet another metalinguistic operator that erases the entire text. However, if the text involves multiple speakers, then *su* will only erase the remarks made by the one who said it, unless that speaker has said nothing. Therefore *susu* is needed to eradicate a whole discussion in conversation.

Note: The current machine parser does not implement either *su* or *susu* erasure.

19.14 Hesitation: Y

The following cmavo is discussed in this section:

> .y. | Y | hesitation noise

Speakers often need to hesitate to think of what to say next or for some extra-linguistic reason. There are two ways to hesitate in Lojban: to pause between words (that is, to say nothing) or to use the cmavo *.y.* (of selma'o Y). This resembles in sound the English hesitation noise written "uh" (or "er"), but differs from it in the requirement for pauses before and after. Unlike a long pause, it cannot be mistaken for having nothing more to say: it holds the floor for the speaker. Since vowel length is not significant in Lojban, the *y* sound can be dragged out for as long as necessary. Furthermore, the sound can be repeated, provided the required pauses are respected.

Since the hesitation sound in English is outside the formal language, English-speakers may question the need for a formal cmavo. Speakers of other languages, however, often hesitate by saying (or, if necessary, repeating) a word ("este" in some dialects of Spanish, roughly meaning "that is"), and Lojban's audio-visual isomorphism requires a written representation of all meaningful spoken behavior. Of course, *.y.* has no grammatical significance: it can appear anywhere at all in a Lojban sentence except in the middle of a word.

19.15 No more to say: FAhO

The following cmavo is discussed in this section:

> fa'o | FAhO | end of text

The cmavo *fa'o* (of selma'o FAhO) is the usually omitted marker for the end of a text; it can be used in computer interaction to indicate the end of input or output, or for explicitly giving up the floor during a discussion. It is outside the regular grammar, and the machine parser takes it as an unconditional signal to stop parsing unless it is quoted with *zo* or with *lo'u ... le'u*. In particular, it is not used at the end of subordinate texts quoted with *lu...li'u* or parenthesized with *to ... toi*.

19.16 List of cmavo interactions

The following list gives the cmavo and selma'o that are recognized by the earliest stages of the parser, and specifies exactly which of them interact with which others. All of the cmavo are at least mentioned in this chapter. The cmavo are written in lower case, and the selma'o in UPPER CASE.

- *zo* quotes the following word, no matter what it is.
- *si* erases the preceding word unless it is a *zo*.
- *sa* erases the preceding word and other words, unless the preceding word is a *zo*.
- *su* is the same as *sa*, but erases more words.
- *lo'u* quotes all following words up to a *le'u* (but not a *zo le'u*).
- *le'u* is ungrammatical except at the end of a "lo'u quotation.
- ZOI cmavo use the following word as a delimiting word, no matter what it is, but using *le'u* may create difficulties.
- *zei* combines the preceding and the following word into a lujvo, but does not affect *zo, si, sa, su, lo'u*, ZOI cmavo, *fa'o*, and *zei*.
- BAhE cmavo mark the following word, unless it is *si, sa,* or *su*, or unless it is preceded by *zo*. Multiple BAhE cmavo may be used in succession.
- *bu* makes the preceding word into a lerfu word, except for *zo, si, sa, su, lo'u*, ZOI cmavo, *fa'o, zei*, BAhE cmavo, and *bu*. Multiple *bu* cmavo may be used in succession.
- UI and CAI cmavo mark the previous word, except for *zo, si, sa, su, lo'u*, ZOI, *fa'o, zei*, BAhE cmavo, and *bu*. Multiple UI cmavo may be used in succession. A following *nai* is made part of the UI.
- *.y., da'o, fu'e,* and *fu'o* are the same as UI, but do not absorb a following *nai*.

19.17 List of Elidable Terminators

The following list shows all the elidable terminators of Lojban. The first column is the terminator, the second column is the selma'o that starts the corresponding construction, and the third column states what kinds of grammatical constructs are terminated. Each terminator is the only cmavo of its selma'o, which naturally has the same name as the cmavo.

be'o	BE	sumti attached to a tanru unit
boi	PA/BY	number or lerfu string
do'u	COI/DOI	vocative phrases
fe'u	FIhO	ad-hoc modal tags
ge'u	GOI	relative phrases
kei	NU	abstraction bridi
ke'e	KE	groups of various kinds
ku	LE/LA	description sumti
ku'e	PEhO	forethought mekso
ku'o	NOI	relative clauses
li'u	LU	quotations
lo'o	LI	number sumti
lu'u	LAhE/NAhE+BO	sumti qualifiers
me'u	ME	tanru units formed from sumti
nu'u	NUhI	forethought termsets
se'u	SEI/SOI	metalinguistic insertions
te'u	various	mekso conversion constructs
toi	TO	parenthetical remarks
tu'u	TUhE	multiple sentences or paragraphs
vau	(none)	simple bridi or bridi-tails
ve'o	VEI	mekso parentheses

Chapter 20

A Catalogue of selma'o

20.1

The following paragraphs list all the selma'o of Lojban, with a brief explanation of what each one is about, and reference to the chapter number where each is explained more fully. As usual, all selma'o names are given in capital letters (with "h" serving as the capital of "'") and are the names of a representative cmavo, often the most important or the first in alphabetical order. One example is given of each selma'o: for selma'o which have several uses, the most common use is shown.

selma'o A (Section 14.6 (p. 324))

Specifies a logical connection (e.g. "and", "or", "if"), usually between sumti.

la djan.	a	la djein.	klama	le	zarci
John	and/or	Jane	goes-to	the	store

Also used to create vowel lerfu words when followed with "bu".

selma'o BAI (Section 9.6 (p. 188))

May be prefixed to a sumti to specify an additional place, not otherwise present in the place structure of the selbri, and derived from a single place of some other selbri.

mi	tavla	bau	la lojban.
I	speak	in-language	Lojban.

selma'o BAhE (Section 19.11 (p. 460))

Emphasizes the next single word, or marks it as a nonce word (one invented for the occasion).

la ba'e .djordj.	klama	le	zarci
George	goes-to	the	store.

It is George who goes to the store.

selma'o BE (Section 5.7 (p. 88))

Attaches sumti which fill the place structure of a single unit making up a tanru. Unless otherwise indicated, the sumti fill the x2, x3, and successive places in that order. BE (p. 468) is most useful in descriptions formed with LE (p. 477). See BEI (p. 468), BEhO (p. 468).

mi		klama	be	ta		troci
I	am-a	(goer	to	that)	type-of	trier.

I try to go to that place.

selma'o BEI (Section 5.7 (p. 88))

Separates multiple sumti attached by BE (p. 468) to a tanru unit.

mi		klama	be	le	zarci	bei	le	zdani	be'o		troci
I	am-a	(goer	to	the	store	from	the	home	)	type-of	trier.

I try to go from the home to the market.

selma'o BEhO (Section 5.7 (p. 88))

Elidable terminator for BE (p. 468). Terminates sumti that are attached to a tanru unit.

mi		klama	be	le	zarci	be'o		troci
I	am-a	(goer	to	the	market	)	type-of	trier.

I try to go to the market.

selma'o BIhE (Section 18.5 (p. 417))

Prefixed to a mathematical operator to mark it as higher priority than other mathematical operators, binding its operands more closely.

li		ci	bi'e		pi'i	vo	su'i	mu	du		li		paze
The-number	3	[priority]	times	4	plus	5	equals	the-number	17.

$3 \times 4 + 5 = 17$

selma'o BIhI (Section 14.16 (p. 343))

Joins sumti or tanru units (as well as some other things) to form intervals. See GAhO (p. 473).

mi	ca	sanli	la drezdn.	bi'i	la frankfurt.
I	[present]	stand-on-surface	Dresden	[interval]	Frankfurt.

I am standing between Dresden and Frankfurt.

selma'o BO (Section 5.3 (p. 82), Section 15.6 (p. 365), Section 18.17 (p. 435))

Joins tanru units, binding them together closely. Also used to bind logically or non-logically connected phrases, sentences, etc. BO (p. 469) is always high precedence and right-grouping.

ta	cmalu		nixli	bo	ckule
That	is-a-small	type-of	(girl	type-of	school).

That is a small school for girls.

selma'o BOI (Section 18.6 (p. 419))

Elidable terminator for PA (p. 482) or BY (p. 469). Used to terminate a number (string of numeric cmavo) or lerfu string (string of letter words) when another string immediately follows.

li	re	du	li	vu'u	vo boi	re
The-number	two	equals	the-number	the-difference-of	four and	two.

selma'o BU (Section 17.4 (p. 400))

A suffix which can be attached to any word, typically a word representing a letter of the alphabet or else a name, to make a word for a symbol or a different letter of the alphabet. In particular, attached to single-vowel cmavo to make words for vowel letters.

.abu	.ebu	.ibu	.obu	.ubu	.ybu
a,	e,	i,	o,	u,	y.

selma'o BY (Section 17.2 (p. 398))

Words representing the letters of the Lojban alphabet, plus various shift words which alter the interpretation of other letter words. Terminated by BOI.

.abu	tavla	by	le	la .ibymym.	skami
A	talks-to	B	about the	of- IBM	computers.

A talks to B about IBM computers.

selma'o CAI (Section 13.4 (p. 292))

Indicates the intensity of an emotion: maximum, strong, weak, or not at all. Typically follows another particle which specifies the emotion.

.ei	cai	mi	klama	le	zarci
[Obligation!]	[Intense!]	I	go-to	the	market.

I must go to the market.

selma'o CAhA (Section 10.19 (p. 235))

Specifies whether a bridi refers to an actual fact, a potential (achieved or not), or merely an innate capability.

ro	datka	ka'e	flulimna
All	ducks	[capability]	are-float-swimmers.

All ducks have the capability of swimming by floating.

selma'o CEI (Section 7.5 (p. 144))

Assigns a selbri definition to one of the five pro-bridi gismu: "broda", "brode", "brodi", "brodo", or "brodu", for later use.

ti slasi je mlatu bo cidja lante gacri cei broda

This is a plastic cat-food can cover, or thingy.

.i le crino broda cu barda .i le xunre broda cu cmalu

The green thingy is large. The red thingy is small.

selma'o CEhE (Section 14.11 (p. 332), Section 16.7 (p. 382))

Joins multiple terms into a termset. Termsets are used to associate several terms for logical connectives, for equal quantifier scope, or for special constructs in tenses.

mi	ce'e	do	pe'e	je	la djan.	ce'e	la djeimyz.	cu	pendo
I	[,]	you	[joint]	and	John	[,]	James		are-friends-of.

I am a friend of you, and John is a friend of James.

selma'o CO (Section 5.8 (p. 91))

When inserted between the components of a tanru, inverts it, so that the following tanru unit modifies the previous one.

mi	troci	co	klama	le	zarci		le	zdani
I	am-a-trier	of-type	(goer-to	the	market	from	the	house).

I try to go to the market from the house.

selma'o COI (Section 6.11 (p. 130), Section 13.14 (p. 309))

When prefixed to a name, description, or sumti, produces a vocative: a phrase which indicates who is being spoken to (or who is speaking). Vocatives are used in conversational protocols, including greeting, farewell, and radio communication. Terminated by DOhU (p. 471). See DOI (p. 471).

coi	.djan.
Greetings,	John.

selma'o CU (Section 9.2 (p. 180))

Separates the selbri of a bridi from any sumti which precede it. Never strictly necessary, but often useful to eliminate various elidable terminators.

le	gerku	cu	klama	le	zarci
The	dog		goes-to	the	store.

selma'o CUhE (Section 10.24 (p. 242))

Forms a question which asks when, where, or in what mode the rest of the bridi is true. See PU (p. 482), CAhA (p. 470), TAhE (p. 484), and BAI (p. 467).

do	cu'e		klama	le	zarci
You	[When/Where?]		go-to	the	store?

When are you going to the store?

selma'o DAhO (Section 7.13 (p. 155))

Cancels the assigned significance of all sumti cmavo (of selma'o KOhA (p. 476)) and bridi cmavo (of selma'o GOhA (p. 474)).

selma'o DOI (Section 13.14 (p. 309))

The non-specific vocative indicator. May be used with or without COI (p. 470). No pause is required between "doi" and a following name. See DOhU (p. 471).

doi	frank.	mi	tavla	do
O	Frank,	I	speak-to	you.

Frank, I'm talking to you.

selma'o DOhU (Section 13.14 (p. 309))

Elidable terminator for COI (p. 470) or DOI (p. 471). Signals the end of a vocative.

coi	do'u
Greetings	[terminator]

Greetings, O unspecified one!

selma'o FA (Section 9.3 (p. 182))

Prefix for a sumti, indicating which numbered place in the place structure the sumti belongs in; overrides word order.

fa	mi	cu	klama	fi	la .atlantas.
x1=	I		go	x3=	Atlanta

fe	la bastn.	fo	le	dargu	fu	le	karce
x2=	Boston	x4=	the	road	x5=	the	car.

I go from Atlanta to Boston via the road using the car.

selma'o FAhA (Section 10.2 (p. 209))

Specifies the direction in which, or toward which (when marked with MOhI (p. 480)) or along which (when prefixed by VEhA (p. 486) or VIhA (p. 486)) the action of the bridi takes place.

le	nanmu	zu'a	batci	le	gerku
The	man	[left]	bites	the	dog.

To my left, the man bites the dog.

selma'o FAhO (Section 19.15 (p. 465))

A mechanical signal, outside the grammar, indicating that there is no more text. Useful in talking to computers.

selma'o FEhE (Section 10.11 (p. 222))

Indicates that the following interval modifier (using TAhE (p. 484), ROI (p. 483), or ZAhO (p. 487)) refers to space rather than time.

ko	vi'i	fe'e	di'i	sombo	le	gurni
You-imperative	[1-dimensional]	[space]	[regularly]	sow	the	grain.

Sow the grain in a line and evenly!

selma'o FEhU (Section 9.5 (p. 187))

Elidable terminator for FIhO (p. 472). Indicates the end of an ad hoc modal tag: the tagged sumti immediately follows.

mi	viska	do	fi'o	kanla	[fe'u]	le	zunle
I	see	you	[modal]	eye	:	the	left-thing

I see you with the left eye.

selma'o FIhO (Section 9.5 (p. 187))

When placed before a selbri, transforms the selbri into a modal tag, grammatically and semantically equivalent to a member of selma'o BAI (p. 467). Terminated by FEhU (p. 472).

mi	viska	do	fi'o	kanla	le	zunle
I	see	you	with	eye	the	left-thing

I see you with my left eye.

selma'o FOI (Section 17.6 (p. 402))

Signals the end of a compound alphabet letter word that begins with TEI (p. 484). Not an elidable terminator.

tei	.ebu	.akut. bu	foi
(	"e"	"acute"	)

the letter "e" with an acute accent

selma'o FUhA (Section 18.16 (p. 434))

Indicates that the following mathematical expression is to be interpreted as reverse Polish (RP), a mode in which mathematical operators follow their operands.

li	fu'a	reboi	re[boi]	su'i	du	li	vo
the-number	[RP!]	two,	two,	plus	equals	the-number	four

2 + 2 = 4

selma'o FUhE (Section 19.8 (p. 456))

Indicates that the following indicator(s) of selma'o UI (p. 485) affect not the preceding word, as usual, but rather all following words until a FUhO (p. 473).

mi	viska	le	fu'e	.ia	blanu	zdani	fu'o	ponse
I	see	the	[start]	[belief]	blue	house	[end]	possessor

I see the owner of a blue house, or what I believe to be one.

selma'o FUhO (Section 19.8 (p. 456))

Cancels all indicators of selma'o UI (p. 485) which are in effect.

mi	viska	le	fu'e	.ia	blanu	zdani	fu'o	ponse
I	see	the	[start]	[belief]	blue	house	[end]	possessor.

I see the owner of what I believe to be a blue house.

selma'o GA (Section 14.5 (p. 322))

Indicates the beginning of two logically connected sumti, bridi-tails, or various other things. Logical connections include "both ... and", "either ... or", "if ... then", and so on. See GI (p. 474).

ga la djan. nanmu gi la djeimyz. ninmu

Either John is a man or James is a woman (or both).

selma'o GAhO (Section 14.16 (p. 343))

Specifies whether an interval specified by BIhI (p. 468) includes or excludes its endpoints. Used in pairs before and after the BIhI (p. 468) cmavo, to specify the nature of both the left- and the right-hand endpoints.

mi	ca	sanli	la drezdn.
I	[present]	stand	Dresden

ga'o	bi'i	ga'o	la frankfurt.
[inclusive]	[interval]	[inclusive]	Frankfurt.

I am standing between Dresden and Frankfurt, inclusive of both.

selma'o GEhU (Section 8.3 (p. 165))

Elidable terminator for GOI (p. 474). Marks the end of a relative phrase. See KUhO (p. 477).

la djan.	goi	ko'a	ge'u	blanu
John	(referred to as	it-1	)	is-blue.

selma'o GI (Section 14.5 (p. 322))

Separates two logically or non-logically connected sumti, tanru units, bridi-tails, or other things, when the prefix is a forethought connective involving GA (p. 473), GUhA (p. 474), or JOI (p. 475).

ge la djan. nanmu gi la djeimyz. ninmu

(It is true that) both John is a man and James is a woman.

selma'o GIhA (Section 14.3 (p. 319))

Specifies a logical connective (e.g. "and", "or", "if") between two bridi-tails: a bridi-tail is a selbri with any associated following sumti, but not including any preceding sumti.

mi	klama	le	zarci	gi'e	nelci	la djan.
I	go-to	the	market	and	like	John.

selma'o GOI (Section 8.3 (p. 165))

Specifies the beginning of a relative phrase, which associates a subordinate sumti (following) to another sumti (preceding). Terminated by GEhU (p. 473) See NOI (p. 481).

la djan.	goi		ko'a	cu	blanu
John	(referred to as	it-1)			is-blue.

selma'o GOhA (Section 7.6 (p. 146))

A general selma'o for all cmavo which can take the place of brivla. There are several groups of these.

A: *mi klama le zarci*

B: *mi go'i*

A: I'm going to the market.

B: Me, too.

selma'o GUhA (Section 14.3 (p. 319))

Indicates the beginning of two logically connected tanru units. Takes the place of GA (p. 473) when forming logically-connected tanru. See GI (p. 474).

la .alis.	gu'e	ricfu	gi	blanu
Alice	is both	rich	and	blue.

selma'o I (Section 19.2 (p. 447))

Separates two sentences from each other.

mi	klama	le	zarci	.i	mi	klama	le	zdani
I	go-to	the	market	.	I	go-to	the	house.

selma'o JA (Section 14.3 (p. 319))

Specifies a logical connection (e.g. "and", "or", "if") between two tanru units, mathematical operands, tenses, or abstractions.

ti	blanu	je	zdani
This	is-blue	and	a-house.

selma'o JAI (Section 9.12 (p. 199))

When followed by a tense or modal, creates a conversion operator attachable to a selbri which exchanges the modal place with the x1 place of the selbri. When alone, is a conversion operator exchanging the x1 place of the selbri (which should be an abstract sumti) with one of the places of the abstracted-over bridi.

mi	jai gau	galfi	le	bitmu	se skari
I	am-the-actor-in	modifying	the	wall	color.

I act so as to modify the wall color.
I change the color of the wall.

selma'o JOI (Section 14.14 (p. 338))

Specifies a non-logical connection (e.g. together-with-as-mass, -set, or -sequence) between two sumti, tanru units, or various other things. When immediately followed by GI (p. 474), provides forethought non-logical connection analogous to GA (p. 473).

la djan.	joi	la .alis.	cu	bevri	le	pipno
John	massed-with	Alice		carry	the	piano.

selma'o JOhI (Section 18.15 (p. 433))

Indicates that the following mathematical operands (a list terminated by TEhU (p. 484)) form a mathematical vector (one-dimensional array).

li	jo'i	paboi	reboi	te'u	su'i	jo'i	ciboi	voboi	du
The-number	array(	one,	two	)	plus	array(	three,	four)	equals

li	jo'i	voboi	xaboi
the-number	array(	four,	six).

$(1,2) + (3,4) = (4,6)$

selma'o KE (Section 5.5 (p. 84))

Groups everything between itself and a following KEhE (p. 476) for purposes of logical connection, tanru construction, or other purposes. KE (p. 475) and KEhE (p. 476) are not used for mathematical (see VEI (p. 485) and VEhO (p. 486)) or discursive (see TO (p. 484) and TOI (p. 484)) purposes.

ta	ke	melbi	cmalu	ke'e	nixli	ckule
That	is-a-(	pretty	little	)	girl	school.

That is a school for girls who are pretty in their littleness.

selma'o KEI (Section 11.1 (p. 247))

Elidable terminator for NU (p. 481). Marks the end of an abstraction bridi.

la djan.	cu	nu	sonci	kei		djica
John		**is-an-(event-of**	**being-a-soldier**	**)**	**type-of**	**desirer.**

John wants to be a soldier.

selma'o KEhE (Section 5.5 (p. 84))

Elidable terminator for KE (p. 475). Marks the end of a grouping.

ta	ke	melbi	cmalu	ke'e	nixli	ckule
That	**is-a-(**	**pretty**	**little**	**)**	**girl**	**school.**

That is a school for girls who are pretty in their littleness.

selma'o KI (Section 10.13 (p. 225))

When preceded by a tense or modal, makes it "sticky", so that it applies to all further bridi until reset by another appearance of KI (p. 476). When alone, eliminates all sticky tenses.

selma'o KOhA (Section 7.1 (p. 139))

A general selma'o which contains all cmavo which can substitute for sumti. These cmavo are divided into several groups.

le	blanu	zdani	goi		ko'a	cu	barda
The	**blue**	**house**	**(referred to as**		**it-1)**		**is-big.**

.i	ko'a	na	cmamau	ti
	It-1	**is-not**	**smaller-than**	**this-thing.**

selma'o KU (Section 6.2 (p. 116), Section 10.1 (p. 207))

Elidable terminator for LE (p. 477) and some uses of LA (p. 477). Indicates the end of a description sumti. Also used after a tense or modal to indicate that no sumti follows, and in the compound NA (p. 480)+ KU (p. 476) to indicate natural language-style negation.

le	prenu	ku		le	zdani	ku	klama
The	**person**	**,**	**to**	**the**	**house**	**,**	**goes.**

The person goes to the house.

selma'o KUhE (Section 18.6 (p. 419))

Elidable terminator for PEhO (p. 482): indicates the end of a forethought mathematical expression (one in which the operator precedes the operands).

li		pe'o		su'i	reboi	reboi	re[boi]	ku'e
The-number		**[forethought]**		**the-sum-of**	**two**	**two**	**two**	**[end]**

du	li		xa
equals	**the-number**		**six.**

selma'o KUhO (Section 8.1 (p. 161))

Elidable terminator for NOI (p. 481). Indicates the end of a relative clause.

le	zdani	poi	blanu	ku'o	barda
The	house	that(	is-blue	)	is-big.

selma'o LA (Section 6.2 (p. 116))

Descriptors which change name words (or selbri) into sumti which identify people or things by name. Similar to LE (p. 477). May be terminated with KU (p. 476) if followed by a description selbri.

la kikeros.	du	la tulis.
Cicero	is	Tully.

selma'o LAU (Section 17.14 (p. 409))

Combines with the following alphabetic letter to represent a single marker: change from lower to upper case, change of font, punctuation, etc.)

tau	sy	.ibu
[single-shift]	"s"	"i"

Si (chemical symbol for silicon)

selma'o LAhE (Section 6.10 (p. 128))

Qualifiers which, when prefixed to a sumti, change it into another sumti with related meaning. Qualifiers can also consist of a cmavo from selma'o NAhE (p. 480) plus BO (p. 469). Terminated by LUhU (p. 478).

mi	viska	la'e	zoi	.kuot.	A Tale of Two Cities	.kuot
I	see	that-represented-by	the-text	"	A Tale of Two Cities	".

I see the book "A Tale of Two Cities".

selma'o LE (Section 6.2 (p. 116))

Descriptors which make selbri into sumti which describe or specify things that fit into the x1 place of the selbri. Terminated by KU (p. 476). See LA (p. 477).

le	gerku	cu	klama	le	zdani
The	dog		goes-to	the	house.

selma'o LEhU (Section 19.9 (p. 457))

Indicates the end of a quotation begun with LOhU (p. 478). Not an elidable terminator.

lo'u	mi du do du mi	le'u	cu	na	lojbo	drani
[quote]	mi du do du mi	[unquote]		is-not	Lojbanically	correct.

"mi du do du mi" is not correct Lojban.

selma'o LI (Section 18.5 (p. 417))

Descriptors which change numbers or other mathematical expressions into sumti which specify numbers or numerical expressions. Terminated by LOhO (p. 478).

li	re	vu'u	re	na	du	li	vo	su'i	vo
The-number	2	minus	2	not	equals	the-number	4	plus	4.

$2 - 2 \neq 4 + 4$

selma'o LIhU (Section 19.9 (p. 457))

Elidable terminator for LU (p. 478). Indicates the end of a text quotation.

mi	cusku	lu	mi	klama	le	zarci	li'u
I	express	[quote]	I	go-to	the	market	[end-quote].

selma'o LOhO (Section 18.17 (p. 435))

Elidable terminator for LI (p. 478). Indicates the end of a mathematical expression used in a LI (p. 478) description.

li	vo	lo'o	li	ci	lo'o	cu	zmadu
The-number	4	[end-number],	the-number	3	[end-number],		is-greater.

$4 > 3$

selma'o LOhU (Section 19.9 (p. 457))

Indicates the beginning of a quotation (a sumti) which is grammatical as long as the quoted material consists of Lojban words, whether they form a text or not. Terminated by LEhU (p. 477).

do	cusku	lo'u	mi du do du ko'a	le'u
You	express	[quote]	mi du do du ko'a	[end-quote].

You said, "mi du do du ko'a".

selma'o LU (Section 19.9 (p. 457))

Indicates the beginning of a quotation (a sumti) which is grammatical only if the quoted material also forms a grammatical Lojban text. Terminated by LIhU (p. 478).

mi	cusku	lu	mi	klama	le	zarci	li'u
I	express	[quote]	I	go-to	the	market	[end-quote].

selma'o LUhU (Section 6.10 (p. 128))

Elidable terminator for LAhE (p. 477) and NAhE (p. 480)+ BO (p. 469). Indicates the end of a qualified sumti.

mi	viska	la'e	lu	barda	gerku	li'u	lu'u
I	see	the-referent-of	[quote]	big	dog	[end-quote]	[end-ref]

I saw "Big Dog" [not the words, but a book or movie].

selma'o MAI (Section 18.19 (p. 438), Section 19.1 (p. 447))

When suffixed to a number or string of letter words, produces a free modifier which serves as an index number within a text.

pamai	mi	pu	klama	le	zarci
1-thly,	I	[past]	go-to	the	market.

First, I went to the market.

selma'o MAhO (Section 18.6 (p. 419))

Produces a mathematical operator from a letter or other operand. Terminated by TEhU (p. 484). See VUhU (p. 487).

ma'o	fy.	boi	xy.
[operator]	f		x

f(x)

selma'o ME (Section 5.10 (p. 95), Section 18.1 (p. 413))

Produces a tanru unit from a sumti, which is applicable to the things referenced by the sumti. Terminated by MEhU (p. 479).

ta	me la ford.	karce
That	is-a-Ford-type	car

That's a Ford car.

selma'o MEhU (Section 5.11 (p. 96))

The elidable terminator for ME (p. 479). Indicates the end of a sumti converted to a tanru unit.

ta me mi me'u zdani

That's a me type of house.

selma'o MOI (Section 5.11 (p. 96), Section 18.18 (p. 437))

Suffixes added to numbers or other quantifiers to make various numerically-based selbri.

la djan.	joi	la frank.	cu	bruna		remei
John	in-a-mass-with	Frank		are-a-brother	type-of	twosome.

John and Frank are two brothers.

selma'o MOhE (Section 18.18 (p. 437))

Produces a mathematical operand from a sumti; used to make dimensioned units. Terminated by TEhU (p. 484).

li	mo'e	re	ratcu	su'i	mo'e	re	ractu
The-number	[operand]	two	rats	plus	[operand]	two	rabbits

cu	du	li		mo'e		vo	danlu
	equals	the-number	[operand]		four	animals.

2 rats + 2 rabbits = 4 animals.

selma'o MOhI (Section 10.8 (p. 216))

A tense flag indicating movement in space, in a direction specified by a following FAhA (p. 471) cmavo.

le	verba	mo'i		ri'u		cadzu		le	bisli
The	child	[movement]	[right]		walks-on	the	ice.

The child walks toward my right on the ice.

selma'o NA (Section 14.3 (p. 319), Section 15.7 (p. 366))

Contradictory negators, asserting that a whole bridi is false (or true).

mi na klama le zarci

It is not true that I go to the market.

Also used to construct logical connective compound cmavo.

selma'o NAI (Section 14.3 (p. 319), Section 15.7 (p. 366))

Negates the previous word, but can only be used with certain selma'o as specified by the grammar.

selma'o NAhE (Section 15.4 (p. 360))

Scalar negators, modifying a selbri or a sumti to a value other than the one stated, the opposite of the one stated, etc. Also used with following BO (p. 469) to construct a sumti qualifier; see LAhE (p. 477).

ta	na'e		blanu	zdani
That	is-a-non-	blue	house.

That is a house which is other than blue.

selma'o NAhU (Section 18.18 (p. 437))

Creates a mathematical operator from a selbri. Terminated by TEhU (p. 484). See VUhU (p. 487).

li		na'u		tanjo	te'u
The-number	the-operator(		tangent	)

vei	pai	fe'i	re	[ve'o]	du	li		ci'i
(	π	/	2	)	=	the-number	infinity.

$\tan(\pi/2) = \infty$

selma'o NIhE (Section 18.18 (p. 437))

Creates a mathematical operand from a selbri, usually a "ni" abstraction. Terminated by TEhU (p. 484).

li		ni'e	ni		clani	[te'u]	pi'i	
The-number			quantity-of	length			times	

ni'e	ni		ganra	[te'u]	pi'i	
	quantity-of	width			times	

ni'e	ni		condi	te'u	du	li		ni'e	ni		canlu
	quantity-of	depth		equals	the-number			quantity-of	volume.

Length × Width × Depth = Volume

selma'o NIhO (Section 19.3 (p. 448))

Marks the beginning of a new paragraph, and indicates whether it contains old or new subject matter.

selma'o NOI (Section 8.1 (p. 161))

Introduces relative clauses. The following bridi modifies the preceding sumti. Terminated by KUhO (p. 477). See GOI (p. 474).

le	zdani	poi	blanu	cu	cmalu
The	house	which	is-blue		is-small.

selma'o NU (Section 11.1 (p. 247))

Abstractors which, when prefixed to a bridi, create abstraction selbri. Terminated by KEI (p. 476).

la djan.	cu	djica	le	nu	sonci	[kei]
John		desires	the	event-of	being-a-soldier.	

selma'o NUhA (Section 18.19 (p. 438))

Creates a selbri from a mathematical operator. See VUhU (p. 487).

li		ni'umu	cu	nu'a va'a		li		ma'umu
The-number		-5		is-the-negation-of	the-number	+5

selma'o NUhI (Section 14.11 (p. 332), Section 16.7 (p. 382))

Marks the beginning of a termset, which is used to make simultaneous claims involving two or more different places of a selbri. Terminated by NUhU (p. 481).

mi	klama	nu'i	ge		le	zarci		le	briju
I	go	[start]	both	to	the	market	from	the	office

nu'u	gi		le	zdani		le	ckule	[nu'u]
[joint]	and	to	the	house	from	the	school.	

selma'o NUhU (Section 14.11 (p. 332))

Elidable terminator for NUhI (p. 481). Marks the end of a termset.

mi	klama	nu'i	ge		le	zarci		le	briju
I	go	[start]	both	to	the	market	from	the	office

nu'u	gi		le	zdani		le	ckule	[nu'u]
[joint]	and	to	the	house	from	the	school.	

selma'o PA (Section 18.2 (p. 414))

Digits and related quantifiers (some, all, many, etc.). Terminated by BOI (p. 469).

mi	speni	re	ninmu
I	am-married-to	two	women.

selma'o PEhE (Section 14.11 (p. 332))

Precedes a logical or non-logical connective that joins two termsets. Termsets (see CEhE (p. 470)) are used to associate several terms for logical connectives, for equal quantifier scope, or for special constructs in tenses.

mi	ce'e	do	pe'e	je	la djan.	ce'e	la djeimyz.	cu	pendo
I	[,]	you	[joint]	and	John	[,]	James		are-friends-of.

I am a friend of you, and John is a friend of James.

selma'o PEhO (Section 18.6 (p. 419))

An optional signal of forethought mathematical operators, which precede their operands. Terminated by KUhE (p. 476).

li		vo	du	li		pe'o		su'i	reboi	re
The-number	four	equals	the-number			[forethought]		sum-of	two	two.

selma'o PU (Section 10.4 (p. 211))

Specifies simple time directions (future, past, or neither).

mi	pu	klama	le	zarci
I	[past]	go-to	the	market.

I went to the market.

selma'o RAhO (Section 7.6 (p. 146))

The pro-bridi update flag: changes the meaning of sumti implicitly attached to a pro-bridi (see GOhA (p. 474)) to fit the current context rather than the original context.

A: mi ba lumci le mi karce
B: mi go'i
A: mi ba lumci le mi karce
B: mi go'i ra'o

A: I [future] wash my car.
B: I do-the-same-thing (i.e. wash A's car).
A: I [future] wash my car.
B: I do-the-corresponding-thing (i.e. wash B's car).

selma'o ROI (Section 10.9 (p. 217))

When suffixed to a number, makes an extensional tense (e.g. once, twice, many times).

mi	reroi	klama	le	zarci
I	twice	go-to	the	market.

selma'o SA (Section 19.13 (p. 463))

Erases the previous phrase or sentence.

mi	klama	sa	do	klama	le	zarci
I	go,	er,	you	go-to	the	market.

selma'o SE (Section 5.11 (p. 96), Section 9.4 (p. 185))

Converts a selbri, rearranging the order of places by exchanging the x1 place with a specified numbered place.

le	zarci	cu	se klama	mi
The	market		is-gone-to-by	me.

Also used in constructing connective and modal compound cmavo.

selma'o SEI (Section 19.12 (p. 461))

Marks the beginning of metalinguistic insertions which comment on the main bridi. Terminated by SEhU (p. 483).

la frank.	prami	sei		gleki	[se'u]	la djein.
Frank	loves	(	[he]	is-happy	)	Jane.

selma'o SEhU (Section 19.12 (p. 461))

Elidable terminator for SEI (p. 483) and SOI (p. 483). Ends metalinguistic insertions.

la frank.	prami	sei		gleki	se'u	la djein.
Frank	loves	(	[he]	is-happy	)	Jane.

selma'o SI (Section 19.13 (p. 463))

Erases the previous single word.

mi	si	do	klama	le	zarci
I,	er,	you	go-to	the	market.

selma'o SOI (Section 7.8 (p. 152))

Marks reciprocity between two sumti (like "vice versa" in English).

mi	prami	do	soi		mi
I	love	you	[reciprocally]		me.

I love you and vice versa.

selma'o SU (Section 19.13 (p. 463))

Closes and erases the entire previous discourse.

selma'o TAhE (Section 10.9 (p. 217))

A tense modifier specifying frequencies within an interval of time or space (regularly, habitually, etc.).

le	verba	ta'e	klama	le	ckule
The	child	habitually	goes-to	the	school.

selma'o TEI (Section 17.6 (p. 402))

Signals the beginning of a compound letter word, which acts grammatically like a single letter. Compound letter words end with the non-elidable selma'o FOI (p. 472).

tei	.ebu	.akut. bu	foi
(	"e"	"acute"	)

the letter "e" with an acute accent

selma'o TEhU (Section 18.15 (p. 433))

Elidable terminator for JOhI (p. 475), MAhO (p. 479), MOhE (p. 479), NAhU (p. 480), or NIhE (p. 480). Marks the end of a mathematical conversion construct.

li	jo'i	paboi	reboi	te'u	su'i	jo'i	ciboi	voboi	du
The-number	array(	one,	two	)	plus	array(	three,	four)	equals

li	jo'i	voboi	xaboi
the-number	array(	four,	six).

(1,2) + (3,4) = (4,6)

selma'o TO (Section 19.12 (p. 461))

Left discursive parenthesis: allows inserting a digression. Terminated by TOI (p. 484).

doi	lisas.	mi	djica	le	nu
O	Lisa,	I	desire	the	event-of

to	doi	frank.	ko	sisti	toi	do	viska	le	mlatu
(	O	Frank,	[imperative]	stop!	)	you	see	the	cat.

Lisa, I want you to (Frank! Stop!) see the cat.

selma'o TOI (Section 19.12 (p. 461))

Elidable terminator for TO (p. 484). The right discursive parenthesis.

doi	lisas.	mi	djica	le	nu
O	Lisa,	I	desire	the	event-of

to	doi	frank.	ko	sisti	toi	do	viska	le	mlatu
(	O	Frank,	[imperative]	stop!	)	you	see	the	cat.

484

Lisa, I want you to (Frank! Stop!) see the cat.

selma'o TUhE (Section 19.2 (p. 447))

Groups multiple sentences or paragraphs into a logical unit. Terminated by TUhU (p. 485).

lo	xagmau	zo'u	tu'e	ganai	cidja	gi	citno
Some	best	:	[start]	If	food,	then	new.

.i	ganai	vanju	gi	tolci'o	[tu'u]
	If	wine,	then	old.	

As for what is best: if food, then new [is best]; if wine, then old [is best].

selma'o TUhU (Section 19.2 (p. 447))

Elidable terminator for TUhE (p. 485). Marks the end of a multiple sentence group.

selma'o UI (Section 13.1 (p. 285))

Particles which indicate the speaker's emotional state or source of knowledge, or the present stage of discourse.

.ui	la djan.	klama
[Happiness!]	John	is-coming.

Hurrah! John is coming!

selma'o VA (Section 10.2 (p. 209))

A tense indicating distance in space (near, far, or neither).

le	nanmu	va	batci	le	gerku
The	man	[medium-distance]	bites	the	dog.

Over there the man is biting the dog.

selma'o VAU (Section 14.9 (p. 328))

Elidable terminator for a simple bridi, or for each bridi-tail of a GIhA (p. 474) logical connection.

mi	dunda	le	cukta	[vau]	gi'e
I	(give	the	book	)	and

lebna	lo	rupnu		vau		do	[vau]
(take	some	currency-units	)		to/from	you.	

selma'o VEI (Section 18.5 (p. 417))

Left mathematical parenthesis: groups mathematical operations. Terminated by VEhO (p. 486).

li	vei	ny.	su'i	pa	ve'o
The-number	(	"n"	plus	one	)

pi'i	vei	ny.	su'i	pa	[ve'o]	du
times	(	"n"	plus	one	)		equals

li		ny.	[bi'e]		te'a	re
the-number		n	[priority]		power	two

su'i	re	bi'e	pi'i	ny.	su'i	pa
plus	two	[priority]	times	"n"	plus	1.

$$(n + 1)(n + 1) = n^2 + 2n + 1$$

selma'o VEhA (Section 10.5 (p. 213))

A tense indicating the size of an interval in space (long, medium, or short).

selma'o VEhO (Section 19.5 (p. 451))

Elidable terminator for VEI (p. 485): right mathematical parenthesis.

li		vei	ny.	su'i	pa	ve'o	pi'i
The-number		(	"n"	plus	one	)	times

vei	ny.	su'i	pa	[ve'o]	du	
(	"n"	plus	one	)	equals	

li		ny.	[bi'e]		te'a	re	su'i
the-number		n	[priority]		power	two	plus

re	bi'e	pi'i	ny.	su'i	pa
two	[priority]	times	"n"	plus	1.

$$(n + 1)(n + 1) = n^2 + 2n + 1$$

selma'o VIhA (Section 10.7 (p. 215))

A tense indicating dimensionality in space (line, plane, volume, or space-time interval).

le	verba	ve'a
The	child	[medium-space-interval]

vi'a		cadzu	le	bisli
[2-dimensional]		walks-on	the	ice.

In a medium-sized area, the child walks on the ice.

selma'o VUhO (Section 8.8 (p. 173))

Attaches relative clauses or phrases to a whole (possibly connected) sumti, rather than simply to the leftmost portion of the sumti.

la frank.	ce	la djordj.	vu'o	noi	gidva	cu	zvati	le	kumfa
Frank	[in-set-with]	George	,	which	are-guides	,	are-in	the	room.

Frank and George, who are guides, are in the room.

selma'o VUhU (Section 18.5 (p. 417))

Mathematical operators (e.g. +, −). See MAhO (p. 479).

li	mu	vu'u	re	du	li	ci
The-number	**5**	**minus**	**2**	**equals**	**the-number**	**3.**

$5 - 2 = 3$

selma'o XI (Section 18.13 (p. 431))

The subscript marker: the following number or lerfu string is a subscript for whatever precedes it.

xy.	xi	re
x	**sub**	**2**

x_2

selma'o Y (Section 19.14 (p. 465))

Hesitation noise: content-free, but holds the floor or continues the conversation. It is different from silence in that silence may be interpreted as having nothing more to say.

doi	.y.	.y.	.djan
O,	**uh,**	**uh,**	**John!**

selma'o ZAhO (Section 10.10 (p. 219))

A tense modifier specifying the contour of an event (e.g. beginning, ending, continuing).

mi	pu'o	damba
I	**[inchoative]**	**fight.**

I'm on the verge of fighting.

selma'o ZEI (Section 4.6 (p. 56))

A morphological glue word, which joins the two words it stands between into the equivalent of a lujvo.

ta	xy.	zei	kantu	kacma
That	**is-an-(X**		**ray)**	**camera.**

That is an X-ray camera.

selma'o ZEhA (Section 10.5 (p. 213))

A tense indicating the size of an interval in time (long, medium, or short).

mi	pu	ze'i	citka
I	**[past]**	**[short-interval]**	**eat.**

I ate for a little while.

selma'o ZI (Section 10.4 (p. 211))

A tense indicating distance in time (a long, medium or short time ago or in the future).

mi	pu	zi	citka
I	[past]	[short-distance]	eat.

I ate a little while ago.

selma'o ZIhE (Section 8.4 (p. 168))

Joins multiple relative phrases or clauses which apply to the same sumti. Although generally translated with "and", it is not considered a logical connective.

mi	ponse	pa	gerku	ku	poi		blabi
I	own	one	dog			such-that	it-is-white

zi'e	noi		mi	prami	ke'a
and	such-that-incidentally		I	love	it.

I own a dog that is white and which, incidentally, I love.
I own a white dog, which I love.

selma'o ZO (Section 19.10 (p. 458))

Single-word quotation: quotes the following single Lojban word.

zo	si	cu	lojbo	valsi
The-word	"si"		is-a-Lojbanic	word.

selma'o ZOI (Section 19.10 (p. 458))

Non-Lojban quotation: quotes any text using a delimiting word (which can be any single Lojban word) placed before and after the text. The delimiting word must not appear in the text, and must be separated from the text by pauses.

zoi	.kuot.	Socrates is mortal	.kuot.	cu	glico	jufra
The-text	"	Socrates is mortal	"		is-an-English	sentence.

selma'o ZOhU (Section 16.2 (p. 376), Section 19.4 (p. 449))

Separates a logical prenex from a bridi or group of sentences to which it applies. Also separates a topic from a comment in topic/comment sentences.

su'o	da	poi	remna
For-at-least-one	X	which	is-a-human,

ro	de	poi	finpe	zo'u	da	prami	de
for-all	Ys	which	are-fish	:	X	loves	Y

There is someone who loves all fish.

Chapter 21
Formal Grammars

21.1 EBNF Grammar of Lojban

Lojban Machine Grammar, EBNF Version, Final Baseline

This EBNF document is explicitly dedicated to the public domain by its author, The Logical Language Group, Inc. Contact that organization at: 2904 Beau Lane, Fairfax VA 22031 USA 703-385-0273 (intl: +1 703 385 0273)

Explanation of notation: All rules have the form:

name $_{number}$= bnf-expression

which means that the grammatical construct "name" is defined by "bnf-expression". The number cross-references this grammar with the rule numbers in the YACC grammar. The names are the same as those in the YACC grammar, except that subrules are labeled with A, B, C, ... in the YACC grammar and with 1, 2, 3, ... in this grammar. In addition, rule 971 is "simple_tag" in the YACC grammar but "stag" in this grammar, because of its frequent appearance.

1. Names in lower case are grammatical constructs.
2. Names in UPPER CASE are selma'o (lexeme) names, and are terminals.
3. Concatenation is expressed by juxtaposition with no operator symbol.
4. | represents alternation (choice).
5. [] represents an optional element.
6. & represents and/or ("A & B" is the same as "A | B | A B").

7. ... represents optional repetition of the construct to the left. Left-grouping is implied; right-grouping is shown by explicit self-referential recursion with no "..."

8. () serves to indicate the grouping of the other operators. Otherwise, "..." binds closer than &, which binds closer than |.

9. # is shorthand for "[free ...]", a construct which appears in many places.

10. // encloses an elidable terminator, which may be omitted (without change of meaning) if no grammatical ambiguity results.

text $_0$=
    [NAI ...] [CMENE ... # | (indicators & free ...)] [joik-jek] text-1

text-1 $_2$=
    [(I [jek | joik] [[stag] BO] #) ... | NIhO ... #] [paragraphs]

paragraphs $_4$=
    paragraph [NIhO ... # paragraphs]

paragraph $_{10}$=
    (statement | fragment) [I # [statement | fragment]] ...

statement $_{11}$=
    statement-1 | prenex statement

statement-1 $_{12}$=
    statement-2 [I joik-jek [statement-2]] ...

statement-2 $_{13}$=
    statement-3 [I [jek | joik] [stag] BO # [statement-2]]

statement-3 $_{14}$=
    sentence | [tag] TUhE # text-1 /TUhU#/

fragment $_{20}$=
    ek # | gihek # | quantifier | NA # | terms /VAU#/ | prenex | relative-clauses | links | linkargs

prenex $_{30}$=
    terms ZOhU #

sentence $_{40}$=
    [terms [CU #]] bridi-tail

subsentence $_{41}$=
    sentence | prenex subsentence

bridi-tail $_{50}$=
    bridi-tail-1 [gihek [stag] KE # bridi-tail /KEhE#/ tail-terms]

bridi-tail-1 $_{51}$=
    bridi-tail-2 [gihek # bridi-tail-2 tail-terms] ...

bridi-tail-2 $_{52}$=
    bridi-tail-3 [gihek [stag] BO # bridi-tail-2 tail-terms]

bridi-tail-3 $_{53}$=
    selbri tail-terms | gek-sentence

gek-sentence $_{54}$=
    gek subsentence gik subsentence tail-terms | [tag] KE # gek-sentence /KEhE#/ | NA # gek-sentence

tail-terms $_{71}$=
    [terms] /VAU#/

terms $_{80}$=
    terms-1 ...

terms-1 $_{81}$=
    terms-2 [PEhE # joik-jek terms-2] ...

terms-2 $_{82}$=
    term [CEhE # term] ...

term $_{83}$=
    sumti | (tag | FA #) (sumti | /KU#/) | termset | NA KU #

termset 85=

    NUhI # gek terms /NUhU#/ gik terms /NUhU#/ | NUhI # terms /NUhU#/

sumti 90=

    sumti-1 [VUhO # relative-clauses]

sumti-1 91=

    sumti-2 [(ek | joik) [stag] KE # sumti /KEhE#/]

sumti-2 92=

    sumti-3 [joik-ek sumti-3] ...

sumti-3 93=

    sumti-4 [(ek | joik) [stag] BO # sumti-3]

sumti-4 94=

    sumti-5 | gek sumti gik sumti-4

sumti-5 95=

    [quantifier] sumti-6 [relative-clauses] | quantifier selbri /KU#/ [relative-clauses]

sumti-6 97=

    (LAhE # | NAhE BO #) [relative-clauses] sumti /LUhU#/ | KOhA # | lerfu-string /BOI#/ | LA #
    [relative-clauses] CMENE ... # | (LA | LE) # sumti-tail /KU#/ | LI # mex /LOhO#/ | ZO any-word #
    | LU text /LIhU#/ | LOhU any-word ... LEhU # | ZOI any-word anything any-word #

sumti-tail 111=

    [sumti-6 [relative-clauses]] sumti-tail-1 | relative-clauses sumti-tail-1

sumti-tail-1 112=

    [quantifier] selbri [relative-clauses] | quantifier sumti

relative-clauses 121=

    relative-clause [ZIhE # relative-clause] ...

relative-clause 122=

    GOI # term /GEhU#/ | NOI # subsentence /KUhO#/

selbri 130=

    [tag] selbri-1

selbri-1 131=

    selbri-2 | NA # selbri

selbri-2 132=

    selbri-3 [CO # selbri-2]

selbri-3 133=

    selbri-4 ...

selbri-4 134=

    selbri-5 [joik-jek selbri-5 | joik [stag] KE # selbri-3 /KEhE#/] ...

selbri-5 135=

    selbri-6 [(jek | joik) [stag] BO # selbri-5]

selbri-6 136=

    tanru-unit [BO # selbri-6] | [NAhE #] guhek selbri gik selbri-6

tanru-unit 150=

    tanru-unit-1 [CEI # tanru-unit-1] ...

tanru-unit-1 151=

    tanru-unit-2 [linkargs]

tanru-unit-2 152=

    BRIVLA # | GOhA [RAhO] # | KE # selbri-3 /KEhE#/ | ME # sumti /MEhU#/ [MOI #] | (number |
    lerfu-string) MOI # | NUhA # mex-operator | SE # tanru-unit-2 | JAI # [tag] tanru-unit-2 | any-
    word (ZEI any-word) ... | NAhE # tanru-unit-2 | NU [NAI] # [joik-jek NU [NAI] #] ...
    subsentence /KEI#/

linkargs 160=

    BE # term [links] /BEhO#/

links 161=
    BEI # term [links]
quantifier 300=
    number /BOI#/ | VEI # mex /VEhO#/
mex 310=
    mex-1 [operator mex-1] ... | FUhA # rp-expression
mex-1 311=
    mex-2 [BIhE # operator mex-1]
mex-2 312=
    operand | [PEhO #] operator mex-2 ... /KUhE#/
rp-expression 330=
    rp-operand rp-operand operator
rp-operand 332=
    operand | rp-expression
operator 370=
    operator-1 [joik-jek operator-1 | joik [stag] KE # operator /KEhE#/] ...
operator-1 371=
    operator-2 | guhek operator-1 gik operator-2 | operator-2 (jek | joik) [stag] BO # operator-1
operator-2 372=
    mex-operator | KE # operator /KEhE#/
mex-operator 374=
    SE # mex-operator | NAhE # mex-operator | MAhO # mex /TEhU#/ | NAhU # selbri /TEhU#/ |
    VUhU #
operand 381=
    operand-1 [(ek | joik) [stag] KE # operand /KEhE#/]
operand-1 382=
    operand-2 [joik-ek operand-2] ...
operand-2 383=
    operand-3 [(ek | joik) [stag] BO # operand-2]
operand-3 385=
    quantifier | lerfu-string /BOI#/ | NIhE # selbri /TEhU#/ | MOhE # sumti /TEhU#/ | JOhI # mex-2 ...
    /TEhU#/ | gek operand gik operand-3 | (LAhE # | NAhE BO #) operand /LUhU#/
number 812=
    PA [PA | lerfu-word] ...
lerfu-string 817=
    lerfu-word [PA | lerfu-word] ...
lerfu-word 987=
    BY | any-word BU | LAU lerfu-word | TEI lerfu-string FOI
ek 802=
    [NA] [SE] A [NAI]
gihek 818=
    [NA] [SE] GIhA [NAI]
jek 805=
    [NA] [SE] JA [NAI]
joik 806=
    [SE] JOI [NAI] | interval | GAhO interval GAhO
interval 932=
    [SE] BIhI [NAI]
joik-ek 421=
    joik # | ek #
joik-jek 422=
    joik # | jek #

gek 807=

 [SE] GA [NAI] # | joik GI # | stag gik

guhek 808=

 [SE] GUhA [NAI] #

gik 816=

 GI [NAI] #

tag 491=

 tense-modal [joik-jek tense-modal] ...

stag 971=

 simple-tense-modal [(jek | joik) simple-tense-modal] ...

tense-modal 815=

 simple-tense-modal # | FIhO # selbri /FEhU#/

simple-tense-modal 972=

 [NAhE] [SE] BAI [NAI] [KI] | [NAhE] (time [space] | space [time]) & CAhA [KI] | KI | CUhE

time 1030=

 ZI & time-offset ... & ZEhA [PU [NAI]] & interval-property ...

time-offset 1033=

 PU [NAI] [ZI]

space 1040=

 VA & space-offset ... & space-interval & (MOhI space-offset)

space-offset 1045=

 FAhA [NAI] [VA]

space-interval 1046=

 ((VEhA & VIhA) [FAhA [NAI]]) & space-int-props

space-int-props 1049=

 (FEhE interval-property) ...

interval-property 1051=

 number ROI [NAI] | TAhE [NAI] | ZAhO [NAI]

free 32=

 SEI # [terms [CU #]] selbri /SEhU/ | SOI # sumti [sumti] /SEhU/ | vocative [relative-clauses]
 selbri [relative-clauses] /DOhU/ | vocative [relative-clauses] CMENE ... # [relative-clauses]
 /DOhU/ | vocative [sumti] /DOhU/ | (number | lerfu-string) MAI | TO text /TOI/ | XI # (number |
 lerfu-string) /BOI/ | XI # VEI # mex /VEhO/

vocative 415=

 (COI [NAI]) ... & DOI

indicators 411=

 [FUhE] indicator ...

indicator 413=

 (UI | CAI) [NAI] | Y | DAhO | FUhO

The following rules are non-formal:

word 1100=

 [BAhE] any-word [indicators]

any-word =

 "any single word (no compound cmavo)"

anything =

 "any text at all, whether Lojban or not"

null 1101=

 any-word SI | utterance SA | text SU

FAhO is a universal terminator and signals the end of parsable input.

21.2 EBNF Cross-Reference

A

    BNF rule #802 (p. 492) $_{802}$

BAI

    BNF rule #972 (p. 493) $_{972}$

BAhE

    BNF rule #1100 (p. 493) $_{1100}$

BE

    BNF rule #160 (p. 491) $_{160}$

BEI

    BNF rule #161 (p. 491) $_{161}$

BEhO

    BNF rule #160 (p. 491) $_{160}$

BIhE

    BNF rule #311 (p. 492) $_{311}$

BIhI

    BNF rule #932 (p. 492) $_{932}$

BO

    BNF rule #52 (p. 490)$_{52}$, BNF rule #383 (p. 492)$_{383}$, BNF rule #385 (p. 492)$_{385}$, BNF rule #371 (p. 492)$_{371}$, BNF rule #135 (p. 491)$_{135}$, BNF rule #136 (p. 491)$_{136}$, BNF rule #13 (p. 490)$_{13}$, BNF rule #93 (p. 491)$_{93}$, BNF rule #97 (p. 491)$_{97}$, BNF rule #2 (p. 490)$_{2}$

BOI

    BNF rule #32 (p. 493)$_{32}$, BNF rule #385 (p. 492)$_{385}$, BNF rule #300 (p. 492)$_{300}$, BNF rule #97 (p. 491)$_{97}$

BRIVLA

    BNF rule #152 (p. 491) $_{152}$

BU

    BNF rule #987 (p. 492) $_{987}$

BY

    BNF rule #987 (p. 492) $_{987}$

CAI

    BNF rule #413 (p. 493) $_{413}$

CAhA

    BNF rule #972 (p. 493) $_{972}$

CEI

    BNF rule #150 (p. 491) $_{150}$

CEhE

    BNF rule #82 (p. 490) $_{82}$

CMENE

    BNF rule #32 (p. 493)$_{32}$, BNF rule #97 (p. 491)$_{97}$, BNF rule #0 (p. 490)$_{0}$

CO

    BNF rule #132 (p. 491) $_{132}$

COI

    BNF rule #415 (p. 493) $_{415}$

CU

    BNF rule #32 (p. 493)$_{32}$, BNF rule #40 (p. 490)$_{40}$

CUhE

    BNF rule #972 (p. 493) $_{972}$

DAhO

    BNF rule #413 (p. 493) $_{413}$

DOI

    BNF rule #415 (p. 493) $_{415}$

DOhU

BNF rule #32 (p. 493) 32

FA

BNF rule #83 (p. 490) 83

FAhA

BNF rule #1046 (p. 493)$_{1046}$, BNF rule #1045 (p. 493)$_{1045}$

FEhE

BNF rule #1049 (p. 493) 1049

FEhU

BNF rule #815 (p. 493) 815

FIhO

BNF rule #815 (p. 493) 815

FOI

BNF rule #987 (p. 492) 987

FUhA

BNF rule #310 (p. 492) 310

FUhE

BNF rule #411 (p. 493) 411

FUhO

BNF rule #413 (p. 493) 413

GA

BNF rule #807 (p. 492) 807

GAhO

BNF rule #806 (p. 492) 806

GEhU

BNF rule #122 (p. 491) 122

GI

BNF rule #807 (p. 492)$_{807}$, BNF rule #816 (p. 493)$_{816}$

GIhA

BNF rule #818 (p. 492) 818

GOI

BNF rule #122 (p. 491) 122

GOhA

BNF rule #152 (p. 491) 152

GUhA

BNF rule #808 (p. 493) 808

I

BNF rule #10 (p. 490)$_{10}$, BNF rule #12 (p. 490)$_{12}$, BNF rule #13 (p. 490)$_{13}$, BNF rule #2 (p. 490)$_2$

JA

BNF rule #805 (p. 492) 805

JAI

BNF rule #152 (p. 491) 152

JOI

BNF rule #806 (p. 492) 806

JOhI

BNF rule #385 (p. 492) 385

KE

BNF rule #50 (p. 490)$_{50}$, BNF rule #54 (p. 490)$_{54}$, BNF rule #381 (p. 492)$_{381}$, BNF rule #372 (p. 492)$_{372}$, BNF rule #370 (p. 492)$_{370}$, BNF rule #134 (p. 491)$_{134}$, BNF rule #91 (p. 491)$_{91}$, BNF rule #152 (p. 491)$_{152}$

KEI

BNF rule #152 (p. 491) 152

KEhE

BNF rule #50 (p. 490)$_{50}$, BNF rule #54 (p. 490)$_{54}$, BNF rule #381 (p. 492)$_{381}$, BNF rule #372 (p. 492)$_{372}$, BNF rule #370 (p. 492)$_{370}$, BNF rule #134 (p. 491)$_{134}$, BNF rule #91 (p. 491)$_{91}$, BNF rule #152 (p. 491)$_{152}$

KI

BNF rule #972 (p. 493) $_{972}$

KOhA

BNF rule #97 (p. 491) $_{97}$

KU

BNF rule #95 (p. 491)$_{95}$, BNF rule #97 (p. 491)$_{97}$, BNF rule #83 (p. 490)$_{83}$

KUhE

BNF rule #312 (p. 492) $_{312}$

KUhO

BNF rule #122 (p. 491) $_{122}$

LA

BNF rule #97 (p. 491) $_{97}$

LAU

BNF rule #987 (p. 492) $_{987}$

LAhE

BNF rule #385 (p. 492)$_{385}$, BNF rule #97 (p. 491)$_{97}$

LE

BNF rule #97 (p. 491) $_{97}$

LEhU

BNF rule #97 (p. 491) $_{97}$

LI

BNF rule #97 (p. 491) $_{97}$

LIhU

BNF rule #97 (p. 491) $_{97}$

LOhO

BNF rule #97 (p. 491) $_{97}$

LOhU

BNF rule #97 (p. 491) $_{97}$

LU

BNF rule #97 (p. 491) $_{97}$

LUhU

BNF rule #385 (p. 492)$_{385}$, BNF rule #97 (p. 491)$_{97}$

MAI

BNF rule #32 (p. 493) $_{32}$

MAhO

BNF rule #374 (p. 492) $_{374}$

ME

BNF rule #152 (p. 491) $_{152}$

MEhU

BNF rule #152 (p. 491) $_{152}$

MOI

BNF rule #152 (p. 491) $_{152}$

MOhE

BNF rule #385 (p. 492) $_{385}$

MOhI

BNF rule #1040 (p. 493) $_{1040}$

NA

BNF rule #802 (p. 492)$_{802}$, BNF rule #20 (p. 490)$_{20}$, BNF rule #54 (p. 490)$_{54}$, BNF rule #818 (p. 492)$_{818}$, BNF rule #805 (p. 492)$_{805}$, BNF rule #131 (p. 491)$_{131}$, BNF rule #83 (p. 490)$_{83}$

NAI

BNF rule #802 (p. 492)$_{802}$, BNF rule #807 (p. 492)$_{807}$, BNF rule #818 (p. 492)$_{818}$, BNF rule #816 (p. 493)$_{816}$, BNF rule #808 (p. 493)$_{808}$, BNF rule #413 (p. 493)$_{413}$, BNF rule #1051 (p. 493)$_{1051}$, BNF rule #932 (p. 492)$_{932}$, BNF rule #805 (p. 492)$_{805}$, BNF rule #806 (p. 492)$_{806}$, BNF rule #972 (p. 493)$_{972}$, BNF rule #1046 (p. 493)$_{1046}$, BNF rule #1045 (p. 493)$_{1045}$, BNF rule #152 (p. 491)$_{152}$, BNF rule #0 (p. 490)$_{0}$, BNF rule #1033 (p. 493)$_{1033}$, BNF rule #1030 (p. 493)$_{1030}$, BNF rule #415 (p. 493)$_{415}$

NAhE

BNF rule #374 (p. 492)$_{374}$, BNF rule #385 (p. 492)$_{385}$, BNF rule #136 (p. 491)$_{136}$, BNF rule #972 (p. 493)$_{972}$, BNF rule #97 (p. 491)$_{97}$, BNF rule #152 (p. 491)$_{152}$

NAhU

BNF rule #374 (p. 492) $_{374}$

NIhE

BNF rule #385 (p. 492) $_{385}$

NIhO

BNF rule #4 (p. 490)$_{4}$, BNF rule #2 (p. 490)$_{2}$

NOI

BNF rule #122 (p. 491) $_{122}$

NU

BNF rule #152 (p. 491) $_{152}$

NUhA

BNF rule #152 (p. 491) $_{152}$

NUhI

BNF rule #85 (p. 490) $_{85}$

NUhU

BNF rule #85 (p. 490) $_{85}$

PA

BNF rule #817 (p. 492)$_{817}$, BNF rule #812 (p. 492)$_{812}$

PEhE

BNF rule #81 (p. 490) $_{81}$

PEhO

BNF rule #312 (p. 492) $_{312}$

PU

BNF rule #1033 (p. 493)$_{1033}$, BNF rule #1030 (p. 493)$_{1030}$

RAhO

BNF rule #152 (p. 491) $_{152}$

ROI

BNF rule #1051 (p. 493) $_{1051}$

SA

BNF rule #1101 (p. 493) $_{1101}$

SE

BNF rule #802 (p. 492)$_{802}$, BNF rule #807 (p. 492)$_{807}$, BNF rule #818 (p. 492)$_{818}$, BNF rule #808 (p. 493)$_{808}$, BNF rule #932 (p. 492)$_{932}$, BNF rule #805 (p. 492)$_{805}$, BNF rule #806 (p. 492)$_{806}$, BNF rule #374 (p. 492)$_{374}$, BNF rule #972 (p. 493)$_{972}$, BNF rule #152 (p. 491)$_{152}$

SEI

BNF rule #32 (p. 493) $_{32}$

SEhU

BNF rule #32 (p. 493) $_{32}$

SI

BNF rule #1101 (p. 493) $_{1101}$

SOI

BNF rule #32 (p. 493) $_{32}$

SU

BNF rule #1101 (p. 493) $_{1101}$

TAhE

BNF rule #1051 (p. 493) $_{1051}$

TEI

BNF rule #987 (p. 492) $_{987}$

TEhU

BNF rule #374 (p. 492)$_{374}$, BNF rule #385 (p. 492)$_{385}$

TO

BNF rule #32 (p. 493) $_{32}$

TOI

BNF rule #32 (p. 493) $_{32}$

TUhE

BNF rule #14 (p. 490) $_{14}$

TUhU

BNF rule #14 (p. 490) $_{14}$

UI

BNF rule #413 (p. 493) $_{413}$

VA

BNF rule #1045 (p. 493)$_{1045}$, BNF rule #1040 (p. 493)$_{1040}$

VAU

BNF rule #20 (p. 490)$_{20}$, BNF rule #71 (p. 490)$_{71}$

VEI

BNF rule #32 (p. 493)$_{32}$, BNF rule #300 (p. 492)$_{300}$

VEhA

BNF rule #1046 (p. 493) $_{1046}$

VEhO

BNF rule #32 (p. 493)$_{32}$, BNF rule #300 (p. 492)$_{300}$

VIhA

BNF rule #1046 (p. 493) $_{1046}$

VUhO

BNF rule #90 (p. 491) $_{90}$

VUhU

BNF rule #374 (p. 492) $_{374}$

XI

BNF rule #32 (p. 493) $_{32}$

Y

BNF rule #413 (p. 493) $_{413}$

ZAhO

BNF rule #1051 (p. 493) $_{1051}$

ZEI

BNF rule #152 (p. 491) $_{152}$

ZEhA

BNF rule #1030 (p. 493) $_{1030}$

ZI

BNF rule #1033 (p. 493)$_{1033}$, BNF rule #1030 (p. 493)$_{1030}$

ZIhE

BNF rule #121 (p. 491) $_{121}$

ZO

    BNF rule #97 (p. 491) $_{97}$

ZOI

    BNF rule #97 (p. 491) $_{97}$

ZOhU

    BNF rule #30 (p. 490) $_{30}$

any-word

    BNF rule #987 (p. 492)$_{987}$, BNF rule #1101 (p. 493)$_{1101}$, BNF rule #97 (p. 491)$_{97}$, BNF rule #152 (p. 491)$_{152}$, BNF rule #1100 (p. 493)$_{1100}$

anything

    BNF rule #97 (p. 491) $_{97}$

bridi-tail

    BNF rule #50 (p. 490)$_{50}$, BNF rule #40 (p. 490)$_{40}$

bridi-tail-1

    BNF rule #50 (p. 490) $_{50}$

bridi-tail-2

    BNF rule #51 (p. 490)$_{51}$, BNF rule #52 (p. 490)$_{52}$

bridi-tail-3

    BNF rule #52 (p. 490) $_{52}$

ek

    BNF rule #20 (p. 490)$_{20}$, BNF rule #421 (p. 492)$_{421}$, BNF rule #383 (p. 492)$_{383}$, BNF rule #381 (p. 492)$_{381}$, BNF rule #91 (p. 491)$_{91}$, BNF rule #93 (p. 491)$_{93}$

fragment

    BNF rule #10 (p. 490) $_{10}$

free

    BNF rule #0 (p. 490) $_{0}$

gek

    BNF rule #54 (p. 490)$_{54}$, BNF rule #385 (p. 492)$_{385}$, BNF rule #94 (p. 491)$_{94}$, BNF rule #85 (p. 490)$_{85}$

gek-sentence

    BNF rule #53 (p. 490)$_{53}$, BNF rule #54 (p. 490)$_{54}$

gihek

    BNF rule #51 (p. 490)$_{51}$, BNF rule #52 (p. 490)$_{52}$, BNF rule #50 (p. 490)$_{50}$, BNF rule #20 (p. 490)$_{20}$

gik

    BNF rule #54 (p. 490)$_{54}$, BNF rule #807 (p. 492)$_{807}$, BNF rule #385 (p. 492)$_{385}$, BNF rule #371 (p. 492)$_{371}$, BNF rule #136 (p. 491)$_{136}$, BNF rule #94 (p. 491)$_{94}$, BNF rule #85 (p. 490)$_{85}$

guhek

    BNF rule #371 (p. 492)$_{371}$, BNF rule #136 (p. 491)$_{136}$

indicator

    BNF rule #411 (p. 493) $_{411}$

indicators

    BNF rule #0 (p. 490)$_{0}$, BNF rule #1100 (p. 493)$_{1100}$

interval

    BNF rule #806 (p. 492) $_{806}$

interval-property

    BNF rule #1049 (p. 493)$_{1049}$, BNF rule #1030 (p. 493)$_{1030}$

jek

    BNF rule #422 (p. 492)$_{422}$, BNF rule #371 (p. 492)$_{371}$, BNF rule #135 (p. 491)$_{135}$, BNF rule #971 (p. 493)$_{971}$, BNF rule #13 (p. 490)$_{13}$, BNF rule #2 (p. 490)$_{2}$

joik

    BNF rule #807 (p. 492)$_{807}$, BNF rule #421 (p. 492)$_{421}$, BNF rule #422 (p. 492)$_{422}$, BNF rule #383 (p. 492)$_{383}$, BNF rule #381 (p. 492)$_{381}$, BNF rule #371 (p. 492)$_{371}$, BNF rule #370 (p. 492)$_{370}$, BNF rule

#134 (p. 491)$_{134}$, BNF rule #135 (p. 491)$_{135}$, BNF rule #971 (p. 493)$_{971}$, BNF rule #13 (p. 490)$_{13}$, BNF rule #91 (p. 491)$_{91}$, BNF rule #93 (p. 491)$_{93}$, BNF rule #2 (p. 490)$_2$

joik-ek

BNF rule #382 (p. 492)$_{382}$, BNF rule #92 (p. 491)$_{92}$

joik-jek

BNF rule #370 (p. 492)$_{370}$, BNF rule #134 (p. 491)$_{134}$, BNF rule #12 (p. 490)$_{12}$, BNF rule #491 (p. 493)$_{491}$, BNF rule #152 (p. 491)$_{152}$, BNF rule #81 (p. 490)$_{81}$, BNF rule #0 (p. 490)$_0$

lerfu-string

BNF rule #32 (p. 493)$_{32}$, BNF rule #987 (p. 492)$_{987}$, BNF rule #385 (p. 492)$_{385}$, BNF rule #97 (p. 491)$_{97}$, BNF rule #152 (p. 491)$_{152}$

lerfu-word

BNF rule #817 (p. 492)$_{817}$, BNF rule #987 (p. 492)$_{987}$, BNF rule #812 (p. 492)$_{812}$

linkargs

BNF rule #20 (p. 490)$_{20}$, BNF rule #151 (p. 491)$_{151}$

links

BNF rule #20 (p. 490)$_{20}$, BNF rule #160 (p. 491)$_{160}$, BNF rule #161 (p. 491)$_{161}$

mex

BNF rule #32 (p. 493)$_{32}$, BNF rule #374 (p. 492)$_{374}$, BNF rule #300 (p. 492)$_{300}$, BNF rule #97 (p. 491)$_{97}$

mex-1

BNF rule #311 (p. 492)$_{311}$, BNF rule #310 (p. 492)$_{310}$

mex-2

BNF rule #311 (p. 492)$_{311}$, BNF rule #312 (p. 492)$_{312}$, BNF rule #385 (p. 492)$_{385}$

mex-operator

BNF rule #374 (p. 492)$_{374}$, BNF rule #372 (p. 492)$_{372}$, BNF rule #152 (p. 491)$_{152}$

number

BNF rule #32 (p. 493)$_{32}$, BNF rule #1051 (p. 493)$_{1051}$, BNF rule #300 (p. 492)$_{300}$, BNF rule #152 (p. 491)$_{152}$

operand

BNF rule #312 (p. 492)$_{312}$, BNF rule #385 (p. 492)$_{385}$, BNF rule #381 (p. 492)$_{381}$, BNF rule #332 (p. 492)$_{332}$

operand-1

BNF rule #381 (p. 492) $_{381}$

operand-2

BNF rule #382 (p. 492)$_{382}$, BNF rule #383 (p. 492)$_{383}$

operand-3

BNF rule #383 (p. 492)$_{383}$, BNF rule #385 (p. 492)$_{385}$

operator

BNF rule #311 (p. 492)$_{311}$, BNF rule #312 (p. 492)$_{312}$, BNF rule #310 (p. 492)$_{310}$, BNF rule #372 (p. 492)$_{372}$, BNF rule #370 (p. 492)$_{370}$, BNF rule #330 (p. 492)$_{330}$

operator-1

BNF rule #371 (p. 492)$_{371}$, BNF rule #370 (p. 492)$_{370}$

operator-2

BNF rule #371 (p. 492) $_{371}$

paragraph

BNF rule #4 (p. 490) $_4$

paragraphs

BNF rule #4 (p. 490)$_4$, BNF rule #2 (p. 490)$_2$

prenex

BNF rule #20 (p. 490)$_{20}$, BNF rule #11 (p. 490)$_{11}$, BNF rule #41 (p. 490)$_{41}$

quantifier

BNF rule #20 (p. 490)$_{20}$, BNF rule #385 (p. 492)$_{385}$, BNF rule #95 (p. 491)$_{95}$, BNF rule #112 (p. 491)$_{112}$

relative-clause

BNF rule #121 (p. 491) $_{121}$

relative-clauses

BNF rule #20 (p. 490)$_{20}$, BNF rule #32 (p. 493)$_{32}$, BNF rule #95 (p. 491)$_{95}$, BNF rule #97 (p. 491)$_{97}$, BNF rule #112 (p. 491)$_{112}$, BNF rule #111 (p. 491)$_{111}$, BNF rule #90 (p. 491)$_{90}$

rp-expression

BNF rule #310 (p. 492)$_{310}$, BNF rule #332 (p. 492)$_{332}$

rp-operand

BNF rule #330 (p. 492) $_{330}$

selbri

BNF rule #53 (p. 490)$_{53}$, BNF rule #32 (p. 493)$_{32}$, BNF rule #374 (p. 492)$_{374}$, BNF rule #385 (p. 492)$_{385}$, BNF rule #131 (p. 491)$_{131}$, BNF rule #136 (p. 491)$_{136}$, BNF rule #95 (p. 491)$_{95}$, BNF rule #112 (p. 491)$_{112}$, BNF rule #815 (p. 493)$_{815}$

selbri-1

BNF rule #130 (p. 491) $_{130}$

selbri-2

BNF rule #131 (p. 491)$_{131}$, BNF rule #132 (p. 491)$_{132}$

selbri-3

BNF rule #132 (p. 491)$_{132}$, BNF rule #134 (p. 491)$_{134}$, BNF rule #152 (p. 491)$_{152}$

selbri-4

BNF rule #133 (p. 491) $_{133}$

selbri-5

BNF rule #134 (p. 491)$_{134}$, BNF rule #135 (p. 491)$_{135}$

selbri-6

BNF rule #135 (p. 491)$_{135}$, BNF rule #136 (p. 491)$_{136}$

sentence

BNF rule #14 (p. 490)$_{14}$, BNF rule #41 (p. 490)$_{41}$

simple-tense-modal

BNF rule #971 (p. 493)$_{971}$, BNF rule #815 (p. 493)$_{815}$

space

BNF rule #972 (p. 493) $_{972}$

space-int-props

BNF rule #1046 (p. 493) $_{1046}$

space-interval

BNF rule #1040 (p. 493) $_{1040}$

space-offset

BNF rule #1040 (p. 493) $_{1040}$

stag

BNF rule #52 (p. 490)$_{52}$, BNF rule #50 (p. 490)$_{50}$, BNF rule #807 (p. 492)$_{807}$, BNF rule #383 (p. 492)$_{383}$, BNF rule #381 (p. 492)$_{381}$, BNF rule #371 (p. 492)$_{371}$, BNF rule #370 (p. 492)$_{370}$, BNF rule #134 (p. 491)$_{134}$, BNF rule #135 (p. 491)$_{135}$, BNF rule #13 (p. 490)$_{13}$, BNF rule #91 (p. 491)$_{91}$, BNF rule #93 (p. 491)$_{93}$, BNF rule #2 (p. 490)$_{2}$

statement

BNF rule #10 (p. 490)$_{10}$, BNF rule #11 (p. 490)$_{11}$

statement-1

BNF rule #11 (p. 490) $_{11}$

statement-2

BNF rule #12 (p. 490)$_{12}$, BNF rule #13 (p. 490)$_{13}$

statement-3

BNF rule #13 (p. 490) 13

subsentence

BNF rule #54 (p. 490)54, BNF rule #122 (p. 491)122, BNF rule #41 (p. 490)41, BNF rule #152 (p. 491)152

sumti

BNF rule #32 (p. 493)32, BNF rule #385 (p. 492)385, BNF rule #91 (p. 491)91, BNF rule #94 (p. 491)94, BNF rule #97 (p. 491)97, BNF rule #112 (p. 491)112, BNF rule #152 (p. 491)152, BNF rule #83 (p. 490)83

sumti-1

BNF rule #90 (p. 491) 90

sumti-2

BNF rule #91 (p. 491) 91

sumti-3

BNF rule #92 (p. 491)92, BNF rule #93 (p. 491)93

sumti-4

BNF rule #93 (p. 491)93, BNF rule #94 (p. 491)94

sumti-5

BNF rule #94 (p. 491) 94

sumti-6

BNF rule #95 (p. 491)95, BNF rule #111 (p. 491)111

sumti-tail

BNF rule #97 (p. 491) 97

sumti-tail-1

BNF rule #111 (p. 491) 111

tag

BNF rule #54 (p. 490)54, BNF rule #130 (p. 491)130, BNF rule #14 (p. 490)14, BNF rule #152 (p. 491)152, BNF rule #83 (p. 490)83

tail-terms

BNF rule #51 (p. 490)51, BNF rule #52 (p. 490)52, BNF rule #53 (p. 490)53, BNF rule #50 (p. 490)50, BNF rule #54 (p. 490)54

tanru-unit

BNF rule #136 (p. 491) 136

tanru-unit-1

BNF rule #150 (p. 491) 150

tanru-unit-2

BNF rule #151 (p. 491)151, BNF rule #152 (p. 491)152

tense-modal

BNF rule #491 (p. 493) 491

term

BNF rule #160 (p. 491)160, BNF rule #161 (p. 491)161, BNF rule #122 (p. 491)122, BNF rule #82 (p. 490)82

terms

BNF rule #20 (p. 490)20, BNF rule #32 (p. 493)32, BNF rule #30 (p. 490)30, BNF rule #40 (p. 490)40, BNF rule #71 (p. 490)71, BNF rule #85 (p. 490)85

terms-1

BNF rule #80 (p. 490) 80

terms-2

BNF rule #81 (p. 490) 81

termset

BNF rule #83 (p. 490) 83

502

text

BNF rule #32 (p. 493)$_{32}$, BNF rule #1101 (p. 493)$_{1101}$, BNF rule #97 (p. 491)$_{97}$

text-1

BNF rule #14 (p. 490)$_{14}$, BNF rule #0 (p. 490)$_{0}$

time

BNF rule #972 (p. 493) $_{972}$

time-offset

BNF rule #1030 (p. 493) $_{1030}$

utterance

BNF rule #1101 (p. 493) $_{1101}$

vocative

BNF rule #32 (p. 493) $_{32}$

Lojban Word Glossary

All definitions in this glossary are brief and unofficial. Only the published dictionary is a truly official reference for word definitions. These definitions are here simply as a quick reference.

a
logical connective: sumti afterthought or.

abu
letteral for a.

a'e
attitudinal: alertness - exhaustion.

a'u
attitudinal: interest - disinterest - repulsion.

ai
attitudinal: intent - indecision - rejection/refusal.

au
attitudinal: desire - indifference - reluctance.

ba
time tense relation/direction: will [selbri]; after [sumti]; default future tense.

ba'a
evidential: I expect - I experience - I remember.

ba'acu'i
evidential: I expect - I experience - I remember.

ba'anai
evidential: I expect - I experience - I remember.

ba'e
forethought emphasis indicator; indicates next word is especially emphasized.

ba'o
interval event contour: in the aftermath of ...; since ...; retrospective/perfect | |----.

bai
bapli modal, 1st place (forced by) forcedly; compelled by force ...

bajra
x_1 runs on surface x_2 using limbs x_3 with gait x_4.

bakrecpa'o
$p_1=r_1$ is a beefsteak.

bakri
x_1 is a quantity of/contains/is made of chalk from source x_2 in form x_3.

balsoi
$s_1=b_1$ is a great soldier of army s_2 great in property b_2 (ka) by standard b_3.

balvi
x_1 is in the future of/later than/after x_2 in time sequence; x_1 is latter; x_2 is former.

bangu
x_1 is a/the language/dialect used by x_2 to express/communicate x_3 (si'o/du'u, not quote).

banli
x_1 is great/grand in property x_2 (ka) by standard x_3.

bapu
time tense: will have been; (tense/modal).

barda
x_1 is big/large in property/dimension(s) x_2 (ka) as compared with standard/norm x_3.

basti
x_1 replaces/substitutes for/instead of x_2 in circumstance x_3; x_1 is a replacement/substitute.

basygau
g_1 (agent) replaces/substitutes b_1 for/instead of b_2 in circumstance b_3.

batci
x_1 bites/pinches x_2 on/at specific locus x_3 with x_4.

bau
bangu modal, 1st place in language ...

bavla'i
$b_1=l_1$ is next after $b_2=l_2$ in sequence l_3.

bavlamdei
$d_1=b_1=l_1$ is tomorrow; $d_1=b_1=l_1$ is the day following $b_2=l_2$, day standard d_3.

baxso
x_1 reflects Malay-Indonesian common language/culture in aspect x_2.

be
sumti link to attach sumti (default x_2) to a selbri; used in descriptions.

be'a
location tense relation/direction; north of.

be'o
elidable terminator: end linked sumti in specified description.

be'u
attitudinal modifier: lack/need - presence/satisfaction - satiation.

bei
separates multiple linked sumti within a selbri; used in descriptions.

bemro
x_1 reflects North American culture/nationality/geography in aspect x_2.

bengo
x_1 reflects Bengali/Bangladesh culture/nationality/language in aspect x_2.

bi'e
prefixed to a mex operator to indicate high priority.

bi'i
non-logical interval connective: unordered between ... and ...

bi'o
non-logical interval connective: ordered from ... to ...

bi'u
discursive: newly introduced information - previously introduced information.

bi'unai
discursive: newly introduced information - previously introduced information.

bilma

x_1 is ill/sick/diseased with symptoms x_2 from disease x_3.

bindo

x_1 reflects Indonesian culture/nationality/language in aspect x_2.

birka

x_1 is a/the arm [body-part] of x_2; [metaphor: branch with strength].

blabi

x_1 is white/very-light colored [color adjective].

blaci

x_1 is a quantity of/is made of/contains glass of composition including x_2.

blakanla

x_1 is an eye of x_2 and has a blue iris

blanu

x_1 is blue [color adjective].

blari'o

c_1 is blue-green.

blaselkanla

x_1 has blue eyes

blolei

k_1 is a ship type/class within ships $b_1 = k_2$, with features k_3.

bloti

x_1 is a boat/ship/vessel [vehicle] for carrying x_2, propelled by x_3.

bo

short scope joiner; joins various constructs with shortest scope and right grouping.

boi

elidable terminator: terminate numeral or letteral string.

bradi

x_1 is an enemy/opponent/adversary/foe of x_2 in struggle x_3.

brazo

x_1 reflects Brazilian culture/nationality/language in aspect x_2.

bredi

x_1 is ready/prepared for x_2 (event).

bridi

x_1 (du'u) is a predicate relationship with relation x_2 among arguments (sequence/set) x_3.

brito

x_1 reflects British/United Kingdom culture/nationality in aspect x_2.

brivla

v_1 is a morphologically defined predicate word signifying relation b_2 in language v_3.

broda

1st assignable variable predicate (context determines place structure).

brode

2nd assignable variable predicate (context determines place structure).

brodi

3rd assignable variable predicate (context determines place structure).

brodo

4th assignable variable predicate (context determines place structure).

brodu

5th assignable variable predicate (context determines place structure).

bu

convert any single word to BY.

budjo

x_1 pertains to the Buddhist culture/religion/ethos in aspect x_2.

bu'a

logically quantified predicate variable: some selbri 1.

bu'e

logically quantified predicate variable: some selbri 2.

bu'i

logically quantified predicate variable: some selbri 3.

bu'o

attitudinal contour: start emotion - continue emotion - end emotion.

bu'ocu'i

attitudinal contour: start emotion - continue emotion - end emotion.

bu'onai

attitudinal contour: start emotion - continue emotion - end emotion.

bu'u

location tense relation/direction; coincident with/at the same place as; space equivalent of ca.

by

letteral for b.

ca

time tense relation/direction: is [selbri]; during/simultaneous with [sumti]; present tense.

cabna

x_1 is current at/in the present of/during/concurrent/simultaneous with x_2 in time.

cadzu

x_1 walks/strides/paces on surface x_2 using limbs x_3.

cafne

x_1 (event) often/frequently/commonly/customarily occurs/recurs by standard x_2.

cagyce'u

x_1 is a farming community with members x_2.

ca'a

modal aspect: actuality/ongoing event.

ca'e

evidential: I define.

ca'o

interval event contour: during ...; continuative |---- -|.

cai

attitudinal: strong intensity attitude modifier.

cakcinki

x_1 is a beetle of species x_2.

calku

x_1 is a shell/husk [hard, protective covering] around x_2 composed of x_3.

carmi

x_1 is intense/bright/saturated/brilliant in property (ka) x_2 as received/measured by observer x_3.

casnu

x_1(s) (mass normally, but 1 individual/jo'u possible) discuss(es)/talk(s) about topic/subject x_2.

ce

non-logical connective: set link, unordered; "and also", but forming a set.

ce'a

2-word letteral/shift: the word following indicates a new font (e.g. italics, manuscript).

ce'e

links terms into an afterthought termset.

ce'i

digit/number: % percentage symbol, hundredths.

ce'o

non-logical connective: ordered sequence link; "and then", forming a sequence.

ce'u

pseudo-quantifier binding a variable within an abstraction that represents an open place.

cei

selbri variable assignment; assigns broda series pro-bridi to a selbri.

centi

x_1 is a hundredth [1/100; 10^{-2}] of x_2 in dimension/aspect x_3 (default is units).

ci

digit/number: 3 (digit) [three].

cidja

x_1 is food/feed/nutriment for x_2; x_1 is edible/gives nutrition to x_2.

cidjrspageti

x_1 is a quantity of spaghetti (long, thin cylindrical pasta)

ci'ajbu

j_1 is a writing desk of material j_2, supported by legs/base/pedestal j_3, used by writer c_1.

ci'e

ciste modal, 1st place used in scalar negation in system/context ...

ci'u

ckilu modal, 1st place on the scale ...

cinfo

x_1 is a lion/[lioness] of species/breed x_2.

cinki

x_1 is an insect/arthropod of species x_2; [bug/beetle].

cipnrstrigi

x_1 is an owl of species x_2

cirla

x_1 is a quantity of/contains cheese/curd from source x_2.

ciste

x_1 (mass) is a system interrelated by structure x_2 among components x_3 (set) displaying x_4 (ka).

citka

x_1 eats/ingests/consumes (transitive verb) x_2.

citmau

$z_1=c_1$ is younger than z_2 by amount z_4.

citno

x_1 is young/youthful [relatively short in elapsed duration] by standard x_2.

ckule

x_1 is school/institute/academy at x_2 teaching subject(s) x_3 to audien./commun. x_4 operated by x_5.

cladakfu

x_1 is a long knife

cladakyxa'i

$x_1=d_1=c_1$ is a sword / long knife weapon for use against $x_2=d_2$ by x_3 with blade of material d_3 long by standard c_3.

clani

x_1 is long in dimension/direction x_2 (default longest dimension) by measurement standard x_3.

cliva

x_1 leaves/goes away/departs/parts/separates from x_2 via route x_3.

cmaci

x_1 is a mathematics of type/describing x_2.

cmalu

x_1 is small in property/dimension(s) x_2 (ka) as compared with standard/norm x_3.

cmaro'i

$c_1=r_1$ is a small rock of type r_2 from location r_3, small by standard c_3. c_1 is gravel.

cmavo

x_1 is a structure word of grammatical class x_2, with meaning/function x_3 in usage (language) x_4.

cmene

x_1 (quoted word(s)) is a/the name/title/tag of x_2 to/used-by namer/name-user x_3 (person).

cmima

x_1 is a member/element of set x_2; x_1 belongs to group x_2; x_1 is amid/among/amongst group x_2.

co

tanru inversion operator; "... of type ..."; allows modifier trailing sumti without sumti links.

co'a

interval event contour: at the starting point of ...; initiative >|< |.

co'e

elliptical/unspecified bridi relationship.

co'i

interval event contour: at the instantaneous point of ...; achievative/perfective; point event >|<.

co'o
> vocative: partings/good-bye.

co'u
> interval event contour: at the ending point of ... even if not done; cessative | >< |.

coi
> vocative: greetings/hello.

coico'o
> vocative: greetings in passing.

cpumi'i
> $l_1=m_1$ is a tractor pulling l_2.

cribe
> x_1 is a bear/ursoid of species/breed x_2.

ctigau
> g_1 feeds c_1 with food c_2.

cu
> elidable marker: separates selbri from preceding sumti, allows preceding terminator elision.

cu'e
> tense/modal question.

cu'i
> attitudinal: neutral scalar attitude modifier.

cu'o
> convert number to probability selbri; event x_1 has probability (n) of occurring under cond. x_2.

cu'u
> cusku modal, 1st place (attribution/quotation) as said by source ...; used for quotation.

cumki
> x_1 (event/state/property) is possible under conditions x_2; x_1 may/might occur; x_1 is a maybe.

cunso
> x_1 is random/fortuitous/unpredictable under conditions x_2, with probability distribution x_3.

cusku
> x_1 (agent) expresses/says x_2 (sedu'u/text/lu'e concept) for audience x_3 via expressive medium x_4.

cutci
> x_1 is a shoe/boot/sandal for covering/protecting [feet/hooves] x_2, and of material x_3.

cuxna
> x_1 chooses/selects x_2 [choice] from set/sequence of alternatives x_3 (complete set).

cy
> letteral for c.

da
> logically quantified existential pro-sumti: there exists something 1 (usually restricted).

dadgreku
> x_1 is a rack used to hang x_2.

dadjo
> x_1 pertains to the Taoist culture/ethos/religion in aspect x_2.

dadysli
> $s_1=d_1$ is a pendulum oscillating at rate/frequency s_2, suspended from d_2 by/at/with joint d_3.

da'a
> digit/number: all except n; all but n; default 1.

da'e
> pro-sumti: remote future utterance; "He'll tell you tomorrow. IT will be a doozy.".

da'i
> discursive: supposing - in fact.

da'inai
> discursive: supposing - in fact.

da'o
> discursive: cancel pro-sumti/pro-bridi assignments.

da'u
> pro-sumti: a remote past utterance; "She couldn't have known that IT would be true.".

dai
> attitudinal modifier: marks empathetic use of preceding attitudinal; shows another's feelings.

dakfu
> x_1 is a knife (tool) for cutting x_2, with blade of material x_3.

dalmikce
> m_1 is a doctor for animal $m_2=d_1$ of species d_2 for ailment m_3 using treatment m_4.

danlu
> x_1 is an animal/creature of species x_2; x_1 is biologically animate.

de
> logically quantified existential pro-sumti: there exists something 2 (usually restricted).

decti
> x_1 is a tenth [1/10; 10^{-1}] of x_2 in dimension/aspect x_3 (default is units).

de'a
> event contour for a temporary halt and ensuing pause in a process.

de'e
> pro-sumti: a near future utterance.

de'i
> detri modal, 1st place (for letters) dated ... ; attaches date stamp.

de'u
> pro-sumti: a recent utterance.

dei
> pro-sumti: this utterance.

dejni
> x_1 owes x_2 in debt/obligation to creditor x_3 in return for x_4 [service, loan]; x_1 is a debtor.

dekto
> x_1 is ten [10; 10^1] of x_2 in dimension/aspect x_3 (default is units).

delno
> x_1 is x_2 candela [metric unit] in luminosity (default is 1) by standard x_3.

denci
> x_1 is a/the tooth [body-part] of x_2; (adjective:) x_1 is dental.

denpa

x_1 awaits/waits/pauses for/until x_2 at state x_3 before starting/continuing x_4 (activity/process).

di

logically quantified existential pro-sumti: there exists something 3 (usually restricted).

di'a

event contour for resumption of a paused process.

di'e

pro-sumti: the next utterance.

di'i

tense interval modifier: regularly; subjective tense/modal; defaults as time tense.

di'inai

tense interval modifier: irregularly/aperiodically; tense/modal; defaults as time tense.

di'u

pro-sumti: the last utterance.

dinju

x_1 is a building/edifice for purpose x_2.

djedi

x_1 is x_2 full days in duration (default is 1 day) by standard x_3; (adjective:) x_1 is diurnal.

djica

x_1 desires/wants/wishes x_2 (event/state) for purpose x_3.

djine

x_1 is a ring/annulus/torus/circle [shape/form] of material x_2, inside diam. x_3, outside diam. x_4.

djuno

x_1 knows fact(s) x_2 (du'u) about subject x_3 by epistemology x_4.

do

pro-sumti: you listener(s); identified by vocative.

do'a

discursive: generously - parsimoniously.

do'anai

discursive: generously - parsimoniously.

do'e

elliptical/unspecified modal.

do'i

pro-sumti: elliptical/unspecified utterance variable.

do'o

pro-sumti: you the listener & others unspecified.

do'u

elidable terminator: end vocative (often elidable).

doi

generic vocative marker; identifies intended listener; elidable after COI.

donma'o

c_1 is a second person pronoun in language c_4.

donta'a

x_1 talks to you (i.e. whoever x_1 is addressing) about x_2 in language x_3

dotco

x_1 reflects German/Germanic culture/nationality/language in aspect x_2.

du

identity selbri; = sign; x_1 identically equals x_2, x_3, etc.; attached sumti refer to same thing.

dubjavmau

x_1 is greater than or equal to x_2.

dubjavme'a

x_1 is less than or equal to x_2

du'e

digit/number: too many; subjective.

du'i

dunli modal, 1st place (equalled by) equally; as much as ...

du'u

abstractor: predication/bridi abstractor; x_1 is predication [bridi] expressed in sentence x_2.

dunda

x_1 [donor] gives/donates gift/present x_2 to recipient/beneficiary x_3 [without payment/exchange].

dunli

x_1 is equal/congruent to/as much as x_2 in property/dimension/quantity x_3.

dy

letteral for d.

dzipo

x_1 reflects Antarctican culture/nationality/geography in aspect x_2.

dzukla

x_1 is a walker-come with destination x_2 with starting point x_3 with route of going x_4 with transportation means -walking limb x_5 with walked on x_6.

e

logical connective: sumti afterthought and.

ebu

letteral for e.

e'e

attitudinal: competence - incompetence/inability.

e'o

attitudinal: request - negative request.

e'u

attitudinal: suggestion - abandon suggest - warning.

ei

attitudinal: obligation - freedom.

fa

sumti place tag: tag 1st sumti place.

fadni

x_1 [member] is ordinary/common/typical/usual in property x_2 (ka) among members of x_3 (set).

fagri

x_1 is a fire/flame in fuel x_2 burning-in/reacting-with oxidizer x_3 (default air/oxygen).

fagyfesti

$x_1 = fe_1$ is the ashes of $x_3 = fa_2$, combusted by fire $x_2 = fa_1$.

fa'a

location tense relation/direction; arriving at/ directly towards ...

fa'o

unconditional end of text; outside regular grammar; used for computer input.

fa'u

non-logical connective: respectively; unmixed ordered distributed association.

fai

sumti place tag: tag a sumti moved out of numbered place structure; used in modal conversions.

fasnu

x_1 (event) is an event that happens/occurs/takes place; x_1 is an incident/happening/occurrence.

fau

fasnu modal, 1st place (non-causal) in the event of ...

fe

sumti place tag: tag 2nd sumti place.

fe'a

binary mathematical operator: nth root of; inverse power [a to the 1/b power].

fe'e

mark space interval distributive aspects; labels interval tense modifiers as location-oriented.

fe'o

vocative: over and out (end discussion).

fe'u

elidable terminator: end nonce conversion of selbri to modal; usually elidable.

femti

x_1 is 10^{-15} of x_2 in dimension/aspect x_3 (default is units).

festi

x_1(s) is/are waste product(s) [left to waste] by x_2 (event/activity).

fi

sumti place tag: tag 3rd sumti place.

fi'a

sumti place tag: place structure number/tag question.

fi'e

finti modal, 1st place (creator) created by ...

fi'i

vocative: hospitality - inhospitality; you are welcome/ make yourself at home.

fi'o

convert selbri to nonce modal/sumti tag.

fi'u

digit/number: fraction slash; default "/n" => 1/n, "n/" => n/1, or "/" alone => golden ratio.

filso

x_1 reflects Palestinian culture/nationality in aspect x_2.

finti

x_1 invents/creates/composes/authors x_2 for function/purpose x_3 from existing elements/ideas x_4.

firgai

g_1 is a mask covering the face of $g_2 = f_2$.

flalu

x_1 is a law specifying x_2 (state/event) for community x_3 under conditions x_4 by lawgiver(s) x_5.

fo

sumti place tag: tag 4th sumti place.

fo'a

pro-sumti: he/she/it/they #6 (specified by goi).

fo'e

pro-sumti: he/she/it/they #7 (specified by goi).

fo'i

pro-sumti: he/she/it/they #8 (specified by goi).

fo'o

pro-sumti: he/she/it/they #9 (specified by goi).

fo'u

pro-sumti: he/she/it/they #10 (specified by goi).

foi

terminator: end composite lerfu; never elidable.

fraso

x_1 reflects French/Gallic culture/nationality/ language in aspect x_2.

friko

x_1 reflects African culture/nationality/geography in aspect x_2.

frinu

x_1 is a fraction, with numerator x_2, denominator x_3 (x_2/x_3).

fu

sumti place tag: tag 5th sumti place.

fu'a

reverse Polish mathematical expression (mex) operator flag.

fu'e

begin indicator long scope.

fu'i

attitudinal modifier: easy - difficult.

fu'ivla

$x_1 = v_1 = f_1$ is a loanword meaning $x_2 = v_2$ in language $x_3 = v_3$, based on word $x_4 = f_2$ in language x_5.

fu'o

end indicator long scope; terminates scope of all active indicators.

fy

letteral for f.

ga

logical connective: forethought all but tanru-internal or (with gi).

gadri

x_1 is an article/descriptor labelling description x_2 (text) in language x_3 with semantics x_4.

ga'e

upper-case letteral shift.

ga'i
> attitudinal modifier/honorific: hauteur - equal rank - meekness; used with one of lower rank.

ga'icu'i
> attitudinal modifier/honorific: hauteur - equal rank - meekness; used with one of equal rank.

ga'inai
> attitudinal modifier/honorific: hauteur - equal rank - meekness; used with one of higher rank.

ga'o
> closed interval bracket marker; mod. intervals in non-logical connectives; include boundaries.

galfi
> x_1 (event) modifies/alters/changes/transforms/converts x_2 into x_3.

galtu
> x_1 is high/up/upward in frame of reference x_2 as compared with baseline/standard height x_3.

ganai
> logical connective: forethought all but tanru-internal conditional/only if (with gi).

ganlo
> x_1 (portal/passage/entrance-way) is closed/shut/not open, preventing passage/access to x_2 by x_3 (something being blocked).

gapru
> x_1 is directly/vertically above/upwards-from x_2 in gravity/frame of reference x_3.

gasnu
> x_1 [person/agent] is an agentive cause of event x_2; x_1 does/brings about x_2.

gau
> gasnu modal, 1st place agent/actor case tag with active agent ...

ge
> logical connective: forethought all but tanru-internal and (with gi).

ge'a
> mathematical operator: null mathematical expression (mex) operator (used in >2-ary ops).

ge'e
> attitudinal: elliptical/unspecified/non-specific emotion; no particular feeling.

ge'i
> logical connective: forethought all but tanru-internal connective question (with gi).

ge'o
> shift letterals to Greek alphabet.

ge'u
> elidable terminator: end GOI relative phrases; usually elidable in non-complex phrases.

gei
> trinary mathematical operator: order of magnitude/value/base; [b * (c to the a power)].

gekmau
> x_1 is happier than x_2 about x_3 by amount x_4

gento
> x_1 reflects Argentinian culture/nationality in aspect x_2.

gerku
> x_1 is a dog/canine/[bitch] of species/breed x_2.

gerzda
> z_1 is a doghouse for dog $z_2 = g_1$.

gi
> logical connective: all but tanru-internal forethought connective medial marker.

gigdo
> x_1 is a billion [British milliard] [10^9] of x_2 in dimension/aspect x_3 (default is units).

gi'a
> logical connective: bridi-tail afterthought or.

gi'e
> logical connective: bridi-tail afterthought and.

gi'i
> logical connective: bridi-tail afterthought conn question.

gi'o
> logical connective: bridi-tail afterthought biconditional/iff/if-and-only-if.

gi'u
> logical connective: bridi-tail afterthought whether-or-not.

girzu
> x_1 is group/cluster/team showing common property (ka) x_2 due to set x_3 linked by relations x_4.

gismu
> x_1 is a (Lojban) root word expressing relation x_2 among argument roles x_3, with affix(es) x_4.

gleki
> x_1 is happy/merry/glad/gleeful about x_2 (event/state).

glico
> x_1 is English/pertains to English-speaking culture in aspect x_2.

go
> logical connective: forethought all but tanru internal biconditional/iff/if-and-only-if(with gi).

gocti
> x_1 is 10^{-24} of x_2 in dimension/aspect x_3 (default is units).

go'a
> pro-bridi: repeats a recent bridi (usually not the last 2).

go'e
> pro-bridi: repeats the next to last bridi.

go'i
> pro-bridi: preceding bridi; in answer to a yes/no question, repeats the claim, meaning yes.

go'o
> pro-bridi: repeats a future bridi, normally the next one.

go'u
> pro-bridi: repeats a remote past bridi.

goi
> sumti assignment; used to define/assign ko'a/fo'a series pro-sumti; Latin 'sive'.

gotro

x_1 is 10^{24} of x_2 in dimension/aspect x_3 (default is units).

gu

logical connective: forethought all but tanru-internal whether-or-not (with gi).

gu'a

logical connective: tanru-internal forethought or (with gi).

gu'e

logical connective: tanru-internal forethought and (with gi).

gu'i

logical connective: tanru-internal forethought question (with gi).

gu'o

logical connective: tanru-internal forethought biconditional/iff/if-and-only-if (with gi).

gu'u

logical connective: tanru-internal forethought whether-or-not (with gi).

gy

letteral for g.

i

sentence link/continuation; continuing sentences on same topic; normally elided for new speakers.

ia

attitudinal: belief - skepticism - disbelief.

ianai

attitudinal: belief - skepticism - disbelief.

ibu

letteral for i.

ie

attitudinal: agreement - disagreement.

ienai

attitudinal: agreement - disagreement.

i'a

attitudinal: acceptance - blame.

i'e

attitudinal: approval - non-approval - disapproval.

i'inai

attitudinal: togetherness - privacy.

ii

attitudinal: fear - security.

ija

logical connective: sentence afterthought or.

ije

logical connective: sentence afterthought and.

io

attitudinal: respect - disrespect.

iu

attitudinal: love - no love lost - hatred.

ja

logical connective: tanru-internal afterthought or.

ja'a

bridi logical affirmer; scope is an entire bridi.

ja'e

jalge modal, 1st place resultingly; therefore result ...

ja'o

evidential: I conclude.

jai

convert tense/modal (tagged) place to 1st place; 1st place moves to extra FA place (fai).

jbena

x_1 is born to x_2 at time x_3 [birthday] and place x_4 [birthplace]; x_1 is native to (fo) x_4.

jdaselsku

c_2 is a prayer of believer $c_1=l_2$ for deity c_3 in medium c_4 according to religion l_3.

jdika

x_1 (experiencer) decreases/contracts/is reduced/diminished in property/quantity x_2 by amount x_3.

je

logical connective: tanru-internal afterthought and.

jegvo

x_1 pertains to the common Judeo-Christian-Moslem (Abrahamic) culture/religion/nationality in aspect x_2.

je'a

scalar affirmer; denies scalar negation: Indeed!.

je'e

vocative: roger (ack) - negative acknowledge; used to acknowledge offers and thanks.

je'enai

vocative: roger (ack) - negative acknowledge; I didn't hear you.

je'i

logical connective: tanru-internal afterthought conn question.

je'o

shift letterals to Hebrew alphabet.

je'u

discursive: truth - falsity.

je'unai

discursive: truth - falsity.

jei

abstractor: truth-value abstractor; x_1 is truth value of [bridi] under epistemology x_2.

jelca

x_1 burns/[ignites/is flammable/inflammable] at temperature x_2 in atmosphere x_3.

jenai

logical connective: tanru-internal afterthought x but not y.

jerxo

x_1 reflects Algerian culture/nationality in aspect x_2.

ji

logical connective: sumti afterthought connective question.

jibni

x_1 is near/close to/approximates x_2 in property/quantity x_3 (ka/ni).

ji'a

discursive: additionally.

ji'i

digit/number: approximately (default the typical value in this context) (number).

ji'u

jicmu modal, 1st place (assumptions); given that ...; based on ...

jinvi

x_1 thinks/opines x_2 [opinion] (du'u) is true about subject/issue x_3 on grounds x_4.

jitro

x_1 has control over/harnesses/manages/directs/conducts x_2 in x_3 (activity/event/performance).

jo

logical connective: tanru-internal afterthought biconditional/iff/if-and-only-if.

jo'a

discursive: metalinguistic affirmer.

jo'e

non-logical connective: union of sets.

jo'i

join mathematical expression (mex) operands into an array.

jo'o

shift letterals to Arabic alphabet.

jo'u

non-logical connective: in common with; along with (unmixed).

joi

non-logical connective: mixed conjunction; "and" meaning "mixed together", forming a mass.

jordo

x_1 reflects Jordanian culture/nationality in aspect x_2.

ju

logical connective: tanru-internal afterthought whether-or-not.

ju'a

evidential: I state - (default) elliptical/non-specific basis.

ju'o

attitudinal modifier: certainty - uncertainty - impossibility.

ju'u

binary mathematical operator: number base; [a interpreted in the base b].

jundi

x_1 is attentive towards/attends/tends/pays attention to object/affair x_2.

jungo

x_1 reflects Chinese [Mandarin, Cantonese, Wu, etc.] culture/nationality/language in aspect x_2.

jy

letteral for j.

ka

abstractor: property/quality abstractor (-ness); x_1 is quality/property exhibited by [bridi].

kadno

x_1 reflects Canadian culture/nationality in aspect x_2.

ka'a

klama modal, 1st place gone to by ...

ka'e

modal aspect: innate capability; possibly unrealized.

ka'o

digit/number: imaginary i; square root of -1.

ka'u

evidential: I know by cultural means (myth or custom).

kai

ckaji modal, 1st place characterizing ...

kalri

x_1 (portal/passage/entrance-way) is open/ajar/not shut permitting passage/access to x_2 by x_3.

kalselvi'i

$x_1=v_2$ is a tear/tear fluid of $x_2=v_1$.

kambla

x_1 is blueness

kanji

x_1 calculates/reckons/computes x_2 [value (ni)/state] from data x_3 by process x_4.

kanla

x_1 is a/the eye [body-part] of x_2; [metaphor: sensory apparatus]; (adjective:) x_1 is ocular.

kanro

x_1 is healthy/fit/well/in good health by standard x_2.

karce

x_1 is a car/automobile/truck/van [a wheeled motor vehicle] for carrying x_2, propelled by x_3

karcykla

x_1 comes/goes to x_2 from x_3 via route x_4 using car x_5

kau

discursive: marks word serving as focus of indirect question: "I know WHO went to the store".

ke

start grouping of tanru, etc; ... type of ... ; overrides normal tanru left grouping.

ke'a

pro-sumti: relativized sumti (object of relative clause).

ke'e

elidable terminator: end of tanru left grouping override (usually elidable).

ke'i

open interval bracket marker; modifies intervals in non-logical connectives; exclude boundaries.

ke'o

vocative: please repeat.

ke'u

discursive: repeating - continuing.

ke'unai

discursive: repeating - continuing.

kei

elidable terminator: end abstraction bridi (often elidable).

kelvo

x_1 is x_2 degree(s) Kelvin [metric unit] in temperature (default is 1) by standard x_3.

ketco

x_1 reflects South American culture/nationality/geography in aspect x_2.

ki

tense/modal: set/use tense default; establishes new open scope space/time/modal reference base.

ki'a

attitudinal question: confusion about something said.

ki'o

digit/number: number comma; thousands.

ki'u

krinu modal, 1st place (justified by) justifiably; because of reason ...

kilto

x_1 is a thousand [1000; 10^3] of x_2 in dimension/aspect x_3 (default is units).

kisto

x_1 reflects Pakistani/Pashto culture/nationality/language in aspect x_2.

klama

x_1 comes/goes to destination x_2 from origin x_3 via route x_4 using means/vehicle x_5.

klesi

x_1 (mass/si'o) is a class/category/subgroup/subset within x_2 with defining property x_3 (ka).

ko

pro-sumti: you (imperative); make it true for you, the listener.

ko'a

pro-sumti: he/she/it/they #1 (specified by goi).

ko'e

pro-sumti: he/she/it/they #2 (specified by goi).

ko'i

pro-sumti: he/she/it/they #3 (specified by goi).

ko'o

pro-sumti: he/she/it/they #4 (specified by goi).

ko'u

pro-sumti: he/she/it/they #5 (specified by goi).

krasi

x_1 (site/event) is a source/start/beginning/origin of x_2 (object/event/process).

krecau

x_1 (body or body part) is hairless

krici

x_1 believes [regardless of evidence/proof] belief/creed x_2 (du'u) is true/assumed about subject x_3.

krinu

x_1 (event/state) is a reason/justification/explanation for/causing/permitting x_2 (event/state).

ku

elidable terminator: end description, modal, or negator sumti; often elidable.

kuarka

x_1 is a quark with flavor x_2.

ku'a

non-logical connective: intersection of sets.

ku'e

elidable terminator: end mathematical (mex) forethought (Polish) expression; often elidable.

ku'i

discursive: however/but/in contrast.

ku'o

elidable terminator: end NOI relative clause; always elidable, but preferred in complex clauses.

kuldi'u

d_1 is a building housing school c_1 teaching subject c_3 to audience c_4.

kurji

x_1 takes-care-of/looks after/attends to/provides for/is caretaker for x_2 (object/event/person).

ky

letteral for k.

la

name descriptor: the one(s) called ... ; takes name or selbri description.

ladru

x_1 is made of/contains/is a quantity of milk from source x_2; (adjective:) x_1 is lactic/dairy.

la'e

the referent of (indirect pointer); uses the referent of a sumti as the desired sumti.

la'edi'u

pro-sumti: the referent of the last utterance; the state described: "IT was fun".

la'i

name descriptor: the set of those named ... ; takes name or selbri description.

la'o

delimited non-Lojban name; the resulting quote sumti is treated as a name.

la'u

klani modal, 1st place (amount) quantifying ...; being a quantity of ...

lai

name descriptor: the mass of individual(s) named ... ; takes name or selbri description.

lanme

x_1 is a sheep/[lamb/ewe/ram] of species/breed x_2 of flock x_3.

lantro

x_1 shepherds flock x_2 composed of sheep x_3

latmo

x_1 reflects Latin/Roman/Romance culture/empire/language in aspect x_2.

lau

2-word letteral/shift: punctuation mark or special symbol follows.

le

non-veridical descriptor: the one(s) described as ...

Lojban Word Glossary

lebna

x_1 takes/gets/gains/obtains/seizes/[removes] x_2 (object/property) from x_3 (possessor).

le'a

klesi modal, 1st place (scalar set) in/of category ...

le'e

non-veridical descriptor: the stereotype of those described as ...

le'i

non-veridical descriptor: the set of those described as ..., treated as a set.

le'o

attitudinal modifier: aggressive - passive - defensive.

le'u

end quote of questionable or out-of-context text; not elidable.

lei

non-veridical descriptor: the mass of individual(s) described as ...

lerfu

x_1 (la'e zo BY/word-bu) is a letter/digit/symbol in alphabet/character-set x_2 representing x_3.

lervla

v_1 is a word which stands for the letter/digit/symbol $v_2=l_1$ in language v_3.

li

the number/evaluated expression; convert number/operand/evaluated math expression to sumti.

libjo

x_1 reflects Libyan culture/nationality in aspect x_2.

li'i

abstractor: experience abstractor; x_1 is x_2's experience of [bridi] (participant or observer).

li'o

discursive: omitted text (quoted material).

li'u

elidable terminator: end grammatical quotation; seldom elidable except at end of text.

lijda

x_1 is a religion of believers including x_2 sharing common beliefs/practices/tenets including x_3.

lijgri

g_1 is a row (group) showing common property (ka) g_2 due to set g_3 linked by relations g_4.

liste

x_1 (physical object) is a list/catalog/register of sequence/set x_2 in order x_3 in medium x_4.

litki

x_1 is liquid/fluid, of composition/material including x_2, under conditions x_3.

litru

x_1 travels/journeys/goes/moves via route x_2 using means/vehicle x_3; x_1 is a traveller.

lo

descriptor: the one, which (is / does) ... / those, which (are / do) ...

logji

x_1 [rules/methods] is a logic for deducing/concluding/inferring/reasoning to/about x_2 (du'u).

lo'a

shift letterals to Lojban (Roman) alphabet.

lo'e

veridical descriptor: the typical one(s) who really is(are) ...

lo'i

veridical descriptor: the set of those that really are ..., treated as a set.

lo'o

elidable terminator: end math express.(mex) sumti; end mex-to-sumti conversion; usually elidable.

lo'u

start questionable/out-of-context quote; text should be Lojban words, but needn't be grammatical.

loi

veridical descriptor: the mass of individual(s) that is(are) ...

lojban

Lojban.

lojbangirz

Logical Language Group (LLG)

lojbaugri

x_1 is the Logical Language Group (LLG).

lojbo

x_1 reflects [Loglandic]/Lojbanic language/culture/nationality/community in aspect x_2.

lu

start grammatical quotation; quoted text should be grammatical on its own.

lubno

x_1 reflects Lebanese culture/nationality in aspect x_2.

lu'a

the members of the set/components of the mass; converts another description type to individuals.

lu'e

the symbol for (indirect discourse); uses the symbol/word(s) for a sumti as the desired sumti.

lu'i

the set with members; converts another description type to a set of the members.

lu'o

the mass composed of; converts another description type to a mass composed of the members.

lu'u

elidable terminator: end of sumti qualifiers; usually elidable except before a sumti.

lujvo

x_1 (text) is a compound predicate word with meaning x_2 and arguments x_3 built from metaphor x_4.

ly

letteral for l.

ma

pro-sumti: sumti question (what/who/how/why/ etc.); appropriately fill in sumti blank.

mabla

x_1 is execrable/deplorable/wretched/shitty/awful/ rotten/miserable/contemptible/crappy/inferior/ low-quality in property x_2 by standard x_3; x_1 stinks/sucks in aspect x_2 according to x_3.

ma'a

pro-sumti: me/we the speaker(s)/author(s) & you the listener(s) & others unspecified.

ma'i

manri modal, 1st place (by standard 2) in reference frame ...

ma'o

convert letteral string or other mathematical expression (mex) operand to mex operator.

ma'u

digit/number: plus sign; positive number; default any positive.

mai

utterance ordinal suffix; converts a number to an ordinal, such as an item or paragraph number.

mamta

x_1 is a mother of x_2; x_1 bears/mothers/acts maternally toward x_2; [not necessarily biological].

matne

x_1 is a quantity of/contains butter/oleo/margarine/ shortening from source x_2.

mau

zmadu modal, 1st place (a greater) exceeded by ... ; usually a sumti modifier.

me

convert sumti to selbri/tanru element; x_1 is specific to [sumti] in aspect x_2.

megdo

x_1 is a million [10^6] of x_2 in dimension/aspect x_3 (default is units).

me'a

mleca modal, 1st place (a lesser) undercut by ... ; usually a sumti modifier.

me'i

digit/number: less than.

me'o

the mathematical expression (unevaluated); convert unevaluated mathematical expression to sumti.

me'u

elidable terminator: end sumti that was converted to selbri; usually elidable.

mei

convert number to cardinality selbri; x_1 is the mass formed from set x_2 whose n member(s) are x_3.

mekso

x_1 [quantifier/expression] is a mathematical expression interpreted under rules/convention x_2.

melbi

x_1 is beautiful/pleasant to x_2 in aspect x_3 (ka) by aesthetic standard x_4.

meljo

x_1 reflects Malaysian/Malay culture/nationality/ language in aspect x_2.

merko

x_1 pertains to USA/American culture/nationality/ dialect in aspect x_2.

mexno

x_1 reflects Mexican culture/nationality in aspect x_2.

mi

pro-sumti: me/we the speaker(s)/author(s); identified by self-vocative.

midju

x_1 is in/at the middle/center/midpoint/[is a focus] of x_2; (adjective:) x_1 is central.

mi'a

pro-sumti: me/we the speaker(s)/author(s) & others unspecified, but not you, the listener.

mi'e

self vocative: self-introduction - denial of identity; identifies speaker.

mi'i

non-logical interval connective: ordered components: ... center, ... range surrounding center.

mi'o

pro-sumti: me/we the speaker(s)/author(s) & you the listener(s).

mi'u

discursive: ditto.

mikce

x_1 doctors/treats/nurses/[cures]/is physician/ midwife to x_2 for ailment x_3 by treatment/cure x_4.

mikri

x_1 is a millionth [10^{-6}] of x_2 in dimension/aspect x_3 (default is units).

milti

x_1 is a thousandth [$1/1000$; 10^{-3}] of x_2 in dimension/aspect x_3 (default is units).

minde

x_1 issues commands/orders to x_2 for result x_3 (event/state) to happen; x_3 is commanded to occur.

misro

x_1 reflects Egyptian culture/nationality in aspect x_2.

mlatu

x_1 is a cat/[puss/pussy/kitten] [feline animal] of species/breed x_2; (adjective:) x_1 is feline.

mleca

x_1 is less than x_2 in property/quantity x_3 (ka/ni) by amount x_4.

mo

pro-bridi: bridi/selbri/brivla question.

mo'a

digit/number: too few; subjective.

mo'e

convert sumti to mex operand; sample use in story arithmetic: [3 apples] + [3 apples] = what.

mo'i

mark motions in space-time.

mo'o

higher-order utterance ordinal suffix; converts a number to ordinal, usually a section/chapter.

mo'u

interval event contour: at the natural ending point of ...; completive | >|<.

moi

convert number to ordinal selbri; x_1 is (n)th member of set x_2 ordered by rule x_3.

mojysu'a

s_1 is a structure of parts s_2 as a monument/memorial to m_3.

mokca

x_1 is a point/instant/moment [0-dimensional shape/form] in/on/at time/place x_2.

molro

x_1 is x_2 mole(s) [metric unit] in substance (default is 1) by standard x_3.

morko

x_1 reflects Moroccan culture/nationality in aspect x_2.

mrostu

s_1 is the grave/tomb of $m_1=s_2$.

mu

digit/number: 5 (digit) [five].

mu'e

abstractor: achievement (event) abstractor; x_1 is the event-as-a-point/achievement of [bridi].

mu'i

mukti modal, 1st place because of motive ...

mu'onai

vocative: over (response OK) - more to come.

mukti

x_1 (action/event/state) motivates/is a motive/incentive for action/event x_2, per volition of x_3.

mulgri

$g_1=m_1$ is a complete set showing common property (ka) g_2, complete by standard m_3.

muslo

x_1 pertains to the Islamic/Moslem/Koranic [Quranic] culture/religion/nation in aspect x_2.

my

letteral for m.

na

bridi contradictory negator; scope is an entire bridi; logically negates in some cmavo compounds.

na'a

cancel all letteral shifts.

na'e

contrary scalar negator: other than ...; not ...; a scale or set is implied.

na'i

discursive: metalinguistic negator.

na'o

tense interval modifier: characteristically/typically; tense/modal; defaults as time tense.

na'u

convert selbri to mex operator; used to create less-used operators using fu'ivla, lujvo, etc.

na'ujbi

x_1 is approximately equal to x_2.

nai

attached to cmavo to negate them; various negation-related meanings.

naja

logical connective: tanru-internal afterthought conditional/only if.

nakykemcinctu

x_1 is a male teacher of sexuality to audience x_2.

namcu

x_1 (li) is a number/quantifier/digit/value/figure (noun); refers to the value and not the symbol.

nanmu

x_1 is a man/men; x_1 is a male humanoid person [not necessarily adult].

nanvi

x_1 is a billionth/thousand-millionth [10^{-9}] of x_2 in dimension/aspect x_3 (default is units).

nau

tense: refers to current space/time reference absolutely.

ne

non-restrictive relative phrase marker: which incidentally is associated with ...

nei

pro-bridi: repeats the current bridi.

ni

abstractor: quantity/amount abstractor; x_1 is quantity/amount of [bridi] measured on scale x_2.

nibli

x_1 logically necessitates/entails/implies action/event/state x_2 under rules/logic system x_3.

ni'e

convert selbri to mex operand; used to create new non-numerical quantifiers; e.g. "herd" of oxen.

ni'i

nibli modal, 1st place logically; logically because ...

ni'o

discursive: paragraph break; introduce new topic.

ni'u

digit/number: minus sign; negative number); default any negative.

nimre

x_1 is a quantity of citrus [fruit/tree, etc.] of species/strain x_2.

ninmu

x_1 is a woman/women; x_1 is a female humanoid person [not necessarily adult].

nitcu

x1 needs/requires/is dependent on/[wants] necessity x2 for purpose/action/stage of process x3.

nixli

x1 is a girl [young female person] of age x2 immature by standard x3.

no

digit/number: 0 (digit) [zero].

nobli

x1 is noble/aristocratic/elite/high-born/titled in/ under culture/society/standard x2.

noda

logically quantified sumti: nothing at all (unless restricted).

no'a

pro-bridi: repeats the bridi in which this one is embedded.

no'e

midpoint scalar negator: neutral point between je'a and to'e; "not really".

no'i

discursive: paragraph break; resume previous topic.

no'o

digit/number: typical/average value.

no'u

non-restrictive appositive phrase marker: which incidentally is the same thing as ...

noi

non-restrictive relative clause; attaches subordinate bridi with incidental information.

nolraitru

t1=n1 is a regent/monarch of t2 by standard n2.

nu

abstractor: generalized event abstractor; x1 is state/process/achievement/activity of [bridi].

nu'a

convert mathematical expression (mex) operator to a selbri/tanru component.

nu'e

vocative: promise - promise release - un-promise.

nu'i

start forethought termset construct; marks start of place structure set with logical connection.

nu'o

modal aspect: can but has not; unrealized potential.

nu'u

elidable terminator: end forethought termset; usually elidable except with following sumti.

nuncti

n1 is an event at which c1 eat(s) c2.

nunctu

x1 (nu) is an event in which x2 teaches x3 facts x4 (du'u) about x5 by means x6; x1 is a lesson given by x2 to x3.

nunkla

n1 is a passage where goer k1 comes/goes to destination k2 from origin k3 via route k4 using means/vehicle k5.

ny

letteral for n.

o

logical connective: sumti afterthought biconditional/iff/if-and-only-if.

obu

letteral for o.

o'u

attitudinal: relaxation - composure - stress.

oi

attitudinal: complaint - pleasure.

oinai

attitudinal: complaint - pleasure.

onai

logical connective: sumti afterthought exclusive or; Latin 'aut'.

pa

digit/number: 1 (digit) [one].

pacru'i

x1 is an evil spirit / demon

pagbu

x1 is a part/component/piece/portion/segment of x2 [where x2 is a whole/mass]; x2 is partly x1.

pa'e

discursive: justice - prejudice.

pa'enai

discursive: justice - prejudice.

pai

digit/number: pi (approximately 3.1416...); the constant defined by the ratio of the circumference to the diameter of all circles.

pamoi

quantified selbri: convert 1 to ordinal selbri; x1 is first among x2 ordered by rule x3.

paso

number/quantity: 19 [nineteen].

patyta'a

p1=t1 complains verbally to p3=t2 about p2=t3 in language t4

pau

discursive: optional question premarker.

paunai

discursive: unreal/rhetorical question follows.

pe

restrictive relative phrase marker: which is associated with ...; loosest associative/possessive.

pe'a

marks a construct as figurative (non-literal/ metaphorical) speech/text.

pe'e

marks the following connective as joining termsets.

pe'i

evidential: I opine (subjective claim).

pe'o

forethought flag for mathematical expression (mex) Polish (forethought) operator.

pei

attitudinal: attitudinal question; how do you feel about it? with what intensity?.

pelnimre

x_1 is a lemon of variety x_2.

pelxu

x_1 is yellow/golden [color adjective].

petso

x_1 is 10^{15} of x_2 in dimension/aspect x_3 (default is units).

pi

digit/number: radix (number base) point; default decimal.

picti

x_1 is a trillionth $[10^{-12}]$ of x_2 in dimension/aspect x_3 (default is units).

pi'a

n-ary mathematical operator: operands are vectors to be treated as matrix rows.

pi'e

digit/number:separates digits for base >16, not current standard, or variable (e.g. time, date).

pi'i

n-ary mathematical operator: times; multiplication operator; $[(((a * b) * c) * ...)]$.

pi'o

pilno modal, 1st place used by ...

pi'u

non-logical connective: cross product; Cartesian product of sets.

pilno

x_1 uses/employs x_2 [tool, apparatus, machine, agent, acting entity, material] for purpose x_3.

piro

number: all of.

piso'a

number: almost all of.

piso'u

number: a little of.

pisu'o

number: at least some of.

pluka

x_1 (event/state) seems pleasant to/pleases x_2 under conditions x_3.

po

restrictive relative phrase marker: which is specific to ...; normal possessive physical/legal.

po'e

restrictive relative phrase marker: which belongs to ... ; inalienable possession.

po'o

discursive: uniquely, only, solely: the only relevant case.

po'u

restrictive appositive phrase marker: which is the same thing as.

poi

restrictive relative clause; attaches subordinate bridi with identifying information to a sumti.

polno

x_1 reflects Polynesian/Oceanian (geographic region) culture/nationality/languages in aspect x_2.

ponjo

x_1 reflects Japanese culture/nationality/language in aspect x_2.

ponse

x_1 possesses/owns/has x_2 under law/custom x_3; x_1 is owner/proprietor of x_2 under x_3.

porto

x_1 reflects Portuguese culture/nationality/language in aspect x_2.

prenu

x_1 is a person/people (noun) [not necessarily human]; x_1 displays personality/a persona.

pritu

x_1 is to the right/right-hand side of x_2 which faces/in-frame-of-reference x_3.

pu

time tense relation/direction: did [selbri]; before/prior to [sumti]; default past tense.

puba

time tense: was going to; (tense/modal).

pu'i

modal aspect: can and has; demonstrated potential.

pu'o

interval event contour: in anticipation of ...; until ... ; inchoative ----| |.

pu'u

abstractor: process (event) abstractor; x_1 is process of [bridi] proceeding in stages x_2.

purci

x_1 is in the past of/earlier than/before x_2 in time sequence; x_1 is former; x_2 is latter.

py

letteral for p.

ra

pro-sumti: a recent sumti before the last one, as determined by back-counting rules.

radno

x_1 is x_2 radian(s) [metric unit] in angular measure (default is 1) by standard x_3.

rafsi

x_1 is an affix/suffix/prefix/combining-form for word/concept x_2, form/properties x_3, language x_4.

ra'a

srana modal, 1st place pertained to by ... (generally more specific).

ra'e

digit/number: repeating digits (of a decimal) follow.

ra'i

krasi modal, 1st place from source/origin/starting point ...

ra'o

flag GOhA to indicate pro-assignment context updating for all pro-assigns in referenced bridi.

ra'u

discursive: chiefly - equally - incidentally.

ra'ucu'i

discursive: chiefly - equally - incidentally.

ra'unai

discursive: chiefly - equally - incidentally.

rakso

x_1 reflects Iraqi culture/nationality in aspect x_2.

ralju

x_1 is principal/chief/leader/main/[staple], most significant among x_2 (set) in property x_3 (ka).

rau

digit/number: enough; subjective.

re

digit/number: 2 (digit) [two].

re'i

vocative: ready to receive - not ready to receive.

re'inai

vocative: ready to receive - not ready to receive.

re'u

converts number to an objectively quantified ordinal tense interval modifier; defaults to time.

reroi

tense interval modifier: twice; objectively quantified tense; defaults as time tense.

ri

pro-sumti: the last sumti, as determined by back-counting rules.

ricfu

x_1 is rich/wealthy in goods/possessions/property/aspect x_2.

ri'a

rinka modal, 1st place (phys./mental) causal because ...

ri'e

attitudinal modifier: release of emotion - emotion restraint.

rinka

x_1 (event/state) effects/physically causes effect x_2 (event/state) under conditions x_3.

risna

x_1 is a/the heart [body-part] of x_2; [emotional/shape metaphors are NOT culturally neutral].

ro

digit/number: each, all.

ro'anai

emotion category/modifier: social - antisocial.

ro'e

emotion category/modifier: mental - mindless.

ro'o

emotion category/modifier: physical - denying physical.

ro'u

emotion category/modifier: sexual - sexual abstinence.

roi

converts number to an objectively quantified tense interval modifier; defaults to time tense.

romai

discursive utterance ordinal: finally; last utterance ordinal.

ropno

x_1 reflects European culture/nationality/geography/Indo-European languages in aspect x_2.

ru

pro-sumti: a remote past sumti, before all other in-use backcounting sumti.

ruble

x_1 is weak/feeble/frail in property/quality/aspect x_2 (ka) by standard x_3.

ru'a

evidential: I postulate.

ru'e

attitudinal: weak intensity attitude modifier.

ru'i

tense interval modifier: continuously; subjective tense/modal; defaults as time tense.

ru'inai

tense interval modifier: occasional/intermittent/discontinuous; defaults as time tense.

ru'o

shift letterals to Cyrillic alphabet.

rusko

x_1 reflects Russian culture/nationality/language in aspect x_2.

ry

letteral for r.

sa

erase complete or partial utterance; next word shows how much erasing to do.

sadjo

x_1 reflects Saudi Arabian culture/nationality in aspect x_2.

sa'a

discursive: material inserted by editor/narrator (bracketed text).

sa'enai

discursive: precisely speaking - loosely speaking.

sa'i

n-ary mathematical operator: operands are vectors to be treated as matrix columns.

sa'unai

discursive: simply - elaborating.

sai

attitudinal: moderate intensity attitude modifier.

sakli

x_1 slides/slips/glides on x_2.

salci

x_1 celebrates/recognizes/honors x_2 (event/abstract) with activity/[party] x_3.

sanli

x_1 stands [is vertically oriented] on surface x_2 supported by limbs/support/pedestal x_3.

saske

x_1 (mass of facts) is science of/about subject matter x_2 based on methodology x_3.

se

2nd conversion; switch 1st/2nd places.

seba'i

basti modal, 2nd place instead of ...

se'a

attitudinal modifier: self-sufficiency - dependency.

se'e

following digits code a character (in ASCII, Unicode, etc.).

se'i

attitudinal modifier: self-oriented - other-oriented.

se'o

evidential: I know by internal experience (dream, vision, or personal revelation).

se'u

elidable terminator: end discursive bridi or mathematical precedence;usually elidable.

sei

start discursive (metalinguistic) bridi.

seja'e

jalge modal, 2nd place (event causal) results because of ...

seka'a

klama modal, 2nd place with destination ...

selbri

$x_2=b_1$ (du'u) is a predicate relationship with relation $x_1=b_2$ among arguments $x_3=b_3$ (ordered set).

selkla

T destination x_1, goes x_2 from x_3 via route x_4 by means x_5.

selma'o

x_1 is the class of structure word x_2, which means or has function x_3 in language x_4.

selsku

c_2 is said by c_1 to audience c_3 via expressive medium c_4.

seltau

x_1 is the modifying part of binary metaphor x_2 with modified part/modificand x_3 giving meaning x_4 in usage/instance x_5

selti'i

x_1 is a suggestion made by x_2 to audience x_3

selti'ifla

$f_1=s_2$ is a bill specifying f_2 (state/event) for community f_3 under conditions f_4, proposed/drafted by s_1.

semau

zmadu modal, 2nd place (relative!) more than ...; usually a sumti modifier.

seme'a

mleca modal, 2nd place (relative!) less than ...; usually a sumti modifier.

semto

x_1 reflects Semitic [metaphor: Middle-Eastern] language/culture/nationality in aspect x_2.

sepi'o

pilno modal, 2nd place (instrumental) tool/machine/apparatus/acting entity; using (tool) ...

seri'a

rinka modal, 2nd place (phys./mental) causal therefore ...

sfofa

x_1 is a sofa/couch (noun).

si

erase the last Lojban word, treating non-Lojban text as a single word.

si'a

discursive: similarly.

si'e

convert number to portion selbri; x_1 is an (n)th portion of mass/totality x_2; (cf. gunma).

si'o

abstractor: idea/concept abstractor; x_1 is x_2's concept of [bridi].

since

x_1 is a snake/serpent of species/breed x_2.

sinso

x_1 is the trigonometric sine of angle/arcsine x_2.

sinxa

x_1 is a sign/symbol/signal representing/referring/signifying/meaning x_2 to observer x_3.

sirxo

x_1 reflects Syrian culture/nationality in aspect x_2.

sisti

x_1 [agent] ceases/stops/halts/ends activity/process/state x_2 [not necessarily completing it].

skari

x_1 is/appears to be of color/hue x_2 as perceived/seen by x_3 under conditions x_4.

skoto

x_1 reflects Gaelic/Scottish culture/nationality/language in aspect x_2.

slaka

x_1 is a syllable in language x_2.

slovo

x_1 reflects Slavic language/culture/ethos in aspect x_2.

softo

x_1 reflects Russian empire/USSR/ex-USSR (Soviet]/CIS culture/nationality in aspect x_2.

so'a

digit/number: almost all (digit/number).

so'e

digit/number: most.

so'i

digit/number: many.

so'imei

quantified selbri: convert many to cardinal; x_1 is a set with many members x_2 of total set x_3.

so'o

digit/number: several.

so'u

digit/number: few.

soi

discursive: reciprocal sumti marker; indicates a reciprocal relationship between sumti.

solri

x_1 is the sun of home planet x_2 (default Earth) of race x_3; (adjective:) x_1 is solar.

solxrula

x_1 is a sunflower of species/variety x_2.

sonci

x_1 is a soldier/warrior/fighter of army x_2.

spageti

x_1 - is spaghetti made out of/containing x_2.

spano

x_1 reflects Spanish-speaking culture/nationality/language in aspect x_2.

sralo

x_1 reflects Australian culture/nationality/geography/dialect in aspect x_2.

srana

x_1 pertains to/is germane/relevant to/concerns/is related/associated with/is about x_2.

srito

x_1 reflects Sanskrit language/Sanskritic/Vedic culture/nationality in aspect x_2.

stali

x_1 remains/stays at/abides/lasts with x_2.

steci

x_1 (ka) is specific/particular/specialized/[special]/a defining property of x_2 among x_3 (set).

stero

x_1 is x_2 steradian(s) [metric unit] in solid angle (default is 1) by standard x_3.

stidi

x_1 (agent) suggests/proposes idea/action x_2 to audience x_3; x_1 (event) inspires x_2 in/among x_3.

stura

x_1 is a structure/arrangement/organization of x_2 [set/system/complexity].

su

erase to start of discourse or text; drop subject or start over.

sudysrasu

x_1 is hay of species x_2

su'a

evidential: I generalize - I particularize; discursive: abstractly - concretely.

su'anai

evidential: I generalize - I particularize; discursive: abstractly - concretely.

su'e

digit/number: at most (all); no more than.

su'i

n-ary mathematical operator: plus; addition operator; $[(((a + b) + c) + ...)]$.

su'o

digit/number: at least (some); no less than.

su'u

abstractor: generalized abstractor (how); x_1 is [bridi] as a non-specific abstraction of type x_2.

sumti

x_1 is a/the argument of predicate/function x_2 filling place x_3 (kind/number).

sutra

x_1 is fast/swift/quick/hastes/rapid at doing/being/bringing about x_2 (event/state).

sy

letteral for s.

ta

pro-sumti: that there; nearby demonstrative it; indicated thing/place near listener.

ta'e

tense interval modifier: habitually; subjective tense/modal; defaults as time tense.

ta'onai

discursive: by the way - returning to main point.

ta'u

discursive: expanding the tanru - making a tanru.

ta'unai

discursive: making a tanru - expanding the tanru.

tai

tamsmi modal, 1st place (like)/(in manner 2) resembling ...; sharing ideal form ...

tamdu'i

d_1 is/are geometrically similar/has the same shape as d_2.

tamsmi

x_1 has form x_2, similar in form to x_3 in property/quality x_4.

tanjo

x_1 is the trigonometric tangent of angle/arctangent x_2.

tanru

x_1 is a binary metaphor formed with x_2 modifying x_3, giving meaning x_4 in usage/instance x_5.

tarmi

x_1 [ideal] is the conceptual shape/form of object/abstraction/manifestation x_2 (object/abstract).

tau

2-word letteral/shift: change case for next letteral only.

tavla

x_1 talks/speaks to x_2 about subject x_3 in language x_4.

te

3rd conversion; switch 1st/3rd places.

teci'e

ciste modal, 3rd place of system components ...

te'a

binary mathematical operator: to the power; exponential; [a to the b power].

te'o

digit/number: exponential e (approx 2.71828...).

te'u

elidable terminator: end conversion between non-mex and mex; usually elidable.

tei

composite letteral follows; used for multi-character letterals.

teka'a

klama modal, 3rd place with origin ...

terbi'a

$x_3=b_1$ is ill/sick/diseased with symptoms $x_2=b_2$ from disease $x_1=b_3$.

tergu'i

x_1 is a light source with lit x_2 with light x_3.

terkavbu

x_1 is a trap/restraint with x_2 being captured/restrained by x_3 (object/event).

tertau

x_1 is the modified part/modificand of binary metaphor x_2 with modifying part x_3, giving meaning x_4 in usage/instance x_5

terto

x_1 is a trillion [10^{12}] of x_2 in dimension/aspect x_3 (default is units).

tezu'e

zukte modal, 3rd place purposefully; (as an action) with goal ...

ti

pro-sumti: this here; immediate demonstrative it; indicated thing/place near speaker.

ti'e

evidential: I hear (hearsay).

ti'o

mathematical expression (mex) operator precedence (discursive).

ti'otci

$t_1=c_2$ is a shade/blind for blocking light coming from/through c_3

tinju'i

$t_1=j_1$ listens to/pays attention to sound $t_2=j_2$ with ambient background t_3.

tirna

x_1 hears x_2 against background/noise x_3; x_2 is audible; (adjective:) x_1 is aural.

to

left parenthesis; start of parenthetical note which must be grammatical Lojban text.

to'a

lower-case letteral shift.

to'e

polar opposite scalar negator.

to'i

open editorial unquote (within a quote); contains grammatical text; mark with editorial insert.

to'o

location tense relation/direction; departing from/directly away from ...

to'u

discursive: in brief - in detail.

toi

elidable terminator: right parenthesis/end unquote; seldom elidable except at end of text.

tolmle

x_1 is ugly to x_2 in aspect x_3 (ka) by aesthetic standard x_4.

tolvri

x_1 is a coward in activity x_2 (event) by standard x_3.

traji

x_1 is superlative in property x_2 (ka), the x_3 extreme (ka; default ka zmadu) among set/range x_4.

tricu

x_1 is a tree of species/cultivar x_2.

troci

x_1 tries/attempts/makes an effort to do/attain x_2 (event/state/property) by actions/method x_3.

tsali

x_1 is strong/powerful/[tough] in property/quality x_2 (ka) by standard x_3.

tu

pro-sumti: that yonder; distant demonstrative it; indicated thing far from speaker&listener.

tu'a

extracts a concrete sumti from an unspecified abstraction; equivalent to le nu/su'u [sumti] co'e.

tu'e

start of multiple utterance scope; used for logical/non-logical/ordinal joining of sentences.

tu'o

null operand (used in unary mekso operations).

tu'u

elidable terminator: end multiple utterance scope; seldom elidable.

ty

letteral for t.

u

logical connective: sumti afterthought whether-or-not.

ua

attitudinal: discovery - confusion/searching.

uanai

attitudinal: discovery - confusion/searching.

ubu

letteral for u.

ue

attitudinal: surprise - not really surprised - expectation.

u'e

attitudinal: wonder - commonplace.

u'u

attitudinal: repentance - lack of regret - innocence.

u'unai

attitudinal: repentance - lack of regret - innocence.

ui

attitudinal: happiness - unhappiness.

uinai

attitudinal: happiness - unhappiness.

uo

attitudinal: completion - incompleteness.

uu

attitudinal: pity - cruelty.

va

location tense distance: near to ... ; there at ...; a medium/small distance from ...

va'a

unary mathematical operator: additive inverse; [-a].

va'e

convert number to scalar selbri; x_1 is at (n)th position on scale x_2.

va'i

discursive: in other words - in the same words.

va'inai

discursive: in other words - in the same words.

vau

elidable: end of sumti in simple bridi; in compound bridi, separates common trailing sumti.

ve

4th conversion; switch 1st/4th places.

vecnu

x_1 [seller] sells/vends x_2 [goods/service/ commodity] to buyer x_3 for amount/cost/expense x_4.

ve'e

location tense interval: the whole of space.

ve'o

right mathematical bracket.

vei

left mathematical bracket.

veka'a

klama modal, 4th place via route ...

veljvo

x_1 is a metaphor [of affix compound] with meaning [of affix compound] x_2 with argument [of affix compound] x_3 with affix compound x_4; x_1 is the tanru/metaphor construct of complex word/ affix compound/lujvo x_4

vemau

zmadu modal, 4th place (relative!) more than/ exceeding by amount ...

veme'a

mleca modal, 4th place (relative!) less than by amount ...

vi

location tense distance: here at ... ; at or a very short/tiny distance from ...

vi'a

dimensionality of space interval tense: 2-space interval; throughout an area.

vi'e

dimensionality of space interval tense: 4-space interval; throughout a spacetime.

vi'u

dimensionality of space interval tense: 3-space interval; throughout a space.

viska

x_1 sees/views/perceives visually x_2 under conditions x_3.

vo

digit/number: 4 (digit) [four].

vo'a

pro-sumti: repeats 1st place of main bridi of this sentence.

vo'e

pro-sumti: repeats 2nd place of main bridi of this sentence.

vo'i

pro-sumti: repeats 3rd place of main bridi of this sentence.

vo'o

pro-sumti: repeats 4th place of main bridi of this sentence.

vo'u

pro-sumti: repeats 5th place of main bridi of this sentence.

voi

non-veridical restrictive clause used to form complicated le-like descriptions using "ke'a".

vorme

x_1 is a doorway/gateway/access way between x_2 and x_3 of structure x_4.

vu

location tense distance: far from ... ; yonder at ... ; a long distance from ...

vu'e

attitudinal modifier: virtue - sin.

vu'i

sumti qualifier: the sequence made from set or composed of elements/components; order is vague.

vu'o

joins relative clause/phrase to complete complex or logically connected sumti in afterthought.

vu'u

n-ary mathematical operator: minus; subtraction operator; $[(((a - b) - c) - ...)]$.

vukro

x_1 reflects Ukrainian language/culture/nationality in aspect x_2.

vy

letteral for v.

xagmau

$xa_1=z_1$ is better than z_2 for xa_2 by standard xa_3, by amount z_4.

xagrai

$t_1=x_1$ is the best among set/range t_4 for x_2 by standard x_3.

xamgu

x_1 (object/event) is good/beneficial/ nice/[acceptable] for x_2 by standard x_3.

xampo

x_1 is x_2 ampere(s) [metric unit] in current (default is 1) by standard x_3.

xance

x_1 is a/the hand [body-part] of x_2; [metaphor: manipulating tool, waldo].

xarci

x_1 is a weapon/arms for use against x_2 by x_3.

xatsi

x_1 is 10^{-18} of x_2 in dimension/aspect x_3 (default is units).

xazdo

x_1 reflects Asiatic culture/nationality/geography in aspect x_2.

xe

5th conversion; switch 1st/5th places.

xebro

x_1 reflects Hebrew/Jewish/Israeli culture/nationality/language in aspect x_2.

xecto

x_1 is a hundred [100; 10^2] of x_2 in dimension/aspect x_3 (default is units).

xeka'a

klama modal, 5th place by transport mode ...

xekri

x_1 is black/extremely dark-colored [color adjective].

xelso

x_1 reflects Greek/Hellenic culture/nationality/language in aspect x_2.

xexso

x_1 is 10^{18} of x_2 in dimension/aspect x_3 (default is units).

xi

subscript; attaches a number of letteral string following as a subscript onto grammar structures.

xindo

x_1 reflects Hindi language/culture/religion in aspect x_2.

xispo

x_1 reflects Hispano-American culture/nationalities in aspect x_2.

xo

digit/number: number/digit/lerfu question.

xrabo

x_1 reflects Arabic-speaking culture/nationality in aspect x_2.

xriso

x_1 pertains to the Christian religion/culture/nationality in aspect x_2.

xu

discursive: true-false question.

xunre

x_1 is red/crimson/ruddy [color adjective].

xurdo

x_1 reflects Urdu language/culture/nationality in aspect x_2.

xy

letteral for x.

y

hesitation noise; maintains the floor while speaker decides what to say next.

ybu

letteral for y.

y'y

letteral for '.

zabna

x_1 is favorable/great/superb/fabulous/dandy/outstanding/swell/admirable/nice/commendable/delightful/desirable/enjoyable/laudable/likable/lovable/wonderful/praiseworthy/high-quality/cool in property x_2 by standard x_3; x_1 rocks in aspect x_2 according to x_3

za'a

evidential: I observe.

za'e

forethought nonce-word indicator; indicates next word is nonce-creation and may be nonstandard.

za'i

abstractor: state (event) abstractor; x_1 is continuous state of [bridi] being true.

za'o

interval event contour: continuing too long after natural end of ...; superfective | ---->.

za'u

digit/number: greater than.

zai

2-word letteral/shift: alternate alphabet selector follows.

zarci

x_1 is a market/store/exchange/shop(s) selling/trading (for) x_2, operated by/with participants x_3.

zbasu

x_1 makes/assembles/builds/manufactures/creates x_2 out of materials/parts/components x_3.

zdani

x_1 is a nest/house/lair/den/[home] of/for x_2.

ze'e

time tense interval: the whole of time.

ze'i

time tense interval: an instantaneous/tiny/short amount of time.

ze'o

location tense relation/direction; beyond/outward/receding from ...

zei

joins preceding and following words into a lujvo.

zenba

x_1 (experiencer) increases/is incremented/augmented in property/quantity x_2 by amount x_3.

zepti

x_1 is 10^{-21} of x_2 in dimension/aspect x_3 (default is units).

zerle'a

l_1 steals l_2 from l_3, which is a crime according to z_2.

zernerkla

x_1 trespasses (illegally enters) into x_2, which is a crime according to x_3

zetro

x_1 is 10^{21} of x_2 in dimension/aspect x_3 (default is units).

zi

time tense distance: instantaneous-to-short distance in time.

zi'e

joins relative clauses which apply to the same sumti.

zi'o

pro-sumti: fills a sumti place, deleting it from selbri place structure;changes selbri semantics.

zmadu

x_1 exceeds/is more than x_2 in property/quantity x_3 (ka/ni) by amount/excess x_4.

zo

quote next word only; quotes a single Lojban word (not a cmavo compound or tanru).

zo'e

pro-sumti: an elliptical/unspecified value; has some value which makes bridi true.

zo'i

location tense relation/direction; nearer than .../inward/approaching from ...

zo'o

attitudinal modifier: humorously - dully - seriously.

zo'u

marks end of logical prenex quantifiers/topic identification and start of sentence bridi.

zoi

delimited non-Lojban quotation; the result treated as a block of text.

zu'a

location tense relation/direction; leftwards/to the left of ...

zu'i

pro-sumti: the typical sumti value for this place in this relationship; affects truth value.

zu'o

abstractor: activity (event) abstractor; x_1 is abstract activity of [bridi] composed of x_2.

zukte

x_1 is a volitional entity employing means/taking action x_2 for purpose/goal x_3/to end x_3.

zuljma

$j_1=z_1$ is/are the left foot/feet of $j_2=z_2$.

zunle

x_1 is to the left/left-hand side of x_2 which faces/in-frame-of-reference x_3.

zy

letteral for z.

General Index

"
word for: 400
"&"
word for: 400
""
word for: 400
"because"
English word
four varieties of: 190
"la"
contrasted with vocatives: 309
"less"
English word
expressing with relative phrases: 196
importance of relative phrase to: 197
"me"
effect of MOI on: 430
"more"
English word
expressing with relative phrases: 196
importance of relative phrase to: 197
"no" quantifier
expanding: 387
"of"
in English
compared with do'e: 189
"or"
"and/or" contrasted with "either ... or ... but not both":
318
"there is a Y"
expression
notation convention: 385
"z" instead of ""
in acronyms names based on lerfu words: 407
' symbol
and consonant cluster determination in lujvo: 56
definition (see also apostrophe): 35
-ek
in name for logical connectives: 320
-er
use of zmadu in forming: 57
-ity: 252
-ness: 252
-ng
Lojban contrasted with English: 43
4-letter rafsi
definition: 56
5-letter rafsi
definition: 56
a
example: 308
a/an
contrasted with the: 308
abbreviated lujvo and plausibility: 273
abduction
example: 303

absolute laws: 264
abstract description: 259
abstract lujvo: 275
abstraction bridi
contrasted with component non-abstraction bridi in
meaning: 95
effect on claim of bridi: 190
abstraction conversion: 259
abstraction of sentences
contrasted with quotation: 256
abstractions
achievement: 250
activity: 250
concept: 258
creating new types: 258
event: 248
experience: 258
forethought connection in: 350
grammatical uses: 248
grouping of connectives in: 350
idea: 258
implicit in sumti: 249
logical connection of: 350
making concrete: 260
mental activity: 255
place structure: 248
point-event: 250
process: 250
simplification to sumti with jai: 260
simplification to sumti with tu'a: 259
speaking
writing, etc.: 256
state: 250
sumti ellipsis in: 249
truth-value and fuzzy logic: 255
vague: 258
with knowing
believing, etc.: 255
with wonder
doubt, etc.: 256
accent mark
a diacritical mark: 402
example: 402
accent marks
proposed lerfu words for: 411
accented letters
considered as distinct from unaccented: 403
achievative event contour: 219
achievement abstraction
place structure: 251
achievement abstractions
definition: 250
related tense contours: 261
achievement event
described: 251
acronym
definition: 407

acronym names from lerfu words
  assigning final consonant: 407
acronyms
  as lerfu strings using "me": 407
  using names based on lerfu words: 407
acronyms names based on lerfu words
  omitting bu: 407
  using "z" instead of "'" in: 407
activity abstraction
  place structure: 251
activity abstractions
  definition: 250
  related tense contours: 261
activity abstractor: 250
activity event
  described: 251
actual events
  explicitly expressing: 236
actual stop
  contrasted with natural end: 221
actuality
  expressing in past/future: 236
  Lojban contrasted with English in implying: 235
addition
  a mathematical operator: 418
addition operator
  contrasted with positive sign: 418
adjective ordering: 85
adjective-noun combination
  with tanru: 80
adjectives
  brivla as Lojban equivalents: 52
adverb-verb combination
  with tanru: 80
adverbs
  brivla as Lojban equivalents: 52
affirmative answer
  quick-tour version: 27
afterthought bridi connectives
  contrasted with forethought bridi connectives: 322
afterthought connection
  contrasted with forethought for grammatical utterances: 337
  definition: 192
  of operands: 435
  of operators: 435
afterthought connectives
  as complete grammatical utterance: 337
  contrasted with forethought connectives: 322
afterthought sentence connection
  modal contrasted with tense: 241
afterthought tense connection
  contrasted with forethought in likeness to modal connection: 241
ailment: 272
algebra of functions
  operator and operand distinction in: 441
alienable possession
  definition: 166

aliens
  communication with: 314
allowable diphthongs
  in fu'ivla contrasted with in gismu and lujvo: 62
  in gismu and lujvo contrasted with in fu'ivla: 62
alpha
  example: 400
alphabet
  Latin used for Lojban: 397
  Lojban: 33
  words for letters in
    rationale: 397
alphabetic order: 33
alphabets
  words for non-Lojban letters
    rationale: 397
alternative guidelines: 264
ambiguity of tanru: 81
American Indian languages and evidentials: 302
Amharic writing: 403
ampersand
  example: 400
ampersand character
  word for: 400
an
  example: 308
anaphora
  definition: 148
  pro-bridi go'i-series as: 148
  pro-sumti ri-series as: 148
  pro-sumti vo'a-series as: 152
anaphoric pro-bridi
  stability of: 155
anaphoric pro-sumti
  stability of: 155
and
  as non-logical connective: 338
  compared with but: 338
  contrasted with cross-product: 342
animal doctor
  example: 271
animal patient: 272
animals
  use of fu'ivla for specific: 60
anomalous ordering of lujvo places: 272
answers
  go'i for yes/no questions: 148
  to operator questions: 439
  to place structure questions: 184
  to tense-or-modal questions: 242
antecedent
  for pro-bridi: 145
  for pro-bridi as full bridi: 145
antecedent of pro-bridi
  definition: 140
antecedent of pro-sumti
  definition: 140
anticipated
  example: 303

any
  as a restricted universal claim: 384
  as a translation problem: 384
  as a universal claim
    later restricted: 384
  as an existential claim: 384
  expressing as existential by variable in subordinate
    bridi: 385
any box: 384
anyone
  contrasted with everyone in assumption of existence:
    384
aorist
  definition: 215
apostrophe
  and consonant cluster determination in lujvo: 56
  as not a consonant for morphological discussions: 50
  as preferable over comma in names: 36
  definition of: 35
  example of: 36
  purpose of: 35
  quick-tour version: 17
  type of letter in word-formation: 35
  use in vowel pairs: 38
  variant of: 35
approximate numbers
  expressing: 424
  expressing some exactness of: 425
Arabian Nights: 449
Arabic alphabet
  language shift word for: 401
argument tags
  based on tenses (see also sumti tcita): 223
arthropod: 270
article
  number: 417
articles
  cmavo as Lojban equivalents: 50
ASCII
  application to lerfu words: 408
aspect
  expressing: 219
  natural languages compared with respect to: 219
assignable pro-sumti
  explicit cancellation of by rebinding: 155
  stability of: 155
asymmetrical tanru: 101
  definition: 101
asymmetrical tanru types
  activity + implement-used: 106
  cause + effect: 103
  characteristic-time + event: 107
  characteristic/detail + object: 102
  effect + causative agent: 103
  elements-in-set + set: 101
  energy-source + powered: 107
  general-class + sub-class: 102
  inhabitant + habitat: 103
  locus-of-application + object: 106
  miscellaneous: 107

object + component/detail: 102
object + place-sold: 106
object + usual-container: 106
object-giving-characteristic + other-object: 105
object-measured + standard-object: 105
object-of-action + action: 101
object-of-purpose-of-instrument + instrument: 103
overriding-property   +   object-with-implicit-
  properties: 105
possessor + object: 103
product + producer: 105
product + source: 104
purpose-of-instrument + instrument: 103
set + element-of-set: 102
similar-appearance-object + object: 105
source + product: 103
source-material + object: 104
typical-place + object: 105
undesired-object + protection-object: 106
whole + part: 105
at least
  contrasted with more than
    less than, at most: 425
at most
  contrasted with more than
    at least, less than: 425
Athens: 251
attitude
  avoidance of expression: 309
  scalar: 293
attitudes
  beginning: 301
  ceasing: 301
  continuing: 301
  empathy contrasted with sympathy: 301
  expressing changes in: 301
attitudinal
  example of scale effect: 293
  signaling as non-propositional: 292
attitudinal answers
  plausibility: 300
attitudinal categories: 294
  example of effect: 295
  mnemonic for: 295
  rationale: 294
attitudinal indicator
  unspecified: 298
attitudinal indicators: 285
  conventions of interpretation: 298
  placement of "nai" in: 298
  placement of scale in: 298
  quick-tour version: 28
attitudinal modifiers: 296
attitudinal questions: 300
  asking about specific attitude: 301
  asking intensity: 300
attitudinal scale
  as axis in emotion-space: 294
  neutral compared with positive + negative: 294
  seven-position: 293

stand-alone usage: 294
usage: 293
attitudinal scales
rationale for assignment: 293
attitudinals
a- series: 290
affecting whole grammatical structures: 299
and logic: 376
at beginning of text: 299
attributing emotion to others: 301
benefit in written expression: 300
categories with nai: 295
categories with scale markers: 295
complexity: 298
compound: 286
contours: 301
contrasted with bridi: 291, 294
contrasted with discursives: 304
contrasted with rationalizations of emotion: 294
design benefit: 294
e- series: 290
emotional contrasted with propositional: 290
emotional/propositional caveat: 290
exceptions: 301
external grammar: 299
grammar of internal compounding: 299
grammar of placement in bridi: 299
i- series: 290
internal grammar
complete: 299
logical language and: 290
negative: 292
neutral: 292
non-speaker attitudes: 301
order of: 294
placement for prevailing attitude: 285
placement in sentences with "nai": 298
positive: 292
prevailing attitude: 285
propositional contrasted with emotional: 290
propositional effect on claim: 290
propositional/emotional caveat: 290
rationale for: 291
referent uncertainty: 299
scale of: 292
stand-alone categories: 295
word-form for primary: 286
audio-visual isomorphism: 33
audio-visually isomorphic: 447
auditoriums: 270
author of this book: 11
ba'e
interaction with bu: 400
ba'o
as futureward of event: 220
derivation of word: 220
explanation of derivation: 220
back-counting pro-sumti: 135
background noise: 268

BAI cmavo
rationale for selection: 189
BAI modal tags
rationale for: 188
BAI selma'o
as short forms for fi'o constructs: 188
effect of conversion on: 188
form of cmavo in: 189
base
assumed: 426
changing permanently: 426
non-constant: 427
specifying: 426
vague: 427
base greater than 16
compound single-digits contrasted with two digits: 427
expressing numbers in: 427
two digits contrasted with compound single-digits: 427
base point
in bases other than 10: 426
base varying for each digit
separator for: 427
base-20 arithmetic
remnants of: 442
basis
example: 304
be'o
effect of ku on elidability of: 91
effect of relative clauses on elidability of: 91
elidability of: 91
beach
example: 252
beefsteak: 274
beetles: 270
begin
contrasted with resume: 221
beginning point
spatial: 223
beverage
example: 157
bi'e
effect on following operator: 419
bibliography: 12
BIhI selma'o
grammar of: 345
binary system
specifying numbers in (see also base): 426
bo
contrasted with ke for tensed logical connection: 350
contrasted with tu'e for tensed logical connection: 350
for right-grouping in tanru: 84
in jeks for operators: 346
in joiks for operators: 346
in logical connectives: 326
right-grouping: 327
bo and forethought connectives: 326
boat class
example: 70

boi
    effect on elidability of me'u: 431
    eliding from lerfu strings: 405
    exception before MAI: 440
    exception before MOI: 431
    exception before ROI: 440
    required between pro-sumti lerfu string and quantifier: 405
bold
    example: 402
books about Lojban: 12
borrowing
    four stages of: 60
borrowing from other language
    fu'ivla as: 53
borrowings
    fu'ivla form with categorizing rafsi: 60
    fu'ivla form without categorizing rafsi: 60
    most common form for: 60
    Stage 1: 60
    Stage 2: 60
    Stage 3: 60
    Stage 3 contrasted with Stage 4 in ease of construction: 61
    Stage 4: 60
    using foreign-language name: 60
    using lojbanized name: 60
bound variable pro-sumti
    stability of: 155
bracketed remark: 462
brackets
    use in IPA notation: 34
bridi
    building from selbri and sumti: 180
    compared with predication: 15
    concept of: 15
    definition: 79
        quick-tour version: 30
    effect of alternate form on sumti order: 180
    effect of using non-standard form: 180
    exception to sumti place structure in: 181
    leaving a sumti place unspecified in with zo'e: 182
    leaving end sumti places unspecified in: 181
    logical connection with negation: 320
    logical connective for: 320
    non-standard form: 180
    omitting the first sumti place: 181
    quick-tour version: 18
    relation to selbri: 79
    selbri-first as exceptional: 181
    standard form of: 180
bridi connection
    use of imperatives in: 337
    use of truth questions in: 337
bridi logical connection
    compared with sumti logical connections: 324
bridi negation
    and DeMorgan's Law: 392
    and negation boundary: 392
    compared with negation between sentences: 388

    multiple: 100
    na before selbri compared to naku in prenex: 385
    naku in prenex compared to na before selbri: 385
    relative order with tense: 100
    two forms of: 385
bridi negation and logical connectives: 388
bridi questions
    quick-tour version: 27
bridi-based comparison
    contrasted with comparison with relative phrase in claims about parts: 197
bridi-tail
    definition: 328
bridi-tail logical connection
    and DeMorgan's Law: 393
bridi-tail modal connection: 193
bridi-tails
    eliding vau in: 329
    forethought tense connection of: 232
brivla
    as one of the 3 basic word classes: 50
    consonant pairs in: 53
    definition: 52
        quick-tour version: 31
    from tanru: 55
    properties of: 52
    recognition of: 52
    relation to bridi: 15
    stress on: 42
    subtypes of: 53
    types: 79
    types of
        quick-tour version: 24
brivla as selbri: 79
brivla equivalents: 93
brivla form
    contrasted with cmavo form: 52
    contrasted with cmene form: 52
broda-series for pro-bridi
    compared with ko'a-series for pro-sumti: 145
broda-series pro-bridi: 145
    assigning with cei: 145
    use as abstract pattern: 145
    use as sample gismu: 145
    with no assignment: 145
    word-form rationale: 145
Brown
    James Cooke: 12
        and "letteral": 397
bu
    and compound cmavo: 400
    effect of multiple: 400
    effect on preceding word: 398
    for extension of lerfu word set: 400
    grammar of: 400
    interaction with ba'e: 400
    interaction with language shift: 401
    omitting in acronyms names based on lerfu words: 407

bu'a-series pro-sumti
    for bound variables: 155
bu'u
    compared with ca: 211
buffer vowel: 40
    and stress: 40
    shortening of: 41
but
    compared with and: 338
    example: 304
but/and equivalence: 29
C string
    as a symbol for a single consonant: 50
C/C string
    as a symbol for a permissible consonant pair: 50
C/CC string
    as a symbol for a consonant triple: 50
ca
    compared with bu'u: 211
    meaning as a sumti tcita: 223
    meaning when following interval specification: 213
    rational for: 211
ca'o
    derivation of word: 220
CAhA selma'o
    making sticky: 236
    order in tense construct: 236
calculator mathematics
    as default in Lojban: 418
canceling letter shifts: 402
cancellation of pro-sumti/pro-bridi assignment
    with da'o: 156
capital letters
    use in Lojban: 399
    use of: 33
capitalization
    for unusual stress in names: 64
    use in names: 64
    use of: 64
cardinal selbri
    definition: 428
    place structure: 428
    place structure effect from subjective numbers: 430
cardinality
    definition: 121
    property of sets: 121
Cartesian product
    with tenses: 239
case
    upper/lower specification: 399
causals
    claiming the relation contrasted with claiming cause
    and/or effect and/or relation: 190
    gismu: 189
    modal: 189
CC string
    as a symbol for a permissible initial consonant pair: 50
CCVVCV fu'ivla
    and rafsi fu'ivla proposal: 76

ce'u
    use in specifying sumti place of property in
    abstraction: 155
cedilla
    a diacritical mark: 402
cei
    for broda-series pro-bridi assignment: 145
cei for broda-series assignment
    compared with goi for ko'a-series assignment: 145
cessitive event contour: 219
ch-sound in English
    representation in Lojban: 35
chapter numbering: 440
chapter titles
    intent of: 10
character codes
    definition: 408
character encoding schemes
    application to lerfu words: 408
characters
    definition: 408
    special: 35
Chelsea Clinton: 265
chemical elements
    use of single-letter shift for: 399
Chilean desert
    example: 76
Chinese characters
    contrasted with alphabets and syllabaries: 403
    representing based on pinyin spelling: 403
    representing based on strokes: 404
circumflex
    a diacritical mark: 402
clamshells: 275
clarity of sounds: 35
Classical Greek aorist tense
    compared with Lojban tense: 215
closed interval: 344
    expressed with mi'i: 437
closings
    letter: 311
cmavo
    as one of the 3 basic word classes: 50
    compound: 51
    contrasted with rafsi in usage: 60
    contrasted with same-form rafsi in meaning: 56
    definition: 50
        quick-tour version: 31
    diphthongs in: 51
    experimental: 51
    for experimental use: 51
    lack of relation of form to grammatical use: 51
    rules for pause after Cy-form: 67
    simple: 51
    stress on: 42, 52
    structure of: 50
cmavo and gismu
    major: 53
cmavo as selbri
    quick-tour version: 24

cmavo form
  contrasted with brivla form: 52
cmavo without rafsi
  method of including in lujvo: 59
cmene
  algorithm for: 65
  alternatives for restricted sequences in: 64
  and analyzability of speech stream: 63
  as one of the 3 basic word classes: 50
  authority for: 64
  avoiding impermissible consonant clusters in: 65
  consonant clusters permitted in: 64
  definition: 63
  examples of: 63
  final letter in: 64
  from Lojban words: 65
  method of including in lujvo: 59
  proscribed syllables in: 65
  purpose of: 63
  rationale for lojbanizing: 63
  requirement for pause after: 64
  restrictions on form of: 64
  rules for: 64
  rules for formation: 64
  rules for pause before: 67
  stress in: 64
  unusual stress in: 64
cmene form
  contrasted with brivla form: 52
co'e
  as selbri place-holder: 151
  rationale for word form: 152
co'e-series pro-bridi: 150
COI selma'o
  effect on pause before name: 309
  effect on referent of "do": 140
  effect on referent of "mi": 140
  ordering multiple with mi'e: 311
Coleoptera: 270
color standards: 283
comma
  definition of: 35
  effect on relative clause in English: 164
  example of: 36
  main use of: 36
  optional: 36
  quick-tour version: 17
  variant of: 36
command
  contrasted with observative form: 181
commands
  quick-tour version: 25
  with ko: 141
commas in numbers
  as numerical punctuation: 416
  effect of other notation conventions: 416
  with elided digits: 416
common abstractor: 248
commutative truth functions: 319

comparative lujvo
  against former state: 282
  and seltau presupposition: 281
  potential ambiguity in: 281
  standardized meanings: 281
comparatives
  use of zmadu in forming: 57
comparison
  claims related to based on form: 197
comparison with relative phrase
  contrasted with bridi-based comparison
    in claims about parts: 197
completitive event contour: 219
complex logical connection
  grouping strategies contrasted: 327
complex logical connectives
  grouping with bo: 327
  grouping with parentheses: 327
complex movements
  expressing: 217
complex negation
  examples: 98
complex numbers
  expressing: 416
components contrasted with mass
  in properties of: 338
compound base
  definition: 427
  expressing digits in: 427
  separator for: 427
compound bridi
  definition: 328
  logical connection of: 328
  more than one sumti in common: 329
  multiple with bo: 330
  multiple with ke...ke'e: 330
  one sumti in common: 328
  separate tail-terms for bridi-tails: 330
  separate tail-terms for forethought-connected bridi-tails: 331
compound bridi with more than one sumti in common
  with common sumti first: 329
  with vau: 329
compound cmavo
  compared with sequence of simple cmavo: 51
  definition: 51
  recognition of: 51
compound emotions: 294
compound letters
  native language
    representing as distinct letters: 403
compound logical connectives
  components: 320
  naming convention: 320
compound of gismu
  lujvo as: 53
compound spatial tense
  as direction with-or-without distance: 211
  beginning with distance only: 210
  effect of different ordering: 210

explanation of: 210
  with direction and distance: 210
compound subscript: 347, 437
compound temporal tense
  beginning with distance only: 212
compound tense
  compared with multiple tenses in sentence: 226
  compared with tense in scope of sticky tense: 226
  definition: 210
  Lojban contrasted with English in order of specification: 210
compound tense ordering
  Lojban contrasted with English: 210
computer interaction: 465
concept abstraction: 258
concept abstractions
  place structure: 258
concept abstractor: 258
concrete terms
  use of fu'ivla for: 60
confusion
  metalinguistic: 307
confusion about what was said: 307
conjunctions
  cmavo as Lojban equivalents: 50
connected tenses
  negation of compared with negation in connective: 238
connecting operands
  with bo in connective: 346
  with ke in connective: 346
connecting operators
  with bo in connective: 346
  with ke in connective: 346
connection
  non-distributed: 340
  simultaneously modal and logical: 198
connection of operands
  grouping: 435
  precedence over operator: 437
connection of operators
  grouping: 435
connective answers
  non-logical: 343
connective question answers
  contrasted with other languages: 337
connective question cmavo
  departure from regularity of: 336
connective questions
  answering: 336
  compared with other languages: 337
  non-logical: 343
connectives
  as complete grammatical utterance: 337
  as ungrammatical utterance: 337
  table by constructs connected: 351
consonant
  definition: 38
  effect on syllable count: 38

consonant clusters
  buffering of: 40
  contrasted with doubled consonants: 38
  contrasted with single consonants: 38
  definition of: 38
  more than three consonants in: 40
consonant pairs
  in brivla: 53
  initial: 39
  letter y within: 53
  restrictions on: 39
consonant triples: 40
  restrictions on: 40
consonant-final words
  necessity for pause after: 66
consonants
  contrasted with vowels: 36
  final: 39
  position of: 39
  pronunciation of
    quick-tour version: 16
  restrictions on: 39
  syllabic: 37
  voiced/unvoiced equivalents: 38
  voicing of: 38
continents
  gismu for: 75
continuitive event contour: 219
continuous
  of tense intervals: 217
contradictory negation
  using naku before selbri: 390
contradictory negation of modals
  explanation of meaning: 200
contradictory negation of tenses
  selma'o allowed with: 235
contributors to this book: 11
conversion
  accessing tense of bridi with jai: 239
  definition: 96, 239
  effect of multiple on a selbri: 186
  effect on BAI: 188
  extending scope of: 186
  modal: 199
  of BAI cmavo: 188
  of operator places: 440
  scope of: 186
  swapping non-first places: 187
  swapping with modal place: 199
conversion and tanru: 96
conversion into sumti from mekso: 418
conversion of mekso into sumti: 418
conversion of operand into operator: 441
conversion of operator into operand: 441
conversion of operator into selbri: 439
conversion of selbri into operand: 437
conversion of selbri into operator: 437
conversion of sentence with quantified variables
  technique: 391
conversion of sumti into operand: 438

conversion of sumti into selbri: 95
conversion with ke: 97
conversion with se
  effect of naku negation boundary on: 390
converted selbri
  as different selbri from unconverted: 185
  as resetting standard order: 185
  compared with selbri with FA in meaning: 185
  contrasted with other similar selbri: 186
  contrasted with selbri with FA in structure: 185
  definition: 185
  forming with SE: 185
  in descriptions: 185
  place structure of: 185
  retention of basic meaning in: 186
  to access non-first place in description: 186
creative understanding: 264
credits for pictures: 11
credits for this book: 11
cross product
  with tenses: 239
cross-dependency: 270
cross-product
  contrasted with and: 342
  of sets: 341
cu
  as selbri separator: 180
  effect of selbri-first bridi on: 183
  effect of tense specification: 208
  effect on elidability of ku: 119
  effect on elidable terminators: 180
  necessity of: 180
  need for
    quick-tour version: 23
  omission of
    quick-tour version: 18
  use of
    quick-tour version: 18
  usefulness of: 180
cu'e
  combining with other tense cmavo: 243
cultural knowledge
  example: 303
cultural words
  rafsi fu'ivla proposal for: 76
culturally dependent lujvo: 308
curious: 256
Cy-form cmavo
  rules for pause after: 67
cycles: 222
Cyrillic alphabet
  language shift word for: 401
  proposed lerfu words for: 410
da
  as a translation for "something": 377
  contrasted with zo'e: 377
da prami da
  contrasted with da prami de: 377
da prami de
  contrasted with da prami da: 377

da'a
  default number for: 423
da'o
  for cancellation of pro-sumti/pro-bridi assignment: 156
  syntax of: 156
da-series
  after third: 454
da-series pro-sumti
  for bound variables: 155
decimal point
  as numerical punctuation: 415
  effect of different notations: 415
  in bases other than 10: 426
deduction
  example: 303
default operator precedence
  contrasted with mekso goal: 418
definable pro-sumti: 134
  sequences of lerfu words as: 136
definite numbers
  combined with indefinite: 424
demonstrated potential
  expressing: 236
demonstrative pro-sumti: 135, 141
  stability of: 155
DeMorgan's Law
  and bridi-tail logical connection: 393
  and distributing a negation: 392
  and internal naku negations: 394
  and logically connected sentences: 392
  and moving a logical connective relative to "naku": 392
  sample applications: 392
dereferencing a pointer
  with la'e: 129
derivational morphology
  definition: 49
derogatory terms: 265
descriptions
  and abstractions: 248
  as based on first place of following selbri: 186
  as possessive sumti: 173
  components of: 116
  importance of selbri first place in: 116
  non-specific: 117
  quick-tour version: 23
  specific: 117
  types of: 116
  use of SE in: 186
descriptions with lo
  teddy bear contrasted with real bear: 118
descriptor
  as part of description: 116
descriptors
  implicit quantifiers for: 125
  omission of: 127
  purpose of: 116
di'e
  effect of tu'e/tu'u on: 343

di'u
contrasted with la'edi'u: 143
contrasted with ta: 143
di'u-series pro-sumti: 142
diacritic marks
proposed lerfu words for: 411
diacritical marks
as lerfu: 402
considered as forming distinct letters: 403
order of specification within tei...foi: 402
problem of position: 402
problem with multiple on one lerfu: 403
specifying with tei...foi: 402
dictionary
superior authority of: 11
digit questions: 431
digit string
definition of: 439
digits
cmavo for: 414
list of decimal: 443
list of hexadecimal: 444
names from: 441
rafsi for: 441
rationale for having 16: 426
digits beyond 9
word pattern: 426
dimension
meaning as sumti tcita: 225
dimensionality
of walking: 216
order with size in spatial tense intervals: 216
dimensionality of interval
as subjective: 216
dimensioned numbers
expressing: 438
diphthongs
classification of: 37
contrasted with vowel pairs: 38
definition of: 36
English analogues of: 46
in fu'ivla: 62
IPA for: 37
list of: 37
pronunciation of
quick-tour version: 17
specific to cmene: 64
specific to names: 64
direct address: 309
direction
following interval in tense construct: 213
interaction with movement specification in tenses: 216
order of relative to distance in spatial tenses: 210
reference frame for: 216
specification with FAhA: 209
directions
multiple with movement: 217
disambiguated instance: 266
disclaimers: 11

discourse
commentary on: 305
expressing utterance relation to: 304
gesture markers: 305
tone of voice markers: 305
discrete
of tense intervals: 217
discursive indicator: 448
discursives
as metalinguistic claims: 304
contrasted with attitudinals: 304
definition: 304
discourse commentary: 305
discourse management: 306
embedded: 462
expressing how things are said: 305
knowledge: 306
placement in sentence: 304
quick-tour version: 29
su'a as: 303
word-level: 305
discursives for consecutive discourse: 304
contrasted: 304
discursives for managing discourse flow: 306
distance
order of relative to direction in spatial tenses: 210
specification with VA: 209
distributing a negation: 392
distribution of quantified sumti: 382
ditto
example: 304
diversified species: 283
do'e
compared with English "of": 189
do'i
compared with zo'e-series as indefinite pro-sumti: 152
dog breathes: 379
dog house
example: 265
doghouse
example: 70
doi
effect on necessity for pause before name-word: 133
effect on pause before name: 309
double negation
and naku: 392
double negatives
effect of interactions between quantifiers and negation on: 388
double underscore notation convention for Quick Tour chapter: 16
doubled consonants
contrasted with consonant clusters: 38
contrasted with single consonants: 38
dream
example: 303
du
as an exception within GOhA selma'o: 94
compared with me in effect: 95
contrasted with dunli: 156

General Index

contrasted with mintu: 156
derivation of: 156
grammar of: 417
meaning of: 156
rationale for selection of selma'o for: 156
with complex mekso on both sides: 418
dunli
contrasted with du: 156
e
contrasted with pi'u: 342
e'o
contrasted with pe'u: 310
e'u
compared with ru'a: 304
Earl
example: 37
editorial commentary: 462
editorial insertion: 462
of text already containing sa'a: 308
with "sa'a: 308
Einsteinian
space-time intervals with 4 dimensions: 216
ek
definition: 320
eks
connecting operands: 346
in sumti forethought logical connection: 324
elementary schools: 270
Elgin
Suzette Haden and evidentials: 302
elidability of be'o: 91
elidability of me'u: 96
elided tense
meaning of: 208
elimination process: 271
ellipsis
quick-tour version: 19
elliptical pro-bridi: 150
elliptical pro-sumti: 150
elliptical sumti: 150
elliptical value
contrasted with typical value for sumti: 150
embarrassment
example: 295
embedded bridi tenses
effect of main bridi tense on: 227
embedded discursive: 462
emotional categories: 294
emotional indicators
noticeable effects of: 315
emotional scale: 293
emotions
compound: 294
cultural bias of expression: 315
insights: 294
recording using indicators: 315
research using indicators: 315
when expressed: 294
emphasis
changing by using non-standard form of bridi: 180

end of file: 465
endpoints
inclusion in interval: 344
English "we"
contrasted with Lojban pro-sumti for "we": 141
English prepositions
contrasted with modal tags in preciseness: 189
equivalents to brivla: 93
erasure
multiple word: 464
names: 464
quotes: 464
total: 465
word: 463
zo: 464
error marking
metalinguistic: 307
event abstractions: 248
types: 250
event contours
achievable: 221
as characteristic portions of events: 220
as sumti tcita: 224
as timeless in perspective: 220
cessative: 220
completitive: 221
continuitive: 220
contrasted with tense direction in implication of extent: 220
definition: 220
division of the event into: 220
implications on scope of event: 220
inchoative: 220
initiative: 220
interruption: 221
order with respect to TAhE and ROI: 220
pausative: 221
perfective: 220
points associated with: 220
resumption: 221
resumptive: 221
strings of: 239
superfective: 221
syntax of: 220
temporal contrasted with spatial: 223
event contours as sumti tcita
contrasted with direction and distance: 224
event types
described: 251
event-relative viewpoint
contrasted with speaker-relative viewpoint: 220
events
considered as a process: 220
duration: 249
place structure: 250
everyone
contrasted with anyone in assumption of existence: 384
everyone bitten by dog: 380

everything
    expressing with "ro da": 378
evidentials
    ba'a scale: 303
    definition: 302
    grammar: 302
    in English: 302
    indisputable bridi: 302
    inspiration for: 302
    ja'o contrasted with su'a: 303
    ka'u contrasted with se'o: 303
    placement in bridi: 303
    quick-tour version: 29
    rhetorical flavor: 302
    scales: 302
    se'o contrasted with ka'u: 303
    su'a contrasted with ja'o: 303
exact number
    expressing: 425
example of examples: 11
examples
    structure of: 11
examples in this book: 10
existential
    mixed claim with universal: 378
existential claims
    definition: 377
    restricting: 379
existential variable
    in abstraction contrasted with in main bridi: 385
    in main bridi contrasted with in abstraction: 385
expanding "no" quantifier: 387
experience abstraction: 258
experience abstractions
    place structure: 258
experience abstractor: 258
experimental cmavo
    definition: 51
    forms for: 51
exponential notation
    with base other than 10: 433
    with gei: 432
exporting negation to prenex
    "naku" contrasted with internal bridi negation: 391
    internal bridi negation contrasted with "naku": 391
external bridi negation
    compared to internal bridi negation: 385
    definition: 385
extrinsic possession
    definition: 166
FA in selbri
    compared with converted selbri in meaning: 185
    contrasted converted selbri with in structure: 185
FA selma'o
    after 5th place: 454
    as a reminder of place in place structure: 182
    avoidance of complex usage of: 184
    compared with zo'e for omitting places: 183
    effect on place structure: 182
    effect on place structure order: 182

effect on subsequent non-tagged places: 183
    for accessing a selbri place explicitly by relative number: 182
    for putting more than one sumti in a single place: 184
    syntax of: 182
FA tags and linked sumti: 90
fa'a
    special note on direction orientation: 246
fa'o
    contrasted with fe'o: 311
    interaction with bu: 400
fa'u
    compared to termsets: 341
    contrasted with .e: 340
face
    specifying for letters: 402
FAhA selma'o
    and direction: 209
    contradictory negation of: 234
    use in specifying space/time mapping direction: 223
fai
    as allowing access to original first place in modal conversion: 199
    effect on numbering of place structure places: 199
false statement
    implications of: 321
fancy A
    notation convention: 319
fancy E
    notation convention: 319
fancy O
    notation convention: 319
fancy U
    notation convention: 319
fe'e
    effect of TAhE/ROI with ZAhO on: 223
fe'o
    contrasted with fa'o: 311
fi'a
    effect on subsequent untagged sumti: 184
fi'o
    and modal conversion: 200
    as modal tag: 187
    effect on following selbri: 187
    mixed modal connection with: 199
    proscribed for sticky modals: 201
    restriction on use: 194
    use in adding places to place structure: 187
fi'o constructs
    short forms as BAI cmavo: 188
fi'o modal followed by selbri
    effect on eliding fe'u: 195
fi'o modals
    negation of by negating selbri: 201
    usage in relative phrases: 197
fi'o tag
    relation of modal sumti following to selbri: 187
fi'o with selbri
    meaning of: 187

figurative lujvo: 308
  place structure: 308
figurative speech: 308
final syllable stress
  rules for pause after: 67
finish
  contrasted with stop: 221
fleas: 265
flexible vocabulary: 52
floating point numbers
  expressing: 433
flow of discourse
  managing with discursives: 306
folk quantifiers
  expressing: 438
font
  specifying for letters: 402
food
  use of fu'ivla for specific: 60
foreman of a jury
  example: 140
forethought bridi connection
  as grammatically one sentence: 322
forethought bridi connectives
  contrasted with afterthought bridi connectives: 322
forethought bridi-tail connection
  special rule for tense: 350
forethought connection
  contrasted with afterthought for grammatical utterances: 337
  definition: 192
  in abstractions: 350
  in tenses: 348
  observatives: 332
  of operands: 435
  of operators: 435
forethought connections
  modal compared with tense in semantics: 241
forethought connectives
  as ungrammatical utterance: 337
  contrasted with afterthought connectives: 322
  with tense: 350
forethought connectives and bo: 326
forethought intervals
  GAhO position: 346
forethought logical connectives
  within tanru: 88
forethought logical connectives in tanru
  effect on tanru grouping: 88
forethought modal sentence connection: 192
  relation to modal of first bridi in: 192
  relation to modal of second bridi in: 192
forethought modal sentence connection for causals
  order of cause and effect: 192
forethought tanru connection: 334
forethought tense connection
  contrasted with afterthought in likeness to modal connection: 241
forethought tense connection of bridi-tails
  order of: 232

forethought tense connection of sentences
  order of: 231
forethought tense connection of sumti
  order of: 232
forethought termsets
  logical connection of: 333
former state: 282
formulae
  expressing based on pure dimensions: 437
fraction
  meaning with elided numerator and denominator: 416
fractions
  expressing with numerical punctuation: 415
  numerator default: 415
fragmentary text: 308
free modifiers
  effects on elidability of terminators: 432
fu'ivla
  algorithm for constructing: 61
  as a subtype of brivla: 53
  as Stage 3 borrowings: 60
  as Stage 4 borrowings: 60
  categorized contrasted with uncategorized in ease of construction: 61
  considerations for choosing basis word: 63
  consonant clusters in: 61
  construction of: 60
  definition
    quick-tour version: 31
  diphthongs in: 62
  disambiguation of: 62
  form for rafsi fu'ivla proposal: 76
  form of: 60
  initial consonant cluster in: 60
  method of including in lujvo: 59
  quick-tour version: 24
  rules for formation of: 60
  stress in: 61
  uniqueness of meaning in: 60
  use of: 60
  with invalid diphthongs: 63
fu'ivla categorizer: 60
  for distinguishing fu'ivla form: 62
  for distinguishing specialized meanings: 62
  selection consideration for: 61
fully reduced lujvo
  definition: 58
function name
  lerfu string as: 406
future event
  possible extension into present: 215
futureward
  as a spatial tense: 216
fuzzy logic and truth-value abstraction: 255
ga'o
  etymology of: 345
gadri
  definition: 115
  GAhO position in forethought intervals: 346

GAhO selma'o
grammar of: 345
ge'a
for infix operations with too many operands: 433
ge'u
effect of following logical connective on elidability: 168
elidability of from relative phrases: 168
gei
as a binary operator: 432
as a ternary operator: 433
rationale for order of places: 432
gek
definition: 322
gek bridi connectives
contrasted with ijeks: 322
geks
connecting operands: 346
in forethought sumti connection: 324
syntax of: 324
General American: 44
general sumti
contrasted with operands: 418
general terms: 283
gihek
definition: 328
giheks
syntax of: 330
gik
as name for compound cmavo: 320
definition: 323
giks
syntax of: 324
gismu
algorithm for: 71
and cmavo
major: 53
as a subtype of brivla: 53
as partitioning semantic space: 53
basic rafsi for: 56
coined: 73
conflicts between: 53
creation
and transcription blunders: 72
considerations for selection after scoring: 72
proscribed gismu pairs: 72
scoring rules: 71
cultural: 74
definition: 53
quick-tour version: 31
ethnic: 75
examples of: 53
exceptions to gismu creation by algorithm: 73
for countries: 74
for languages: 74
for Lojban source languages: 74
geographical: 75
length of: 53
level of uniqueness of rafsi relating to: 56
Lojban-specific: 73

place order
rationale: 284
place structures: 283
rationale: 283
quick-tour version: 24
rationale for choice of: 53
religious: 75
rules for: 53
scientific-mathematical: 73
selection of: 53
source of: 53
source-language weights for: 72
special: 53
too-similar: 72
glottal stop
as pause in Lojban: 35
glue in lujvo
n-hyphen as: 56
r-hyphen as: 56
y-hyphen as: 56
go'i
as affirmative answer to yes/no question: 148
compared with mo in overriding of arguments: 153
contrasted with mi'u: 304
go'i ra'o
contrasted with go'i: 149
go'i with xu
quick-tour version: 27
go'i-series pro-bridi: 148
as main-bridi anaphora only: 148
assigning for permanent reference: 148
compared with ri-series pro-sumti in rules of reference: 148
effect of sub-clauses on: 148
effect of sumti of referent bridi on: 148
in narrative about quotation: 150
in quotation series: 150
in quotations: 150
referent of: 148
goal of this book: 10
goer-house
example: 264
GOhA selma'o
as component in tanru: 93
as selbri: 93
goi
rationale for non-inclusion in relative clause chapter: 168
use in assigning lerfu as pro-sumti: 146
use in assigning name: 146
goi assignment of ko'a-series pro-sumti
use in speech contrasted with writing: 145
goi for ko'a-series assignment
compared with cei for broda-series assignment: 145
grammatical categories
use of upper case for: 11
grammatical terms
quick-tour version: 30
Greek alphabet
language shift word for: 401

Greek-Americans own restaurants: 122
grouping
  of connection in abstractions: 350
  of connection in tenses: 348
grouping parentheses: 84
guhek
  definition: 334
guheks
  connecting operators: 346
  syntax of: 334
guheks for tanru connection
  rationale: 334
happy face
  example: 400
having
  of properties: 251
hearsay
  example: 303
heartburn
  example: 308
Hebrew alphabet
  language shift word for: 401
hereafter known as
  example: 145
hesitation sound: 465
hexadecimal system
  specifying numbers in (see also base): 426
hierarchy of priorities for selecting lujvo form: 69
hiragana
  contrasted with kanji: 403
hospitality
  example: 310
hundred
  expressing as number: 414
hyphen letter
  definition: 58
hyphens
  use of: 58
hyphens in lujvo
  proscribed where not required: 68
hypothetical world: 289
  contrasted with real world
    example: 307
hypothetical world point of view: 306
i
  regarding forethought bridi connection: 322
ICAO Phonetic Alphabet
  proposed lerfu words for: 412
ice'o
  contrasted with .ibabo: 343
idea abstraction: 258
idea abstractions
  place structure: 258
identity
  expressing with po'u: 166
identity predicate: 156
if
  English usage contrasted with Lojban logical
    connective: 321
  expressing hypothetical world: 306
  expressing real world: 306
  meaning in logical connections: 321
if ... then
  compared with only if: 321
  logical connectives contrasted with other translations:
    323
ijek
  definition: 320
ijek bridi connectives
  contrasted with geks: 322
ijek logical connectives
  connecting bridi: 320
ijeks
  syntax of: 322
ijoik
  as name for compound cmavo: 320
  definition: 343
imaginary journey
  and spatial tense: 209
  ending point: 209
  origin in tense forethought bridi-tail connection: 232
  origin in tense forethought sentence connection: 231
  origin in tense forethought sumti connection: 232
  origin of in tense-connected sentences: 231
  stages of in compound tenses: 210
  starting at a different point: 223
  starting point: 209, 223
  with interval direction: 214
imaginary journey origin
  with sticky tenses: 225
imperatives
  and truth: 337
  attitude: 296
  English contrasted with Lojban in presence of subject
    of command: 141
  quick-tour version: 25
  with ko: 141
implausible: 273
implicit quantifier
  for quotations: 124
  on quotations
    discussion of: 124
importance of point
  scale with ra'u: 306
inalienable
  distinguishing from alienable: 166
inalienable possession
  definition: 166
  expressing with po'e: 165
inchoative event contour: 219
incidental association
  expressing with ne: 167
incidental identification
  expressing with no'u: 167
incidental relative clause
  as a parenthetical device: 164
  definition: 163
inclusion
  property of sets: 121

indefinite description
    as needing explicit outer quantifier: 127
    as prohibiting explicit inner quantifier: 127
    compared with restricted variable: 382
    definition: 127, 382
indefinite numbers
    combined with definite: 424
indefinite portions
    subjective: 424
indefinite pro-bridi: 150
    stability of: 155
indefinite pro-sumti: 135, 150
    implicit quantifier for: 135
    stability of: 155
indefinite sumti
    as implicit quantification: 391
    compared to sumti with lo: 383
    meaning when multiple in sentence: 382
    multiple in sentence: 382
indefinite values
    subjective: 424
indicator scope: 448
indicators: 286
    evolutionary development of: 314
    grammar for compounding: 298
    meaning when compounded: 298
    placement of: 289
    quick-tour version: 28
    ramifications: 314
    rationale for selection: 314
    scope effect of new paragraph: 448
    types of: 286
indirect question: 309
indirect question involving sumti: 257
indirect questions
    "ma kau" contrasted with "la djan. kau": 257
indirect questions without "kau": 257
indisputable bridi: 302
individual descriptors
    different implicit outer quantifiers among: 126
individual objects
    multiple: 119
individuals
    expressing relation with mass formed: 428
    expressing relation with set formed: 428
individuals into mass
    by non-logical connection: 339
individuals into set
    by non-logical connection: 339
individuals of set
    expressing measurement standard for indefinites: 428
indivisible: 251
induction
    example: 303
inexact numbers with bounds: 425
inexact portions with bounds: 426
infix notation mixed with Polish: 436
    example: 436
initial consonant pairs
    list of: 39

initiative event contour: 219
innate capabilities
    expressing implicitly: 235
innate capability
    expressing explicitly: 236
innate properties
    extension of from mass to individuals: 236
    extension to individuals not actually capable: 236
inner product: 434
inner quantifier
    contrasted with outer quantifier: 125
    definition: 125
    effect of on meaning: 125
    explicit: 125
    implicit on descriptors: 125
    in indefinite description: 127
inner sumti
    referring to from within relative clause within relative clause: 177
integral
    architectural concept
        example: 62
    mathematical concept
        example: 62
interactions between quantifiers and negation
    effect: 388
interjections
    quick-tour version: 28
intermediate abstraction: 259
internal bridi negation
    compared to external bridi negation: 385
    definition: 385
internal naku negations
    and DeMorgan's Law: 394
internal world: 289
International Phonetic Alphabet (see also IPA): 34
intersect: 259
intersection
    of sets: 341
intersection of sets
    compared with and: 341
interval
    closed: 344
    followed by direction in tense construct: 213
    inclusion of endpoints: 344
    open: 344
    relation to point specified by direction and distance: 213
    relative order with direction and distance in tense: 213
    specifying relation to point specified by direction and distance: 213
interval continuousness
    meaning as sumti tcita: 225
interval direction
    specifying: 213
interval properties
    meaning as sumti tcita: 225
    strings of: 239
interval size
    as context-dependent: 214

meaning as sumti tcita: 225
  unspecified: 215
  vague: 215
interval spread
  expressing English "intermittently": 218
  mutually contrasted: 217
  negation with nai: 218
  with unspecified interval: 218
intervals
  effect of nai on: 345
  expressed as center and distance: 344
  expressed as endpoints: 343
  expressing by endpoints with bi'o: 238
  forethought: 346
  spread of actions over: 217
intrinsic possession
  definition: 166
  expressing by using place in some selbri: 166
  expressing with po'e: 165
introduce oneself: 311
invalid diphthongs
  in fu'ivla: 63
invalid speech
  marking as error with na'i: 307
inversion of quantifiers
  definition: 386
  in moving negation boundary: 386
inversion of quantifiers on passing negation boundary
  rationale for: 387
invertebrate: 275
inverted tanru
  effect on sumti after the selbri: 92
  effect on sumti before the selbri: 92
inverting quantifiers
  with movement relative to fixed negation: 390
  with movement relative to naku: 390
IPA: 34
IPA pronunciation
  description: 44
irony
  example: 306
  expressing: 306
irrelevant
  specifying of sumti place: 151
isomorphism
  audio-visual: 33
IT
  as notation convention in relative clause chapter: 162
italic
  example: 402
iy diphthong
  in cmene: 64
j-sound in English
  representation in Lojban: 35
jai
  for modal conversion: 97
jai with tense
  as equivalent of SE in grammar: 239
jai without modal
  meaning: 200

jargon
  use of fu'ivla for: 60
je'e
  contrasted with vi'o: 311
jei
  place structure: 255
jek
  definition: 320
jeks
  connecting abstractors: 350
  connecting operators: 346
  syntax of: 334
Jesus: 259
ji'i
  effect of placement: 424
  with elided number: 425
jo'i
  precedence of: 433
jo'u
  contrasted with ce: 339
  contrasted with ce'o: 339
  contrasted with joi: 339
  result of connection with: 339
joi grammar
  contrasted with eks: 338
  contrasted with jeks: 338
joigik
  as name for compound cmavo: 320
  definition: 346
joigiks
  connection types: 346
  syntax of: 346
joik
  as name for compound cmavo: 320
  definition: 338
joiks
  effect of nai on: 343
  grouping: 342
  syntax of: 345
  use of "se" in: 339
jokes: 10
ju'u
  grammar of: 427
ka'o
  as special number compared with as numerical
  punctuation: 416
kanji
  contrasted with alphabets and syllabaries: 403
  representing based on romaji spelling: 403
  representing based on strokes: 404
kau
  "ma kau" contrasted with "la djan. kau": 257
ke
  contrasted with bo for tensed logical connection: 350
  for conversion of tanru: 97
  for expanding scope of scalar negation: 98
ke in sumti grouping
  where allowed: 328
ke'a
  ambiguity when omitted: 154

and abstract descriptions: 154
  as referent for relativized sumti: 162
  contrasted with ri in relative clauses: 154
  effect of omission of: 162
  for relativized sumti in relative clauses: 154
  meaning in relative clause inside relative clause: 177
  non-initial place use in relative clause: 162
  stability of: 155
  subscripting for nested relative clauses: 154
ke'a with subscript
  use for outer sumti reference: 177
ke'i
  etymology of: 345
ke'o
  compared to ki'a: 311
ke'u
  contrasted with va'i: 306
KEI selma'o
  eliding: 248
ki
  with no tense: 227
ki'a
  compared to ke'o: 311
killing Jim: 250
klama
  place structure of: 179
know who
  contrasted with know that: 257
knowledge discursives: 306
  compared with propositional attitudes: 306
ko
  in later selbri place in imperative: 141
  in sub-clause of main bridi: 141
  use for commands: 141
  use for imperatives: 141
ko'a-series
  after tenth: 454
ko'a-series for pro-sumti
  compared with broda-series for pro-bridi: 145
ko'a-series pro-sumti: 144
  as assignable: 144
  assigning with goi: 144
  assignment with goi as symmetrical: 144
  contrasted with lerfu as pro-sumti in explicit assignment of: 145
ku
  as elidable terminator for descriptions: 119
  effect of following selbri on elidability of: 119
  effect of possessive sumti on elidability of: 173
  effect on elidability of be'o: 91
  effect on of omitting descriptor: 127
  quick-tour version: 23
  uses of: 119
  with tense: 208
KU selma'o
  quick-tour version: 23
ku'o
  effect of vau on elidability: 173
  elidability for relative clauses: 163

Kzinti
  communication with: 314
l-hyphen
  use of: 61
la
  compared with le in specificity: 117
  contrasted with lai in implications: 121
  contrasted with le in implications: 118
  contrasted with lo in implications: 118
  implications of: 117
  use with descriptions contrasted with use before Lojbanized names: 117
LA selma'o
  contrasted with LE in use of name-words: 133
  effect on necessity for pause before name-word: 133
la'e
  as short for le selsinxa bele selsinxa be: 129
  effect of on meaning: 129
la'e lu
  compared with me'o: 405
la'edi'u
  contrasted with di'u: 143
la'i
  as set counterpart of lai: 121
la'o
  interaction with bu: 400
la-series descriptors
  compared with le-series in implicit quantification: 125
Láadan evidentials: 302
LAhE selma'o: 128
  effect of relative clause placement with: 174
lai
  as mass counterpart of lai: 120
  contrasted with la in implications: 121
lambda calculus
  operator and operand distinction in: 441
language shift
  based on name + bu: 401
  choice of Lojban-lerfu-word counterpart: 401
  compound: 401
  effect on following words: 401
  formation of shift alphabet name: 401
  interaction with bu: 401
  rationale for: 401
  standardization of: 402
languages
  abbreviations for: 101
Laplace
  example: 64
large-base decimal fraction
  expressing: 427
latent component: 280
Latin
  alphabet of Lojban: 397
Latin alphabet: 33
  language shift word for: 401
lau
  effect on following lerfu word: 403
LAU selma'o
  grammar of following BY cmavo: 409

le
  and specificity: 116
  and truth of selbri: 116
  compared with English the: 116
  compared with la in specificity: 117
  contrasted with lo in implications: 119
  contrasted with lo in implicit quantification: 126
  contrasted with lo in specificity: 117
  contrasted with lo in truth requirement: 117
  implications of: 116
  implicit outer quantifier for: 126
  in false-to-fact descriptions: 117
  meaning of in the plural: 119
le nu
  definition: 248
LE selma'o
  contrasted with LA in use of name-words: 133
le'e
  relationship to le'i: 122
le'i
  as set counterpart of lei: 121
  relationship to le'e: 122
le-series cmavo
  as encompassing le-series and la-series descriptors for quantification discussion: 125
  definition: 125
  rationale for implicit inner quantifier: 125
  rule for implicit inner quantifier: 125
le-series descriptors
  compared with la-series in implicit quantification: 125
learning Lojban
  magnitude of task: 53
left-grouping rule
  definition of: 82
legal jargon
  example: 145
legal system: 255
lei
  contrasted with loi in specificity: 120
lerfu
  as assignable pro-sumti: 145
  contrasted with lerfu word: 398
  definition: 397
  reference to: 405
  referring to with me'o: 405
lerfu as pro-sumti
  contrasted with ko'a-series in explicit assignment of: 145
  explicit assignment of antecedent: 146
  implicit assignment of antecedent: 145
lerfu juxtaposition interpretation
  contrasted with mathematical interpretation: 407
lerfu shift scope
  exception for mathematical texts: 407
lerfu string
  as function name: 406
  as mathematical variable: 406
  as pro-sumti: 404
    assumption of reference: 404
  as pro-sumti assigned by goi: 404

  as quantifier: 406
  as selbri: 406
  as subscript: 406
  as utterance ordinal: 406
  definition: 404
  interpretation
    contrasted with mathematical interpretation: 407
lerfu strings
  as acronyms using "me": 407
  as pro-sumti
    for multiple sumti separated by boi: 404
  as quantifiers
    avoiding interaction with sumti quantified: 407
  in mathematical expressions: 419
  interpretation of contrasted with normal mathematical interpretation: 419
  uses in mathematics: 406
  with numerical selbri: 430
lerfu word
  contrasted with lerfu: 398
  for "": 398
lerfu word cmavo
  list of auxiliary: 409
lerfu word set extension
  with bu: 400
lerfu words
  as a basis for acronym names: 407
  composed of compound cmavo: 398
  composed of single cmavo: 398
  consonant words contrasted with vowel words: 398
  effect of systematic formulation: 398
  for consonants: 398
  for vowels: 398
  formation rules: 398
  forming new for non-Lojban letters using bu: 403
  list of proposed
    notation convention: 409
  Lojban coverage requirement: 398
  proposed for accent marks: 411
  proposed for Cyrillic alphabet: 410
  proposed for diacritic marks: 411
  proposed for multiple letters: 411
  proposed for noisy environments: 412
  proposed for radio communication: 412
  table of Lojban: 398
  using computer encoding schemes with se'e: 408
  vowel words contrasted with consonant words: 398
lerfu words ending with "y"
  pause after
    rationale: 399
lerfu words for vowels
  pause requirement before: 398
lerfu words with numeric digits
  grammar considerations: 403
less than
  contrasted with more than
    at least, at most: 425
letter
  alphabet: 397
  contrasted with word for the letter: 398

letter encoding schemes
  application to lerfu words: 408
letteral
  definition: 397
letters
  non-Lojban
    representation of diacritical marks on: 402
    representation with consonant-word + bu: 401
    representation with consonant-word + bu, drawback: 401
    representation with language-shift: 401
    representation with names: 400
  sound contrasted with symbol for spelling: 401
  symbol contrasted with sound for spelling: 401
li
  as converter of mekso into sumti: 418
  contrasted with me'o: 438
  relation to me'o compared with la/zo relation: 439
  terminator for: 436
LI selma'o: 137
lined up: 273
linguistic behavior: 256
linguistic drift: 10
linguistic drift in Lojban
  possible source of: 67
linked arguments: 453
linked sumti
  definition: 89
  in tanru: 89
linked sumti and FA tags: 90
linked sumti and sumti tcita: 90
Linnaean names
  rules for: 65
list
  as a physical object: 339
  contrasted with sequence: 339
lists
  use of tu'e/tu'u in: 343
literally: 308
LLG: 11
lo
  and truth of selbri: 117
  contrasted with le in implications: 119
  contrasted with le in implicit quantification: 126
  contrasted with le in specificity: 117
  contrasted with le in truth requirement: 117
  contrasted with loi and lo'i: 121
  implications of: 117
  implicit outer quantifier for: 126
  omission of: 127
lo'a
  contrasted with na'a: 402
lo'e
  relationship to lo'i: 122
lo'i
  as set counterpart of loi: 121
  contrasted with lo and loi: 121
  relationship to lo'e: 122
  with elided quantifiers: 428

lo'o
  effect of logical connective on elidability of: 436
lo'u
  interaction with bu: 400
lo-series cmavo
  rationale for implicit inner quantifier: 125
  rule for implicit inner quantifier: 125
lo-series description
  caution on exact numbers as inner quantifiers on: 126
logic
  and attitudinals: 376
  limits of: 376
  resolving ambiguities of "nobody": 376
logic and Lojban
  more aspects: 395
logical connection
  effect on elidability of lo'o: 436
  grouping strategies for complex cases contrasted: 327
  in abstractions
    inner bridi contrasted with outer bridi: 350
  in mathematical expressions: 346
  in tanru
    contrasted with unconnected version: 333
    expandability of: 334
    grouping with bo: 334
    grouping with ke: 334
  inside abstractions
    contrasted with outside: 350
  interaction with tenses: 347
  negation in connecting more than 2 sentences: 325
  of bridi-tail as opposed to tanru: 334
  of bridi-tails
    forethought: 331
    restriction on ke: 330
  of forethought termsets: 333
  of modals: 201
  of more than 2 sentences
    all or none: 325
    forethought: 326
    things to avoid: 325
  of observatives
    relation of first places: 329
  of selbri: 328
  of sumti
    grouping with parentheses: 328
    restriction on ke: 328
  of tanru
    caveat: 335
  of tanru as opposed to bridi-tail: 334
  termsets: 332
  transformation between forms: 324
  with bo
    precedence: 326
logical connection of abstractors: 350
logical connection of more than 2 sentences
  mixed "and" and "or": 325
logical connectives: 317
  associative: 325
  bridi-tail connection: 329

cmavo
   format for each selma'o: 320
effect on elidability of ge'u from preceding relative
phrase: 168
equivalence relation on 3 sentences: 325
grouping with bo: 326
in tanru: 85
more than 2 sentences: 325
negated first sentence as a potential problem for
understanding: 323
non-associative: 325
observative sentence connection: 329
pairing from left: 326
rationale for multiple sets in grammar: 319
recipes
   simplified for logic chapter discussion: 388
relation to truth functions: 319
relative precedence with me'u: 96
right-grouping with bo: 327
selma'o
   enumerated: 320
syntax rules summary: 352
table by truth function value: 351
tensed: 232
logical connectives and bridi negation: 388
logical connectives and negation
   caveat for logic chapter discussions: 388
logical connectives in tanru: 333
   ambiguity of: 86
   effect on formal logical manipulations: 87
   effect on tanru grouping: 86
   usefulness of: 86
logical connectives within negation
   effects of expansion on: 392
logical language
   truth functions: 317
Logical Language Group
   example: 70
   relation to Lojban: 9
logical variables
   creating more by subscripting: 395
   effect of global substitution: 377
   effect of order in prenex: 378
   effect of using multiple different: 377
   explicitly placing in outer prenex: 385
   for selbri: 394
   implicit placement in smallest enclosing bridi prenex:
   385
   notation convention: 377
   when not in main bridi: 378
   with multiple appearances in bridi: 377
   with poi
      in multiple appearances: 381
   with ro
      in multiple appearances: 381
logically connected sentences
   and DeMorgan's Law: 392
logically connected tenses
   definition: 347
   expansion to sentences: 237

with JA: 237
Loglan: 12
logograms
   words for: 400
loi
   as mass counterpart of lo: 120
   contrasted with lei in specificity: 120
   contrasted with lo and lo'i: 121
Lojban
   features of: 9
   history of: 9
   stability of: 10
Lojban alphabet: 33
Lojban letters
   IPA for pronouncing: 35
   list with IPA pronunciation: 35
Lojbanistan: 10
long rafsi
   definition: 56
long rafsi form
   compared with short form in effect on lujvo meaning:
   55
loose association
   expressing with pe: 165
lower case letters
   use in Lojban: 399
lower-case
   lerfu word for: 399
lower-case letters
   English usage contrasted with Lojban: 399
   Lojban usage contrasted with English: 399
lower-case word
   effect on following lerfu words: 399
lu
   contrasted with me'o for representing lerfu: 405
lu'a
   effect of on meaning: 129
lu'e
   as short for "le sinxa be": 129
   effect of on meaning: 129
lu'i
   effect of on meaning: 129
lu'o
   effect of on meaning: 129
lu'u
   as elidable terminator for qualified sumti: 128
lujvo
   abbreviated: 273
   abstract: 275
   algorithm for: 68
   and consonant pairs: 59
   and plausibility: 68
   and seltau/tertau relationship: 266
   and the listener: 68
   as a subtype of brivla: 53
   as suppliers of agent place: 283
   asymmetrical: 268
   based on multiple tanru: 68
   cmavo incorporation: 264
   comparatives: 280

compared with tanru: 263
consideration in choosing meaning for: 67
considerations for retaining elements of: 68
construction of: 55
definition
  quick-tour version: 31
design consideration for relationship: 266
dropping elements of: 67
dropping SE rafsi: 273
examples of making: 69
from cmavo with no rafsi: 59
from tanru: 55
fully reduced: 58
guidelines for place structure: 264
interpreting: 266
invention of: 56
meaning drift of: 67
meaning of: 55
multiple forms of: 55
place structure of figurative lujvo: 308
pro-sumti rafsi effect on place structure of: 156
quick-tour version: 24
rationale for: 264
recognizing: 58
rules for formation of: 56
scored examples of: 69
scoring of: 69
selection of best form of: 69
shorter for more general concepts: 68
summary of form characteristics: 58
superlatives: 280
symmetrical: 267
ultimate guideline for choice of meaning/place-structure: 67
unambiguity of: 67
unambiguous decomposition of: 55
unreduced: 56
unsuitability of for concrete/specific terms and jargon: 60
with zei: 59
zi'o rafsi effect on place structure of: 157
lujvo creation
  interaction of KE with NAhE: 275
  interaction of KE with SE: 275
  use of multiple SE in: 275
lujvo form
  consonant cluster requirement in: 58
  final letter of: 58
  hierarchy of priorities for selection of: 69
  number of letters in: 58
  requirements for hyphen insertion in: 58
  requirements for n-hyphen insertion in: 59
  requirements for r-hyphen insertion in: 59
  requirements for y-hyphen insertion in: 59
lujvo place order: 271
  asymmetrical lujvo: 271
  based on 3-or-more part veljvo: 272
  comparatives: 281
  rationale for standardization: 271
  superlatives: 282

superlatives as exceptions: 282
symmetrical lujvo: 271
lujvo place structure
"ni" lujvo: 276
"nu" lujvo: 275
basis of: 267
comparative lujvo: 281
cross-dependent places: 270
dependent places: 269
dropping "KE": 274
dropping "KEhE": 274
dropping cross-dependent places: 270
dropping dependent places
  caveat: 270
dropping dependent seltau places: 269
dropping dependent tertau places: 270
dropping redundant places: 266
effect of "SE": 268
effect of "SE"-dropping in tertau: 274
explicated walk-through: 266
guidelines: 264
multi-place abstraction lujvo: 276
notation conventions: 266
rationale for standardization: 267
selecting tertau: 270
superlatives: 282
when first place redundant with non-first: 268
when first places redundant: 267
when first places redundant plus others: 268
ma
  as sumti question: 153
  for tense questions: 242
ma'o
  potential ambiguity caveat: 441
ma'u
  with elided number: 424
mai
  contrasted with mo'o: 440
MAI selma'o
  exception on use of boi before: 440
male sexual teacher
  example: 71
man biting dog: 209
marathon: 251
Mars road
  example: 186
mass
  compared with set as abstract of multiple individuals: 121
  contrasted with ordered sequence: 339
  contrasted with set in attribution of component properties: 121
  contrasted with set in distribution of properties: 339
  expressing measurement standard for indefinites: 428
  expressing relation with individuals forming: 428
  expressing relation with set forming: 428
  joining elements into a: 338
mass contrasted with components
  in properties of: 338

mass name
  use of: 120
mass object
  and logical reasoning: 120
  as dependent on intention: 120
  contrasted with multiple individual objects: 120
  properties of: 120
mass objects
  peculiarities of English translation of: 120
masses
  rule for implicit outer quantifier: 125
mathematical equality
  expressing: 417
mathematical expression
  referring to: 438
mathematical expressions
  connectives in: 346
  implicit quantifier for: 137
  tensed connection in: 350
mathematical expressions in tanru: 94
mathematical intervals: 347
mathematical notation
  and omitted operators: 414
  and operator precedence: 419
  infix: 417
  international uniqueness of: 413
mathematical operators: 418
mathematical texts
  effect on lerfu shift scope: 407
mathematical variables
  lerfu strings as: 406
mathematics
  use of lerfu strings in: 406
matrices
  use as operands: 434
  use of parentheses with: 434
matrix
  as combination of vectors: 433
  definition: 433
  with ge'a for more than 2 rows/columns: 433
  with more than 2 dimensions: 434
matrix column operator: 433
matrix row operator: 433
mau
  avoiding in favor of seme'a: 197
Mayan mathematics
  as a system with base larger than 16: 427
me
  compared with du in effect: 95
  explicitly specifying: 311
  place structure of: 95
  used with names: 96
me'a
  avoiding in favor of semau: 197
me'i
  with elided number: 426
me'o: 137
  compared with la'e lu: 405
  contrasted with li: 438
  contrasted with lu...li'u for representing lerfu: 405

contrasted with quotation for representing lerfu: 405
  relation to li compared with la/zo relation: 439
me'u
  relative precedence with logical connectives: 96
me/du equivalence: 95
measurements
  expressing: 418
medieval weapon: 272
mei
  place structure formed for objective indefinites: 428
mekso
  and literary translation: 441
  complex used as quantifier: 435
  design goals: 413
mekso chapter
  completeness: 414
  table notation convention: 414
mekso goal
  coverage: 413
  expandable: 413
  for common use: 413
  for mathematical writing: 413
  precision: 413
  unambiguous: 413
mekso goals
  and ambiguity: 413
  and non-mathematical expression: 413
  mathematical notation form: 413
melting: 283
membership
  property of sets: 121
mental activity: 255
mental discomfort
  example: 295
metalinguistic comment
  with embedded discursive: 462
metalinguistic levels: 463
metalinguistic levels or reference: 463
metalinguistic pro-sumti: 135
  implicit quantifier for: 135
metalinguistic words
  quick-tour version: 29
mi'e
  contrasted with other members of COI: 311
  effect of ordering multiple COI: 311
mi'u
  contrasted with go'i: 304
mi-series
  of pro-sumti: 140
mi-series pro-sumti
  lack of pro-bridi equivalent: 141
mintu
  contrasted with du: 156
misinterpretation: 275
mixed claim
  definition: 378
mixed modal connection
  afterthought: 198
  as proscribed in forethought: 198
  definition: 198

of bridi-tails: 198
of sentences: 198
of sumti: 198
mo
  as selbri question: 153
  compared with go'i in overriding of arguments: 153
mo'e
  terminator for: 437
mo'o
  contrasted with mai: 440
modal bridi-tail connection: 193
modal causals
  implication differences: 189
modal cmavo
  basis in gismu place structure: 203
  position relative to selbri: 101
  regular form for derivation: 202
  table with English equivalents: 203
modal cmavo table
  format of: 203
modal connection
  simultaneous with logical: 198
modal connection of selbri
  using bridi-tail modal connection: 193
modal connectives
  fi'o prohibited in: 194
modal conversion
  access to original first place with fai: 199
  grammar of: 199
  place structure of: 199
  with no modal specified: 200
modal conversion with fi'o: 200
modal conversion without modal
  as vague: 200
modal conversions
  in descriptions: 200
modal followed by selbri
  compared with tanru modification in meaning: 194
  contrasted with tanru modification in grammar: 194
  effect on eliding cu: 194
modal operand connection: 193
modal place
  definition: 187
  on description selbri: 189
  rationale for term name: 187
  relation of to selbri: 187
modal place relation
  importance of first place in: 187
modal sentence connection: 191
  condensing: 192
  effect on modal: 191
  forethought: 192
  relation to modal of first sentence in: 191
  relation to modal of second sentence in: 191
  table of equivalent schemata: 241
  with other than causals: 191
modal sumti
  and FA marking: 187
  as first place of modal tag selbri: 187
  definition (see also seltcita sumti): 187

effect on place structure: 187
  leaving vague: 194
  position in bridi: 187
  unspecified: 194
modal sumti connection: 192
modal tag
  definition (see also sumti tcita): 187
  fi'o with selbri as: 187
  for vague relationship: 189
modal tags
  contrasted with English prepositions in preciseness: 189
  short forms as BAI cmavo: 188
modal tags and sumti tcita: 90
modal-or-tense question
  with cu'e: 242
modal-or-tense questions
  pre-specifying some information: 243
modals
  compared with tenses in syntax: 240
  contradictory negation of: 200
  contrasted with tenses in semantics: 240
  expanding scope over inner modal connection: 195
  expanding scope over logical connection with ke ... ke'e: 195
  expanding scope over multiple sentences with tu'e...tu'u: 195
  expanding scope over non-logical connection: 195
  for causal gismu: 189
  importance of 1st sumti place for sumti tcita use: 240
  improving relative phrase preciseness with : 196
  making long-scope: 201
  making sticky: 201
  negation of: 200
  scalar negation of: 200
  termset connection: 192
modals often attached with relative phrases
  list: 197
modifier
  seltau as: 81
modifying brivla (see also seltau): 54
MOI selma'o
  use of boi before: 431
more than
  contrasted with less than
    at least, at most: 425
morphology
  conventions for: 49
  definition: 49
  derivational: 49
  simplicity of: 49
  symbolic conventions for discussing: 49
movement
  order in tense constructs: 216
  time: 217
  with multiple directions: 217
movement specification
  interaction with direction in tenses: 216
mu'e
  place structure: 251

multiple compound bridi
  restriction on ke: 330
multiple conversion
  avoiding: 186
  effect of ordering: 186
multiple indefinite sumti
  effect of re-ordering in sentence: 383
  expressing with equal scope: 383
  meaning: 382
multiple indefinite sumti scope
  in termset: 383
multiple indicators: 299
multiple individual objects
  contrasted with mass object: 120
  meaning of: 119
multiple letters
  proposed lerfu words for: 411
multiple logical connectives
  within tanru: 87
multiple ma
  as multiple questions: 154
multiple mo
  as multiple questions: 154
multiple quantification
  effect on selbri placement among sumti: 391
multiple questions in one bridi
  expressing: 154
multiple relative clauses
  attaching with zi'e: 168
  connecting different kinds with zi'e: 168
multiple SE
  effect of ordering: 186
multiple speakers: 465
multiple sumti in one place
  avoiding: 184
  meaning: 184
multiple tanru inversion
  effect on grouping: 92
multiple tenses
  effect of order in sentence: 226
myth
  example: 303
n-hyphen
  contrasted with r-hyphen in requirements for use: 59
  use of: 56, 59
na
  and negation boundary: 392
  order in logical connectives with se: 322
na and tense
  multiple: 100
na writing convention
  in eks: 324
na'a
  contrasted with lo'a: 402
na'e
  before gu'e: 100
  contrasted with na'e ke: 98
na'u
  terminator for: 437
  use in asking operator questions: 439

NAhE selma'o: 128
  effect of relative clause placement with: 174
nai
  effect on intervals: 345
  effect on joiks: 343
  placement in afterthought bridi connection contrasted with forethought: 323
  placement in forethought bridi connection contrasted with afterthought: 323
naku
  as creating a negation boundary: 390
  compared with sumti in grammar: 390
  effect on moving quantifiers: 390
  in linked sumti places: 392
  multiple in sentence: 392
  outside of prenex: 390
naku negation
  rationale for considering an advanced technique: 390
naku negation boundary
  effect on conversion with se: 390
naku su'oda
  as expansion of noda: 387
naku zo'u
  and negation boundary: 392
name equivalent for typical
  rationale for lack of: 123
name words
  recognition of: 132
name-words
  limitations on: 133
  pause requirements before: 133
  permissible consonant combinations: 133
names
  algorithm for: 65
  alternatives for restricted sequences in: 64
  as possessive sumti: 173
  assigning with goi: 146
  authority for: 64
  borrowing from other languages: 134
  examples of: 63
  from Lojban words: 65
  in vocative phrase: 132
  multiple: 133
  pause requirement in lerfu words: 400
  purpose of: 63
  quick-tour version: 17
  rationale for lojbanizing: 63
  requirement for pause after: 64
  restrictions on form of: 64
  rules for: 64
  rules for formation: 64
  stress in: 64
  stress on: 42
  two kinds of: 132
  unusual stress in: 64
  uses of: 132
  using rafsi: 133
  with LA descriptor: 132
names from vowel-final base
  commonly used consonant endings: 134

names in Lojban (see also cmene): 63
names with la
  implicit quantifier for: 134
naming predicate: 118
natural end
  continuing beyond: 221
  contrasted with actual stop: 221
nau
  effect on sticky tenses: 230
  syntax: 230
Navajo
  example: 63
ne
  compared with pe: 167
Nederlands
  example: 64
need any box: 384
negated intervals
  meaning of: 345
negating a forethought-connected bridi-tail pair: 331
negating a forethought-connected sentence pair: 331
negating a sentence
  and truth value: 317
negation
  complex examples: 98
  form for emulating natural language negation: 390
  of operand: 441
  of operator: 440
  of tenses: 234
negation and logical connectives
  caveat for logic chapter discussions: 388
negation between sentences
  compared with bridi negation: 388
  meaning of: 388
negation boundary
  and zero: 387
  effect of moving: 386
negation cmavo
  position relative to selbri: 101
negation in prenex
  effects of position: 386
negation manipulation
  "na" contrasted with "naku" in difficulty of: 391
  "naku" contrasted with "na" in difficulty of: 391
negation of fi'o modals
  by negating selbri: 201
negation of modals: 200
  contradictory: 200
  scalar: 200
negation of tenses
  meaning of: 234
negation sumti qualifiers
  meanings of: 130
negations with logical connectives
  effects on expansion of sentence: 392
negative answer
  quick-tour version: 28
negative numbers
  expressing: 415

negative sign
  contrasted with subtraction operator: 417
negator
  movement from bridi to sumti: 392
new notation: 266
ni'e
  terminator for: 437
ni'o
  effect on pro-sumti/pro-bridi assignments: 156
ni'u
  with elided number: 424
no'i
  effect on pro-sumti/pro-bridi assignments: 156
no'u
  compared with po'u: 167
  contrasted with po'u: 167
nobody
  ambiguous interpretations of: 376
  interpretation of: 375
  Lojban contrasted with English: 376
noda
  expanding to naku su'oda: 387
noisy environments
  proposed lerfu words for: 412
non-logical connection
  and elidability of terminators: 338
  in mathematical expressions: 346
  in tanru
    distinguishing from connection of sumti: 338
  of individuals into mass: 339
  of individuals into set: 339
  of modals: 201
  of operands: 436
  of operators: 436
  of sumti
    distinguishing from connection in tanru: 338
  of termsets: 342
non-logical connectives
  effect of nai on: 343
  grouping: 342
  including tense: 350
  intervals: 343
  ordered intervals: 344
  sentence: 343
  syntax rules summary: 352
  un-ordered intervals: 344
  within tanru: 88
non-logical forethought termsets
  connecting tagged sumti: 342
non-logically connected tenses: 348
non-Lojban quotation: 136
non-Lojban text
  rules for pause with: 67
non-restrictive relative clause
  definition (see also incidental relative clause): 163
non-specific descriptions: 117
non-standard orthographies
  caveat: 47
  Cyrillic: 47
  Tengwar: 47

nonagenarian: 281
normal circumstances: 249
notation conventions
  for Quick Tour chapter: 16
nouns
  brivla as Lojban equivalents: 52
nu
  definition: 248
  place structure: 250
nu'a
  use in answering operator questions: 439
null operand
  for infix operations with too few operands: 432
null operator
  for infix operations with too many operands: 433
number article
  explanation of use: 417
number questions: 431
  answers to: 431
number sumti
  syntax of: 136
  with li: 136
  with li contrasted with me'o: 137
  with me'o: 137
  with me'o contrasted with li: 137
number words
  pattern in: 414
numbers
  as compound cmavo: 414
  as grammatically complete utterances: 431
  as possessive sumti: 173
  cmavo as Lojban equivalents: 50
  English contrasted with Lojban on exactness: 382
  expressing simple: 414
  greater than 9: 414
  implicit quantifier for: 137
  list of indefinite: 444
  list of special: 444
  Lojban contrasted with English on exactness: 382
  on logical variables: 381
  rafsi for: 58
  special: 416
  talking about contrasted with using for quantification: 417
  using for quantification contrasted with talking about: 417
numeric digits in lerfu words
  grammar considerations: 403
numerical punctuation: 415
  undefined: 417
numerical selbri
  alternative to compensate for restriction on numbers: 430
  based on non-numerical sumti: 430
  complex: 430
  grammar: 430
  restriction on numbers used for: 430
  special: 428
    with lerfu strings: 430
  use of "me" with: 430

numerical tenses
  effect on use of boi: 440
observation evidential
  contrasted with observative : 303
observative
  contrasted with observation evidential: 303
  definition: 181
observative form
  contrasted with command: 181
observative with elided CAhA
  convention: 237
observatives
  and abstractions: 248
  quick-tour version: 19
octal system
  specifying numbers in (see also base): 426
octogenarian: 281
old topic: 448
omission of descriptor
  effect on ku: 127
omitting terminators
  perils of: 99
on right
  contrasted with toward right: 216
one-third of food: 429
only if
  compared with if ... then: 321
open interval: 344
  expressed with mi'i: 437
operand
  converting from operator: 441
  converting into operator: 441
  converting selbri into: 437
  converting sumti into: 438
operand connection
  afterthought: 435
  forethought: 435
operand modal connection: 193
operands
  connecting: 346
  contrasted with general sumti: 418
  too few for infix operation: 432
  too many for infix operation: 433
operator
  converting from operand: 441
  converting into operand: 441
  converting into selbri: 439
  converting selbri into: 437
operator connection
  afterthought: 435
  forethought: 435
operator derived from selbri
  effect of selbri place structure on: 437
operator left-right grouping
  as Lojban default: 418
operator precedence
  and mathematical notation: 419
  effect of pragmatic convention: 419
  generalized explicit specification: 419
  in Lojban default: 418

plans for future: 440
rationale for default left-grouping: 419
scope modification with bi'e: 419
specifying by parenthesis: 419
operator precedence in other languages: 419
operators
    analogue of tanru in: 346
    connecting: 346
    list of simple: 443
operators of VUhU
    grammar of operands: 418
order of variables
    in moving to prenex: 382
ordered sequence
    by listing members: 339
    contrasted with mass: 339
    contrasted with set: 339
ordinal selbri
    definition: 429
    place structure: 429
    place structure effect from subjective numbers: 430
ordinal tense: 222
orthography
    non-standard: 47
    relation to pronunciation: 33
outer product: 434
outer quantifier
    contrasted with inner quantifier: 125
    definition: 125
    effect of on meaning: 125
    implicit on descriptors: 125
    in indefinite description: 127
outer quantifiers
    for expressing subsets: 126
    rationale for differences in implicit quantifier on descriptors: 126
outer sumti
    prenex for referring to from within relative clause within relative clause: 177
    referring to from within relative clause within relative clause: 177
PA selma'o
    exception on use of boi with MOI: 431
    members with rafsi: 441
paragraph separation
    spoken text: 449
    written text: 448
paragraphs
    effects on scope: 448
    separator: 448
parasitic worms
    example: 275
parentheses
    for complex mekso used as quantifier: 435
parenthesis
    mathematical: 419
partial quotation: 308
parts of speech: 50
passive voice: 20

past event
    possible extension into present: 215
pastward
    as a spatial tense: 216
paternal grandmother
    example: 55
pau
    placement in sentence: 308
pausative event contour: 219
pause
    and cmene: 67
    and consonant-final words: 66
    and Cy-form cmavo: 67
    and final-syllable stress: 67
    and non-Lojban text: 67
    and vowel-initial words: 67
    between words: 66
    contrasted with stop: 221
    contrasted with syllable break: 35
    proscribed within words: 66
    representation of in Lojban: 35
    requirement between stressed syllables: 52
    symbol for: 400
    word for: 400
pause before name
    effect of doi: 309
    effect of vocatives of COI: 309
pauses
    before vowels: 51
    rules for: 66
pe
    as loose association: 165
    compared with ne: 167
    compared with poi ke'a sranapoi ke'a srana: 165
    contrasted with po: 165
pe'u
    contrasted with e'o: 310
peace symbol: 408
percent
    as numerical punctuation: 416
perfective event contour: 219
perils of omitting terminators: 99
period
    definition of: 35
    example of: 36
    optional: 35
    quick-tour version: 17
    within a word: 35
personal pro-sumti: 134
    implicit cancellation of by change of speaker/listener: 155
    implicit quantifier for: 134
    stability of: 155
personal pronouns
    with ko'a-series for he/she/it/they: 144
    with mi-series for I/you: 140
personal pronouns for he/she/it/they
    English contrasted with Lojban in organization: 144
Pheidippides: 251
phonetic alphabet: 34

Phonetic Alphabet
  proposed lerfu words for: 412
physical distress
  example: 295
pi'u
  contrasted with .e: 342
  use in connecting tenses: 239
pictures
  credits for: 11
pinyin
  as a basis for Chinese characters in Lojban lerfu
  words: 403
piro
  explanation of meaning: 126
pisu'o
  explanation of meaning: 126
place structure
  adding new places to with modal sumti: 187
  definition: 179
  definition of: 16
  effect of FA on: 182
  effect of modal conversion on: 199
  empty slots in: 179
  explicitly mapping sumti to place with FA: 182
  gismu: 283
  instability of: 180
  leaving a sumti place unspecified in with zo'e: 182
  notation conventions: 179
  re-ordering by conversion: 96
place structure and tanru inversion: 91
place structure of selbri
  determining: 179
place structure order
  effect of FA on: 182
place structure questions: 184
place structures
  omitting places with FA: 183
  omitting places with zo'e: 182
plants
  use of fu'ivla for specific: 60
plausibility
  in abbreviated lujvo: 273
playgrounds: 270
pleases: 25
plural
  Lojban equivalent of: 425
plural masses
  possible use for: 126
plurals
  Lojban contrasted with English in necessity of
  marking: 117
plurals with le
  meaning of: 119
pluta
  contrasted with ve klama: 186
po
  as restrictive possession: 165
  compared with poi ke'a se steci sranapoi ke'a se steci
  srana: 165
  contrasted with English possession: 165

  contrasted with pe: 165
  contrasted with po'e: 166
po'e
  as intrinsic possession: 165
  compared with poi ke'a jinzi ke se steci sranapoi ke'a
  jinzi ke se steci srana: 165
  contrasted with po: 166
po'o
  placement in sentence: 305
po'u
  as identity: 166
  compared with no'u: 167
  compared with poi ke'a dupoi ke'a du: 166
  contrasted with no'u: 167
  relative phrase of contrasted with relativized sumti of:
  166
poi
  discussion of translation: 163
  dropping from multiple appearances on logical
  variables: 381
  syntax of: 162
point
  event considered as: 221
point-event abstraction
  place structure: 251
point-event abstractions
  definition: 250
  related tense contours: 261
point-event abstractor: 250
pointing
  reference by: 141
pointing cmavo
  quick-tour version: 17
police lineup: 431
Polish notation
  and mekso goals: 413
Polish notation mixed with infix: 436
  example: 436
politeness
  thank you and you're welcome: 310
  you're welcome: 310-311
portion
  on set contrasted with on individual: 126
portion selbri
  definition: 429
  place structure: 429
  place structure effect from subjective numbers: 430
positive numbers
  explicit expression: 415
positive sign
  contrasted with addition operator: 418
possessed in relative phrases
  compared with possessor: 167
possession
  expressing with po: 165
  intrinsic
    expressing with po'e: 165
  Lojban usage compared with French and German in
  omission/inclusion: 167

Lojban usage contrasted with English in omission/ inclusion: 167
  quick-tour version: 25
possession not ownership
  quick-tour version: 25
possessive sumti
  compared with relative phrase: 172
  contrasted with relative phrases in complexity allowed: 173
  definition: 172
  effect on elidability of ku: 173
  relative clauses on: 173
  syntax allowed: 173
  with relative clauses on possessive sumti: 173
possessive sumti and relative clauses
  development history: 173
possessive sumti with relative clauses
  effect of placement: 173
possessor in relative phrases
  compared with possessed: 167
possessor sumti
  definition: 172
potential
  expressing in past/future: 236
potential events
  expressing implicitly: 235
precedence
  mathematical default: 418
precise erasures: 464
predicate answers: 452
predication
  as a relationship: 15
  compared with bridi: 15
prenex
  considerations for dropping: 380
  dropping for terseness: 381
  effect of order of variables in: 380
  explanation: 377
  internal to a bridi: 385
  purpose of: 380
  removing when numeric quantifiers present: 382
  syntax of: 377
  use for outer sumti reference: 177
prenex manipulation
  exporting na from left of prenex: 389
  importing na from selbri: 389
  moving naku past bound variable: 389
  rules: 389
prenex scope
  for sentences joined by .i: 395
  for sentences joined by ijeks: 395
  in abstractions: 395
  in embedded bridi: 395
  in relative clauses: 395
  informal: 395
prepositions
  cmavo as Lojban equivalents: 50
pretty
  English ambiguity of: 83

pretty little girls' school
  forty ways: 108
previous topic: 449
primitive roots
  gismu as: 53
principle of consistency
  of logical-if statements: 321
pro-bridi
  as abbreviation for bridi: 145
  broda-series: 145
  compared to pro-sumti as means of abbreviation: 140
  definition: 140
  overriding sumti of antecedent bridi for: 145
  scope effect of new paragraph: 448
pro-bridi assignment
  explicit cancellation of with da'o: 156
  no'i effect on: 156
  stability of: 155
pro-bridi rafsi
  as producing context-dependent meanings: 157
pro-sumti
  and discursive utterances: 463
  as possessive sumti: 173
  classes of: 134
  compared to pro-bridi as means of abbreviation: 140
  compared to pronouns in usage as abbreviations: 140
  contrasted with description: 115
  definition: 140
  di'u-series: 142
  for listener(s): 140
  for listeners and/or speakers and/or others: 140
  for relativized sumti in relative clauses: 154
  for speaker(s): 140
  implicit quantifier for: 134
  ko'a-series: 144
  lerfu as: 145
  lerfu string
    effect on reference to lerfu itself: 405
  lerfu strings
    interaction with quantifiers and boi: 405
  mi-series: 140
  quick-tour version: 17
  rafsi for: 156
  referring to place of different bridi with go'i-series: 152
  referring to place of same bridi with vo'a-series: 152
  scope effect of new paragraph: 448
  series: 140
  ti-series: 141
  typical: 150
  unspecified: 150
  vo'a-series: 152
pro-sumti assignment
  explicit cancellation of with da'o: 156
  no'i effect on: 156
  stability of: 155
pro-sumti for "we"
  contrasted with English "we": 141
pro-sumti for speaker/listener/others
  as masses: 141

relation to joi: 141
pro-sumti for utterances: 142
pro-sumti rafsi
  anticipated use of for abbreviating inconvenient forms: 157
  effect of on place structure of lujvo: 156
probability selbri
  definition: 429
  place structure: 429
  place structure effect from subjective numbers: 430
  values: 429
process abstraction
  place structure: 251
process abstractions
  definition: 250
  related tense contours: 261
process abstractor: 250
process event
  described: 251
pronouns
  as anaphora: 148
  compared to pro-sumti in usage as abbreviations: 140
pronouns in English
  as independent of abbreviations: 139
  as noun abbreviations: 139
pronunciation
  IPA for Lojban: 35
  quick-tour version: 16
  relation to orthography: 33
  standard: 34
properties
  place structure: 253
property abstraction
  specifying sumti place of property with ce'u: 155
property abstractions
  specifying determining place by sumti ellipsis: 252
  specifying determining place with ce'u: 252
  sumti ellipsis in: 252
  use of multiple ce'u for relationship abstraction: 253
property description: 252
proposed law: 273
proposed lerfu words
  as working basis: 409
propositional
  of attitudinals: 289
propositional attitudes: 255
  compared with knowledge discursives: 306
protocol
  computer communications using COI: 311
  parliamentary using COI: 311
  using vocatives: 311
pu
  meaning as a sumti tcita: 223
  meaning when following interval specification: 214
PU selma'o
  compared with FAhA: 211
  contradictory negation of: 234
PU tenses
  contrasted with ZAhO tenses in viewpoint: 220

pu'o
  as pastward of event: 220
  derivation of word: 220
  explanation of derivation: 220
pu'u
  place structure: 251
punctuation
  in numbers: 415
  list of numerical: 444
punctuation lerfu words
  interaction with different alphabet systems: 403
  mechanism for creating: 403
  rationale for lau: 403
punctuation marks
  cmavo as Lojban equivalents: 50
qualified sumti
  contrasted with unqualified sumti: 128
quantification
  before description sumti compared with before non-description sumti: 124
quantificational pro-sumti: 134
  implicit quantification rules: 134
quantified space: 219
quantified sumti
  different types contrasted for scope for distribution: 383
quantified temporal tense
  definition: 218
  negating with nai: 219
quantified temporal tense with direction
  Lojban contrasted with English in implications: 218
quantified temporal tenses
  "once" contrasted with "only once": 219
  caveat on implication of: 219
quantified tenses
  as sumti tcita: 225
quantifier
  lerfu string as: 406
  on previously quantified variable: 395
quantifier scope
  in multiple connected sentences: 389
quantifiers
  effect of moving naku: 390
  with logical variables: 381
  with sumti: 124
question pro-sumti: 135
  implicit quantifier for: 136
questions
  answering with go'i: 148
  connection: 336
  digit: 431
  fill-in-the-blank: 451
  marking in advance: 308
  multiple: 452
  number: 431, 452
  operator: 439
  place structure position: 184
  quick-tour version: 26
  rhetorical: 308
  selbri: 153, 452

sumti: 153, 451
  truth: 451
  with "xu": 308
quotation
  contrasted with me'o for representing lerfu: 405
  contrasted with sentence abstraction: 256
  four kinds: 136
  implicit quantifier for: 136
quotations
  as possessive sumti: 173
  implicit quantifier for: 124
r-hyphen
  contrasted with n-hyphen in requirements for use: 59
  use of: 56, 59
ra'u
  scale of importance: 306
radio communication
  proposed lerfu words for: 412
radix
  decimal (see also base): 426
rafsi
  as fu'ivla categorizer: 60
  based on pro-sumti: 156
  considerations restricting construction of: 58
  contrasted with cmavo in usage: 60
  contrasted with same-form cmavo in meaning: 56
  contrasted with words: 60
  conventional meaning for cu'o: 441
  conventional meaning for frinu: 441
  definition: 55
    quick-tour version: 31
  forms of: 56
  four-letter
    requirement for y-hyphen: 59
  lack of
    effect on forming lujvo: 59
  level of uniqueness of relation to gismu: 56
  long: 56
  multiple for each gismu: 67
  multiplicity of for single gismu: 56
  possible forms for construction of: 57
  rationale for assignments of: 57
  rules for combining to form lujvo: 56
  selection considerations in making lujvo: 56
  short: 57
  uniqueness in gismu referent of: 56
  use of: 56
rafsi assignments
  non-reassignability of: 58
rafsi for numbers: 58
rafsi form
  effect of choice on meaning of lujvo: 55
rafsi fu'ivla: 76
rafsi space: 57
re-ordering logical variables with se: 381
real world
  contrasted with hypothetical world
    example: 307
real world point of view: 306
Received Pronunciation: 44

reciprocal
  expression of mathematical: 415
reciprocal pro-sumti: 152
reciprocity
  expressing with soi: 153
  expressing with vo'a-series pro-sumti and soi: 152
recital rooms: 270
redundancy
  effect on vocative design: 309
reference
  ambiguity of ti/ta/tu: 161
  and discursive utterances: 463
  quick-tour version: 24
  to relativized sumti with ke'a: 162
  use of relative clause for: 162
reference frame
  specifying for direction tenses: 216
reference frame for directions in tenses: 216
reference grammar: 10
referent
  of operand: 441
  referring to with la'e: 129
referent of pro-bridi
  definition: 140
referent of pro-sumti
  definition: 140
reflexive pro-sumti: 134, 152
  stability of: 155
relation of first places in logical connection of observatives
  rationale: 329
relationship
  active/static/attributive compared: 15
  as basis of sentence: 179
  objects of: 179
relationship abstraction: 253
relative clause
  compared with tanru: 164
  connecting to relative phrase with zi'e: 168
  contrasted with tanru: 164
  effect of omission of ke'ake'a on: 162
  restrictive (see also restrictive relative clause): 163
  use for reference: 162
relative clause scope
  extending to preceding sumti with vu'o: 175
relative clauses
  as part of name: 172
  effect of commas in English: 164
  effect on elidability of be'o: 91
  impact of indefinite sumti on placement: 172
  impact of la on placement: 172
  impact of LAhE on placement: 174
  impact of NAhE on placement: 174
  kinds of: 163
  list of cmavo for: 177
  on connected sumti: 174
  on names: 172
  on number: 174
  on possessive sumti: 173
  on quotation: 174

on vocative phrases: 176
  placement with vocative phrases: 176
  relative clauses within: 176
  restricted contrasted with incidental: 163
  restricted contrasted with incidental in English expression: 164
  syntax with indefinite sumti: 172
  use in restricting existential claims: 379
  use in restricting universal claims: 379
  use of ke'a for referral to relativized sumti in: 154
relative clauses and indefinite sumti
  placement considerations: 172
relative clauses and LAhE
  placement considerations: 174
relative clauses and NAhE
  placement considerations: 174
relative clauses and names
  placement considerations: 172
relative clauses and possessive sumti
  development history: 173
relative clauses on complex sumti
  Lojban contrasted with English: 175
relative clauses on indefinite sumti
  syntax considerations: 172
relative clauses on lo
  syntax suggestion: 172
relative clauses with possessive sumti
  effect of placement: 173
relative phrase
  as an abbreviation of a common relative clause: 165
  compared with possessive sumti: 172
  connecting to relative clause with zi'e: 168
  rationale for: 165
  syntax of: 165
relative phrases
  contrasted with possessive sumti in complexity allowed: 173
  contrasted with relative clauses in preciseness: 196
  improving preciseness with modals: 196
relative phrases with modals
  compared to relative clauses in preciseness: 196
relative pro-sumti: 135
relativity theory
  relation to Lojban tense system: 212
relativized sumti
  definition: 162
  in relative clauses within relative clauses: 177
remembered
  example: 303
repeating decimals
  expressing with numerical punctuation: 415
  marking start of repeating portion: 415
representing lerfu
  lu contrasted with me'o: 405
respectively
  specifying with fa'u: 340
  with different relationships: 342
restricted claims
  definition: 379

restricted variable
  compared with indefinite description: 382
restrictive relative clause
  definition: 163
resume
  contrasted with begin: 221
resumptive event contour: 219
revelation
  example: 303
reverse Polish notation
  and mekso goals: 413
  definition: 434
  marker: 434
  number of operands: 435
  operands of: 435
  parentheses in operands of: 435
  terminator: 434
  use of parentheses in: 434
  with too few operands: 435
  with too many operands: 435
reviewers of this book: 12
rhetorical question: 308
ri
  contrasted with ke'a in relative clauses: 154
ri-series pro-sumti: 148
  in narrative about quotation: 150
  in quotation series: 150
  in quotations: 150
right-grouping in tanru
  with bo: 84
right-grouping rule
  definition of: 84
righteous indignation
  example: 296
ro
  dropping from multiple appearances on logical variables: 381
  effect of order when multiple in sentence: 383
ro'anai
  example: 295
roger
  example: 311
ROI selma'o
  effect of ZAhO on fe'e flag: 223
  exception on use of boi before: 440
  scalar negation of: 235
romaji
  as a basis for kanji characters in Lojban lerfu words: 403
Roman Empire: 250
rounded numbers
  expressing: 425
rounded/unrounded vowels: 35
RP
  as abbreviation for reverse Polish notation: 434
ru'a
  compared with e'u: 304
sa
  interaction with bu: 400

sa'a
  editorial insertion of text already containing sa'a: 308
  interaction with li'o: 308
  interaction with sei: 308
  interaction with to'i: 308
Sapir-Whorf effects
  and emotional indicators: 315
sarcasm
  example: 306
  expressing: 306
scalar attitude: 293
scalar negation
  effect on selbri: 98
scalar negation of modals
  explanation of meaning: 200
scalar negation of non-logical connective: 343
scalar negation of tenses
  selma'o allowed with: 235
scale
  granular contrasted with continuous: 429
scale selbri
  definition: 429
  place structure: 429
  place structure effect from subjective numbers: 430
scientific names
  rules for: 65
scientific notation
  rationale for order of places: 432
  with gei: 432
score
  as 20-year span: 442
  as alternate base for years: 442
se
  as grammatical in JOI compounds: 339
  in logical connective to exchange sentences: 321
  order in logical connectives with na: 322
  use with operators: 440
  using to re-order logical variables: 381
se du'u: 256
se klama
  place structure of: 185
SE selma'o
  after 5th place: 454
  effect of multiple on a selbri: 186
  effect on place structure numbering: 185
  effect on selbri place structure: 185
  extending scope of: 186
  for converting place structure: 185
  rationale for no 1st place conversion: 185
  scope of: 186
  word formation of cmavo in: 185
se writing convention
  in eks: 324
se'e
  and number base convention: 408
se'u
  as elidable terminator for soi: 153
  elidability considerations: 153
section numbering: 439

selbri
  as part of description: 116
  brivla as: 79
  converting into an operand: 437
  converting into an operator: 437
  converting operator into: 439
  definition: 79, 179
    quick-tour version: 30
  lerfu string as: 406
  omitting with co'e: 151
  place structure of: 179
  place structure of converted operator: 439
  relation to bridi: 79
  scalar negation of: 98
  with GOhA: 93
selbri from sumti: 95
selbri list for quick tour: 17
selbri logical variables: 394
selbri place structure
  effect on operator formed by: 437
selbri placement among sumti
  effect of multiple quantification on: 391
selbri questions
  quick-tour version: 27
selbri variables
  form when not in prenex: 394
  prenex form as indefinite description: 394
  quantified: 394
selbri-first bridi
  effect on sumti places: 181
  effect on use of cu: 183
  specifying first sumti place in with fa: 182
self-orientation
  example: 296
selma'o
  cross-reference list of
    selma'o catalog: 467
  definition: 50
    quick-tour version: 31
seltau
  compared with English adjective: 54
  compared with English adverb: 54
  definition: 91
  definition of: 81
  effect on meaning of tanru: 81
  filling sumti places in: 89
seltcita sumti
  definition (see also modal sumti): 187
sentence
  basic Lojban: 179
sentences
  close grouping: 448
  connecting non-logically: 343
  connecting with tense: 230
  forethought tense connection of: 231
  separator for joining: 448
  tenseless
    quick-tour version: 29
separate questions
  quick-tour version: 27

separately tensed sentences
  contrasted with tense connected sentences: 231
sequence
  as an abstract list: 339
  contrasted with list: 339
  contrasted with set: 129
sequence of events
  expressing non-time-related sequences: 343
sequence of tense rules
  Lojban contrasted with English: 229
set
  as specified by members: 339
  by listing members with ce: 339
  compared with mass as abstract of multiple individuals: 121
  contrasted with mass in attribution of component properties: 121
  contrasted with mass in distribution of properties: 339
  contrasted with ordered sequence: 339
  expressing measurement standard for indefinites: 428
  expressing relation with individuals forming set: 428
  expressing relation with mass formed from set: 428
set operations: 341
sets
  properties of: 121
  rule for implicit outer quantifier: 125
  use in Lojban place structure: 121
sexual discomfort
  example: 295
sexual teacher
  male
    example: 71
shared bridi-tail sumti
  avoiding: 193
shellfish: 275
shift
  single-letter
    grammar of: 399
shift word
  for single letter: 399
  scope: 399
shift words
  canceling effect: 402
  for face: 402
  for font: 402
shoehorn: 270
short rafsi: 57
short rafsi form
  compared with long form in effect on lujvo meaning: 55
si
  interaction with bu: 400
signed numbers
  expressing: 415
signs on numbers
  grammar: 415
simple sumti: 115
sinful
  example: 296

single consonants
  contrasted with consonant clusters: 38
  contrasted with doubled consonants: 38
single-letter shift
  as toggle: 400
single-word quotation: 136
size
  order with dimensionality in spatial tense intervals: 216
slinku'i test
  definition: 61
slowdown: 251
smiley face
  example: 400
  word for: 400
soi
  use in expressing reciprocity: 153
  use in expressing reciprocity with vo'a-series pro-sumti: 152
soi with one following sumti
  convention: 152
somebody
  contrasted with somebody else: 377
something
  contrasted with someone: 379
  expressing using "su'o": 381
  unspecified definite with "zo'e": 376
sounds
  clarity of: 35
  complex: 35
  difficult: 35
sounds for letters
  Lojban contrasted with English: 35
source languages
  use in creating gismu: 71
space
  as time-based metaphor: 223
  contrasted with time in number of directions: 211
space intervals
  compared with time intervals in continuity: 222
space location
  as part of tense system (see also tense spatial tense): 208
space tenses
  quick-tour version: 30
space/time metaphor
  expressing direction mapping for: 223
spaghetti: 60
Spanish ch
  example: 403
Spanish ll
  example: 403
spatial contours
  as sumti tcita: 224
  contrasted with temporal event contours: 223
  expressing: 222
spatial directions
  list of: 245
spatial information
  adding to a sentence with tense sumti tcita: 223

spatial interval modifiers
  order in tense: 222
spatial intervals
  expressing degree of continuity over: 222
spatial tense
  4-dimensional interaction with temporal tense: 216
  as an imaginary journey: 209
  as optional in English: 209
  compared with temporal tense in elidability: 209
  contrasted with temporal in dimensionality: 215
  definition: 209
  direction: 209
  distance: 209
  four-dimensional: 216
  linear: 215
  one-dimensional: 215
  order relative to temporal: 211
  planar: 215
  reference frame: 209
  referent of: 209
  three-dimensional: 215
  two-dimensional: 215
spatial tense intervals
  order of size and dimensionality in: 216
  order of VEhA and VIhA in: 216
spatial tenses
  as sumti tcita: 223
  order of direction and distance specifications: 210
speaker's state of knowledge: 306
speaker-listener cooperation: 27
speaker-relative viewpoint
  contrasted with event-relative viewpoint: 220
specific descriptions: 117
specific terms
  use of fu'ivla for: 60
specificity
  expressing with po: 165
speech rhythm
  for grouping in English: 82
spelling out words
  Lojban contrasted with English in usefulness: 398
spiritual discomfort
  example: 295
square brackets
  use of in notation: 11
standard bridi form
  definition: 180
standard for subjective numbers
  specifying: 430
standard pronunciation: 34
starting marker: 464
state abstraction
  place structure: 251
state abstractions
  definition: 250
  related tense contours: 261
state abstractor: 250
state event
  described: 251
steady speed: 251

stereotypical
  as not derogatory in Lojban: 122
  compared with typical: 122
stereotypical objects: 122
sticky modals
  canceling: 201
  definition: 201
  fi'o proscribed from: 201
sticky tenses
  and CAhA: 236
  canceling: 227
  definition: 225
  effect of nau on: 230
  effect on future tense meaning: 225
  from part of a multiple tense: 226
stop
  contrasted with finish: 221
  contrasted with pause: 221
stories
  flow of time in: 227
story tense
  Lojban convention contrasted with English convention: 228
story time
  as a convention for inferring tense: 227
  definition: 227
  rationale for: 227
  tenseless sentences in: 227
  with no initial sticky time: 229
stress
  definition of: 42
  effect of buffer vowel on: 40
  effect of syllabic consonants on: 37
  example: 295
  final syllable
    rules for pause after: 67
  irregular marked with upper-case: 399
  levels of: 42
  on cmavo: 52
  primary: 42
  quick-tour version: 17
  rules for: 42
  secondary: 42
  showing non-standard: 33
stressed syllable
  compared with stressed vowel: 42
stressed vowel
  compared with stressed syllable: 42
structure of examples: 11
structure of this book: 10
structure words: 50
su
  interaction with bu: 400
su'e
  with elided number: 426
su'o
  as implicit quantifier for quotations: 124
  with elided number: 426
sub-subscripts: 432

subjective amounts
  expressing: 424
subjective numbers
  effect on place structure for cardinal selbri: 430
  effect on place structure for ordinal selbri: 430
  effect on place structure for portion selbri: 430
  effect on place structure for probability selbri: 430
  effect on place structure for scale selbri: 430
  rationale for effect on place structure: 430
  specifying standard for: 430
subjective portions
  expressing: 424
subordinate clause tense
  effect of main bridi tense on: 229
  Lojban compared with Esperanto: 229
  Lojban compared with Russian: 229
  Lojban contrasted with English: 229
subordinate clauses
  tense usage rules in English: 229
subscripted topics: 449
subscripting: 453
subscripts
  and fuzzy truths: 455
  and names: 455
  and paragraph separators: 455
  and pro-sumti: 454
  and sumti re-ordering: 454
  and tense: 455
  before main expression: 432
  effects on elidability of terminators: 432
  external grammar of: 431
  for sticky tense: 227
  internal grammar of: 431
  lerfu string as: 406
  mathematical: 455
  multiple as sub-subscript: 432
  multiple for same base word: 437
  on ke'a for nested relative clauses: 154
  terminator for: 432
  to form matrices of more than 2 dimensions: 434
  use with ke'a for outer sumti reference: 177
  use with logical variables: 395
subscripts on lerfu words
  effect on elidability of boi: 432
subsets
  expressing with outer quantifiers: 126
subtraction operator
  contrasted with negative sign: 417
subtypes of words: 52
sumti
  as having implicit quantifiers: 124
  as objects in place structure slots: 179
  beginning with "ke": 328
  between descriptor and description selbri: 172
  classified by types of objects referred to: 119
  converting into an operand: 438
  definition: 115, 179
    quick-tour version: 30
  descriptions as: 115
  dropping trailing unspecified: 181

explicitly mapping into place structure with FA: 182
  for individual objects: 119
  for mass objects: 119
  for set objects: 119
  forethought tense connection of: 232
  irrelevant to relationship: 151
  kinds of: 115
  multiple in one place with FA: 184
  names as: 115
  numbers as: 115
  omitted first place in selbri-first bridi: 181
  order in selbri: 181
  order in selbri-first bridi: 181
  pro-sumti as: 115
  quotations as: 115
  re-ordering with FA: 182
  relation with bridi: 15
sumti connection
  afterthought: 324
  forethought: 324
sumti into selbri: 95
sumti logical connection: 324
  compared with bridi logical connections: 324
  contrasted with tanru logical connection: 335
  rationale for: 324
sumti modal connection: 192
sumti placement
  variant
    quick-tour version: 19
sumti qualifiers
  as short forms for common special cases: 128
  elidable terminator for qualified sumti: 128
  external syntax of: 128
  for negation: 130
  internal syntax of: 128
  list of: 128
sumti questions
  quick-tour version: 26
sumti reordering
  quick-tour version: 20
sumti tcita
  based on event contours: 224
  based on spatial contours: 224
  based on tense direction: 223
  based on tense distance: 223
  based on tenses: 223
  definition (see also modal tag): 187
  event contours contrasted with direction/distance as basis for: 224
sumti tcita and linked sumti: 90
sumti tcita and modal tags: 90
sumti tcita and tense tags: 90
sumti tcita based on dimension: 225
sumti tcita based on event contours
  relation of main bridi to sumti process in: 224
sumti tcita based on interval continuousness: 225
sumti tcita based on interval properties: 225
sumti tcita based on interval size: 225
sumti tcita based on quantified tenses: 225

sumti with lo
  compared to indefinite sumti: 383
sumti with tense
  effect of main bridi tense on: 227
sumti with tenses
  quick-tour version: 30
sumti-based description
  definition: 127
  inner quantifier on: 127
  outer quantifier on: 127
sumti-based descriptions with le
  as increasing restricting to in-mind: 128
sunburn
  example: 252
superfective event contour: 219
superscripts: 432
supervising
  as a contribution to mass action: 338
supplementary information: 270
sword blade: 272
syllabaries
  lerfu word representation: 403
syllabic consonant
  effect on stress determination: 64
syllabic consonants: 37
  effect on stress: 37
  final in word: 37
syllabic l
  considered as a consonant for morphological
  discussions: 50
syllabic m
  as a consonant for morphological discussions: 50
syllabic n
  as a consonant for morphological discussions: 50
syllabic r
  as a consonant for morphological discussions: 50
syllabication
  and names: 42
  definition of: 41
  examples of: 42
  rules for: 41
syllable break
  contrasted with pause: 35
  representation in Lojban: 35
  symbol for: 400
  word for: 400
symbol
  for operand: 441
  referring to with lu'e: 129
symmetrical tanru: 107
symmetrical tanru types
  both separately true: 107
  one or other true: 108
  using crucial/typical parts: 108
  using more inclusive class: 108
symmetrical veljvo: 268
sympathy
  example: 301
ta
  contrasted with di'u: 143

tables
  format of: 11
tagged sumti termsets
  connecting with non-logical forethought connectives:
  342
TAhE selma'o
  effect of ZAhO on fe'e flag: 223
  scalar negation of: 235
tail-terms
  definition: 329
tanru
  ambiguity in: 55
  ambiguity of: 54, 81
  and abstractions: 248
  and conversion
    quick-tour version: 22
  and creativity: 54
  as ambiguous: 81
  asymmetrical: 101
  combination of: 54
  containing mathematical expressions: 94
  default left-grouping of: 82
  definition: 80
    quick-tour version: 31
  expanding: 305
  explanation of: 54
  explicating: 305
  explicitly defining: 305
  expression of: 55
  meaning of: 81
  place structure of: 264
    quick-tour version: 22
  place structures of: 89-90
  possible meanings of: 265
  primary meaning of: 81
  purpose: 264
  quick-tour version: 21
  reducing logically connected sumti to
    caveat: 335
  simple: 80
  to lujvo: 55
  with GOhA: 93
tanru and conversion: 96
tanru connection
  connotation of non-logical: 338
tanru connection grouping
  guheks unmarked tanru: 335
tanru conversion
  effect on place structure
    quick-tour version: 22
tanru default grouping
  quick-tour version: 21
tanru grouping
  complex: 83
  effect of jeks: 334
  effect of tanru inversion on: 92
  guheks compared with jeks: 335
  three-part: 82
  with bo: 84
  with ke: 84

with ke and bo: 85
tanru grouping with JA+BO
  effect on tanru grouping: 87
tanru inversion: 91
  definition: 91
  effect on tanru grouping: 92
  in complex tanru: 92
  multiple: 92
  rule for removing: 92
  where allowed: 92
tanru inversion and place structure: 91
tanru logical connection
  contrasted with sumti logical connection: 335
tanru nested within tanru: 82
technical terms: 11
telephone conversation
  hello: 310
television: 44
template: 258
temporal direction
  exception in meaning when following ze'e: 219
temporal information
  adding to a sentence with tense sumti tcita: 223
temporal tense
  as mandatory in English: 207
  compared with spatial tense in elidability: 209
  historical definition: 207
  interaction with 4-dimensional spatial tense: 216
  Lojban contrasted with English in necessity: 207
  order relative to spatial: 211
  quantified with direction: 218
  real relationship to time in English: 207
temporal tense elision
  compared with spatial tense elision in meaning: 209
temporal tenses
  compared with spatial tenses: 211
ten
  expressing as number: 414
tense
  aorist: 215
  as observer-based: 212
  as subjective perception: 211
  connecting sentences in with: 230
  contradictory negation contrasted with scalar negation of: 234
  effect of different position in sentence: 209
  effect of sticky tense on: 226
  emphasizing by position in sentence: 209
  explanation of presentation method: 207
  expressing movement in: 216
  handling multiple episodes: 227
  in forethought bridi-tail connection
    special rule: 350
  interval contrasted with point: 213
  Lojban contrasted with English in implications of completeness: 215
  Lojban contrasted with English in implying actuality: 235
  Lojban contrasted with native languages: 207
  numerical: 440

on embedded bridi: 227
order of direction
  distance and interval in: 213
order of direction specification in: 210
order of distance specification in: 210
order of movement specification in: 216
order of spatial interval modifiers in : 222
order of temporal and spatial in: 211
overriding to speaker's current: 230
point contrasted with interval: 213
position in sentence alternative: 208
position of in sentence: 208
quantified: 218
rationale for relative order of temporal and spatial in: 211
relation of interval to point specified by direction and distance: 213
relation of point specified by direction and distance to interval: 213
relative order with bridi negation: 100
scalar negation contrasted with contradictory negation of: 234
scalar negation of with NAhE: 234
scope effect of new paragraph: 448
scope of: 225
selbri types applicable to: 208
space-time dimension for intervals: 216
speaker's current: 230
specifying relation of interval to point specified by direction and distance: 213
static contrasted with moving: 216
subscripting: 227
sumti tcita form contrasted with connected sentences: 231
with both temporal and spatial: 212
with ku: 208
tense afterthought connection forms
  selma'o allowed: 232
tense and na
  multiple: 100
tense as sumti tcita
  contrasted with tense inside sumti: 225
tense cmavo
  position relative to selbri: 101
tense connected sentences
  contrasted with separately tensed sentences: 231
  forethought mode: 231
  importance of bo in: 231
tense connection
  equivalent meanings: 232
  expansions of: 232
tense connection of bridi-tails
  meaning of: 232
tense connection of sentences
  contrasted with sumti tcita form: 231
  order of: 231
tense connection of sumti
  meaning of: 232
tense conversion
  accessing original first place with fai: 240

accessing tense of bridi with jai: 239
of temporal tenses: 240
use in sumti descriptions: 240
with jai: 97
tense direction
as sumti tcita: 223
contrasted with event contours in implication of extent: 220
implications on scope of event: 215
tense direction/distance as sumti tcita
contrasted with event contours: 224
tense distance
as sumti tcita: 223
tense forethought connection forms
selma'o allowed: 232
tense in scope of sticky tense
compared with compound tense: 226
tense inside sumti
contrasted with tense as sumti tcita: 225
tense on main bridi
effect on embedded bridi tenses: 227
effect on embedded sumti with tenses: 227
tense questions
by using logical connective question: 243
methods of asking: 242
tense questions with ma: 242
tense selma'o
summary of: 244
tense sentence connection
table of equivalent schemata: 242
tense specification
effect on "cu": 208
effect on elidability of terminators: 208
tense system
and space location: 208
tense tags and sumti tcita: 90
tense with sumti tcita
asymmetry of: 230
tense-or-modal questions
pre-specifying some information: 243
with cu'e: 242
tensed connectives
in mathematical expressions: 350
tensed logical connection: 348
tensed logical connectives: 232
forethought: 350
in ek...bo: 349
in ek...ke: 349
in gihek...bo: 349
in gihek...ke: 349
in ijek...bo: 349
in ijek...tu'e: 349
in ijoik...bo: 349
in ijoik...tu'e: 349
in jek...bo: 349
in joik...bo: 349
in joik...ke: 349
with ke...ke'e: 233
with tu'e...tu'u: 233

tensed logically connected bridi-tails: 233
with grouping: 234
tensed logically connected sentences: 233
with grouping: 234
tensed logically connected sumti: 233
with grouping: 234
tensed non-logical connectives: 350
forethought: 350
tenseless sentences in story time: 227
tenses
compared with modals in syntax: 240
connected
with negation: 238
contradictory negation of with nai: 234
contrasted with modals in semantics: 240
forethought connection in: 348
forethought logical connections: 238
grouping of connectives in: 348
importance of 2nd sumti place for sumti tcita use: 241
logically connected with JA: 237
multiple in sentence: 226
multiple in sentence compared with compound tense: 226
negating: 234
non-logical connection of: 238
non-logical connection of for sub-events: 238
possible groupings of: 238
quick-tour version: 29
use as sumti tcita: 223
viewpoint of PU contrasted with viewpoint of ZAhO: 220
tenses with elided CAhA
meaning: 237
term
definition: 332
terminators
eliding ku in non-logical connections: 338
termset
effect on scope of multiple indefinite sumti: 383
formation: 332
termset logical connection
unequal length: 332
termset modal connection: 192
termsets
compared to fa'u: 341
non-logical connection of: 342
tertau
definition: 91
definition of: 81
effect on meaning of tanru: 81
text
division numbering with -mai: 440
sub-division numbering with -mai: 439
text quotation
as internally grammatical: 136
syntax of: 136
thank you
example: 310
the
contrasted with a/an: 308

example: 308
for talking about numbers themselves: 417
this
  adjective expression with ti noi: 142
  adjective expression with vi: 142
  adjective usage contrasted with pronoun usage: 142
  as utterance reference in English: 142
  pronoun expression with ti: 142
  pronoun usage contrasted with adjective usage: 142
this book
  author of: 11
  contributors to: 11
  credits for: 11
  examples of: 10
  goal of: 10
  reviewers of: 12
  structure of: 10
this/that in English
  compared with ti-series pro-sumti: 141
thus
  example: 303
ti
  as pronoun expression for English this: 142
ti noi
  as adjective expression for this: 142
ti-series pro-sumti
  3 degrees of distance with: 142
  as pointing referents only: 141
  compared with English this/that: 141
  contrasted with di'u-series pro-sumti: 143
  conversational convention for: 142
  lack of pro-bridi equivalent: 142
  problems in written text: 142
tilde
  a diacritical mark: 402
time
  as part of tense system (see also tense
    temporal tense): 208
  as space-based metaphor: 223
  contrasted with space in number of directions: 211
time tenses
  quick-tour version: 29
time travel: 217
times
  explicit expression of: 423
  implicit expression of: 423
title
  specifying with tu'e...tu'u: 448
to the market from the office: 332
to'o
  special note on direction orientation: 246
Tolkien
  and non-standard Lojban orthography: 47
too
  example: 304
too many rats
  example: 430
topic-comment
  description: 449

topic/comment
  multiple sentence: 450
tosmabru test: 68
toward right
  contrasted with on right: 216
transformations with logical connectives
  steps: 393
triumph: 250
truncation of number
  expressing: 425
truth
  in imperative sentences: 337
truth functions: 317
  16 possible: 318
  commutative: 319
  creating all 16 with Lojban's basic set: 319
  fundamental 4 in Lojban: 319
  relation to logical connectives: 319
  table of logical connectives: 351
truth questions: 308
  answering "no": 335
  answering "yes": 335
  as yes-or-no questions: 335
  contrasted with connection questions: 336
  simple: 335
truth table
  explanation: 318
truth tables
  abbreviated format: 318
  for 4 fundamental Lojban truth functions: 319
  list of 16 in abbreviated form: 318
  notation convention: 318
truth-value abstractions
  place structure: 255-256
ts-sound in Russian
  representation in Lojban: 35
tu
  archaic English yon as equivalent of: 142
tu'a
  as being deliberately vague: 129
  effect of on meaning: 129
  use for forming abstractions: 129
tu'e
  contrasted with bo for tensed logical connection: 350
  effect on di'e: 343
  use in lists: 343
tu'o
  for infix operations with too few operands: 432
types and subtypes of words: 52
typical
  compared with stereotypical: 122
typical objects
  and instantiation: 122
  determining characteristics of: 122
typical Smith
  example: 123
typical sumti: 150
typical value
  contrasted with elliptical value for sumti: 150

umlaut
a diacritical mark: 402
unabridged dictionary: 461
unconditional signal: 465
unconnected tanru
contrasted with logically connected version: 333
undemonstrated potential
expressing: 236
underscore notation for Quick Tour chapter: 16
unequal termset connection
compared with compound bridi connection with unequal separate bridi-tails: 333
unfilled places of inverted tanru: 92
Unicode: 408
union
of sets: 341
union of sets
compared with or: 341
units of measurement
expressing: 418
universal
mixed claim with existential: 378
universal claims
dangers of using: 380
explanation: 378
restricting: 379
unqualified sumti
contrasted with qualified sumti: 128
unreduced fractions
use in granular scales: 429
unreduced lujvo
definition: 56
unspecified breed
example: 269
unspecified direction
temporal contrasted with in spatial: 212
unspecified emotion: 298
unspecified level of emotion: 298
unspecified sumti
non-trailing: 181
using zo'e as place-holder for: 182
unspecified trailing sumti
dropping: 181
unstated emotion: 298
unusual characters
words for: 400
unvoiced consonants
contrasted with voiced in allowable consonant pairs: 40
unvoiced vowel glide
apostrophe as: 35
upper-case
lerfu word for: 399
upper-case letters
English usage contrasted with Lojban: 399
Lojban usage contrasted with English: 399
utterance
expressing relation to discourse: 304
utterance ordinal
lerfu string as: 406

utterance pro-sumti
stability of: 155
utterance pro-sumti (see also di'u-series pro-sumti): 142
utterances
non-bridi: 453
uy diphthong
in cmene: 64
V
as a symbol for a single vowel: 49
VA selma'o
and distance: 209
relation of words to ti ta, tu: 209
va'i
contrasted with ke'u: 306
vague abstraction: 258
vague abstractions
place structure: 258
vague abstractor: 258
vague relationship
modal tag for: 189
valid speech
marking as error with jo'a: 308
variables
logical: 377
vau
effect on elidability ku'o: 173
vau for shared bridi-tail sumti
avoiding: 193
ve klama
contrasted with pluta: 186
vector
components of: 433
definition: 433
vector indicator: 433
terminator for: 433
vectors
use as operands: 434
use of parentheses with: 434
veljvo
symmetrical: 267
verbs
brivla as Lojban equivalents: 52
vi
as adjective expression for English this: 142
vi'o
contrasted with je'e: 311
vice versa
English
expressing with vo'a-series pro-sumti and soi: 152
virtue
example: 296
vo'a-series pro-sumti
use in expressing reciprocity with soi: 152
vocative phrase
effect of position on meaning: 132
elidable terminator for: 132
explicit quantifiers prohibited on: 131
forms of: 131
implicit descriptor on: 131

implicit quantifiers on: 131
purpose of: 130
with complete sumti: 131
with sumti without descriptor: 131
vocative phrase terminator
elidability of: 132
vocative phrase with name
placement of relative clause on: 176
vocative phrase with selbri
placement of relative clause on: 176
vocative phrases
as a free modifier: 130
relative clauses on: 176
vocative word
phrase following: 131
vocatives
and definition of "you": 309
contrasted with "la": 309
definition: 309
grammar overview: 309
notation convention symbol "X": 309
quick-tour version: 25
rationale for redundancy: 309
voiced consonants
contrasted with unvoiced in allowable consonant pairs: 40
voiced/unvoiced consonants
restrictions on: 39
vowel
buffer: 40
vowel buffer
contrasted with y sound: 41
vowel pairs
contrasted with diphthongs: 38
definition of: 38
grouping of: 38
involving y: 38
list of: 38
use of apostrophe in: 38
vowel-initial words
necessity for pause before: 67
vowels
contrasted with consonants: 36
definition of: 37
length of: 41
pronunciation of
quick-tour version: 16
vu'i
effect of on meaning: 129
use for creating sequence: 129
VUhU operands: 418
VV string
as a symbol for a double vowel: 49
whole time interval
expressing: 219
wine-dark sea: 264
word classes: 50
word forms
as related to grammatical uses: 49
in Lojban (see also morphology): 49

word quotation
as morphologically valid: 136
internal grammar of: 136
words not in the dictionary: 18
wrong concept: 270
x1
in place structure notation: 179
notation convention
quick-tour version: 18
y
considered not to be a vowel for morphological discussions: 49
letter
between letters of consonant pair: 53
prohibition from fu'ivla: 61
use in avoiding forbidden consonant pairs: 39
y sound
contrasted with vowel buffer: 41
y-hyphen
and consonant cluster determination: 56
and stress determination: 56
use of: 56
yes/no questions: 308
quick-tour version: 27
yielding the floor: 465
yon
as archaic English equivalent of tu: 142
you
defining: 309
you're welcome
fi'i contrasted with je'e: 310
je'e contrasted with fi'i: 310
you-cmavo
example: 156
you-talk
example: 156
za'e
interaction with bu: 400
use to avoid lujvo misunderstandings: 67
za'i
place structure: 251
za'u
with elided number: 426
ZAhO selma'o: 224
contradictory negation of: 234
effect on fe'e flag for TAhE and ROI: 223
ze'e
effect on following PU direction: 219
ze'eba
meaning of: 219
ze'eca
meaning of: 219
ze'epu
meaning of: 219
ze'o
special note on direction orientation: 246
zei
interaction with bu: 400
zero
relation to negation boundary: 387

ZI selma'o
  compared with VA: 211
zi'e
  compared with English and: 168
  contrasted with logical connectives: 168
  use in connecting relative phrase/clause to relative phrase/clause: 168
zi'o: 151
  as creating new selbri: 151
zi'o rafsi
  effect of on place structure of lujvo: 157
Zipf's Law: 67
zo
  interaction with bu: 400
zo'e
  as a translation for "something": 376

as place-holder for sumti: 150
as place-holder for unspecified sumti: 182
compared with FA for omitting places: 183
contrasted with da: 377
zo'e-series
  compared with do'i as indefinite pro-sumti: 152
zo'e-series pro-sumti: 150
zo'i
  special note on direction orientation: 246
zoi
  interaction with bu: 400
zu'a
  derivation of word: 209
zu'o
  place structure: 251

Lojban Words Index

.a: 50, 325, 351
.a'enai: 290
.a'o: 286
.a'u: 343
.a'ucu'i: 291
.abu: 398, 400, 404-406, 409-411
.ai: 286, 311
.au: 50, 286, 297
.e: 50, 324, 351
.ebu: 398, 402, 409-411
.ei: 50, 286
.eicai: 294
.eicu'i: 294
.einai: 294
.eiru'e: 294
.eisai: 294
.i: 50, 320, 323, 326, 338, 343, 348
.i'anai: 292
.i'enai: 292
.i'inai: 300
.ia: 50-51, 286, 289
.ianai: 286, 292, 306
.ibu: 51, 398, 403, 409-411
.ie: 51, 286, 289, 311
.ienai: 367
.ii: 51, 286, 293
.ija: 388
.ije: 388, 395
.ijebabo: 348
.io: 51, 286, 296
.iu: 51, 286
.o: 50, 351
.obu: 398, 409-411
.oi: 286, 288, 293, 298
.oinai: 298
.onai: 436
.u: 50, 351
.u'u: 288
.u'unai: 297
.ua: 51, 286
.uanai: 307
.ubu: 398, 410-411
.ue: 51, 286
.ui: 51, 286, 400, 462
.uinai: 367
.uo: 51, 286, 288
.uu: 51, 286, 288
.y'y: 398, 410-411
.y'y.: 38, 398
.y.: 51, 465-466
.y.bu: 407, 410-411
.ybu: 398
a: 320, 325, 351, 388
A selma'o: 324, 338, 346, 349, 435
a'e: 290
ai: 426
ai.: 136

au: 426
ba: 30, 50, 149, 211, 214, 220, 226, 233, 238, 241, 347-348
ba'a: 303
ba'acu'i: 303
ba'anai: 303
ba'e: 400, 461
ba'o: 220, 227, 261
bai: 194-195, 201, 332
bai ke: 195
BAI selma'o: 199
bajra: 17
bakrecpa'o: 274
bakri: 57
balsoi: 267-268, 271, 277
balvi: 211, 241
bangu: 133
banli: 267-268, 271
bapu: 348
barda: 81
basti: 278
basygau: 278
batci: 381
bau: 194, 199, 201
bavla'i: 272
bavlamdei: 272
baxso: 75
be: 88-93, 98, 100, 189, 264, 361, 364, 392, 453, 462
be'a: 222
be'o: 88-92, 96, 99, 264
be'u: 297
bei: 88-92, 98, 264, 361, 392, 453, 462
bemro: 75
bengo: 75
bi'e: 419, 436
bi'i: 343-344, 346-347
bi'o: 238, 343-344, 346, 436
bi'u: 308-309
bi'unai: 308-309
BIhI selma'o: 346
bilma: 60
bindo: 75
birka: 166
blabi: 170
blaci: 57-58
blakanla: 274
blanu: 89, 91, 308, 372
blari'o: 17, 24
blaselkanla: 274
blolei: 70
bloti: 70, 142
bo: 82-88, 92, 98, 108, 128, 130, 191, 231-233, 264, 326-327, 330, 334, 342, 346, 348-350, 362, 441, 448, 457
BO selma'o: 435
boi: 347, 405-406, 420-421, 431-432, 434, 440, 455
bradi: 73
brazo: 75
bredi: 73

bridi: 16, 30, 44, 73, 253
brito: 75
brivla: 24, 31, 42, 52, 56, 59
broda: 53, 73, 145, 455
brode: 53, 73, 145, 455
brodi: 53, 73, 455
brodo: 53, 73, 455
brodu: 53, 73, 455
bu: 398, 400-401, 403, 407, 409, 466
bu'a: 157, 394-395
bu'e: 394-395
bu'i: 394-395
bu'o: 301
bu'ocu'i: 301
bu'onai: 301
bu'u: 212
bubu: 400
budjo: 76
by: 398, 409-410
by.: 60, 398, 404
ca: 30, 211, 214, 223, 230, 236, 347
ca'a: 236
ca'e: 303
ca'o: 220, 261
cabna: 211
cadzu: 97-98, 100, 275
cafne: 260
cagyce'u: 106
cai: 293-294
cakcinki: 270
calku: 270
carmi: 293
casnu: 342
ce: 50, 339
ce'a: 402-403
ce'e: 202, 332, 383
ce'i: 415, 441
ce'o: 339, 343, 347, 437
ce'u: 154-155, 252-254
cei: 145, 148, 155
centi: 73
ci: 123, 126, 417-418, 420, 434
ci'ajbu: 106
ci'e: 372
ci'u: 197, 283, 364-365, 372
cidja: 61
cidjrspageti: 61
cinfo: 283
cinki: 270, 284
cipnrstrigi: 108
cirla: 62
ciste: 364, 372
citka: 277
citmau: 281
citno: 280-281
ckule: 82, 90, 270
cladakfu: 272
cladakyxa'i: 107, 272-273
clani: 272
cliva: 270

cmaci: 62
cmalu: 81-82, 84, 90
cmaro'i: 104
cmavo: 20, 31, 42, 53, 73
cmene: 63
cmima: 421
co: 91-92, 362
co'a: 220, 223, 261
co'e: 151-152, 157, 159
co'i: 221, 261
co'o: 25, 367
co'u: 220, 261
coi: 25, 50, 131
COI selma'o: 140, 175, 309
coico'o: 310
cpumi'i: 102
cribe: 118
ctigau: 277-278
cu: 18, 20, 23-24, 28, 30, 119, 180, 183, 194, 208, 248, 355, 367
cu'e: 242-243, 453
cu'i: 286, 288, 293-294
cu'o: 429, 441-442
cu'u: 50, 196
cumki: 293
cunso: 441, 445
cusku: 196, 279, 459
cutci: 17
cuxna: 339
cy: 399, 410-411
cy.: 51, 398
da: 134, 257, 330, 356, 377-383, 385, 389-391, 394-395, 454
DA selma'o: 454
da'a: 423-424, 441
da'e: 135, 143
da'i: 306
da'inai: 306
da'o: 156, 448, 466
da'u: 135
dadgreku: 103
dadjo: 76
dadysli: 102
dai: 64-65, 133, 301
dakfu: 272
dalmikce: 272
danlu: 272
de: 134, 356, 377-380, 382-383, 390-391, 394-395
de'a: 221, 261
de'e: 135, 143
de'i: 197
de'u: 135
decti: 73
dei: 135, 143
dejni: 331
dekto: 74
delno: 74
denci: 107
denpa: 400
di: 50, 134, 356, 377, 379, 381-382, 394-395
di'a: 221, 261

di'e: 135, 143, 343
di'i: 217
di'inai: 218
di'u: 24-25, 135, 143
dinju: 62
djedi: 272
djica: 274, 450-451
djine: 411
djuno: 256-257
do: 25, 28, 90, 126-127, 134, 140-142, 145, 149, 156-157, 184, 278, 292, 309, 329, 462
do'a: 306
do'anai: 306
do'e: 152, 189, 202, 204
do'i: 64-65, 133, 135, 143, 152
do'o: 134, 140
do'u: 132, 309
doi: 25, 64-65, 67, 131, 133, 154, 157, 309-310, 453, 460
DOI selma'o: 175
donma'o: 156
donta'a: 156
dotco: 75
du: 94-95, 156-157, 222, 417-418, 421, 442
du'e: 297, 424, 430
du'i: 197
du'u: 256
dubjavmau: 421
dubjavme'a: 421
dunda: 184, 329, 331
dunli: 156, 421
dy: 409-410
dy.: 398
dzipo: 75
dzukla: 275, 333
e: 337, 340, 351, 388, 464
e'e: 298
e'o: 310
e'u: 44, 304
ei: 426
fa: 182-184
fa'a: 246
fa'o: 311, 400, 465-466
fa'u: 339-340, 452
fadni: 121
fagri: 264
fagyfesti: 264
FAhA selma'o: 235
fai: 184, 199-200, 240, 277
fasnu: 204
fau: 204
fe: 90, 182, 184
fe'a: 436
fe'e: 222-224
fe'o: 311
fe'u: 187, 195
femti: 74
festi: 264
fi: 90, 182, 184, 329
fi'a: 184, 199, 453
fi'e: 196

fi'i: 310
fi'o: 187, 195, 201
fi'u: 415, 441
filso: 75
finti: 196
firgai: 106
flalu: 273
fo: 50, 90, 182-183, 430
fo'a: 134, 157-158
fo'e: 134, 158
fo'i: 134, 158
fo'o: 134
fo'u: 134
foi: 402-404, 409
fraso: 75
friko: 75
frinu: 441
fu: 90, 182
fu'a: 434
fu'e: 457, 466
fu'i: 297
fu'ivla: 31
fu'o: 457, 466
fy: 406, 410, 464
fy.: 398, 421, 441
ga: 322, 351, 392-393
GA selma'o: 324, 346, 435
ga'e: 399
ga'i: 296
ga'icu'i: 296
ga'inai: 296
ga'o: 344-345, 347, 437
gadri: 115
GAhO selma'o: 238, 345-346
galfi: 278
galtu: 411
ganai: 323-324
ganlo: 345
gapru: 411
gasnu: 277-278, 283
gau: 189
ge: 70, 351, 392-393
ge'a: 432-433, 435
ge'e: 298-300, 309
ge'i: 337, 453
ge'o: 401
ge'u: 145, 168
gei: 432-433, 435
gekmau: 275
gento: 75
gerku: 18, 70, 146, 170, 265-266, 268-269, 279-280
gerzda: 70, 266, 268-271, 274
gi: 88, 100, 192, 231, 322-324, 336, 346, 351-352, 392-393
GI selma'o: 320
gi'a: 351
gi'e: 271, 320, 328, 337, 351
gi'i: 453
gi'o: 351
gi'u: 351
gigdo: 74

GIhA selma'o: 330, 349
girzu: 71, 421
gismu: 16, 31, 53, 72
gleki: 275
glico: 74, 459
go: 351
go'a: 146, 148
go'e: 148-149
go'i: 24, 27, 93-94, 146, 148-149, 305, 335-336, 369
go'o: 149
go'u: 146, 148
gocti: 74
GOhA selma'o: 140
goi: 134, 144-147, 155, 404, 454
gotro: 74
gu: 50, 320, 323, 351
gu'a: 351
gu'e: 88, 100, 351
gu'i: 337, 453
gu'o: 351
gu'u: 351
GUhA selma'o: 334-335, 346
gy: 409-410, 459, 464
gy.: 146, 398, 464
i: 21, 47, 191-192, 230-231, 303-304, 320-322, 336, 343, 351-352, 388, 395, 447-448, 457, 464
I selma'o: 322, 349
i'a: 289
i'e: 289, 292
ja: 87, 108, 320, 323, 326, 351, 388, 421
JA selma'o: 237, 320-322, 334-335, 338, 346, 349-350
ja'a: 369, 453, 455
ja'e: 189
ja'o: 303
jai: 97, 199-200, 239, 260, 276-277, 459
jbena: 283
jdaselsku: 271, 279
jdika: 280, 282
je: 85-88, 107-109, 198, 202, 243, 264, 326, 338, 348, 351, 388
je'a: 369-370
je'e: 310-311
je'enai: 311, 367
je'i: 453
je'o: 401
je'u: 306
je'unai: 306
jegvo: 76
jei: 254-256, 455
jelca: 308
jenai: 243
jerxo: 75
ji: 453
ji'a: 304
ji'i: 424-425
ji'u: 372
jibni: 421
jinvi: 351
jitro: 279
jo: 87, 109, 351

jo'a: 307-308, 373
jo'e: 339, 341
jo'i: 433, 437
jo'o: 401
jo'u: 339-340, 343
joi: 88, 338-340, 343, 400
JOI selma'o: 238, 320, 342-343, 345-346, 349, 436
jordo: 75
ju: 87, 351
ju'a: 304
ju'o: 306
ju'u: 426-427
jundi: 268
jungo: 74
jy: 410
jy.: 398
ka: 64, 154, 253, 276
ka'a: 188
ka'e: 236
ka'o: 416
ka'u: 303
kadno: 75
kai: 372
kalri: 345
kalselvi'i: 103
kambla: 276
kanji: 403
kanla: 187, 274
kanro: 18
karce: 268
karcykla: 268
kau: 257
ke: 71, 84-86, 88, 92, 97-99, 108, 186, 199, 233, 264, 274-275, 327-328, 330, 334, 342, 346, 349-350, 361-362, 369, 435, 448, 457
ke'a: 135, 154-155, 162, 0, 162-163, 177
ke'e: 84-86, 88, 92, 97-99, 108, 186, 199, 233, 264, 274-275, 327, 330, 334, 346, 361-362, 369, 435, 448
ke'i: 344-345, 347, 437
ke'o: 311
ke'u: 305-306
ke'unai: 306
kei: 94, 247-248, 259, 276
kelvo: 74
ketco: 75
ki: 201, 225-228, 236, 245
ki'a: 50, 307, 311, 371
ki'o: 416
ki'u: 189, 198
kilto: 74
kisto: 75
klama: 17, 22, 97-98, 179-182, 185-186, 188, 249, 264, 270, 275, 284, 333, 360, 362, 384, 454
klesi: 70
ko: 25-26, 116, 124, 134, 141, 337
ko'a: 134, 144-145, 148, 156, 177, 404
ko'e: 134, 177, 404
ko'i: 134
ko'o: 134
ko'u: 134

krasi: 205
krecau: 363
krici: 351
krinu: 189
ku: 23-24, 91, 96, 119, 127, 170-173, 194, 208, 210, 223, 338, 452
ku'a: 339, 341
ku'e: 420-421, 436
ku'i: 304, 338
ku'o: 162-163, 170-171, 173, 379
kuarka: 62
kuldi'u: 270
kurji: 18
ky: 43, 409-411
ky.: 398
la: 17, 64-65, 67, 96, 115, 117, 120-121, 125-126, 132-134, 172, 309, 408, 460-461, 464
LA selma'o: 185
la'e: 129, 143, 174, 405, 441, 460
la'edi'u: 25, 143
la'i: 67, 121, 125, 132-133, 460
la'o: 60, 65, 400, 460
la'u: 243, 372
ladru: 107
lai: 64-65, 67, 120-121, 125, 132-133, 460
lanme: 279
lantro: 280
latmo: 76
lau: 403
le: 24-25, 52, 91, 115-119, 125-127, 131, 149, 169-171, 248, 309, 338, 363, 371, 376, 383, 418, 465
LE selma'o: 185, 240
le'a: 364, 372
le'e: 122-123, 125-126
le'i: 121-122, 125
le'o: 296
le'u: 115, 136, 457-460, 466
lebna: 329, 331
lei: 64, 120-121, 125
lerfu: 62, 397-398
lervla: 398
li: 115-116, 136-137, 417-418, 430, 435-436, 438-439, 442
li'i: 258
li'o: 308
li'u: 116, 136, 405, 457-458, 465
libjo: 75
lijda: 279
lijgri: 102
liste: 339
litki: 278
litru: 270
lo: 117-118, 120-122, 125-127, 135-137, 169-172, 363, 371, 383, 436
lo'a: 401-402
lo'e: 122-123, 125-126
lo'i: 121-122, 125, 428
lo'o: 436
lo'u: 136, 400, 457-460, 464, 466
logji: 133
loi: 120-121, 125, 169

lojban.: 53
lojbangirz: 71
lojbaugri: 71
lojbo: 73
lu: 115-116, 136, 405, 457-458, 465
lu'a: 126, 129
lu'e: 129, 256, 441, 460
lu'i: 129
lu'o: 129
lu'u: 128, 174, 260
lubno: 75
lujvo: 31, 55, 73
ly: 64-65, 133, 409-411
ly.: 398
ma: 26-27, 135, 153-154, 242, 257, 451-452
ma'a: 134, 140-141
ma'i: 216, 430
ma'o: 406, 421, 434, 440-441
ma'u: 415, 418, 424-425
mabla: 295
mai: 440, 456
mamta: 58, 89
matne: 120
mau: 196-197
me: 95-96, 407, 430
me'a: 196-197
me'i: 425
me'o: 137, 405, 438-439, 442
me'u: 95-96, 430-431
megdo: 74
mei: 340, 428, 441-442
mekso: 73
melbi: 17, 83-84
meljo: 75
merko: 75, 407
mexno: 75
mi: 23, 28, 90, 92, 115-116, 124, 134, 140-142, 145, 148, 150, 156, 164, 173, 180, 182, 184-185, 199, 296, 311, 331, 333, 362, 428
mi'a: 134, 140-141
mi'e: 140, 309-311
mi'enai: 311
mi'i: 343-344, 437
mi'o: 50, 124, 134, 140-141
mi'u: 304
midju: 411
mikce: 272
mikri: 73
milti: 73
minde: 280
misro: 75
mlatu: 88
mleca: 196, 280-282, 421
mo: 27, 153-154, 361, 439, 452
mo'a: 297, 424, 430
mo'e: 254, 438, 442
mo'i: 216-217, 245
mo'o: 440, 456
mo'u: 261
moi: 429-431, 441-442

MOI selma'o: 94
mojysu'a: 106
mokca: 411
molro: 74
morko: 75
mrostu: 106
mu: 123, 171, 431, 434
mu'e: 250-251, 261
mu'i: 189, 240
mu'onai: 311
mukti: 189, 240-241
mulgri: 102
muslo: 76
my: 149, 409-411
my.: 398
na: 28, 100, 320-325, 330-331, 334-336, 351-352, 355-357, 360, 367-369, 371, 385, 388-393, 421, 453, 455
na'a: 402
na'e: 98-100, 200, 275, 360-365, 368, 370-371
na'i: 307-308, 371-372
na'o: 217
na'u: 437, 439-440
na'ujbi: 421
NAhE selma'o: 174, 234, 440
nai: 288, 293, 295, 298-299, 309, 320, 322-324, 330, 334, 343, 345-346, 351-352, 366-367, 388, 392, 453, 466
naja: 87, 109
nakykemcinctu: 71
namcu: 421
nanmu: 175, 189, 335, 394
nanvi: 73
nau: 230
ne: 167, 196-197
nei: 149
ni: 254-255, 437
ni'e: 437-438, 440
ni'i: 189
ni'o: 21, 156, 448-449, 455, 457
ni'u: 415, 420, 424-425
nibli: 189
nimre: 80
ninmu: 335
nitcu: 384
nixli: 82, 90
no: 44-45, 135, 337, 387, 414, 423, 427
no'a: 149
no'e: 365
no'i: 156, 448-449, 455, 457
no'o: 423
no'u: 167
nobli: 65
noda: 387
noi: 162-164, 167-168, 172, 196
nolraitru: 103
nu: 247-251, 264, 276-277, 454
NU selma'o: 94, 260, 350
nu'a: 94, 439
nu'e: 310
nu'i: 193, 243, 333, 383
nu'o: 236

nu'u: 193, 243, 333, 383
nuncti: 108, 277
nunctu: 101
nunkla: 276, 454
ny: 409-411, 419-420
ny.: 398, 407
o: 351
o'u: 50, 295
pa: 65, 123, 382, 415, 420, 422-423, 426, 430-431
pa'e: 306
pa'enai: 306
pacru'i: 108
pagbu: 421
pai: 416
pamoi: 98, 430
paso: 427
patyta'a: 59
pau: 308, 453
paunai: 308
pe: 165, 167, 172-173, 196
pe'a: 308
pe'e: 332-333
pe'i: 29, 304
pe'o: 421
pei: 50, 293, 300-301, 453
pelnimre: 80
pelxu: 80
petso: 74
pi: 126, 415-416, 423-424, 426-427, 441
pi'a: 433-434
pi'e: 427
pi'i: 418-419, 434
pi'o: 188
pi'u: 239, 339, 341
picti: 74
pilno: 187-188, 280
piro: 123, 125-126, 423, 426
piso'a: 423
piso'u: 423
pisu'o: 123, 126, 134, 426
pluka: 18
pluta: 186
po: 165
po'e: 165-166
po'o: 305
po'u: 166-167
poi: 162-164, 168-170, 196, 371, 379-381
polno: 75
ponjo: 75
ponse: 451
porto: 75
prenu: 81, 119, 417
pritu: 411
pu: 30, 100, 208-209, 211, 215, 220, 223, 225-227, 230, 332, 347-348
pu ge: 350
PU selma'o: 219, 235
pu'i: 236
pu'o: 220, 261
pu'u: 250-251, 261

puba: 227
purci: 211
py: 409-411
py.: 398
ra: 130, 135, 146-148
ra'a: 205
ra'e: 415
ra'i: 205
ra'o: 149-150
ra'u: 306
ra'ucu'i: 306
ra'unai: 306
radno: 74
rafsi: 31, 53, 55
rakso: 75
ralju: 65
rau: 297, 424, 430
re: 52, 123-124, 127, 171, 194, 340, 411, 420, 425, 434
re'i: 310
re'inai: 310
re'u: 219, 222
reroi: 239
ri: 129-130, 135, 146-148, 154, 450, 458
ri'a: 189-191, 201
ri'e: 297
ricfu: 329
rinka: 189, 191-192, 260, 278, 283, 323
risna: 308
ro: 124-127, 134-135, 171, 378, 380-383, 386, 389, 405, 422-423, 426, 441
ro'anai: 295
ro'e: 295
ro'o: 343
ro'u: 298
roi: 217-219, 440
romai: 456
ropno: 75
ru: 135, 146-148
ru'a: 29, 304
ru'e: 293
ru'i: 217-218
ru'inai: 218
ru'o: 401
ruble: 293
rusko: 74
ry: 410-411
ry.: 398
sa: 299, 400, 458, 464-466
sa'a: 308, 372, 462-463
sa'enai: 306
sa'i: 433-434
sa'unai: 306
sadjo: 75
sai: 343
sakli: 57
salci: 58
sanli: 344
saske: 62

se: 20, 23, 34, 96-97, 185, 188, 195, 197, 203, 264, 274-275, 320-322, 324, 330, 334, 339, 344-346, 351-352, 381, 390-392, 429, 440, 454
SE selma'o: 96, 199, 239, 454
se te: 186
se'a: 297
se'e: 408
se'i: 297
se'o: 303
se'u: 153, 462-463
seba'i: 197
sei: 308, 314, 440, 462-463
seja'e: 189
seka'a: 188
selbri: 16, 30, 179
selkla: 275
selma'o: 31, 50
selsku: 279
seltau: 81, 264
selti'i: 273
selti'ifla: 273
semau: 197
seme'a: 197
semto: 76
sepi'o: 188
seri'a: 190
sfofa: 44
si: 299, 400, 458-459, 463-466
si'a: 304
si'e: 429, 442
si'o: 258
since: 62
sinso: 74
sinxa: 129
sirxo: 75
sisti: 373
skari: 372
skoto: 75
slaka: 400
slovo: 76
so'a: 422, 424, 441
so'e: 422-423, 441
so'i: 422, 441
so'imei: 108
so'o: 422, 441
so'u: 422, 441
softo: 75
soi: 152-153
solri: 65
solxrula: 104
sonci: 267-268
spageti: 62
spano: 74
sralo: 75
srana: 205
srito: 76
stali: 18
steci: 165
stero: 74
stidi: 273

stura: 421
su: 299, 400, 458, 465-466
su'a: 303, 306
su'anai: 303
su'e: 425, 441
su'i: 94, 418, 434, 439, 442
su'o: 124-126, 134-137, 171, 381-382, 386, 394, 425-426, 441
su'u: 258-259
sudysrasu: 104, 108
sumti: 16, 30, 179
sutra: 17, 80-81, 93, 98-99
sy: 410-411
sy.: 53, 398
ta: 17, 135, 141-143, 161, 209
ta'e: 217, 357
ta'onai: 306
ta'u: 305
ta'unai: 305
tai: 205
tamdu'i: 421
tamsmi: 205
tanjo: 74, 437
tanru: 21, 31, 81
tarmi: 62, 206, 421
tau: 399-400
tavla: 17-18, 22-23
te: 20, 23, 96, 203
te'a: 419
te'o: 416, 425
te'u: 433, 437, 441-442
teci'e: 364
tei: 402-404, 409
teka'a: 188
terbi'a: 103
tergu'i: 103
terkavbu: 101
tertau: 81, 264
terto: 74
tezu'e: 189
ti: 17, 30, 116, 135, 141-143, 147, 161-162, 170, 209
ti'e: 303
ti'o: 440
ti'otci: 103
tinju'i: 268
tirna: 268
to: 462
to'a: 399
to'e: 275, 364-366
to'i: 308, 462
to'o: 246
to'u: 306
toi: 462
tolmle: 365
tolvri: 108
traji: 280, 282
tricu: 62
troci: 92
tsali: 293
tu: 17, 135, 141-143, 161, 209

tu'a: 129, 259-260
tu'e: 195, 199, 233, 327-328, 343, 349-350, 395, 448, 450
tu'o: 432, 435
tu'u: 195, 199, 233, 327, 343, 395, 448, 450
ty: 401, 410
ty.: 398, 401, 411
u: 351
u'e: 50-51
u'u: 290
UI selma'o: 456
va: 209
va'a: 420, 432, 435, 439
va'e: 429
va'i: 305-306
va'inai: 305-306
vau: 170, 173, 193, 248, 329, 379, 453, 457
ve: 20, 96, 203
ve klama: 186
ve'e: 219
ve'o: 194, 347, 406-407, 419-421
vecnu: 17, 23, 188
vei: 194, 347, 406, 419-421
veka'a: 188
veljvo: 264
vemau: 281
veme'a: 281
vi: 30, 209-210
vi'a: 216
vi'e: 216
vi'u: 216
viska: 187
vo: 123, 403, 434
vo'a: 134, 152
vo'e: 134, 152
vo'i: 134
vo'o: 134
vo'u: 134
voi: 169
vorme: 260
vu: 30, 209
vu'e: 296
vu'i: 129
vu'o: 173, 175
vu'u: 420
vukro: 75
vy: 410-411
vy.: 398
xagmau: 282
xagrai: 282
xamgu: 89, 282
xampo: 74
xance: 280
xarci: 272
xatsi: 74
xazdo: 75
xe: 20, 96, 203, 453
xebro: 76
xecto: 74
xeka'a: 188
xekri: 283

Lojban Words Index

xelso: 76
xexso: 74
xi: 347, 395, 406, 431, 453
xindo: 74
xispo: 76
xo: 431, 452
xrabo: 74
xriso: 76
xu: 21, 27, 308, 335-336, 367, 372, 451
xunre: 88, 364
xurdo: 75
xy: 406, 410
xy.: 398, 405, 421, 455
za'a: 29, 303
za'e: 67, 400, 461
za'i: 250-251, 261
za'o: 221, 261
za'u: 425
zabna: 295
ZAhO selma'o: 222
zai: 401, 403
zarci: 18, 116-117
zbasu: 151
zdani: 70, 89, 91, 186, 264-266, 268-269, 274, 465
ze'e: 219
ze'i: 214

ze'o: 246
zei: 59-60, 76, 400, 466
zenba: 280, 282
zepti: 74
zerle'a: 101
zernerkla: 274
zetro: 74
zi: 212
zi'e: 168-169
zi'o: 135, 151, 157
zmadu: 57, 196-197, 280-282, 421
zo: 115, 133, 299, 400, 405, 458-460, 464-466
zo'e: 19, 135, 150-152, 182-183, 257, 329, 376
zo'i: 246
zo'o: 306
zo'u: 177, 377, 449-450
zoi: 115, 400, 459-460, 464
zu'a: 209-210, 231, 243
zu'i: 135, 150-151
zu'o: 250-251, 261
zukte: 283
zuljma: 59
zunle: 209, 411
zy: 409-411
zy.: 398, 421

Examples Index

"a" is letteral: 405
$: 408
$(n + 1)(n + 1) = n^2 + 2n + 1$: 419
(n+1)-th rat: 430
$+1 + -1 = 0$: 418
-1: 415
$1 + 1 = 2$: 417
10^{20}: 433
12-point: 402
123: 414
$2 + 2$: 254
2 rats + 2 rabbits = 4 animals: 438
2/7: 415
$3 * 10^8$: 432
3 grams: 418
3.1415: 415
8 out of 10: 430
A gives B to C: 405
A gives BC: 404
A loves B: 404
ABC base 16: 426
Abraham Lincoln: 338
Acer: 62
addition problems: 94
afraid of horse: 172
after sleep: 291-292
aleph null: 416
Alexander Pavlovitch Kuznetsov: 404
all-th: 429
always and everywhere: 222
American dollars: 408
Amsterdam: 40
and earlier: 349
and simultaneously: 349
and then: 232-233, 349
anyone who goes
   walks: 384
Appassionata: 196
approximately 40: 425
Armstrong: 43
Arnold: 63
Artur Rubenstein: 195-196
assumption: 304
at least: 425
at least two: 425
at most: 425
at most two: 425
attend school: 217
Avon: 188
bear wrote story: 118
Bears wrote book: 121
beautiful dog: 24
beefsteak: 274
Beethoven: 196
beetle: 270
being alive: 251
better: 282

between Dresden and Frankfurt: 344-346
bicycle race: 259
big boat: 55
big nose: 162
big nose-pores: 162
big person: 162
big red dog: 85
Bill Clinton: 265
blue
   as sad: 308
blue and red: 339
blue house: 186, 333
blue-eyed: 274
boat sailed: 224
bomb destroyed fifty miles: 344
bone bread: 41
Boston from Atlanta: 180
both dogs: 424
bovine: 274
breathe: 348
brie: 62
Brooklyn: 89
brothers: 340
Brown
   John: 64
Bulgarian: 63
butter is soft: 120
butterfly
   social: 22
can see: 236
car goer: 269
carried piano: 338
carry sack: 199
carry sack and dog: 233
carry the piano: 346
Carthage destroyed: 304
cat of plastic: 154
Catherine: 64
Cathy: 64
cause death: 260
cave: 228
Chief: 65
child on ice: 213
choose from: 339
Chrysler: 96
CIA: 407
cobra: 62
coffee mixed with tea: 343
coffee or tea: 337
coin heads: 429
condescension: 296
continues: 220
cup's friend: 167
curious: 256
deference: 296
Devanagari: 401
die after living: 224

discuss in language: 342
DNA: 407
doctor and then rich: 349
dog bites: 380
dog or cat: 336
doghouse: 267
dogs bite: 382
Dong: 271
Doyle: 133
ducks swim: 235
eat in airplane: 217
eat themselves: 423
eight out of ten: 430
empathy: 301
engineering: 18
Englishman in Africa: 120
enough currency: 424
enough-th: 429
ete: 402
everybody loves something: 386
everything breathes: 379
everything loves everything: 378
everything sees me: 378
everything sees something: 378
except from 10 to 12: 345
experienced: 303
F.8 base 16: 426
far away from the nearby park: 224
fast talker: 21
fast-talker shoe: 21
father: 15
father mother: 55
fewsome: 428
Fido: 380
field rations: 56
finished: 220
first rat: 429
firstly: 439
fish eat: 450
fish on right: 214
flashbacks in story time: 228
font: 402
formal requirement: 293-294
former market: 227
four "e"s: 405
Four score and seven: 442
fourteen "e"s: 397
Frank is a fool: 255-256
friend's cup: 167
from one to two o'clock: 344
function f of x: 406
German rich man: 328
Gettysburg Address: 442
girls' school
   little: 82
give: 16
give or receive: 184
giving the horse: 253
go: 180
go to Boston from Atlanta: 180

go to market: 208
go to Paris or Rome: 392
go to the store: 10
goer table: 81
good house: 89
grasp water: 192
great soldier: 267, 271
had earlier: 226
han4zi4: 403
hands in pockets: 168
handwriting: 402
happiness: 155
has a heart: 251
have never: 219
healthy: 27-28
Helvetica font: 402
hepatitis: 59-60
hiragana: 402
hit cousin: 305
hit nose: 305
hits: 15
Hollywood: 123
hours
   minutes
      seconds: example: 427
huh?: 307
husband and wife: 303
IBM: 407
if coffee
   bring tea: 338
in the aftermath: 224
individual: 428
infant ducks: 236
inferior: 296
infinity: 416
inflammable: 237
intermittently: 218
irrational number: 174
James: 39
Jane: 63
Japanese hiragana: 402
Japanese katakana: 401
Jesus: 259
Jim: 63
John and Sam: 15
John Brown: 64
John is coming: 286
John Paul Jones: 133
John says that George goes to market: 229
Jupiter life: 350
juror 5: 173
katakana: 401
Kate: 64
Katrina: 63
kept on too long: 221
killing Jim: 250
kissing Jane: 249
know: 255
know who: 256
Korean: 63

Lady: 65
large meal: 297
lemon tree: 80
Length * Width * Depth = Volume: 438
Lepidoptera: 22
less than: 425
less than two: 425
likes more than: 197
lion in Africa: 122
lions in Africa: 120
list: 339
list of things to do: 343
listen attentively: 268
living things: 151
Livingston: 304
long ago and far away: 212
long-sword: 273
Lord: 65
Lottie: 133
love more: 252
lukewarm food: 130
Lyra: 133
magic square: 434
man or woman: 317
man-woman: 335
manhole: 210
manysome: 429
maple sugar: 62
maple trees: 62
meat slice: 274
mice: 258
Mitsubishi: 404
mixed with: 339
Mon Repos: 269
more than: 425
more than two: 425
mother father: 55
my: 172
my chair: 169
n people: 406
NATO: 407
near the faraway park: 224
near the park: 224
nearby in time: 212
New York city: 167
New York state: 167
Newport News: 133
news: 449
nothing sits: 386
Nth rat: 406
nth rat: 430
Nthly: 406
NYC: 407
observation: 304
ocean shell: 275
Old McDonald: 36
on two occasions: 239
on verge: 220
once: 218
once and future king: 348

One
    the: 65
only: 305
only once: 219
opinion: 304
opposite-of-minus: 441
owe money: 331
Persian rug: 59
person's arm: 166
Pete: 63
piano-moving: 119
place of eating: 240
plant grows: 190-191, 200
prayer: 271
Preem Palver: 94
pregnant sister: 307
pride of lions: 438
probability .5: 429
pronouncement: 303
property of loving: 252
quack: 401
quadratic formula: 436
quality and quantity: 350
quark: 62
quick runner: 80
Ralph: 378
rat eats cheese: 219, 224
rat eats cheese in park: 239
rats are brown: 121
rats in park: 428
Red Pony: 128
red pony: 174
regularly: 217
respectively: 340
rich and German: 341
rock face: 223
Roman Empire: 250
room which he built: 177
rounded down: 425
rounded up: 425
rug
    Persian: 59
runner shoe: 21
said John: 463
salad ingredients: 222
scale of redness: 430
school building: 270
schooner: 80
see with eye: 195
see with left eye: 187
set of all rats: 428
set of rats: 129-130
shell worm: 275
shellfish: 275
Sherman tank: 59
ship sank: 301
shook stick: 139
Simon says: 143
simultaneously: 349
singular me: 428

sister pregnant: 307
six-shooter: 239
sneak in: 274
snow falls: 225
snowball's chance: 430
social butterfly: 22
Socrates: 190
some do not go to school: 389
some relationship: 394
somebody loves self: 377
somebody loves somebody: 377
somebody's dog: 377
something is loved by everybody: 386
something sees everything: 378
something sees me: 376, 381
south face: 223
sow grain: 222
sowed grain: 243
spaghetti: 61
SQL: 407
Steven Mark Jones: 404
stroke cat then rabbit: 232-233
Sun
    the: 65
supper: 57
Susan: 462
syllabic pronunciations of consonants
    in fu'ivla: 61-63
    in fu'ivla category attachment: 61-63
syllabication
    variants of: 44
Take care!: 26
Talk!: 25
talker: 22
taller: 15
tan(pi/2) = infinity: 437
tank
    Sherman: 59
the destination: 186
the go-er: 185
The men are women: 117
the two of you: 127
thingy: 145
this boat: 142
three bears: 128
three cats white
    and two big: 395
three dogs bite two men: 382

Three Kings: 95
three of four people: 346
three or four people: 435
three rats: 428
title of book: 129
to movie
    house
        office: example: 184
to-do list: 343
tomorrow: 272
too long: 221, 224
toward her right: 216
toward my right: 216
transfinite cardinal: 416
traveling salesperson: 188
try the door: 259
try to go: 92
twice today: 225
two brothers: 94
two dogs are white: 124
typical Englishman: 122
typical Lojban user: 122
ugh: 343
under compulsion: 194
under conditions: 250
unspecified route: 181
veterinarian: 272
vice versa: 152-153
walk to market: 97
want to be a soldier: 248
wash self: 152
weapon against self: 381
went and bought: 348, 350
what is your name: 153
when: 242
when else: 243
when/where/how: 242
where: 242
whether criminal: 255
window: 319
word "abu": 405
word "bu": 400
x sub b,d: 347
x sub k: 406
X-ray: 59
x-sub-3: 431
younger: 281
zero to one: 347

CPSIA information can be obtained at www.ICGtesting.com
Printed in the USA
BVOW06*1410260516

449685BV00011B/43/P

9 780966 028324